The Heritage of Great Britain and Ireland

BLENHEIM PALACE   Courtesy of: Blenheim Palace

Front Cover: BUNRATTY CASTLE   Courtesy of: Shannon Heritage

Back Cover: Warwick Castle   Courtesy of: Warwick Castle

KENSINGTON WEST PRODUCTIONS
LONDON
ENGLAND

ACKNOWLEDGEMENTS

The Heritage of Britain and Ireland 1992 has been a compelling project to work on. It should be underlined that without the hard work and sheer determination of all our researchers, editors and other contributors we would not have been able to produce such an informative and well-illustrated book which we sincerely hope our readers enjoy.

Each and every stately home, castle, garden and an assortment of galleries and museums deserve special thanks for their time and co-operation with the extensive research which has made this book as comprehensive as possible.

A sincere thank you for all the efforts of our hard working production team from typesetter to printer to repro house and cartographer who forfeited many an evening and weekend to finish the book on time. Without them the task would have seemed impossible.

We have received assistance from many sources including the Historic Houses Association, National Trust and English Heritage, all of which is gratefully appreciated. Amongst many excellent photographic contributions we would particularly like to thank David Noble, Ronald Weir, Historic Royal Palaces, English Heritage and especially Brian Lynch for his spectacular front cover shot of Bunratty Castle. All have contributed to a wonderful collection of photographs and paintings.

We would, of course, appreciate any constructive comments or suggestions on the layout and contents of our book, so please do write to us and air your views.

On a final note we hope you find our first edition of The Heritage of Britain and Ireland a useful, informative but above all enjoyable publication.

Kensington West Productions
338 Old York Road, Wandsworth, London, SW18 1SS. Tel : 081 870 9394, Fax: 081 870 4270

Editors
Melanie Bradley-Shaw and Jacqui Hawthorn

Consultant Editors
Eric Blair, Janet Blair, Tom Hawthorn, Nova Jayne Heath, David MacLaren, Jason McCreight, Anne Sutherland

Hotel Editors
Giles Appleton, Sally Conner, Jacqui Hawthorn, Tom Lawrence, Mathew Rowlands, James Tucker

Cartography
Ecoscape Associates, St Judes, Barker Street, Shieldfield, Newcastle upon Tyne

Typesetting
Wandsworth Typesetting Ltd., 205a St Johns Hill, London SW11

Origination
Trinity Graphics (Hong Kong)

Printing
Cronion S.A. (Spain)

FOLLOWING THE HERITAGE TRAIL

In 1975 Mr James Lees-Milne wrote:

"The English country house is as archaic as the Osprey. The few left fulfilling the purpose for which they were built are inexorably doomed"

Sixteen years later there are more pairs of Ospreys nesting in the United Kingdom than ever before. Those country houses which have survived have gone through a metamorphosis, attracting many millions of visitors and in many cases are still homes to their original families.

It is well known that the most popular houses are those in which the old families are still present. Yet Mr Lees-Milne's warning has substance and should not be ignored.

Every four years a hundred historic houses are sold by their original owners. Their collections are dispersed. Almost a third are converted for commercial purposes. Many of the country house hotels shown between these covers are cases in point. Others are converted into flats - some very successfully. The most disturbing group are those which are sub-divided, losing their historically related land and estate buildings. They can never be re-assembled.

There are now only 1,450 historic houses in the whole of the United Kingdom which have been occupied by the same family for two generations or more, supported by a land holding.

The rate of attrition will continue unless the British Government appreciates these unique buildings cannot, in normal circumstances, be maintained out of taxable income.

The pleasure which this book will give its readers is to 'waysign' the astonishing variety and styles of historic houses in the United Kingdom. Nowhere in the world are there so many country houses as in this country. They are a supreme example of a collective work of art, ranging from rich interiors to collections of pictures, sculptures, libraries housing volumes of beautifully bound books and archives containing the secrets of generations, all tied together by the grounds and gardens which reflect nature's influence upon these great creations.

Stepping back in time to explore and understand the evolution of our heritage helps to clarify the perspective of contemporary life as we hurtle into the 21st century. Not only should this book be a guide to the past but also an influence on the future.

The Rt. Hon Earl Of Shelburne

Bowood House

CONTENTS

FEATURED STATELY HOMES, CASTLES AND GARDENS

INDEX BY REGION

5

INDEX BY REGION

INDEX BY REGION

Florence Court   (The National Trust)

GREAT BRITAIN AND IRELAND

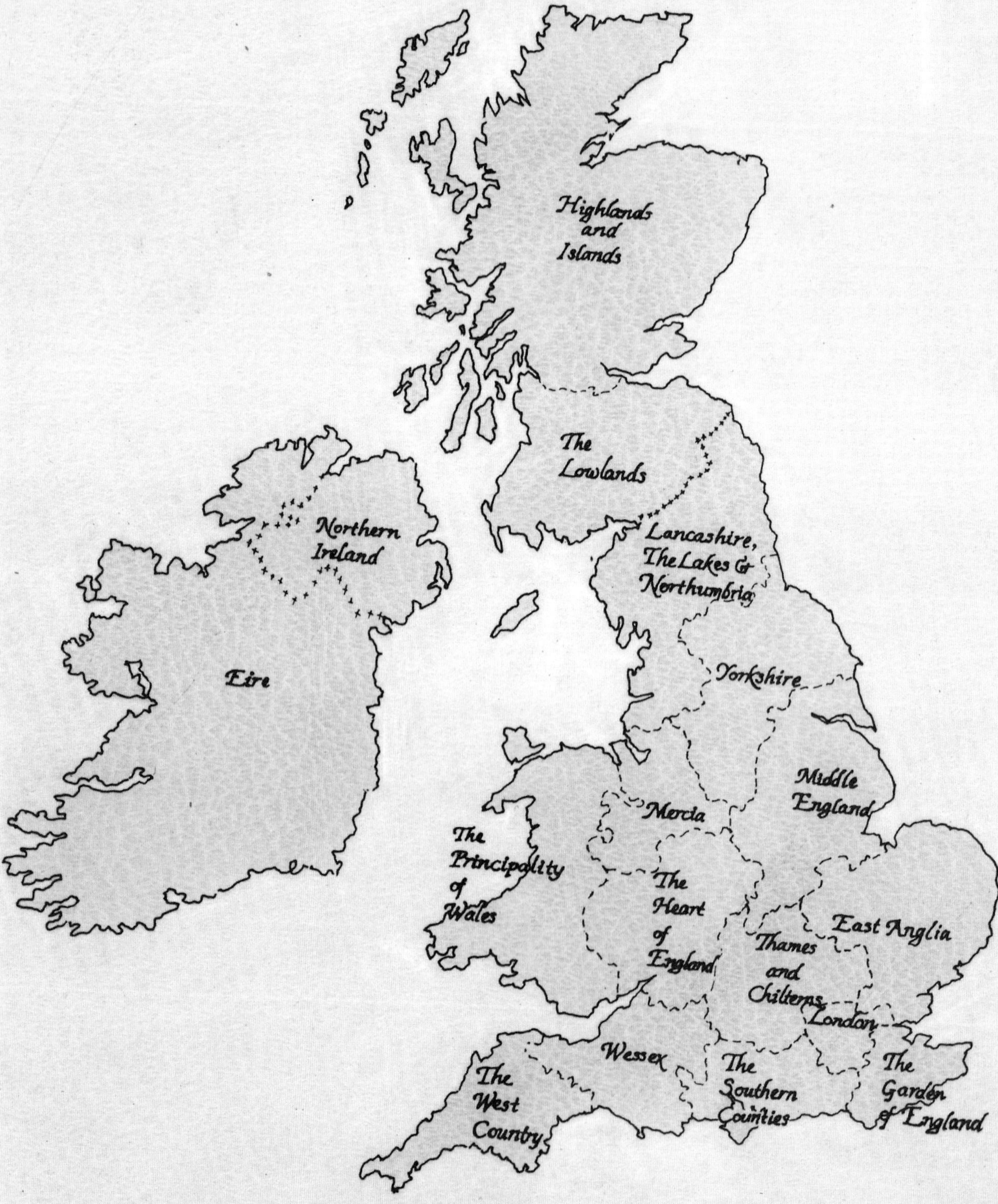

Highlands
and
Islands

The
Lowlands

Northern
Ireland

Lancashire,
The Lakes &
Northumbria

Eire

Yorkshire

Middle
England

Mercia

The
Principality
of
Wales

The
Heart
of
England

East Anglia

Thames
and
Chilterns

London

Wessex

The West Country

The
Southern
Counties

The
Garden
of England

INTRODUCTION

The Heritage of Britain and Ireland is surely one of the most colourful, exciting and accessible collections in the world.

As we edge towards the end of the twentieth century, these valuable heirlooms become all the more precious in our chaotic world.

So many tourists marvel at our buildings and historical collections with their fascinating history and yet many more of us take our rich history for granted. We hope that this book will encourage the reader to make their own excursions into the heritage of Britain and Ireland.

The book is not exhaustive. Such a tome would be both impractical and extremely weighty! The book is, however, an appraisal of the major stately homes, castles, houses and monuments open to the public. To assist you in planning your visit, we have included at the back of the book a directory which gives you details of opening times and a guide to entrance charges.

The main body of the book takes the reader on a journey through England, from the south west, through her shires to the Principality of Wales, north to bonnie Scotland and on to Ireland.

The book is easy to use and clearly laid out with many featured houses described in detail. Hand drawn maps at the front of each section will enable you to plan your route easily. Museums, gardens and many other places of special interest are also detailed in the book but obviously, the list is not exhaustive and we suggest you contact your local tourist board for further information if required. They will be delighted to help you plan your trip to maximise your enjoyment.

In the hope that many people will wish to stay locally, we have included a wide selection of establishments. These range from the very luxurious to cosy inns and friendly bed & breakfasts. All those mentioned offer a first class service and most are of some historical importance themselves whether it is a haunted cellar or 12th century bar. Once again, we would urge you to contact these establishments in advance of your trip as they are extremely popular.

In an age of constant change, it is rewarding to dwell on the rich tapestry weaved by our ancestors. The Heritage of Britain and Ireland has given us huge pleasure in its creation and we hope that our efforts provide you with a similar sense of satisfaction whenever and wherever you travel within Britain and Ireland.

Sherborne Castle

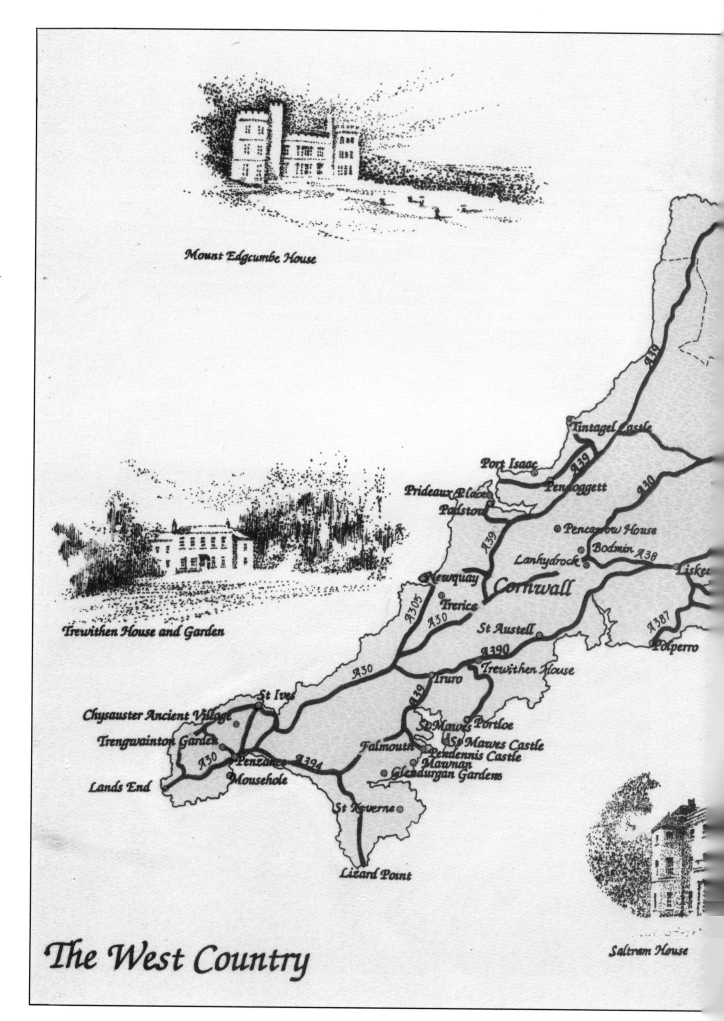

Mount Edgcumbe House

Trewithen House and Garden

Tintagel Castle

Port Isaac

Pendoggett

Prideaux Place

Padstow

Pencarrow House

Bodmin

A38

A39

Lanhydrock

Lisket

Newquay

Cornwall

A3058

Trerice

A30

St Austell

A390

Trewithen House

Polperro

A387

A30

Iruro

A39

St Ives

St Mawes Portloe

Chysauster Ancient Village

St Mawes Castle

Trengwainton Garden

Falmouth

Pendennis Castle

A30

Mawnan

Penzance

A394

Glendurgan Gardens

Lands End

Mousehole

St Keverne

Lizard Point

Saltram House

The West Country

10

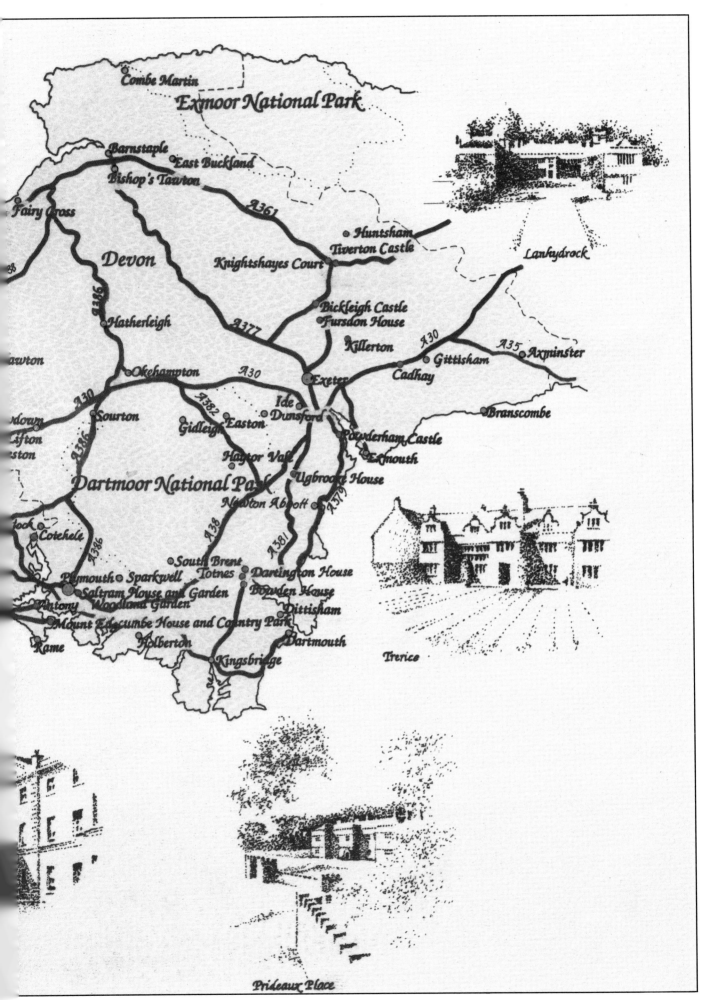

Combe Martin

Exmoor National Park

Barnstaple
East Buckland
Bishop's Tawton

Fairy Cross

A361

Devon

Huntsham
Tiverton Castle

Knightshayes Court

Lanhydrock

A386

Hatherleigh

A377

Bickleigh Castle
Fursdon House

Killerton

A30

Gittisham

A35 Axminster

Okehampton

A30

Exeter

Cadhay

A382

Ide
Dunsford

Sourton

A386

Gidleigh

Easton

Powderham Castle

Branscombe

Haytor Vale

Exmouth

Dartmoor National Park

Ugbrooke House

A379

Newton Abbott

Cotehele

A38

A381

A386

South Brent
Totnes

Darlington House

Plymouth

Sparkwell

Bowden House

Saltram House and Garden
Antony   Woodland Garden

Dittisham

Mount Edgcumbe House and Country Park

Trerice

Rame

Yealberton

Dartmouth

Kingsbridge

Prideaux Place

THE WEST COUNTRY

The south west counties of Devon and Cornwall offer a fascinating mixture of spectacular coastlines with unspoilt moorland conjuring up images of romance and intrigue. The breathtaking cliffs run along the whole length of the north Cornwall and north Devon coasts - secluded caves hidden away on miles of beautiful beaches. The picturesque fishing towns of Padstow and Boscastle on the north coast of Cornwall remain unspoilt, as do the traditional fishing villages of Mevagissey, Fowey and Looe on the south coast.

Enjoy the beautiful scenery at Bodmin Moor and Dartmoor and visit the smugglers' haunts in the caves on the beaches. Visit the 18th century Poldark tin mine which is on three levels with a major heritage section. On a clear day see the striking sight of St Michael's Mount. At high tide it becomes an island, but when the causeway re-appears it is possible to walk to this romantic place.

Visit the astonishing Braunton Burrows in Devon which cover an area of about 2,000 acres at the northern end of the Taw and Torridge Estuary. It is thought that the burrows are the largest in the country. Enjoy the flowers of the heather at the Lizard peninsular which are unique to this area of heathland, visit the lighthouse and then go to the pretty village of Landewednach situated to the north. Stand at the most south west point in England, Lands End, and watch the Atlantic waves crashing on the rocks below. On a clear day you can see the peaceful Isles of Scilly, a group of islands 28 miles south west of Lands End. The warm climate enables exotic flowers and palm trees to flourish. When you visit these beautiful islands make sure you enjoy the unique subtropical waters of **Tresco Abbey** gardens. Notable for fishing are the palm tree lined resorts of Torquay, Paignton and Brixham.

With its rich heritage all around and the strong call of the sea, this is the land of legend, the land of King Arthur. Enjoy the peaceful countryside, remember the tragic Cornish romances of 'Lorna Doone' and Daphne du Maurier's 'Jamaica Inn' and 'Frenchmans Creek'. You cannot fail to enjoy your time in the unspoilt beauty of Devon and Cornwall.

MOORLAND CORNWALL

Bodmin Moor, although much smaller than Exmoor or Dartmoor, is still as mysterious and beautiful in its own way. John Betjeman, the eccentric author, who was passionate about north Cornwall once described the moors as 'that sweet brown home of Celtic saints, that haunted thrilling land of ghosts, of ancient peoples whose hut circles, beehive dwellings and burial mounds jut out above the ling and heather'. Whether driving or walking, famous landmarks can be reached like Brown Willy, the moor's highest point which with Roughton dominate these bleak northern moors each ranging over 1,300 feet. **Dozmary Pool,** an intriguing lake, is said to be the last resting place of King Arthur's Sword Excalibur, yet another of the moor's mysteries. The moor is exposed to harsh winds and for many centuries the eerie curfew bell used to be sounded in Bodmin Town to call people off the moor. Nevertheless, despite the general opinion that the moors are bleak even though very beautiful, it is still a very thrilling place to explore.

Situated close to Bodmin, is the beautiful Georgian house and gardens at **Pencarrow** which has a superb collection of 18th century paintings including works by Samuel Scott, Arthur Devis, Richard Wilson and Henry Raeburn. Pencarrow also has some exceptional pieces of furniture and china which are well worth a look. The house was completed by Sir John Molesworth, 5th Baronet, c1770. In 1882 Sir Arthur Sullivan composed much of the music for 'Iolanthe' whilst staying at Pencarrow. The music room, which was obviously of great inspiration to Sir Arthur, has a fine plaster ceiling portraying the four seasons, with simulated bird's-eye maple grained walls. The gardens were laid out by Sir William Molesworth, the Victorian statesman in the 1840s. Altogether there are 50 acres of formal and woodland gardens with an ancient British Encampment and lake. Huge rhododendrons and camellias provide a wonderful display of colour and aroma in the spring, and specimen conifers stand smartly along the mile long drive. The sunken Italian Garden lies at the front of the house centred on a fountain and a wonderful granite rockery. Within a pretty woodland setting is the lake and the sheltered valley, containing the American Gardens which were originally planted with species from Western America but now also have an abundance of rhododendrons and conifers. Travelling south east of Bodmin is **Lanhydrock House**, the National Trust property which overlooks the valley of the River Fowey. Lanhydrock House gives the impression that time has stood still and gives the wonderful feeling of living in the Victorian period. The house was re-built in 1881 after a disastrous fire and the survival of the north wing affords a taste of the original interiors.

It was designed by London architect Richard Coad who not only incorporated luxuries such as radiators in nearly every room, but designed the exterior reflecting the house built by Sir Richard Bobartes and his son between 1630 and 1642. One of the features of the house is the 116ft long gallery in the original north wing which has an outstanding plaster ceiling illustrating in intricate detail early scenes from the Old Testament. The ceiling was created in 1650 by local craftsmen. You can still visit the dairy and the huge kitchen which are fascinating. Lanhydrock's 19th century garden is also very Victorian with magnolias, rhododendrons and camellias providing colourful displays beyond the well which was used by the monks of St Petroc's Priory at Bodmin. The wooded valley of the River Fowey gives magnificent views from the top of the garden with Bodmin Moor on the horizon.

To the east of the moor, high on a hill stands the majestic **Launceston Castle**. Originally built in the aftermath of the Norman Conquest, the castle is a well known and popular landmark. The views from the topmost wall overlook Bodmin Moor and are particularly breathtaking. The ancient parish of St Stephen, which pre-dates Launceston, can also be seen. The remains of parts of the castle have stood on the same spot since the 13th century. It was originally a very basic motte-and-bailey castle established by Robert of Mortain, the half-brother of William the Conqueror, when he became Earl of Cornwall just after 1066. It is believed that Richard built the present structure between 1227 and 1272. These were glorious days for Launceston! After the Civil War when the castle fell into disrepair one of the towers was used as a prison. One of its inmates was the famous Quaker leader George Fox who was incarcerated there for eight months in 1656, charged with distributing 'subversive' literature.

There are many wonderful sights in Launceston including the church of St Mary Magdalene which has an intricate granite exterior. **Lawrence House** is a smart 18th century house which has a small museum full of local curios and artefacts. There is also a two float steam railway which is a steady walk downhill from the castle. Launceston is definitely worth a visit and as John Betjeman said 'Travellers lift up their hearts at the sight of Launceston'.

THE FAL ESTUARY

Falmouth is known to many as the grandest harbour in the English Channel. What was once a tiny hamlet is now Cornwall's largest port. It was the Pope's threatened crusade against him that drove Henry VIII to protect this coastline which resulted in the **Castles of Pendennis and St Mawes.**

Pendennis Castle, situated at the mouth of the River Fal, stands 200 feet above sea-level which was an ideal position to defend Cornish roads. With the exception of Raglan, Pendennis was the last fortress to hold out for King Charles in the Civil War. The Parish church is dedicated to King Charles, the Martyr. The original part of the castle is a circular tower or keep surrounded by a curtain wall. Elizabeth I added a large outer enclosure in 1598 when there were rumours that the Spanish were preparing to launch another Armada against England. The castle was used for military purposes as late as the Second World War when it became a coastal defence post.

The entrance to Pendennis is through an impressive gateway, above which is the Royal Arms carved magnificently in stone. The room from where the draw-bridge and portcullis were operated is above this entrance and the two stalls through which the chains passed can still be seen. Guns and armour which were used in the Civil War are displayed in a separate museum.

On the opposite shore is **St Mawes Castle**, which although built for the defence of the estuary, did not suffer the gunfire and bloodshed of the Civil War. It is an unusual Tudor Castle shaped like a clover leaf with a substantial tower and rests contentedly among shrubs and rock plants.

We travel now between Truro and St Austell to the village of Probis where you will find **Trewithen House** and gardens, whose name means 'House of Trees' which perfectly sums up this beautiful early Georgian house. Set in magnificent wooded parkland and described by Country Life as 'one of the outstanding West Country Houses of the 18th century', Trewithen's origins travel back to the 17th century. It has been lived in and treasured by the same family for over 250 years. Thomas Edwards, an architect from Greenwich, was responsible for the stunning building we see today. After it was bought in 1715 by Philip Hawkins, the house was substantially re-built and it was some 40 years before it was completed. The Hawkins family encouraged the mining of tin and china clay in Cornwall and as well as being eminent landowners they built a railway and harbour. Christopher Hawkins was created a baronet in 1799 and was MP for Grampound; he later became Father of the House of Commons. The Hawkins were great collectors and you can't fail to notice this when you wander round Trewithen. The Gardens are internationally famous, attracting visitors from as far away as New Zealand, Japan and North America. They were created at the beginning of the century by George Johnstone, a direct Hawkins descendant, with rare and beautiful shrubs. Many were developed from seed in the 1920s sent from Tibet, China and Nepal and provide spectacular flowers

in the mild Cornish climate. The scent from the magnolias and rhododendrons is quite heady. The gardens provide wonderful inspiration, you can even buy a wide variety of shrubs and plants so there's no excuse! A useful tip for parents - Trewithen has a children's playground.

LAND'S END AND POINTS WEST

Lands End is the most South Westerly point of mainland Britain. Everyone at some stage should stand at Lands End and see the magnificent views with the jagged rocks and reefs, the longships and Wolf Rock lighthouse. On a clear day you could be lucky to see the Scilly Isles which are 28 miles west. You can even have refreshments at the first and last house which has been there since Victorian times. Northwards along the coastal path is the beautiful beach which is Sennen Cove; there is also a famous Iron Age hill-fort on the Mayon cliff. Cape Cornwall, a famous mining area, also has prehistoric remains. Several of these can be reached from the road leading from Madron to Morvah. Two miles north west of Penzance, half a mile west of Heamoor on the B3312 Penzance-Madron road are the **Gardens of Trengwainton** which are owned by the National Trust. Although not fully matured, it has a remarkable collection of tender and half hardy trees. Parts of Trengwainton are much older, the tall beeches and oaks shelter the rambling Victorian mansion (not open to the public), without which the little valley would be open to the full force of the westerly gales. Yards of scarlet rhododendrons, and a fifty foot magnolia sargentiana robusta are the high spots of a spring visit to Trengwainton. There is a beautiful view of St Michael's Mount in the bay below which can be seen when standing on the lawns in front of the house. **Chysauster Ancient Village,** two and a half miles north west of Gulval, near Penzance, has stone houses erected by our pre-historic ancestors half way up a hillside, through a stone passage. The village had existed for two centuries by the time the Romans came.

THE ATLANTIC COAST

If you enjoy visiting smaller houses with a degree of sophistication then **Trerice**, the National Trust property which is three miles south east of Newquay, would be of interest. Built in the Elizabethan period of local buff limestone, it escaped fashionable alterations in the prosperous times of the 18th and 19th centuries. It belonged to one of the great families of Cornwall for 400 years, the Arundel's, before it was passed in 1802 to the Aclands. Trerice is an unpretentious house, however, it does have a splendid south-facing drawing room on the first floor, which is thought to have been created out of a medieval solar by Sir John Arundel.

Of the gardens that surrounded Trerice until 1915 little remains. There are now fruit trees set out in the quincunx pattern used in the seventeenth century, where every tree is in line with its neighbour from wherever it is viewed.

Still in the Elizabethan period we visit **Prideaux Place**, which is still owned and inhabited by the family who built it in 1585. This splendid house opened to the public for the first time in 1987. Visit the great chamber which has an intricate embossed plaster ceiling which dates back to 1585. You can trace the Prideaux marriages in the library with its amazing heraldic stained glass windows. Looking out from the gatehouse is the beautiful deer park. The herd of fallow deer is one of the oldest in the country and legend has it that if the herd dies out so do the Prideauxs. There are stable yards and a quaint dairy which leads to the woods (featured later). On to Tintagel, where despite the fact that **Tintagel Castle** was built 600 years after King Arthur, legend still has it that this was his stronghold. The setting of the castle is breathtaking on this spectacular Cornish Coast. Isolated on a rock known as 'The Island', the ruins of this medieval castle cling to the edge of a cliff face. Many other remains which are easy to explore are strewn all over the island.

The castle was built in the 12th century by the Earl of Cornwall, a bastard son of Henry I; later it belonged to the Black Prince. It was a prison for a time and then fell into decay. Now safe in the hands of English Heritage, it is wonderful to stand and dream of the mystery, romance and legend while the Atlantic waves crash below.

THE SMUGGLERS COAST

Situated on the west bank of the River Tamar, which separates Devon and Cornwall, and eight miles south west of Tavistock is the National Trust property **Cotehele House**. Built from granite this lovely house stands in beautiful gardens. It is a fine example of an early Tudor manor house built by Sir Richard Edgcumbe and his son Sir Piers between 1485 and 1540. Armour, weaponry and hunting trophies decorate the hall with 17th century tapestries hanging floor to ceiling in most rooms.

The spectacular grounds are over 1000 acres, where azaleas, rhododendrons and ferns provide wonderful colour, thriving in the exceptionally mild climate. There is also a medieval dovecote and stewpond which once provided meat and fish for a large self-sufficient community.

Also owned by the National Trust is **Antony House**, one of the finest Georgian houses in Cornwall. The traditional way of approaching Antony House is by boat crossing to Cornwall by the Torpoint ferry from Plymouth. Built from granite between 1711 and 1721 by Sir William Carew, Antony House is a simple two storey rectangular building faced with silver grey stone. It is a small but very appealing house with exceptional furnishings; there are family and other portraits, including a wonderful portrait of Charles I which hangs in the hall.

Yew trees feature to the west of the lawns leading down to the Tamar. There is a pretty summer display of flowers in the sheltered garden, and for tree enthusiasts, there are a number of unusual trees including a large ginkgo and a huge cork oak.

Mount Edgcumbe House stands proudly above a tree-lined avenue overlooking Plymouth Sound. It was re-built to its original 16th century design by Kenelm 6th Earl of Mount Edgcumbe and architect Adrian Gilbert Scott after the house was burnt to a shell in 1941 from incendiary bombs. The interior has a Georgian character. Family portraits hang in the balcony with an Armada display in the garden room. The beautiful garden that surrounds the house has streams and summer houses. It has colourful rhododendrons and unusual shrubs and a lovely Lucombe Oak. Mount Edgcumbe also has a grade I Historic Garden which was the creation of the family and consists of English, French and Italian style gardens which are surrounded by huge hedges, some being in existence since the 17th century.

THE ENGLISH RIVIERA

Powderham Castle, situated near Exeter, was first built between 1390 and 1420. It has a beautiful interior with many fascinating features. You can also meet Timothy the Tortoise who has lived in the garden since 1880. (featured later).

You will certainly enjoy a visit to **Ugbrooke House** and parks. It is the home of the Clifford family and has a very lived-in feeling. The original house and chapel were built about 1200 and re-designed by Robert Adam, with beautiful embroideries, period furniture and paintings. There are also nostalgic exhibits with a fascinating collection of early gramophones and wireless, firearms and weapons from the past. The Cardinal's bedroom is also another attraction, complete with four poster bed. There are lovely walks in the grounds by 'Capability' Brown, and delicious cream teas in the Wyvern Cafe which is in the original 18th century Stable block. Ugbrooke House and the grounds are also used for hosting dinners, receptions, seminars, launches and filming. **Bowden House** is situated about a mile from Totnes. This delightful house dates back to the 9th century when Bowden became the residence of the De Broase family who were the builders of Totnes Castle in the 13th century; parts of the house date from this period. An Elizabethan mansion was created in 1510 with a Queen Anne facade added in 1704 and a Neo-classical Baroque style decoration in the Grand Hall. At Bowden all the guides are dressed in Georgian costume which adds authenticity to the visit. You can also visit the photographic museum and enjoy a delicious cream tea!

Ugbrooke House

THE WEST COUNTRY

DARTMOOR AND THE BLACKDOWN HILLS

Dartmoor could not fail to impress any visitor with its beautiful variety of landscapes. Formed by volcanic action, the moor is full of bogs and frequent mist and rain. It has a vast expanse of green, broken only by rocky tors. There is an abundance of wildlife, including foxes, otters and badgers and of course the ponies who roam freely. There are interesting prehistoric relics of the communities who lived on the moor long before Celtic, Roman and Saxon times. A good example of an isolated moor settlement is Widecombe which is famous for its fair. The 16th century church house nearby, is well worth a visit and the Lydford Gorge is a spectacular sight on the western side of the moor. The main attraction here is where the River Lyd descends for two miles between walls up to 60ft high.

There is also Spinsters Rock, near Drewsteignton, which is a megalithic form dating from Neolithic times, and the remains of many villages. A fairy tale atmosphere is created by Wistman's Wood, Black Tor Beare and Piles Copse which are ancient uplands oak copses covered with mosses and ferns. Wherever you go on Dartmoor, you will enjoy its wild beauty which is free to all.

There are several National Trust properties in the area that are well worth a visit. **Saltram House** dates from the 18th century and the original contents of the rooms show this era in elegant detail. The house was re-modelled originally by John and Lady Catherine Parker but it was their son, John Parker who invited the famous architect Robert Adam to Saltram, who designed everything including the door handles. Four fabulous looking glasses are set off by the blue damask lining the walls; cherubs make music in the rococo plaster ceiling; beautiful pictures and paintings adorning the walls. There is an extensive deer park which was formed in the mid-18th century. The gardens are a lovely mixture of wooded glades and shrubs with displays of colour by the magnolias and rhododendrons. There is a mass of daffodils in the spring, patches of cyclamen in September, and citrus fruits surround the fountain in the summer. **Fursdon House** is nine miles north west of Exeter. Primarily a family home, it is set in farmland with magnificent views across the estate. Fursdon, a Georgian fronted manor house has been the home of the Fursdon family for over 700 years of unbroken male succession. There is an interesting Regency library and lots of family portraits, costumes and mementoes. The intriguing history of **Bickleigh Castle** spans nine centuries. This romantic medieval building is the former home of the heirs of the Earls of Devon (featured later).

We travel now to **Tiverton Castle** which was originally a Royal Castle built in 1106. It has seen turbulent days of war and romance and when considering its stormy past, it is amazing that so much of the castle still remains. Henry I came to the throne in 1100 when he was troubled by disturbing dreams of the Three Estates of the Realm - Lords, Church and Commons all plotting against him. Land was then granted to his followers for the building of protective castles. Richard de Redvers was ordered to build a castle at Tiverton. With its strong position above the River Exe, it dominated the crossing of the river, which formed a natural defence to the west. The castle changed hands many times in nearly 900 years of continuous occupation. It became the house of Princess Katherine, daughter of Edward IV in 1495 on her marriage to William Courtenay, later Earl of Devon. The Gifford family acquired the castle in the

16th century and during the Civil War it was held for Charles I, but on 19th October 1645 it fell to the Roundhead General, Sir Thomas Fairfax. The castle was bought by Peter West after it had been restored and he built a beautiful house within the walls. The Carews, by marriage, then owned Tiverton for nearly 200 years. There is much to see at Tiverton Castle; Civil War Armoury, Medieval Gatehouse and Towers, entrances to secret passageways which extend throughout the town. There are romantic ruins of the towers, wall and chapel where one can dream back in time. There is a wonderful Campbell clock collection, fine furniture and pictures. If you visit in July and August you can end your day with a delicious cream tea.

The National Trust's property, **Knightshayes,** is situated two miles north of Tiverton and is not a particularly beautiful building. John Heathcoat-Amory, 1st Baronet, purchased the Knightshayes Estate and built this Gothic house which looks down the valley on the little town below. It is an example of domestic architecture by William Burges, the high Victorian Medievalist who is better known for his churches. This rather miserable exterior was planned to conceal its outstanding interior. The designs by Burges were never put into practice, and his replacement John Diblee Crane's designs were by no means dull even though he was more conventional! There are many beautiful sights to see inside at Knightshayes which include the collection of Old Masters built up after the Second World War by Sir John Heathcoat-Amory, 3rd Baronet, and his wife. They were also the inspiration behind the gardens which are well worth a visit.

Tiverton Castle

THE WEST COUNTRY

The gardens of the National Trust at **Killerton** are spectacular, they are laid out on Killerton Clump which are steep slopes of volcanic outcrop. The original design was by John Veitch, a Scotsman, in the 1770s who went on to become one of the great nurserymen and landscape gardeners of his time. The late 18th century house contains the Paulise de Bush collection of costume which is displayed on dummies in a setting showing life and society of the day. The interiors of the house have altered substantially over the years. The library now houses the collection of the Rev. Sabine Baring Gould (1834 -1924) who is best known for his hymn 'Onward Christian Soldiers'. The music room is dedicated to the wife of the 10th Baronet, who took lessons from Sebastian Wesley on the chamber organ. Back to the garden where you really must visit the magnificent stables at the foot of the drive.

Cadhay at Ottery St Mary is first mentioned in the reign of Edward I and was held by a de Cadhay. It stands in a beautiful listed garden (featured later).

On the golden coast you will find the beautiful **Chambercombe Manor**. Held in the cleft of a secluded, wooded valley, the Manor House has much to offer, its history and legends compensating for its small size. This delightful white-painted, rose-covered farmhouse with its tall chimneys retains much of its former grandeur both in the fabric of the building and its furniture and decoration. Chambercombe Manor dates from the 11th century and was owned by the Champernon family for some 400 years, passing eventually to the Duke of Suffolk and thence to the Crown. It is not certain when the house fell from its high estate but its furniture ranges from Elizabethan to Victorian times. Amongst the predominantly Tudor furniture in the beamed Great Hall, a fine example is the heavily carved oak cupboard dated 1595 and an excellent

example of a Cromwellian refectory table. The limed ash floor, which resembles polished granite, is over 300 years old and is one of the finest of its kind. The Victorian Bedroom has a fine four poster bed of that period, complete with the original hangings and hand-made lace, and is charmingly furnished with furniture of the same period.

The Coat of Arms Bedroom, with its fine wagon roof and Tudor plaster frieze, has a beautiful Elizabethan tester bed of handsomely carved oak depicting the three wise men. This was Lady Jane Grey's room and bears the Grey family arms above the fireplace. The room adjoining this one is at the centre of the legend of Chambercombe - so pause first and take courage - for in 1865 in this small chamber the skeleton of a woman was discovered on the bedstead. She was believed to be a lady visiting relatives at the house, who, having been wrecked on the rocks at Hele, was carried up to this room where she later died. Her jewellery was taken and the room sealed off from the outside world. Rumours also abound concerning the secret passage which leads to an underground footway used by smugglers who, it seems, had a very good working arrangement with Manor Farm. This lovely house also has its own tiny chapel - only 10 feet by 6 feet - which was one of only four in the west country mentioned in Domesday. The grounds extend to over four acres of complete peace and tranquillity with delightful herbaceous borders and rose and herb gardens. Across the wooden bridge lie the water gardens where a variety of water fowl dip and dive. The peaceful courtyard, with its pools and fountains is the perfect spot to enjoy coffee or afternoon tea.

Devon and Cornwall are counties of many attractions which will inspire you - you cannot fail to enjoy the splendours of the sea and surrounding countryside.

Chambercombe Manor

PRIDEAUX PLACE

In the shelter of the hill above the delightful little harbour at Padstow, Prideaux Place commands wonderful views over the Camel Estuary. The house has changed little in the last two centuries and there have been Prideauxs living here since the time of Elizabeth I. Politically unlucky, the family always backed the wrong side in both the Civil War in the 1640s and Monmouth's Rebellion of 1685, but somehow managed to survive - often by judicious marriages. Just such a marriage secured a Royal Pardon for their activities in the Civil War and the staggering fine of £15,000 paid to Judge Jeffrey, the Hanging Judge, atoned for Edmund Prideaux's part in Monmouth's Rebellion.

Like so many of our historic houses, Prideaux Place would never have been built if Henry VIII's ambitions to marry Anne Boleyn had not necessitated taking over the Church and its lands. The land at Padstow belonged to the wealthy Prior of Bodmin and when, in 1536, it became obvious that the King would confiscate all church possessions, he was fortunate to have as his right hand man a sharp witted lawyer called Nicholas Prideaux.

Nicholas engineered a marriage between his nephew and the Prior's niece and managed to buy the freehold of the manor and thriving port of Padstow, sold off by the thwarted King after a legal action which, astoundingly, Henry VIII lost.

The house was built by Nicholas's great nephew Sir Nicholas Prideaux who wanted a grand modern house to reflect his growing importance. His impressive E-shaped Elizabethan manor, completed in 1592, with three pointed gables and castellated bays remained unaltered until the 18th century.

The original Great Hall, now the Dining Room, has a mixture of Elizabethan and Georgian panelling, the former of Spanish oak with a carved frieze of small animals.

The Morning Room contains some of the best pictures in the house. Several are by the Regency Court painter John Opie who grew up on the estate. One, a rare self-portrait, was left by Opie as a tip for the housekeeper. A most romantic picture is the pastel of Humphrey Prideaux by the celebrated Italian artist Rosalba Carriera. She fell hopelessly in love with him and wrote of her feelings for him in a letter concealed behind the frame. Sadly, Humphrey never knew - the letter was only discovered in 1914.

The Drawing Room has a particularly fine collection of satinwood furniture, and also contains examples of Sevres, Meissen and Royal Worcester porcelain, together with exceptional 19th century Japanese Satsuma plates. Among the miniatures is an interesting relic of the Civil War, which on one side depicts Charles I and on its reverse a likeness of Cromwell - one could never be too careful in those days!

The beautiful Grenville Room is in reality the dining room of the Earl of Bath taken from his grand manor house at Stow. The house was built and demolished in one generation, and the ever-enterprising Prideauxs removed his dining room lock, stock and barrel to Prideaux Place, complete with inset paintings by Verrio, Grinling Gibbons carving and the latest 17th century gadget - the Earl's wine cooler. Now hanging in this room is the important collection of Royalist Caroline paintings.

The glorious Library, with its ribbed ceiling, is pure Regency Gothic, its stained glass windows representing the history of the many heiresses whose fortunes have contributed much to Prideaux.

The Great Chamber is the crowning glory of this lovely house with its original 16th century plaster ceiling depicting the story of Susannah and the Elders. It was known as the hidden ceiling as in the 18th century another ceiling was hung below it.

The Hall, with its fine cantilevered staircase which also comes from the Grenville house, has one of the oldest pieces of furniture, a chest inlaid with mother of pearl which was salvaged from an Armada ship that foundered in Padstow estuary in 1585. A portrait on the staircase is worthy of close inspection for its subject, Honor Fortescue, may have been encountered elsewhere in the house. She is the lady in green, who according to legend haunts Prideaux Place.

The formality of the gardens designed by Edmund Prideaux in the 1730s was largely swept away by the more natural style favoured by his son Humphrey who built the fortifications in front of the house. In Victorian times the wheel of gardening fashion had come full circle in the form of a formal Italian flower garden which has been restored. Much of the gardens, particularly the recently discovered Green Walk, was so overgrown that the present owner managed to trace it only with the help of a large-scale map, a compass and a very long piece of string! One of the most exciting features of the garden, at the top of the lawn, is an ancient Celtic Cross in a remarkable state of preservation, which has stood on this spot since at least the 9th century. A range of charmingly unspoilt farm buildings around the stableyard houses a Gift Shop and Terrace Tea Rooms.

Prideaux Place

POWDERHAM CASTLE

Powderham Castle was built between 1390 and 1420 by Sir Philip Courtenay, 6th son of the 2nd Earl of Devon and Margaret, daughter of Humphrey de Bohun, Earl of Hereford and Essex and grand-daughter of Edward I. The present Earl is the direct descendent of Sir Philip. The castle was extensively damaged during the Civil War and fell to the Parliamentary forces. When the family returned to Powderham early in the 18th Century, they embarked on a series of re-building and restoration which continued into the 19th Century.

The Castle contains a large collection of portraits by many famous artists, including Reynolds, Kneller and Hudson, as well as some charming works by the Courtenay family's drawing master and his pupils. The Ante-Room is part of the medieval castle and has a lovely 18th Century rococo ceiling and most unusual fireplace with a window over it. When the room is in use in the evening a mirror can be rolled across the window. The very handsome pair of bookcases are made of rosewood inlaid with brass and are signed and dated J. Channon 1740.

One of the most beautiful rooms in the castle is the Music Room designed for the 3rd Viscount by James Wyatt, the most fashionable architect of the day. The walls are divided by Corinthian pilasters and in the alcoves between are alabaster vases on marble stands. The lovely fireplace is of Carrara marble, opposite which hangs a portrait of Louis XIV by Callet which came from the French Embassy at the time of the French revolution. The gilt furniture was almost certainly made by Edward Marsh and Tatham, upholsterers to the Prince Regent, and the beautiful carpet is Axminster. The organ was built by Brice Seede in 1769 and was specially designed for the room and the medallions around the walls were painted by the 3rd Viscount and some of his thirteen sisters. He was one of the most gifted members of the family but his life was touched by tragedy. When still a boy he was involved in a scandal with the notorious William Beckford which undoubtedly overshadowed his later life. As a rich and talented young man he entertained on a lavish scale but gave Powderham a bad name. Later he left England for good, living first in New York and then in Paris where he died, unmarried in 1835. Much of the contents of Powderham were sold in 1825 to pay his debts. Four years before he died, the 3rd Viscount successfully claimed the Earldom of Devon which had been in abeyance since Edward Courtenay died in exile in 1556.

The Staircase Hall is the upper part of the original medieval Great Hall and was refurbished by the 1st Viscount in the 18th Century manner, including the installation of the mahogany staircase in 1754 which has been described as among the half dozen or so most sumptuous surviving examples of rococo plasterwork in England. It is remarkably beautiful, with a great profusion of birds, animals, flowers, fruit, foliage and musical instruments set in panels against a vivid blue-green background. The coat of arms at the bottom of the stairs is said to have added four guineas to the final bill.

The Marble Hall is one of the most interesting rooms in the house and was the lower half of the original Great Hall. It contains two delicately worked tapestries, one 17th Century Brussels and the other probably Soho, circa 1700. The incredible clock, which stands 13 feet high is by Stumbels of Totnes and still plays its full tunes at 4, 8 and 12 o'clock. The Courtyard and the Dining Hall are Victorian additions to the Castle, built by Charles Fowler for the 10th Earl. The handsome linenfold panelling was put in by the 11th Earl who also installed the fascinating series of coats of arms tracing the family history from the French Knight Athon, who founded the Castle of Courtenay to the present day.

The gardens at Powderham Castle are informal. The Rose Garden is planted mostly with older, sweet scented varieties and enjoys fine views over the terraces and beyond. A herd of fallow deer share the beautiful park with many other species of birds and wildfowl. Heron can be seen fishing the River Kenn which meanders through the delightfully peaceful surroundings with lovely views of the Exe estuary and the little village of Lympstone. In the garden one might see Powderham's oldest inhabitant, the extremely sociable Timothy, who came to England in 1880 from Turkey when he was already fully grown which puts his age at around 160. An industrious tortoise, he ensures that the Castle lawns are always weed free.

Powderham Castle's ease of access from the M5 which is 7 miles away (junction 30 then follow A379 towards Dawlish) makes it the perfect setting for functions ranging from new car launches to clay pigeon shoots, from candle-lit dinners to international conferences. Some of the elegant State Rooms are available for wedding receptions.

BICKLEIGH CASTLE

Bickleigh Castle, in the beautiful thickly wooded Exe valley, comes as something of a surprise. Across the small stone bridge over the moat the Courtyard is surrounded not by battlements and baileys, towers and turrets but by small thatched cottages of great charm and a series of barns. The original castle dates from Norman times and in about 1410 became the property of the Courtenays, heirs to the Earls of Devon. When Sir Philip Courtenay's son died, leaving an orphaned daughter Elizabeth, he asked his cousin William Carew and his wife to live in the castle and look after her. When Elizabeth grew up, William's younger brother fell in love with her and the couple ran away to marry against her grandfather's wishes. After Thomas Carew distinguished himself in the battle of Flodden Field he was reconciled with Sir Philip Courtenay who gave Bickleigh Castle to Elizabeth as her marriage settlement. For the next two centuries the Castle became the home of the Carew family.

During the Civil War Sir Henry Carew supported the Royalist cause and the Castle was 'sleighted' by General Fairfax and the Roundheads, leaving only the south wing, Gatehouse and Chapel still standing. Sir Henry restored the Gatehouse and added the typical Devon farmhouse of cob and thatch as all attempts to rebuild a fortified manor were thwarted by Cromwell. Poor Sir Henry died broken-hearted in 1681, partly because of the devastation of the castle and partly because his young son and nephew died tragically on the same day. As he left no heir the buildings fell into disrepair until early this century when a succession of owners began to restore Bickleigh, thus saving it from complete ruin, and their endeavours are maintained by the present owners, Mr and Mrs Noel Boxall.

The oldest remaining part of the Castle is the thatched Chapel, built between 1090 and 1110, and thought to be the oldest complete building in Devon. The nave and chancel are the original Norman work, and the barrel roof and some of the windows were added in the 15th century. The peaceful simplicity of this small chapel is enhanced by its furnishings, almost all of which date before 1600. The collection of alabaster was found, together with two skeletons thought to be Thomas and Elizabeth Carew, when the floor was excavated by a previous owner. The sermon timer could perhaps be put to practical use today.

The Gatehouse was part of the fortified manor built by the Courtenays late in the 14th century. The Armoury now contains a collection of arms including a Cromwellian suit of armour and the Guard Room, furnished mainly with Tudor pieces, has some fine portraits.

The Farmhouse wing dates from the Stuart period and contains some fine examples of seventeenth century furniture and Mrs Boxall's lovely collection of period samplers. One fascinating small room was originally a bacon-curing chamber, rarely found in the West Country.

The Garden Room has a remarkable carved overmantle which almost certainly came from the original hall. It survived the Civil War intact because it was removed to the village rectory for safe keeping.

The Gardens at Bickleigh are delightfully informal. The original moat is now a water garden and the old Castle Courtyard is now a smooth green lawn beyond which rises a huge mound thickly covered in rhododendrons which frame the building with colour in early summer.

Across the Courtyard in the thatched barn is the Mary Rose exhibition. Her commander, Vice-Admiral Sir George Carew lived at Bickleigh for about ten years.

Another Carew, one Bampfylde, distinguished himself by running away from school and becoming king of the local gypsies. His portrait hangs in the Guardroom and he is buried in an unmarked grave in the churchyard. Bickleigh village at midnight on midsummer's night is possibly not the place to be - for on that night only Sir Alexander Cruwys (also a Carew), who was run through by a sword, rides out across the bridge in full armour with his head under his arm!

There are tales of a nun bricked up, secret passages, buried treasure which give the castle an atmosphere all its own. But it is the feeling of timelessness, the blending of centuries which gives Bickleigh its particular charm.

CADHAY

Set in meadows watered by the River Otter about a mile from Ottery St. Mary, Cadhay is approached along an avenue of ancient limes. Serene and traditional, it reflects its quiet history.

The Tudor manor house was built around 1550 by John Haydon who had married the De Cadhay heiress. This was the time of Henry VIII's Dissolution of the Monasteries and it would seem that the demolished Priest's College nearby provided a ready supply of building materials. Built around an oblong courtyard, the house is mainly constructed from Salcombe sandstone with dressings from the famous quarry of Beer which supplied the stone for Exeter Cathedral.

In 1587 Robert Haydon added the long gallery without which no Elizabethan home was complete. He was also responsible for what is probably the most striking feature of the house, the Court of Sovereigns. The walls of the courtyard are patterned with an irregular chequering of sandstone and flint and above the doors stand four statues of Henry VIII, Edward VI, Mary and Elizabeth, the latter dated 1617.

In the early 18th century the Great Hall with its open-timbered roof would have seemed old-fashioned in the extreme and so a floor was inserted, causing considerable damage to the beautiful original hammer beams and carved braces. At this time the Tudor mullioned casement windows were torn out to make way for Georgian sashes, except for those of the east facade which escaped this fate for some reason. The north front was refaced with a thin skin of Beer stone giving an air of great dignity.

For much of the 18th and 19th centuries the house was sadly neglected, occupied by a tenant with parts of the building used as a farmhouse. Fortunately the house was acquired by W.C. Dampier Whetham under whose careful conservative eye it was restored to its present state. Tudor open hearths were uncovered, an entrance forecourt was built, a lawn was laid down to the large pond with fine views over Ottery St. Mary and the imposing Irish yews were planted.

Since Mr Whetham's time the house belonged to the William-Powlett family who have continued to maintain and care for their historic home in its lovely gardens. Although none of the original contents remain at Cadhay, the house contains some very fine furniture and pictures.

THE WEST COUNTRY

The remoteness of England's West Country has ensured its status as one of the most unspoilt areas of Britain's countryside. The temperate climate also allows for some superlative plant collections in the many beautiful gardens. The coastline has its own haunting history and the National Trust walks criss-cross coves, beaches and headlands.

In the summer months, Cornwall and Devon are far from deserted as many tourists make their way to this special corner of the country. To enjoy the real beauty of nature it is worth visiting the area out of season when the beaches are deserted and country lanes quiet. Only then can you appreciate the real peace and tranquillity of the place.

All manner of accommodation is to be found here, ranging from country house hotels to bed & breakfast in the local inn.

Devon, but more especially Cornwall, were the haunts of many smugglers, smuggling in contraband from across the Channel. Jamaica Inn may be the most famous hidey-hole, but everywhere you go there is much evidence of this shady past and tales of wrecking and intrigue are an integral part of the history of the country folk. The community centres around the sea and many small fishing villages remain unpoilt despite their often tragic history.

It was here the press gangs rampaged through the villages, pressing men into naval service. It is from here that many fishermen have sadly been lost at sea yet the stories of heroism are countless. It is here where the lifeboats put out to sea so often to rescue the unsuspecting from the clutches of the merciless waves.

Coastal paths link inlets and coves enjoying some of the most stunning coastal scenery.

In contrast to the sheltered coves and cosy pubs is the vast and unspeakable bleakness of Dartmoor and Exmoor. Beautiful in their own way, these awesome tracts of uncultivated scrubland are home to much wildlife. This is the home of Tarka the otter, Lorna Doone and many other feted characters.

The charm of Devon and Cornwall lies in its mystery. Sweep aside the swirling mists of Dartmoor and the coastal frets of the seaside and you will discover one of the most beautiful areas of Britain.

HOTELS OF DISTINCTION

ALSTON HALL, Holbeton, Devon. Tel:(075530) 555
Alston hall is a substantial Edwardian manor house, complete with oak-panelled hall and ballustraded minstrels' gallery. Set in formal gardens only 20 minutes drive from Plymouth.

ALVERTON MANOR, Truro, Cornwall. Tel: (0872) 76633
Alverton Manor, once a chapel, dates back over 150 years. This Grade II listed building is both elegant and comfortable, lovingly restored to its former glory. The Terrace Restaurant is first-class, serving 'English' food in a modern style.

THE ARUNDELL ARMS, Lifton, Devon. Tel:(0566) 84244
A 250 year old former coaching inn near Dartmoor, the Arundell Arms is one of England's best-known sporting hotels, with twenty miles of private fishing on the river Tamar and its own shooting.

THE BEL ALP HOUSE, Haytor, Devon. Tel:(0364) 661217/8
An elegant country retreat on the edge of Dartmoor with beautiful views towards the coast, twenty miles away. This is a relaxing family hotel, ideally located for exploring Devon and Cornwall.

COMBE HOUSE, Gittisham, Devon. Tel:(0404) 42756
A peaceful and secluded fourteenth-century Elizabethan mansion set in its own estate. The finely proportioned rooms are filled with antiques and the hotel makes an ideal retreat from which to explore Devon.

THE CORNISH ARMS, Pendogget, Cornwall.
Tel: (0208) 880263
This is an interesting old inn situated beside the B3314 road. It boasts beams, stone floors and considerable character. There are well furnished bedrooms mostly with ensuite bath or shower.

COULSWORTHY HOUSE HOTEL, Combe Martin, Devon.
Tel:(0271) 882463
A charming small hotel on the edge of the Exmoor National Park with commanding views to the sea. Offering family run comfort with a very high standard of cooking.

COURT BARN COUNTRY HOUSE HOTEL, Clawton, Devon.
Tel:(0409) 27219
A lovely Victorian manor house on a 14th century site, set in five acres of informal gardens. The hotel has won many awards for its outstanding cuisine and is luxuriously furnished with antiques.

DANESCOMBE VALLEY HOTEL, Calstock, Cornwall.
Tel: (0822) 832414
Built for Lord Ashburton, proudly shown and comfortable with good furniture, great views. Do book if you want to eat in the small restaurant with its superb and popular local produce.

DUNSFORD MILLS COUNTRY HOUSE HOTEL, Dunsford, Devon. Tel: (0647) 52011
A fully restored mill on the River Teign, inside the Dartmoor National Park, this hotel is an ideal base for visiting historic Exeter. A comfortable place, offering high-quality cuisine.

EASTON COURT HOTEL, Chagford, Devon.
Tel:(0647) 433469
A Grade II listed thatched country house with many historic and literary connections. The hotel has been lovingly restored and the many comforts include a superb library. It is conveniently situated for Castle Drogo.

FAIRWATER HEAD COUNTRY HOUSE HOTEL, Hawchurch, Devon. Tel: (0297) 349
Set in magnificent gardens on the borders of Dorset and Devon, this Edwardian country house enjoys panoramic views over the Axe valley. Convenient for many historic houses and gardens in the area.

FAIRWATER HEAD HOTEL

Tucked away amidst magnificent countryside on the borders of Dorset and Devon, the village of Hawkchurch with its flower filled lanes, sits high above the Axe Valley, just five miles from the coast.

Fairwater Head is a welcoming country house with 21 luxury ensuite bedrooms, award winning gardens and noted family hospitality. Superb food prepared by award winning chefs, and an absolute haven of peace and tranquility.

Within easy driving distance you can visit some of Britain's finest gardens and National Trust properties including Montacute, Killerton, Knightshayes, Forde Abbey and the sub-tropical gardens at Abbotsbury. The choice is endless.

The Lyme Regis Golf Club is just a short distance away and considered to be the most improved course in the West Country. The views across Lyme Bay are spectacular and the greens a joy to 'Putt' on. An expert greens staff and enthusiastic committee are aiming to create a championship course. Guests of Fairwater Head are given reduced green fees. Also worth playing are Honiton, Yeovil, and the East Devon at Budleigh Salterton.

Fairwater Head Country House Hotel
Hawkchurch
Axminster
Devon EX13 5TX
Tel: (029 77) 349

TREBREA LODGE

Overlooking the North Cornish Coast, renowned for its unparalleled beauty and grandeur, stands Trebrea Lodge.

Built in a dominant position and set in four and a half acres of wooded hillside, the house was lived in and improved by successive generations of the Brays for almost six hundred years. In the late 18th century John Bray enlarged the house and added the formal Georgian facade. However, the interior retains the feeling and warmth of an old Cornish Manor House.

Because of its historical and architectural interest, the house is now Grade II** listed.

Whilst maintaining the atmosphere of a private house, we have ensured that each of our eight bedrooms has all the conveniences of modern living. All have a private bathroom and an uninterrupted view across open fields to the Atlantic Ocean, less than a mile away.

A full English breakfast and four-course dinner is served in our oak panelled dining room. The menu changes daily and all the food is prepared and cooked by ourselves using the finest local ingredients; these include sea trout and wild salmon from the River Tamar.

There are many varied and interesting walks from Trebrea Lodge including some of the most spectacular and dramatic stretches of the Cornish coastal path. Nearby is Tintagel Island with its 12th century ruins, built, according to legend, on the site of King Arthur's birthplace.

A short distance inland is windswept Bodmin Moor, with many archaeological sites and stone circles.

Trebrea Lodge
Trenale
Tintagel
Cornwall PL34 OHR
Tel: (0840) 770410

THE WEST COUNTRY

FINGALS AT OLD COOMBE MANOR, Dittisham, Devon. Tel:(080422) 398
This elegant Queen Anne manor house provides the highest standards and comfort. The hotel offers many sporting activities and is conveniently situated for exploring the historic towns of Dartmouth and Totnes.

THE GEORGE, Hatherleigh, Devon. Tel: (0837) 810454
This cob and thatch building was founded in 1450 as a retreat for monks. It later became a coaching inn and is now widely frequented by farmers from the busy nearby market.

GIDLEIGH PARK, Chagford, Devon. Tel:(0647) 432367/225
Gidleigh Park in Dartmoor is renowned for its comfort and gastronomy, with many top culinary awards to its credit. Set in forty acres in the Teign Valley it offers numerous sporting facilities including fourteen miles of fishing.

GLAZEBROOK HOUSE HOTEL, South Brent, Devon. Tel:(0364) 73322
Resting in a four acre site within the beautiful Dartmoor National Park, this spacious mid-Victorian country house provides an elegant retreat for the discerning lover of tranquillity and seclusion.

GREAT TREE HOTEL, Chagford, Devon. Tel: (06473) 2491
Adapted from a hunting lodge, On the edge of Dartmoor, this adapted hunting lodge provides a quiet and secluded refuge amidst eighteen acres of gardens, orchards and paddocks. Delicous five course dinners and comfortable rooms. Central for racing, golfing, walking and exploring Devons heritage.

HALMPSTONE MANOR, Bishops Taunton, Devon. Tel:(0271) 830321
This country house hotel is set in 200 acres and provides an ideal escape with luxurious service, accommodation and cuisine. A perfect base for exploring the West Country.

HAMLYNS, Blacklands, Devon. Tel:(075537) 219
Isambard Kingdom Brunel not only designed this hotel, but stayed here during the building of his historic Great Western Railway. The beauty of the Devonshire countryside is just outside the door.

HOTEL TRESANTON, St Mawes, Cornwall. Tel:(0326) 270544
Time slows as one enters this charming Cornish village and the picturesque Tresanton is ideal for those seeking pure relaxation. Nearby are National Trust gardens, St Mawes castle and the sleepy harbour.

HUNTSHAM COURT, Huntsham, Devon. Tel: (039 86) 210
A highly relaxed hotel within a rather gaunt Victorian building. The interior has a wonderful atmosphere, from the splendid furniture in the panelled Great Hall to pre-war radios in the rooms.

LEWTRENCHARD MANOR, Lewdown, Devon. Tel:(0566) 83256
An imaginatively restored 17th century country manor house set in eleven acres of grounds. The splendid panelled restaurant has a fine reputation and the hotel offers many sporting and leisure facilities.

LOBSTER POT, Mousehole, Cornwall. Tel: (0756) 731251
A warren of rooms posing as an inn, its darkened mysterious corners and hidden spaces fill it with character. Very popular restaurant with a veranda overhanging the harbour.

LOWER PITT, East Buckland, Devon. Tel: (059 86) 243
The delightful seclusion of this ancient stone farmhouse restaurant makes the difficulty of finding it all the more charming on arrival. Resting in its North Devon hamlet, the homeliness is accentuated by real log fire.

THE LUGGER HOTEL, Portloe, Cornwall. Tel:(0872) 501322
Originally a 17th century smuggler's inn, this hotel sits at the very water's edge of a beautiful Cornish cove. With four crowns from the English Tourist Board, the Lugger commands fabulous seaward views from the Roseland Peninsula.

MASONS ARMS, Branscombe, Devon. Tel: (029780) 300
700 years of drinking and eating have left their mark on this old inn - quaint and with comfortable bedrooms in rolling Devon.

MEUDON HOTEL, Mawnan Smith, Cornwall. Tel: (0326) 250541
This former manor house, set in 'Capability Brown' designed sub-tropical gardens, has been stylishly refurbished to provide comfort, warmth and considerable charm. A new bedroom wing has been added in which modernity takes over, so there are ensuite bathrooms and TV. Menus are French and English.

NANSIDWELL COUNTRY HOUSE, Mawnan Smith, Cornwall. Tel:(0326) 250340
An unspoilt country mansion set in sub-tropical gardens leading to the sea, and surrounded by National Trust coastline, this hotel is tastefully furnished and specialises in excellent local seafood cuisine. There are several historic houses nearby.

OLD MILL, Ide, Devon. Tel: (0392) 59480
In the heart of this charming little village, this pretty 16th century mill provides very pleasant surroundings for the enjoyable sea-food which features prominently on the menu.

POLHAWN FORT, Rame, Cornwall. Tel:(0752) 822864
Originally a Napoleonic sea fortress, this carefully preserved hotel is a haven amidst the remote wilds of the breathtaking Cornish coastline. The bedrooms have flag-stoned floors and hold magnificent views over the sea.

RISING SUN, Lynmouth, Devon. Tel: (0598) 53223
A former pub has been transformed along with adjacent cottages into a charming hotel. There are terraced gardens, thatched roof and some fine sea views. The bedrooms are comfortable and include a delightful, self-contained private suite. Local seafood and game are a feature of the menus.

THE ROYAL BEACON, Exmouth, Devon. Tel: (0395) 264886
Originally a Georgian posting house, the Royal Beacon maintains a tradition of hospitality. Facing south, the hotel affords views across the gardens down to the beach and the Devon coastline.

THE BEL ALP HOUSE

Through the changing seasons, The Bel Alp House, owned and personally run by Roger and Sarah Curnock, enjoys breathtaking views from one of England's most spectacular and beautiful positions at 900 feet on the South Eastern edge of Dartmoor.

The Bel Alp was originally built as a private house and retains the atmosphere of a large family home. Since the Curnock family purchased it in 1983, they have restored the house to its former elegance. The beautiful arches that are such a feature of the house, the large, airy, light-filled rooms and the friendly atmosphere have all been enhanced by the careful use of warm colours, comfortable furniture, family antiques and paintings and an abundance of house plants.

The nine bedrooms are decorated and furnished in quiet, restful colours with the emphasis on comfort rather than glossy design. All have private bathrooms, colour television and direct dial telephones, with the majority enjoying the wonderful view. Two of the bedrooms are on the ground floor and there is a lift giving easy access to the others and to the beautiful garden.

One of Bel Alp's greatest attractions is Sarah's mouth-watering food, for which she has such a high, and growing, reputation. Each evening she prepares a different five course set dinner using the finest, fresh local produce and including a board of a dozen or so delicious Devon famhouse cheeses.

Dartmoor, Southern England's last great wilderness, is a wonderful area to explore by car, foot or horse. There are an abundance of pretty towns and villages and the famous names of Widecombe and Princetown are brought to life after travelling over tracts of open moorland. Throughout the year Dartmoor has its own magical beauty. In Summer and Autumn the tor-topped hills explode into colour with gorse and heather flower, while in Winter drifting mists roll away leaving crisp blue skies.

Being only 10 minutes from the A38, Bel Alp House is ideally situated for exploring the history and beautiful countryside of Devon and into Cornwall with many National Trust houses and gardens. It is perfect for attending racing at Devon and Exeter (10 miles) and Newton Abbot (8 miles). All of the very excellent South Devon Golf Courses are within easy reach, the nearest being St-over, near Newton Abbot, (5 miles) and The Manor House, near Moretonhampstead, (10 miles).

The Bel Alp House
Haytor
Nr. Bovey Tracey
Devon TQ13 9XX

Tel: 0364 661217

THE WEST COUNTRY

TREBREA, Trenale, Cornwall. Tel: (0840) 770410
This Grade II listed building is set in four and a half acres of wooded hillside, overlooking the North Cornish Coast. Nearby is Tingagel Island with its 12th century ruins.

TYTHERLEIGH COT HOTEL, Chardstock, Devon. Tel:(0460) 21170
A charming 14th century listed village house delightfully located in idyllic Devon landscape this, hotel has a friendly and relaxing atmosphere with outstanding modern cuisine.

ACCOMMODATION OF MERIT

BRIDGE FARM, Bridge Reeve, Devon. Tel: (0769) 80792
This classic thatched farmhouse, complete with the original beams, faces a courtyard surrounded by stables, barns and cottage garden within fifty acres of breathtaking countryside. Nearby is Tiverton Castle and numerous other interesting places. Booking essential.

CRUGSILLICK MANOR, St Mawes, Cornwall. Tel: (0872) 501214
A listed manor house built in the early 18th century and situated in the Roseland Peninsular with lovely views. Ideally placed for touring all the major Cornish historical houses and gardens, together with the beautiful coastline.

EAST CORNWALL FARMHOUSE, Fullaford Road, Cornwall. Tel: (0579) 50018
A former Court House set in the beautiful Silver Valley. All bedrooms have colour TV and tea/coffee making facilities and two are ensuite. Cotehele House is only two miles away, whilst for golfers the tremendous St Mellion complex is only ten minutes drive.

ERTH BARTON, Saltash, Cornwall. Tel: (0752) 842127
This beautiful manor house has been inhabited since Edward III's reign. Standing on the private peninsular of the Lynher Estuary. It has massive oak doors, stone mullions, and is a Site of Special Scientific Interest. Central for touring Cornwall and Devon. Booking essential. (See photograph).

GATE HOUSE, North Bovey, Devon. Tel: (0647) 40479
Fine medieval thatched Devon Longhouse, built mid-fifteenth century. Original beams, granite fireplace and bread oven all add to the welcoming atmosphere. North Bovey, a classic Dartmoor village, is central for most historical sites of Devon. Booking essential.

MIXTON HOUSE, Lerryn, Cornwall. Tel: (0208) 872781
Classical Georgian country house in two acres of secluded gardens overlooking the beautiful Lerryn River Valley. Grass tennis court and a boat are available and it is conveniently situated for exploring the south coast and all of Cornwall's fascinating heritage.

OAKFIELD, Chudleigh, Devon. Tel: (0626) 852194
This large country house, built in 1850, still retains the original woodwork on the eaves. It is in Chudleigh, an ancient wool town, and with its heated pool, orchards, formal garden and paddocks is a perfect stop for Exeter, Dartmoor and Southern coast. Booking essential.

ROSEBUD COTTAGE, Bossiney, Cornwall.
Tel: (0840) 770861
Picturesque Cornish stone cottage with a peaceful garden, near Bassiney Cove. Ideally situated for exploring Tintagel Castle on the Atlantic coast and other places of heritage in Cornwall, with exciting forays into Devon.

Erth Barton

ROYAL BEACON HOTEL

Situated in Exmouth, the oldest seaside resort in Devon, the Royal Beacon has long been established as a premier hotel. An elegant building, it was originally a Georgian posting house. The early traditions of hospitality, good fare and comfort have continued throughout the years, adapting, evolving and modernising to meet the expectations of today's sophisticated guests.

The quiet location is magnificent, facing south and looking down across our own gardens immediately to the beach, the sea and the Devon coastline.

Beautiful surroundings and comfortable furnishings are not everything - our staff create the real atmosphere. Courtesy, friendliness and professionalism are a matter of pride for them all.

The lounge and bar are spacious and there is a superb snooker room for the enthusiast ... and outside there's Devon! The perfect place for windsurfing, bird-watching, fishing, walking, visiting the theatre or playing a round of golf. Exmouth is an ideal centre from which to explore an area rich in natural and man-made beauty from the estuary's flocks of sea birds and the beautiful flower and tree displays at Bicton Gardens to the colour and excitement of Exeter Maritime Museum or the splendour of Exeter Cathedral.

End the day at the hotel's exceptional Fennels Restaurant which reflects the Victorian period in its charm and elegance. Traditional Devon cream teas are served in the afternoon and in the evening you are invited to choose from our thoughtfully planned table d'hotel or extensive a la carte menu complemented by fine wines.

Retire for the night to one of the Royal Beacon's superbly appointed, spacious rooms, many of which enjoy sea views. All have en suite facilities and colour television, radio, direct line telephone, tea and coffee making facilities, hair drier and trouser press. Each room has its own distinctive style and individuality.

Royal Beacon Hotel
The Beacon
Exmouth
Devon
EX8 2AF
Tel: (0395) 264886/265269
Fax: (0395) 268890

THE WEST COUNTRY

SILKHOUSE, Drewsteignton, Devon. Tel: (064 723) 267
Near Drewsteignton this 16th century longhouse, named by the Huguenots, creates a peaceful retreat with beamed ceilings, granite fireplaces, beautiful cottage gardens and acres of fields, woods and streams. This is a delightful and romantic base for exploring Devon. (See photograph).

INNS OF CHARACTER

BLUE ANCHOR, Helston, Cornwall.
Formerly a monks' rest home, this 15th century brewing house is now probably the oldest of its kind. Still serving its own brew along with a variety of snacks, this fascinating inn is well worth visting.

BUSH, Morwenstow, Cornwall.
This warm and inviting little pub is one of Britain's very oldest, parts of it dating back to the 10th century. In an idyllic location within a short walk of the Cornish coast it offers good bar food, traditional ales and local cider.

CARPENTER ARMS, Methwell, Cornwall.
Good value bar food and fine ales are available at this delightful 15th century village pub. Beams, flagstones and thick walls abound to create a rustic and warm atmosphere. The close proximity of Cotehele, a National Trust Tudor house, adds a further attraction to this well-located inn.

THE CHERUB, Dartmouth, Devon.
Heavy creaky beams from ships' timbers dominate this superb old pub dating back to around 1830. It certainly merits its official Grade I status, offering splendid food, a selection of fine ales and 52 malt whiskies.

CORNISH ARMS, St Merryn, Cornwall.
Dating back some 700 years this pub is full of character. The simple, yet delightful, furnishings of flagstones and ancient stonework contrast with the robust mahogany bar to create a quiet, homely atmosphere. Reliable bar food and real ale come at sensible prices.

NOBODY INN, Doddiscombleigh, Devon.
This atmospheric 16th century pub has a reputation for its impressive selection of wines, whiskies and fine ales, not to mention the outstanding bar food. Attractively furnished in contemporary style, the pub also offers views over the spectacular local scenery.

PILCHARD, Burgh Island, Devon.
A cosy atmosphere is the hallmark of this popular, family-owned 12th century pub. With a panoramic view across local sands, the pub is heavily beamed and is lit by old ships' lamps hanging from the ceiling. Reliable bar food and evening seafood are most popular.

Silk House

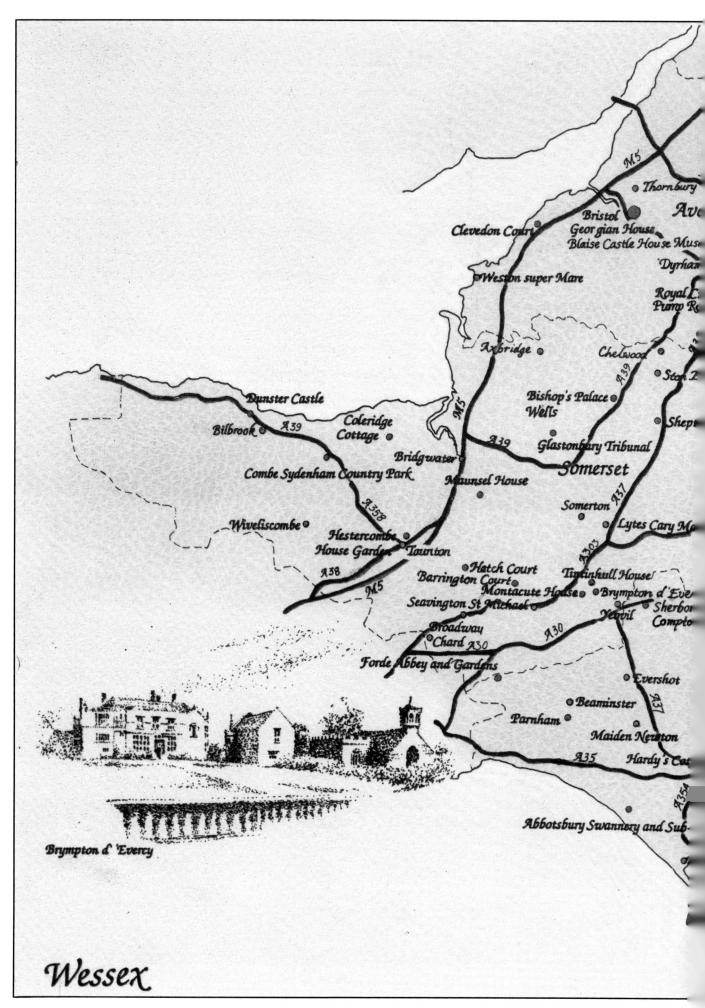

Thornbury

Ave

Bristol
Clevedon Cotri
Georgian House
Blaise Castle House Muse

Dyrham

Weston super Mare

Royal E.
Pump R.

Axbridge
Chelwood

Sto. 2

Bishop's Palace
Wells

Shep

Dunster Castle

Bilbrook
A39
Coleridge
Cottage

Glastonbury Tribunal

Bridgwater
Somerset

Combe Sydenham Country Park

Maunsel House

Somerton

Lytes Cary M.

Wiveliscombe
A358

Hestercombe
House Garden
Taunton

Tintinhull House

A38
Hatch Court
Barrington Court
Montacute House
Brympton d'Eve
M5
Seavington St Michael
Sherbo.
Compto.
Yeovil

Broadway
Chard
A30
A30
Forde Abbey and Gardens

Evershot

Beaminster
Parnham
A37
Maiden Newton
A35
Hardy's Cot.
A35A

Abbotsbury Swannery and Sub.

Brympton d'Evercy

Wessex

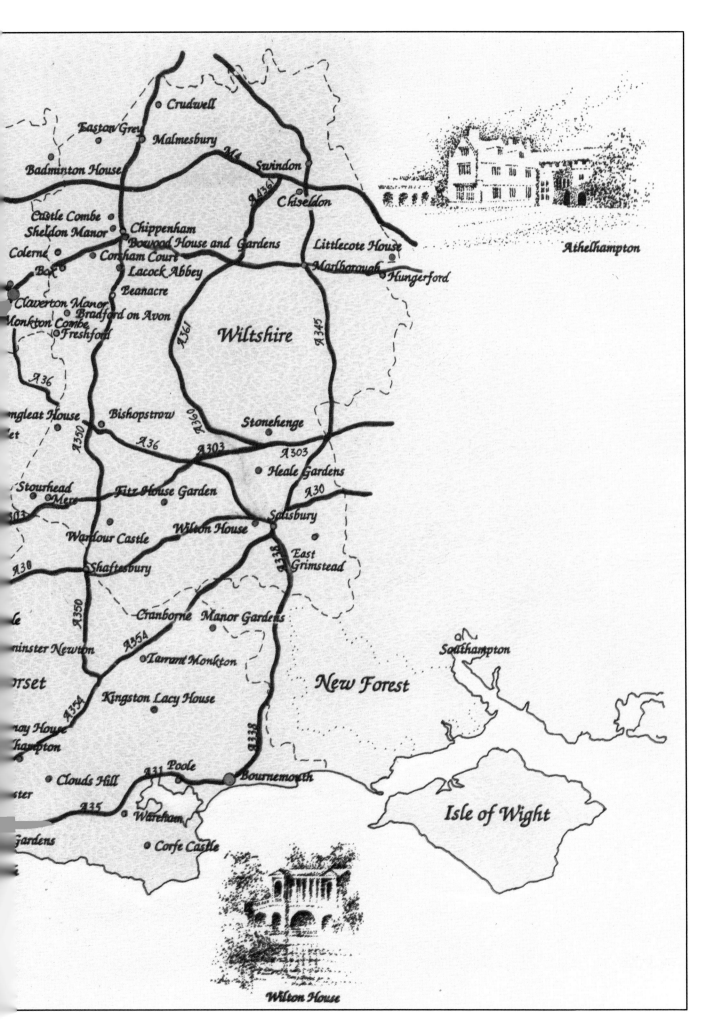

Crudwell

Easton Grey
Malmesbury

M4

Badminton House Swindon

A4361

Chiseldon

Castle Combe
Sheldon Manor Chippenham
Bowood House and Gardens Littlecote House
Colerne Corsham Court
Box Lacock Abbey Marlborough
Hungerford
Beanacre
Claverton Manor
Monkton Combe Bradford on Avon
Freshford A361 Wiltshire A345

A36

A350

Bishopstrow A360
Stonehenge
ngleat House A36
et A303 A303

Stourhead Heale Gardens
Mere Fitz House Garden A30

A303 Salisbury
Wardour Castle Wilton House
A338 East
A30 Grimstead

A350 Shaftesbury

A354 Cranborne Manor Gardens

Southampton
minster Newton Tarrant Monkton

A354 New Forest

orset
A354 Kingston Lacy House

A338

ay House
hampton

A31 Poole
Clouds Hill Bournemouth
ster

A35 Wareham Isle of Wight

Gardens Corfe Castle

Athelhampton

Wilton House

29

WESSEX

ROMAN BATHS TO BADMINTON

The Roman spa city of Bath is one of the most beautiful cities in England. Situated on the river Avon between the Cotswold and Mendip Hills, with its 2000 years of history Bath will not cease to amaze you. Primarily the origins of Bath come from the hot springs when the Romans discovered that the water had healing powers. It was at this time that the sophisticated Baths were built and, apart from Hadrian's Wall, remain Britain's greatest monument to the Roman Empire.

Bath has not always been an attractive place despite the many visitors the Roman Baths attracted, which eventually created more wealth than the established wool industry. The sanitation was appalling and thieving was a great problem, but in the 18th century this started to change, the Baths became a social centre as well as a place for healing.

Beau Nash, a stylish young man, controlled the social scene for Bath, but it was Ralph Allen and architect John Ward who were responsible for the creation of the beautiful Georgian city. Ralph Allen purchased two limestone quarries and with the building material available they built an unforgettable city.

The Baths are situated in the centre of the town adjacent to Bath Abbey which provide a fascinating history of Roman times, the many treasures retrieved from the ground are in the adjoining **Roman Baths Museum**.

Part of the great Bath complex is the Pump Room, whose building dates back to 1796 when the town hall decided a bigger room was needed than the one used in the dandy days of Nash.

The interior remains unchanged, and one can enjoy drinking spa water here whilst listening to soft chamber music. What a wonderful experience! When the Pump Room was re-built in 1790 the first significant traces of Roman public buildings were discovered after the uncovering of the temple steps and parts of the highly ornamented temple front. It was the beginning of the exciting rediscovery of Roman Baths. Apart from the hot waters which still flow today and the Roman remains, the museum contains fine carvings from the temple of Sun's Minerva and the head of the cult statue.

Those interested in architecture must visit the spectacular **Royal Crescent** which consists of thirty very sophisticated houses, fronted by Ionic columns. This was the first terrace to be built as a crescent and remains a fine example of its kind in Europe. Visit **Number 1 Royal Crescent** whose interior has been restored in an authentic setting displaying Georgian furnishings.

Sir Winston Churchill made his first political speech at **Claverton Manor** just outside Bath on July 26 1897. The house, built of Bath stone, is situated above the valley of the River Avon and was designed by George IV's architect, Sir Jeffrey Wyatville, in 1820. Claverton Manor has the only comprehensive Museum of Americana in Europe. It shows through a series of completely furnished rooms how Americans lived from the 17th to the 19th centuries.

There are beautiful gardens which feature unusual items of interest such as one stage waggon and an Indian teepee. There is the art collection in the Old Stables and a replica of George Washington's magnificent rose and flower garden at Mount Vernon, Virginia.

Number 1 Royal Crescent

WESSEX

Another interesting museum well worth a visit is the **Holburne Museum** at the far end of Pulteney Street, one of Bath's most elegant Georgian streets, where a unique combination of ancient and modern can be discovered. The magnificent building was originally built as the Sydney Hotel in the late 18th century and then adapted for the purposes of a museum by Sir Reginald Blomfield between 1913 and 1916. It stands in its own grounds and contains a superb collection of decorative and fine art made by Sir Thomas William Holburne (1792-1874).

The collection includes English and Continental silver and porcelain, Italian maiolica and bronzes together with glass, furniture, miniatures and Old Master paintings by artists such as Gainsborough, Stubbs, Turner and Zoffany, to name but a few. Since Holburne's time the collection has been added to by gifts and bequests, with the emphasis still on the 17th and 18th centuries. This historic collection is displayed together with work by 20th century artist-crafts people in the Crafts Study Centre which opened within the museum in 1977. It contains a superb collection and archive of ceramics, woven and printed textiles, calligraphy and furniture mainly built up from donations. Bernard Leach gave the Centre nearly 100 of his pots together with pieces he had collected in Japan, Korea and China and also bequeathed all his papers to the collection. In 1987 the Crafts Council agreed to place on long loan some 100 exhibits from their collection now on display within the museum. This substantial addition means that the Holburne is able to lead the field in showing work by British artist-crafts people from 1900 to the present day.

Dyrham Park is the property of the National Trust. The house, built between 1691 and 1702 overlooks a spectacular 263 acre

Holburne Museum

deer park. The furnishings in the house remain the same as when William Blathwayt, who was Secretary of War to William III, first completed them. Blathwayt frequently visited Holland purchasing furnishings and the famous blue and white Delftware. Enjoy the beautiful bird painting by Hondecoeter, leather wall hangings from The Hague and from the west front of the house glorious views towards the Bristol countryside. Blathwayt used the services of William Talman who was Wren's second in command to construct the east wing, where you can see the state rooms and the Blathwayt Eagle. Resembling Versailles with its massive Tuscan columns is the Orangery which is attached to the house. There are formal gardens featuring terraces and fountains and the deer park dating from the 18th century remains unchanged.

Moving on to the Three Day Event at Badminton in April or May, gives you the chance to see the magnificent Palladian **Badminton House** which is rarely open.

If you is interested in beautiful historic costumes then the **Museum of Costume** is a must. Situated close to The Circus are the **Assembly Rooms** which were built in 1769 by architect John Wood who was popular in the 18th century. The ground floor houses the internationally famous museum of costume which has a splendid collection of fashions from the late 16th century to the present. Included in this collection is the awesome rare silver dress of c.1660. The chandeliers in the Assembly Rooms are original and quite stunning.

BRISTOL

We travel now to the ancient port of Bristol, which is still a busy port; in the summer there are festivals and water events of all kinds.

St Mary Redcliffe, one of England's greatest parish churches can be visited in Bristol's old city centre. The cathedral, with its many treasures, stands on College Green and if you enjoy spectacular ruins then go to Cabot Tower - you will not be disappointed. Whilst visiting Bristol drive west along the Avon Gorge to the elegant suburbs of Clifton, and Brunel's dramatic Clifton Suspension Bridge which spans the Gorge 250 feet up. At Clifton enjoy walking around York Crescent and visit the Roman Catholic Cathedral whose interior, although modern, is brilliant. By crossing the Suspension Bridge - hold tight - you will reach the Avon Gorge Nature Reserve and Leigh Woods which both have lovely walks.

Just outside Bristol is the spectacular **Blaise Castle Estate** which adjoins the village of Henbury and has over 400 acres of wonderful varied scenery. Human occupation dates back to c.3000-c.2000 BC and during the Iron Age there was a hill fort on **Blaise Castle Hill** which, in the Middle Ages, was thought to have been the site of a chapel dedicated to St Blaise, the patron saint of Woolcombers. This is how the estate has its name. The house was designed in 1796 by Paty and there is a museum which displays many aspects of everyday life, including domestic furnishings and equipment. The collection of packaging from the chocolate manufacturers J.S.Fry & Son, watches and many other exhibits illustrate in great detail some of the industries of Bristol. Pictures and prints in the Dining Room convey Blaise Estate's history.

The Georgian House in Great George Street is well worth a visit to savour the atmosphere of this merchant's town house. Completed in 1791 it is furnished in the style of the period both above and below stairs.

If you travel one and a half miles east of Clevedon on the Bristol road you will come to the National Trust's **Clevedon Court**. It is an amazing 14th century manor house with a chapel and tower. The house remains virtually unchanged, although in the 18th century its owner provided the great hall with an upper storey. The Eton family who were the former owners were

Museum of costume & fashion, Bath.

quite a literary family and Thackeray, the novelist, was a visitor. Arthur Hallam, a close friend of the poet Tennyson, was buried in Clevedon church a fact which Tennyson recorded in 'In Memoriam'. Clevedon has beautiful gardens, also dating back to the 18th century and a fascinating collection of glass for which nearby Nailsea was famous.

DORSET: HARDY COUNTRY

We travel now to Dorset which is quite often known as Hardy country; inland Dorset is the home of Thomas Hardy and it was here he found inspiration for novels like 'The Mayor of Casterbridge'. At Higher Bockhampton you can see the cottage where Hardy was born. The pretty thatched villages, lovely heaths, ancient trackways and rolling chalk hills have not changed much from the landscape he wrote about. Almost the whole of Dorset is designated as an Area of Outstanding Natural Beauty. The pretty sandy bays and rich coastline of Weymouth, which is the county's most popular resort, are wonderful for long walks and were a great favourite with George III. The pebbled ridge of Chesil Beach can be reached by walking from Studland and on to Lyme Regis where you will find many fossil hunters. This glorious county has something beautiful for everyone to enjoy. Visit **Athelhampton**, which is one of the loveliest medieval houses in England, with 10 acres of formal and landscape gardens to enjoy (featured later).

When Lawrence of Arabia, the legend of the First World War, was in the RAF in 1925 at Bovington he bought a little brick and tile cottage on the slopes of **Clouds Hill**. Used as a peaceful retreat, the rooms with their simple furnishings remain very much as Lawrence left them, particularly the book room which is packed full of his books. The old wind-up gramophone that played his favourite Beethoven and Mozart can be found in the Music Room. When he was discharged from the airforce in 1935 at the age of 46 it was to Clouds Hill that he returned, only to be tragically killed five days later in a motorcycle accident.

After mourning the tragic Lawrence of Arabia we move on to the home of the famous author Thomas Hardy. Hardy's cottage is three miles north east of Dorchester, half a mile south of the A35 in a pretty village called **Higher Bockhampton**. Hardy was born in 1840 in a bedroom which looks east towards Egdon Heath. Every day he walked six miles to Dorchester to attend school. After his success with 'Far from the Madding Crowd', published in 1874, Hardy devoted his time to writing. Also at this time he left the cottage for a disastrous marriage to Emma Gifford, which provided him with inspiration for many of his moving poems. The pretty garden is full of pansies, lupins, marigolds and much more, giving a warm country feeling.

On the South Downs of Dorset you can see a monument to Vice Admiral Sir Thomas Masterman Hardy, Flag Captain of the Victory at Trafalgar, who was immortalised by Nelson's dying words. Erected in 1846 and designed by A.D. Troyte, it stands on the Black Downs.

Located on the western end of Chesil Beach is the picturesque village of Abbotsbury. Made up of pretty yellow stone and thatched cottages it offers many attractions. There is a fascinating medieval tithe barn which is the only remains of a Benedictine abbey. Behind the village on a hill stands St Catherine's

WESSEX

Chapel which was built by the monks in the 15th century. This vantage point gives a view of the beautiful surrounding countryside. The monks also established the Swannery which is today the largest in England. Existing now for more than six centuries, the Swannery is a safe place for breeding for the hundreds of mute swans and species of wild fowl. The subtropical gardens provide early spring displays of camellias, azaleas, rhododendrons and magnolias. There are also unusual trees and rare shrubs to see whilst watching the peacocks strutting proudly.

THE BLACKMOOR VALE

Up into the hills we travel into the rich country of the Blackmoor Vale.

Parnham House, just south of Beaminster, offers more to look at than the history of the house. It is the home of John Makepeace, the internationally renowned maker and designer of fine furniture. Pieces of his outstanding furniture are shown in the house. Originally re-built in 1540, Parnham was enlarged with great guidance from architect John Nash in 1810. The Tudor oak-beamed ceiling in the Great Hall along with the huge fireplace is very grand and there are intricate plaster ceilings and friezes from several periods. This rather mellow house is set in fourteen acres of beautiful gardens, some very formal with a lions head fountain and others more intimate. The Italian Garden is especially pretty with a lily pool and a colourful display of azaleas and rhododendrons.

Forde Abbey and gardens near Chard are well worth a visit. This Cistercian monastery , founded in 1140, was converted into a private house in the mid 17th century (featured later).

Sherborne Castle is an impressive 16th century mansion built by Sir Walter Raleigh which has been in continuous occupation since 1617 by the Digby family (featured later).

Compton House for the past 25 years, has been the home of many unrivalled species of butterflies. This grand 16th century Tudor-style front is set in peaceful surroundings complete with its own 13th century church. If you are a butterfly fanatic you can see all the stages of their development, and if you want to start your own collection you can buy the eggs and caterpillars. Another attraction here is the **Lullingstone Silk Farm** which produced the silk for the Prince and Princess of Wales' wedding.

DORSET DOWNS

All garden lovers should take a trip to **Cranborne Manor Gardens** in Wimborne. These especially lovely gardens were laid out by John Tradescant in the 17th century and somewhat enlarged in the 20th century. They feature a variety of gardens such as a White garden, Herb, Mount and Knot garden which is planted with Elizabethan flowers and the beautiful wild and water gardens. Rare and uncommon plants and old fashioned species roses can be purchased.

Kingston Lacy, owned by the National Trust, is one of the most beautiful properties to visit. It originates from the 17th century but in the 18th and 19th centuries changes were made by experts to the house and park. William John Bannes (1786-1855) was responsible for the Italianate Palazzo look with the

pictures and works of art he acquired whilst travelling. There is a magnificent marble staircase which leads up to the principal rooms on the first floor. The Spanish Room is outstanding with wonderful gilded leather hangings and a coffered ceiling.

In the centre of Kingston Lacy is the beautiful 250 acre park which is landscaped in 18th century style. The Trust restored the Edwardian Garden where to the west of the house, forget-me-nots and wallflowers grow in spring time. There are many enjoyable guided walks around this lovely estate.

SOMERSET

We take you now to the varied landscape of Somerset with the wildness of Exmoor Park and the pretty scenery of Sedgemoor it has much to offer, including the unspoilt villages of Dunster, Dulverton and Porlock and the picturesque harbour town of Watchet, further east lies Taunton in the Vale of Taunton. At the foot of the Quantocks is England's smallest cathedral city, Wells, which is north of the county. Set against the impressive background of the Mendip Hills, is the magnificent Cheddar Gorge and Wookey Hole caves; travelling south the pretty town of Glastonbury with its mysterious Abbey ruins complete with legendary tales can be found. The towns of Wincanton and Ilminster, all situated in this lovely countryside, offer many historic sites to enjoy.

YEOVIL TO THE VALE OF TAUNTON

Brympton d'Evercy is an outstanding mansion house with 17th century south front and Tudor west front. There are impressive state rooms, extensive gardens, a vineyard and much more (featured later).

Montacute House, owned by the National Trust, is in Montacute Village, four miles west of Yeovil. This magnificent house was built of Ham Hill stone in the 1590s by Sir Edward Phillips and it was probably finished in 1601. This Elizabethan house was designed by William Arnold, a local stone mason, includes wonderful carved statues, open stone parapets, twisted pinnacles and a decorated entrance porch. The Gallery, which has a reputation for being the largest of its kind in England, has on permanent loan from The National Portrait Gallery, a collection of Tudor and Jacobean portraits. The Great Hall is very impressive with its stained glass and stone screen. There is a formal walled garden which looks out on to open parkland.

We move to **Barrington Court**, Montacute's neighbour, also owned by The National Trust. Built in the 16th century this house, although not as grand as Montacute, is still very charming with a hint of romance and fantasy. Although few internal features have survived, Barrington has displays of period and reproduction furniture. There is a magical garden which is laid out within the Elizabethan courtyards in a series of outdoor rooms. You can still see the inspirational work of Gertrude Jekyll in the raised beds and the various colour schemes with marigolds, azaleas, wallflowers and dahlias.

Hatch Court near Taunton is a very grand Palladian-style mansion made of Bath stone, designed by Thomas Prowse of Axbridge in 1755. Much of the interior decoration was carried out in around 1800 along with the erection of the magnificent stone staircase. Hatch Court has an outstanding collection of pictures and a rather interesting semi-circular China Room; complete with Deer Park it commands fabulous views of Somerset.

Lytes Cary Manor bears the name of the family who lived here for 500 years from the 13th to the 18th century. Owned by the National Trust it is a mile north of the Ilchester bypass. This rather magical house is built round a courtyard, with the Lyte family swan crowning the entrance porch, wings half raised as if to defend. The oldest feature of Lytes Cary is the simple chapel attached to the house, built in c.1343 by Peter Lyte. After the Lytes departed in 1748 and the house was neglected, Sir Walter Jenner rescued it this century and furnished it with 17th and 18th century oak pieces and medieval fabrics. Sir Walter was the inspiration behind the Elizabethan style garden.

Travel five miles north west of Yeovil and half a mile south of the A303 to find **Tintinhull**, the beautiful gardens owned by The National Trust. There are many varied borders and walled gardens divided by clipped hedges. The 17th and early 18th century house can be seen overlooking one of Tintinhull's wonderful features, a grassy walled forecourt guarded by stone eagles, high on a gate. This charming garden was created this century by Mrs Reiss who moved here in 1933. To the keen plantsman there are many individual species to enjoy. The overall effect of the garden is magnificent and well worth a visit.

THE QUANTOCKS

Combe Sydenham Hall

The Quantock Hills lie west of Bridgewater and north of Taunton, rising to 1,250 feet. This once bleak and dreary moorland is now well wooded and if you enjoy hill walking then the Quantocks will definitely present a challenge. At the foot of the hills there are charming villages and churches to explore, such as Stogarsey, a Norman survival, Goathurst, Spaxton and Combe Florey. The hills have had their share of famous people, 'The Ancient Mariner' and 'Christabel' were written between 1796 and 1803 when Samuel Taylor Coleridge lived north of the Quantock Hills in Nether Stovey. William and Dorothy Wordsworth lived in Alfoxton Park in 1797 which resulted in the book 'Lyrical Ballads'.

Four miles north east of Taunton there are lovely views across the Vale of Taunton Deane from **Hestercombe House and Garden**. The house, dating back from the 1870s, has a magnificent hallway and wooden staircase. Hestercombe's main attraction is the historic multi level garden laid out at the turn of this century by Sir Edwin Lutyens; Miss Gertrude Jekyll was responsible for all the planting. Somerset Council over the last ten years have restored the gardens to their original form. On the east side of the garden is the magnificent Orangery and there is attractive stonework with a long pergola supported by stone pillars.

If visiting Hestercombe one could combine it with a visit to **Combe Sydenham Hall** which is near Taunton. Built on the site of a monastic settlement in 1580, it was the home of Elizabeth Sydenham and her husband Sir Francis Drake. The Cannon Ball associated with their wedding and the beautifully restored courtroom are of interest. There are lovely walks in the woodland and. Combe Sydenham also has a beautiful deer park and corn mill to enjoy.

The unspoilt village of Dunster two miles from Minehead is dominated by the National Trust's **Dunster Castle**. Commanding excellent views of the Bristol Channel, Quantock Hills and Exmoor the castle is surrounded by trees. It was created by Antony Salvin in from 1868 to 1872 for George Fownes Luttrell. There are beautiful 17th century plasterwork ceilings and a lovely carved balustraded staircase depicting a stag hunt. The 17th century painted leather hangings illustrate the story of Anthony and Cleopatra and can be found in Salvin's gallery. In the gardens there are olive trees, palms and a lemon tree which in summer is laden with fruit. Despite being exposed to westerly winds, the mild climate allows tender plants and shrubs to grow.

Coleridge Cottage is where Samuel Taylor Coleridge lived with his wife Sara and son Hartley for three years from 1797. Although once a pretty thatched cottage, it was altered quite substantially at the end of the 19th century. Some of Coleridge's best poems were written here including 'Tears in Solitude', 'This Lime Tree Bower my Prison' and 'Frost at Midnight'. There are many mementoes of the poet displayed in this charming cottage.

We travel now to the home of Sir Benjamin and Lady Slade, **Maunsel House** which is in North Newton, near Bridgewater. Parts of the house were built before the Norman Conquest but most of it is built around a Hall erected in 1420. In 1086 the manor was called 'Mannsel', being derived from the French meaning 'Sleave of land'. It was then granted to Count Eustace of Boulogne, kinsman of William the Conqueror. Geoffrey

WESSEX

Chaucer wrote part of 'The Canterbury Tales' whilst on one of his frequent visits.

NORTH TO THE MENDIPS

On now to Glastonbury where, if you are feeling energetic, you can climb the steep conical hill Glastonbury Tor, which rises up out of the flat Somerset Plain. From the top it will be worth it for the magnificent views. You can see Brean Down and the island of Sleep Holm, the Quantocks, Exmoor and much of Dorset. At the foot of the Tor is Chalice Well, where Joseph is supposed to have buried the Holy Grail.

One of Glastonbury's main attractions is the ruined **Abbey**, although little of its history is known it is one of the richest and most famous in England. St Mary's Chapel, the abbey church and various monastic buildings make up the ruins we see today. Abbots Kitchen is the fascinating kitchen, built in the 14th century, it still stands intact with its vaulted domed roof and a fireplace in each corner. In the gatehouse is a model of the abbey as it was in 1539. Relics of pre-mechanised farming in Somerset can be seen in the Somerset Rural Life Museum in what was once the principal Tithe Barn of the abbey. Both King Arthur and Queen Guinevere were supposed to have been buried in the abbey, and another story says that St Patrick was one of the first abbots here.

The Bishop's Palace in Wells is not to be missed, with its fortified walls and moat, Jocelins Hall (early 13th century), the Bishop's Chapel and the Banqueting Hall ruins. The Bishop's residence is outstanding. Wells derives its name from the wells in the gardens at Bishop's Palace. The grounds, in a beautiful setting, have many lovely herbaceous plants, roses, shrubs, mature trees and the Jubilee Arboretum. On the moat the swans and water fowl make elegant viewing.

Set against the background of the Mendips is the spectacular **Cheddar Gorge** and nearby **Wookey Hole Caves**. A guided tour leads through the caverns and becomes slightly eerie when it reaches a strangely shaped rock known as The Witch of Wookey, so beware! The River Axe emerges at Wookey Hole and these limestone caverns have been a magnet for explorers everywhere. After visiting the caves one can see the long established paper mill, which will show a recreation of a traditional fairground by night.

WILTSHIRE

Wiltshire is the home of ancient man, evidence of the earliest inhabitants can be seen at prehistoric sites throughout, including Avebury and Stonehenge. The rolling hills and lush green valleys are the homes of many great houses, often set in beautiful parklands. Wiltshire, noted for its open spaces and wonderful landscapes, has many historic attractions. Note the 404 foot high Cathedral spire which dominates the historic city of Salisbury. In the south lies the vast expanse of Salisbury Plain, on the edge of which a huge white chalk horse has been carved out into the steep slope of Bratton Down. This original saxon horse was re-modelled in 1778 from 'cartbreed' to blood breed.

The Marquis of Bath claims there is something for everyone at Longleat. This definitely applies to the beautiful county of Wiltshire.

STONEHENGE & SALISBURY PLAIN

Stonehenge, one of the most impressive megalithic monuments in Europe is situated on the broad expanse of Salisbury Plain, to the west of Amesbury (featured later).

Stourhead House and gardens are definitely worth visiting. One could spend days here and still not see everything. The fine Palladian mansion built for wealthy banker Henry Hoare in the early 18th century stands on a ridge of the Wiltshire Downs, somewhat overshadowed by the magical gardens. Created by Henry Hoare in 1741, they are acknowledged as having one of the finest layouts in Europe.

In the late spring the rhododendrons provide a mass of exotic colour to this 2,600 acre estate. There are many magnificent trees, beeches, oaks, Norwegian maple, tulip trees, cedars and many other exotics. You will find that every tree, shrub or flower is planted overlooking splendid views. There are classical temples, lakes, grottoes, statues, pretty bridges expressing a taste of ancient Greece and Rome and creating the impression of a painting come to life. The view from King Alfred's tower, which is said to mark the spot where he stood against the Danes in 879 is worth the 150 foot climb on to Kingsettle Hill. The mansion built in 1721 by Colin Campbell is worth a visit. Both the mansion and park are part of the village of Stourton which stands at the park entrance. They are all now in the safe hands of The National Trust.

As a child I would be a constant source of annoyance by nagging my parents to take me to Longleat, but that was for the Safari Park which is still thrilling, not **Longleat House** itself. Now under my own steam I still visit Longleat House every time I am in Wiltshire. Known as one of the grandest country houses in England it was built in Italian Renaissance style (featured later).

Lacock Abbey, owned by the National Trust, is three miles south of Chippenham. Situated on the banks of the River Avon, it was founded in 1232 by Ela, Countess of Salisbury in memory of her husband William Longespee. Only the Cloisters and the Chapter House survive from the original Abbey. Lacock was converted into a Tudor dwelling house shortly after its suppression in 1539 by Sir William Sharrington. An addition by Sir William included the Octagonal Tower, in which there is a photostat of the Lacock Magna Carta of 1225. In the middle of the 18th century architectural changes were made when John Ivory Talbot, a descendant of Sharrington's niece, added the Gothic-style Entrance Hallway and the Great Hall. The South Gallery has many beautiful family portraits to see. There is also a museum at the Abbey gates commemorating William Henry Fox Talbot's photographic work.

Corsham Court is a beautiful Elizabethan house built in 1582. It was purchased by Paul Methuen in the mid 18th century to house a collection of 16th and 17th century Italian and Flemish master paintings and statuary. It is now the home of Lord Methuen. In the middle of the 19th century Corsham Court was enlarged to make room for a second collection of fashionable masters, rare Italian primitives and stone inlaid furniture.

Alterations took place at the house and architects were instructed. 'Capability' Brown set the style in the 1760s by incorporating the Elizabethan Stables and Riding School. He also rebuilt the Gateway, retaining the Elizabethan stone front.

The East wing was designed around this time as Staterooms and picture galleries. The other Staterooms, which include the Music Room, are fascinating and, with the Dining Room, provide the setting for an amazing collection of over 150 paintings, statuary, bronzes, and furniture.

From the gardens there are magnificent views to the north, south, and particularly east. The lake originally created by 'Capability' Brown in 1763 on the north side of the house provides a tranquil setting. It was moved by Repton in 1796 to its present location. There are many beautiful trees in these secluded gardens, you will enjoy the herbaceous borders and the beautiful scent of the rose gardens.

Situated in Chippenham is the surviving **Manor House** of a long deserted medieval village **Sheldon Manor**. The magnificent porch and parvis above date back to the last quarter of the 13th century. The separate little Chapel from the 15th century has three of its original windows and windbreaks in the roof. Inside is the most wonderful collection of ornaments, oddments, oak furniture and glass, and a quilt made out of the skins of duck billed platypuses. Another interesting feature of the house is a stone cistern in the thickness of the Plantagenet wall, fed by a wooden pipe from a valley in the roof. There are many other attractions at Sheldon Manor including Nailsea glass, porcelain, Persian saddlebags and memorabilia of the American War of Independence. The gardens are also beautiful with many features and unusual plants and flowers.

The best time to see the magnificent gardens of **Bowood House** is in the spring, when daffodils, narcissi and bluebells cover 100 acres of grounds created by 'Capability' Brown in the 1760s. There is a long 40 acre lake which provides the centre piece to this magnificent garden. Additions to this were the cascade, hermits cave and little Doric temple. The beautiful terraced gardens stocked with roses and clipped yew trees all add to the tranquil atmosphere of these lovely surroundings. Bowood is the family home of the Earl of Shelburne, eldest son of the Marquis of Landsdowne. Originally built in 1725 it was never completed. After the 2nd Earl of Shelburne purchased Bowood in 1754, over the next century architects such as Henry Keene,

Robert Adam, David Cockerell, Smirke and Barry were commissioned to adapt the house to the trends of the time. On the ground floor there are some superb rooms such as the laboratory in which Dr J Priestley discovered oxygen gas in 1774 and the Orangery which is now a picture gallery. You can also see famous Landsdowne sculptures in the Sculpture Gallery. The west wing has a series of exhibition rooms which unfold the family history from Georgian times to the present day.

We travel now to **Littlecote** near Hungerford. To imagine oneself in the Tudor period is very easy here. This impressive Tudor country home, built between 1490 and 1520, has beautiful panelling and intricate plaster ceilings. The Great Hall contains a huge shovelboard table, measuring 30 feet long, it is probably one of the largest in the world. There is a large collection of Cromwellian armour to be seen from the Civil War. Wander through the street of the re-created period village which is bursting with craftsmen and villagers in historical costume. Enjoy the Tudor sporting events by taking part in the falconry displays and jousting contests. Make sure you see the excavations at Littlecote's ancient Roman site which includes the amazing orphans mosaic, first discovered in the 18th century.

Close to Littlecote is **Farleigh Hungerford Castle** whose 14th century ruins are as fascinating as the turbulent history of its owners, the Hungerfords. The Castle is owned by English Heritage.

CRANBORNE CHASE

The high ground of Cranborne Chase lies south east of Shaftesbury and north east of Blandford. The National Trust's Win Green Hill at 911 foot is the highest point of the Chase. From here there are fabulous views of the Quantock Hills stretching west and to the Isle of Wight stretching south.

Heale House Gardens are near Salisbury in Middle Woodford. This early Carolean manor house was where King Charles II hid during his escape. The house is set in an unusually beautiful garden; the water garden has been planted with magnolia and acers; and surrounds the Wikko bridge. Many of the unusual plants can be purchased in the plant centre.

Corsham Court

WESSEX

Wilton House, three miles west of Salisbury is the magnificent home of the Earl of Pembroke with superb 17th century state rooms by Inigo Jones (c.1650) (featured later).

Fitz House Garden at Teffont Magna is an attractive garden set on a hillside around a listed group of fascinating stone buildings. There are uniform borders of yew and beech hedges with a stream burbling in this tranquil setting. Spring bulbs and blossom add stunning colour along with azaleas, roses and clematis of all types. There is also a variety of mixed borders, honeysuckles and vines to enjoy.

English Heritage own **Old Wardour Castle**, the 14th century castle that, surrounded by woods, stands on the edge of a beautiful lake. The recently restored Gothic Pavilion and the 18th century rockwork grotto give wonderful feelings of mystery.

During the Civil War, Old Wardour was seriously damaged and has not been inhabited since but a great deal of the original building can still be seen. The castle has a unique architectural aspect to it. It was built in one symmetrical construction, therefore containing everything, unlike other castles of that time where chambers and household were dispersed in towers and separate buildings. Old Wardour's destiny was to be as a fascinating ruin. A scheme to build a new house on the other side of the park by architect John Paine took place. Sensitive to the old castle's architecture it was beautifully landscaped to enhance the romantic and mysterious effect. Josiah Lane added the final touch by building an elaborate grotto.

From the Roman spa city of Bath on to the ancient port of Bristol with the dramatic Clifton Suspension Bridge, travelling to Thomas Hardy land in Dorset and walking in the Blackmoor Vale on to the varied landscape of Somerset, and then journeying to Wiltshire, home of ancient man, these are just a few of the fascinating attractions you can enjoy in Wessex.

Roman Baths

FORDE ABBEY

'Nobody that could stay here would go from hence. Nobody is so well anywhere else as everybody is here.'

For four centuries Forde Abbey, home of the Roper family, was a Cistercian monastery and it is rare to see so much of a monastery in use as a private house. Thomas Chard, the last of thirty-two abbots who had spent many years restoring the 12th century buildings, handed Forde over to Henry VIII upon his Dissolution of the Monasteries in 1539. The abbey and its lands was leased by the Crown for over a hundred years and suffered sad neglect at the hands of absentee landlords.

In 1649 Edmund Prideaux, Attorney General to Oliver Cromwell, bought the abbey and set about transforming it in the Italian style for which its monastic layout was curiously well suited. He did not sweep away the work of Abbot Chard, merely imposing his own ideas of style and decoration on the buildings he found. The abrupt collision of architectural styles might have seemed strange, but the patina of age has drawn the old and new together and the whole front is subtly united by the crenellated parapets running from end to end. The interiors of the principal rooms were lavishly transformed with panelling and plasterwork, and their external appearance was updated with large mullioned windows.

In 1702 the Abbey passed through the female line to Francis Gwyn, Secretary at War to Queen Anne, whose descendants lived here throughout the 18th century and created the lovely gardens. In 1846 the last Gwyn died and the estate was sold with all its contents. In 1864 it was bought by Mrs Bertram Evans and came thence to the Roper family by marriage, who continue to farm as the monks did five centuries ago.

Entered under Abbot Chard's perpendicular tower, the Great Hall has a magnificent oak panelled roof, possibly installed after the Dissolution. The richly carved staircase with its elaborate plaster ceiling was entirely the work of Edmund Prideaux in 1658, and rises gently to the Saloon, formerly the monks gallery. Here the rich plasterwork is exceptional for the skill and imagination of its unknown craftsmen. It repays a long

look. The Mortlake tapestries were commissioned for the room by Sir Edmund, but his death and the arrest of his son for supporting the Duke of Monmouth's cause, delayed their delivery. Eventually they were presented to Sir Francis Gwyn, married to Prideaux's granddaughter, by Queen Anne in recognition of his services as Secretary of State for War. They are the most important works of art in the Abbey and are in exceptionally good condition.

The monks' Upper Refectory, which retains its 15th century roof, became a library in 1890. The screen below the gallery is made from a collection of Breton bedsteads. Above the Abbot's elegant cloister Edmund Prideaux built a series of state rooms. All have the most intricate plaster ceilings which depict plants turning into people. The Chapel, once the Chapter House of the Abbey, has a fine early 12th century vaulted ceiling. Sir Edmund put in the delicately carved screen and the Gwyns the intricate and unusual pulpit.

The great sale of 1846 dispersed most of the contents of Forde. Despite this, the combination of monastic peace and simplicity with the comfortable elegance of a family home gives the Abbey a unique charm.

The garden is worthy of the house it surrounds and was created by the Roper family using the legacy of 18th century landscape and 19th century trees as a framework. There are great yews and ancient lime trees and the Mount is dominated by the incense cedar, rising like Cleopatra's Needle, flanked by giant redwoods. No garden once tended by monks would be complete without water. At Forde there are four ponds connected by a series of cascades from the Great Pond which covers four acres. There is a Rock Garden, Bog Garden, an Arboretum, rare and tender shrubs and great vistas of herbaceous plants. Every season provides something of interest and the keen gardener would be well advised to bring notebook and pen.

Forde Abbey is three miles from the A30 between Chard and Crewkerne.

SHERBORNE CASTLE

With its sweeping acres of deer park, a shimmering lake stretching as far as the eye can see, beech, cedar and rare ornamental trees landscaped to form its frame, Sherborne Castle is a lofty biscuit-coloured faerie place. Heraldic griffins, ostriches and monkeys perch on slender balustrades and gaze from gateways, columns and even from its eight angled turrets giving the castle its twin image of fantasy and fortification.

Sherborne has been the country home of the two distinguished families of Raleigh and Digby. Linked coincidentally by kinship, they shared the gifts of handsome good looks, courage, wit and daring but most of all a great love of the sea. Built by Sir Walter Raleigh (Raw-ly please) in the early 1590s, the estate was lost when, thrown into the Tower on a charge of high-treason, he was forced to relinquish his lease to the Crown. By an error of omission in his will, his son was prevented from inheriting what Sir Walter referred to as his 'fortunes fold'.

In 1617 the estate was given to Sir John Digby by his grateful sovereign James I in recognition of his services as Ambassador to Spain. To Sherborne came the masters Robert Adam, 'Capability' Brown, Gainsborough, Reynolds and Chippendale together with fine porcelain, rare books, priceless collections and ancient treasures. Each succeeding generation has left its imprint with well chosen artists.

Sherborne is in fact not one, but two castles about a quarter of a mile apart, separated by the lake and standing on opposite ridges of high ground. Built in the 12th Century, the old castle became a casualty of the Civil Wars when, as a Royalist stronghold, it was stormed by General Fairfax in 1645. The original Norman Keep, Banqueting Hall and graceful Cloisters were reduced to a pile of rubble.

The 'new' castle or Sherborne Lodge as it was known then, was the home created by Sir Walter Raleigh when he was first ostracised from the court of Queen Elizabeth I upon his secret marriage to her lady-in-waiting. The house Raleigh built is said to be one of the earliest versions of plastered exterior walls which have now faded to a subtle ochre. Recent restoration has revealed a light and well proportioned home with a profusion of leaded glass windows - many of them obscured by later Digby enlargement schemes. On the top floor a crude lead sink and pipes pumped fresh spring water from nearby Jerusalem Hill.

Sir Walter then turned his attentions to the grounds. He designed water gardens with hanging terraces, planted orchards and laid down a bowling green. Some of the trees he planted were new and exotic species which he or his friends brought from the Mediterranean and beyond. Giant Virginia cedars still make the view from the new castle to the old profoundly majestic. Near the cedar grove is Raleigh's stone platform with benches from where he would enjoy the panoramic views and a pipeful of his favourite tobacco. On one such sweet occasion - so the story goes - he was doused with ale by an anxious manservant convinced his master was on fire.

When John Digby, later 1st Earl of Bristol, acquired Sherborne Castle he was quick to put to good use the remnants of the old castle in the rebuilding of the new. To Raleigh's central, four-storied building with its four angled turrets he added four more, connected by new wings which formed the north and south courtyards and gave the castle the configuration H. Later,

when 'good Lord William' Digby built the elegant Adam stable block he too used the fallen masonry from the ruined castle.

The castle interior somewhat belies the very grand impression created by the outside. Many of the rooms are of smaller proportions and a refurnished with a quiet restraint. The Library is a wonderful example of Strawberry Hill Gothic with classical sculptures surmounting the bookcases, fine Georgian and Regency furniture.

The Blue Drawing Room (now faded to a lovely green) contains a wealth of furniture - Regency, Louis XV and Georgian - but has a strong oriental flavour borne out by the 18th Century cabinet in Chinese coromandel lacquer and valuable examples of Kakeimon, Arita and K'ang Hsi porcelain, more of which are displayed in the Porcelain Room. In the Green Drawing Room (formerly Blue, and the source of much confusion) four pieces of furniture are particularly worth a second look; a pair of George III commodes, a Louis XIV kingwood writing table and a walnut despatch box believed to have carried documents for the proposed marriage between Charles I and the Spanish Infanta.

Raleigh's kitchens and cellars - now a museum- form the oldest part of the house. The old bakehouse in the basement turret is believed to have been built in the time of Henry II. The brick, fan-vaulted wine cellar and the barrel-roofed beer cellar are Jacobean but all have been skilfully incorporated by Sir Walter, who widened the doorways to accommodate larger barrels. The Jacobean underground passage now leads to a charming tea shop.

Sherborne Castle is surrounded on all sides by its protective landscape giving a sense of peaceful, private grandeur and there is little that is formal about the castle grounds. The lake, 50 acres of glistening water, stretches between the two castles. Heron, Canada geese, mallard and visiting swans dip their beaks into its dark depths where, even now, hide massive pike and eels.

Inspiration for the lake came to Edward, 6th Lord Digby, as he watched the rising floodwater of the River Yeo from the rooftops. He commissioned the landscape expert of the day, 'Capability' Brown, to embark upon an adventurous project to include not only a lake but a cascading waterfall below the Norman ruins - a project which took over 20 years to complete. The lake is bordered on the castle side by the Adam Orangery, Boat House and Tea Garden Lawns and is spanned by a charming little Georgian bridge built after Admiral Sir Henry Digby suggested that the family should 'chip in' to pay for its construction. The focal point of the lawns which sweep down to the lakeside is a rare ghinko tree, one of the largest in England and a lakeside walk leads round to Raleigh's Seat where he pondered on his 'fortunes fold'.

BRYMPTON D'EVERCY

'There are greater, more historic, more architecturally impressive buildings in grander scenery; but I know of none of which the whole impression is more lovely.' So wrote the late Christopher Hussey in Country Life.

Brympton d'Evercy, two miles from Yeovil in the soft Somerset countryside, gives the impression of permanent summer. It is still very much a family home containing fine furniture and portraits in its simple elegant rooms, together with the famous I Zingari cricket club collection.

The first impression of Brympton is of a cluster of butter-coloured stone buildings around well-kept lawns. The west front is a fine example of Tudor design and bears the arms of Henry VIII. The estate was acquired by John Sydenham in about 1520 and much of the main house dates from this time.

The Sydenham's family fortune ebbed and flowed and within a hundred years they were the largest landowners in England, and in the next hundred, the estate had shrunk to its existing size. During this period successive generations had added bits, removed wings, built turrets, culminating in the final extravagance - the splendid south front. Built in 1678 by Sir John Posthumous Sydenham, it is a fine example of the classical style; apart from the asymetry of the windows and the central drainpipe that is, which simply add to the character and charm of the house.

However it proved to be the family's financial undoing for Sir

John's son put the house on the market in 1697 as a 'very large New Built Mansion', offers in the region of £16,000. A buyer was not forthcoming so the house passed into the hands of the Receiver General of Somerset, who built the Clock Tower, the front porch and put new doors in the Priest House in 1722. He in turn foolishly lost Brympton for being 'remiss in his returns to the Exchequer'. At auction the house fetched £15,492.10s.

Francis Fane, a prosperous barrister, bought the estate in 1731 and it is his descendants who live there still. In 1857 Lady Georgiana Fane took over the running of the estate and established the formal layout of the gardens. She never married because she lost her heart to a dashing young subaltern, considered totally unsuitable by her father. The 'lowly soldier' became better known as the Duke of Wellington! (Perhaps if Georgiana had got her husband, Brympton would not have got its garden).

Behind the Clock Tower a vineyard has been planted and Brympton d'Evercy produces its own excellent white wine. Apple orchards fringe the cricket ground and supply the cider distillery, which now also produces Brympton Apple Brandy. Cream teas are a delicious alternative for the less adventurous visitor who might like to stroll through Lady Georgiana's lovely gardens to the peaceful little church.

As Christopher Hussey said 'None that summarises so exquisitely English country life.'

ATHELHAMPTON

Athelhampton remains essentially medieval, surrounded by walls and courts, much as in former days. The River Piddle almost encircles it and first sight of the house is through the Great Gate in the massive protecting wall. It is a quiet, private place.

Sir William Martyn, Lord Mayor of London, was granted a license to enclose 160 acres of deer park and to build a battlemented house with towers in about 1485. The Wars of the Roses had ended and the Tudor era was just beginning. The house Sir William built, though not grand, was befitting for a wealthy merchant gentleman. His son added the south west wing which projects from the main house at a rather curious angle and, in about 1600 a gable was built above the line of the battlements which can be seen to disappear where they meet the window and emerge again on the other side.

At the end of the 16th century Athelhampton passed in equal share to the four daughters of the last Martyn and eventually passed to George Wood who founded a school at Athelhampton. The house had been neglected and he set about restoring it although some sections, including the gatehouse, had to be pulled down. Wood employed the local Hardy family firm of builders and Thomas Hardy's poems The Dame of Athelhall and The Children and Sir Nameless were both written about Athelhampton.

Robert Cooke, a great collector of antiques, had long resolved to restore an historic house to display his collection and to that end he bought Athelhampton in 1957. His son, Sir Robert, took over the house in 1966 and, together with his wife, he set about completing the restoration begun by George Wood. The result is probably one of the finest examples of Early Tudor domestic architecture in the country, perfectly illustrated in the Great Hall. The timbered roof remains substantially as it was built before 1500 and much of the heraldic glass in the windows here

and throughout the house dates from this time. The Flemish tapestry above the delicate linenfold panelling depicts Samson slaying the Philistines with the jawbone of an ass. The fire-dogs in the great fireplace are by Pugin and the oak furniture includes some fine Jacobean armchairs.

The Great Chamber has finely-figured oak panelling with Elizabethan carved panels over the fireplace in the Italian manner. The handsome William Kent display cabinet contains some lovely Worcester porcelain.

The fifteenth century newel staircase suddenly changes from stone, in its lower flights, to solid slabs of oak as one climbs to the King's Room - so called because the Manorial Court was held here in the name of the king. The timbered ceiling, linenfold panelling and Ham stone fireplace combine with an oriel window to form a worthy replacement of an earlier structure. A rare feature of the Green Parlour, a lovely cosy room which is obviously still in use (note the television) is the fine carving on the 15th century beams and surrounding cornice.

The Athelhampton gardens are full of variety; the formal and architectural balanced by woodland and riverside walks. The formal gardens are a series of walled courts grouped around a central circular Corona which is in the Elizabethan manner with tall obelisks and a fountain. A backdrop of dark clipped yew emphasises the warm russet Ham stone walls. North of the Corona is the Private Garden with a central lawn on two levels. The sunken part contains a long fish pond, shaped to echo the design of the Great Hall roof, with a fountain. This leads to the White Garden through which the river twists and turns. South of the Corona steps lead to the Great Court with its twelve huge clipped yews in the shape of giant pyramids imitating the obelisks in the Corona itself - and yet another fountain. The gentle, soothing sound of running water is never far away at Athelhampton.

STONEHENGE

Rising out of Salisbury Plain, silhoutted by the setting sun, Stonehenge is an awe-inspiring sight. Images of magic, mystery and ritual surround it, for 5,000 years after it was built the reasons for its existence are still a matter for conjecture. It is one of the world's most amazing feats of prehistoric engineering and the most famous ancient monument in Britain.

The inner horseshoe is surrounded by slightly smaller stones in a perfect circle, all erected between 3100 and 1100 BC. What incredible lengths the builders went to in constructing such a monument. It is impossible for us to imagine, in our mechanised world, how men cut and shaped these huge stones, with only primitive tools to help them. Even more extraordinary, the massive stone lintels are mortice-and-tenored to the uprights upon which they rest, and are curved to follow the circumference of the circle. Nor were they stones from the immediate surrounding area - some were brought from the Marlborough towns 20 miles away, but the smaller blue stones came from the Preseli Mountains in South West Wales. Without machines or roads as we know them, it was an exceptional feat of organisation.

Many reasons have been advanced as to the origin and purpose of the stones, some more fanciful than others; Roman Temple, spaceship launch pads, architects from ancient Greece or Druid shrine. There is no evidence to support any of these but one fact is certain - the major axis of stonehenge was carefully aligned with the midsummer and midwinter sun. There are other alignments with the rising and setting of the moon, all of which point to ceremonies which mark the seasons and the annual calendar.

From afar Stonehenge may seem disappointingly small, for we are used to being dwarfed by our modern buildings. Close to, its grandeur is clear and its enchantment almost overpowering. Some of the stones making up the outer ring and inner horseshoe of uprights with lintels weigh over 50 tons each. These are the hard, cold facts which show what astonishing things the earliest inhabitants of these islands could achieve. The mystery surrounding Stonehenge is as perpetual as the stones themselves.

LONGLEAT

At the head of its long drive, tucked among cushioning hills, **Longleat House** is an impressive sight. This huge square house, a typical example of the restrained exuberance of Elizabethan architecture at its best, has been home to successive generations of the Thynne family for over 400 years.

Longleat was built by John Thynne on the site of an Augustinian Priory acquired in 1540. Thynne, or 'the builder' as he was known, was a man whose determination and single mindedness saw his rapid rise from Kitchen Clerk to Henry VIII to Steward to the powerful and influential Duke of Somerset, Lord Protector to Edward VI. Wounded during Somerset's victory over the Scots at Pinkie in 1547, Thynne was knighted by the grateful Duke on the battlefield itself. In the same year Sir John began to build, but when his house was nearing completion it was destroyed by fire. Again displaying the tenacity which was to serve him well throughout his somewhat chequered career, Sir John simply started again, this time with the help of probably the best architect of the day. Despite two periods of incarceration in the Tower, Sir John saw his house completed in 1580. Sadly, that same year this amazing man died - but not before he had enjoyed the privilege of entertaining his Queen, Elizabeth I, at Longleat. By 1682, Sir Thomas Thynne was created Viscount Weymouth and just over 100 years later, the 3rd Viscount became Marquess of Bath. Ambitious Sir John would have been a proud man.

The Great Hall at Longleat remains more Elizabethan in character than the rest of the house despite the addition of a minstrels gallery in 1600 and the small gallery around 1663. Further extensive refurbishment was carried out by the 2nd Marquess and his architect, Sir Geoffrey Wyatville which included the replacement of the original Wren staircase and the creation of the lower east corridor.

The three State Rooms are furnished with fine examples of French furniture, rare porcelain, silver, tapestries and paintings and all have elaborately painted ceilings in the Italian manner. In the State Dining Room where family members gaze down from leather-covered walls, the beautiful ceiling incorporates a series of paintings of the school of Titian. The saloon, at 90 feet long the largest room in the house, has a ceiling inspired by one in the Massimo Palace in Rome. The ceiling in the State Drawing Room however, must be considered the most exquisite, adapted from an original in St Mark's Cathedral, Venice.

An outstanding feature of Longleat must surely be its magnificent collection of books, some 40,000 volumes, housed in a series of libraries - seven in all. These rooms range in size from the cool, green intimacy of the Ante-Library with its refreshingly informal study of the present Marquess by Sutherland, to the glowing splendour of the Red Library. The most famous of Longleat's apparitions is that of Louisa Carteret, second wife of the 2nd Viscount. Her portrait hangs beside the fireplace in the Lower Dining Room.

The beautiful park at Longleat is thought by many to be one of 'Capability' Brown's greatest achievements. Employed by the 3rd Viscount he swept away formality in favour of wooded areas and created lakes from the Long Leat which flowed gently through the park. In the 1950s the present Marquess, with the help of Russell Page, reinstated the Formal Gardens and Azalea Drive which can now be enjoyed in all their former splendour. The Secret Garden, behind Wyatville's Orangery is a lovely sight in high summer filled with the subtle shades and scents of old fashioned roses.

However, the innovative development which aroused considerable controversy in 1966 was the introduction of the now world-renowned Lions of Longleat who pad around the park along with other animals not normally associated with rural Wiltshire. More than just a zoo in a particularly splendid setting, Longleat is in the forefront of the conservation of endangered species.

WILTON HOUSE

Wilton House rises majestically from the rolling Wiltshire landscape where the River Nadder meets the River Wylye, three miles from historic Salisbury. In 1544 Henry VIII gave the Saxon Abbey at Wilton and its lands to William Herbert, his brother-in-law. Already a rich and powerful man, he pulled down the abbey and began to build a house worthy of his status. In 1551 he became Earl of Pembroke and continued to find favour with his Royal master, a situation enjoyed by succeeding Earls who were to hold high office under future monarchs. A second parallel thread which runs through the rich fabric of Wilton's history was a great love and patronage of the arts. Indeed Mary Sidney, 2nd Countess of Pembroke, was considered to be 'the greatest patroness of wit and learning of any lady of her time'. Her brother Philip wrote his Arcadia at Wilton and Shakespeare's first folio edition of plays, published in 1623, was dedicated to William and Philip Herbert, Mary's sons.

These brothers made alterations to the house and greatly added to its contents. Philip, the 4th Earl, became Lord Chamberlain to Charles I who 'loved Wilton above all places and went there every summer.'

In 1647 a disastrous fire destroyed all but the centre of the east front, and almost all the contents. Philip immediately began the daunting task of rebuilding. The work was started by Inigo Jones and completed by his nephew John Webb in 1653.

The family continued to flourish under continued royal patronage until the time of the 7th Earl, the black sheep in an otherwise completely white flock. He was a good-for-nothing spendthrift, was twice accused of murder and found guilty of manslaughter and committed to the Tower. On his death many of Wilton's treasures were sold to pay his debts. He was succeeded by his brother Thomas, who more than redeemed the family honour and was largely responsible for the fine art collection including the celebrated Wilton Diptych now in the National Gallery. He also founded the Wilton Royal Carpet Factory!

George, 11th Earl of Pembroke, employed James Wyatt, the fashionable architect of the late Georgian period, to alter his house in order to make it more convenient and warmer, and give more room for pictures. Wyatt's Gothic style sits comfortably with the earlier work of Inigo Jones, whose series of grand State Rooms are an important feature of the house. The Single Cube Room, as its name implies, is as long and wide as it is high - in this case 30 feet - a perfect cube. The panelling is pine painted white with carving from the dado to the cornice enriched with gold leaf. The ceiling is richly painted and the four walls are hung with scenes from Sir Philip Sidney's Arcadia. The opulence of this room serves as an overture to Inigo Jones' masterful creation, the Double Cube Room, which is simply breathtaking. Double the size of the preceding room, everything appears to have doubled; the reds of chairs and sofas are now deepest crimson; the white panelled walls, elaborately decorated with swags of fruit, flowers and foliage, flame with different shades of gold; the family portraits are of grand proportions. Dominating the room is Van Dyck's group portrait of the Herbert family, measuring a massive 17 feet long by 11 feet high which almost eclipses the other fine works in this room. Most of the elaborate furniture is by William Kent and Thomas Chippendale and was made for this room between 1730 and 1770.

In the Great Ante Room the different style which Wyatt brought to the house is thrown into sharp, and pleasing, focus. Rembrandt's delightful study of his ageing mother hangs in this room. The Corner Room contains some of the best paintings from what is undoubtedly one of the finest collections of art still in private hands. The work of Rubens, Van Dyck, Breughel, Gellee, Rembrandt, Reynolds and many more are represented. The Large Smoking Room contains a unique set of 55 paintings in gouache of the Spanish 'Haute Ecole' riding school in their original frames. They were painted in 1755 by a famous Austrian riding master for the 10th Earl, an expert horseman, who built the indoor riding school at Wilton (and a tennis court) and wrote books on military equitation.

Wilton House is set amidst natural parkland which replaces the more stylised formality of the 16th and 17th centuries. Immense cedars of Lebanon shade the lawns around the house and oaks, planes, limes and tulip trees frame the beautiful Palladian Bridge of 1737 which spans the Nadder where it was specially widened. The forecourt gardens were laid out around a central fountain by the 17th Earl of Pembroke as a memorial to his father.

WESSEX

The Kingdom of Wessex, once a powerful seat of England, is now a more tranquil place to while away the hours. It offers the visitor a tremendous amount, from King Alfred's capital city of Winchester to the Roman city of Bath and the ancient Stonehenge and Glastonbury Tor. This is a place of mystery and powerful magic.

The countryside is one of contrasts, flatlands rise suddenly into hillside and craggy cliffs. Cheddar Gorge and the caves of Wooky are yet more examples of the patient hand of mother nature carving out her path through obstacles in her way.

The general landscape is one of gently undulating green fields darkened every now and then with woodland. The summer months are naturally busy but there are pockets of tranquillity off the beaten track, even in the very height of summer.

In Hardy Country, many of the villages are delightfully unspoilt and it is here one can find some of the finest bed & breakfasts in the country. The villages, many of which contain historical buildings, are charming and have remained virtually unchanged for centuries. There are castles, houses and gardens galore in this pleasant countryside and a visit to the county of Somerset would not be complete without a trip to one of the many cider presses from some locally produced scrumpie.

Stonehenge is a constant cause of debate and mystery. How did those stones get there? Why are they there? Despite much discussion it remains an unsolved mystery.

Wiltshire, Dorset and Somerset, even the names paint a picture; rose covered cottages, rolling countryside and romance.

Thomas Hardy feared the age of mechanisation as it reached southward to ravage the fields and lanes. However, whilst it cannot be denied much has changed since his day, the atmosphere in these hideaway villages remains the same; peaceful and friendly.

HOTELS OF DISTINCTION

APSLEY HOUSE HOTEL, Bath, Avon. Tel: (0225) 336966
An elegant Georgian Hotel, reputedly built for the Duke of Wellington in 1830, offers the highest standards of comfort and cuisine within easy reach of the centre of Bath.

BATH SPA HOTEL, Bath, Avon. Tel: (0225) 444006
Spacious, grand, elegant, marvellous, with attention to details all in one splendid country house hotel in historic Bath. How the Romans would have lived if they had had the facilities.

BEECHFIELD HOUSE, Beanacre, Wiltshire. Tel: (0225) 703700
Built in 1878 of mellow Bath stone, Beechfield House stands in 8 acres of beautiful gardens and is elegantly furnished with antiques. Ideally situated for exploring Bath, Bowood House and Lacock.

BRIDGE HOUSE HOTEL, Beaminster, Dorset. Tel: (0308) 862200
This hotel makes an ideal base for exploring Hardy country. Complete with stone mullioned windows and its own priesthole the history of this hotel is uncertain but it offers extremely comfortable accommodation with fresh local food.

BUCKLAND TOUT SAINTS, Kingsbridge, Devon. Tel: (0548) 853055
This 17th century manor house is one of the finest examples of Queen Anne architecture in the South West of England. Lovingly restored it stands in 6 acres of gardens and is an ideal base for touring Devon.

CASTLE HOTEL, Castle Combe, Wiltshire. Tel: (0249) 782461
White-walled and black-beamed, this centuries-old stone house has lost none of its ancient charm, with exposed stone walls, uneven floors, open fireplaces and rustic, period furniture.

CHARLTON HOUSE HOTEL, Shepton Mallet, Somerset. Tel: (0749) 342008
This 17th century Manor House stands in 6 acres of landscaped grounds which feature a trout lake and historic surrounding countryside.

CHEDINGTON COURT, Chedington, Dorset. Tel: (0933589) 265
A fine manor house built in the 1840s with great views. Well and solidly furnished, it boasts a croquet lawn and helicopter landing facilities. The food is excellent in the spacious restaurant.

CHELWOOD HOUSE, Bristol, Avon. Tel: (0761) 490730
Built in 1681 Chelwood House retains many original features and affords uninterrupted views that stretch as far as Bath. Furnished with antiques, the hotel offers a relaxed atmosphere with first class service.

CHISELDON HOUSE, Wiltshire. Tel: (0793) 741010
A charming early Regency house set in 3 acres of mature gardens, Chiseldon makes an ideal base for exploring the ancient sites of Avebury and Stonehenge whilst Salisbury, Bath and Cirencester are only a short drive.

CLOS DU ROY AT BOX HOUSE, Bath, Avon. Tel: (0225) 744447
A handsome Georgian mansion set in 7 acres of beautiful gardens. Its restaurant has an excellent reputation with regular gourmet evenings. Box House is an ideal base for exploring the historical West Country.

COMBE GROVE MANOR, Bath, Avon. Tel: (0225) 834644
An exclusive 18th century country house hotel set in 68 acres of formal gardens and woodlands 2 miles from Bath. The hotel offers many sporting facilities, including tennis and golf.

DRAGON HOUSE HOTEL, Bilbrook, Somerset. Tel: (0984) 402215
Very pleasant roadside hotel, cottagey and traditional it offers a good standard of service. Near the typical seaside town of Minehead, a little faded but charming.

EASTBURY HOTEL, Sherborne, Dorset. Tel: (0935) 813131
In the heart of Thomas Hardy's Dorset rests this elegant hotel, originally a townhouse built in 1740 during the reign of George II. It is close to Sherborne Abbey and Castles.

WESSEX

FOUNTAIN HOUSE HOTEL SUITES, Bath, Avon. Tel: (0225) 338622

An elegant Georgian mansion with comfortably appointed suites in the heart of Bath with its Roman Spas, Circus and Assembly Rooms. The Cotswolds, Longleat, Castle Combe and Laycock are a short drive away.

HOMEWOOD PARK, Freshford, Avon. Tel: (0225) 723731

A truly elegant Victorian House with rooms exuding an air of discreetly gracious pride and charm. The setting is soothing and tranquil, in ten acres of beautifully tended gardens and ground.

IVY HOUSE HOTEL, Marlborough, Wiltshire.
Tel: (0672) 515333

An 18th century listed building set in a charming cobbled courtyard. The Ivy House has been imaginatively restored and is an ideal base for touring Avebury, Stonehenge and the Marlborough Downs.

KINGS ARMS INN, Montacute, Somerset. Tel: (0935) 822513

A handsome Elizabethan coaching inn in this unspoilt village. This hotel is attractively and comfortably decorated. It has a reputation for fine English food, and it is well located for Brympton d'Evercy and Sherborne Castle.

LANGLEY HOUSE, Wiveliscombe, Somerset.
Tel: (0984) 23318

The excellent restaurant is enhanced by its beautiful setting in this 16th century hotel. The set menus are interesting and the standard of food extremely high. The chef makes full use of home-grown produce from the hotel's gardens. The accommodation is equally attractive with delightful public rooms and charming bedrooms.

LANGTRY MANOR HOTEL, Bournemouth, Dorset.
Tel: (0202) 23887

Edward VII built this house for his beautiful Lillie, the memontoes are well displayed. Typical of the romantic royal Edwardian era.

LUCKNAM PARK, Colerne, Wiltshire. Tel: (0225) 742777

A magnificent Georgian mansion beautifully furnished with fine antiques, a mere 6 miles from Bath. This hotel offers many first class facilities including a leisure spa, and is perfectly located for exploring the West Country.

LYNCH COUNTRY HOUSE, Somerton, Somerset.
Tel: (0458) 72316

In the heart of rural Somerset this elegant Georgian Grade II listed country house is set in its own beautifully kept grounds and provides an excellent base from which to visit the numerous local stately homes.

MANOR HOUSE, Castle Combe, Wiltshire.
Tel: (0249) 782206

The Manor House is idyllically set in 26 acres of grounds with a trout stream and terraced Italian garden. The hotel offers five star luxury in a relaxed atmosphere with excellent cuisine and is close to the fascinating city of Bath.

MANSION HOUSE, Poole, Dorset. Tel: (0202) 685666

Quietly resting in the heart of the ancient town of Poole is this beautifully restored Georgian building. The Isle of Purbeck,

Corfe Castle and a maritime museum are all close by.

MORTONS HOUSE HOTEL, Corfe Castle, Dorset.
Tel: (0929) 480988

A 16th century 'E' shaped house linked by underground tunnels to Corfe Castle, Mortons House is steeped in history. Offering high quality British cooking, it is a perfect base for Lulworth Cove, Durdle Dour, Kingston Lacy Estate, Compton Acres and Hardy Country.

OAK HOUSE, The Square, Axbridge, Somerset.
Tel: (0934) 732444

Medieval setting for this Somerset hostelry with its own well, stone walls and a very warm hearted welcome and log fire. Good sized bedrooms, some en suite, all with modern amenities.

OLD BELL HOTEL, Malmesbury, Wiltshire.
Tel: (0666) 822344

A grade I listed building, this could easily be England's oldest hotel. Each of the bedrooms capture the hotel's fascinating history and the traditional English cuisine complements a fine wine list.

OLD SHIP, Mere, Wiltshire. Tel (0747) 860258

Located in the middle of the town, this attractive stone built inn offers comfortable accommodation and its panelled and beamed bars add to the cosy atmosphere.

PEAR TREE AT PURTON, Purton, Wiltshire.
Tel: (0793) 772100

The Pear Tree is an imaginatively and caringly run hotel with an award winning restaurant. All the bedrooms are tastefully and individually decorated, each one named after an historic character with an association with the village of Purton.

PHEASANT HOTEL, Seavington St Mary, Somerset. Tel: (0460) 40502

A former 17th century farmhouse, the Pheasant is now a pleasing and well restored hotel. The bedrooms, mainly in what were outbuildings, are luxurious, as are the bathrooms. The food is imaginative, British and Continental in style.

PLUMBER MANOR, Sturminster Newton, Dorset.
Tel: (0258) 72507

This Jacobean Manor has been held by the owner's family since the 17th century and portraits hang in a fascinating gallery. In the heart of Hardy's Dorset it is the perfect base for exploring the historic surrounding countryside.

PRIORY HOTEL, Wareham, Dorset. Tel: (0929) 551666

Close to Corfe Castle and historic Poole, in the heart of idyllic Dorset, the Priory has sheltered travellers since the 16th Century. It commands 4 acres of landscaped gardens sloping down to the River Frome.

PRIORY HOTEL, Bath, Avon. Tel: (0225) 331922

This well run former private residence has retained many of the early 19th century gentlemen's necessities - croquet lawn, orangery, lovely furniture. There is also a wonderful and widely acclaimed restaurant featuring local produce.

ROYAL CRESCENT HOTEL, Bath, Avon. Tel: (0225) 319090

Part of the Grade I listed, much renowned, original terrace,

46

CHELWOOD HOUSE HOTEL

Just minutes from beautiful Chew Valley Lake, Chelwood House enjoys an enviable location between Bristol, Bath and Wells - all cities of exceptional historic and cultural interest. A former dower house dating from 1681, the upper rooms of the hotel enable visitors to take in far-reaching views over the meadows and rolling Mendip Hills. An impressive staircase leads up to the distinctively designed guest rooms; three have four-poster beds of different national styles - French, Victorian and Chinese. Antique furniture, ornaments and paintings from the personal collection of owners, Rudi and Jill Birk, enhance the relaxed ambience of the two lounges. Rudi Birk's Bavarian origins are a key influence on his first-class cuisine - in addition to an English a la carte menu a selection of traditional Bavarian dishes can be prepared. In 1990 the hotel's 'Restaurant in a Garden' opened, consisting of a conservatory dining room with plants, fountain, gazebo and hand-painted murals, creating a lush setting for dinner. The hosts take credit for inspiring a convivial family atmosphere at this professionally run hotel which represents good value for money. The hotel is ideally situated for a variety of leisure pursuits and there are many places of natural, historic and sporting interest close at hand.

One of the best fishing lakes in Britain, Chew Valley Lake, is just 10 minutes away and Blagdon Lake is also closeby.

There are approximately 15 Golf Courses within a radius of 20 miles and, for the racing enthusiast, Bath Races can be reached in 20 minutes and Chepstow and Wincanton within an hour.

Chelwood House
Chelwood
Avon BS18 4NH
Tel: (0761) 490730

STON EASTON

THE PEAR TREE AT PURTON

Less than five miles from the centre of thriving Swindon, this beautiful Cotswold stone house has been converted and extended into a small English Hotel of character and style.

The Pear Tree features eighteen elegant rooms and suites, all tastefully and individually decorated. Each is named after an historic character with an association with the village of Purton, such as Anne Hyde, the mother of Queen Mary and Queen Anne; James Kibblewhite, the runner; Nevil Maskelyne, the astrologer royal and E.H. Budd the cricketer.

Every conceivable comfort can be found in the rooms including private bathrooms with showers, direct dial telephone, colour television with teletext and video channel, hairdryer and trouser press.

The Pear Tree is imaginatively and caringly run by the proprietors Francis and Anne Young, with the award-winning restaurant under the skilled control of Janet Pichel-Juan. The fixed-price menus offer the best of seasonal produce featuring the excellent local beef, lamb and pork.

A range of weekend and three night breaks have been formulated to enable guests to take advantage of these sumptuous culinary delights and the John Veysey Suite is additionally available for meetings, dinners, weddings and product launches.

Despite its proximity to the hustle and bustle of city life, the Pear Tree is set in seven and a half acres of tranquil countryside and looks out over a traditional Victorian garden to the Cotswold Hills beyond.

The hotel nestles in the famous Vale of the White Horse, at the southern extremity of the Cotswolds and therefore provides an ideal base for exploration of the surrounding countryside. The vibrant Marlborough Downs lie to the south and offer easy access to the historic sites of Avebury and Stonehenge. The many and varied delights of Bath, Cirencester, Oxford, Blenheim Palace, Woodstock and Swindon are all within relatively short travelling distance and together provide a wealth of attractions for the most indefatigable visitor.

The Pear Tree is easily reached from junction 16 of the M4. Follow the signs from Purton, proceed through the village, turn right up the hill and the hotel will be found some fifty yards past The Tithe Barn.

The Pear Tree at Purton
Church End, Purton
Swindon,
Wiltshire SN5 9ED
Tel: (0793) 772100
Fax: (0793) 772369

known to Jane Austen (although not so well appointed then), often seen in photographs. Excellent cooking and wines complement the great views in the restaurant.

STON EASTON PARK, Bath, Avon. Tel: (0761) 21631
An internationally famous Grade I listed Palladian Mansion, this superb hotel offers the height of luxury and comfort and has won innumerable awards for its decor, service and food. Set in beautifully landscaped grounds it is the perfect place to relax.

SUMMER LODGE HOTEL, Evershot, Dorset. Tel: (0935) 83424
A charming Georgian building now a luxurious hotel, Summer Lodge offers every comfort in an idyllic location in the heart of Hardy country. There are many National Trust houses within easy reach.

THORNBURY CASTLE, Nr Bristol, Avon. Tel: (0454) 418511
The only Tudor castle in England used as a hotel. It was begun in 1310 and used by Henry VIII and Anne Boleyn. The architecture and furnishings are of the grandest style and personally guided tours are available.

WHATLEY MANOR, Malmesbury, Wiltshire. Tel: (0666) 822888
A luxurious Grade II listed manor house on the banks of the Avon. Largely furnished in period style the hotel offers many leisure facilities and is within easy reach of Bath, Bristol, Wells and the Cotswolds.

WOOLLEY GRANGE, Bradford-on-Avon, Wiltshire. Tel: (02216) 4705
Woolley Grange is set in formal gardens and has a warm and friendly atmosphere. Children are very welcome and well catered for. It is an ideal base for visiting Bath, Longleat and Stonehenge.

YALBURY COTTAGE, Dorchester, Dorset. Tel: (0305) 262 382
A small country house hotel tastefully refurbished whilst retaining many original features. Offering the best English cuisine in a relaxing atmosphere Yalbury is an ideal base for visiting Parham, Athelhampton, the Kingston Lacy Estate and much more.

ACCOMMODATION OF MERIT

ALWARD HOUSE, Alderbury, Wiltshire. Tel: (0722) 710371
This large, late Victorian, dower house was built originally for Longford Castle nearby. Beautiful oak floors and oak roof cladding were all made from trees on the estate, together with airy high ceilings complete with ornate cornices. Perfect for exploring Wessex.

AUDLEY HOUSE, Bath, Avon. Tel: (0225) 333110
Classic early Victorian house, built in 1842, and set in an acre of sweeping lawns. A mere walk to Royal Crescent, the Circus and central Bath with Longleat, Stonehenge and West Country a short drive away.

Jews Farm House

LUCKNAM PARK

Lucknam Park is a magnificent Georgian country house six miles from Bath, set in extensive parkland of two hundred and eighty acres. A focus of fine society and gracious living for over 250 years, Luckham Park now recreates as a luxurious hotel the elegance and style of an era long ago.

Guests approach the hotel along a mile-long avenue lined with beech trees, leading to the house and its honey-toned stonework. Wide lawns, abundant fresh flowers and an aura of quiet and calm promise a very individual welcome. Whether you are a traveller, a gourmet or simply a romantic, guests will find at Lucknam Park an elegance and tranquility born out of a sense of everything being right and well ordered.

The nine suites and thirty bedrooms are furnished with a delicate sense of historical context, but also with the luxury and facilities demanded of a first class country-house hotel. Individually designed, with generous space and splendid views, each one enjoys the comfort and charming service which help to make Lucknam Park a special hotel. The restaurant is set with exquisite porcelain, silver and glass, reflecting the sumptuous but discreet atmosphere and service. The highly acclaimed menu offers Modern English cuisine using only the freshest ingredients and complemented by an excellent wine cellar.

The leisure facilities at Lucknam Park are second to none. Within the walls of the old garden the Leisure Spa opens up another world: indoor swimming pool and jacuzzi, saunas and steam room. A fully equipped gymnasium, snooker room, beauty salon and tennis courts are all of the highest standards.

Guided tours with a personal guide can be arranged to explore the splendours of the glorious Georgian city of Bath and surrounding countryside. The delightful villages of Castle Combe, Lacock and the stately homes of Bowood House and Corsham Court are all close by. Many other activities are available too. Take your pick from hot-air ballooning, golf, racing, riding, clay pigeon shooting, fishing, archery and boating. The magnificent Theatre Royal in Bath even holds private seats for guests at Lucknam Park.

Lucknam Park epitomises a country house hotel at its best. The hotel is less than two hours drive from London and guests can be sure that their memories of Lucknam Park will stay with them for a long time to come.

Lucknam Park
Colerne
Wiltshire SN14 8AZ

Tel: Bath (0225) 742777
Telex: 445648   Fax: (0225) 743536

WESSEX

CERNE ABBEY, Dorchester, Dorset. Tel: (0300) 341284
Founded in 9th century, and later becoming a Benedictine Abbey in 987 AD, this is the scene of a Miracle of St Augustine. In the gardens the old abbey guest house an Ancient Monument, is open for viewing. All in all a fascinating base for historical Dorset.

CHANTRY, Mere, Wiltshire. Tel: (0747) 860264
A beautiful 15th century house with stone walls, stone mullioned windows, heavy oak doors and a Great Hall, complete with refectory table. Convenient for Stonehenge, Salisbury, Bath and many other sites. Booking essential.

JEWS FARM HOUSE, Huish Champflower, Somerset.
Tel: (0984) 24218
High in the Brendons, on the edge of Exmoor, this historic farm house was built in 1248 by John d'Jeu, hence its name. Central, not only for Exmoor, but also for all various historical sites in Somerset and Devon. Booking essential.

MAIDEN NEWTON HOUSE, Maiden Newton, Dorset. Tel: (0300) 20336
Originally built in 1842 a Rectory, this unusual and beautiful house is set in 21 acres of parkland with trout streams and ornamental gardens. This family home is ideal for touring Dorset and its many historical places of interest.

MERFIELD HOUSE, Rode, Avon. Tel: (0373) 830298
Large Georgian house, in 30 acres of parkland, overlooking the River Frome and 10 miles from Bath. The high ceilings and large windows give a light airy feel. Bristol and other historical areas nearby are easily reached.

OLD HOUSE, Sutton Veny, Wiltshire. Tel: (0985) 40344
hatched, 300 year old stone house set in attractive gardens on the western edge of Salisbury Plain. Obviously within easy reach of Stonehenge this comfortable house is also convenient for Stourhead, Longleat and many others.

OLD SCHOOL HOUSE, Bathford, Avon. Tel: (0225) 859593
Bathford is a pretty walled village in a conservation area and this was the schoolhouse built in 1837. Central for touring West Country and only three miles from Georgian Bath.

OLD VICARAGE, Burbage, Wiltshire. Tel: (0672) 810495
Spacious Victorian 'Gothic' Rectory built of local flint and brick, next door to the church and set in charming village with it many thatched cottages. Stonehenge, Marlborough, and many country houses and gardens are within easy reach.

WHITTLES FARM, Beercrocombe, Somerset. Tel:(0823) 480301
Farmhouse, on 200 acre working farm, built in 16th century with a 19th century facade. Convenient for many country houses and gardens together with the West Country and its coast and historical sites.

INNS OF CHARACTER

CROSS GUNS, Bradford on Avon, Wiltshire.
With gardens overlooking the river Avon and a maze of bridges and aquaducts, this old fashioned pub is beautifully located. Stone walls, low 17th century beams and oak tables add to the traditional atmosphere. Good food and ales are renowned here.

CROSS KEY, Fovant, Wiltshire.
Antique furniture and brassware dominate this secluded but atmospheric 15th century pub. Excellent wines and bar food are good value at this unspoilt resting place.

THE GEORGE, Norton Street, Somerset.
Charming rustic simplicity abounds at this 600 year old pub characterised by thick stone walls and courtyard and even a Norman stone turret. A similarly historic atmosphere greets customers inside where traditional food and ales may be enjoyed.

THE GLOBE, Appley, Somerset. Tel: (0823) 672372
Green, Somerset pastures surround this delightful 500 year old country pub. Generous portions of bar food and a fine local brew can be enjoyed here, deep in the Somerset countryside.

LANGTON ARMS, Tarrant Monkton, Dorset.
Outstanding bar food, a whole host of fine ales and popular wines are the main delights of this 17th century pub. Such is the friendly atmosphere here that it is very popular with locals as well as visitors. Accommodation is also available.

THE PACK HORSE, South Stoke, Somerset.
Heavy black beams and stone-mullioned windows are some of the many distinctive charms at this 14th century inn renowned for its attractively priced bar food and friendliness. This former priory is delightfully set above a wooded valley.

THE RED LION, Avebury, Wiltshire.
Neolithic stones dating back to around 2,400 BC surround this beautifully thatched and half timbered pub. Extensive restoration has not altered the delightful atmosphere of this busy inn.

RING O'BELLS, Compton Martin, Avon.
Flagstone floors, wooden beams and a huge ingle-nook fire are among the charms in this traditional country pub. Good bar food and fine ales can be enjoyed at this attractively placed inn.

SHAVE CROSS INN, Shave Cross, Dorset.
Good bar food, fine ales, cider and country wines contribute towards the friendly atmosphere within this characterful partly 14th century pub. The timbers and flagstones below the thatched roof add to this pub's distinctive charms.

SMITHS ARMS, Godmanstone, Dorset.
England's smallest inn was reputedly granted a licence by Charles II. This tiny 15th century ex-smithy, built of flint and with a deep thatched roof, has real ales, traditional food and a character all of its own.

THE SHIP, Porlock, Somerset.
Stunning views across the sea and local moors await visitors to this 13th century cottage. Low beams, old benches and a flagstone floor contribute towards a simple but charmingly friendly atmosphere in which to enjoy local ales and cider.

THE WAGGON AND HORSES, Beckhampton, Wiltshire.
This heavy-stoned and thatched Tudor coaching inn featured in Charles Dickins 'Pickwick Papers'. Visitors to the inn today will be similarly impressed by the ales and home made food available at this characterful pub.

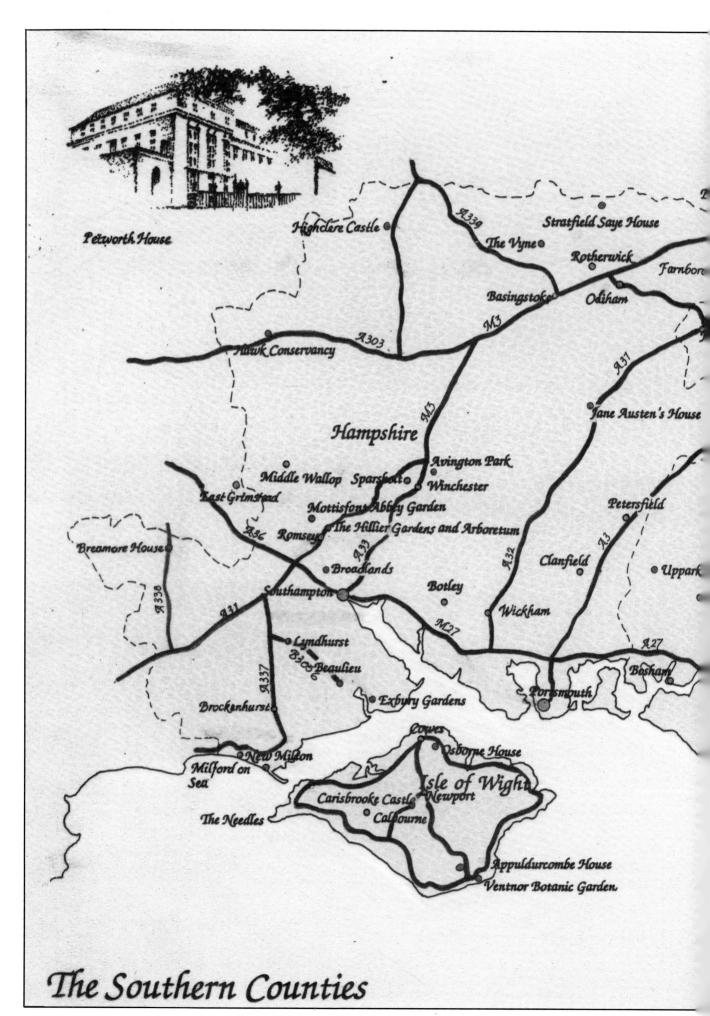

Petworth House

Highclere Castle

Stratfield Saye House

The Vyne

Rotherwick

Farnboro

A339

Basingstoke

Odiham

M3

A31

A303

Hawk Conservancy

Jane Austen's House

M3

Hampshire

Avington Park

Middle Wallop

Sparsholt

Winchester

Petersfield

East Grimstead

Mottisfont Abbey Garden

The Hillier Gardens and Arboretum

A36

Romsey

A33

A3

Breamore House

A32

Clanfield

Uppark

Broadlands

Botley

A338

Southampton

Wickham

A31

M27

A337

Lyndhurst

B30

Beaulieu

M27

A27

Portsmouth

Bosham

Brockenhurst

Exbury Gardens

Milford on Sea

New Milton

Cowes

Osborne House

Isle of Wight

Carisbrooke Castle

Newport

The Needles

Calbourne

Appuldurcombe House

Ventnor Botanic Garden

The Southern Counties

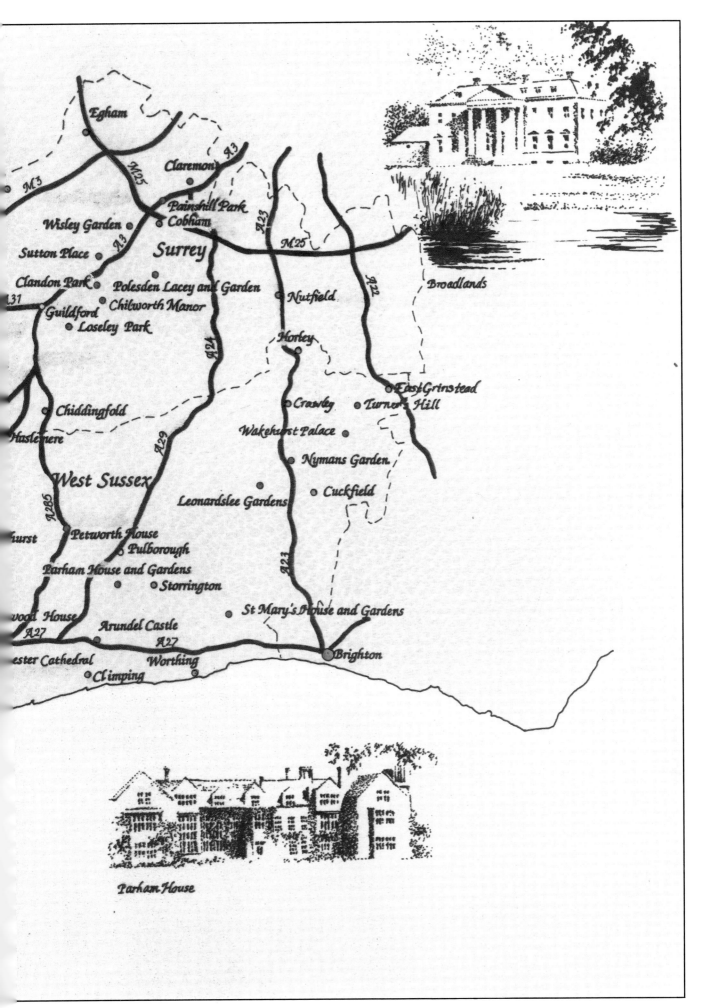

Egham

M3

M25

Claremont

A3

Painshill Park
Cobham

Wisley Garden

Sutton Place

A3

Surrey

Clandon Park

A31

Polesden Lacey and Garden

Chilworth Manor

Guildford

Loseley Park

Nutfield

M25

A23

A22

Broadlands

Horley

A24

Chiddingfold

A29

Haslemere

East Grinstead

Crawley

Turner's Hill

Wakehurst Palace

West Sussex

Nymans Garden

A285

Leonardslee Gardens

Cuckfield

Petworth House

A23

Pulborough

Parham House and Gardens

Storrington

wood House

St Mary's House and Gardens

A27

Arundel Castle

A27

ester Cathedral

Worthing

Brighton

Climping

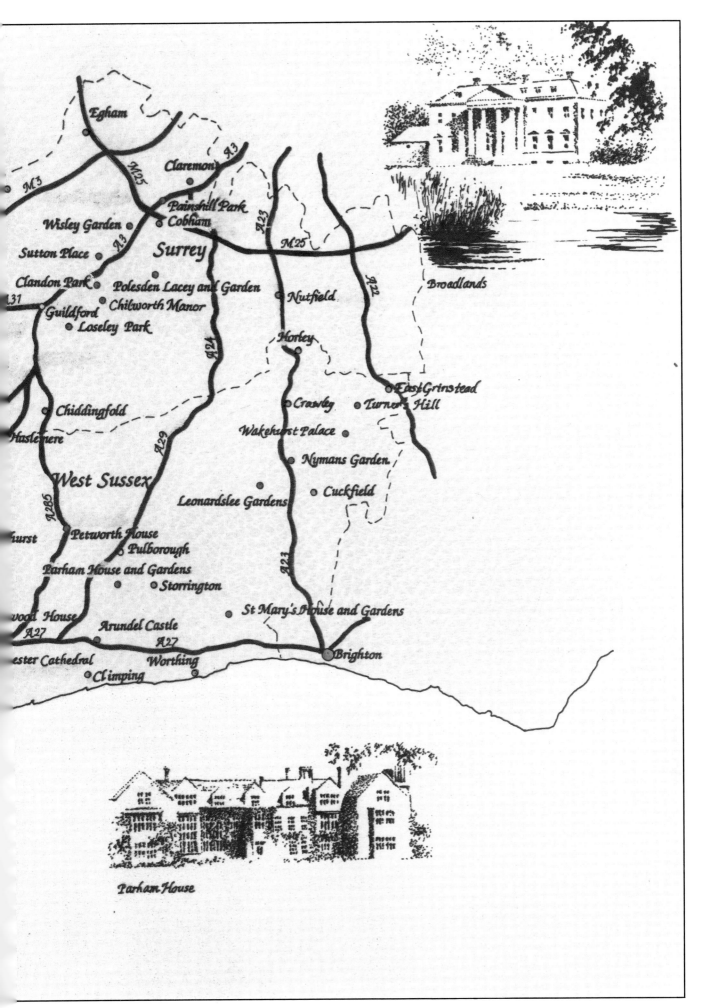

Parham House

53

THE SOUTHERN COUNTIES

The Southern Counties combine the inland splendour of the New Forest with its unspoilt beauty to the west of the region through the South Downs and beyond. They contrast on the coastline from the bustling ports of Portsmouth and Southampton, with its spectacular sailing waters, to the quaint harbours of Lymington and Chichester. The Isle of Wight is separated from the mainland by the Solent and known to many as the 'jewel' of Hampshire.

There are many enjoyable and famous walks in these beautiful counties, including The Pilgrims Way which is the ancient track that Pilgrims once travelled from Winchester across Southern England to Canterbury to visit the shrine of Thomas Beckett. Part of the walk will take you along the Downs Way (north between Farnham to the west and Dover to the east) from where you will see magnificent views across the Surrey countryside.

You can visit the pretty market town of Farnham, with its castle standing high on a hill and boasting in Castle Street one of the best examples of Georgian street architecture. Saxon Winchester has many legends and a beautiful cathedral. The Isle of Wight offers a variety of sights to see including Queen Victoria's holiday home, Osborne House. West Sussex, as well as providing us with spectacular scenery from the South Downs also has the beautiful historic City of Chichester.

BEAULIEU AND THE NEW FOREST

William the Conqueror ordered the planting of the New Forest in AD 1078 for his favourite sport of deer hunting. The forest stretched from the Avon on the west to Southampton water on the east, and from the borders of Wiltshire to the English Channel -that was 700 years ago. Now the area has reduced considerably although still covering 144 square miles. The forest is divided into three areas, all with very different characters. Open moorland, heather, furze and bracken make up the northern region which is split into five parallel ridges by streams heading for the River Avon. The middle part of the forest lives up to the true meaning of the word 'forest' with old woods and thickets and plantations of young trees. There is cultivated land around Lyndhurst, Minstead and Burley, and wonderful walks, whether on foot or horseback. The southern part of the forest is overgrown in places consisting mainly of bare heathland. The Court Verderers administer the laws of the forest as they have done for hundreds of years. There is a great variety of wildlife in the forest which would be hard to find anywhere else in Britain. Birdwatchers will be in their element. In the winter the forest is far from being a lonely place with siskins and bramblings to keep it company. The coastal haunts of the forest attract waders and occasionally rarely seen birds such as osprey, avocet and spoonbills.

The New Forest remains a place of outstanding and unspoilt beauty which gives a great deal of pleasure to all who travel here.

Beaulieu, situated in the heart of the New Forest is the family home of Lord Montagu. As a memorial to his father who was one of the pioneers of motoring in Great Britain, there is now a world famous **National Motor Museum** (featured later). **Exbury Gardens** are situated in a beautiful 200 acre woodland garden. Created by Lionel de Rothschild, Exbury Gardens are famous for their magnificent displays of rhododendrons, azaleas, camellias and other beautiful floral plantings. After

wandering round these lovely gardens you can enjoy refreshments in the tea room.

Broadlands was the home of Lord Mountbatten of Burma. This magnificent example of Palladian architecture is set in Capability Brown parkland by the banks of the River Test (featured later).

The **Sir Harold Hillier Gardens** and **Arboretum** will be found near Romsey. The gardens contain the largest collection of woody trees and shrubs in the British Isles. They are planted in an attractive landscape of 160 acres of Hampshire countryside. Truly a garden for all seasons there is something of considerable interest and beauty to enjoy in every month of the year. In spring time there are magnificent floral displays from rhododendrons, azaleas and camellias followed by pretty pastel shades of summer flowering shrubs. Autumn then takes over as colourful leaves fall, and the midwinter colour and scent are provided by Chinese witch hazels.

Breamore House, built in 1583 of rose coloured brick stands in the most beautiful parkland surrounded by Home farms, providing a tranquil atmosphere. It has been the home of only two families, the Dodingtons who built it, and the Hulses who bought it in 1748, and is now the family home of the present Baronet, Sir Weston Hulse. The house features fine collections of paintings and tapestries with a beautiful display of porcelain and furniture. Although many rooms are furnished in sophisticated Georgian style, the house has managed to main-

Sir Harold Hillier Gardens

tain its Tudor character. There is an impressive picture collection including works by Dutch masters, Van Dyck, Teniers, Janssens and Lievens. You can also enjoy the Carriage Museum housed in the Queen Anne Stable Block. The Red Rover, the last stage coach to travel between London and Southampton is a great favourite. The gardens are beautiful with a mass of daffodils covering grassy banks. In the formal yew garden you will see fine 17th century statues of the four seasons by Francesco Franchi.

SAXON WINCHESTER

King Alfred designated Winchester the Capital of England, and he is now commemorated in a statue in The Broadway. Since this time Winchester has been an important city both historically and administratively, having the oldest public school in England. The magnificent **Cathedral** dates back as far as the 7th century to St Peter's church which once occupied the site. When the Normans came to Britain, William the Conqueror arranged for the Cathedral to be built in the Norman's distinctive architectural style; this is reflected in the tower, transepts and the crypt. Legend has it that Winchester was a contender for Camelot, the capital of King Arthur. You can see the Round Table when you visit the Great Hall which is all that remains of the Norman Castle. Another legend born in Winchester comes from the expression that if it rains on St Swithin's Day it will rain for the next forty days. St Swithin was one of the Cathedral's Bishops, who wished to be buried in the churchyard where rain would not fall on him. His wish wasn't granted therefore he caused it to rain for forty days.

The Cathedral is one of the longest in Europe measuring 556 feet. You can see Pilgrims' hall where in the middle ages Pilgrims used to rest on their journey to Canterbury. The remains of **Wolvesey Castle**, the former residence of the Bishop of Winchester, lie next to Cathedral Close. It was reduced to ruins during the Civil War. Further along from Cathedral Close is **Winchester College**, which was founded in 1382 and is now one of the country's leading schools for boys. Inside is a school room designed by Sir Christopher Wren.

Mottisfont Abbey, situated near Romsey is owned by the National Trust. It was granted after the Dissolution to William, Lord Sandys, Lord Chamberlain to Henry VIII in exchange for the villages of Chelsea and Paddington. It was unusual that the monastery was adapted to incorporate the church and gives the impression of a wonderful blend of medieval priory and 16th century mansion. Sash windows were inserted as part of the Georgian alterations, in fact few traces of the Tudor interior remain. The main feature of the house is the drawing room known as the Whistler's Room which takes its name from Rex Whistler's elaborate trompe l'oeil. The gardens are beautiful with a lovely variety of plants. Visitors especially enjoy the national collection of pre-1900 shrub roses set in walled gardens. The aroma is wonderful from this colourful display.

William Cobbett once wrote of **Avington Park** that it was 'one of the prettiest places in the country', this is certainly true. The house was enlarged in 1670 for George Brydes, when two wings were added and a classical portico, surmounted by three statues. The architect was possibly a follower of Sir Christopher Wren. You can visit the Staterooms which include the Ballroom and Salon, boasting their magnificent early 18th century painted ceilings. Pompeiian style painted figures can be seen in the Red Drawing Room and Library. By prior arrangement you can see the state bed and dressing rooms. **St Mary's Church** is one of the finest Georgian churches in England. It is in the grounds close by and must be visited. After your visit to Avington Park you can enjoy afternoon tea in the large Victorian Orangery.

Jane Austen's House, Chawton near Alton, contains many personal relics of herself and family. Most of her admired novels were written or revised at this red brick building where the author spent the last eight years of her life from 1809 until 1817.

WATERSHIP DOWN

Watership Down are the magnificent downs near Kingsclere which apart from the many beautiful walks are renowned for their rabbits!

The Vyne is situated between Bramley and Sherborne St John, four miles north of Basingstoke. One of the most beautiful Tudor houses of its time, it was built in the early 16th century by William Sandys, who later became Lord Chamberlain. Its appearance is low, U-shaped red brick surrounded by woodland. A century later a classical portico was added and the original mullions have been replaced with Georgian sash windows. The Vyne overlooks lawns and a picturesque lake with waterlilies. From the other side of the lake on the north side of the house you can see the chapel - this is one of the most perfect private oratories in England; rising to the height of two stories, it remains as it was built between 1518 and 1527. It features magnificent stained glass windows which depict Henry VIII and Catherine of Aragon amongst its most noble. After the Civil War, Lord Sandys moved to Mottisfont Abbey and the new owner John Chute made many interior alterations during the 18th and early 19th centuries. One of the outstanding features is the Palladian style Staircase Hall with its fluted columns, panelling and a decorative plaster ceiling. Many furnishings collected over the years include Queen Anne furniture, tapestries, porcelain figures and Venetian painted glass plates.

Stratfield Saye House, although originally built in 1630 by Sir William Pitt, it was in 1817 that the nation purchased the house for the first Duke of Wellington after his victory at Waterloo (featured later).

Avington Park

THE SOUTHERN COUNTIES

The Hawk Conservancy situated at Weyhill near Andover is a specialist centre for birds of prey from all over the world. Set in a beautiful wild garden on the edge of Salisbury Plain the birds are trained using traditional methods. You can see hawks, falcons, eagles and owls in flight where you can appreciate their great beauty and splendour. This takes place several times a day, weather permitting.

ISLE OF WIGHT - THE 'JEWEL' OF HAMPSHIRE

The Isle of Wight is a small island thirteen miles from Cowes, south to St Catherine's Point, and seventeen miles from the Needles east to Bembridge. With its miles of sandy beaches, rugged cliffs and unspoilt countryside it has much to offer its visitors. Queen Victoria and Prince Albert enjoyed many summer holidays here at their home, Osborne House, just outside Cowes, which is now open to the public. Cowes, although full of lovely Georgian and Victorian buildings, is famous for its yachting tradition. Home of the Royal Yacht Club, the club house stands on the site of a castle originally built by Henry VIII. Outside Newport you can see Carisbrooke Castle where Charles I was held prisoner for almost a year. The **Tennyson Trail** runs for 15 miles from Carisbrooke to the western side of the island at Alum. Passing through **Brighstone Forest** the trail emerges on Brighstone Down and then on to East Afton Down to Freshwater Bay and the Bird Sanctuary on Tennyson Down. The Down is held in memory of the poet who walked there daily. You can see wonderful views off the jagged chain of cliffs known as **The Needles** from the Tennyson Monument, where a fort of 1861 called **The Needles Old Battery** has been restored.

Painshill Park

Ryde, Sandown and Shanklin are the island's popular seaside resorts along with Ventnor where you can visit the **Botanic Gardens**. Pretty postcard villages such as Brighstone and Godshill have lovely thatched cottages, cafes and gift shops, there is also **Winkle Row**, a group of ancient cottages which is a wonderful subject for the camera, situated in the unspoilt village of Calbourne.

With the island's beaches, magnificent countryside and abundance of historical attractions you will definitely enjoy your time here.

Osborne House, just outside Cowes, was the holiday home of Queen Victoria and her beloved Prince Albert. Here they spent many happy summers with their children enjoying the sea air. Built by Thomas Cubitt mostly between 1845 and 1851, overlooking the Solent, the house was designed as an Italianate Villa with two tall towers and a first floor loggia or balcony, of which Albert partly designed and supervised all the construction work. King Edward VII, Queen Victoria's son, presented Osborne to the nation and requested that it be preserved as a sacred memory to his parents. You can visit the rooms where the Royals lived which have hardly changed: photographs, paintings, gifts from visitors and many mementoes can be seen everywhere. Note the intricate Indian plaster decoration in the Dunbar Room and the furniture made from deer antlers in the Horn Room. The Billiard Room has a magnificent painted billiard table and the Royal Nursery has been restored on the second floor, allowing visitors a fascinating insight into the royal children's early years. Queen Victoria died at her beloved Osborne in 1901 and left behind many treasures for us to enjoy.

Appuldurcombe House, near Wroxall was never a house but a status symbol. The house was begun in 1702 by Sir Robert Worsley but he ran out of money. The east facade dates from this year with its beautiful example of English baroque architecture. Set in beautiful parkland designed by 'Capability' Brown, the house was completed at the end of the century. It was damaged by a German landmine in 1943 and is now an empty shell. Once an important estate in the Isle of Wight, the remains of this grand house now owned by English Heritage are well worth visiting.

Carisbrooke Castle, also owned by English Heritage, has many attractions but the most popular one with children is the donkeys, which work a 16th century wheel, pulling water from the 161 foot deep well. The oldest parts of the castle are 12th century but there was also a wooden castle before that - 71 steps high, up the great mound. There are still fragments of a Roman wall at its base. The castle although fortified against the French, then the Spaniards, is well known as the prison of Charles I from 1647 to 1648. You can enjoy finding evidence of the castle's 11th century origins and of the 16th century modernisations. The impressive gatehouse is set into the walls through which you pass when you enter the castle.

SURREY HEATHLANDS AND ROYAL HUNTING GROUNDS

Loseley Park near Guildford is the home of the More-Molyneux family whose ancestors built the house in the reign of Elizabeth I. Apart from being a beautiful Elizabethan Mansion it is famous for its dairy farm with a Jersey herd producing renowned additive free dairy products (featured later).

THE SOUTHERN COUNTIES

Still in the Guildford area we visit **Chilworth Manor** whose beautiful gardens were laid out in the 17th century on the site of an 11th century monastery. There is a lovely walled garden dating back to the 18th century where you can enjoy an abundance of spring flowers, a variety of flowering shrubs and herbaceous borders and also the 11th century stewponds with colourful displays of flowers. The house is open but at very limited times.

Clandon Park owned by the National Trust is a magnificent Palladian house built between 1731 and 1735 by Giacomo Leoni, and looks as if it should be in Venice not set in Surrey countryside. Clandon is one of the five remaining buildings by this Venetian architect whose interior is as beautiful as its exterior, with the highly decorated formal marble hall being its most impressive feature. Built for Thomas, 2nd Baron Onslow, to replace an Elizabethan house his family acquired in 1641, it has remained in the family ever since. Although few of the original contents remain, Clandon still has impressive furniture, porcelain, textiles and a wonderful collection of 17th and 18th century Chinese birds.

The recently restored **Claremont Landscape Garden** at Esher, owned by the National Trust, is the earliest surviving English landscape garden. Famous gardening names such as Bridgeman, 'Capability' Brown, William Kent and Vanbrugh have all worked on Claremont's designs. It is said to be one of the first gardens designed in the natural manner and it even pre-dates Stourhead by some twenty years. You can see beautiful exotic trees and avenues, an island with a pavilion, grotto and turf amphitheatre. Rhododendrons and laurel provide beautiful displays of colour. **Polesden Lacy,** the National Trust's

property near Dorking, was originally a Regency Villa which was altered in the Edwardian period. It has a beautiful 18th century garden (featured later).

Painshill Park at Cobham is one of the most visited 18th century landscape gardens in England. Charles Hamilton designed this lovely ornamental garden between 1738 and 1773 by creating gardens of different moods and variety. You can enjoy long views across the Surrey countryside between the trees and the mysterious lake which is never completely visible at any point. The best way to enjoy Painshill Park is to take a leisurely circuit walk, that way you won't miss any of the wonderful sights. A Gothic temple, a 'Chinese' arched bridge, a ruined abbey, a grotto, a spectacular water wheel - all disappear and reappear as the walk proceeds. The Park boasts breathtaking vistas, a serpentine lake and many beautiful buildings and follies.

Coverwood Lakes at Ewhurst are pretty landscaped water and cottage gardens in a beautiful setting between Holmbury Hill to the north and Pitch Hill to the south. There are colourful displays of rhododendrons, azaleas, primulas and both mature and young trees to see. There are four small lakes, a bog garden and a young thirty one and a half acre arboretum, along with a herd of pedigree Poll Hereford cattle and a flock of Mule sheep in the adjoining farm. After wandering around these lovely gardens you can enjoy tea and home-made cakes.

WEST SUSSEX - THE SOUTH DOWNS

Goodwood House lies in magnificent gardens which are notable for the trees planted by successive Dukes of Richmond.

Coverwood Lakes

THE SOUTHERN COUNTIES

In 1750 Goodwood consisted of 1100 acres, by 1806 the estate boasted 17,000 acres, of which 12,000 remain today.

Adjacent to the racecourse on the crest of the South Downs is the wonderful **Goodwood Country Park** which measures sixty acres. Goodwood House was first purchased by the 1st Duke of Richmond, son of King Charles II, and has remained the home of the Dukes of Richmond ever since and acquired many wonderful treasures collected by all ten Dukes. There are pictures by Canaletto, Van Dyke, Stubbs, and Reynolds, wonderful French tapestries and porcelain. Smaller treasures such as the silver plate from which Napoleon ate his breakfast on the morning of the Battle of Waterloo and an emerald ring given by Charles II to Louise de Querrouaille are fascinating.

Chichester, built by the Romans, is nowadays famous for its Festival Theatre and Arts, but the **Norman Cathedral** is still a sight to be seen with its tall 277 feet slim spire. It dominates the skyline and is visible from the sea at almost every point in the city. In 1245 St Richard of Chichester became Bishop and was adopted as the town's saint. The old spire collapsed in a gale in 1861 but was successfully reconstructed, preserving its original design, by Sir Gilbert Scott. Features of the Cathedral include double aisles of the nave with its fine Norman arches and 14th century choir stalls. More modern works of art include the brightly coloured altar tapestry designed by John Piper in 1966 and the oil painting by Graham Sutherland, depicting the appearance of Christ to Mary Magdalene on the first Easter morning. Recently discovered Roman remains under the foundations of the Cathedral can be seen in the Guildhall museum. Composer Gustav Holst is buried in the north transept.

Arundel Castle, situated in magnificent grounds overlooking the River Arun is the ancestral home of the Dukes of Norfolk (featured later).

Parham at Pulborough, is a beautiful Elizabethan Country House built of local stone in 1577 for Sir Thomas Palmer. In 400 years it has been the home of only three families and is now lived in by Mrs P A Tritton. There are many wonderful rooms to see including the Great Hall with its panels, original carved oak screen and Elizabethan fire place which was discovered between 1946 and 1947 behind three others. Portraits include that of Henry Frederick, Prince of Wales, by Robert Peake in 1611 and a portrait possibly of Queen Elizabeth I. In the panelled Great Parlour you can see intricate needlework, carpets and 17th century royal portraits. As well as having fine furniture and pictures in many beautiful settings spanning over four centuries, there is also a very rare early embroidery and tapestry collection that is unique. The garden is a joy with magnolias, cherries and wisteria leading to the outstanding walled garden. Colourful shrub borders, a herb garden enclosed by a yew hedge and a romantic orchard lead to a wonderful display and aroma in the rose garden with a unique feature being the new brick and turf maze. These gardens are a delight to walk round and afterwards you can enjoy tea served in the kitchen amongst a wonderful display of the copper 'batterie de cuisine'.

Petworth House owned by the National Trust is set in a beautiful deer park and was re-built from 1688 to 1696 by the 6th Duke of Somerset (featured later).

St Mary's House at Bramber is definitely worth a visit as it is

St Mary's House, Bramber

THE SOUTHERN COUNTIES

one of the most ancient and distinguished houses of its kind in Britain. The foundations of St Mary's go back to the 12th century when land at Bramber was granted to the Knights Templar. The present house was re-fashioned c1470 by William of Waynflete, Bishop of Winchester and founder of Magdalen College, Oxford. Classified as 'the best late 15th century timber framing in Sussex' the house came into private ownership after the Dissolution of the Monasteries. There is much to see at St Mary's: fine panelled rooms, including the unique 'painted room' which was elaborately decorated for the visit of Queen Elizabeth I; the King's Room which has connections with Charles II's escape to France in 1651; and the rare 16th century painted wall-leather with splendid carved oak fire places are just a few of the features. The Library contains the largest book collection of first editions and illustrated books by the celebrated 19th century comic poet and engraver, Thomas Flood. The gardens are also part of St Mary's charm. A lovely end to your visit would be to have tea, which is served in the Music Room.

Situated high up on the Downs is the National Trust's property **Uppark** which has remained almost unaltered since the 18th century. The beautiful interior was the work of Sir Matthew Fetherstonhaugh, who bought Uppark in 1747. A wealthy man, he redecorated most of the principal rooms and enriched the house with collections of furniture and works of art. Sir Matthew's wife, Sarah, introduced a Queen Anne doll's house which is housed in a room off the dining room. You can still see some of Uppark's 18th century damask curtains and flock wallpaper, and imagine what life was like for those servants by visiting its Victorian kitchens and domestic quarters. Part of Uppark's charm comes from its fabulous setting with views across a picturesque landscape to the sea.

Stansted Park is the beautiful home of the Earl of Bessborough, situated on the borders of Hampshire and Sussex set in glorious parkland. Surrounded by part of the ancient forest of Bere,

Stansted House was built on its present site in 1688 about the same time as nearby Uppark. In 1900 the main part of the house was destroyed by fire and rebuilt in 1903. The 9th Earl of Bessborough purchased the estate in 1924 and arranged for H.S. Goodhart-Rendel to restore the chapel as it is now. John Keats was inspired there to write some of his finest verse. There are beautiful and elegant rooms to see with collections, portraits and a fascinating **Museum of Theatrical Costumes** and artefacts. There are over 30 acres of grounds which include walled gardens and an arboretum containing many trees including the cedar of Lebanon which was probably planted about 1575.

Also owned by the National Trust is the magnificent 30 acre garden, **Nymans,** which is at Handcross four and a half miles south of Crawley. Surrounded by the Sussex Weald, this fabulous garden was created over more than half a century from 1890 by Ludwig Messel and his son Leonard. Here you will find rare and beautiful shrubs and plants from all over the world. There is something of interest all year round from spring time daffodils to the scarlet and gold of maples in autumn. There are amazing views to the heights of the Weald and to the South Downs from the terrace overlooking the park. While on the subject of gardens, we travel north west of Ardingly to **Wakehurst Place**, owned by the National Trust and managed by the Royal Botanic Gardens, Kew. Here you will discover a wonderful collection of exotic trees, shrubs and various other plants and the extensive water gardens are magical. Designed in a horseshoe to follow the valley, the garden is never far from water. Other features include the Winter Garden, Rock Walk and the Loder Valley Nature Reserve.

Here we leave these beautiful southern counties with their mixture of countryside and stately homes in the hope that you have enjoyed your travels through a truly glorious part of England.

Stansted Park

BEAULIEU

Lord Montagu's home, set in the heart of the beautiful woodlands of the New Forest, has been owned by his family since the 16th century. In 1538 Sir Thomas Wriothesley, later Earl of Southampton, acquired the 8,000 acre estate after the Dissolution of the Monasteries. The 13th century Beaulieu Abbey was in ruins but for the Great Gatehouse which Sir Thomas altered into a modest manor house, known as Palace House.

Following the death of the 4th Earl of Southampton in 1667, the Beaulieu estate passed into the family of the Duke of Montagu who had married his youngest daughter. At the end of the 18th century the estate passed, again by marriage to the Dukes of Buccleuch and in 1867 Beaulieu was given by the 5th Duke to Lord Henry Scott, the present owners grandfather, as a wedding present.

Henry decided that Palace House was too small and cramped and engaged Sir Arthur Blomfield to carry out extensive alterations. Major rebuilding was begun in 1871 and completed in 1874. The style was Victorian Gothic, but wherever possible Blomfield incorporated the monastic remains, even in the attics. This is particularly evident in the Dining Hall and Lower Drawing Room with their fine fan-vaulted ceilings. Today, Palace House, with all the atmosphere of a lived in home, offers an insight into the past with many fascinating family treasures, portraits and photographs. Costumed figures depict notable events in the family's history.

Beaulieu Abbey was founded in 1204 when King John made a gift of land to the Cistercian Monks. Although much was destroyed during Henry VIII's Dissolution some buildings have survived besides the Great Gatehouse, now Palace House. The scale of the great Abbey church can still be seen and the arches of the Cloisters evoke the peace and solitude of Cistercian life. The Domus now houses an exhibition illustrating the daily life of the monks.

Beaulieu is famous as the home of the National Motor Museum, one of the finest of its kind in the world. It is a fascinating collection of more than 250 vehicles and displays which illustrate how motoring has been part of our daily lives since the 1890s. The museum's origins date back to 1952 when Lord Montagu displayed a handful of veteran cars in Palace House as a memorial to his father, a motoring pioneer.

'Wheels' is an exciting journey in electronically-controlled pods through amazing displays that bring alive 100 years of motoring; a trip through time from an Edwardian picnic to the possibilities of motoring in the 21st century. One wonders what the monks would have thought of all this!

There are pleasant grounds in which to stroll beside the Mill Pond with its family of swans, and the Brabazon Suite provides everything from snacks to delicious meals. The grounds can be enjoyed from the Monorail which also travels through the roof of the Motor Museum providing a bird's-eye view of the historic vehicles below.

BROADLANDS

Standing amidst lawns which slope gently down to the River Test, Broadlands enjoys uninterrupted views across the meadows to the sweep of wooded hills beyond. The family home of Lord Mountbatten until his tragic death in 1979, and now the home of his grandson Lord Romsey, this beautiful house is an example of the finest mid-Georgian design.

A previous owner, the 2nd Viscount Palmerston engaged the services of 'Capability' Brown who, in 1766 landscaped the grounds and altered and improved the house. He squared the house in the classical Palladian style and encased it in pale coloured brick to give the appearance of stone and added the imposing South Portico. In 1788 a second portico was added by Henry Holland. The main rooms were decorated in the style of Robert Adam.

The octagonal Domed Hall has a coffered ceiling which, together with its colour scheme suggests gently falling snow. Here and in the adjoining Sculpture Hall, pieces from the Broadlands collection of ancient Greek and Roman marbles are displayed to great effect. The dining room, with its walls of clear, vibrant yellow forms a perfect setting for the three magnificent Van Dyck portraits which hang here. This sophisticated room demonstrates Lady Romsey's skill at incorporating modern principles of design within the elegant framework of the house.

The delicate plasterwork of the white and gold Saloon is an example of neo-classical design at its finest. This classical theme extends to the fine English furniture. There is a wonderful collection of Sevres and Meissen porcelain. The lovely intricate ceiling in the Drawing Room is inset with oval panels painted by Angelica Kauffman and this room was a particular favourite of Edwina, Lady Mountbatten.

The Library contains many family portraits, as well as the most famous of Broadlands paintings, The Iron Forge by Joseph

Wright, bought by the 2nd viscount Palmerston in 1772. The paintings on the North Staircase trace the direct descent of Lord Mountbatten through the male line and his connections with the Russian Royal family can be seen in the Oak Room.

The Palmerston Room, with its more sombre Victorian atmosphere is a permanent tribute to the life and work of the 3rd Viscount Palmerston, the great 19th Century Prime Minister and possibly the most popular in Britain's history. The room seems filled with his presence - plans for the Crimea campaign remain on his desk at which he always stood when working.

Broadlands has seen many distinguished owners with strong political and naval traditions - a theme evident in the many collections on display lending an unusual and informal atmosphere to the house. Of the many important guests here, several have been members of the Royal family with whom it has always been a favourite - especially for honeymoons.

The Mountbatten exhibition is on permanent display in the stable block and provides a fitting memorial to the life and service of one of our most respected and warmly regarded public figures.

Broadlands rolling Hampshire parkland, just ½ mile from the village of Romsey off the A31, needed only minimal enhancement from 'Capability' Brown. The River Test, renowned for its fishing, flows through the park for over 3miles. In 1736, the 1st Viscount Palmerston wrote to his son '.... I have two salmons caught out of the river by me!'

There are no formal gardens at Broadlands which serves to emphasise the graciousness of this lovely home.

A restaurant, shop and delightful picnic area can be found close to the Japanese stream.

STRATFIELD SAYE HOUSE

In the heady days of victory after the long and arduous campaign at Waterloo a grateful nation voted a sum of money for the purchase of a house worthy of the heroic Duke of Wellington. After considering - and rejecting - many grander houses, in 1817 the Great Duke chose Stratfield Saye. It is clear that from the outset he intended to demolish the house and build 'Waterloo Palace' which would rival Blenheim Palace, built 100 years before in similar circumstances.

As it became apparent that the available funds were insufficient for his plans, the practical Duke set about making his modest home convenient and comfortable and was well satisfied. Not so his friends who considered Stratfield Saye small, poky and unworthy of him. Sir Robert Peel was positively scathing and Queen Victoria was not enthusiastic although she found the house convenient, if rather hot. She presumably referred to the central heating in the passages and the blue patterned china water closets which the Duke had installed in every room.

The main part of the house and stable blocks were built in 1630 by Sir William Pitt and the house remains relatively unchanged, but the interior was extensively remodelled, particularly between 1730 and 1790 by George Pitt, Baron Rivers. At this time the red-brick was covered with stucco and painted white. The Great Duke added the Conservatory in 1838 and two outer wings in 1846, taking care to match the existing gables.

The impressive galleried Hall has Roman mosaic pavements brought from Silchester and the portraits on the upper wall are all Dukes and Duchesses of Wellington. In the Staircase Hall is one of the Great Duke's early radiators - still in working order, though now fired by oil.

The beautiful Gallery, which looks out across the River Loddon to the park, is decorated with prints edged with gilded wooden beading applied to the walls, with gold leaf covering the spaces between. This unusual technique was copied by the Great Duke in the Print Room and several of the bedrooms. The Small Drawing Room contains a lovely collection of miniatures, drawings and watercolours, mostly of the family.

The presence of the Great Duke is even now apparent throughout the house, perhaps nowhere more so than in the Library. He was often to be found in here and much of the furniture, ornaments and personal mementoes are still here including a lock of hair from Copenhagen, his favourite charger. The faithful old war horse carried his master the entire day at the Battle of Waterloo and the Music Room is largely devoted to his memory.

The Wellington Exhibition in the Stables depicts the life and times of Arthur, 1st Duke of Wellington, and houses a profusion of mementoes of this great man's long life as soldier and statesman - including of course the famous boots! Also on view is the massive Funeral Car commissioned by the Prince Consort for the Great Duke's state funeral procession in 1852.

On each side of the house lie the Pleasure Grounds with many rare and interesting trees with a particularly fine group of Wellingtonias, named in honour of the Great Duke in 1853. In the Ice House Paddock lies the grave of Copenhagen, buried with full military honours after living out his days in retirement at Stratfield Saye, frequently ridden by his master and a multitude of children. The spreading Turkey Oak which shelters his grave grew from an acorn planted by Mrs Apostles, the Duke's housekeeper.

The Wellington Country Park offers nature trails, fishing, boating, wind surfing and a host of other family activities in 550 acres of unspoilt countryside astride the A32.

LOSELEY PARK

Loseley Park is a stunning Elizabethan mansion built in 1562 by Sir William More, an ancestor of the present owner and occupier, James More-Molyneux, from stone brought from the ruins of Waverley Abbey, now 850 years old. Visitors to Loseley Park often comment on the very friendly atmosphere of the house - it is a country house, a family home, rather than a museum. The Latin inscription over the inner door of the Entrance Hall, 'Invidiae claudor, pateo sed semper amico', roughly translated as 'I am shut to envy, but always open to a friend' sums up the welcome that visitors can expect.

Dignified and beautiful, the house is set amid magnificent parkland scenery, with the garden terrace and moat walk also open to visitors. The house is open from Wednesday to Saturday during the months of June to September, between 2 and 5pm. In a tour that begins in the Great Hall, there is much of historical and family interest to take in. Each succeeding generation of the family has added its contribution of furniture, books and paintings, down to the photographs of the present generations.

Fine paintings, including full length portraits of King James I and his Queen hang in the Great Hall, together with a portrait of the Holbein school, of the boy King Edward VI. In the Library, a carved piece of wood above the mantelpiece bears the arms and initials of Queen Elizabeth I to commemorate her visits to Loseley. The beautifully proportioned Drawing Room has a gilded ceiling decorated for King James I's visit and a unique chimneypiece, intricately carved out of a solid block of chalk. Fine period furniture is to be found throughout the house, such as a rare inlaid Wrangleschrank cabinet, dating from the 16th century. These are all just a small taste of what the house has to offer. As well as Elizabeth I and James I,

H.M. Queen Mary has visited Loseley and the house has been featured in films for cinema and television.

Loseley Park also functions as a thriving agricultural estate. Some 700 head of Jersey cattle are kept at Loseley providing milk and cream for the famous Loseley dairy products. There is a farm shop where visitors can indulge in such temptations as Loseley Cereal Products, including stone ground wholemeal flour, quiches, bread and vegetables. Farm tours are available from April to October and must be booked in advance. These are planned to include the famous Jersey herd, cows and calves, and many rare breeds of sheep and pigs, peacocks and poultry. Trailer rides provide a rather more novel way of touring the farm. Other special events planned include Spring, Summer, Autumn and Christmas Craft Fairs to be held in the grounds in 1992.

There is yet more to Loseley Park. Loseley Tithe Barn, a 17th century timbered barn, originally two barns moved from farms on the estate, has been superbly rebuilt and modified to provide a uniquely attractive venue for many types of private and business functions. It is especially suitable for Wedding Receptions - with a beautiful setting of the backdrop of Loseley House for photographs. Excellent catering facilities and fine wines are supplied for each event, with menus created individually as required. Also housed within the Barn is a restaurant serving delicious lunches, snacks and teas.

Loseley Park is a truly magnificent experience. Situated just outside Guildford, this historic home is a rare treat and definitely worth the journey!

POLESDEN LACEY

Polesden Lacey is beautifully situated on high ground with fine views from the south terrace across the park-like landscape to the Ranmore Woods on the far side of the valley. To the east lie the steep slopes of Box Hill.

The present mansion was begun in 1821 on the site of a house once owned by the playwright Richard Sheridan. Designed by Thomas Cubitt around an open central courtyard, it is a charming two storey building with roughcast yellow washed walls. Though the interior of the house has been entirely reconstructed, the exterior preserves somthing of its Regency flavour.

In 1906, it was bought by Captain the Hon. Ronald Greville and his wife, Margaret, a celebrated Edwardian hostess. The atmosphere of Polesden Lacey is almost entirely due to Mrs Greville and the luxurious setting which she created for herself and her guests in the twilight years of country house society. Daughter of the McEwan brewing family, her father's fortune provided for her lavish lifestyle and her bequest of Polesden Lacey to the National Trust was made in his memory.

From her wealthy but obscure background, Mrs Greville burst into society upon her marriage in 1891, and began to consolidate her position in a calculated and determined fashion. Polesden Lacey provided the essential base from which she ran her campaign. Although she added only the Study to the house, the interior was remodelled by the architects of the Ritz Hotel. She achieved notable success and entertained Edward VII on a number of occasions, as well as many crowned heads of Europe and famous contemporaries such as Beverley Nichols and Harold Nicholson.

Possessed of a venomous wit, Mrs Greville talked little about her wonderful art collection, but if she did not have an acute artistic sensibility, she understood perfectly what was needed to create a richly appointed house of the period. The porcelain furniture, pictures and silver were combined in an eclectic manner and though perhaps lacking the discrimination of the connoisseur, it is easy to recognise the opulence and comfort which was precisely the required effect.

Beverley Nichols captured the social context in which Mrs Greville operated,' The hostesses of the twenties were like great galleons, sailing the social seas with all flags flying and all guns manned', and apparently not above stealing each other's chefs and gardeners. During the London season, flowers, fruit, vegetables and dairy produce had to be supplied from Polesden Lacey and sent daily to her house in London. She also had a penchant for violets which had to be produced in November.

The Dining Room at Polesden Lacey, the scene of some of Mrs Greville's most memorable triumphs, is neo-classical in style and hung with crimson silk brocade. Her collection of English portraits including works by Raeburn, Lawrence and Reynolds is to be found in this room.

The Drawing Room, resplendent with carved and gilt panelling, contains the sumptuous French furniture and oriental porcelain brought from Mrs Greville's London home, while in the Study the fine porcelain is Meissien and Furstenburg.

The Corridor around the central courtyard contains the major part of Mrs Greville's collection of pictures. Among the paintings is a group of early Italian works and a collection of Dutch landscapes.

It was always Mrs Greville's intention that Polesden Lacey should be a memorial to her father, but the house and its magnificent contents also paints a very vivid picture of this remarkable lady herself.

ARUNDEL CASTLE

This great castle, situated in magnificent grounds overlooking the River Arun and the Sussex Downs was built at the end of the llth century by Roger de Montgomery, Earl of Arundel. Through the Fitzalan family the castle passed by marriage to the Dukes of Norfolk who have held it ever since. The Duke of Norfolk is the premier Duke and hereditary Earl Marshall of England.

In 1556 Mary Fitzalan, daughter of the 12th Earl of Arundel married the 4th Duke of Norfolk who was beheaded for treason by order of Queen Elizabeth I on Tower Hill in 1572, thus forfeiting his title. Thomas, 14th Earl of Arundel was restored to many of the family honours, but spent much time abroad. In his absence during the Civil War, Arundel Castle was besieged by Roundheads in 1643 who mounted their guns on top of the church tower and were thus able to fire down inside the castle walls. Parts of the barbican still bear the marks of cannon ball attacks.

The 16th Earl was restored to the Dukedom after the War by Charles II, but chose not to live at Arundel which had been extensively damaged. The 8th Duke carried out repairs and the llth Duke, an amateur architect, began to reconstruct the castle to his own design in 1787.

The major rebuilding took place between 1875 and 1900 when the 15th Duke engaged C A Buckler as his architect, resulting in the present Victorian Gothic style of the castle. It has amongst its treasures a fascinating collection of fine furniture dating from the 16th century, tapestries, clocks and portraits by Van Dyck, Gainsborough, Reynolds, Mytens and Lawrence. Personal possessions of Mary Queen of Scots and a selection of heraldic items from the Duke of Norfolk's collection are on display.

The Picture Gallery was added to the castle c.1716 and here are hung portraits of the Dukes and Duchesses of Norfolk and some of the Earls of Arundel. One of of the great historic groups of family portraits, they include several of individual merit, such as the 6th Duke and Duchess by Lely and the 13th Duchess by Lawrence.

The Library is the principal survivor of the 11th Duke's work and is one of the most important Gothic rooms c.1800 in the country. It is entirely fitted out in carved Honduras mahogany as if it were a church with slender clustered columns supporting the vaulted ceiling. The ten thousand volumes are rich in manuscripts and Catholic history.

The grand and lofty Dining Room was the private chapel in the 18th century and was converted for its present use by the 11th Duke in 1795. He embellished it with a huge stained glass window showing the Queen of Sheba being entertained by Solomon. In 1846 this was removed prior to Queen Victoria's visit in case she failed to be amused. Displayed here are the Earl Marshal's baton and the gold cups presented at their coronation by Sovereigns since George II.

The elegant Drawing Room has a large heraldic chimney piece carved in Painswick stone. Buckler, as well as being an architect was Surrey Herald Extraordinary and worked out the heraldic decorations throughout the castle. The pier tables are of ormolu, not gilt wood, and for that reason extremely rare.

PETWORTH HOUSE

Although there has been a house on the site of Petworth since at least 1309, it owes its appearance today to Charles Seymour, 6th Duke of Somerset, nicknamed the 'Proud Duke'. It was he who in 1688 set about rebuilding the ancient house of the Percy family, which had been acquired on his marriage to the daughter and heiress of the last Earl of Northumberland in 1682. Of the earlier building only the chapel and cellars survive. In 1750 the estate passed by marriage to the Wyndham family, and in the following year Charles Wyndham, 2nd Earl of Egremont, employed the young 'Capability' Brown to landscape the park. During the long tenure of his son, the 3rd Earl, the great collections of pictures and sculpture for which Petworth is renowned were augmented by works of contemporary British artists, many of whom were his friends and frequent visitors to his house.

The Marble Hall dates almost entirely from the time of the Duke of Somerset and is the only important 17th century interior in the house to have survived both the fire of 1714 and the alterations of the 3rd Earl. The decoration is full of baroque French and Dutch features found only rarely in English houses of this date which suggests that Daniel Marot might have been involved in the remodelling of Petworth in 1688. Most of the paintings in this room are by Reynolds.

The 2nd Earl of Egremont, during the course of the Grand Tour, acquired the Old Master paintings and antique sculpture which today form the backbone of the Petworth collection. He also played a considerable role in 18th century politics and his official duties as Secretary of State for the South involved many banquets and he was heard genially to say, 'Well I have but three turtle dinners to come and if I survive them I shall be immortal.' Sadly he did not, and was succeeded by his young son.

The 3rd Lord Egremont introduced a golden age at Petworth and the North Gallery was largely his creation. It contains paintings and sculpture acquired earlier by his father. Among the artists represented in the Gallery are Turner, Gainsborough, Reynolds, Wilson, Zoffany, Romney and Fuceli. The Turner Room is devoted entirely to the works of the artist who was

a constant visitor to Petworth in the 1830's. He was given the old library as his studio and became deeply attached to his friend and patron, now in his 80's. The square Dining Room contains paintings by Van Dyck and the family silver, mainly by Paul Storr, and the Beauty Room is so called after the series of portraits by Sir Godfrey Kneller and Michael Dahl of the Ladies of the Court of Queen Anne, amongst whom the Duchess of Somerset was a familiar figure.

In 1837 he was succeeded by his natural son, later created Lord Leconfield, and in 1947 the 3rd Lord Leconfield gave Petworth to the National Trust.

Perhaps even more than for its fabulous collections, Petworth is famous for its park, 'Capability' Brown's masterpiece immortalised in Turner's paintings. The great sweep of parkland away from the west front of the house towards the lake, the smooth downland contours of the hills, and the perfectly balanced clumps of beeches, chestnuts and oaks owe more of their perfection to 'Capability' than to nature. The Pleasure Ground, woodland garden, was relatively unaltered by Brown except for the addition of a Doric Temple and the Ionic Rotunda. Between 1870 and 1914 the 2nd and 3rd Ladys Leconfield carried out some new planting, taking advantage of the sandstone soil to grow plants not seen in the surrounding chalk downs.

'Capability' Brown's greatest triumph at Petworth is the Serpentine Lake, created from a series of small ponds by damming the stream which fed them, thus creating the incomparable view from the house. On a pedastal in the shallow waters is a large stone hound, a memorial to one of the 3rd Earl's favourite dogs which is said to have drowned here.

Real Tennis has been played at Petworth House since the 16th century. The present court, one of the few remaining in the country attached to a private house, dates from 1872 and replaces an earlier court. The game is still played by the Petworth House Tennis Club - members only - but anyone interested should apply to the Secretary.

SOUTHERN COUNTIES

The south of England is considered to be the wealthiest area in Britain. This may or may not be the case, but what is certain is that it possesses an number of very fine country houses and gardens. These have been lovingly restored to their original state; small islands of splendour as the 20th century hurtles by.

Surrey often surprises as the Stockbroker Belt yields a treasure trove of historical houses and Royal hunting grounds.

Much of Sussex is downland and there are few more appealing places on a quiet summers' day. Its proximity to London does lead to some congestion but if you stray off the main roads you are more than likely to stumble on a peaceful village pub on a village green. There are all manner of hotels from which to explore the surrounding countryside, plus an ever increasing number of first class bed & breakfasts.

Hampshire is home to some fine chalk streams, flowing through sleepy villages and here, the dense woodlands contrast sharply with the expanse of the downs. The historic, cathedral city of Winchester is well worth a visit. However, this county is probably best known for its picturesque coastline and harbours so popular with the sailing fraternity. Full of contrast, Hampshire is also home of the New Forest and there are plenty of good hotels in this area from which to explore.

The North Downs of Surrey were initially settled by the Romans and were used as a 'pit stop' en route from London to Chichester. The Pilgrims Way is marked by the spot where the River Wey crosses the Downs. Although many people continuously passed through the county it was not until the heathlands were made popular by Royalty that it became a fashionable place to live. This is 'Tudor country' and many of the buildings are evidence of Tudor architectural development.

Coastal Sussex is a delightful part of England. One of the first areas to be settled, the remains of fortresses dating from the Iron Age have been discovered as has other evidence of settlement dating back before Christ. Numerous celebrated families made their homes here and these are now open to the public or have been converted into luxurious hotels.

The affluence of the area in some instances leads to comparatively higher prices, but do not be put off. There is a huge variety of charming establishments in this area should you wish to explore further.

HOTELS OF DISTINCTION

AMBERLEY CASTLE, Amberley, West Sussex.
Tel: (0798) 831992
A spectacular medieval fortress nestling in the South Downs provides the setting for this unique country castle hotel. Steeped in history, its battlements afford breathtaking views, while its 14th century curtain walls and portcullis tell tales of its fascinating history.

BAILIFFSCOURT, Climping, West Sussex. Tel: (0903) 723511
A 1930's replica of a 13th century courthouse which has been cleverly constructed from derelict properties from all over the South of England, this hotel offers many facilities. Basing itself on a medieval manor it is furnished accordingly with four poster beds and open log fires.

CAREYS MANOR HOTEL, Brockenhurst, Hampshire.
Tel: (0590) 23551
An elegant country house on the site of a royal hunting lodge and used by Charles II, Careys Manor is within easy reach of Stonehenge, Beaulieu, Broadlands, Salisbury and Winchester. The hotel is set in its own landscaped gardens in the glorious New Forest.

CHEQUERS HOTEL, Pulborough, West Sussex.
Tel: (07982) 2486
This historic Grade II listed building dates from the time of Queen Anne and is ideally placed for exploring the ancient Roman City of Chichester, as well as Arundel Castle and other stately homes.

CHEWTON GLEN HOTEL, New Milton, Hampshire.
Tel: (0425) 275341
Chewton Glen is situated in parkland between the New Forest and the sea and guarantees peace and quiet. The hotel offers many sporting facilities and its own team of highly trained therapists to pamper you.

CISSWOOD HOUSE, Lower Beeding, Sussex.
Tel: (0403) 891216
Built in 1928 as the country house for the then Chairman of Harrods, Cisswood is a friendly, family run hotel with an emphasis on quality. It is set in 12 acres of beautiful gardens.

CROWN INN, Chiddingford, Surrey. Tel: (024879) 2255
Creaking floor and stairs, this really is one of the oldest hostelries, established in 1383. All the best in linenfold panelling, inglenooks and the usual fascinating design.

FARRINGFORD HOTEL, Freshwater, Isle of Wight.
Tel: (0983) 752500
Set in attractive parkland and once the home of Lord Tennyson, this 18th century mansion counters the exterior grandeur of country living with an interior of endearing simplicity and comfort.

FIFEHEAD MANOR, Middle Wallop, Hampshire.
Tel: (0264) 781565
Part medieval, this comfortable hotel has been both a nunnery and family home. It is ideally placed for Salisbury and Winchester Cathedrals, Wilton House and Stonehenge.

GEORGE HOTEL, Odiham, Hampshire. Tel: (0256) 702081
This is an old coaching inn which dates from the 16th century. and still retains many of its original features, including an array of antiques. There are two distinct styles of food, either a tempting array of bar snacks or a wider choice in the restaurant which was earlier the home of the local assizes.

GHYLL MANOR, Rusper, West Sussex. Tel: (0293) 871571
Originally Elizabethan and now extended, Ghyll Manor is set in 40 acres of well tended grounds. There are conference and banqueting facilities available in this proudly maintained hotel.

GRAVETYE MANOR, East Grinstead, West Sussex.
Tel: (0342) 810567
One of the first Elizabethan manor houses to be converted to a

CHEWTON GLEN

In verdant parkland on the southern edge of the New Forest stands a magnificent country house hotel. Chewton Glen and its combination of splendour, elegance and comfort affords the discerning visitor every amenity they could wish for. The public areas are beautiful decorated, such as the light, airy main sitting room looking out onto the garden and the cosy inner lounge with its marble fireplace.

Our suites and double bedrooms have bathrooms ensuite, colour television, direct dial telephone and radio. They are furnished with antiques, attractive painted furniture and luxurious fabrics.

Guests can stroll around the thirty acre grounds or play tennis, croquet, golf or alternatively bathe in the heated outdoor swimming pool or off the shingle beach nearby. The hotel has an indoor tennis centre, health club with indoor pool, and its own nine-hole golf course.

Once the appetite has been whetted, the Marryat Room, the Hotel's Michelin-rosetted restaurant offers sumptuous fare. Our distinguished modern only by the quality of the service.

To find us leave the A35 on the Walkford Road and once through Walkford turn left down Chewton Farm Road.

Your stay will be a pleasant one; we hope it will be a long one. Whether you have enjoyed a day at the races or a round of golf at one of the many nearby golf courses we know that Chewton Glen will make your day that extra special.

Chewton Glen
New Milton
Hampshire

Tel: (0425) 275341
Fax: (0425) 272310

hotel, this is still one of the finest examples. The gardens are beautifully maintained, and the interior is rich with oak panelling, ornate plasterwork and a beautiful restaurant of outstanding reputation.

GREAT FOSTERS, Egham, Surrey. Tel: (0784) 433822
Originally built as a Royal hunting lodge, the hotel retains its imposing facade and has catered in the past for an impressive list of notable guests, stretching back over 400 years.

LAINSTON HOUSE HOTEL, Winchester, Hampshire. Tel: (0962) 63988
This elegant William and Mary country house stands in 63 acres of beautiful countryside which includes a reputedly haunted 12th century chapel, a country herb garden and dovecote. Historic Winchester and the New Forest are close by.

LANGRISH HOUSE, Petersfield, Hampshire. Tel: (0730) 66941
A former, possibly Carolean, manor house is the setting for Langrish House. The reception rooms offer splendid views of the beautifully maintained gardens. The bedrooms, some of them fairly new and single, have ensuite bath or shower.

LANGSHOTT MANOR, Horley, Surrey. Tel: (0293) 786680
A beautifully restored, Grade II listed Elizabethan manor house in 3 acres of gardens close to Gatwick Airport. This lovely hotel with its oak panelled reception rooms exudes warmth and character.

LITTLE THAKEHAM, Storrington, West Sussex. Tel: (0903) 744416
A splendid example of Sir Edwin Lutyen's memorable style including delightful gardens in the fashion of Gertrude Jekyll. Mullioned windows, minstrels' gallery and huge fireplaces add to the atmosphere, while the elegant dining room and tempting desserts here are especially good.

LYTHE HILL HOTEL, Haslemere, Surrey. (0428) 651251
An enchanting Tudor building and entire ancient hamlet nestling in the Surrey foothills is the setting for this luxurious hotel which offers many sporting facilities and fine cuisine. It is well situated for Goodwood, Cowdray and London.

MILL HOUSE HOTEL, Ashington, West Sussex. Tel: (0903) 892426
The road to this old coaching inn has not improved much since the 17th century, but the comfort here definitely belongs to the 20th century in this small hostelry.

MILLAND PLACE, Liphook, Hampshire. Tel: (0428) 76633
Close to historic Winchester on the slopes of a natural amphitheatre this lovingly restored country house commands 7 acres of stunning landscaped gardens with waterfalls, fountains and streams, all culminating in a lake.

NEW PARK MANOR, Brockenhurst, Hampshire. Tel: (0590) 23467
This beautiful King Charles manor house retains many original period features whilst offering every comfort and convenience and many sporting facilities. It is ideally based for Beaulieu and Broadlands.

MILLSTREAM HOTEL, Bosham, West Sussex. Tel: (0243) 573234
A most attractive small hotel on the banks of Chichester harbour, this hotel has been restored to an exceptionally high standard of comfort. An excellent mix of English and French cuisine using local specialities is available.

MONTAGU ARMS HOTEL, Beaulieu, Hampshire. Tel: (0590) 612324
Situated at the head of the River Beaulieu in the heart of the New Forest, this hotel makes a fine holiday spot. It offers award-winning English cuisine and is ideally situated for visiting the National Motor Museum, Exbury Gardens or Bucklers Hard.

NORFOLK ARMS HOTEL, Arundel, West Sussex. Tel: (0903) 882101
Near Arundel Castle, seat of the Dukes of Norfolk and originally part of the Ducal Estate, this hotel offers both ancient and modern bedrooms, all comfortably appointed.

NUTFIELD PRIORY, Redhill, Surrey. Tel: (0737) 822072
Towers, elaborate carvings, cloisters, stained glass, a uniquely architectured restaurant and antique-furnished all library make for fascinating visit. The hotel commands 40 acres of gardens and parkland with views across the Surrey and Sussex countryside.

OCKENDEN MANOR, Cuckfield, West Sussex. Tel: (0444) 416111
A 16th century manor house set in 9 acres of gardens, this hotel retains some striking period features. Ockenden Manor is famous for its modern English cuisine and outstanding cellar of 300 bins!.

OLD HOUSE, Wickham, Hampshire. Tel: (0329) 833049
This Georgian Hotel stands in the square of the lovely village. The rooms are elegantly furnished with many antiques, however, it is the restaurant which is so memorable. French 'regional' cuisine is superbly prepared and served, complemented by an excellent wine list.

OLD MANOR HOUSE, Romsey, Hampshire. Tel: (0794) 517353
Oak beams and huge fireplaces contribute to the atmosphere of this excellent restaurant. The menus are kept deliberately brief by the Chef patrons, but the food is memorable, as is the extensive wine list.

PARKHILL HOTEL, Lyndhurst, Hampshire. Tel: (0703) 282944
A graceful 18th century manor house in the grounds of a Roman fort in the New Forest, the hotel provides peace and relaxation with the highest standards of comfort and cuisine. There is also an outdoor swimming pool and coarse fishing is available.

PENNYHILL PARK HOTEL AND COUNTRY CLUB, Bagshot, Surrey. Tel: (0276) 71774
Great care has been taken to preserve the period atmosphere of this Victorian mansion, set in 112 acres of grounds. Individually furnished bedrooms and superb cuisine contribute to the luxury of this beautiful hotel.

THE SPREAD EAGLE

The Spread Eagle at Midhurst has been welcoming guests since its origin as a Tavern in 1430, and throughout its long and well documented history as a famous coaching inn. Today in private ownership, the Hotel has been sympathetically extended and renovated, and 20th century comforts incorporated. Yet over 550 years of history pervade the atmosphere of this Inn. Guy Fawkes enjoyed his visits, and in 1906 the King's horses were stabled here. Wander through the courtyard to the echoes of Cromwell's men and down to the mill pond that served the great South Mill in days gone by. The oldest part of the hotel has medieval foundations, whilst the newer 1650 part of the hotel has a Georgian influence. Tudor bread ovens, a wig powder closet and a series of Flemish stained glass windows, are just some of the features which create its very special atmosphere.

Traditional Sussex Christmas puddings compete with the copperware in decorating a lovely restaurant which features a large inglenook fireplace and dark oak beams. With the emphasis on quality and seasonal produce, the talented chefs offer both classic and innovative cooking. A choice from the well-devised and extensive wine list will complement your meal.

Careful thought has been given to the individual furnishings and fabrics for each of the 41 bedrooms. All have bathrooms, colour televisions and direct dial telephones. The perfect setting for those with something very special to celebrate is the Queen Elizabeth I four-poster suite.

Log fires welcome guests in colder months while summer drinks can be enjoyed in the walled courtyard, flanked by climbing roses and clematis.

It is all too easy to relax at the Spread Eagle, but guests can also explore the old country town of Midhurst or browse around Petworth, the recognised antique centre of the South. Chichester, with its sailing harbours, magnificent cathedral and acclaimed Festival Theatre, offers a wealth of English heritage and culture. Fishbourne Roman Palace and the Weald and Downland Museum are unique attractions close by. Goodwood House and Petworth House as well as Jane Austen's home at Chawton are all within easy reach. Cowdray Park Polo Club is a mere mile away, and the R.H.S. Wisley Gardens are just 25 miles away. The nearby South Downs offer wonderful walks, all in all, Midhurst is the perfect base from which to explore this beautiful, unspoilt area of the South East.

The Spread Eagle Hotel
South Street
Midhurst
West Sussex GU29 9NH
Tel: (0730) 816911
Fax: (0730) 815668
Telex: 86853 SPREAG G

PENNYHILL PARK

Just 50 minutes from central London in the full splendour of the English countryside lies the little village of Bagshot and Pennyhill Park.

At the end of the winding driveway the stone-fronted, creeper-clad house stands surrounded by 112 acres of parkland and lake. This is Pennyhill Park, built in 1849 by the pioneering Canadian bridge-builder, James Hodge. The building has been altered several times to suit the individual tastes and requirements of its various owners.

The total commitment to service at Pennyhill complement the traditions of its historic past. On entering the main hallway and with the stately sweep of the period staircase a warm welcome awaits you from attentive staff. Trained to Edwardian standards of courtesy they provide impeccable and discreet service.

Peace and tranquillity surround this house which, though old, provides every modern amenity.

You can watch polo at Smiths' Lawn Windsor; Sunningdale and Wentworth are just two of the nearby prestigious golf courses. Pennyhill Park also has its own nine-hole golf course and other sporting facilities including tennis courts, a Roman-styled swimming pool, clay pigeon shooting and horse riding stables with professional coaching. The sauna and solarium are housed in the Pennyhill Park orangery, and the three-acre lake is annually stocked with brown and rainbow trout for those in search of more tranquil pursuits.

The award winning Latymer restaurant provides all the elegance amd quiet dignity expected of its surroundings. The food, of mainly British produce, is served in the traditional way; and the service, known to many, is complemented by an outstanding selection of fine wines.

There are 76 bedrooms and suites in this fine example of the English country house, all individually designed and beautifully furnished. Each room is named after a shrub or flower, save for the most luxurious Hayward suite, the namesake of the last permanent occupant of this English country manor house. Every room at Pennyhill Park is furnished and decorated using soft, elegant fabrics and comforting themes such as walnut and oak.

Pennyhill Park Hotel and Country Club,
London Road,
Bagshot,
Surrey. GU19 5ET
Tel: (0276) 71774

SOUTHERN COUNTIES

RHINEFIELD HOUSE, Brockenhurst, Hampshire.
Tel: (0590) 22922
A substantial Victorian mansion offering tremendous flexibility with its many recreational facilities including a leisure club and tennis courts. Set in its own gardens with ornamental drive it is a perfect base for exploring the New Forest.

THE ROYAL BERKSHIRE, Sunninghill, Berkshire.
Tel: (0344) 23322
Previously the home of the Churchill family, this Queen Anne mansion is set in 15 acres of gardens with many recreational facilities and a leisure complex. It offers superb food and is well placed for Heathrow.

SOUTH LODGE, Lower Beeding, Hampshire.
Tel: (0403) 891711
An elegant country house with one of the finest Victorian rock gardens in England. The light and spacious bedrooms have fine views over the South Downs and the hotel is well situated for Glyndbourne, Chartwell, Goodwood and Leonardslee.

SPREAD EAGLE HOTEL, Midhurst, West Sussex.
Tel: (0730) 816911
The Spread Eagle is one of England's oldest hotels dating from 1430 and has been beautifully restored in keeping with its past. It is an ideal base for visiting Chichester Cathedral, Fishbourne Roman Palace and Downland Museum.

SWAINSTON MANOR HOTEL, Calbourne, Isle of Wight.
Tel: (0983) 521121
A Georgian style hotel, part 11th century, and built on a grand scale with amazing views. The local population is the most stable in the UK. No wonder, the island is lovely and has many regal connections with Queen Victoria and modern boating royals.

TYLNEY HALL, Rotherwick, Hampshire. Tel: (0256) 764881
Grade II listed, with 66 private acres this hotel sets standards for elegance with its forecourt fountain, floodlit exterior and wood panelled library bar.

WESTOVER HALL, Milford-on-Sea, Hampshire.
Tel: (0590) 643044
An attractive country house overlooking the Solent and Isle of Wight on the edge of the New Forest. Meeting the highest standards of comfort with award-winning cuisine, the hotel offers many leisure facilities too.

WHITE HORSE INN, Chilgrove, West Sussex. Tel: (024359) 219
Lovely downland setting for simple and excellent cooking. Wonderful cellar, worth coming for this alone with the best of wines at refreshing prices.

WINTERBOURNE HOTEL, Bonchurch, Isle of Wight.
Tel: (0983) 852535
Once the home of Charles Dickens, Winterbourne is set in its own grounds with a path leading to an uncrowded beach. Offering excellent cuisine it enjoys one of the most beautiful settings on the island.

ACCOMMODATION OF MERIT

BULMER FARM, Holmbury St Mary, Surrey.
Tel: (0306) 730210
A delightful beamed farmhouse built in the 1600s, together with a quaint inglenook fireplace, around a courtyard. It is convenient for London, Gatwick, Heathrow while an exploration of the Sussex/Surrey heritage sites is a must.

CHURCH FARM, Barton Stacey, Hampshire.
Tel: (0962) 960268
A Tudor tithe barn, with Georgian additions, set in the heart of Wessex. The adjacent, recently converted, coach house can accommodate up to five on a self-contained basis. Nearby are Winchester, Salisbury, Stonehenge, Oxford and Goodwood.

DEERFELL, Haslemere, Surrey. Tel: (0428) 53409
This old stonebuilt coach house to Blackdown House, has breathtaking views across the hills and valleys of Sussex. Haslemere is a pretty town with easy access to London by train. It also borders on Hampshire and Sussex.

KNAPHILL MANOR, Woking, Surrey. Tel: (0276) 857962
Dating from the 18th century this family home is set in 6 acres of pretty grounds, with a tennis court and croquet lawn. It makes for a delightful beginning or ending to a holiday as Heathrow and Gatwick are not far away.

NIRVANA HOTEL, Bassett, Hampshire. Tel (0705) 760474
Personally run by the proprietors, Douglas and Eileen Dawson, guests are assured of a warm and friendly welcome at this comfortable hotel. As well as the extensive facilities, one recent addition is the superb conference room.

OLD RECTORY, Headley, Hampshire. Tel: (0428) 714123
Beautiful Georgian Rectory, with classic well-proportioned architecture and private walled garden, providing elegant accommodation with excellent fare. Chawton, Petworth and Selborne are nearby, together with a great deal of conservation land for enjoyable walks.

OLD MARKET HOUSE, Broughton, Hampshire.
Tel: (0794) 301249
Midway between Salisbury and Winchester, this 16th century building is a marvellous base for visiting Stonehenge and many other historic sites. Full of character with its log fires in the inglenook fireplace, sloping floors and low doorways.

INNS OF CHARACTER

CAT AND FIDDLE, Hinton Admiral, Hampshire.
Cob walls and a deep thatched roof dominate the exterior of this 11th century former hospice, recorded in the Domesday Book, which has long provided shelter for travellers to the New Forest. Traditional bar food and fine ales compliment this ancient place.

CROWN, Shorwell, Isle of Wight.
Old wooden settles and tables combine to provide a comfortable atmosphere in this attractive old pub. Good home cooked food and well kept ales may be enjoyed here. The garden with its trout stream and willow trees offers a picturesque setting.

SOUTHERN COUNTIES

CROWN INN, Chiddingfold, Surrey.
Based on a 13th century hospice for Winchester monks on pilgrimage to Canterbury, this is one of the country's oldest licensed inns. Extensive oak beams and panelling are in keeping with the deep sense of history. Good food and ales are served at this attractively rural location.

FOLLY, Cowes (East), Isle of Wight.
Originally based on a sea barge beached here but not recorded as a building until 1792 this popular pub retains a nautical flavour with a VHF radio-telephone, wind speed indicator and chronometer among its charms. Good bar food, ales and rums can be enjoyed within the old timbered walls.

THE GEORGE INN, Vernham Dean, Hampshire.
With its undulating tiled roof supported by weathered timbers, this peaceful 17th century village inn has a relaxed and rambling feel. Good value, traditional bar food and fine ales may be enjoyed at this homely spot.

SHEPHERD AND DOG, Fulking, West Sussex.
Two sixteenth century cottages blended to form this delightful village pub in 1735. Low ceilings and panelled walls prevail in these rustic surroundings. Excellent food and numerous fine ales make it rather popular.

SWAN, Fittleworth, West Sussex.
Parts of this old pub date from the 15th century and earlier. Constable's brother George often lodged here on painting expeditions and examples of his work abound. Fine ales and good bar food are complimented by friendly service.

THREE HORSESHOES, Laleham, Surrey.
The past uses of this 13th century inn include a coroner's court, post office and even a parish vestry. The preponderance of beams, alcoves and traditional furnishing has maintained a 'villagey' atmosphere. Highly praised food and good wines and ale make it a popular retreat.

WHITE HART, Stopham, West Sussex.
Standing next to a charming 14th century bridge in very picturesque country scene, this pub is built of delightful mellow stone. Excellent bar food, good ales and fine wines can be enjoyed within these unspoilt walls.

WHITE HORSE, Petersfield, Hants.
Elegance is not the word to describe this remote but characterful 17th century pub. Instead, a charming unassuming character prevails among the old pictures, farm tools, rugs and drop leaf tables. Interesting wines, many fine ales and traditional food provide further attraction.

WHITE LION, Warlingham, Surrey.
Not far from London, this 15th century pub remains pleasantly unspoilt. Low beams, black panelled rooms, wood-block floors and a Tudor fireplace contribute to its charming character. Simple bar food and well kept handpumped ales are most enjoyable.

Lainston House Hotel

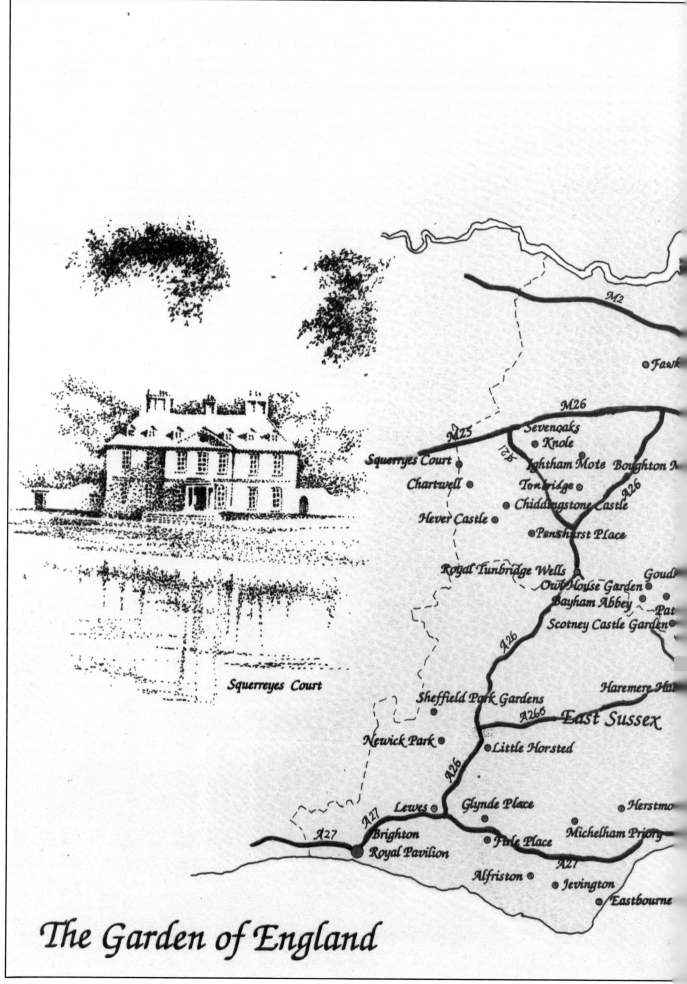

Squerreyes Court

The Garden of England

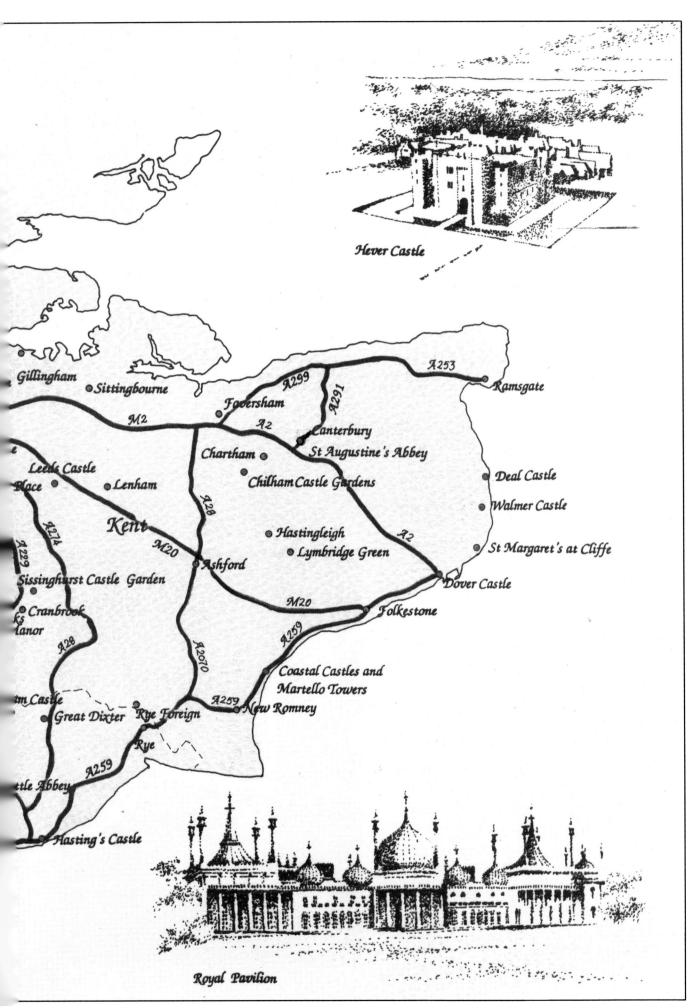

Hever Castle

Gillingham
Sittingbourne
Faversham
A299
A291
A253
Ramsgate
M2
A2
Canterbury
Chartham
St Augustine's Abbey
Leeds Castle
Lenham
Chilham Castle Gardens
Deal Castle
Place
Walmer Castle
A274
Kent
A28
Hastingleigh
A2
A229
M20
Lymbridge Green
St Margaret's at Cliffe
Sissinghurst Castle Garden
Ashford
Cranbrook
M20
Dover Castle
lanor
A28
Folkestone
A259
A2070
Coastal Castles and
Martello Towers
m Castle
A259
Great Dixter
Rye Foreign
New Romney
Rye
A259
ttle Abbey
Hasting's Castle

Royal Pavilion

THE GARDEN OF ENGLAND

Kent has been famous for its fruit growing since Roman times, and is well known for its hops and fertile farms. The landscape conjures pictures of rolling hills, green and lush gardens with oast houses dotting the landscape.

THE WEALD

The Weald of Kent, to the west of the county, also has its fair share of pretty houses and unspoilt villages.

Bidborough is often reckoned to be Kent's best kept village and offers lovely views over the Weald and the North Downs. The village of Penshurst is dominated by **Penshurst Place**, ancestral home of the Sidneys since 1552, and one of England's great houses. The Great Hall, built in 1340, is 'a unique survivor of medieval domestic splendour' and the gardens, toy museum and venture playground are all fun to visit. Do take a look at the village as well though.

Chartwell, the country home of Sir Winston Churchill is a popular stopover for visitors. The house has been preserved as a museum to the statesman and contains many of his paintings. On the outskirts of Westerham, nestling amidst tall trees, **Squerryes Court** looks out over a lake to wooded hills beyond, and has been the home of the Warde family since John Warde bought it from the 3rd Earl of Jersey in 1731. The present house was built in 1680 during the reign of Charles II but is a perfect example of a typical William and Mary house. The rooms are beautifully proportioned, light and airy and the quality of the brickwork is superb, having mellowed to a soft shade of russet.

The simple elegance of the architecture is mirrored in the simplicity of the interior which provides a perfect setting for the lovely furniture, porcelain and paintings collected by generations of the Warde family. The Entrance Hall has several family portraits, one of which is of Sir Patience Warde. It seems his father, having had six sons and one daughter, insisted that if he had another son he would call him Patience. He proved to be a man of his word. It was Sir Patience's great-nephew who bought Squerryes.

The undulating parkland at Squerryes, dotted with ancient limes, rises to the Gazebo which was built about 1740 as a shelter from which to watch the training gallops used by the race-horses owned by John Warde at that time. The lake, which in those days would have supplied carp for the table, has been enlarged and is now stocked with trout. The Darent River rises from springs in the lake and Squerryes is supplied with water from a spring in the Park.

The Elizabethan village of **Chiddingstone** is kept by the National Trust. The 19th century neo-gothic castle stands near the village's original 'chiding stone' where chattering women could be chided by villagers. It is most noted for the collections of Denis Eyre Bower, a Derbyshire bank clerk who retired here. He was passionately interested in the Stuarts and Jacobites and art from Egypt and Japan which is apparent in his large collections on display.

Hever Castle, is a popular haunt for tourists. It dates back to the 13th century. Anne Boleyn spent her childhood here and the Astor family bought it in 1903 and laid out extensive gardens overlooking the 35 acre lake (featured later).

Knole, at Sevenoaks, is one of the largest private houses in England, and was given by Elizabeth I to Thomas Sackville. It is noted now as the former home of the novelist Vita Sackville-West, whose upbringing at Knole was described in her diaries and her biography. **Sissinghurst Castle** also has connections with Vita Sackville-West, and her husband Harold Nicholson. The gardens there were created in the 1930s by the couple, and are lovely at all times of the year. Sissinghurst is particularly renowned for its wonderful collection of sweet-smelling old-fashioned roses, its white garden and perhaps most famous of all, the dazzling red border.

Rochester upon Medway is a lovely city to visit which boasts 2,000 Roman established fortifications to defend their bridge over the River Medway. The city has had an important role to play at crucial stages in the development of the nation. Rochester's most striking remains today were bequeathed by the Normans, the magnificent castle, built between 1126 and 1139, boasts what many historians believe is the finest keep of that period in the country. Across from here is the great cathedral. Bishop Anndulf of Bec, chief castle builder to William the Conqueror was responsible for replacing the Saxon church, the lower part of the tower is all that remains from the 11th century. The rest of the cathedral is largely 12th century, with additions from the 13th and 15th centuries, much of the restoration and re-building happened after the depradations of the Civil War. Interesting features include the elaborate Romanesque carving of the west door, the choir stalls, the chapter house doorway of 1340 and a series of Bishops' tombs spanning seven centuries. Charles Dickens spent his boyhood here; many of the city's older buildings feature in his novels and the famous Dickens Chalet which was shipped to his home in Gads

Hever Castle

76

THE GARDEN OF ENGLAND

Hill Place has been transferred to its present position in the high street.

In the heart of the Kentish Weald, at Ivy Hatch near Sevenoaks, is **Ightham Mote**, a very pretty medieval moated manor house. The house still has its original great hall, chapel and crypt and its museum on conservation is an important one.

Finchcocks situated in Goudhurst near Cranbrook, Kent is a beautiful house with a fine example of Georgian baroque architecture; it is noted for the outstanding quality of its brickwork. Finchcocks was named after the family who lived on the site in the 13th century and despite having changed hands several times over the years, it has suffered remarkably little alteration. Richard Burnett the pianist acquired Finchcocks in 1970 and it now houses his wonderful collection of historical keyboard instruments, most of which have been restored to full playing condition. Finchcocks with its many items of musical interest, pictures and furniture provides a fascinating collection of things to enjoy. The house, with its high ceilings, provides the perfect setting where music is performed on the instruments for which it was written. Now a musical centre of high international repute, many musical events are held here. The extensive parkland and gardens are beautiful with a lovely orchard of ornamental fruit trees, it also offers stunning views over the Kentish landscape of parkland, farmland and hop gardens.

THE ROYAL SPA

Perhaps the best known of Kent's villages is **Royal Tunbridge Wells**, one of England's most elegant towns. In Regency days it was an important spa town, drawing visitors from near and far to take its waters. The 18th century Pantiles, a lovely shopping walk, evokes memories of those days. The Pantiles take their name from the dutch tiles that originally paved it. Bath Square, at one end of the Pantiles, is where the medicinal springs were discovered by Lord North and the waters can still be drunk today. Or you could take a picnic at High Rocks, which has been a popular local picnic area for hundreds of years.

Nearby Pembury has lovely woods which are popular with walkers, and Lamberhurst is known as a wine producing region - not many places in England can claim that! Lamberhurst is also famous for having produced the famous iron railings that surround St Paul's Cathedral.

The National Trust now administers the neo-gothic **Scotney Castle** and its gardens. In 1835 Edward Hussey created the most romantic of gardens around the ruined tower of Scotney Castle. In summer the garden is full of purple buddleias, pink calico and masses of royal fern, while white rambler roses cascade over the old castle walls. The **Owl House**, owned by the Marchioness of Dufferin and Ava, a 16th century timber framed 'Owlers' (wool smuggler's) cottage, is surrounded by the most delightful gardens. There are thirteen acres of rare shrubs, romantic leafy glades, azaleas, roses, camellias and much more.

MAIDSTONE AND ITS SURROUNDS

Still more stately homes and old buildings must be mentioned as worthy of note. Near Ashford is **Godington Park**, a Jacobean mansion with interesting wood panels and carvings. **Old Soar Manor** at Plaxtol is a lovely 13th century home and West Malling has the ruins of a Benedictine Abbey founded in 1080.

Maidstone's history is associated with Wat Tyler and Jack Cade. Now a bustling commuter town, its industries have traditionally included brewing and paper making. Its 14th century All Saints Church is flanked by the Archbishop's Palace, whose stables are now a Carriage Museum. **Chiddingstone Manor** is a Municipal Museum in the town centre.

Near Maidstone, don't miss **Leeds Castle**, which you will spot nestling in the trees, by its magnificent lake. Keep an eye out for local notices, as the castle hosts some spectacular open air concerts, sometimes with fireworks to add to the splendour of the occasion (featured later).

At Chilham, eight miles from Charing, stands **Chilham Castle**, built by Inigo Jones in 1616, but including a Norman Keep

Rochester Castle

THE GARDEN OF ENGLAND

on Roman foundations. There are lovely gardens by John Tradescant with lakeside walks and extensive woodlands to enjoy. The castle itself is not open to visitors.

Four miles from Maidstone we find **Boughton Monchelsea Place**, an Elizabethan Manor of great interest, which has a fine collection of Mortlake tapestries and the 13th century **Allington Castle** is where Sir Thomas Wyatt was executed for his part in the rebellion against 'Bloody Mary' in 1554.

CANTERBURY TALES

Canterbury, Kent's county town, is famous for many things. It is the chief cathedral city of England, its archbishop bears the title Primate of all England, and it is visited each year by thousands of pilgrims.

The first cathedral was built there in AD 597 when St Augustine arrived from Rome to baptise Kent's King Ethelbert, and thus began the spread of Christianity from the South. None of this survives, however, and the present cathedral was begun in 1067. The murder of Thomas á Becket took place there, and the cathedral has suffered other indignities since. However, it still attracts many visitors and its surviving stained glass is among the finest in the country.

The city has many other attractions including the surviving parts of its walls and the West Gate, Kings School with its unusual external Norman staircase, its new Marlow Theatre, its Royal Museum and the nearby ruins of a Norman castle.

COASTAL CASTLES

The original Cinque ports were Hastings, Sandwich, Dover, Romney and Hythe, but the ancient towns of Winchelsea and Rye were added later. As well as being important for trade, the coastal towns were also important for the nation's defence, and many relics of the fortresses that protected us from invasion remain. **Martello Towers**, built to protect us from Napoleon and his forces, are a feature of much of the coast from Folkestone to Seaford, taking their names from a fort in Corsica. There is also a Royal Military Canal, which bends its way from Romney Marsh via Hythe to Winchelsea.

Henry VIII built about 20 forts along the south coast, following his break with Rome, and he regarded the low-lying areas around Deal and Romney Marsh as being especially vulnerable. The castle at Deal was one of his most powerful, and survives well. **Walmer** and **Sandown Castles** are also interesting to visit. Walmer Castle, built in the 1530s, became the official residence of the Warden of the Cinque Ports. Its furnishings date from the mid-19th century when the Duke of Wellington was warden.

Sandwich lost its importance as a port as its river silted up, but remains a pretty little town with narrow streets and timbered houses. **Richborough Castle** on the Stour, with its huge walls, is a very formidable reminder of the Roman occupation, and has an interesting Museum.

Dover is much in the news as we watch the progress of the Channel Tunnel, with Shakespeare Cliff, the first sight of land, a welcome sight to many a weary traveller. **Dover Castle** with its massive keep built by Henry II, dominates the town. One of the largest and best preserved castles it has been called the 'Key of England' and was of great strategic importance. It was captured by Cromwell during the Civil War, and many of its towers were adapted to take artillery during the Napoleonic Wars. The Town Hall with the Maison Dieu Hall are of interest. Chatham has an interesting 'Living Museum' of Naval History and is also famous as being the town where Charles Dickens spent his schooldays. Sandgate has the remains of a castle overlooking the shore; **Saltwood Castle** and **Stutfall Castle** lie further along the coast; and the Romney, Hythe & Dymchurch Railway attracts visitors from far and wide, travelling more than 13 miles to Dungeness Lighthouse.

REGENCY BRIGHTON

Described variously as 'an extravaganza of pinnacles, piers and promenades' and the home of 'peers, queers and racketeers', Brighton clearly means different things to different people.

Its attractions are certainly very broadly based. It became a fashionable seaside resort in Regency times, when the Prince Regent, son of George III became attracted to what was then Brighthelmstone. With its attractive Regency and Victorian architecture, its proximity to the rolling South Downs, and its seaside attractions, it is not hard to find plenty to do here. The five miles of beach feature the West Pier, built in 1886 and the Palace Pier opened in 1901, with many amenities including a theatre at its end.

Certainly Brighton's best known building is its extraordinary **Royal Pavilion** (featured later). This was commissioned in 1783 by the Prince Regent, in a sort of quasi-Oriental style. Its on-

Chilham Castle

THE GARDEN OF ENGLAND

ion-shaped dome is much commented on. Satirist Sydney Smith commented 'The dome of St Paul's must have come to Brighton and pupped'. Nash added the Banqueting Room and Music Room.

Brighton is also a super shopping centre, with a reputation for art and antiques. Do visit the Lanes, the little windy roads crammed with shops, which hark back to the old Brighton. A huge new marina development has been added to the town, as an attraction for those of a nautical bent.

SUSSEX WEALD

The Weald of Sussex is a favourite haunt for visitors. The Blue-bell Railway, one of Britain's few surviving steam railways, runs between Horstead Keynes and **Sheffield Park**, a National Trust garden. Visit Sheffield to see the five lakes, each on different levels and linked by cascades of water.

The Augustinian monks who built **Michelham Priory** diverted the River Cuckmere to form the six and a half acre moat, one of the largest in England. A superb example of Elizabethan architecture is **Glynde Place**, which also has a small aviary and collections of needlework and bronzes. **Firle Place**, seat of the Gage family since the 15th century is a Tudor mansion, extensively altered between 1713 and 1754. There is a fine Palladian drawing room with white and gold panelling surrounding full length family portraits. Other treasures include Sevres porcelain and Teniers painting 'The Wine Harvest' with a lovely panelled gallery.

The administrative centre of East Sussex is **Lewes**, a pretty town next to the Ouse which retains many relics of its ancient past. The Castle, now a ruin, was once one of the strongest in the country.

1066 AND ALL THAT

The Norman Conquest, which began with the Battle of Hastings (actually six miles from the existing town) has had a lasting impact on the area. **Hastings Castle** was an important strategic link for William and fragments of his castle remain among the present ruins. Battle, the actual location of the defeat of King Harold, is bordered on its south by the Abbey wall. The Abbey was built by William to fulfil a promise on the eve of the battle. Head on to **Bodiam Castle**, with its moats and curtain walls, built in 1386 as protection against marauding Frenchmen. The village of Northiam is worth a visit, as is **Great Dixter**, a manor house restored and extended by Lutyens in 1911.

Haremere Hall in Etchingham, East Sussex dates from the 12th century when Miles de Haremere was mentioned in local records. The present house was built by John Bussbridge, but is well remembered as the home of Sir John Lade who apart from frequently entertaining the Prince Regent at his parties was also a notorious gambler and practical joker. There are many beautiful treasures to see, including Samurai swords, antique ginger jars given by the Lama of Tibet and many lovely pieces of chinese porcelain. In the Great Hall you can see carved tables from the Mandarins Palace in China; carved doors and flemish fireplaces. In the gardens you will find beautiful conifers, mature trees and shrubs, with rolling views over the parkland. **Newick Park** is a magnificent country house set in spectacular Sussex countryside, the original house was built in the 16th century by one of the Ironmasters. (featured later).

The Garden of England, as its name implies, has much to commend it to the inquisitive and expectant. It is of little surprise that such a picturesque part of the country draws visitors to it like a magnet and of even less wonder that all are enchanted by its splendid array of treasures.

Firle Place

HEVER CASTLE

This enchanting, double-moated castle in the heart of the Kent countryside, once the childhood home of Anne Boleyn, dates back to 1270 when the massive gatehouse, outerwalls and inner moat were first constructed.

Some 200 years later the Bullen or Boleyn family built a comfortable Tudor house within the walls, the same house which stood witness to Henry VIII's long, romantic courtship of Anne. Finally, she succumbed to his fatal charm and became his second wife and mother of the future Queen Elizabeth I. An exhibition in the Tudor Long Gallery, inspired by Victorian engravings on display in the castle, depicts the Boleyn family gathered to greet the King and his courtiers. Life sized figures of the King and Anne with Katherine of Aragon, Jane Seymour, Cardinal Wolsey and Sir Thomas Moore, all in sumptuous court dress form the focal point of the exhibition. There are also portraits of the young Queen and the Book of Hours which Anne carried to the scaffold.

After her execution, Henry gave the castle to his fourth wife, Anne of Cleeves in whose ownership it remained until her death in 1557. Since that time, the castle passed through many hands and suffered long years of neglect. In 1903, William Waldorf Astor, a wealthy American who later became the 1st Viscount Astor of Hever, acquired the estate and invested time and considerable amounts of money on an extensive programme of restoration to the house and grounds. He used only the finest craftsmen and materials and within an incredible five years had meticulously recreated Hever's carved wood panelling and decorative plasterwork. The Astor family's part in there-birth of the castle can now be appreciated through the superb collections of furniture, paintings and objets d'art as well as the quality of workmanship throughout. The 'Astor's of Hever' exhibition traces their contribution to the recent history of the castle and gardens during four generations of Astor stewardship.

The gardens and grounds, planned and planted by Lord Astor between 1903 and 1908, are an outstanding feature of this warm and welcoming house extending over 30 acres, with a further 300 acres of meadow and woodland. An ambitious project, the huge 35 acre lake was dug by hand by 800 men and the course of the River Eden diverted to fill it. An outer moat was excavated and a series of charming formal gardens planted between the moats, brimming with water-lilies. Fittingly, a small garden is dedicated to Anne Boleyn with a yew maze and a small herb garden fresh with the aroma of the many culinary varieties grown. On the far side of the lake there is also Anne Boleyn's walk through shady, mature trees.

Pergolas support a dazzling array of climbing roses, sweet-scented jasmine and clematis, as do the castle walls themselves. Another garden contains Tudor chessmen meticulously clipped from yew. Perhaps the most spectacular is the Italian garden named, not for its plant varieties, but for the collection of classical statuary and sculpture dating from Roman to Renaissance times amassed by Lord Astor when American Ambassador to Rome. The pieces have been carefully arranged - each within a bay built into a long stone wall over which plants scramble and fall in a delightful blend of subtle colour.

At the same time as restoring the castle, William Astor built a Tudor Village country house to extend the castle and accommodate family and guests. Today, this has become a highly efficient conference facility providing peace and security combined with unobtrusive service. The Tudor Suite is available for non-residential meetings, receptions and dinners whilst the Tudor village itself is used for accommodation for residential and incentive weekends.

The Dining Hall of the Castle formerly the Great Hall in Anne Boleyn's time, with its linenfold panelling, carved minstrels Gallery and crackling open fire is a magnificent and historic setting for a celebration meal or special occasion. The Inner Hall may be used for drinks and special theme evenings - even a murder can be arranged! Guests have the use of an outdoor heated pool and hard tennis court, croquet lawn and billiard room. Within the castle grounds many sports can be arranged including clay pigeon shooting, archery, fishing, horse riding and falconry displays.

LEEDS CASTLE

'Leeds, beheld among the waters on an autumnal evening when there is a faint blue mist among the trees - the loveliest castle in the whole world.' Leeds Castle, rising from its two small islands in the midst of the still waters of its lake, is one of the most ancient and romantic castles in the Kingdom. Enveloped by acres of thickly wooded parkland, this former Norman stronghold became a Royal Palace at the hands of Henry VIII.

Royal ownership of the castle began in 1278 when Leeds was conveyed to King Edward I who carried out extensive alterations. To strengthen the castles defences he built a great dam to enable the valley of the Len to be flooded in times of danger. In order to protect the dam and the Mill which conveyed the water from the lake he devised one of the most unusual barbican systems ever. A wall rising sheer from the water, was built around the largest island, strengthened at intervals by D-shaped turrets.

It was Edward I who granted Leeds to his Queen, inaugurating the custom that the castle became part of the dower of the queens and was retained by them during widowhood. Leeds Castle became 'the Ladies' castle and was a favourite of six medieval queens. Edward III carried out continuous works, particularly to the royal apartments in the Gloriette (keep) and in the enlargement of the park, but perhaps the most important improvements were carried out by Henry VIII. Clearly Henry was very fond of Leeds Castle and expended large sums in beautifying it. He transformed the Gloriette by adding centred bay windows to the royal apartments and built the Maiden's Tower to house the royal maids-of-honour. Anne Boleyn who lived at nearby Hever Castle could well have been one of them. In 1552 Leeds passed out of royal ownership and in the early 17th century the main buildings were rebuilt in the Jacobean style. In the 18th century the castle was given a 'Strawberry Hill' Gothic appearance. By 1824 the castle had regained its medieval style, thanks to the judicious restoration of the Wykeham-Martin family, who were also responsible for much of the present layout of the Park.

For some 100 years the Wykenham-Martins settled back to enjoy their castle, so when Lady Olive Baillie bought Leeds in 1926 much needed to be done. She set about her task with characteristic imagination and vigour and the castle as we see it today is an elegant tribute to what became her life's work. Over almost thirty years she collected magnificent medieval furnishings, wonderful fabrics, tapestries and fine paintings.

The Queen's Room and Bathroom are prepared as they might have been in the year 1430, authentic to the last detail. The walls are covered with damask, and the rich canopy of the bed and simple white hangings of the bath are suspended from the ceiling. Those royal apartments of the 13th century Gloriette are linked to the main building on the larger island by a magnificent two-storied stone bridge which leads to the elegant 18th century Yellow Drawing Room and Thorpe Hall Drawing Room, both of which contain beautiful collections of chinese porcelain.

The grounds surrounding Leeds Castle are a delight. The Woodland Garden, created by Lady Baillie, is bordered by the little streams of the River Len. In spring great masses of daffodils, narcissi and anemones form a multi-coloured carpet beneath the ash, alder and willows.

The Culpeper Garden is an old English cottage garden - poppies and lupins, lavender and roses, a profusion of herbs. The scent on a warm summer morning is wonderful. The Lady Baillie Aviary is housed in a progressive modern aviary designed by Vernon Gibberd, and among the exotic occupants are her favourite parakeets. The Maze ends in a fascinating underground grotto and Leeds Castle boasts one of two vineyards in Kent recorded in the Domesday Book. After a five century lapse grapes are once again being grown and the castle now has its one wine label.

When Lady Baillie generously gave Leeds Castle to the nation she intended it to be used for the advancement of medicine and the arts and for meetings at an international level. With its high level of security, proximity to London and easy access from Gatwick and Heathrow Airports, it is now one of the world's most outstanding conference and residential facilities. Modern technical conference aids are available; secretarial and simultaneous translation facilities can be arranged as well as social or sight-seeing programmes for delegate's husbands and wives. Special events and entertainments take place throughout the year, many with a seasonal theme. A variety of light meals, snacks and cream teas are available in and around the Fairfax Hall. There are also picnic sites around the park and the Castle Shop, which stocks a wide range of quality gifts and souvenirs. Guide books to the castle are available in French, German and Japanese, and there is a 9-hole golf course in the castle grounds for guest to enjoy.

THE ROYAL PAVILION

The Royal Pavilion, the famous seaside Palace of George, Prince of Wales, is possibly the most dazzling and exotically beautiful buildings in the British Isles. It began life as little more than a 'modest farmhouse' which the Prince of Wales rented when he first began to visit Brighton to enjoy the bracing sea air in 1783. He also enjoyed the informal atmosphere after the strictures of life at Court and so in 1787 he asked Henry Holland to create a classically styled villa known as the Marine Pavilion.

The Dome was originally constructed as the Royal Stables, which prompted the people of Brighton to comment that the horses were better housed than their owner. This caused George, now Prince Regent, to embark on a lavish rebuilding programme from 1815 to 1822 which transformed the villa into the Royal Pavilion. He and the architect John Nash created an Indian fantasy in the heart of Brighton with domes and minarets everywhere. The interiors were decorated in the Chinese taste carried to unique heights of splendour and magnificence.

The tent-shaped Octagon Hall leads via the cool green of the Entrance Hall to The Corridor which runs the length of the building connecting the two main entertaining rooms, the Banqueting Room with the Music Room. With its bright pinks and blues, the Chinese theme dominates with a mixture of real and imitation bamboo furniture. The famous cast-iron staircase at each end also have the appearance of bamboo.

The Nash Banqueting Room was designed to be as spectacular as possible for the Prince's dinner guests. It is dominated by the magnificent central light, originally gas, suspended from the blue-green dome of the ceiling by a fire-breathing silver dragon. Around the room is one of the most important collections of Regency silver-gilt on public view.

The Music Room is a spectacular fantasy which moved George to tears when he first saw it. Its domed ceiling depicts gilded, scallop-shaped shells and the wall paintings are of rich reds and gold. The Drawing Rooms, by contrast, have a relaxed atmosphere and were used for card games, chess or backgammon. Here George would regale his guests with stories and serve late suppers of wine and sandwiches.

The Great Kitchen was one of the most modern of its day. The high ceiling and decorative canopies of burnished copper would draw away heat and cooking smells, making conditions far more pleasant for the cooks who toiled to produce the most elaborate dishes. The structural cast-iron columns have been disguised as palm trees and the gleaming collection of copper pots and pans contains over 500 pieces.

George's niece, Queen Victoria, apparently did not find the Pavilion to her taste and felt Brighton to be 'far too crowded'. She sold the Pavilion to Brighton in 1850 and today the main state rooms are available in the evening for private entertaining on the grand scale - exactly as the Prince Regent intended.

NEWICK PARK

Constructed on the site of an earlier house, little remains of the original Elizabethan building although the date 1563 or 1568 is said to be on one of the cellar walls and elsewhere, 1584 has been found on the foundations. The south west angle of the house, which contains the study and mullion window on the second floor, gives an indication of the importance of the original building. Built for an Iron Master, the quality of craftsmanship and fine panelling surrounding the fireplace would suggest that Newick Place, as it was then known, was a substantial property. The south front is probably of early 18th century design and construction with five bays, whilst the front elevation with its semi-circular bays was added between 1765 and 1783. It was probably during this period that the Bossi fireplaces were installed. The exterior has remained largely unaltered over the last 200 years and is clearly identifiable from a drawing made by Lambert in 1783.

Surprisingly little is known of the history of the house or park. It is believed to have fallen into disuse during Elizabeth I's reign when the mining of iron ceased. At the end of the 17th century, the house was rescued from decay by Francis Millington and then inherited by Baron Mansell. It is at this point that the earliest description of the house and grounds can be found. A list of pictures found in the house in 1713 would indicate that once again it was owned by a wealthy family.

The house consisted of about seven rooms on each floor besides the usual outhouses, stables and dairy. The gardens were of considerable importance with a formal flower garden and walled garden planted with a vast number of fruit trees and bushes. Avenues were planted as walks and the park to the south of the lake was mainly wooded.

During the period 1795 to 1873, considerably more emphasis was placed on the importance of farming and the formal design of the old park disappeared to be replaced by the field structure and parkland of today.

Constructed of brick and slate, the main part of the house dates from 1783. Here are an unusual number of outstanding chimney pieces including the stone chimney piece in the Library, circa 1720. The marble chimneypiece in the drawing room and Longford Room are by Bossi. The Bossi brothers are known to have been working in Dublin in the 1780's and to have been involved in undertaking work for Robert Adams.

The decorative detail in all the rooms is outstanding and whilst the individual rooms are too important and too numerous to mention, features include original Elizabethan panelling, woodblocked floors and plus many other delightful features.

The property, located in some of the most unspoilt and scenic countryside in Sussex with far reaching views to the South Downs. Set in the heart of the 253 acre estate, this magnificent grade II listed building is one of the most exclusive business entertainment centres in Southern England.

THE GARDEN OF ENGLAND

There are huge expanses of isolated land over the vast stretches of the Weald and much of England's Garden remains surprisingly uncrowded. It boasts a splendid array of orchards and hop-fields and the oast houses are a cheery reflection of one of England's more interesting agricultural enterprises.

In contrast to this, are the chalk cliffs, rich marshlands around the coast which boasts the Cinque Ports and castles a plenty.

The city of Canterbury dates from Saxon times and the centre piece is the Cathedral. The timber-framed buildings merge happily with the more modern weatherboard houses. Today's pilgrims are ensured a warm welcome in the many local pubs, often with a history of their own.

The sea ports, with castles and cobbled streets, are stunningly quaint and although the small streets are busy during the summer months, the ports have managed to retain their charm.

Regency Brighton with its Royal Pavilion is a curious contrast to the villages of Kent but it offers a great range of hotels. The streets are alive and shopping here is renowned. In fact, the bustle of Brighton might well make you yearn for those quiet Kentish villages.

Whether you are camping in the wake of Chaucer's Pilgrims or relaxing with a view of the downs, The Garden of England will provide you with a fascinating insight into the rich heritage of Britain. Pilgrim or not, there is much to please in this characterful countryside.

HOTELS OF DISTINCTION

BRANDSHATCH PLACE, Ash Green, Kent. Tel: (0474 872239)
An elegant Georgian house set in 12 acres of gardens and woodland. This hotel offers excellent facilities including use of a sports club, and boasts food of an exceptional standard.

CHILSTON PARK COUNTRY HOUSE, Lenham, Kent. Tel: (0622) 859803
A magnificent Grade I listed mansion set in 250 acres of Kent parkland. Filled with antiques the hotel is reminiscent of a bygone era and enhanced by the lighting of 200 candles at dusk each day.

COUNTY HOTEL, Canterbury, Kent. Tel: (0227) 766266
Set in the centre of this historic city, the bedrooms of this fine hotel feature hand-made funiture and four-poster beds. Antique, mirror-panelled walls give an air of formality to 'Sully's' restaurant.

EASTWELL MANOR, Eastwell Park, Kent. Tel: (0233) 635751
This ancient manor house has a courtyard, panelling, antiques, enormous fireplaces and magnificent cornices all complemented by tasteful 1990's comfort and amenities. Croquet and tennis on the lawn.

FALSTAFF HOTEL, Canterbury, Kent. Tel: (0227) 462138
Many years ago, the pilgrims to this holy city relied on the friendly hospitality of this ancient inn. The beamed lounge with leaded windows matches the character of the heavy wood furniture.

THE GRAND, Brighton, East Sussex. Tel: (0273) 21188
Thoroughly renovated to show off the original features which were the pride of a truly Grand Hotel. Very smart and extremely well appointed, with stunning views and wonderful shopping in The Lanes and small shops.

HORSTED PLACE, Little Horsted, East Sussex. Tel: (0825) 75581
This is a truly grand hotel, splendidly furnished, with outstanding views to the Downs from every room. The hotel offers fine English and French cuisine with impeccable and unobtrusive service.

HOWFIELD MANOR, Chartham Hatch, Canterbury. Tel: 0227) 738294
Originally part of the Priory of St Gregory this charming manor house dates back to the 11th century and stands in 5 acres of grounds with a formal English rose garden, a mere 2 miles from the city of Canterbury.

MERMAID INN, Rye, East Sussex. Tel (0797) 223065
An inn of considerable historical character dating back to 1420, with oak beams, open fires and leaded windows. The food and hospitality are good and the charming bedrooms have the advantae of modern amenities.

NETHERFIELD PLACE, Battle, East Sussex.
Tel: (04246) 4455/4024
This floral, peaceful, Georgian hotel is well established in beautiful and historic East Sussex and conveniently close to the Channel ports 'Garden' sports are available and fresh produce is the norm in elegant the restaurant.

ROSE & CROWN, Tonbridge, Kent. Tel: (0732) 357966
The Rose & Crown is a 16th century coaching inn, now renovated to become a popular hotel. Traditional furnishings include oak beams and furniture.

STOCK HILL HOUSE, Gillingham, Kent. Tel: (0747) 823626
A peaceful hotel set in ten acres of its own mature and well-tended gardens. The interior is grand and extravagant with gilt mirrors, antiques and huge carved animals adorning the public rooms.

SUNDIAL, Herstmonceux, East Sussex. Tel: (0323) 832217
The food is notably classical French in this pleasant restaurant contained within a 17th century cottage with beautifully tended gardens.

TANYARD HOTEL, Boughton Monchelsea, Kent.
Tel: (0622) 744705
With a history stretching back to the 14th century, this charming hotel boasts the beauty of open beams, inglenook fireplace, and a lovingly maintained garden.

THACKERAY'S HOUSE, Tunbridge Wells, Kent.
One of the homes of the writer William Makepeace Thackeray, this clapboard house is filled with many interesting items and

THE GARDEN OF ENGLAND

curios. Chef Patron Bruce Wass has created an imaginative menu in both the more formal restaurant and in the cosy bistro downstairs.

THROWLEY HOUSE, Faversham, Sedwich. Tel: (0795) 539168
A handsome Georgian style mansion with Adam features, Throwley House has a warm atmosphere and stands in 16 acres of mature parkland. Welcoming children, it makes an ideal family hotel.

THRUXTED OAST, Chartham, Kent. Tel: (0227) 730080
This old oast house where hops were stored for almost two centuries, has now been converted to make three hotel bedrooms, with the charming interior of open beams. Said to test the best of map readers.

WALLETT'S COURT, St Margaret's Cliffe, Kent. Tel: (0304) 852424
Tradditionally a 17th century house, the decor and furniture are in trend with the building. The bedrooms vary considerably in size, with all the modern amenities. The restaurant is excellent and the menus imaginative.

WHITE LODGE COUNTRY HOUSE, Alfriston, Sussex. Tel: (0323) 870265
Exquisitely furnished with period pieces, White Lodge offers style and luxury with every facility, and spectacular views over the Cuckmere Valley. Within easy reach of Brighton, Eastbourne and Newhaven.

THE WISH TOWER, Eastbourne, East Sussex. (0323) 22676
This attractive and comfortable hotel stands on the promenade, looking over the sea and the Wish Tower, a martello tower that is now a fascinating Napoleonic and World War II museum.

WOODMANS ARMS AUBERGE, Hastingleigh, Kent. Tel: (023 375) 250
This homely restaurant concentrates on the personal touch. The restaurant seats only ten, so the service and food is completely individual. There are 3 rooms available in this peaceful 17th century house.

ACCOMMODATION OF MERIT

EGYPT FARM, Hamptons, Kent. Tel: (0732) 810584
A beautiful example of carefully converted oast house, and 300 year old barn. Set in four acres of garden amidst the farmlands of the Kentish Weald, it is wonderfully convenient for researching Kent's fascinating history. Booking essential. (See photograph).

FRITH FARM HOUSE, Otterden, Kent. Tel: (079 589) 701
A Late Georgian farmhouse in six acres of gardens, near Canterbury, on the North Downs. Ideally situated for easy access to all of the major places of historical interest in Kent.

LITTLE ORCHARD HOUSE, Rye, East Sussex.
Tel: (0797) 223831
This Georgian townhouse and garden stands at the very heart

Egypt Farm

of the unique Conservation Area that is ancient Rye. Although recently renovated to provide central heating and bathrooms, the house retains its inherent period character.

LITTLE MYSTOLE, Mystole, Kent. Tel: (0227) 738210
Near Canterbury and Dover, this charming little Georgian house is a perfect place from which to explore Kent's heritage, or perhaps to play some golf. Surrounded by parkland, orchards and hop gardens.

MAPLEHURST MILL, Frittenden, Kent. Tel: (0580 80) 203
Near to Sissinghurst, Maplehurst Watermill skilfully blends enchanting guest accommodation amidst the original machinery. Dine on delicious dishes and home-grown produce by candlelight in the medieval miller's house, and walk in the rural peace of 11 acres of garden and meadow. (See photograph).

THE OLD CLOTH HALL, Cranbrook, Kent. Tel: (0580) 712220
This listed Tudor Manor house is set in 12 acres, with oast house, open-air pool, tennis court and croquet lawn. Close to Sissinghurst, Rye and Leeds Castle. Queen Elizabeth I dined here too.

POWDERMILLS, Battle, East Sussex. Tel: (04246) 2035
Once a famous gunpowder works and part of the Battle Abbey Estate, set in 150 acres of park, woods and lakes, this Georgian house offers quality en suite accommodation. The elegant Orangery Restaurant, open to non-residents, serves traditional English and French country cooking. (See photograph).

SMALLBERRY HILL, Hadlow Down, East Sussex. Tel: (082 585) 302
Originally built in 1542, this Tudor ironmaster's house has beautiful views over the surrounding countryside. Convenient for either exploring historical Sussex and Kent or for attending Glyndebourne Opera with a hamper prepared by the hostess.

WALNUT TREE FARM, Upper Hardres, Kent. Tel: (0227) 87375
A 14th century thatched farmhouse set in 6 acres and offering hearty farmhouse breakfasts. Beautifully situated to enjoy, not only the local countryside but also Canterbury and Dover, with the historic town of Royal Tunbridge Wells only a few miles away.

INNS OF CHARACTER

BELL INN, Burwash, East Sussex.
Rudyard Kipling, a village inhabitant, described this Jacobean inn and the surrounding countryside in his novel 'Puck of Pook's Hill'. The atmosphere remains unapologetically traditional and the outstanding food holds the main attraction. A range of fine ales further complements this unspoilt inn.

THE CASTLE INN, Chiddingstone, Kent.
National Trust owned - like the rest of this delightful village - this ancient building became an inn in 1730. Its charming interior with oak floors, sturdy wall benches and latticed windows, boasts a collection of over 140 wines. Traditional bar food and fine ales may also be enjoyed at this beautiful location.

Maplehurst Mill

THE GARDEN OF ENGLAND

GEORGE & DRAGON, Speldhurst, Kent.
Originally a manor house, enormous flagstones, heavy beams, and tiny alcoves characterise this now half-timbered building dating back to 1212. One of Southern England's oldest pubs, the traditional food and numerous fine ales.

MERMAID, Rye, Kent.
Rebuilt after a raid by the French in 1420, this beautiful ancient smugglers' inn has changed surprisingly little. Situated on a narrow cobbled hill, the rooms have characteristic panelling and heavy timbering. Traditional bar food and fine ales may be enjoyed at this unspoilt location.

STAR, Alfriston, Sussex.
This famous medieval inn was once run by monks for travelling pilgrims. Today the timber-framed frontage and heavy oak interior reflect its full historical past. Traditional home-made food and fine ales add to the many delights here.

STAR & EAGLE, Goudhurst, Kent.
This 14th century former monastery retains a striking medieval look. Jacobean style seats under heavy beams are the interior characteristics. Atmospheric, and very popular, it serves good food and well kept ales.

Powdermills

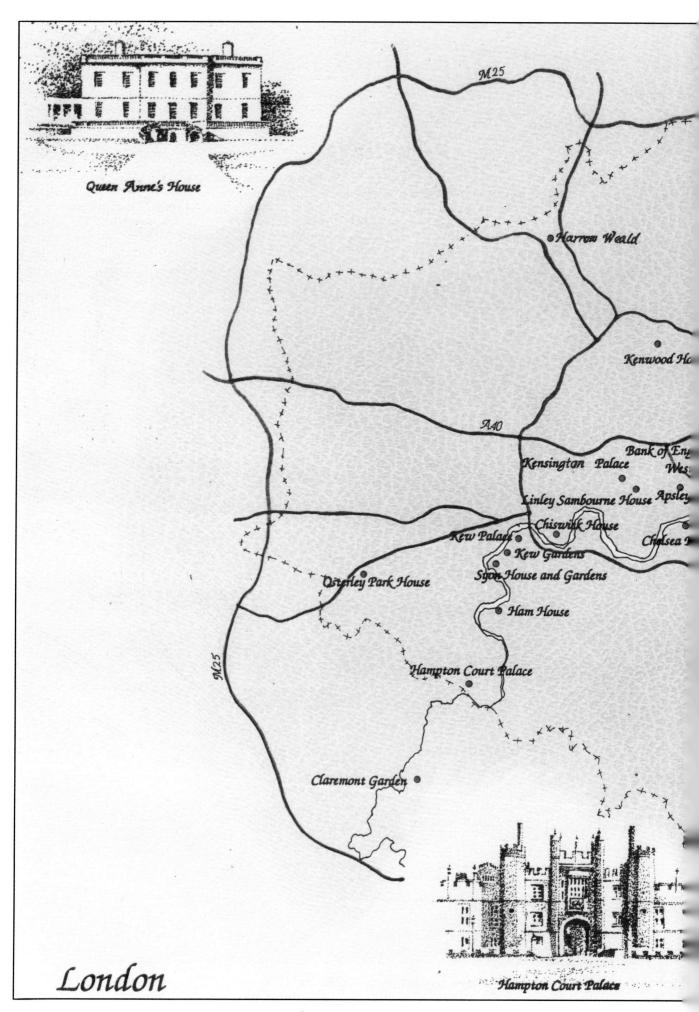

Queen Anne's House

M 25

Harrow Weald

Kenwood Ho

A40

Bank of Eng
Wes

Kensington   Palace

Linley Sambourne House   Apsley

Chiswick House

Kew Palace

Kew Gardens   Chelsea

Syon House and Gardens

Osterley Park House

Ham House

M 25

Hampton Court Palace

Claremont Garden

Hampton Court Palace

London

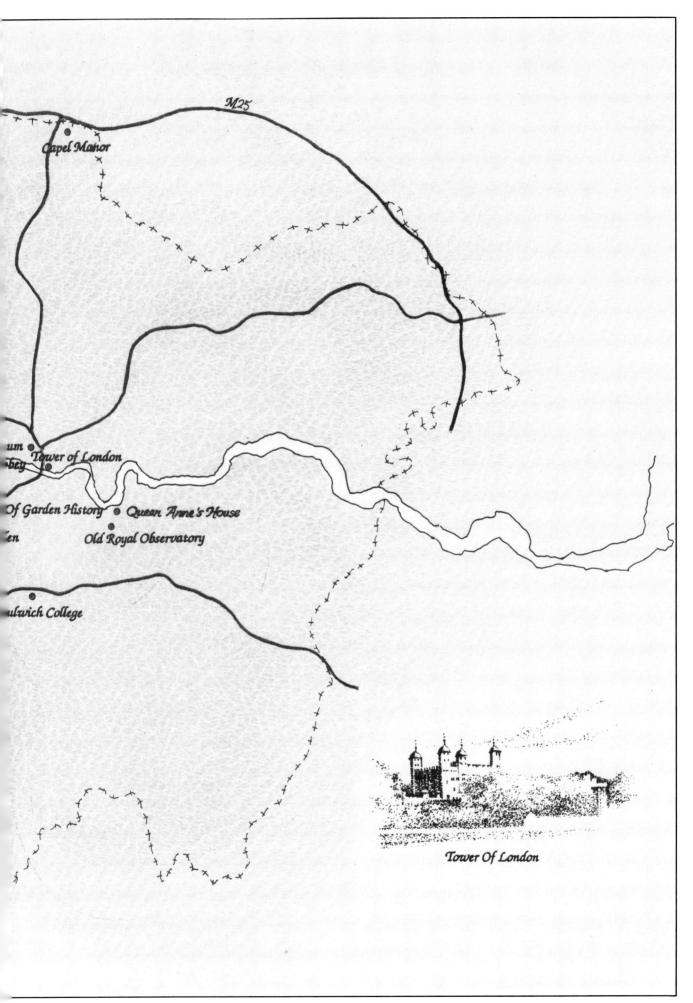

M25

Capel Manor

um
Tower of London
bey

Of Garden History   Quean Anne's House

en   Old Royal Observatory

ulwich College

Tower Of London

LONDON

'When a man is tired of London, he is tired of life;for there is in London all that life can afford.'

London has so much to offer its visitors that the problem can be knowing where to start. The capital boasts a seemingly endless variety of attractions - the royal and historic heritage of the country, museums and art galleries, theatres and cinema, parks, pubs and restaurants, shops and markets, architectural and literary treasures - it's all here. The visitor's problem is the happy one of deciding which aspects of London can be fitted into a given schedule.

PALACES AND PRISONS

London is perhaps best known for its royal connections, so this is a good place to start. **Buckingham Palace** is perhaps the most famous of all the royal homes, and no trip to London would be complete without at least driving past. It is best approached from **The Mall**, which will give a taste of the view from the many royal processions which follow this historic route.

The palace itself was built in 1703 by the Duke of Buckingham, was bought by George III in 1762 and was remodelled by Nash in 1825 for George IV. Though visitors are not allowed inside, the Changing of the Guard and the symbolic handing over of the Palace keys, which takes place daily at 11.30 is always very popular, especially with children. Get there early for a good view through the railings, or follow the 'Old Guard' which begins grouping at 11am at St James's Palace and marches up The Mall led by the Drums Corps.

While at **St James's Palace**, look out for the initials of Henry VIII and Anne Boleyn which are carved over its doors.

One of London's best known pageants is Trooping the Colour, on the second Saturday in June, which celebrates the Queen's official birthday. The five Foot Guards regiments troop their standards (colours) before the Queen.

Kensington Palace, the birthplace of Queen Victoria, and residence of Princess Margaret, was remodelled by Sir Christopher Wren for William III and Mary II. The State Apartments and Court Dress Collection make interesting viewing for royal followers.

Another of the famous palaces, though this one requires a trip out from London, is **Hampton Court Palace**, a stately home which was built by Cardinal Wolsey and given to Henry VIII. Fire damaged parts of the building and some of the treasures it houses, but major repairs have been carried out to restore it. Don't forget to visit the gardens, and the famous maze while you are there (featured later).

If you expect a royal connection for **Lambeth Palace**, you'll be disappointed. For more than 700 years this has been the London residence of the Archbishops of Canterbury. The Gatehouse dates back to 1490, and the Lollards Tower to 1436.

You certainly won't however, be disappointed by **The Tower of London**, which has a rather gloomy place in England's history (featured later). The Keep or White Tower, from which the whole place takes its name, was begun by William the Conqueror in about 1078 and the Chapel of St John still presents a fine example of Norman architecture.

Many famous people arrived by the River Thames through Traitor's Gate, and were held prisoner there, and some of the less fortunate met their death nearby - at Tower Green for the Royal prisoners or on the public scaffold at nearby Tower Hill for the 'commoners'.

The Yeoman Warders, or Beefeaters, as they are better known, still wear uniforms designed in the reign of Henry VII.

From the Tower, you can't help noticing **Tower Bridge**, which looms up above you. This was built in 1894, and still uses much of its original equipment to raise and lower its central sections to allow tall ships to pass below - a really impressive sight if you are lucky enough to catch it. The high level walkways are now open to the public, but should definitely be avoided by those who suffer from vertigo. Those willing to brave the heights will, however, be rewarded with some spectacular views of London and the Thames.

For a welcome break from sight-seeing, a good place to relax would be St Katharine's Dock. Here you may be able to spot a Thames Barge, recognisable by its brown sails, or you could browse around the shops followed by a drink at the historic Dickens Inn.

CHURCHES AND STEEPLES

The **Palace of Westminster**, or **Houses of Parliament**, as it is better known, is the home of both the House of Commons and the House of Lords. **Big Ben**, the clock at the top of the

Westminster Abbey

LONDON

316 foot tower, is certainly one of London's most photographed sights, though actually the name Big Ben refers to the 13.5 ton bell which strikes the hours. Visitors can enter the 'Strangers Galleries' while the houses are in session, or visit when Parliament is in recess.

While you are at Westminster, cross over the road to **Westminster Abbey,** where all of England's monarchs since William the Conqueror have been crowned, and buried. Edward the Confessor is believed to have founded the Abbey, which was consecrated in 1065 (features later). Further up Victoria Street, **Westminster Cathedral,** the principal Roman Catholic Cathedral in England was completed much later, in 1903 in an imposing early Byzantine style.

St Paul's Cathedral in Ludgate Hill is a must for London's visitors. One of the finest examples of the architecture of Sir Christopher Wren, it was begun in 1675, and is built out of Portland Stone. The central dome rises to 365 feet at the top of the cross, and the Whispering Gallery is very well known. Go with a friend and prove for yourselves that a message whispered on one side can be heard quite clearly 112 feet away on the other side. Your reward for climbing all the steps to the external galleries will be great views over London. Down below, the crypt houses many famous tombs.

If you are interested in Wren churches, walk down Ludgate Hill into Fleet Street, which till recently was the home of many of England's famous newspapers, and visit **St Bride's**. This lovely church was rebuilt by Wren after the Great Fire. Some Roman relics are housed in its crypts, and the church has a long association with printers and members of the press.

Another Wren church, **St Clement Danes**, is situated in the Strand. Now the church of the Royal Air Force, every third hour it rings out the tune of the nursery rhyme 'Oranges & Lemons say the bells of St Clements'. Other churches worth a visit for enthusiasts include **Southwark Cathedral**, one of London's oldest buildings with a part-Norman nave; **All Souls** in Langham Place, built by John Nash in 1824; **Temple,** The Round Church, built by the Knights Templar has an interesting history; **Brompton Oratory** is built in an Italian Renaissance style and **St Bartholomew the Great** in Smithfield, the oldest church in London apart from the Tower.

THE SQUARE MILE

The City of London, or The Square Mile as it is locally known, offers many major sights of interest, and it is fun to wander through its little winding streets and observe the bustle. The **Monument** in King William Street commemorates the beginning of the Great Fire of London in 1666, and for anyone feeling fit enough to climb the 311 steps, there is a good view of the City. **The Bank of England** in Threadneedle Street, is storehouse of the nation's gold and official bank to the Government by royal charter (featured later).

The Guildhall dates from 1411, and houses much of the City's administration, as well as an unrivalled collection of books, manuscripts and prints of London in **The Guildhall Library**, and more than 700 exhibits in **The Guildhall Clock Museum**. **The Royal Exchange** at Cornhill dates back to 1568 as a meeting place, and the nearby **Stock Exchange** in Throgmorton Street offers guided visits to the viewing gallery to witness the buying and selling of stocks and shares. Also worth a look is Richard Rogers' **Lloyds Building** which has a viewing area and an exhibition on the insurance giant's 300 years in the City.

The **Inns of Court** - Gray's Inn, Lincoln's Inn and Temple, are the only three surviving inns housing and educating lawyers. These offer fine architecture, pretty gardens and courtyards, and a glimpse of a way of life gone by.

GALLERIES AND MUSEUMS

As well as being rich in history, London offers a seemingly endless selection of art galleries and museums. Here again, the trick is to pick out the ones that appeal to you, rather than wearing yourself out trekking round to see everything.

Trafalgar Square is the location of two of our best known art galleries - the **National Gallery** and the **National Portrait Gallery**, each of which offers hours of browsing around the famous and not-so famous exhibits. The **Tate Gallery** at Millbank contains the National Collections of British Painting, Modern Foreign Paintings and Modern Sculpture.

The **Royal Academy of Arts** in Piccadilly is famous for its summer exhibitions as well as its collections, and the **Courtauld Institute** in Woburn Square contains pictures bequeathed to the University of London by many including Botticelli and Bellini. The **Sir John Soane's Museum** is a lovely 19th century house with pictures, sculptures and antiquities and more than 20,000 architectural drawings. Leighton House Museum is adjacent to Holland Park in Kensington, this group of remarkable studio houses was built by some of the leading figures of the Victorian Art World (featured later). The **Wellington Museum**, at **Apsley House** was built between 1771-1778 and houses Spanish, Dutch and Flemish paintings, together with many personal relics of the First Duke of Wellington. The **Wallace Collection** in Manchester Square makes a welcome refuge from shopping in nearby Oxford Street, and has an admirable collection of art which will appeal to many tastes.

Like its galleries, many of London's museums need little introduction. The **Science Museum** is always popular with children as there is plenty for them to do, as well as look at; **Madame Tussauds** waxworks contains historic and current figures as well as the famous Chamber of Horrors which is not for the faint-hearted, and next door, the **Planetarium** is always popular with youngsters. Fans of the Chamber of Horrors will probably also care for the London Dungeon, in Tooley Street, which looks at the more unpleasant side of London's history, made all the more sinister by the dark, vaulted building which houses the collection.

The **Victoria and Albert** is our national museum of art and design covering all countries, areas and styles. The **British Museum** offers a vast store of art treasures including the Elgin Marbles. The Reading Room, which can only be used by ticket holders, can accommodate 500 people, and the famous **British Library** is entitled to a copy of every book published in the UK.

The **National History Museum** is well worth a visit, it has a vast collection of animals, reptiles, birds, plants, fossils and minerals, and the **Museum of London** at London Wall is devoted entirely to London, its people and their history. It is one

LONDON

of our few new large museums.

The **Imperial War Museum**, housed in the former Bedlam hospital, records Britain's military history through an exhibit of souvenirs and relics. As well as the large and well-known museums, there are many specialised collections which are of great interest (featured later).

The **Museum of Garden History** at St Mary-at-Lambeth, houses a small but fascinating collection of artefacts and books which is constantly growing. It is run by the Tradescant Trust after the two John Tradescants who imported many of the plants we know today. A recently added collection of rare gardening books and antique garden tools makes this a must for keen gardeners. Another must for the greenfingered is the **Chelsea Physic Garden**, set up in 1673 by the Society of Apothecaries. Its three and a half acres form one of Europe's oldest botanic gardens, and Europe's oldest rock garden dating back to 1772.

OUT OF TOWN

We cannot talk about gardens without mentioning **The Royal Botanic Gardens at Kew** (featured later). Its 121 hectares contain magnificent glasshouses and historical buildings as well as a splendid collection of plants and trees throughout the year. One of our most attractive museums is at Greenwich, which can be reached by car, train or boat from the centre. Here, the **National Maritime Museum**, illustrates our naval history from Tudor times. It is housed in the Queens House, which was built by Inigo Jones as part of the original Greenwich Palace. Another part of this museum, the **Old Royal Observatory** is

to be found in nearby Greenwich Park. The Observatory exhibits items of astronomical, horological and navigational interest. Children and adults alike are fascinated by the **Cutty Sark**, the tea clipper built in 1869 and reckoned to be the fastest of her day, once covering a distance of 363 miles in a day.

A little further down the Thames, the **Thames Barrier Centre** displays the world's largest moveable flood barrier, a £480m project aimed at saving London from flooding.

A little north of the centre of London, **Kenwood House** in Hampstead, is a stately home which offers a fine example of the work of architect Robert Adam. It also houses the Iveagh Bequest of furniture and pictures and in the summer hosts a series of outdoor musical concerts in its popular gardens. Kenwood lies next to **Hampstead Heath** which is a lovely open park offering extensive views of London.

Hampstead village is fun for tea, and lots of famous people live there. **Highgate Cemetery**, a little further north, is well known as the burial place of Karl Marx. However, on certain Sundays in the year, the older part of the cemetery, across the road from Marx's grave, offers some fascinating examples of old family mausoleums with creaking trees and creeping ivy to complete the effect. Look out for some famous graves there too, such as George Eliot's, and those of Charles Dickens' family.

Syon Park at Isleworth, was laid out in the 16th century by Capability Brown. **Syon House**, a former monastery, built by Henry V, has magnificent interiors which belie its somewhat sombre exterior. In 1604 James I granted Syon to the

Syon House

LONDON

Northumberlands and in 1762 the 1st Duke commissioned the young Robert Adam, who created the spectacular State Rooms thought to be among his best work. The Red Drawing Room is hung with crimson silk from Spitalfields and the superb carpet is signed and dated in the corner. The 19th century Great Conservatory, built for the 3rd Duke, was the first of its kind and the inspiration for the Crystal Palace.

Like Syon and Kenwood, **Osterley Park** was redecorated and refurbished by Robert Adam, The elegant rooms are almost as he left them and many of Adam's drawings for the furniture are on display. In the lovely park the semi-circular garden house is again the work of Robert Adam and the delightful old stables - now the tea room - are all that remains of the original Tudor house.

If you are a dedicated gardener seeking inspiration or just a vaguely interested visitor, there is little to compare with the gardens of **Capel Manor**. Just minutes from the M25 lies a garden of national repute, with a collection of some of the finest plants and examples of plantings in the region. The 30 acre grounds are set around Capel Manor, a superb Georgian building. The grounds present well over two dozen richly planted 'theme' gardens including historical, demonstration, rock, walled, water, woodland through to modern. There is a special garden for the physically disabled and a sensory garden for the visually impaired. An Italianate maze has recently been added to the collection, as have a range of new gardens sponsored by the Consumers Association.

Richmond Park, has herds of deer, which are a spectacular site, a delight to the visitor, and its ponds provide facilities for anglers and those with model boats.

RELAXING

After all the sight-seeing, London has plenty to offer as entertainment. The West End's theatres and cinemas are well known, and the capital is also full of restaurants and pubs, many with historic connections or of architectural interest. The **Telecom Tower**, for example is London's tallest building, and has a revolving restaurant at its top.

London is also famous for its shops. Stroll along **Oxford Street,** into **Regent Street** taking in department stores such as Selfridges, Libertys and Dickins & Jones. Wander down Carnaby Street, which became famous for its boutiques in the 60's. Visit Covent Garden, where the former fruit and vegetable markets have been converted into a thriving shopping centre with market stalls, bars, restaurants and street entertainment.

Also, not to be missed are Knightsbridge, which boasts stores such as Harrods and Harvey Nichols, Sloane Street and Kings Road.

Or simply sit in one of London's parks - **Regents Park** overlooked by Nash terraces, complete with its zoo, its open air theatre (only in summer), and its canal; **St James's Park** with a Chinese style lake and Duck Island; **Kensington Gardens**; **Hyde Park** whose Serpentine lake is well known; and **Green Park**, London's smallest park.

Whatever you want to do or see, London is sure to have it on offer somewhere.

Capel Manor

TOWER OF LONDON

One of the most famous and most visited fortified buildings in the world, the Tower of London spans over 900 years of British history. Standing on the north bank of the River Thames, between London and Tower Bridges, it has been fortress, palace, prison, arsenal, garrison and zoo.

After his coronation in Westminster Abbey in 1066, William the Conqueror withdrew to the safety of Barking, 'while certain fortifications were completed in the city against the restlessness of the huge and brutal populace. For he realised that it was of the first importance to over awe the Londoners!' The new royal castle was at first an enclosure within the surviving Roman city walls, but within about ten years palatial accommodation was provided for the King in the White Tower which dominates the castle and gives the Tower its name. The massive walls are between 12 and 15 feet thick and the entrance was by means of wooden steps at first floor level which could be destroyed in times of siege, although the Tower has never fallen to assault or siege. Inside the White Tower is the beautiful 11th century Chapel of St John, oldest complete ecclesiastical building in London and one of the best preserved examples of Norman architecture. Below the Chapel is the tiny dungeon, the smallest in the Tower measuring only four feet square, where Guy Fawkes was imprisoned. Also in the White Tower are the Royal Armouries, founded by Henry VIII and containing one of the most comprehensive collections of arms and armour. It includes four suits of Henry VIII's own armour, each larger than the previous one as the King's great frame increased in girth.

During the reign of Henry III and Edward I the Tower assumed its present form with the White Tower enclosed within two fortified walls and a huge moat. Entrance to the Tower from the river was through Traitor's Gate, and many an unfortunate prisoner must have experienced a terrible fear and dread as the gates closed behind the boat on what was probably their last journey.

Many prominent prisoners were held in the Bell Tower, nota-

bly Sir Thomas Moore in 1535 and Princess Elizabeth in 1554. As would befit her royal rank she was allowed to walk on the ramparts, hence its name Elizabeth Walk. The Bloody Tower, built by Henry VIII as the Garden Tower, was renamed in the reign of Elizabeth I when the 8th Earl of Northumberland shot himself here. It is also thought that the Little Princes were murdered here in 1483, and Sir Walter Raleigh spent thirteen years in the Bloody Tower charged with high treason. He seems to have enjoyed a certain degree of privilege not accorded to all prisoners for his wife lived with him and his second son was born in the Tower. The portcullis of the Bloody Tower is the only one in the country still in working order.

The Beauchamp Tower was built between 1275 and 1285 to house prisoners of noble rank. The walls bear the coats of arms and last messages carved during the long days of anxious waiting. The Bowyer Tower displays a gruesome collection of instruments of torture and the executioner's block and 16th century axe last used for the execution in 1747 of Lord Lovat.

The Jewel House in the Waterloo Barracks houses the most spectacular collection in the world. The present regalia dates from the time of Charles II, much of the old regalia having been destroyed by Cromwell after the Civil War. Among the breathtaking symbols of the English monarchy are the Imperial State Crown, St Edward's Crown used for the actual coronation ceremony, the Orb, the Sceptre set with the First Star of Africa, the largest cut diamond in the world and the Crown of Queen Elizabeth the Queen Mother with the famous Koh-in-noor diamond. A thousand tiny points of light flash and glint from these exquisite stones.

The famous Tower ravens always number at least six, and their presence may date back to the Royal Menagerie of Henry III's time when lions, leopards, a polar bear and even an elephant were kept at the Tower. According to legend, if the ravens ever leave then both the Tower and England will fall.

KEW GARDENS

The Royal Botanic Gardens cover 300 acres on the south bank of the River Thames. Here every season brings its own display of colour and interest from over 50,000 different plants, both in open ground and in the many specialist display glasshouses.

The Gardens were founded in 1759 by Princess Augusta, Dowager Princess of Wales and mother of George III. After the death of her husband, Frederick, she had continued to develop their estate surrounding Kew Palace, and started the first botanic garden on a site close to the present Orangery. It had become fashionable by the mid 18th century to have decorative buildings erected in large gardens, and Kew was no exception.

In 1757 Sir William Chambers became Princess Augusta's official architect and over the next five years he designed over two dozen buildings which were erected at Kew. Many, such as the Mosque, the Palladian Bridge and the Menagerie, have since disappeared, but amongst those remaining are the Orangery, the Ruined Arch and the Temple of Bellona as well as the Pagoda.

One of the best known featues in the Kew landscape, the Pagoda was completed in 1762 as a surprise for Princess Augusta. The previous summer Horace Walpole, then living in Twickenham wrote 'we begin to perceive the tower of Kew from Montepelier Road; in a fortnight you will be able to see it in Yorkshire'. Its ten storey octagonal structure, nearly 50 metres high was at that time the most accurate imitation of a Chinese building in Europe.

The eight sides of each storey, except the top one, have round headed recesses, alternate recesses being glazed. The walls are constructed of multi-coloured bricks. Originally the roofs were covered with varnished iron plates, with an iron dragon sitting at each edge. Each of the eighty dragons was covered in coloured glass and had a bell in its mouth. The whole building must have glinted and glittered in the sun and chimed in the wind, until George IV removed the metal plates and the dragons to pay off his debts.

In 1859 the Government of the day commissioned Decimus Burton, co-architect of the Palm House, to draw up plans for a Tempera House to house tender woody plants. The chosen site was set deep in the then new arboretum and the octagons were completed in 1861, followed by the central block in 1862 but the two wings were not finished until 1898.

Plants were quickly established in the new glass house which was twice the size of the Palm House. The main block contained fruit trees such as guava, mango, papaya and tree tomato, while the north wing was planted with Himalayan rhododendrons.

In 1882 the Marianne North Gallery was opened to the public. The Gallery was provided by Miss North to house the paintings she had presented to Kew. Born in 1830 Marianne North devoted her life to flower painting after the death of her father in 1889. She travelled widely, often enduring considerable discomfort in order to paint flowers in their natural habitat. Her many journeys took her to the United States, Canada, Jamaica, Brazil, Japan, Sarawak, Java, Sri Lanka and India. In later life and despite failing health she travelled to South Africa, the Seychelles and Chile. On display are 832 of her beautiful paintings.

HAMPTON COURT PALACE

Thomas Wolsey would undoubtedly have approached his new mansion in the country by barge. Begun in 1514, early in the reign of Henry VIII, the site he chose was on the north bank of the River Thames where he could enjoy the peace and clean air of the green Surrey countryside. He was a powerful, ambitious man, later Cardinal Wolsey, and built his fine red-brick house accordingly. It was grand enough to rival many a royal residence, with a piped supply of fresh water and splendid apartments for himself and for his royal master Henry VIII and his first Queen, Catherine of Aragon. By 1525, when building was almost complete, Wolsey, fearing the King's envy, wisely presented Henry with Hampton Court Palace in exchange for Richmond Palace.

Henry immediately began to enlarge the already enormous Palace, replacing Wolsey's Great Hall with an even greater one, remodelling the Chapel Royal and adding vast new kitchens and wine cellars to cater for the King's great love of food. Tennis courts, bowling alleys and a tiltyard, together with the surrounding parkland stocked with deer and game catered for Henry's great love of sport. He built a gateway in honour of his second wife, Anne Boleyn who was beheaded in 1536 and in 1537, amidst great joy and celebration, his only son Edward was born here to Jane Seymour. Tragically his third Queen died shortly afterwards. His 5th wife, Catherine Howard was held prisoner here before her trial and execution and Henry's sixth, and last marriage to Catherine Parr took place in the Palace chapel.

Elizabeth I seems not to have shared her father's liking for the Palace, perhaps understandably, having almost died of smallpox here, and although James I spent his first Christmas as King at Hampton Court, he too seems to have preferred other Palaces. Charles 1 was imprisoned by Cromwell's army, who then retained the Palace for his own use after the King's execution.

The second great period of building began in 1659 when William of Orange and his wife Mary commissioned Sir Christopher Wren to replace the old fashioned Tudor Palace with a building to rival the new Versailles. Cleverly, Wren created the illusion of a new Palace by screening the existing buildings with his new Baroque East Front and Fountain Court. During the reigns of George I and II, Hampton Court became a favourite summer residence of the Court with a constant round of lavish balls, parties and boating trips, before ceasing to be a royal residence in the time of George III.

In 1986 fire devastated Sir Christopher Wren's elegant south wing, but despite the extensive damage many treasures were rescued and much new information has been discovered about the Palace and its construction. This forms the basis of the Fire Exhibition in the King's Guard Chamber.

The wonderful gardens at Hampton Court date from around 1700 when Queen Anne redesigned the formal Tudor plantings of Wolsey and Henry VIII in the then fashionable French manner. The formal areas were very elaborate with parterres, ponds and fountains, clipped yews and long shaded walks. The famous, ever-frustrating Maze in the Wilderness dates from around this period and the Great Vine of Black Hamburg grapes, planted in 1768 by 'Capability' Brown is still a major attraction. The Tudor Tiltyard is now a rose garden and there are also Tudor and Elizabethan Knot Gardens, the King's Privy Garden, Great Fountain and Broad Walk.

Hampton Court is still a Royal Palace and, as such, is used for state functions attended by the Royal Family.

LEIGHTON HOUSE

Leighton House can be found in a lovely location near Holland Park in Kensington. Built between 1864-66 to designs by George Aitchison, it was the home of Frederic Lord Leighton who was the great nineteenth century classical painter and president of the Royal Academy.

The detail of this splendid house reflects Leighton's concern to create a 'House Beautiful'. The rooms are richly decorated with ebonised woodwork and gilding which were the earliest, and remain one of the most important, expressions of the Aesthetic Movement in England. The Arab Hall was added in 1877 - 79. This centre piece was designed to house Leighton's collection of Islamic tiles which are one of the most impressive in the world. The Arab Hall has remained completely intact and is a remarkable monument to eclectic Victorian taste. You can enjoy the decorations by Walter Crane and Randolf Caldecottand carvings by Edgar Boehm.

In its prime time Leighton House, filled with beautiful objects was very much a miniature palace of art. Leighton's love of music established a great tradition of concerts, at which Joachim, Charles Halle and Pauline Viardot performed. The tradition continued when, on Leighton's death in 1896, the museum was founded to perpetuate his memory.

There is a fascinating collection of pre-Victorian and pre-Raphaelite art with important paintings by Burne-Jones and Millais as well as Leighton himself. Loans from private and public collections enhance the permanent collection. The Drawings collection is the most important corpus of work by Leighton and may be viewed, in part, on the walls, and studied in full by appointment. these works, together with sculpture and furniture of the period are displayed in rooms restored to their original opulence.

Leighton House has a full programme of concerts, lectures and exhibitions. Contemporary art and music are especially encouraged, to continue the tradition of patronage established by Leighton.

The house may be booked for concerts, lectures, exhibitions, receptions, small conferences and private funtions. Guided tours are available by appointment for parties of not more than 25. The museum is open to the public Monday to Friday, 11.00 a.m. to 5.00 p.m., additionally until 6.00 p.m during exhibitions and Saturdays from 11.00 a.m. to 5.00 p.m. Closed Sundays and Bank Holidays.

BANK OF ENGLAND MUSEUM

The Bank of England Museum traces the history of the Bank from its foundation by Royal Charter in 1694 to its role today as the nation's central bank.

Before the Bank of England, the business of banking was largely in the hands of the goldsmiths who made extensive loans to merchants and to the Crown. By the end of the 17th century, however, the need for a more broadly based national bank had become increasingly apparent. The government welcomed the new Bank as a means of financing the costly war against France that had broken out in 1688.

One of the principle features of the Museum is a splendid reconstruction of a late 18th century banking hall, the Bank Stock office. Originally completed in 1793 by Sir John Soane, the leading English architect of the period, it stood on this site until the rebuilding of the Bank in its present form between the wars.

The Museum takes the visitor through numerous important incidents in the Bank's - and the Nation's - history and has a variety of exhibits. These include correspondence with famous stockholders of the 18th century such as George Washington and Horatio Nelson, (facsimile) Roman and modern gold bullion bars as well as examples of forgeries and early printing machines. Also on display is a Roman mosaic floor, one of two discovered during the interior rebuilding at the Bank.

The tour culminates in an interactive video display, used both to explain the work of the Bank and to test the user's knowledge of money and banking. You can then sit at a dealing desk similar to those in use in the Bank's dealing rooms with up-to-the-minute information displayed on the screens and listen to telephone commentaries on the work of a dealer in the foreign exchange, gilt (government stock) or money markets.

Bank of England Museum
Threadneedle St
London EC2R 8AH
Tel: 071-601 5545

THE IMPERIAL WAR MUSEUM

The Imperial War Museum - Museum of the Year 1990

The Cabinet War Rooms - Churchill's secret underground headquarters during the Second World War

HMS Belfast - moored on the Thames near Tower Bridge

Duxford Airfield - a Second World War airbase

The Imperial War Museum tells the story of 20th century warfare. The Museum's art galleries display a selection of paintings from the second largest collection of British 20th century works of art in the country, and the dramatic Large Exhibit Hall displays weapons from the world wars and more recent conflicts.

You can learn what it was like to fly with the RAF on a daring bomber raid over occupied Europe or experience a walk through a trench complete with sounds, smells and other special effects to get some idea of what it was like to be a soldier on the western front.

The Imperial War Museum has three outstations, one of which is HMS Belfast. She is the last survivor of the Royal Navy's big gun ships, and is permanently moored in the River Thames as a floating museum.

A clearly marked route has been laid out to enable visitors to explore the ship thoroughly. Among the areas to be discovered are the Bridge, the Boiler and Engine Rooms, the Galley, the Punishment Cells and two 6-inch gun turrets.

Another, the Cabinet War Rooms, located in the heart of ceremonial London. Visitors can view them exactly as they were when British history was shaped within them. Some of the most important and far-reaching decisions of the Second World War were taken here.

The third of the Imperial War Musuem's outstations is Duxford. As well as the finest collection of military and civil aircraft in the country there's a ride simulator - in which children of all ages will enjoy having a go - and an incredible variety of tanks, vehicles and guns - even a lifeboat and midget submarines.

Imperial War Museum
Lambeth Road
London SE1 6HZ
Tel: 071-416 5000
Fax: 071-416 5374

WESTMINSTER ABBEY MUSEUM

On the east side of the Great Cloister is a range of buildings that formed part of the medieval Benedictine monastery. The monks slept in the dormitory which extended over the existing Chapter House Vestibule, Pyx Chamber and Undercroft and from which they could reach the Abbey for night prayers by a gallery across St Faith's Chapel and down a wooden staircase into the South Trancept.

They spent much of the day, when not in church, either in the Cloister or in the Undercroft and attended a daily meeting in the Chapter House - the meeting was called Chapter because it involved the reading of a chapter from the Rule of St Benedict. The Pyx Chamber and Undercroft date from shortly after the Norman Conquest and are among the first monastic buildings added to Edward the Confessor's foundation. On the dissolution of the monastery in 1540 the Chapter House was taken over by the Exchequer to house the great mass of documents that it had accumulated over the centuries, including the Domesday Book.

The Westminster Abbey Museum, together with the Pyx Chamber and the Chapter House are a rewarding attraction to visitors to the East Cloister of Westminster Abbey.

The museum is housed in the magnificent vaulted undercroft beneath the former monks dormitory. The centrepiece of the museum exhibition is the Abbey's collection of royal and other effigies. From the late 13th century onwards funeral effigies of dead monarchs were carried in the funeral procession, on the coffin, beneath a canopy. The effigy was generally wearing full coronation regallia, the robes being lent by the Great Wardrobe.

On arrival at the Abbey, the effigy was placed within a hearse at the foot of the Sanctuary steps and displayed for weeks after the burial. The effigy was later stacked away in a chantry chapel in the Abbey. Several effigies have disappeared altogether but the collection includes the effigy of King Charles II made at the time of his death in 1685, but not carried at his funeral. This was dressed in his own Garter robes which have recently been cleaned and restored in the textile conservation workshop of the Victoria and Albert Museum. The collection also includes the head of the funeral effigy of King Henry VII who

died in 1509, taken from a death mask, and an effigy of Horatio Nelson, deemed by his contemporaries to be a remarkable likeness.

The early effigies were made of wood and were hollowed out behind to reduce their weight. Real hair wigs were placed on the models and eyebrows were rebuilt with the hair of small dogs. Later effigies were made from plaster and canvas moulded over a framework and later still partly from wax. Other items on display include replicas of the coronation regalia; armour, including the Funeral Achievements of King Henry V; a bronze portrait of Sir Thomas Lovell, almost certainly by the sculptor Pietro Torrigiano; alabaster carvings by Grinling Gibbons and some panels of medieval glass.

The Pyx Chamber is also part of the eleventh century vaulted undercroft. It was divided off around 1200 and for over 400 years was used as a royal treasury. Today, it is once again in use as a treasury, housing a fine display of plate from the Abbey and St Margaret's Church. Like most of the churches and cathedrals in this country the Abbey lost all its plate either at the reformation in the 16th century or during the Commonwealth period in the 17th century. After the Reformation it acquired a splendid Communion set for the High Altar in chased and embossed silver gilt. Also in the chamber is a shallow curved chest made in the late Middle Ages to store copes. In it, is displayed a cope of cloth of gold made in the 17th century for Abbey clergy and possibly worn at the coronation of Charles II in 1661. The two rectangular chests dating from the 13th and 14th centuries are too large to get through the door and were evidently made in the Chamber.

The Chapter House, a large octagonal chamber dating from 1257 is one of the finest in England and is still owned by the crown. Above the entrance doorway is one of the most important set pieces of medieval sculpture to have survived in England. The life-size figures represent the Annunciation, with Gabriel and Mary separated by winged angels. Also in the Chamber are a fascinating series of wall paintings.

In 13th century England the art of the tiled pavement was highly developed. The one in the Chapter House dates from the 1250's and is by far the most complete surviving example.

WESTMINSTER ABBEY

An architectural masterpiece of the thirteenth to sixteenth centuries, Westminster Abbey also presents a unique pageant of British history; the Confessor's shrine, the tombs of Kings and Queens and countless memorials to the great and famous.

The Abbey has been the setting for every coronation since 1066 and for numerous other royal occasions. Nine hundred years ago the Abbey was a Benedictine Monastery, offering the traditional Benedictine hospitality to its visitors, until its dissolution in 1540 . Today, it is still a church dedicated to regular worship and the celebration of the Nation's great events.

The history of the Abbey during those nine hundred years is too rich and varied to be committed to such a small passage but just a few of the more fascinating parts of the Abbey are described below.

Elizabeth I is buried in the North Aisle of the Chapel of Henry VII. Elizabeth died in 1603 and she lies in the same vault as her half-sister, Mary Tudor. The monument contains an effigy which bears a faithful likeness to the Queen. The Chapel itself was completed in 1519 and its vaulted roof is an outstanding example of spectacular Tudor architecture. Since 1725, the Chapel has been used as the Chapel of the Order of Bath and gaily coloured banners, crests and mantlings of the Knights adorn the 16th century wooden stalls. Behind the altar lies Henry VII and his consort Elizabeth of York.

The Abbey Church was consecrated in 1065. Its founder, the saintly King Edward was too ill to be present and died a few days later. Two hundred years later, Henry III began rebuilding the Church to house a shrine worthy of the King. It is this building you see today.

Westminster Abbey is home to the coronation chair. This oak chair was made for King Edward I by Master Walter of Durham. It was designed to hold the ancient stone of Scone seized from the Scots in 1296. For coronations, the chair is moved into position in the Sanctuary. Since 1308, it has been used by every sovereign. Only two, King Edward V and Edward VIII were never crowned.

It is not just royalty who are buried within the Abbey. Poets' corner is the resting place of some of Britian's finest authors and poets. The tomb to which the corner owes its origin is that of Geoffrey Chaucer, the first great English poet. He was buried here in 1400 and transfered to a grander tomb in 1556. The placing of memorials to poets began here in earnest in the 18th century with a full-length statue of William Shakespeare. Eliot, Auden, Dylan Thomas and Lewis Carroll are among the most recent.

The focal point of the Abbey's architecture was originally St Edwards Shrine which was screened off in mid 15th century. Its life today is the High Altar, framed by three tombs, medieval wall paintings and a masterpiece of Italian Renaissance painting.

The beautiful Gothic Nave, the tallest in Britain, with the grave of the Unknown Warrior and memorials to statesmen, scientists and servicemen is a moving tribute to those who have had a great influence on the history of the Nation.

The Great Cloister is medieval and Little Cloisters was rebuilt in

the 17th century. In the East Walk is the Chapter House. It is one of the largest in the country reflecting the large size of the monastery. It was used regularly as a Parliament House for the Commons for over a century.

The Abbey welcomes over 3½ million visitors every year but worship and prayer remain the primary function of the Abbey community. A priest is always available and you are invited to share in acts of prayer at the Abbey. Many vistiors spend only a short time in the Abbey, but those who are able to share in the worship contribute to the historic witness of this great church.

SELSDON PARK

Set high in the rolling hills of the Surrey countryside Selsdon Park combines the ancient virtues of hospitality and courtesy with the modern attributes of efficiency and friendliness.

The estate was purchased by the present owner's father and converted into an hotel in 1925. Additions were made during the thirties, and again in the eighties to include a modern courtyard wing and a tropical leisure complex. The hotel now has 170 bedrooms and suites and a considerable range of conference and banqueting rooms.

An outstanding asset to Selsdon Park is the 18 hole championship golf course laid out in 1929 by five-times British Open Champion, J H Taylor. Originally cut out of the thick forest which clothed this part of the Surrey Hills, the course has been extended over the years, but the layout remains substantially as it was sixty years ago. Covering 6402 yards, this course is not perhaps for the novice, although it provides a stimulating challenge to low and high handicappers alike.

A round or two on this interesting course prepares the golfer to sample the pleasures of luncheon or dinner in the Restaurant, or the more informal cuisine of the Phoenix Brasserie and Grill which is open from Monday to Friday The traditional Bar Lounge, warmed in winter by crackling logs, provides old world comfort while the contemporary atmosphere of the Phoenix Bar makes it an ideal place to sample the wide range of cocktails available.

Golfing weekends here are a delight, and there is plenty to occupy the time of a non-golfing partner. There is a heated outdoor swimming pool (open from May to September), a jogging trail, two hard tennis courts and two grass courts (floodlit as necessary), boules pitch and croquet lawn. A large billiard room containing four full sized snooker tables remains open for the use of resident guests until 1 am. Horse riding can be organised at a stables nearby. The architect-designed Leisure Complex contains a well-equipped gymnasium and squash courts, providing opportunities for vigorous exercise, while the tropical swimming pool, sunbeds, steambath, sauna and jacuzzi provide less strenuous pleasures.

Selsdon Park Hotel has an almost unbeatable combination of sporting and leisure facilities to offer the golfer and non-golfer alike, together with all the amenities of a 4-star hotel.

Selsdon Park Hotel
Sanderstead
South Croydon
Surrey CR2 8YA
Tel: 081-657 8811
Fax: 081-651 6171

LONDON

It is a peculiar irony that many of the vast hotels in London have a less memorable heritage than their country cousins. Indeed, many of the outstanding hotels are of a contemporary design and others date from the 18th and 19th centuries - mere babes in arms!

What really adds to the charm of London is the heritage of the people as much as the place. As a capital city, London has seen and endured so much; coronations, world wars, fires, plagues, pomp and ceremony, cheers and tears.

Many of the old London clubs are particularly fascinating in their origins. The Wig and Pen Club, Pratts, Whites, The Turf Club are just a few. These establishments have witnessed political revolution, those walls have been party to economic discourse, political backstabbing and much sporting banter.

The streets of London are awash with history. The former homes of the famous are marked by blue plaques; Ghandi in lowly W14 and Thomas Hardy in less than fashionable SW12. While the face of London may be ever changing, there are a number of historic hostelries where time has stood still although many breweries have bowed to modern day pressures, insisting on fairly alarming modernisation.

London is a treasure trove of museums, markets, galleries and even palaces but it is also a working capital. The old Covent Garden has gone but in its place is a thriving market and fashionable shopping area. However, it is not too difficult to conjure up images of the barrows loaded with fruit, vegetables and flowers and the real characters of the piece hawking their wares.

The thrill of the theatre, the splendour of St Paul's and Parliament, Old Father Thames and the sombre beauty of Westminster Abbey are an intrical part of our heritage. As of course, are the Royal Family whose history is ours and whose legacy includes the Tower of London and the spectacle of Buckingham Palace.

Love it or hate it, London is one of the most fascinating and colourful capital cities of the world.

HOTELS OF DISTINCTION

BASIL STREET HOTEL, Basil Street, S.W.3, Tel: 071-581 3311
A classical tranquility exudes throughout this gracious, awfully English hotel. Ideally placed for exploring the bustle of the West End and Knightsbridge, the interior is tastefully designed and furnished.

THE BEAUFORT, 33 Beaufort Gardens, S.W.3,
Tel: 071-584 5252
An oasis of peace and tranquility a hundred yards from Harrods. The Beaufort is furnished in traditional English chintzes and wallpapers, and houses the largest collection of original English floral watercolours in the world.

BROWN'S HOTEL, Albemarle and Dover Streets, W.1,
Tel: 071-493 6020
Long established as one of the more civilised of the London hotels. Definitely the rendezvous for afternoon tea, its beautiful furnishings and service are pure elegance.

CADOGAN HOTEL, 75 Sloane Street, S.W.1,
Tel: 071-235 7141
Owned by Historic House Hotels, the building is the combination of two late Regency houses and an 1880s building. The classic period features, such as the moulded ceilings, have been preserved. The hotel maintains its strong connections with Lillie Langtry and Oscar Wilde.

CANNIZARO HOUSE, Wimbledon, S.W.19, Tel: 081-879 1464
Originally an 18th century country house, this magnificent hotel presides over Wimbledon Common. The drawing-room is ornately decorated with a combination of flowers, antiques and oil paintings.

CHESTERFIELD HOTEL, 35 Charles Street, W.1,
Tel: 071-491 2622
Courtesy is one of the hallmarks of this charming hotel. Another of the extremely English set, the charm is established from the moment one enters the foyer, with its sparkling chandelier and leather chesterfield. A pianist performs nightly in the bar.

CLARIDGE'S, Brook Street, W.1, Tel: 071-629 8860
Need one say more than the name? Liveried hall porters, beautiful decor, perfect service, not to mention the famous pink and green reading room and the Hungarian quartet that still plays in the colonnaded lounge.

THE CONNAUGHT, Carlos Place, W.1, Tel: 071-499 7070
Caught in a Twilight Zone of its own, refusing to move from the elegance of the 20s and 30s, this is probably the most discreet and exclusive of London's great hotels. Situated in the heart of Mayfair, sophistication is the key here.

THE DORCHESTER, Park Lane, W.1, Tel: 071-629 8888
Recently lavishly refurbished and restored for its long-awaited re-opening. Bedrooms have been modelled and re-built in the style of a classic English country house.

DORSET SQUARE HOTEL, 39 Dorset Square, N.W.1,
Tel: 071-723 7874
Created from the tasteful blending of two Regency houses, this hotel boasts a beautiful chintz-filled lounge with a well-stocked honesty bar in a magnificent antique cabinet. Antique and reproduction furniture decorates the bedrooms.

DUKES HOTEL, 35 St James Place, S.W.1,
Tel: 071-4591 4840
In the heart of civilised St James, this traditional hotel is tastefully furnished with a conservative collection of antiques, period furniture and chintz fabrics.

THE FENJA, 69 Cadogan Gardens, S.W.3, Tel: 071-589 7333
The conversion from grand Victorian house to a rather stylish hotel has been accomplished here with a great deal of style and thought. The individual bedrooms are decorated with antiques, paintings and fresh flowers.

THE GORING, 17 Beeston Place, SW1, Tel: 071-834 8211
Noted in history as the first hotel to offer private bathrooms and central heating throughout. Still owned by the original family since 1910, the decor has a comfortable feel to it, with wood, brass and marble in tasteful use throughout.

LONDON

GROSVENOR HOUSE, Park Lane, W.1, Tel: 071-499 6363
Beautifully decorated, with spacious and carefully designed day rooms with solid furniture leading to the airy bedrooms, complete with double beds and marble tiled bathrooms.

THE HALCYON, 81 Holland Park, W.11, Tel: 071-727 7288
Very attractively placed for the visiting antique dealer, this hotel has been built from two Victorian town houses, carefully combined to leave the beautiful architecture intact. The ornate plaster cornices and fireplaces are enhanced by a collection of period antiques.

HYDE PARK HOTEL, 66 Knightsbridge, S.W.1,
Tel: 071-235 2000
Intended as 'residential chambers for gentlemen', this imposing hotel not only offers an ideal position in Knightsbridge, but the interior is also highly impressive. Sparkling chandeliers hang from gold, ornate ceilings, lighting the marble walls.

THE MARLBOROUGH, Bloomsbury Street, W.C.1,
Tel: 071-636 5601
Skilfully managing to combine old-fashioned comfort with the modern amenities that the discerning traveller has come to expect, the bedrooms here are decorated with porcelain, polished brass lamps and light oak furniture.

LE MERIDIEN, Piccadilly, W.1, Tel: 071-734 8000
A very elegant building, exuding more the aura of a private gentleman's club than a hotel. The sounds of the harpist playing under the chandeliers in the lounge adds to the general exclusive ambience.

THE MONTCALM, Great Cumberland Place, W.1,
Tel: 071-402 4288
Some of the friendliest staff in London greet you as you enter this hotel, behind a listed Georgian frontage. A traditionally masculine style of decor gives the place the solid atmosphere of a gentleman's private club.

THE PORTLAND BLOOMSBURY HOTEL, 7 Montague Street, WC1, Tel: 071-323 1717
A small and charming hotel in a fashionable area of Bloomsbury retaining many original Regency features with a wealth of antiques. Its pretty garden backs onto the British Museum and Covent Garden is only a short walk away.

THE RITZ, Piccadilly, W.1, Tel: 071-493 8181
The simple name of this hotel has become so much a part of the national heritage that it seems hardly worth noting as one of London's more elegant hotels. The bedrooms are ornately decorated and offer the ultimate in luxury, including marble fireplaces and gilded plasterwork.

THE SAVOY, Strand, W.C.2, Tel: 071-836 4343
Again, the name says it all. Over a hundred years of providing some of the best hospitality in the world has left this hotel in a special position in English history. Afternoon tea in the Thames Foyer is a must; or try a cocktail, possibly just invented, in the American Bar.

STAFFORD, St James's Place, S.W.1, Tel: 071-493 0111
Very much a clubland address, this hotel maintains the expected air of civilised discretion. Very attractive and very English, except for the amusingly loud American bar decorated with baseball caps, badges and ties.

WHITES HOTEL, Lancaster Gate, W.2, Tel: 071-262 2711
Originally an early Victorian house, the decor is opulent to say the least. The elegant reception room leads onto graceful bedrooms in a variety of styles.

ACCOMMODATION OF MERIT

ABER HOTEL, 89 Crouch Hill, Hornsey, Tel: 081-340 2847
A medium-sized, family-run hotel, the Aber offers a peaceful night's sleep within easy reach of the bright lights and loud noises of central London.

BELGRAVE HOUSE HOTEL, 28-32 Belgrave Road, S.W.1,
Tel: 071-828 1563
The Belgrave House is centrally located with easy access to Victoria station, Buckingham Palace and the West End. All bedrooms are centrally heated and some have private facilities.

BYRON HOTEL, 36-38 Queensborough Terrace, W.2,
Tel: 071-243 0987
Opposite Kensington Gardens, this acclaimed hotel aims to recapture some of the charm and elegance of Victorian England. Whatever the objectives, the results are excellent, with particularly fine interior decor.

CHASE LODGE, 10 Park Road, Hampton Wick,
Tel: 081-943 1862
This excellent and high-quality establishment, close to Kempton and Sandown racecourses is a perfect base for avid tourists. A multitude of places of interests are within easy travelling diatance, including Syon Park, Kew Gardens, Wisley, Hampton Palace, Windsor Castle, Osterley House and Royal Bushy Park.

CHESHAM HOUSE HOTEL, 64-66 Ebury Street, S.W.1,
Tel: 071-730 8513
The Chesham has undergone recent and extensive refurbishment, and looks set to reap immense benefits. Service too, is consistently courteous and helps to create an atmosphere of well-being.

CLEARVIEW HOUSE, 161 Fordwych Road, N.W.2,
Tel: 081-452 9773
Guesthouses in the capital set in quiet residential areas are not always over-easy to find, but this example is well worth seeking out. Accommodation is both modern and tasteful.

CRANBROOK HOTEL, 24 Coventry Road, Ilford,
Tel: 081-554 6544
The occasion to pamper oneself without spending a small fortune does not arise frequently. However this extremely comfortable suburban hotel offers some rooms with ensuite facilities and jacuzzi and, most importantly, is not excessively priced.

KNIGHTSBRIDGE HOTEL, 10 Beaufort Gardens,
Tel: 071-589 9271
The first-time visitor to the Knightsbridge will immediately be impressed by its elegant facade. Entering the hotel will most definitely not prove a let-down, with stylish and appropriate furnishings the order of the day.

LONDON

STONEHALL HOUSE, 35-37 Westcombe Park, SE3,
Tel: 081-858 8706
Stonehall is a traditional guesthouse that will make its visitors more than welcome. The TV lounge and garden are both well thought of.

WIMBLEDON HOTEL, 78 Worple Road, SW19,
Tel: 081-946 9265
Cosy and family-run, this popular hotel is always highly praised by previous residents. Local amenities are within walking distance.

WINCHESTER HOTEL, 12 Belgravia Road, S.W.1,
Tel: 071-828 2972
The elegance of the area is matched by this well-appointed hotel. Rooms are of a uniformly high standard and guests will leave feeling refreshed and invigorated.

INNS OF CHARACTER

ANCHOR, 34 Park Street, Rotherhithe, S.E.16
This rambling and creaking old inn dates back to around 1750 and is historically suspected to be the very one from which the diarist, Samuel Pepys, watched the Great Fire ravaging the city. Lovingly restored in the 1960s.

CITTIE OF YORKE, 22 High Holborn, W.C.1
People have been drinking on this spot since 1430, though the original pub was reconstructed in Victorian times using 17th century materials. Complete with the longest bar in Britain, thousand gallon wine vats and beautiful ornately carved cubicles offering some welcome privacy.

DOVE, 19 Upper Mall, Hammersmith
This quaint old pub holds a place in the "Guinness Book Of Records" as having the smallest bar room, a tiny 4'2" by 7'10". James Thomson is said to have written parts of his work here, and a manuscript of his most famous - 'Rule Brittania' - hangs on the wall.

FREEMASONS, Downshire Hill, Hampstead, N.W.3
Close to the Heath, the beauty here is the old rambling garden with its fountain and fishpond. Worth visiting to see the only lawn billiards court left in England.

GEORGE, Southwark, S.E.1,
One of the most genuinely historic pubs in the country. Many years ago, when Southwark was London's entertainment centre, all manner of performers would ply their trade here, including the rather well known 'Lord Chamberlain's Men' - Shakespeare's strolling players. Noted in 1598 as one of London's "fair Inns for the receipt of travellers".

HOLLANDS, 9 Exmouth Street, Stepney, E.1
Most of the decorations here are original early-Victorian, complete with antique mirrors, Vanity Fair pictures, old cartoons and interesting photographs. The pub was opened back in Queen Victoria's reign by the present landlord's great-grandfather.

LAMB & FLAG, 33 Rose Street, Covent Garden, W.C.2
When Charles Dickens was working in nearby Catherine Street, he would write about the Middle Temple lawyers he would watch frequenting this pub. Little has changed here since those times. It is considearbly more civilised now though than it was when the poet Dryden was beaten nearly to death in its courtyard.

OLDE CHESHIRE CHEESE, Wine Office Court, E.C.4
The building here dates back to the 17th century and its list of distinguished clientele includes Congreve, Pope, Voltaire, Thackery, Dickens, Conan Doyle, Yeats and Dr Johnson. The friendly bustle of the place invites this kind of discussion.

PRINCESSE LOUISE, 208 High Holborn, W.C.1
This old-fashioned gin-palace boasts a deeply elaborate decor. One of the most interesting features - oddly enough - is the magnificent gents' lavatory, the subject of a separate preservation order.

Cannizaro House

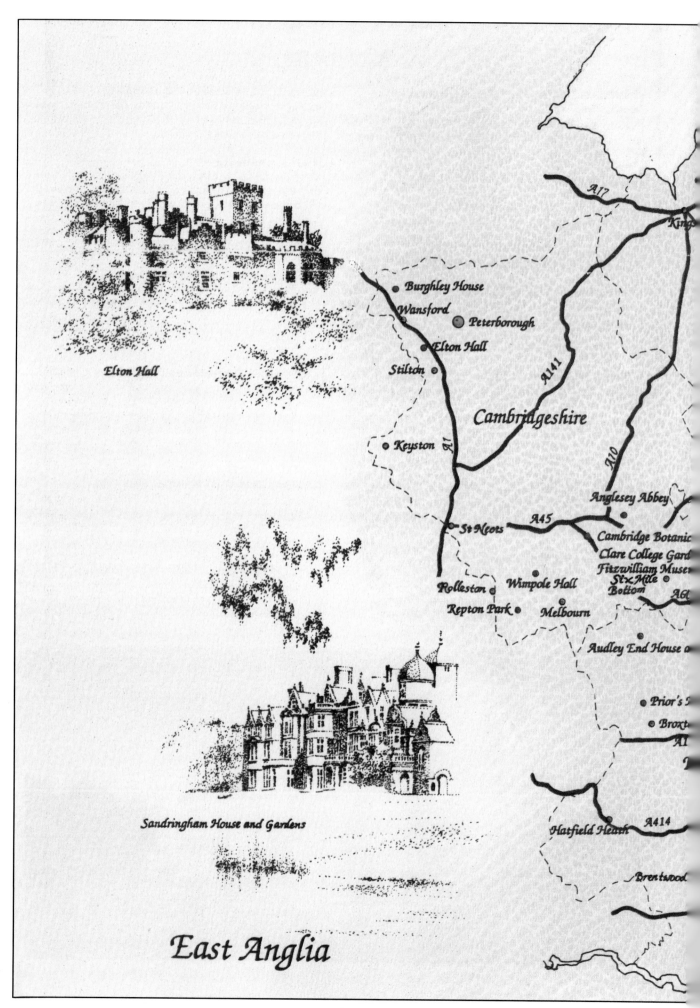

Elton Hall

Burghley House
Wansford
Peterborough
Elton Hall
Stilton

Cambridgeshire

Keyston

A17

King

A141

A10

Anglesey Abbey

St Neots
A45
Cambridge Botanic
Clare College Gard
Fitzwilliam Muser
Rolleston
Wimpole Hall
St × Mile
Bottom
Repton Park
Melbourn
A4

Audley End House

Prior's

Broxt

A1

Hatfield Heath
A414

Brentwood

Sandringham House and Gardens

East Anglia

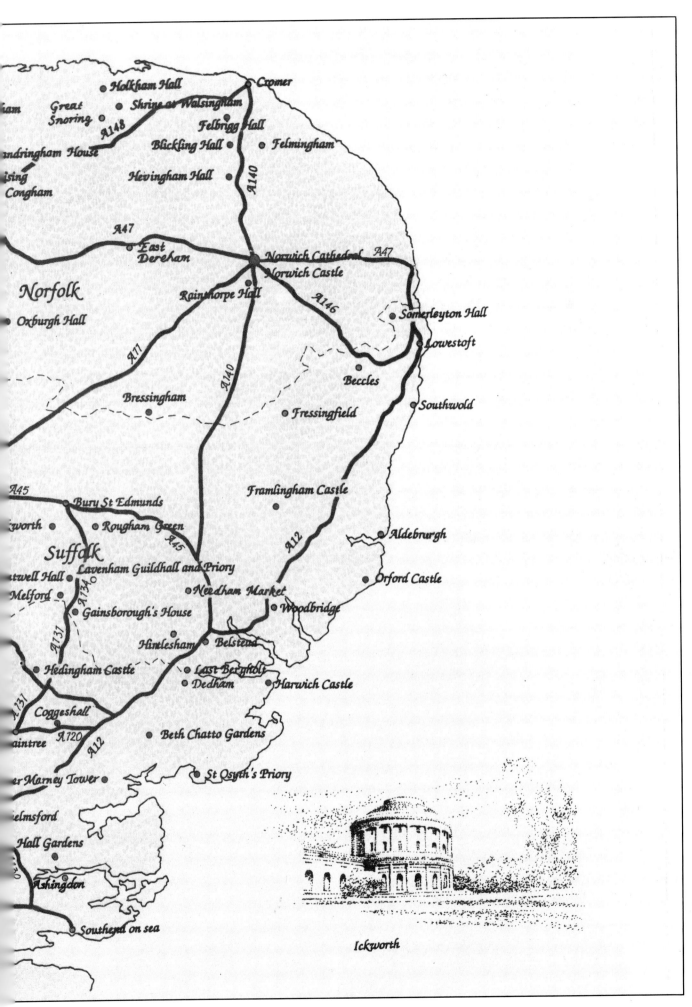

Holkham Hall

Cromer

Great
Snoring

Shrine at Walsingham

A148

Felbrigg Hall

...ham

Blickling Hall

Felmingham

...ndringham House

A140

...ising

Hevingham Hall

Congham

A47

East
Dereham

Norwich Cathedral

A47

Norfolk

Norwich Castle

Rainthorpe Hall

A146

Oxburgh Hall

Somerleyton Hall

A77

Lowestoft

A140

Bressingham

Beccles

Fressingfield

Southwold

A45

Framlingham Castle

Bury St Edmunds

...xworth

Rougham Green

A45

Aldeburgh

Suffolk

A12

Lavenham Guildhall and Priory

...atwell Hall

A134

Orford Castle

...Melford

Needham Market

A131

Gainsborough's House

Woodbridge

Hintlesham

Belstead

Hedingham Castle

East Bergholt

A131

Dedham

Harwich Castle

Coggeshall

...aintree

A720

A12

Beth Chatto Gardens

...r Marney Tower

St Osyth's Priory

...elmsford

...Hall Gardens

...Ashingdon

...Southend on sea

Ickworth

107

EAST ANGLIA

The counties of Cambridgeshire, Suffolk, Norfolk and Essex make up a curious mixture of fenland, coastline, broad and village. Cambridge stands out as a beacon of learning and the Suffolk wool towns are pleasingly unspoilt. The low-lying countryside which was once waterlogged now provides some of the finest arable lands in the country. Although the popular conception of East Anglia is one of tedious regularity, there are highlights to witness. The streets and colleges of Cambridge are a delight and to the north, Ely Cathedral, the 'Ship of the Fens' beckons you to this beautiful old town.

Norfolk is criss crossed by dykes and ditches, many of which date from Roman times. The Norfolk Broads which were created by the flooding of the peat diggings contrast with the arcing coastline. The county is much loved by the Royal Family and Sandringham remains one of the Queen's favourite residences.

The countryside of East Anglia has inspired many landscape artists, none more celebrated than Constable. The countryside that now bears his name offers a myriad of river views, thatched cottages and villages. Cathedrals and churches abound and many of the local churches date back to the 14th century and reveal a precious insight to the area's development.

Although Essex is a busier county, it too has splendid examples of preserved English villages, complete with pond and thatched pub. The village names also conjure up an image of past eras; Saxons, Romans, Danes, Vikings and Normans. Each had a lasting effect on the history of the region. **Colchester** is England's oldest recorded town and was the capital of Roman Britain. The town bustles today, but Roman remains are still to be seen and 20th century Colchester follows the original Roman street plan.

The region is blessed with an abundance of English 'quaintness' and beauty. Villages, each with their own history, spatter a countryside where peace and tranquillity are still commonplace. From abundant Fenland to rich academia, the peatlands, coast line and ecclesiastical sanctuary, the very fabric of this society, offers a wealth of different attractions for the visitor.

CAMBRIDGE AND THE COLLEGES

The Cambridge Colleges have gained their treasures from many sources, from monarchs and merchants, travellers and scribes. The scholastic origins of the town date from the 13th century when the monasteries and Cathedrals which housed a variety of religious orders developed schools for their number.

Peterhouse is the oldest Cambridge College, founded in 1284 by Hugh Balsham, Bishop of Ely. He bought two houses on this site for his scholars but bequeathed them more money enabling them to build a hall. The college takes its name from the neighbouring St Peter's Church and together they were the first of the collection of buildings that today give Cambridge its unique beauty. St Peter's was rebuilt in the 14th century and its name changed to St Mary's. There are many churches in Cambridge but the most notable University church is that of Great St Mary's. If you climb to the top of the tower you will have a splendid view of the bustling market place and many of the colleges. The clock tower chimes composed for the Cambridge Church are the same as those of Big Ben. Little remains of the original hall as it was renovated and altered during the

15th and 19th centuries. The Chapel was completed in 1632 and is a particular delight.

Kings College was founded by Henry VI in 1441. He established the celebrated Eton School at the same time and they share the same coat of arms but despite the Monarch's ambitions, only the Chapel was completed. The rest of the Front Court dates from 1723 and 1823. The former works make up the Fellow's building, designed by James Gibbs and the latter saw the completion of the hall and screen which today face the street. The Chapel itself remains the centrepiece of the buildings and has been built on in stages. The great fan-vaulted ceiling was completed in 1515. The carved coats of arms on the walls are those of Henry VIII and his initials, with those of Anne Boleyn, can be clearly seen on the screen. Renaissance windows depict the New Testament story and above each one, the equivalent story from the Old Testament is recorded. Ruben's magnificent painting 'Adoration of the Magi' is another treasure to behold here - in pride of place behind the altar.

The Chapel is open from 9am to 4pm during term time and until 5pm during vacation. On Sundays it is open from 2pm to 3pm and from 4.30pm to 5.45pm during term and during vacation is open between 10.30am and 5pm. The Chapel may be closed occasionally for rehearsals and recordings. Choral services are held at 5.30pm during term (Tuesday to Saturday) and at 10.30am and 3.30pm on Sundays. Members of the public are welcome to attend these services. There are few more delightful places in which to find peace in truly majestic surroundings.

Queens College was founded by Margaret of Anjou, wife of Henry VII, and Elizabeth Woodville, wife of Edward IV. It dates from the mid 15th century and hides a number of treasures. One of the most fascinating is the Mathematical Bridge which dates from 1749. The bridge, so called because it was allegedly constructed without bolts, was dismantled by curious Victorians who were unable to rebuild it without the use of iron nails and bolts. That will teach us to tamper with history! The oldest parts of the college date from the 15th century and the half timbered President's Gallery dates from the following century. The elaborate sundial dates from the 17th century. Of the many celebrated academics who have stayed at the college perhaps Erasmus, the Renaissance Humanist, is the most famous. We can not tell you whether the learned thinker was charged for overnight accommodation in 1511 or what the tariff was. You will be admitted between 1.45pm and 4.30pm and also from 10.15am to 12.45pm from late June to early October.

Also on the shortlist are the colleges of **Trinity and St John's**, which are worthy of a visit. Two exceptional features of the former are the library built by Sir Christopher Wren and the fountain which date from 1602.

Trinity was founded by Henry VIII in 1546 and replaced two older colleges. The front gate and that next to the Chapel, belonged to one of these colleges and commemorate Edward III. Dr Thomas Neville designed the Great Court during the reign of Elizabeth I. The Chapel contains memorials to many celebrated members of this college including Sir Isaac Newton, Tennyson and Bacon. The Wren Library is open to the public on weekdays from noon to 2pm and on Saturdays in term between 10.30am and 12.30pm.

EAST ANGLIA

St John's was founded in 1511 by Margaret, mother of Henry VII. Her coat of arms can be seen on the front gate together with a statue of St John. The large Chapel dates from 1869 and was designed by George Gilbert Scott. There are a number of courts in the college and the third leads to the Kitchen Bridge which affords a wonderful view of the more vaunted Bridge of Sighs, modelled on the Venetian design.

Magdalene, founded in 1350, is a fascinating reminder of one of the tragedies of Britain, the Black Death. The terrible disease wiped out almost one third of the population including many priests and professional men. The college's sole purpose was to train men in law after the cessation of the disease.

Samuel Pepys was a student at Magdalene College and left his famous library to the college. The library is open from 2.30pm to 3.30pm.

Jesus College was built in 1496, on the premises of an existing convent where at the time only two nuns remained. The Chapel contains work by William Morris and is open daily from 6.00am to 10am. Also try to visit **Sydney Sussex** where Cromwell was a student, or **Christ's College** where Milton studied.

Americans should make their own pilgrimage to **Emmanuel** where university founder, John Harvard was a student.

Clare College was founded in 1338 by the widowed Lady Elizabeth de Clare. The College coat of arms shows her shield, with tears on a black border of mourning. However, the present buildings date from the 17th century as does the Bridge, the oldest in Cambridge.

St Catherine's College was founded in 1473 but the majority of the buildings date from the 17th and 18th centuries. Thomas Hobson lived on this site. His custom of hiring out his horses in rotation led to the saying 'Hobson's Choice.'

Finally, **Pembroke College,** founded in 1347 by the Widow of Pembroke boasts some of the most attractive gardens in Cambridge. The earliest buildings are medieval but the Chapel is the first architectural design of Sir Christopher Wren, completed about 1666. Nicholas Ridley, the Protestant Martyr, was the Master here and the poet Thomas Grey a member of the college.

Tours of the colleges can be arranged throughout the year through the Tourist Information Centre (0223) 358977. It goes without saying that the colleges are places of learning and visitors should respect this at all times.

In addition to the colleges, visitors to the town should endeavour to visit **Fitzwilliam Museum** on Trumpington Street which houses artifacts bequeathed by the 7th Viscount Fitzwilliam to the University. The collection is one of the finest outside London and contains paintings, prints, music and other treasures. The University's Botanic Garden and specialist museums are also worth a look. These establishments are generally open from 10am but details are available from the Tourist Office.

The River Cam itself is a great source of history and has been an integral part of the development of Cambridge. The Backs pass behind the college and punts and rowing boats can be hired - a tremendous way to see some of the colleges. Lovers of terra firma will enjoy the riverside walks and picnic spots along the towpaths.

Cambridge revolves around the beautiful buildings and their history with memories of Milton and Newton and there are many delights to behold in this varsity town.

BEYOND CAMBRIDGE

There are a number of houses of note to consider, all within a twenty mile radius of Cambridge. **Anglesey Abbey** is situated in the village of Lode, some six miles north east of Cambridge on the B1102. Built on the site of an Augustinian Abbey it contains the celebrated Fairhaven collection of paintings and furniture. The Abbey is surrounded by an outstanding 100 acre garden and arboretum with a large collection of statuary. The interior of the house is a treasure trove of priceless furniture, silver, paintings, porcelain, tapestries and statuary. It includes works by Gainsborough, an Egyptian bronze dating from 500BC, and a fabulous array of other rare trinkets. The gardens boast majestic avenues and walks, and a geometric framework of horsechestnuts is filled with a delightful composition of trees, grasses and flowers. Many rare species are displayed in the arboretum, including the Hungarian oak, the Indian chestnut, the Judas tree and the Japanese hop hornbeam. Gardens of hyacinth and dahlia are watched over by busts of Roman Emperors, Father Time and stone griffins - a splendid sight. The house and gardens are particularly attractive when seen against the powerful East Anglian skies, whose towering cloudscapes form and dissolve over the distant Fens.

The most spectacular mansion in Cambridgeshire is that of **Wimpole Hall**. When the house was in the possession of the 2nd Earl of Oxford it hosted Swift and Pope among others. A baroque Chapel merits particular attention, the east wall is filled with Thornhill's 'Adoration of the Magi'. The Long Library is equally splendid. Harley's collection of books and manuscripts was the largest and most important in England and now forms the nucleus of the British Library. Wimpole's crowning glory is however, John Soane's Yellow Drawing Room. The elegance of the room renders the visitor speechless. In contrast to this, Soane's Bath House with a tiled pool is another remainder of 18th century 'good' life.

Wimpole's setting within extensive wooded parkland contributes to the splendour of the house. 'Capability' Brown excelled himself here and others such as Repton have added to the grounds. The farm to the north of the House has a 150 foot Great Barn which houses a museum of architectural implements. The thatched barn is surrounded by paddocks and pens making up Wimpole's farm for rare breeds.

We set sail again now for the 'Ship of the Fens'. **Ely Cathedral** is unique in its gothic architecture. Ely, the capital of the Fens is where Hereward the Wake, 'The Last of the English', held out against William The Conqueror. Half timbered buildings, attractive Georgian houses in St Mary's Street and the 12th century remains of the Chapel of St John are also of interest in this market town. However, nothing can dim the impact of the Cathedral. Work on the present building began in 1083. In 1322 the Norman Crossing Tower collapsed and was replaced by a larger, octagonal tower, surmounted by a timber vault carrying an octagonal lantern. The 12th century decoration on the exterior of the north wall of the nave is the Cathedral's finest carving. Three doorways which date from 1130 survive and the quality of carving and their excellent condition make them some of the most important survivors of Norman architecture in Britain.

THE NENE VALLEY

Elton Hall merits a special visit when you are considering places of interest in East Anglia (featured later) as do the nearby National Trust properties at Houghton Mill and Longthorpe Tower.

Houghton Mill is located in the village of Houghton, off the A1123, the St Ives to Huntingdon Road. There has been a cornmill on this site since Domesday. The mill's inland setting is very picturesque and the present day building dates from the 17th century. The restored machinery gives a valuable insight into times gone by and is well worth a visit.

Longthorpe Tower is another interesting spectacle. The edifice is an interesting 13th century fortified manor house. There are some fascinating wall paintings which date from the 14th century and were discovered in 1946. They show, amongst other scenes, 'The Seven Ages Of Man', 'The Labours Of The Monster' and 'The Three Quick and The Three Dead'.

COLCHESTER AND CONSTABLE COUNTRY

'Constable' Country has much to offer in addition to its riverscapes and thatched villages. The area is within easy striking distance of London and one of the most splendid Jacobean houses in England is at **Audley End** (featured later).

If you are planning a trip here it would be a good idea to tie it in with a journey to **Hedingham Castle.** The village of Castle Hedingham is situated near to the Essex/ Suffolk border and is of exceptional historical interest. It was built in 1140 by Aubrey de Vere, son of one of William The Conqueror's leading noblemen. The majestic Norman keep stands as a monument to the Earls of Oxford who owned the castle for 550 years. The building is beautifully preserved and retains its original stone floors and roof. The interior reveals a great variety of decorative stonework, cut many centuries ago by Norman hands. The Banqueting Hall has a Minstrels' Gallery and possesses one of the finest Norman arches in England. The castle is approached by a beautiful Tudor bridge built in 1496 by the 13th Earl of Oxford. This now spans the dry moat and replaces the original drawbridge. The castle is situated off the B1058.

Colchester stands in the midst of rolling East Anglian countryside. Today, it is very much a bustling 20th century town but its heritage is both rich and fascinating. There was thought to be a settlement at Colchester in the 5th century BC, and in the first century AD, Cunolebin was King at Cumnlodunum. Literary buffs will know it was this King on whom Shakespeare based his Cymbeline. The invading Romans occupied Colchester in AD43 and in the following years developed a major colony here. In AD60, the Britons under Queen Boadicea revolted and overthrew the Roman invaders. In the Dark Ages, Danes frequently raided the town and by the late 11th century the Normans had built a castle round the former Roman Temple. The town's charter was granted by Richard I in 1190. Today, one can see the gate house of St John's Abbey and St Botolph's Priory, ruined during the Civil War. Evidence of the earth works which protected pre-Roman Colchester can be seen to the west

St Osyth's Priory

of the town. The Balkerne Gate survives from Roman times. Later occupations are marked by the Norman Castle which ironically was built with Roman brick. The Keep, the largest ever built in Europe, is all that remains and now houses the fascinating Castle Museum. The old Siege House is another fascinating relic, the timbers are riddled with Civil War bullets and bear witness to further tumultuous times. There are few towns in Britain which can boast such a rich and varied heritage and visitors will be enthralled by the remains which stand as testament to so many different periods of English history.

South of Colchester, one finds two further places of interest. In **Layer Marney,** one finds the Church of St Mary The Virgin, a brick building dating from the 16th century. It has an impressive mural of St Christopher and several family tombs. Layer Marney Tower was a mansion designed by the 1st Lord Marney. The house was never completed to its original scale and as a result the enormous gatehouse is rather incongruous. A seven storey building with other buildings 'clinging' on to it, it follows an earlier trend of castle building and is a good example of 16th century building based on much earlier designs.

St Osyth's Priory is the centre piece of the little village of St Osyth, a charming old English community. The Priory was founded in the 12th century by Augustinian Canons and was named after the martyred daughter of Frithenwald, first Christian King of East Anglia. Only limited parts of the building remain but they include an impressive late 15th century gatehouse, complete with patterned stone and battlements. A more lasting tribute to St Osyth can be seen in the extensive grounds and gardens which surround the Priory. Peacocks strut across the shady lawns and fallow deer roam the park. The gatehouse, which was restored in the 15th century, houses an art collection which includes ceramics and jade carvings   an impressive sight.

Lovers of gardens will find **Hyde Hall Gardens,** Rettendon, particularly satisfying. There is interest throughout the year with bulbs, flowering shrubs and an abundance of roses. Ornamental greenhouses are well cared for and two well stocked ponds complete the picture.

BROADLY SPEAKING!

Norwich has its roots in Saxon times as first records of a settlement here begin 1,000 years ago. It has been well preserved and a curious mixture of architectural styles from numerous periods complement each other beautifully. Norwich has a Cathedral, 33 pre-Reformation churches , a Norman castle, a 15th century Guildhall and Georgian Assembly Rooms. The Cathedral and castle are the centre points of the city and an ideal point from which to start our tour of the city.

The Cathedral rises in Norman splendour from the Cathedral Close which surrounds it. Today, the building leaves you breathless - imagine what those who saw it consecrated in 1278 must have felt! The architecture is predominantly Norman and the survival of the semi-circular East End is unique in Northern Europe. The stone Bishop's throne is thought to date from the 10th century. Ornate, gilded and painted bosses decorate the vaulting and those in the cloisters are outstanding examples of medieval craftsmanship. Subsequent changes include the replacement of the Norman roof by stone vaults and the building of the magnificent spire which was added in the 15th cen-

tury. The Close is entered by four gateways. Three are elaborate gates but the fourth is a 15th century water gate at Pull's Ferry. This is a beautiful spot and marks the entrance to a small canal which was built to transport building material to the Cathedral. The Close also houses Edward VI Grammar School - it was here that one Horatio Nelson was put through his academic paces.

The large Keep of the Norman Castle stands on a hill above the market place. It was built in 1130 and replaced in the 1830s. From 1220 the castle was the county prison but today it is the home of the city museum and art gallery. The gallery has a marvellous collection of works from the Norwich school, most notably those of John Sell Cotman. There is a wealth of fascinating collections in the museum and the more morbid will be intrigued to inspect a skull which shows the after effects of a battle axe! Norwich is a fascinating city and other places you should try and visit are St Peter Hungate Church Museum of Church Artefacts, dating from 1380. The Church of St Peter Mancrost is perhaps the most interesting of Norwich's numerous churches and Strangers Hall gives a captivating insight into English domestic life. The House has 14th century origins and rooms which vary in style from early Tudor to late Victorian. There are 15th century Flemish tapestries in the Great Hall and Parlour and 17th century stumpwork embroidery in the large bedroom. Finally, consider Bridewell Museum, it is housed in part of a 14th century merchant's house and was used as a prison for tramps and beggars in 1583. The courtyard has an array of dates and initials all scratched by prisoners.

Norwich is a delightful city and it is a pleasure to wander round its medieval streets, the most famous of which is Elm Hill, now home to many of the city's antique shops.

The Norfolk Broads which consist of more than 200 miles of waterways reveal a number of other delights. **Holkham Hall,** a Palladian Mansion built in the mid 18th century is particularly impressive. Visitors to Holkham Hall are given an ample opportunity to visit numerous other gardens, buildings and ecclesiastical monuments and the following trio is intended just to whet the appetite. Holkham Hall is featured later.

Blickling Hall, located off the A140, is a fire-red brick Jacobean and 18th century mansion. The house was completed in 1628 and comprised a large central block with long wings on either side terminated with corner turrets. In the 18th century, the open ends of the court were filled in. The house combines the Jacobean and Georgian architecture beautifully. The long gallery is the most spectacular room with intricate plasterwork running 123 feet down the East Front. At approximately the time of the second Jacobite rebellion the gallery was converted into a library in order to house a remarkable collection of inherited books. Presents from Catherine the Great, including a magnificent tapestry, are especially worth seeing.

The parkland which rolls away from the house contains an artificial lake bounded by mature oaks. Other features include parterre beds set around a 17th century fountain. As the island of herbaceous plants blossom in contrasting yellows, oranges, purples and blues it makes for a marvellous display. A secret garden and orangery date from the 18th century but sadly little of Sir Henry Hobart's formal Jacobean garden survives.

Blickling Hall is now in the safe hands of the National Trust as

EAST ANGLIA

is **Felbrigg Hall** which lies north of Blickling. A noted collection of pictures, including small Dutch and Italian canvasses is situated in the West Wing. The building is essentially 17th century but the interiors were beautifully fashioned by James Paine in the 18th century. Felbrigg's south entrance is a perfect example of a Jacobean exterior and is probably the work of Robert Lyminge of nearby Blickling. The Library here is also impressive and Dr Johnson is commemorated in books once owned by the renowned lexicographer.

There is a superb walled garden with a large octagonal dovecote. Fruit trees and vines merge with displays of dahlias and roses while herbaceous borders complete the picture. A nationally renowned collection of colchicums form a dazzling fringe to the shrubbery which lines the paths. Trees in the garden date back to William Windham I whose intention was to shield the house from the bitter winds off the North Sea. The work is excellent and has been continued through the generations. The last Squire of Felbrigg planted some 200,000 trees and formed the V shaped rides commemorating VE Day.

Beeston Hall near Wroxham, is a charming house close to the Norfolk Broads which has been owned by the same family for 350 years. It was built in 1786 in Gothic style by the Preston family and is now the home of Sir Ronald and Lady Preston. The house has a medieval monastery-like appearance from the outside but the hall has the ground plan of a typical Georgian mansion with classical interiors contrasting charmingly with the Gothic. 'Capability' Brown's follower, Richmond, was responsible for the landscaping with wonderful views. The house and its contents reflect the life style of a Norfolk family over generations, most of whose members were Country Squires.

Our final thought for the area is located at Walsingham. **Walsingham Priory** was founded by Richeldis de Favarques for a community of Augustinian Canons. By the 13th Century, the Chapel containing the Shrine of Our Lady had become a place of pilgrimage. The Shrine was built in 1061 to commemorate a vision of the Lady of the Manor and around this, the Priory was built. Both Henry III and Edward I were frequent visitors. The monastic buildings were destroyed in the 15th century and the visible ruins date from this, and later centuries. In more recent times an Anglican Church has been built adjacent to the former priory wall and at Houghton St Giles, a Roman Catholic Church was developed around the 14th century Chapel known as the Slipper Chapel. Walsingham today attracts many pilgrims who walk barefoot to the shrine.

ROYAL NORFOLK

The Royal Family's love of Norfolk is well known and **Sandringham** is one of the jewels in the crown of their country estates (featured later). Aside from the Royal residence, there are a number of interesting sights to see. Two of the most renowned are **Castle Rising** and **Oxburgh Hall**.

The former stands on some of the most spectacular earthworks in England. The castle itself was built by William de Albini and dates from the mid 12th century. The Great Keep is one of the largest to survive in England and the exterior walls are impressive, decorated with ornate arches. The main moat is nearly 60 feet deep and is crossed by a brick bridge while the gatehouse looks solemnly on. Castle Rising is surrounded by an immense earth rampart about 64 feet high and the surrounding works are circular in shape and measure over 1,000 yards.

Beeston Hall

EAST ANGLIA

Oxburgh Hall is located some seven miles west of Swaffham and on a fine day one can see the Octagon of Ely Cathedral ,some 26 miles away across the Fenland. Although the land is now cultivated, when Sir Edward Bedingfield built this fortification it was set upon an island in marshland. It has a magnificent setting, rising from the waters of the moat. The fortified Gatehouse boasts turrets and mullioned windows and is a most impressive sight. The interior of the house includes Tudor survivals and Victorian rooms. The King's Chamber in the gatehouse tower has a splendid original medieval fireplace. This room is where Henry VII slept when he visited Oxburgh in 1487. The Bedingfield family remained at Oxburgh for 500 years and the house was unaltered throughout the 16th and 17th centuries. A Priest's Hole in the floor is a reminder of the family's religious sympathies and goes part way to explaining their poverty during this period. The most prized possession at the house is needlework by Mary Queen of Scots which is displayed in a suitably darkened room. In contrast to this sombre period of history, the 19th century interiors are splendid examples of Catholic High Victorian taste. Victorian and medieval craftsmanship are beautifully combined in the little chapel - a most pleasing part of this fascinating place. The grounds boast a Victorian Kitchen Garden while roses, clematis and other climbers marry well with the striking red brick buildings.

Euston Hall, near Thetford, is the family home of the Dukes of Grafton and has been for more than 300 years. You can enjoy the splendour of the formal rooms and the fascinating collection of pictures, including the portrait of Charles II in Garter robes by Sir Peter Lely, painted towards the end of his life. The walk through the pleasure tranquil grounds leads you to the church and around the river basin which was designed especially for the Third Duke by William Kent.

THE WEALTHY WOOLTOWNS

The old Suffolk wool towns are some of the most unspoilt towns in England. Lavenham, Long Melford and Bury St Edmunds are just three examples. Within their boundaries, or nearby, are some interesting houses, themselves surrounded by idyllic villages.

Ickworth (featured later) which lies near Bury St Edmunds is perhaps the most noted but there are several others to mention.

Bury St Edmunds itself is a town rich in history. The Abbey, which dates from 1021 now stands in ruins. Its two great gateways and Angel Hill on the West Side, together with the Cathedral Church of St James and St Mary's Church form the heart of medieval Bury St Edmunds.

The town was named after Edmund, King of East Anglia in about 850. His body was incorporated into a shrine and the High Altar, which is still discernible, is where the Barons of England met in 1214 and swore to force King John to sign the Magna Carta. The rest, as they say, is history.

Long Melford is one of the outstanding small towns in Suffolk. The High Street is dominated by the 15th century church of the Holy Trinity, a wonderful sight which combines pillar work and stained glass to marvellous effect. At the upper end of Melford Green one finds Melford Hall, a turreted, brick Tudor mansion which has seen little change since its completion in 1578. In this year, the house saw many visitors, the most noted being Queen Elizabeth I. Although the house was ransacked in the Civil War and suffered a disastrous fire in 1942 it re-

Euston Hall

Gainsborough House

EAST ANGLIA

mains a splendid sight. Family portraits, Chinese porcelain and fine furniture grace the rooms. Beatrix Potter is also remembered here and one can see the model for Jemima Puddleduck amongst other memorabilia. Intriguing topiary and the delightful small gardens should also be seen.

To the north of Long Melford, **Kentwell** is another distinguished house. A Tudor Manor House based on an E plan, it boasts magnificent brickwork, a broad moat, interconnecting gardens and a bricked, paved maze. There are many re-creations of Tudor life here, plus open air theatres featuring the works of Shakespeare.

Lavenham is one of the most photographed villages in England. Oak timbers with clay and whattle are almost irresistible it seems! Some of the houses date from the 18th century when the town first established itself as a wool trading town. In those days, wool was a very valuable commodity and the Lord Chancellor still sits on a woolsack!

The Church of St Peter and St Paul is charming, dating from the 15th century. The tall West Tower and the Nave are of particular interest. The half-timbered Guildhall, originally the headquarters of the Guild of Corpus Christi, dates from 1529. It has since been used as a prison workhouse and almshouse. Dr Rowland Taylor, Archbishop Cranmer's Chaplain, was held here before being burnt at the stake.

Although there are many other delights to witness in Suffolk, **Thomas Gainsborough's** house is one not to be missed. As you would expect, the house contains a magnificent collection of his work and also holds both contemporary and historic exhibitions of artwork, which are of great inspiration to all budding artists.

THE HERITAGE COAST

Heading towards the Suffolk coast there are a number of castles, Churches and Houses open to the public. **Heveningham Hall** is described by many as the loveliest Palladian house in England and aside from this property, three gems are shortlisted here.

Somerleyton Hall is a magnificent red brick mansion which was rebuilt in Anglo-Italian style in 1846 and is surrounded by beautiful gardens. The interior boasts rich panelling, delightfully carved furniture and tapestries. The Bell Tower is enchanting and the three storey porch an impressive welcome. The gardens include a maze, nature trail, shrubbery and rare trees.

Framlingham is a pleasant old market town. The Castle was built in the late 12th century by the 2nd Earl of Norfolk and was, at the time, the most modern defence of its type in the country. As a result, it has seen a turbulent history. In 1215 it was attacked and taken by King John in his struggle with the Barons and later, as the sanctuary for Mary Tudor, it became the rallying point for her supporters. In the 17th century, Pembroke College received the castle as a bequest and was instructed to build a poor house which still exists on the site of the Great Hall.

East Anglia has great appeal for a holiday week-end away or even a shorter visit. It remains one of the most unspoilt and peaceful corners of England. From academic Cambridge to Roman Colchester, Norman Norwich and the plethora of churches and monuments and houses, East Anglia offers the choice for visitors which many counties can only dream of.

Somerleyton Hall

ELTON HALL

Nestling in the lovely Nene Valley on Cambridgeshire's border with Northamptonshire, Elton Hall is a charming family home. There has been a house on this site since the Norman Conquest and the Proby family has lived here for over 300 years when Sir Peter Proby, Lord Mayor of London, was granted the land by Elizabeth I. In 1789, the title Earl of Carysfort was conferred upon the Proby family and was held until the 5th Earl died in 1909 and the Earldom with him. The house then passed through the female line to the present branch of the Proby family.

Elton Hall is an engaging mix of architectural styles. In fact, when viewed from any aspect no one facade is similar to another.

When Sir Thomas Proby acquired the house in the mid 17th Century he incorporated the tower and chapel into the south front and built on a north wing. Minor alterations were carried out in the mid 18th Century but the house was extensively enlarged and modified during the period 1780 to 1815. The gatehouse was joined to the rest of the house by a two storey block - the upper room of which is now the library. It has a Jacobean mullioned bay window taken from another house which was pulled down in 1807. Much of the work at this time is thought to have been done by French prisoners of war from the prison camp at Norman Cross. Also at this time the west front was faced with stucco and given a gothic castellated appearance - not entirely what it seems. To save expense, the battlements and turret tops were made of wood and simply painted to give the appearance of stone.

With his architect, Sir Henry Ashton, the 3rd Earl of Carysfort removed much of the gothic trimmings from the west front to give a simpler, more classical appearance but left them intact on the south front, so retaining its gothic look. Finally, the 4th Earl built the central tower, a billiard room and new kitchens on the east side of the gatehouse. The 5th Earl collected many of the best paintings and furniture in the house including early 15th Century Old Masters, works by Constable, Gainsborough and Reynolds and the remarkable pre-Raphaelite work of Alma Tadema and Millais.

The Drawing Room is the largest room in the house and was originally the medieval chapel. The decoration dates from 1860 and is in the style of a French chateau but retains its elegant 18th Century ceiling. Most of the paintings here are by Sir Joshua Reynolds and include a self-portrait. The charming unfinished study of Kitty Fisher was banished to the housekeepers room in Victorian times because its subject was considered to be a lady of ill-repute. The pair of cabinets in this room were made from an imperial Japanese lacquer box and are extremely rare as it was a capital offence to export lacquer from Japan.

The State Dining Room, built by the 3rd Earl, evokes a time gone by when food had to be carried across an open courtyard by a small army of servants. It has a fine marble fireplace, original to the house but not to this room and three large gothic windows copied exactly from those in the chapel. The old county boundary used to run through the middle of the room which gave rise to some wry comment concerning the separate dining arrangements of the Earl and Countess. In 1983 the pictures were rehung in the 18th Century manner, to show at its best the very fine collection of Old Masters including one which has been attributed to Leonardo da Vinci.

The Library contains one of the finest private collections in the country and represents the continuing interest in art through generations of the family from as early as 1634. The magnificent manuscripts, liturgical works and bibles are especially outstanding - in particular Henry VIII's Prayer Book which includes writings by Catherine Parr, Thomas Seymour, Princess Mary and Edward VI as well as Henry himself.

Close to the house, in a small spinney, a furtive presence has sometimes been seen. He is said to be one Robert Sapcote, philanderer and inveterate gambler whose family once lived here. He frequently lost large sums of money to his guests and on such occasions he would lie in wait for his hapless friends in the guise of a common highwayman and rob them of their winnings as they left the park. The gardens have been extensively restored to include a Knott Garden, Sunken Garden, Arboretum and a Rose Garden - resplendent in July with the warm tea-scent of old roses.

Elton Hall is suffused with the welcoming atmosphere of an elegant yet comfortable family home, qualities which make it an excellent location for a variety of business entertaining. The grounds are also available for shooting or coarse fishing.

AUDLEY END HOUSE

The impressive facade of Audley End is uniquely beautiful. The appearance of this Jacobean country mansion is palatial with its regular arrangement of windows, delicate turquoise caps of the turrets and elaborate porches which make a striking composition when seen from across the park. Yet the house is less than half its original size.

Of the original house nothing remains but its name - that of its builder Sir Thomas Audley created Baron Audley of Walden in 1538. The present house was built between 1605 and 1614 by Thomas Howard de Walden, later the 1st Earl of Suffolk in recognition of his part in defeating the Spanish Armada. He was appointed Lord Treasurer to James I and built a grand mansion to reflect his high office. It was the largest house built in the Jacobean period and King James is reputed to have said that Audley End was too large for the King but not for the Lord Treasurer.

A house of this size must have cost the Earl a great fortune and when certain irregularities were discovered at the Treasury he found himself in the Tower. His mansion had indeed cost him dear. Over the next 150 years or so the house was gradually reduced in size and by the latter half of the 18th century had assumed its present size.

The house was remodelled in the 18th and 19th centuries and the richly decorated interiors, with notable collections of furniture and pictures are now displayed as they were then. Entrance to the house is by the North Porch which leads into the splendid Great Hall. At one end is a massive Jacobean screen, exquisitely carved with a profusion of detail. It is typical of great houses of this period. Standing opposite, in complete contrast is a simple stone screen with cleaner classical lines. The whole is finished by an elegant double staircase and a timbered ceiling enriched with plaster panels painted with heraldic devices.

The Little Drawing Room is a particularly charming room. Designed by Robert Adam, the gilded mouldings and intricate wall paintings are a splendid example of his sense of proportion and colour. One of the most attractive rooms is Lord Braybrooke's Sitting Room, which houses the finest of the extensive collection of pictures at Audley End. The Chapel, with its beautiful painted glass window of the 'Last Supper', and delicate ceiling is a remarkably complete example of the 'Strawberry Hill Gothic' style.

The magnificent 18th century park surrounding the house was the work of 'Capability' Brown, who was engaged to transform the earlier formal gardens into his own style of open pastoral landscape, which he did with spectacular results.

There is a delightful woodland grove, fountains and a rose garden with a number of garden buildings in the classical style, many of which were designed by Robert Adam. A particularly good example is his lovely Palladian Bridge which spans the River Carr which meanders through the park.

HOLKHAM HALL

'An Englishman's home is his castle'. So said Sir Edward Coke, founder of the family fortune which resulted in the building of Holkham Hall. Some 200 years later, having spent six impressionable years on the Grand Tour, Thomas Coke returned to Norfolk not only with new-found knowledge from Europe, but with a substantial collection of treasures.

Realising that the Elizabethan manor house he had inherited was too small, he demolished it and in 1734 set about building Holkham in its place. The design was inspired by Palladio and was really a joint venture between Coke, his friend Lord Burlington and William Kent, one of the great 18th century architects. The result, a central block flanked by four wings, is one of the finest examples of neo-classical style in the country.

In 1744 Thomas Coke was created Earl of Leicester, but sadly died in 1759 before his grand mansion was completed. His widow faithfully executed his wishes and finally in 1762 Holkham was complete. As the Earl had no sons the title died with him, but the estates went to his nephew and thence to his son, also Thomas Coke.

The epitome of the country squire, he was a great patron of agricultural inventions, but perhaps his greatest legacy was the four course rotation of crops. Known simply as 'Coke of Norfolk', his agricultural achievements were rewarded by Queen Victoria with a peerage in 1837. The title he took was Earl of Leicester, and such was the esteem in which he was held that, when he died aged 88, his tenants erected a monument in the grounds. He was succeeded by his son, the 2nd Earl who added the porch and Orangery and the impressive Perseus Fountain.

After entering the house through the unpretentious vestibule, the entrance hall is stunning. Nowhere is the influence of Palladio more apparent. The domed ceiling is supported by magnificent fluted alabaster columns and around the walls are displayed classical Greek and Roman statues. However the major part of Holkham's collection of classical sculpture, one of the finest still in private hands, is found in the Statue Gallery.

The collection of 18th century art is also outstanding and includes works by Rubens, Van Dyck, Claude, Poussin and Gainsborough, most of which are hung as they were in 1773. Possibly the most famous painting in the collection 'The Return of the Holy Family' by Rubens, hangs in the Saloon. The ceiling here is the grandest in the house and the walls are covered in the original caffoy - a type of velvet. Throughout the house much of the fine 18th century furniture is by William Kent and was designed for the house. In fact it is unusual to find a house so little altered in its contents and decoration.

The North Dining Room is a classically beautiful room with two fine chimney pieces and a finely executed plaster ceiling, the design of which is reflected in the carpet. Until 1939, dinner was a white tie affair, with servants making the 70 yard dash from the kitchens every evening. Then with the advent of War, the servants left and never returned. The Old Kitchen itself, gleaming with copper and pewter is well worth a second look.

Holkham Hall is set in extensive parkland with a lake almost a mile long, surrounded by nine miles of wall. Close to the house are formal Victorian Gardens and the 18th century walled kitchen garden is now the garden centre.

SANDRINGHAM

'Dear old Sandringham, the place I love better than anywhere else in the world.' So wrote King George V for whom it was, above all, home.

The Norfolk estate was purchased by the Prince of Wales, later King Edward VII, so that he should have a private house well away from London, to which he could escape when duty permitted and enjoy the benefits of a country life. He engaged the architect A.J. Humbert to replace a much smaller Georgian house, and his new home was completed in 1870. All that remains of the previous house is the old conservatory, now the billiard room. The Ballroom was built on in 1881 and the Bachelor Wing in 1891, both designed by Colonel R.W. Edis. The largest room in the house, known as the Saloon, is two storeys high and it is here that the Royal Family spend the evening with their guests after dinner. Beyond one of the two fireplaces hangs a fine portrait of the Prince and Princess of Wales with two of their children painted by Heinrich von Angeli.

The Main Drawing Room, considered 'handsome' by Queen Victoria, is hung with many more portraits of the Prince of Wales, his wife and their children. There are also two outstanding tables, one made in Paris in the 18th century and the other made for Sandringham in 1863 by Holland and Sons. The elegant green Dining Room contains fine tapestries from Spain and a display case in the Ballroom Corridor contains guns used by various members of the Royal Family, each labelled with the owners name. The Ballroom itself is now used for cinema shows and parties.

The grounds of Sandringham House were originally laid out by W.B. Thomas, soon after the estate was purchased in 1862. There are two lakes and extensive woodland walks which contain a wealth of shrubs, such as camellias, hydrangeas, azaleas and rhododendrons among mature trees, mainly Scots and Corsican Pine, Oak, Beech and Maple. Especially beautiful is

the rhododendron, 'Polar Bear', which flowers in July, and the delightful scent of lilies lingers until the end of August. During the summer over eighty varieties of hardy fuchsias add splashes of colour throughout the grounds and there is a very rare specimen of the Handkerchief Tree.

York Cottage is situated in the grounds and was the home of Prince George, later King George V, from his marriage in 1893 until he and Queen Mary moved to Sandringham House on the death of his mother, Queen Alexandra, in 1925.

Sandringham Country Park covers 600 acres bordering the designated Area of Natural Beauty adjacent to the Wash Coastline. The area consists of wood and heathland and contains numerous varieties of broadleaf and coniferous trees. Two Nature Trails meander through remote woodlands and sunny glades, where visitors may picnic. There is also a Childrens' Adventure Play Area.

Sandringham Museum occupies buildings formerly used as Coach Houses, Fire Station, Queen Mary's Carving School and the Estate Power House. Four galleries house Big Game Trophies, the majority of which were shot by various members of the Royal Family between 1880 and 1930.

Two galleries house gifts presented to the Royal Family during overseas tours, part of the Royal Doll Collection and a fine collection of commemorative china and glass relating to Coronations and Jubilees.

The display of vehicles used by members of the Royal Family includes King Edward VIII's 1900 Daimler Tonneau which was the first car to be purchased by a Royal.

Sandringham House is off the A148 Kings's Lynn to Cromer road.

ICKWORTH

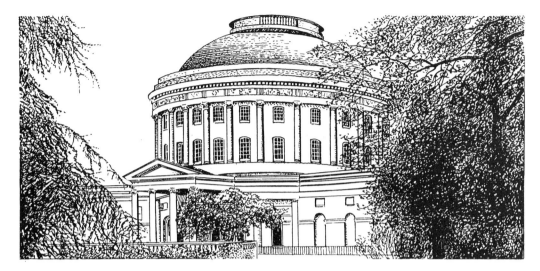

Begun about 1794, the elliptical rotunda of Ickworth makes this fine mansion one of the most extraordinary in England. Built by the Bristol family, the unusual architecture features curved corridors to flanking wings and sumptuous state rooms with opulent late Regency and 18th century French furniture.

John Hervey, created Earl of Bristol in 1714, was the real founder of the family fortunes, marrying two heiresses and becoming a staunch Whig in the early years of the Glorious Revolution. He consulted architects with a view to rebuilding the modest manor house he had inherited on a site near Ickworth church, but his plans were never put into practice. Quite why Lord Bristol's grandiose schemes were never achieved remains something of a mystery, but may have been due in part to the extravagance of his numerous and mostly unsatisfactory sons.

His eldest son by his second marriage, John, Lord Hervey, was perhaps the most brilliant member of an exceptionally gifted family, becoming Lord Privy Seal, and remembered today for his outspoken memoirs of the Court of George II. Lord Hervey, despite his somewhat ambivalent nature (which caused the conclusion that there were three human species - 'men, women and Herveys'). made a love match with the delightful Molly Lepel who bore him eight children. The three eldest sons became the 2nd, 3rd and 4th Earls of Bristol and it was Frederick, the genial 4th Earl Bishop of Derry who began to build in 1794. The Bishop had already been able to indulge his passion for travel and collecting works of art and he soon became a well-known figure bowling along the roads of Germany and Italy in his great coach, causing Hotels Bristol to spring up in towns all over the Continent. His other consuming interest was in building and his vast Irish houses at Downhill and Ballyscullion were conceived more as museums to contain his collections, than for domestic comfort. Ickworth, his next venture, was to be his grandest of all and work on the oval rotunda was begun in 1795, inspired by Belle Isle in Lake Windermere built some twenty years earlier. Its execution was supervised by Francis and John Sandys to designs thought to be the work of Mario Asprucci the younger.

The Earl-Bishop was denied the satisfaction of seeing his finished mansion for he died in 1803 whilst travelling in Italy, in the outhouse of a peasant who could not admit a heretic prelate into his cottage. His final journey home to the family vault at Ickworth was tinged with an irony that would have delighted him. His coffin was shipped back disguised as a packing case containing a statue, the superstitious sailors refusing to sail with a corpse on board. The Earl-Bishop's son, who was to become 1st Marquess in 1826, decided to reverse the original scheme so that the east wing became the family residence, while the rooms in the rotunda were used for entertaining and as a setting for the collections.

Apart from the Pompeian Room, decorated in 1879, the last major alterations were made by the 4th Marquess who commissioned Reginald Blomfield to remodel the east wing and the main staircase. The splendid contents of the house include paintings by some of the world's greatest artists including Titian, LeBrun, Velasquez, and portraits by Gainsborough, Hogarth, Lawrence and Reynolds. In the East Corridor a large cabinet contains some of the best porcelain including a gold and white chinoiserie service made at Meissen about 1730 and some fine examples of Doccia, the porcelain factory near Florence. The West Corridor now displays the Bristol family silver, a collection almost unrivalled in England both for its quantity and quality. A large number of early 18th century pieces are by Huguenot makers working in London such as Pierre Harrache, Philip Rollos, Simon Pantin, Pierre Platel, Paul Crespin and Paul de Lamerie. There are also fine examples of the rococo period - sugar bowls, salt cellars, meat and dessert dishes, and the early 19th century is equally well represented by tea urns and entree dishes made by Paul Storr. Probably the most outstanding single piece is the magnificent Baroque wine cistern made in London in 1680 by Robert Cooper.

From the house, the Orangery with its fatsias, fuchsias and scented geraniums leads to the semi-formal Italian garden. Plantations of evergreens edged with tall box hedges, sweep up close to the house on the south, while a central path from the rotunda leads up through mulberry trees to a curving terrace walk dividing the garden from the park. There are several miles of marked walks through the park which is planted with magnolias, fine copper beeches and many rare trees. The Grand Tour - all seven miles of it - rewards the energetic with fabulous views of Ickworth's Rotunda.

Ickworth is in Horringer village, three miles south west of Bury St Edmunds on the A143. Since 1956 it has been administered by the National Trust.

EAST ANGLIA

This is the land of Constable and Cromwell, of picture book cottages and Cathedrals. It is also one of the least spoiled areas of England.

The Fens are generally quiet and the Norfolk Broads, although popular with holidaymakers, are a haven for wildlife. There are a number of country house hotels, bed & breakfasts and self-catering accommodation for the visitor to this area which, although lacking in landscape, makes up for it in character.

The colleges of Cambridge are alive with history. With many famous graduates, the University town sits smugly on the edge of the Fens, an island of academia and architectural beauty in a sea of somewhat uniform landscape. There are many buildings here of great interest both architecturally and historically. There are, however, few hotels with similar appeal although farther afield in Suffolk and Norfolk there is a greater selection of good establishments. The wool towns are particularly pleasant and Mildenhall, Lavenhall, Long Melford and Bury St Edmunds are four to be recommended.

Suffolk's villages are a reminder of prosperous times gone by but their very peace and quiet is special and draws many looking for a haven from the bustling 20th century.

Norfolk is no less fertile than neighbouring Suffolk and it too boasts a fascinating history, much of it naval as the county is bordered on the east by beautiful and remote beaches. Norfolk too has royal connections, it is a county much loved by The Queen who spends time at Sandringham.

Norfolk's relatively isolated location has protected it, to some degree, from many visitors and has preserved its tiny villages where time genuinely appears to have stood still.

HOTELS OF DISTINCTION

ANGEL HOTEL, Bury St Edmunds, Suffolk. Tel: (0284) 753926
The 12th century vaults house one of the restaurants in this hotel, much loved by Dickens. Polished comfort and care show in lovely furnishings and extras.

THE BELL INN, Stilton, Cambridgeshire. Tel: (0733) 24066
An historic coaching inn situated on the old A1, the Great North Road. Renowned in the 18th century for serving Stilton and now lovingly renovated to include comfortable bedrooms, an elegant dining room and friendly bars.

BELSTEAD BROOK HOTEL AND RESTAURANT, Ipswich, Suffolk. Tel: (0473) 684241
Originating in Saxon times with subsequent additions in the reign of King James and World War II, this fascinating hotel lies in six acres of garden and woodlands and is well situated for the Suffolk coastline.

THE BLACK LION, Long Melford, Suffolk. Tel: (0787 312356
Situated on the green is this fully retsored 17th century coaching inn, you will find a family run hotel, where nothing is too much trouble. A veritable home from home, famed for its 'Countrymen Restaurant'.

BRENTWOOD MOAT HOUSE, Brentwood, Essex. Tel: (0277) 225252
Originally the home of Catherine of Aragon, the Moat House was built in 1512 and is mentioned in the diaries of Samuel Pepys. The hotel contains many original Tudor features including an impressive baronial dining hall.

CHIMNEYS, Long Melford, Suffolk. Tel: (0787) 79806
Long Melford is an architecturally delighful village in which the 16th century Tudor facade of Chimneys sits pleasingly. This is an outstanding restaurant which varies its menus regularly and complements them with a wine list to further tempt its visitors.

CONGHAM HALL COUNTRY HOUSE HOTEL, Grimston, Norfolk. (0485) 600250
A Georgian manor house nestling in 40 acres of grounds converted to a luxury hotel. With its internationally renowned herb garden Congham Hall offers the finest cuisine and is an excellent base to visit Sandringham.

THE SWAN, Southwold, Suffolk. Tel: (0502) 722186
Previously a 17th century inn, the Swan stands in the market place of this delightful Suffolk town, providing good value and comfortable accommodation. The restaurant has a strong local following and specialises in English cuisine.

THE CROWN, Southwold, Suffolk. Tel: (0502) 722275
A splendid restaurant takes centre stage at this sophisticated and welcoming high street hotel. Characterful bedrooms and a welcoming bar are other excellent reasons for visiting.

ELMINGHAM HALL COUNTRY HOUSE HOTEL, Elmingham, Norfolk. Tel: (0692) 69631
A peaceful and secluded Elizabethan manor house in 15 acres of grounds, this hotel provides a perfect base for visiting Blickling Hall, Felbrigg Hall, the Broads and Norwich.

HAYCOCK HOTEL, Near Peterborough, Cambridgeshire. Tel: (0780) 782223
Complete with its own cricket pitch and beautifully preserved hotel sign, the celebrated 17th century Haycock coaching inn has been extensively refurbished and yet carefully retains the character of a bygone age.

HINTLESHAM HALL, Hintlesham, Suffolk. Tel: (047387) 334
The Georgian facade faces the front, while the Tudor rear part overlooks gardens and lawns. Effortless luxury is the air of this highly impressive hotel. The adjoining restaurant is equally gracious.

HOLLY LODGE HOTEL, Heacham, Norfolk. Tel: (0485) 70790
A 16th century listed building of great historic interest, Holly Lodge Hotel is well placed for touring the Halls at Houghton, Blickling and Sandringham with Norwich, Ely and Cambridge within an hour's drive.

KING'S HEAD HOTEL, East Dereham, Norfolk. Tel: (0362) 693842
This imposing red brick town-centre inn was originally a coach-

ing stop-over in the 17th century; a fact visitors staying in the converted bedrooms of the former stable block are pleasantly reminded of.

OLD RECTORY, Great Snoring, Norfolk Tel: (0328) 820597
Built around 1500, this restful old Rectory provides a haven of tranquility. From the stone-mullioned windows to the old grandfather clock in the hall, the emphasis is quietly and peacefully elegant.

OLD BRIDGE HOTEL, Huntingdon, Cambridgeshire. Tel: (0480) 52681
An attractive Georgian hotel on the River Ouse with views over meadows and parkland. The restaurant has an excellent reputation and the individually designed bedrooms offer every comfort.

THE PHEASANT, Keyston, Cambridgeshire. Tel: (080 14) 241
This charming building combines the elegance and professionalism of a restaurant with the homely atmosphere and rural portions of a country pub.

RAVENWOOD HALL, Bury St Edmunds, Suffolk. Tel: (0359) 70345
This fine Tudor building with elaborate oak carvings is now an excellent hotel, conveniently situated for exploring Cambridge and Newmarket, and offers many sporting facilities.

SCOLE INN, Scole, Norfolk. Tel: (0379) 740481
This inn of character was built in 1655. It still retains its early features only the essentials have been tastefully modernised. This is a busy place with a thoroughly pleasing restaurant.

SECKFORD HALL, Woodbridge, Suffolk. Tel: (0394) 385
Built in 1530 and set in 34 acres of parkland, the hotel is in the heart of Constable country. Its architecture boasts the splendour of English oak combined with the beauty of ancient stone. Guests may fish in the private trout lake.

SHIPDHAM PLACE, Shipdham, Norfolk. Tel: (0362) 820303
This Former 17th century rectory offers a combination of informality and old English charm. The restaurant and wine list are further attractions as are the interesting and well appointed gardens.

SWYNFORD PADDOCKS HOTEL, Near Newmarket, Suffolk. Tel: (0638) 70234.
The poet Lord Byron lived and wrote in this charming country house, formerly known as the Lodge, during his illustrious love affair with his half sister, Augusta. It is ideally placed to explore East Anglia, including historic Cambridge.

UPLANDS HOTEL, Aldeburgh, Suffolk. Tel: (0728) 452420
A small and jolly hotel near the sea. Comfortable and homely, with a stunning garden and close to festivals and local arts activities.

WAVENEY HOUSE HOTEL, Puddingmoor, Suffolk. Tel: (0502) 712270
On a riverbank setting where the moorings can be kept in sight. This lovely hotel is ideal for boating persons who prefer dry land. Very pretty market town, near Aldeburgh and other artistically interesting locations.

WHITE HART HOTEL, Coggeshall, Essex. Tel: (0376) 561654
An old-fashioned hotel with layers of history from the 1400's and boasting two ghosts among its regular guests. Nicely up-to-date in the essential areas, with an excellent beamed and darkly furnished restaurant.

WHITEHALL, Stansted, Essex. Tel: (0279) 890603
This charmingly small manor has its origins back in 1151 with beams, open fireplaces and vaulted timbered ceilings. Surrounded by delightful Tudor villages, it is also convenient for London and Cambridge.

ACCOMMODATION OF MERIT

BRIDGE HOUSE, Great Shelford, Cambridgeshire. Tel: (0223) 842920
This pretty, early Victorian farmhouse with large colourful garden is a family home within easy reach of the Nene Valley and Cambridge itself. It is close to counties of Hertfordshire, Bedfordshire and Essex.

CALDREES MANOR, Ickleton, Essex. Tel: (0799) 30253
Attractive and unusual Georgian manor house with 25 acres of parkland and lakes adjoining its gardens. Only 15 minutes from Cambridge and Newmarket, it is also convenient for exploring much of Essex, Hertfordshire and Bedfordshire.

ELM HOUSE, Earls Colne, Essex. Tel: (0787) 222197
A fine red-brick Queen Anne house in a village of great architectural interest. Colchester is a mere 10 miles away, while the specialist gardens and vineyards of East Anglia are easily reached, together with Constable country. Coggeshall, Long Melford and Lavenham are antique collectors' delights.

ELMDON LEE, Littlebury Green, Essex. Tel: (0763) 838237
Set in a quiet corner on a 900 acre estate, this is a warm and comfortable 18th century farmhouse. Saffron Walden, originally a Quaker settlement and wool market town, is close to Cambridge, Duxford Aircraft Museum and Audley End.

HILL HOUSE, Dullingham, Suffolk. Tel: (0638) 507214
A large Victorian farmhouse in a lovely rural setting with an extensive landscaped garden. East Anglia's many sites of historical interest are within easy reach, as is the racing at Newmarket. London is also under an hour away by train.

THE MANOR HOUSE, Dersingham, Norfolk. Tel: (0485) 540228
Next to the church in Dersingham, this delightful old farmhouse has land next to the royal estate of Sandringham. The sea is a mere two miles away, and with a bird sanctuary at Brettisham this is clearly a beautiful base for touring Norfolk.

MAYFIELD FARM, Long Stratton, Norfolk. Tel: (0508) 31763
A carefully restored and now listed Tudor farmhouse with preserved old beams and large fireplaces adding to the warmth and comfort. The splendour of the surrounding countryside embraces one after a day touring Norfolk's hidden treasures.

OTLEY HOUSE, Otley, Suffolk. Tel: (0473) 890253
Delightful 17th century country house with Georgian aspect, in mature gardens complete with lake and wildfowl. Framlingham Castle, Lavenham and Snape Concert Hall are all close.

THE BLACK LION

Situated on the green, in this fully restored 17th century coaching inn, you will find a family run hotel where nothing is too much trouble. A veritable home form home, famed for its Countryman restaurant.

Classically influenced, mouthwatering dishes are freshly made to your order by Stephen, who trained at the Dorchester Hotel. He uses fresh locally grown Suffolk produce, seasoned with herbs cultivated in his own garden. There are two menus at lunch and dinner to stimulate your tastebuds, and these are changed each month. To compliment this epicural delight, Janet his wife, can offer you a selection from 150 carefully chosen wines. Apart from her long standing interest in the subject, she has been awarded several higher certificates in wine, to give you expert guidance in making the perfect choice. After an agonising decision of which luscious dessert to choose, comes the cheeseboard. Expect to find at least 14 different cheeses, a speciality of the house. Retire from the intimate dining room to relax in the informal and delightful surroundings of either of the two lounges, equipped with books, magazines and games. Perhaps even a sip of liqueur from a selection of over 100.

And so to bed. From this vantage point, there are panoramic views of the hamlet of Long Melford and you can be forgiven for thinking that you have stepped back in time a couple of centuries. Each of the 10 spacious bedrooms are equipped with its own private bathroom, direct dial telephone, colour TV, radio and tea and coffee facilities. If you are lucky you could be sleeping soundly in one of the two four poster beds or the mahogany half tester. There is a family suite, and well behaved children are catered for. Dogs are accepted by appointment.

Long Melford is famous for its quaint architecture and a wealth of antique shops. A stones throw away are two country houses, 15th century Kentwell Hall, restored lovingly to its original state and National Trust Melford Hall, the family seat of the Hyde-Parkers, who are still in residence. Other places of interest nearby are the wool villages of Lavenham, historic Bury St Edmunds, winner of 'England in Bloom', Sudbury, the home of Gainsborough, horse racing at Newmarket, a preserved steam railway at Castle Headingham and Constable country.

The Black Lion Hotel and Countryman Restaurant is featured in all recognised guides and the Errington family wish you a warm and pleasant stay.

The Black Lion Hotel
The Green
Long Melford
Suffolk CO10 9DN
Tel: (0787) 312356

EAST ANGLIA

TANNINGTON HALL, Tannington, Suffolk. Tel: (072876) 226
A former monastery, now a beautifully appointed moated hall, used as a working farm. Norwich, Constable country, Lavenham, Aldeburgh, Snape Maltings and Stowmarket's Museum of East Anglian Life are all local.

INNS OF CHARACTER

THE BULL, Long Melford, Suffolk.
Originally a medieval manor hall, this attractive black and white timbered building became an inn in 1580. Similarly impressive oak timbers and dark heavy beams dominate the interior. Very popular bar food and several fine ales add to the attraction of this delightful old inn.

CHEQUERS, Foulmere, Cambridgeshire.
Heavy beams, exposed timber and old-fashioned furnishings create a discreet atmosphere within this 16th century former coaching inn. Great attention is given to the splendid range of vintage ports and liqueurs while the barfood menu is ambitious and excellent.

FOUNTAIN HOUSE, East Bergholt, Suffolk.
At the back of the airy flagstoned bar, a lounge leads onto an old and charming little cottage restaurant, where tables are manoeuvred around the ancient beams that characterise this house.

FOX & GOOSE, Fressingfield, Suffolk.
Next door to a church, this restaurant offers the best in old English traditional food. The delightful black and white exterior contains an unpretentious dining room with tiled floor and exposed beams, serving simple and honest food.

THE KING'S HEAD, Laxfield, Suffolk.
Tucked behind a cemetery, this thatched Tudor pub in rural East Suffolk is decidedly unspoilt. Old seats, barrelled ales (although there is no bar) and authentic tasty food within a timeless atmosphere make this a true gem.

KING'S HEAD, Orford, Suffolk.
Parts of this predominantly Tudor inn date back 700 years. The heavily carved and blackened oak beams and old wooden chairs maintain the very traditional, cosy atmosphere. A variety of excellent seafood and fine ales can be enjoyed at this delighful pub.

LE TALBOOTH, Dedham, Essex.
From riverside garden in summer to winter log-fires, the tranquility of this setting remains undisturbed throughout the year. Superb food complements the idyll of this Constable - country restaurant.

LIFEBOAT, Thornham, Norfolk.
Overlooking the marshes where smugglers landed in centuries past, this delightful pub is characterised by great oak beams, carved tables and many other old charms. Good food, fine ales and the beautiful location make this atmospheric pub very popular.

OLD RECTORY, Great Snoring, Norfolk.
Built around 1500, this restful old rectory provides a haven of tranquility. From the stone-mullioned windows to the old grandfather clock in the hall, the emphasis is quietly and peacefully elegant.

OLDE FERRY BOAT, Needingworth, Cambridgeshire
This 10th century thatched inn, set in a remote part of the Fens, is one of the oldest in the country. Recent expensive refurbishment has not altered the rambling atmosphere. Fine ales and an extensive menu add to its distinctive attraction.

OSTRICH, Castle Acre, Norfolk.
Situated overlooking the village green beside the ruins of a Norman castle, this 18th century pub has a wonderfully intimate atmosphere. Exposed oak beams, trusses and 16th century masonry capture considerable attention.

ROSE & CROWN, Snettisham, Norfolk.
With its old-fashioned beamed bar, this cosy 14th century pub is very characterful. Farm tools and carpentry maintain the rural look. The excellent food, assorted ales and own house wines have an impressive reputation.

SEABRIGHTS BARN, Great Baddow, Essex.
This converted 16th century barn retains its rustic charm. Its attraction derives from the wide range of delicious food combined with good fine ales and wines.

WHITE HART, Great Yeldham, Essex.
Heavy beams and oak panels create a traditional and cosy atmosphere at this striking Tudor house built in 1505. As popular today as it was when Samuel Pepys supposedly endorsed its licence application, it serves good bar food and ales.

The George at Stamford

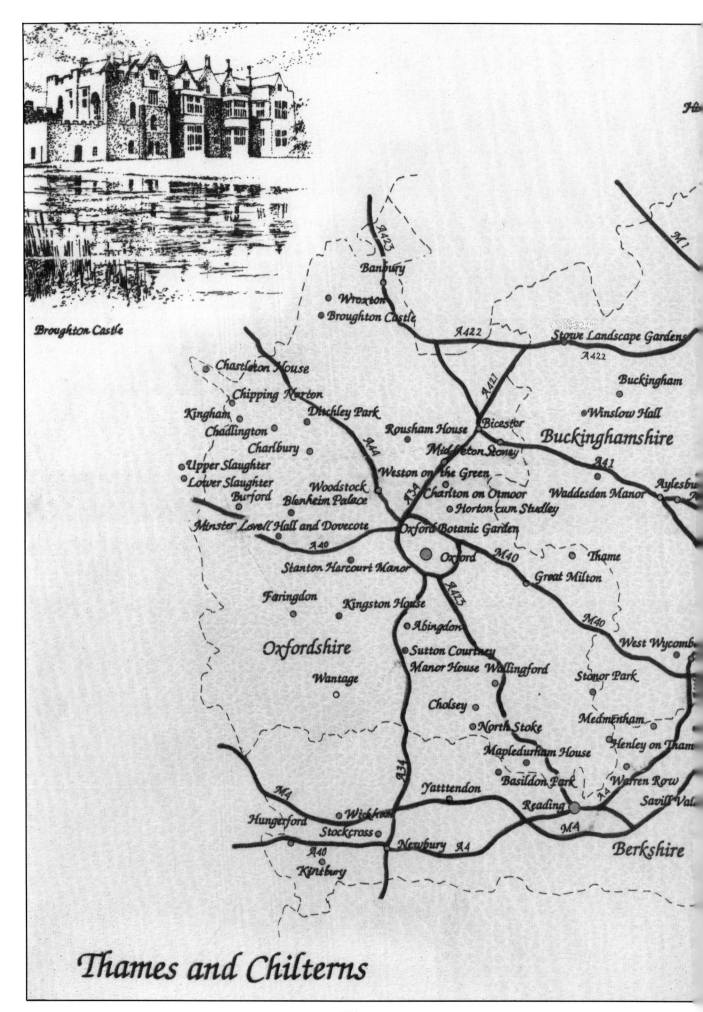

Broughton Castle

Banbury
Wroxton
Broughton Castle

A423

A422

Stowe Landscape Gardens
A422

Buckingham

Winslow Hall

A421

Chastleton House
Chipping Norton
Kingham
Chadlington
Charlbury
Ditchley Park

Bicester

Buckinghamshire

Rousham House
Middleton Stoney
Weston on the Green

A44

A41

Upper Slaughter
Lower Slaughter
Burford
Woodstock
Blenheim Palace

A34

Charlton on Otmoor
Horton cum Studley

Waddesdon Manor

Aylesbu

Minster Lovell Hall and Dovecote
A40

Oxford Botanic Garden

Stanton Harcourt Manor

Oxford

M40

Thame

Great Milton

M40

West Wycomb

Faringdon
Kingston House

Oxfordshire

Wantage

A423

Abingdon
Sutton Courtney
Manor House Wallingford

Cholsey

North Stoke

Mapledurham House

Stonor Park

Medmenham

Henley on Tham

Warren Row

Savill Val.

M4
Hungerford
Wickham
Stockcross
A40
Kintbury

A34

Yatttendon

Basildon Park

Reading

A4

M4

Newbury   A4

Berkshire

Thames and Chilterns

124

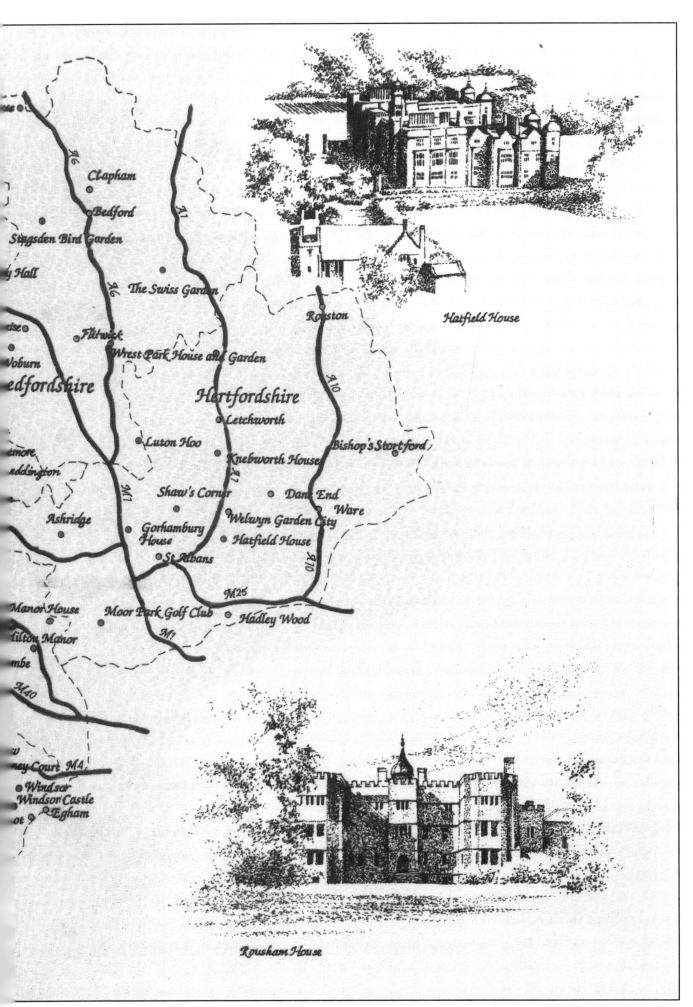

Clapham

Bedford

Stagsden Bird Garden

y Hall

The Swiss Garden

A6

Flitwick

Wrest Park House and Garden

Royston

Hatfield House

Bedfordshire

Voburn

Hertfordshire

Letchworth

Luton Hoo

Knebworth House

Bishop's Stortford

Shaw's Corner

Dane End

Ware

Welwyn Garden City

Ashridge

Gorhambury House

Hatfield House

St Albans

M25

Manor House

Moor Park Golf Club

Hadley Wood

ilton Manor

M1

mbe

M40

ney Court M4

Windsor

Windsor Castle

Egham

Rousham House

THE THAMES VALLEY AND THE CHILTERNS

BUCKINGHAMSHIRE AND THE VALE OF AYLESBURY

Buckinghamshire has been called the Queen of the Home Counties. Stretching from the Ouse and the Grand Union Canal in the north to the Thames to the south, the county has the Chiltern Hills running like a spine through its centre - its glorious beechwoods are all that remain of the woods which once covered the whole county.

There are many country houses, especially around the Vale of Aylesbury, with the town of Aylesbury at its heart.

Aylesbury itself is now very much a modern town, but has areas of interest within it. **The King's Head** is one of the few inns to be owned by the National Trust, and is entered through a medieval gateway, while the Hickman's Almshouses and Prebendal House, both date back to the 17th century.

Several of the homes of the Rothschild family are to be found here, the most famous of which is **Waddesdon Manor**, a French Renaissance style chateau built by Ferdinand de Rothschild in 1874 to 89, and now run by the National Trust. Waddesdon Manor is well worth a visit, inside you will find a magnificent collection of furnishings, paintings and personal mementoes of the family, the clocks are of particular interest as well as the two writing tables, one made for Marie Antoinette and another for Louis XVI. In the bachelor room you will discover a museum of small arms. The grounds have fountains and sculptures collected from france, Italy and the Netherlands, there is also a sizeable aviary and two deer enclosures.

Chicheley Hall can be found at Newport Pagnell, it is the rather grand home of the Honourable Nicholas Beatty, grandson of Admiral the Earl Beatty Commander of the Battle Cruiser Squadron at the Battle of Jutland in 1916. The house built between 1719 and 1723, is one of the finest 18th century houses and remains remarkably unaltered. Designed by Francis Smith of Warwick who was a well known architect and master builder, it has many outstanding features, including the doors and windows which were inspired from four of the leading architects of Baroque Rome. There are also lovely pieces of furniture and a magnificent collection of sea pictures. The garden has wide open lawns, which are surrounded by a three sided formal canal attributed to George London who was also one of the designers of Hampton Court, there are many fine trees which include a magnificent Cedar of Lebanon.

One of Europe's finest landscape gardens is to be found near Buckingham at **Stowe School**. Surrounding the magnificent 18th century mansion is one of Britain's most amazing landscape gardens, it covers 250 acres and contains a staggering six lakes and thirty two garden temples. Including works by Banburgh, Ken, Gibbs and Leoni, Stowe is of great historic importance. The style English Garden comes from William Kent, when in the 1730s he laid out in the Elysian fields one of the first natural landscapes. 'Capability' Brown worked here as head gardener for 10 years and in 1744 he was married in the church hidden in the trees. The gardens remain relatively unchanged and are still enjoyed as described in the 18th century as 'the faire majestic paradise of Stowe.' The pretty little village of Winslow, with its thatched cottages and overhanging gables also boasts **Winslow Hall**, which was probably designed by Wren. It was built in 1698 to 1702 for William Cowndes who was secretary of the Treasury under William III, the house has

Stowe

suffered very little structural alteration and retains most of its original features and many lovely pieces of furniture. Winslow Hall has attractive decor, a warm homely feel and is still occupied by the owners.

Ascott House, situated in the picturesque village of Wing, this lovely 17th century farm house belonged to the Rothschild family and contains fine examples of French furniture, Chinese porcelain and Anthony de Rothschild's notable collection of English and Dutch paintings.

Buckingham, the county town before Aylesbury, was host to Catherine of Aragon, and **Long Crendon's Court House** at **Long Crendon** near Thame began life in the 14th century as a modest wool store. In the 15th century manorial courts were held regularly in this charming half timbered building.

Mentmore Towers situated near Leighton Buzzard, is an example of the Victorian 'Jacobethan' romantic house, reminding us of the wealth and power of the Rothchilds in the 19th century (featured later).

THE CHILTERNS

Though much of Buckinghamshire has become commuterland, many of the towns and villages have taken care to retain their character. Lovely trees adorn the Chilterns, and the area is rich in history.

West Wycombe was the headquarters of the Hellfire Club, rakes and gamblers who were thought to have an interest in witchcraft. **West Wycombe Park** is a Palladian mansion, the former

Toll House at Chiltern Open Air Museum

home of the 18th century eccentric and dilettante Sir Francis Dashwood. The house is lavishly decorated with frescoes and painted ceilings. Nearby High Wycombe has a long association with chair making and boasts a museum devoted to this subject.

Chalfont St Giles has various claims to fame. It is home to the **Chiltern Open Air Museum** which rescues historic buildings facing destruction. They are re-erected at the site to reflect the vernacular heritage of the Chilterns region and illustrate the lives and work of local people over the past five centuries.

Also at Chalfont St Giles is Old Jordans, a 17th century farmhouse where the early Quakers held their first meetings. The Mayflower Barn was built in 1624, and is claimed to include timbers taken from the ship which carried the Pilgrim Fathers to America in 1620. **Milton's Cottage** was the home of the poet from 1665, when he sought refuge from the plague. Here he completed 'Paradise Lost' and began 'Paradise Regained'.

Chenies Manor House is close to Amersham and a delightful house has a warm homely feeling. With amazing chimneys and a pretty garden, this red brick Tudor House definitely deserves a visit.

The War Memorial at Coombe Hill near Wendover marks the highest point of the Chilterns, and nearby, but not open to the public, is Chequers, the Prime Minister's official country residence.

Winslow Hall

Cliveden, near Taplow, is the former home of Nancy Astor. It sits on cliffs 200 feet above the River Thames, and was built in

THE THAMES VALLEY AND THE CHILTERNS

1851, with 375 acres of magnificent gardens including a parterre, a water garden and other lovely formal gardens (featured later).

Princes Risborough has a pretty town centre with a 17th century manor house, and Pyrton is a secluded village with some fine thatched and Georgian houses and a fine Elizabethan manor house.

BEDFORDSHIRE - PILGRIM'S PROGRESS

John Bunyan wandered the village greens of Bedfordshire, preaching. He was born in Harrowden, but grew up in Elstow, now part of Bedford and here the **Moot Hall** now houses an exhibition on rural life in Bunyan's time. Bedford has many reminders of its favourite son.

Houghton House, near Ampthill, is believed to be Bunyan's 'House Beautiful'. The ruins of this red-brick house, built for the Dowager Countess of Pembroke, are all that has remained of the house since the end of the 18th century when all but the outer walls were pulled down. Inigo Jones has been suggested as its architect and the house was thought to have inspired John Bunyan. Nearby **Stagsden Bird Gardens**, is fun for a change of theme. This specialist Bird Garden, in a lovely country setting, is home to over 150 species including birds of prey, waterfowl, pheasant, owls, cranes and exotic flamingos. There are old and rare breeds of poultry and some of the more precocious inhabitants-myrahs in particular - are liable to answer back.

Nearby Dunstable Downs, much of which is owned by the National Trust, is home to Whipsnade Zoo, and the turf of the western slope is cut into the white chalk Whipsnade lion.

Lions are also a big feature at nearby **Woburn Abbey**. The original Abbey was founded in 1145, but the present house was rebuilt between 1747 and 1761. The Abbey is set in 300 acres of lovely deerpark, landscaped by Humphry Repton. The Wild Animal Kingdom is home to elephants, giraffes and many other species, as well as the lions for which it is most famous (featured later).

Luton Hoo is an example of the work of Robert Adam, although it was never finished according to his plans. It has gardens landscaped by 'Capability' Brown and is a treasury of Old Master paintings, tapestries, jewellery, bronzes and porcelain. It also houses a fabulous collection of Faberge jewellery, as well as portraits and mementoes of the Russian Imperial Family.

Wrest Park at Silsoe, owned by English Heritage is well worth a visit for its noble formal gardens, with attractive features including fountains and elegant statuary. The park illustrates many styles of gardening which have been in vogue from about 1850. The Swiss Garden near Old Warden, takes its name from the tiny thatched Swiss Cottage at its heart. The gardens form an extension to the gardens of Old Walden Park, and were developed in the early 1800s. Do also visit the Lodge Reserve at Sandy, home of the Royal Society for the Protection of Birds, which is set around a magnificent Tudor-style house built in 1870.

Dorney Court

THE THAMES VALLEY AND THE CHILTERNS

BERKSHIRE - THE WESTERN DOWNS

Royal Berkshire is one of the smallest of the English Shire Counties, stretching from London out to Wiltshire and including Windsor, Maidenhead and Bracknell as well as plenty of unspoilt countryside. Reading was once the home of a powerful Benedictine monastery, and is now a university town, with attractions including its Museum of English Rural Life, Forbury Gardens and the ruined 12th century abbey.

Basildon Park has a lovely setting overlooking the Thames Valley. Made of Bath stone, and built in 1776, it overlooks 400 acres of parks and woodlands. **Highclere Castle**, south of Newbury, is well-known for its collections of Egyptian treasures, booty of the fifth earl who discovered Tutankhamen's tomb with Howard Carter (featured later).

ROYAL WINDSOR

The Wren Guildhall and the Church rich with engravings by Grinling Gibbons seem almost incidental to the massive castle at **Windsor** which dominates the surrounding countryside. Windsor has been the home and burial place of English kings and queens for the last 900 years, and the castle is one of the largest and oldest inhabited castles in the world. However, most of what we see today is the result of the 19th century rebuilding by George IV. St George's Chapel, within the palace grounds, is one of the oldest churches in England, dating back to 1475 and monarchs who lie buried there include Henry VIII and George VI (featured later). **Frogmore Gardens** and Mausoleum, in the 400 acre Home Park are major attractions as are the **Valley Gardens** within Windsor Great Park, covering 400 acres of woodland. A notable feature is the large heather garden, providing interest and subtle colour in all seasons. The Royalty & Empire Exhibition, the Racecourse and the Safari Park are also very popular with Windsor's tourists.

ETON AND BEYOND

Eton, just across the bridge from Windsor, is famous worldwide for its public school, **Eton College**. This was founded in 1440 by Henry VI and has lovely cloisters and a 15th century Chapel which is quite beautiful.

On your way from Windsor to Dorney, you must stop off to see the **Savill Gardens**, a few miles of south of Windsor and presenting a glorious display of rhododendrons, magnolias and camellias. Once at Dorney, visit **Dorney Court** its enchanting many-gabled, timbered Manor house of warm terracotta Tudor brick. Built around 1440 and lived in by the present family for over 400 years, the inviting atmosphere is very much that of a family home. Twelve generations of Palmers have loved this house and added to its furniture and paintings giving a real feeling of continuity. Its unpretentious rooms are filled with a sense of history drawn from generations of family portraits; fine furniture from the earliest oak of the 15th and 16th centuries, lacquered examples from the 17th century to mahogany pieces from the 18th and 19th centuries; needlework stitched by Palmer ladies to record family events - the accumulated personal treasures of hundreds of years. Inside the house is little changed since 1500 and the rooms are still used for their intended purpose which serves to reinforce the feeling of stepping backwards into history.

AROUND HERTFORDSHIRE

St Albans is a thriving combination of old and picturesque with modern shops and commuter traffic. The former Roman city of Verulanium lies to the west, and the museum there houses an important collection of Roman remains including part of a theatre. The presence of a cathedral highlights the importance of St Albans in the history of Christianity. In AD304, the Roman St Alban was martyred for his conversion to the Christian faith, and the town has been important to pilgrims ever since. A Clock Tower and the City Museum are both worth a visit.

Gorhambury House, two miles west of St Albans, was the home of the Earls of Verulam from 1777 to 1784. It was built by Sir Robert Taylor in the 1780's, it was Sir Francis Bacon's country house and part of the older house still survives.

Ayot St Lawrence, near Welwyn, was the home of playwright George Bernard Shaw for 40 years, and his home Shaw's Corner is open to the public. The Ashridge Estate stretches across 4,000 acres including woodlands, commons and the area up the Ivinghow Beacon. The house, in early gothic-revival style, was begun in 1808 by James Wyatt.

Letchworth and Welwyn, the first and second garden cities respectively, were developed according to plans by Ebenezer Howard. South of Welwyn is **Hatfield House**, built in 1611 beside the ruins of the Tudor palace of the bishops of Ely, and containing a wealth of Tudor and Jacobean treasures (featured later). **Knebworth House**, three miles north of Welwyn, was built in the 1500s by the Lytton family (featured later).

Moor Park is more than just a golf club. Built in the 1680s for the Duke of Monmouth, it was extensively refurbished by Benjamin Styles around 1720. The imposing entrance hall has a painted and gilded ceiling with a magnificent dome not unlike that in St Peter's in Rome. Several notable Italian craftsmen were employed on the lavish interiors including Cipriani, whose mark can be seen in the lovely coffered ceiling in the dining room. Altogether a splendid 19th hole!

OXFORDSHIRE

The county of Oxfordshire is famous for many things. Its county town Oxford, has been a centre for learning and scholarship for more than 700 years, as well as being a bustling market town. The county is also famous for other reasons. Wantage was the birthplace of King Alfred, Banbury is famous for its cakes and its nursery rhyme, and Sir Winston Churchill was born at Blenheim Palace and lies buried at Bladon near Woodstock. There's also the regatta at Henley, the railway at Didcott and numerous other attractions.

CITY OF DREAMING SPIRES

It was Matthew Arnold who coined this phrase in the 19th century, but the City of Oxford dates back before the Norman Conquest and there are references to a university from the 12th century. There are more than 600 listed buildings in Oxford, and you will pleased to hear that I will not even attempt to list them all here. Suffice it to say that most of the colleges open their chapels and quadrangles to visitors in the afternoons. The **Bodleian Library** is worthy of a mention , being one of the world's greatest, with a staggering five million books. And apart

THE THAMES VALLEY AND THE CHILTERNS

from the university, look out for interesting churches and municipal buildings and the lovely riverside walks of Oxford.

BEYOND OXFORD

Blenheim Palace, the country's largest private house, is well known because of its connections with Churchill, but is worthy of merit in its own right. It is a classical mansion, designed by Sir John Vanburgh and set in 2,000 acres of gardens (featured later).

Milton Manor House, south of Abingdon, is a lovely 17th century house designed by Inigo Jones, built in 1663 for Thomas Calton, this elegant pink-brick house is unusual in that back and front are exactly alike, even its roof elevations are equal - an exercise in perfect symmetry. In 1764 two Georgian wings, a bakery, brewhouse and stables were added by Bryant Barrett whose descendants live there today. The house has an outstanding Strawberry Hill 'Gothic' library.

Broughton Castle, 20 miles from Oxford, the home of Lord Saye and Sele, is not truly a castle in the literal sense of a military fortress. On this site in about 1300 Sir John de Broughton built a manor house on an island within a wide moat. In 1554 Richard Fiennes completed a great reconstruction in the 'Court' style of Edward VI and after his death in 1573 his son, also Richard, continued to embellish and refine and thus the medieval manor house was transformed into a Tudor Mansion.

The building activity of the 16th century gave way to political activity in the 17th century, when the family became caught up in events which were to lead inevitably to the dark days of Civil War. Great houses had to choose sides and Broughton and the Fiennes family came down strongly on the side of Parliament. Sir William Fiennes raised his own regiment of bluecoats and four troops of horse and fought shoulder to shoulder with his four sons at the nearby battle of Edgehill in 1642. After the battle the castle was captured and occupied by Royalist forces.

The 18th century, by contrast, afforded a welcome respite before the tribulations of the 19th century caused by the frivolous and extravagant life-style of the 15th Baron who was one of the Prince Regent's set. He chose not to live in unfashionable Oxfordshire and let the castle slide ever further into dilapidation and disrepair, culminating in a sale of most of the contents of the castle - even down to the swans which bobbed on the moat. What strange irony that the squandering of this family fortune probably saved Broughton from the architectural excesses of the Victorians, and fortunately left much of the medieval structure intact. Several rooms have beautiful original plasterwork ceilings and both Queen Anne's Room and the King's Chamber have magnificent fireplaces. Through the Gatehouse, built in 1405, lies the church of St. Mary which holds the tombs and memorials of many of the Fiennes family.

A Royalist in the civil war built **Rousham House** at Steeple Aston, which boasts the only surviving garden landscaped by William Kent. The house, with gardens dipping down to the River Cherwell, was built in 1635 for Sir Robert Dormer and remains in the ownership of the same family today. The original house was in the shape of an H with mullioned windows and gables, but was completely transformed by Kent in 1738. He added low wings complete with statuary and replaced the

Mapledurham House

THE THAMES VALLEY AND THE CHILTERNS

gables with straight battlements and a central cupola. The windows were glazed with octagonal panes, but these were replaced by sash windows in Victórian times which had a somewhat deadening effect - William St. Aubyn is thought to be responsible. William Kent made few structural alterations inside the house which retains some of its 17th century panelling and the original Jacobean staircase. The massive oak door into the Entrance Hall is another relic of the Jacobean house and still bears the holes through which Sir Robert would train his musket on any advancing Roundheads.

There are also some fine family portraits by Lely and Kneller together with William Kent's sketches for the gardens.

The gardens of Rousham Park were remodelled by Kent and remain almost as he left them. Many of the features which delighted 18th century visitors are still there, and with its sylvan glades and classic features goes far to confirm William Kent as the father of the English art of landscape design.

Pangbourne is a pretty village, famous for its public school and its thatched cottages and Goring and Streatley, both on the Thames, attract many visitors. Not to be missed is **Mapledurham** with its 17th century Almshouses and 16th century mansion house. The nearby Catholic chapel and ancient watermill are interesting too.

In the Oxfordshire Cotswolds, villages such as **Minster Lovell**, Burford, Chadlington and Chastleton are well worth exploring. And do visit the 18th century **Ditchley Park**, designed in

Kingston House

THE THAMES VALLEY AND THE CHILTERNS

the 18th century by James Gibbs with magnificent interiors by Henry Flitcroft and William Kent. During the Second World War it was the weekend headquaters of Winston Churchill's War Cabinet.

Five miles north of Henley, in the Chilterns, is **Stonor Park**, historic home of the Stonor family for more than 800 years (featured later), and **Kingston House**, the home of Lord and Lady Tweedsmuir, is something of a mystery. Exactly when the present house was built, or by whom it was designed, is not known. The Baroque feeling of the house and its resemblance to work by Gibbs and Wren has led some authorities to attribute it to one of their followers in about 1710. However old deeds show that the house was in existence in 1670 when John Latton sold it to Edmund Fettiplace.

An important feature of the house is the magnificent cantilevered staircase and gallery in the pine panelled entrance hall, leading some to suggest Sir Roger Pratt as the possible architect. From the Saloon the beautiful proportions of the house, with its symmetry of design, high rooms and fine architectural detail, can be appreciated to the full. This room contains some very good paintings, fine 18th century English and French furniture and some lovely Chinese Famille Vert porcelain.

The house stands within a framework of mellow brick walls, enclosing herbaceous and shrub borders, and lawns with fine trees. The early 18th century gazebo was built above an Elizabethan cockpit and the grounds also contain the old schoolhouse.

Waterperry Gardens near Wheatly are spacious, peaceful ornamental gardens set in a 83 acre Estate. There are many interesting plants and fine trees, with riverside walks. At the end of your visit you can enjoy home made refreshments.

THE VALE OF THE WHITE HORSE

The white horse carved in ancient times onto the Berkshire downs give this area its name. The area is full of myth and legend, and also has a rich literary heritage, with names like William Morris, Alexander Pope and Matthew Arnold having local associations.

William Morris illustrated his 'News From Nowhere' with a woodcut of the Elizabethan Kelmscott Manor, and the writer was buried at Kelmscot. Stanton Harcourt is famous for its associations with John and Charles Wesley, and Pope's Tower, one of the few remaining parts of the manor, is where Alexander Pope completed the fifth volume of his translation of 'The Iliad'.

Waterperry Gardens

MENTMORE TOWERS

Mentmore is one of the finest early Victorian houses and an exceptional example of the Jacobean Revival at its best. Built between 1851 and 1855 for Baron Meyer Amschel de Rothschild, Mentmore Towers is a reminder of the enormous wealth and power of the Rothschilds in the 19th century.

Baron Rothschild, fourth son of Nathan Mayer de Rothschild, founder of the famous banking firm, had two passionate interests in life - art collecting and horse racing. Mentmore was built as a fitting setting for his vast collection of art treasures including Old Master paintings, silver, tapestries, Limoges enamels and 18th century French furniture. No expense was spared and it was by far the grandest of all the Rothschild mansions. To indulge his other passion he built a stud farm and a large racing stable.

The architect chosen was Sir Joseph Paxton who revolutionised Victorian architecture by his extensive use of glass, and whose reputation had been made by his design for the Crystal Palace. Both in the romantic character of its composition and the beauty of its detail, Mentmore is unique. It is the sole surviving example of Paxton's domestic architecture in the country. It was modelled on Wollaton Hall, a large Elizabethan mansion, but instead of a central tower the Grand Hall at Mentmore is covered entirely with glass.

No expense was spared in the construction. The exterior is faced with golden Ancaster stone, while stone for the interior came from Caen in France and marble for the staircases was shipped from Italy. At the time there was a flourishing trade in 18th century interiors which were removed by enterprising art dealers from the grand houses of Europe to be incorporated in new Victorian mansions. Many found their way to Mentmore.

The Entrance Hall, paved with Sicilian and Rouge Royale marble, has a magnificent staircase of white Sicilian marble in the grand Renaissance style leading from the Grand Hall. Here the enormous black marble chimney piece supported by two white marble rams is reputed to have been designed by Rubens for his house in Antwerp. At first floor level the Grand Hall is surrounded by an arcaded gallery with a balustrade of pink alabaster and green marble. Above this the cornice is elaborately carved by Raphaele Monti and supports the coved glass ceiling divided by moulded walnut ribs and suspended from the ridge and furrow roof. On three sides of the Hall are huge doors and windows of plate glass in narrow walnut frames, and a further immense pane of glass in the South Entrance framing spectacular views of the Vale of Aylesbury, Ivinghoe Beacon and the long line of the Chilterns.

The main interiors can be roughly divided between 'Italian Palazzo' in the public places, and 'French Versailles' in the reception and private rooms. The Dining Room is perhaps the most lavish, lined with gilded boiseries made originally for the Hotel de Villars in Paris in 1731 framing superb panels of rich 16th century Genoese velvet. The library, octagonal in shape, has a domed ceiling and 'secret' doors disguised by false book backs. The white marble fireplace, Italian Renaissance, is the oldest one in the house and is thought to have been made in Florence in the 16th century.

In 1877 Mentmore was inherited by Baron Rothschild's daughter, Hannah, who married the 5th Earl of Rosebery in 1878.

Lord Rosebery was an eminent Liberal politician and was Foreign Secretary twice and Prime Minister in 1895. He also shared the Baron's love of the turf and owned three Derby winners - the family racing trophies can be seen on the Grand Staircase. The 5th Earl was succeeded by his son in 1929 whose family owned Mentmore until his death in 1974.

Mentmore became the focus of world-wide attention in 1977 when Sothebys sold the contents of the house for over six million pounds. At the time of the sale a trap door was discovered in a corridor which led to a strong room where silver valued at hundreds of thousands of pounds was discovered. Though the contents have been dispersed all the beautiful interiors remain intact.

The 4,000 acre estate includes Mentmore Village itself, a model village of 'Jacobean' cottages created by Baron Rothschild. The lovely park is laid out in the style of Humphrey Repton and planted with fine exotic trees, many planted by famous visitors to Mentmore Towers.

CLIVEDEN

Cliveden, built in 1850 by Charles Barry for the Duke of Sunderland, is the third house to occupy this idyllic riverside site since the 17th century. The previous building, which was destroyed by fire, is commemorated in large carved stone lettering beneath the parapet. It was built in the 17th century by William Winde for the second Duke of Buckingham and its essential character was preserved by Barry in the present house wherever possible. Winde's elegant terrace with its twenty-eight arches survived below Barry's grand main house linked to two 18th century wings by curved corridors.

The magnificent gardens, stretching down to the River Thames, are largely the work of William, first Viscount Astor, who bought Cliveden in 1893. A double staircase leads from the terrace to the famous Borghese balustrade, splendidly elaborate, which was brought from the villa Borghese in Rome. The first Lord Astor was an avid collector of classical statuary, and there are urns and sarcophagi throughout the gardens.

Below the balustrade the vast formal parterre runs almost as far as the eye can see. The simple pattern of the beds of lavender edged with clipped box makes a sharp contrast to the ornate balustrading. Lord Astor's Italian garden, bordered with box hedges and topiary, is the perfect setting for a collection of classical statues.

A Japanese garden surrounds the small lake bordered by irises and day lilies, azaleas and rhododendrons. Deep red acers contrast sharply with yellows and greens of the moisture-loving shrubs which trail into the water. Across a bridge of stepping stones on a tiny island is the garden's focal point - a brightly painted pagoda crowned by a golden dragon which was made for the Paris exhibition of 1867.

The drive, flanked by an avenue of mature limes leads to a fountain in the form of a huge shell and the steep Yew Walk leads down to the Thames. To the west of the house is an open air theatre, the Blenheim Pavilion built in memory of the first Duke of Marlborough and also in the grounds is a charming little temple with a green copper dome.

Although Cliveden is now a hotel, part of it are open to the public including the oak-panelled hall with its 17th century Brussels tapestries. The second Viscount Astor and his wife Nancy entertained many famous and important guests including Sir Winston Churchill, Henry James, Rudyard Kipling, Lord Curzon and many others. Tradition has it that George Canning, the eminent statesman, was very fond of these gardens, and of one spot in particular from where he could sit and watch the Thames below, under the shade of an ancient tree still known as Canning's Oak.

WOBURN ABBEY

Woburn Abbey has been the home of the Dukes of Bedford since it was bequeathed to the 1st Earl of Bedford by Henry VIII. Built on the site of the 12th century Cistercian Abbey, it was rebuilt between 1747 and 1761 by Henry Feitcroft who added the west wing with its central pediment. At the end of the 18th century Henry Holland was commissioned to build the south and east wings, thus giving the Abbey its quadrangular form. Sadly in 1950 the whole of the east wing succumbed to the ravages of dry rot and had to be pulled down, and with it the Indoor Riding School and the Real Tennis Court.

In the vanguard of great houses who opened their doors to the public, Woburn Abbey contains one of the most important private collections of works of art with English and French furniture, silver, European and oriental porcelain and paintings by many of the world's great artists including Reynolds, Van Dyck and Velasquez. There are over twenty specially commissioned views of Venice in the Canaletto Room and the famous Armada Portrait of Elizabeth I by Gower painted after the defeat of the Armada in 1588. The lovely porcelain includes the fabulous dinner service by Sevres, a gift from Louis XV to the 4th Duchess.

The interiors of Flitcroft and Holland are sumptuously furnished, and throughout the Abbey there is a very strong oriental feeling. The Chinese Room designed by Henry Flitcroft is still hung with the original wallpaper brought from China over 200 years ago, and there are some magnificent examples of chinese porcelain on display.

In the Stables is the unique Antiques Centre, with 40 shops housed within frontages which have all been salvaged from demolition sites up and down the country. This is probably one of the largest centres of its kind outside London.

The 3,000 acre Deer Park was landscaped by Humphrey Repton in the 19th century and is the home to nine species of deer. The Pere David were preserved from extinction at Woburn by the 11th Duke and the Park now boasts the largest breeding herd in the world. In the 40 acres of grounds around the house there are many fine specimen trees, with ponds and a rock garden approached through a stone archway. Also in the grounds is Henry Holland's lovely Chinese Dairy, and in the private gardens the maze has not escaped the chinese influence. Designed by the 6th Duke of Bedford and planted about 1831, the Hornbeam maze leads those with a good sense of direction to the Chinese Temple built in 1833 to a design dating from 1757.

It would be impossible to think of Woburn without its famous Safari Park. Throughout the 350 acres children and adults alike are transported from the countryside of Bedfordshire to Big Game country where tigers, lions, elephants, camels, monkeys and zebras roam freely.

An altogether safer diversion is the Woburn Golf and Country Club which has two 18 hole championship courses and hosts several prestigious tournaments.

HIGHCLERE CASTLE

The Earl of Carnarvon, a wealthy and important man aware that his simple Georgian house did not convey his position in fashionable society engaged Sir Charles Barry to remedy the matter. He transformed Highclere Castle into the huge, exuberant mansion which caused Disraeli to exclaim 'How Scenical!' With its huge pinnacles and tall central tower providing an Italianate flourish Barry was well pleased, preferring Highclere to the Houses of Parliament which he was building at the same time. The Earl now had a home commensurate with his wealth and power.

Several architects had a hand in the interior design of the house and as a result, each room is quite different in style from the next, an extravagant mix much-favoured by the Victorian gentleman.

The entrance hall is pure church gothic with stone columns and fan-vaulting and a sophisticated early central heating system. If the comfortable double library with its golds and faded crimsons suggests the masculine appearance of a gentleman's club this could be because Barry also designed the library at the Reform Club. One can imagine why this room was a favourite of the 4th Earl and his many distinguished guests. The exotic desk and chair in this room once belonged to Napoleon and the family portraits by Beechey are exceptional.

By complete contrast, the music room is light and feminine. Its baroque ceiling painted in 1776 was moved here from the original house along with the Italian embroidered and gilded panels. In the drawing room the predominant style is rococo revival. The furniture is a mix of French, Italian and Chinese pieces dating from 1720 to 1900. The Victorians muddled periods and styles with complete equanimity. In the smoking room with its muted tones and leather chairs, we return to the tradi-tional preserve of the Victorian gentleman once more.

Occupying the centre of the house, the saloon is true Victorian gothic, splendidly theatrical with its high vaulted ceiling and ornate gallery. The dining room is Stuart revival dominated by Van Dyck great equestrian portrait of Charles I.

Highclere has been filled with the accumulated treasures of generations of collectors. Possibly the most famous was the 5th Earl who, with Howard Carter, first gazed into the tomb of Tutankhamun in 1922 - the pinnacle of his illustrious career. His vast collection of Egyptian artefacts is now in the

Metropolitan Museum in New York with the exception of some of his earliest finds discovered in 1987 by the present Earl. They were concealed in a series of small compartments in the thickness of the wall between the drawing room and smoking room where they had lain undisturbed since the 1920s. In order for this grand household to run smoothly an army of servants was housed in the warren of rooms and passageways below stairs.

The earliest record of a garden at Highclere is from 1218 when the Bishop of Winchester planted an orchard. The gardens of the earlier Georgian house have all but disappeared, leaving only a collection of temples and arches which can be seen from the drive. What followed was a more natural landscape in the manner of Capability Brown. The massive cedars were grown from seed brought back from Lebanon in the 18th Century.

In Victorian times the gardens produced all the fruit and vegetables for the table. Today, grapefruit, figs, oranges, grapes, bananas, rice coffee and eucalyptus flourish in the tropical house behind the Victorian fernery. A relatively recent addition is the secret garden.

WINDSOR CASTLE

For over nine centuries this Royal Palace and fortress, still under the direct control of the Soverign, has provided an awesome background to the great Ceremonies of State, and is by far the oldest royal residence still in use. It was originally built as a fortress by William the Conqueror, one of a series all 20 miles (one day's march) from the centre of London and from each other. An isolated escarpment overlooking the River Thames was chosen as the site, and the slope of the escarpment resulted in its somewhat elongated narrower shape.

Soon after it was built this military post was used as a royal residence and in 1110 King Henry I held court in the Castle. During the reign of Henry II State Apartments were built, those in the Upper Ward for domestic use and those in the Lower for ceremonial purposes, and the castle's defences were considerably stregthened. The lower half of the Round Tower which dominated both the Castle and the surrounding town of Windsor probably dates from this period.

King Edward III carried out a grand programme of reconstruction, resulting in many of the two storey buildings seen today. The King, who was born at Windsor, founded England's Premier Order of Chivalry, the Order of the Garter in 1348. To provide a worthy setting for the gatherings of the new order, he demolished the residence of Henry III and erected a new and more spacious range of apartments which included the original St George's Hall. These apartments were still standing when King Charles I spent his last Christmas in captivity at the Castle in 1648, shortly before his execution.

After the Restoration, Charles II replaced them with a new palace in the fashionable Baroque style, the basic structure of which survives in the present State Apartments. Three of its rooms still retain much of their original decoration, including fabulous ceilings painted by Antonio Verrio.

One hundred and fifty years later, standards of comfort had once more changed and a monarch came to the throne whose visions of grandeur eclipsed any of his predecessors. King George IV commissioned Sir Jeffry Wyatville who carried out the castle's last and greatest reconstruction. To preserve the elegant rooms of Charles II he had the smaller rooms converted to house visiting royalty, and built new private apartments on the other two sides of the Upper Ward. The larger rooms were remodelled for ceremonial use, all in the Gothic style. The external additions included an extra storey on the Round Tower, several new towers and a profusion of elaborte machicolations on both old and new, giving the castle its dramatic air of romantic medievalism.

The earliest chapel of which traces remain was built by Henry III. In 1745 King Edward IV began the present chapel of St George which took 50 years to complete, and replaced its predecessor as the chapel of the Order of the Garter. Meanwhile the earlier chapel had been reconstructed by King Henry VII for use as a Lady Chapel which was later remodelled by Queen Victoria as a memorial to her husband, Prince Albert, who died at Windsor in 1861.

The State Apartments contain a bewildering display of priceless furniture, tapestries, paintings, carvings, statuary and armour. The Waterloo Chamber was conceived by George IV to commemorate the victory at Waterloo. Having commissioned Sir Thomas Lawrence to paint a series of portraits of everyone who had played a part in Napoleon's defeat, Wyatville was given the task of providing a gallery grand enough to accommodate such a large collection. His solution was to build a roof over an open courtyard in the centre of the State Apartments with a clerestory designed to give adequate lighting to the portraits. The immense table is laid for the Waterloo Banquet held each year on 18th June, the date of the glorious victory.

The King's Dressing Room contains a remarkable series of portraits by various artists including Holbein, Durer, Rembrandt and Rubens and one of the most famous portraits of King Charles I. The triple portrait by Van Dyck was painted to enable Bernini to carve a bust of the King without making the journey from Rome. The Castle also houses a collection of master drawings of incomparable richness and variety, begun when the famous series of drawings came into the possession of King Henry VIII. Works by Leonardo da Vinci, Michelangelo and Raphael were added in the following century by the Stuarts.

KNEBWORTH HOUSE

Knebworth House was transformed 150 years ago by the romantic Victorian novelist Edward Bulwer-Lytton into a gothic fantasy house. Its turrets, domes and gargoyles silhouetted against the sky line conceal a red brick house dating back to Tudor times.

Sir Robert Lytton purchased Knebworth in 1490 and ten years later began to build on to the 15th century gatehouse a new four-sided house enclosing a central courtyard. Successive generations have moulded the house to their own highly individual needs, building, demolishing, decorating but never quite obliterating the work of their predecessors.

In 1810 it was Mrs Elizabeth Bulwer-Lytton's turn to stamp the house with her own personal taste. Finding the building old-fashioned and too large, she simply demolished three sides of it, including the medieval gatehouse, part of which she then re-erected as a lodge in the park. She then concealed the red brick of the remaining wing with stucco, replaced the windows in the gothic style and added eight towers, battlements and a porch. Her son, the famous novelist, succeeded her in 1843 envisaging a gothic palace complete with domes, turrets and gargoyles.

The Banqueting Hall is reputed to be one of the finest rooms in England. The oak decoration of the ceiling which hides the Tudor roof timbers, the screen and the minstrels gallery all date from about 1600. This room was used as a theatre and in 1850 Charles Dickens performed here. On another occasion, Dickens made a speech which proved to be strangely prophetic. Referring to Sir Edward, his host and fellow novelist "....... crowds of people will come to see the place where he lived and wrote." More recently, Winston Churchill, a frequent guest, painted the Banqueting Hall. The painting now hangs at one end of the room.

The Library contains various editions of over seventy volumes of the plays, poems and essays of Edward Bulwer-Lytton. His son Robert, the 1st Earl who later became Viceroy of India, was also a poet but was discouraged by his father. Nevertheless, he

is said to have written his dispatches from India in verse as he found it easier than prose.

In the study where he always worked are books, letters and pictures relating to the work of Edward Bulwer-Lytton. The portrait over the fireplace shows him smoking an incredibly long pipe which reaches almost to the floor, a pastime of which he wrote: 'blue devils fly, before its honest breath. It ripens the brain...' He would also gaze for hours into a crystal ball.

Over 100 letters written to Edward by his great friend Dickens are on display here. Outside this room, on the staircase landing, hangs the best known painting of Bulwer-Lytton by his friend Daniel Maclise and beside it the most delightful sketch of a small girl - his daughter Emily.

The Hampden Room was Edward's bedroom as a child and contains a charming collection of children's furniture, toys and books including some rare Japanese clockwork toys.

A special exhibition of the Lytton connection with India is housed in the former squash court. As Viceroy it was Robert, 1st Earl of Lytton, who proclaimed Victoria Empress of India. The exhibition contains a unique collection of treasures, mementoes and photographs covering the period of the 1870s, the 2nd Earl of Lytton's Governorship of Bengal in the 1920s and the friendship of Winston Churchill and Pamela, 2nd Countess, who was reputed to have been his first great love.

Sir Edward's romantic embellishment of the house extended to the gardens which became elaborate and formal with ornate foundations, statues and shrubbery walks. In 1908, Lutyens decided that the exterior of Knebworth needed a simpler setting which was achieved by planting avenues of bleached limes and a broad yew hedge with gardens and brick built pergola behind. A new herb garden has been added which was designed by Gertrude Jekyll but was not built until later. The gardens are surrounded by 250 acres in which herds of deer roam freely.

HATFIELD HOUSE

The history of Hatfield House begins about 1497 when Cardinal Morton, Bishop of Ely finished building the Old Palace. Built of rich russet-coloured brick, the Banqueting Hall remains at the west of the present house. When Henry VIII seized the possessions of the Church he kept Hatfield chiefly as a residence for his children. Here Edward, Mary and Elizabeth shared a troubled childhood, and when, in 1558, Elizabeth heard of her accession to the throne she was reading beneath an oak tree in the park. Her first act was to send for William Cecil, later Lord Burghley, and appoint him her Chief Minister which he remained for the rest of his life.

Elizabeth I's successor James I did not care for the Old Palace as a house, preferring Theobalds, the home of Burghley's son Robert Cecil, afterwards 1st Earl of Salisbury. James proposed an exchange and, having little or no say in the matter, Robert agreed. He had been brought up to succeed his father as Chief Minister to the Crown and in the tradition of his family served James all his life. Small, sickly and with a crooked back, yet he dominated English politics and was responsible for the discovery of the Gunpowder Plot.

His favourite pastime was building. Accordingly in 1608 he pulled down three sides of Hatfield Palace and built himself the present house, designed mainly by Robert Lyminge with advice from others thought to include the young Inigo Jones. The central block was given up to State Rooms suitable for entertaining the King and splendidly decorated. The two wings were for his family and although Jacobean, the house was in the Elizabethan form of a letter E. The gardens were elaborately planned with fountains and a lake and rare plants brought from abroad by John Tradescant, the famous botanist. A walled vineyard was established in the park.

Just before the house was finished in 1612 Lord Salisbury died and Hatfield was not prominent again until, in the second half of the 18th century, it was the home of George III's Lord Chamberlain, the 1st Marquess of Salisbury. He was somewhat overshadowed by his beautiful wife, the leading Tory hostess of her day.

A hundred stories are told of her eccentricities. She rode the estate scattering guineas to the poor from a velvet bag carried by the groom; she held gambling parties till dawn when the floor was ankle-deep in discarded packs of cards; she hunted hounds till nearing eighty and partly blind. Sadly this indomitable old lady was to meet a tragic end in a fire which destroyed a large part of the west wing.

Her grandson, the 3rd Marquess, was three times Prime Minister and during his time in office England attained her most powerful position in history. Among other notable guests at Hatfield were Gladstone, Disraeli and Lewis Carroll who must have been a little taken aback when the family would nonchalantly hurl cushions to quell the fires when the new electric wires along the ceiling occasionally burst into flames.

The State Rooms are rich in world-famous paintings, fine furniture, rare tapestries and historic armour. In the splendid Marble Hall with its rich panelling and ceiling hang two of the most celebrated paintings of Elizabeth I - the Rainbow Portrait and the Ermine Portrait by Hilliard. Also at Hatfield are her garden hat, her yellow silk stockings and her gloves together with a great mass of her letters.

The Grand Staircase is one of the finest examples of the period in existence. It is an adaptation of the Italian Renaissance style of the English oak staircase. It is elaborately carved, and each pillar is surmounted by a figure. The beautifully carved gates at the bottom were to prevent dogs running about the upper floors of the house.

The formal gardens created by John Tradescant for Robert Cecil were swept away by the tide of landscaping which brought the parkland up to the very walls of the house. In the last years the present Marchioness has recreated the gardens (as far as possible), with their planting and design in the 17th century manner. A Knot Garden has been made in the courtyard and the lower West Garden has been made into a delightful scented garden with a herb garden at its centre. The West Garden is filled with roses, irises and peonies with a number of rare and unusual plants.

Within the gardens stands the surviving wing of the Old Palace, now used for corporate and private entertainment as well as for Elizabethan banquets.

BLENHEIM PALACE

'The cumulative labours of Vanbrugh and 'Capability' Brown have succeeded at Blenheim in setting an Italian Palace in an English Park without incongruity.' This was Sir Winston Churchill's opinion of the house in which he was born in 1874.

A celebration of victory, Blenheim Palace marks the nation's gratitude to John Churchill, 1st Duke of Marlborough, who defeated the French at the Battle of Blenheim in 1704. On behalf of the nation Queen Anne gave the estate of Woodstock and £240,000 to the Duke in order that a suitable house might be built for him. The architect entrusted with this task was Sir John Vanbrugh, unconventional and theatrical, aided by the somewhat more practical, though no less talented, Nicholas Hawksmoor.

Built in the English Baroque style between 1705 and 1725, its sheer size and grandeur are breathtaking. Corinthian columns support a lofty portico approached by a double flight of steps from a vast entrance court; great clusters of chimneys are surmounted by grenades shooting tongues of flame skywards.

It is thought by many to be Vanbrugh's masterpiece, though the Duchess was not entirely happy. She is said to have favoured Sir Christopher Wren, and when she gained control after the Duke suffered a stroke, poor Vanbrugh could stand her interference no longer and resigned in 1716. During its construction the finest craftsmen of the day were employed including Grinling Gibbons whose fine carving can be seen, particularly in the Saloon.

The entrance hall is imposing with two tiers of stone archways and its lofty ceiling, painted by Sir John Thornhill, depicts the victorious Duke as a Roman general. The Palace contains a wealth of treasures including French and English furniture, Chinese porcelain, paintings by Kneller, Sargent, Reynolds and Van Dyck, rare bronzes including works by Susini and Soldani and the famous Blenheim tapestries. Depicting scenes from the Duke's victorious campaigns, these Brussels tapestries hang in the State Apartments. The Banqueting Hall has walls and ceilings painted by Louis Laguerre which show the Duke riding the heavens in a chariot.

Of outstanding beauty is the Long Library containing 10,000 volumes, with lovely views over the gardens to the lake. By contrast the room in which Sir Winston Churchill was born is refreshingly simple. Four other rooms are devoted to an exhibition of Churchill memorabilia.

Blenheim's gardens are renowned for their beauty and range from the formal Water Terraces and Italian Garden to the natural charm of the Arboretum Pleasure Grounds and Cascade. The 2,000 acres of Parkland were landscaped by 'Capability' Brown in 1784. He created two beautiful lakes by damming the River Glyme and planted great avenues of trees which stretch for two miles beyond the Palace. Below the house Vanbrugh's Bridge crosses the lake. The 9th Duke employed Duchene who designed the Italian Garden with the Waldo Storey Fountain and created the Water Terraces with the river-god fountain by Bernini. The Temple of Diana by William Chambers was the romantic spot chosen by Winston Churchill to set the scene when he proposed to Clementine Hozier.

The Palace is eminently suitable for a wide range of functions from conferences to concerts, exhibitions to equestrian events.

STONOR

Stonor is hidden by encircling beechwoods in a fold of the Chilterns five miles from the Thames at Henley, with commanding views of the surrounding park. Fallow deer, never far from sight, have grazed these slopes since medieval times when fragrant, thyme-flavoured, Stonor venison was much prized at Court.

The house, an extended Tudor E-shape, has a facade of honey-coloured brick which unites the underlying framework of much older buildings. On the south-east corner is the 14th century chapel of flint and stone with a brick tower. The atmosphere is at once unpretentious and yet grand, remote and private, due as much to family history as to geographical considerations. The Stonor family has lived here for eight hundred years and prospered from sheep and the wool trade for the first four hundred, during which time the house was rebuilt and improved.

Then came the Reformation. The Stonors held firmly to the old religion and refused to take the Oath Supremacy. The chapel is one of only three in England where Mass has been celebrated without a break. Stonors were imprisoned and penalised for their beliefs, their lands were confiscated, they paid enormous fines, were deprived of public office and were forced to send their children abroad for a Catholic education. Stonor became a great centre for Catholic policy and the library contains one of the most important private collections of Catholic books; many were secretly printed in the house by Edmund Campion in a secret room in the roof around 1581. Over a period of more than 150 years life at Stonor was focused inwards for the safety of the family and the priests to whom a refuge was never denied. Little was done to the house during these dark days. As the religious climate slowly began to change, so did Stonor, and in the 18th century the Gothicization of the interior had begun. After the Catholic Emancipation Act of 1829 the family once more held office and in 1838 Thomas Stonor ('Old Tom') was granted the ancient Barony of Camoys by Queen Victoria. He served for 32 years as Lord-in-Waiting to the Queen and co-founded Henley Royal Regatta.

The house contains many items of rare furniture, paintings, drawings, tapestries and sculptures from Britain, Europe and America. In the Main Hall there is a rare Tudor banqueting table and the Drawing Room contains family portraits by the Court painter, Sir Godfrey Kneller.

The most remarkable feature of the Dining Room is the 1816 wallpaper by Defours which gives the impression of a leisurely cruise down the River Seine, passing all the important landmarks of Paris along the way. The set of four 18th century American wall sconces are very rare.

The Study has some excellent Italian Drawings by Carracci, Tiepolos and Tintoretto and two magnificent Venetian globes complete with stands which is unusual.

The Gothic bridge and a flight of steeply narrow steps lead to The Edmund Campion room tucked away in the gable over the main door. Here the secret printing of books went on hidden in the space behind the chimney. Campion was captured near Wantage and executed in 1581 and a raid on Stonor resulted in the arrest of John Stonor and his mother and the confiscation of the printing press.

The Park still retains the 18th century planting and layout and the peaceful hillside garden is still enclosed in its old walls. Today Stonor appears largely as it has done since 1760.

LE MANOIR AUX QUAT'SAISONS

Le Manoir aux Quat'Saisons is situated in 27 acres of gardens and parkland in the Oxfordshire village of Great Milton. Easily accessible from London or Birmingham via the M40 motorway, this internationally acclaimed country house hotel and restaurant is one of only nine establishments in the World to be awarded the Relais & Chateaux Gold and Red shields. This is their highest classification and confirms the overall standard of excellence and hospitality at this magnificent 15th century Cotswold manor house.

There are nineteen elegant bedrooms at Le Manoir aux Quat'Saisons. Each one has been individually designed and captures the atmosphere of warmth and friendliness by the use of beautiful fabrics and antique furnishings. Many of the luxurious bathrooms feature whirlpool baths or steam showers. In the converted stable block, most of the bedrooms have a private terrace overlooking the gardens and orchard. Even the medieval dovecote has been transformed into a romantic suite.

Chef/Patron Raymond Blanc is one of the World's finest chefs

and Le Manoir is widely acknowledged as Britain's finest restaurant. The extensive vegetable and herb gardens in the grounds provide the kitchen with a great variety of produce. An extensive wine list, the work of Restaurant Director, Alain Desenclos, complements Raymond Blanc's cuisine.

Before or after your meal, a stroll through the gardens at Le Manoir is a delight. Colourful herbaceous borders line the paths, the water gardens and lake attract wildlife and, in the private swimming pool garden, residents can relax, sip a cool drink and soak up the sun. More energetic guests can enjoy a game of tennis.

Private lunch or dinner parties can be held in the Cromwell Room where up to 46 guests can enjoy the specially priced party menus created by Raymond Blanc.

Le Manoir aux Quat'Saisons - a unique combination of exceptional cuisine and comfort.

Le Manoir aux Quat'Saisons
Great Milton
Oxford
OX9 7PD
Tel: (0844) 278881
Fax: (0844) 278847

THE THAMES & CHILTERNS

The Thames meanders its way through a number of Britain's busiest counties. Here, despite the inevitable overspill from London, there are still many unspoilt villages and market towns.

Bedfordshire's history is closely entwined with witchcraft but despite a 'black' past it remains an area of great beauty. Woburn Abbey is the jewel in the crown and in the work of John Bunyan's Pilgrims Progress we are constantly reminded of Bedfordshire's pleasant countryside. Today, the Tudor buildings are pubs and inns, all extending a very warm welcome.

The Vale of Aylesbury is also full of England's heritage and here, a number of splendid houses are open to the public whilst others have been converted into hotels of character.

The country lanes of South Buckinghamshire weave a tapestry through beechwoods and rolling hills and the Ichnield Way threads its way through the county. Florence Nightingale and Benjamin Disraeli are just two of the famous folk who hail from Buckinghamshire and their love of the county is shared by many who have settled here.

Berkshire is rich with royal history. Windsor Castle lies to the east of the county and to the west the rolling downs tumble into the towns of Lambourn, Newbury and Hungerford. The Thames is an ever present companion and provides the perfect setting for many pubs and inns who make the most of their riverside locations. The area has some of the country's most luxurious hotels - their palatial elegance makes for both a memorable and sometimes costly stay!

Hertfordshire boasts a number of Roman sites dotted around the countryside. The Grand Union Canal, linking London to the Midlands, runs through some glorious countryside - a surprise to many. Unfortunately, there are few hotels of excellence in Hertfordshire but there are all manner of smaller establishments which are good.

Oxfordshire certainly has its fair share of hotels. Although the University town itself cannot boast of too many such establishments, it is packed full of fascinating buildings and a living history that must be experienced. Again, this is a county of rolling countryside dotted with many pretty villages and much that is the epitomy of England. Amongst other attractions, Blenheim Palace should be near the top of the list of historical places to visit.

Despite their proximity to the capital, these counties have remained largely unspoiled and it is their very location which has contributed to their rich and varied history.

HOTELS OF DISTINCTION

BAY TREE HOTEL, Burford, Oxfordshire. Tel: (099382) 2791
A cleverly refurbished Tudor hotel with oak panelled rooms, huge stone fireplaces and a galleried staircase. The Bay Tree has a relaxed atmosphere whilst offering every modern facility.

THE BEAR, Woodstock, Oxfordshire. Tel: (0993) 81151
This old stone country inn in the centre of Woodstock is full of character. Blackened beams, log fires and antique furniture are everywhere and there are some fabulous four-posters in the comfortable bedrooms.

BEAR AT HUNGERFORD, Hungerford, Berkshire. Tel: (0488) 682512
The Bear is one of England's most historic inns, dating back and indeed owned by Henry Vlll. The comforts are modern however, in these most interesting of surroundings.

BEETLE & WEDGE, Moulsford on Thames, Oxfordshire. Tel: (0491) 651381
A beautifully renovated building providing comfortable accommodation on the banks of the Thames. Outbuildings are also used effectively as a public bar. The public rooms are imaginatively furnished and the setting is superb.

THE BELL, Charlbury, Oxfordshire. Tel: (0608) 810278
Cotswold stone which has mellowed over the centuries to give a lovely warm colour, is the hallmark of this old inn. Warm inside too and extremely carefully run, giving access to beautiful countryside and frequented by Oxford College graduates and undergraduates.

BELL INN, Aston Clinton, Buckinghamshire. Tel: (0296) 630252
A famous inn, renowned in the lovely Buckinghamshire countryside for its service and food. Elegant with antiques and great thoughtfulness for the traveller.

BELL INN, Woburn, Bedfordshire. Tel: (0525) 290280
A mixture of architectural styles add to the charm of this old coaching inn. The bar and restaurant are heavily beamed and very cosy, whilst the reception area and many bedrooms are located in the Georgian part. There are some rooms in the older part which are very interesting.

CLIVEDEN, Taplow, Berkshire. Tel: (06286) 68561
The former home of the Astors is set in 350 acres of beautiful gardens and parkland and is surrounded by history. The rooms are both opulent and elegant, full of interesting antique furniture.

CROWN & CUSHION, Chipping Norton, Oxfordshire. Tel: (0608) 642533
15th century inn, smartened up and now with spacious bedrooms, and some positively splendid bathrooms. Cosy feel and a snooker table is available.

DANESFIELD HOUSE, Marlow, Buckinghamshire. Tel: (0628) 891010
A stunning Victorian Gothic hotel in 65 acres of grounds overlooking the Thames. The hotel offer numerous sporting facilities and an exceptional cuisine. It is only a short drive from the Chilterns.

THE THAMES & CHILTERNS

DUNDAS ARMS, Kintbury, Berkshire. Tel: (0488) 58263
Flanked by the Kennett and Avon canal, as well as a wild colony of ducks, this solid 18th century inn has a few rooms available in a pleasantly converted stable block.

FEATHERS, Woodstock, Oxfordshire. Tel: (0993) 812291
Parts of the hotel date back to the 17th century and the building has been tastefully restored and elegantly furnished with interesting antiques. Panelled rooms, huge open fireplaces and flagstone floors all add to the 'old world' charm whilst outside there is an attractive cobbled courtyard used by guests during the summer months.

FLITWICK MANOR, Flitwick, Bedfordshire. Tel: (0525) 712242
A delightful 17th century manor house in 50 acres of parkland with an ironstone church, grotto and lake. The manor houses a collection of silver and pewter dish covers and antiques. Well positioned for Oxford, Cambridge and Woburn.

FOLEY LODGE HOUSE, Stockcross, Berkshire. Tel: (0635) 528770
This former Victorian hunting lodge has been converted into a luxury country house hotel with all modern facilities. Oxford, Newbury Racecourse and Highclere Castle are all nearby.

GOLDEN PHEASANT HOTEL, Burford, Oxfordshire. Tel:(099382) 3223
A charming historic Cotswold hotel with an enclosed courtyard garden. The hotel offers excellent cuisine and a special old-world atmosphere. Ideally located for Blenheim, Oxford and the Burford Wildlife Park.

GREEN END PARK HOTEL, Dane End, Hertfordshire. Tel: (0920) 438344
The decoration in this 18th century manor house is elaborate to say the least, with gilt and crystal chandeliers, luxurious drapes and Dutch blinds covering tall windows. All set in eight acres of splendid grounds.

HANBURY MANOR, Thurbridge, Nr Ware, Hertfordshire. Tel: (0920) 487722
From beamed ceilings and oak panelling to fascinating tapestries this hotel is nothing less than impressive, and with its huge range of facilities caters for nothing less than the civilised aesthetic.

HARTWELL HOUSE, Aylesbury, Buckinghamshire. Tel: (0296) 747444
This beautiful 13th century house has been sympathetically restored and stands in 80 acres of gardens landscaped by a pupil of Capability Brown. Ideally located for Blenheim Palace, Woburn Abbey and Waddesdon Manor.

HATTON COURT, Milton Keynes, Buckinghamshire. Tel: (0908) 510044
A splendid Victorian house skilfully restored yet retaining many fine architectural features such as the oak panelled dining room. Well situated for visiting Woburn Abbey and Silverstone.

LE MANOIR AUX QUAT'SAISONS, Great Milton, Oxfordshire. Tel: (0844) 27881
The history of this outstanding manor dates back 750 years. Set in 27 acres of beautiful landscaped gardens and woodland it is just a short drive away from Oxford, Woodstock and Blenheim Palace.

MANSION HOUSE AT GRIM'S DYKE, Harrow Weald, Middlesex. Tel: 081 954 4560
Once the home of W. S. Gilbert (of Gilbert and Sullivan fame), this tastefully maintained hotel has a particularly cosy library bar, decorated with prints of opera costumes.

MILL HOUSE HOTEL, Kingham, Oxfordshire. Tel: (060 871) 8188
This lovingly restored old mill possesses a warm cosy atmosphere, which the local stone, exposed beams and open atmosphere of the public rooms do much to enhance.

MILL HOUSE HOTEL, Kingham. Tel: (0608) 658188
A delightful former mill set in 7 acres of gardens bordered by a trout stream. The cuisine is of a very high standard. This is an ideal base for touring Blenheim Palace, Stratford-upon-Avon and the Cotswolds.

MONKEY ISLAND HOTEL, Bray-on-Thames, Berkshire. Tel: (0628) 23400
Set on an island in the Thames this hotel is steeped in history. It offers comfortable accommodation and imaginative cuisine and is an ideal base for touring Royal Windsor, Eton College, Henley and London.

MOORE PLACE, Milton Keynes, Buckinghamshire. Tel: (0908) 282000
An elegant Georgian mansion with a locally acclaimed restaurant, Moore Place offers mainly facilities and is an ideal base for visiting Woburn Abbey, Whipsnade Zoo and Dunstable Downs.

OAKLEY COURT, Windsor, Berkshire. Tel: (0628) 7414
In 35 acres of gardens sloping down to the Thames the architectural grandeur of this hotel is quite breathtaking. Built in 1859 it holds exclusive fishing rights to the famous river.

OLD SWAN, Minster Lovell, Oxfordshire. Tel: (0993) 775614
A stunning, half-timbered Cotswold inn surrounded by beautiful countryside. The building dates back from the 15th century and the interior still has many original features, including large open fires.

PARIS HOUSE, Woburn, Bedfordshire. Tel: (0525) 290692
Set in Woburn Park, this lovely old house has been converted to an equally excellent restaurant. The food is mainly French, but is highly imaginative and the house specialities are recommended. The wine list is excellent.

PINK GERANIUM, Melbourn, Hertfordshire. Tel: (0763) 60215
A pretty 16th century thatched cottage houses this superb restaurant. The intimate atmosphere is an added attraction and the food first class, complemented by an excellent wine list.

THE ROYAL BERKSHIRE

One of the most beautiful hotels in the country. The Royal Berkshire combines traditional elegance with superb facilities and personal service.

Once the home of the Churchill Family for over 100 years, this handsome Queen Anne mansion (built in 1705) is set in 15 acres of glorious gardens and woodlands, and positioned between Ascot Racecourse and the Polo Club.

This deluxe hotel proudly boasts 82 individual bedrooms and a whole host of individual extras.

Leisure facilities abound in the gardens and surrounding areas, with an indoor pool, saunas and squash complex.

The Royal Berkshire has rapidly established a high reputation for its cuisine and Stateroom Restaurant. Chef Andrew Richardson produces a range of epicurean and contemporary dishes that add a new dimension to the enjoyment of food.

Fresh seasonal ingredients from local markets and suppliers ensure natural flavours – freshness and creativity whatever you choose.

You are assured of a very special welcome at The Royal Berkshire.

The Royal Berkshire
Operated by Hilton International
London Road
Sunninghill
Ascot
Berkshire SL5 0PP

Tel: (0344) 23322
Fax: (0344) 27100

OAKLEY COURT

Just three miles from Royal Windsor, set amongst thirty five acres of beautifully landscaped gardens sloping gently down to the banks of the River Thames, stands Oakley Court.

Built in 1859, this turreted Victorian Gothic Mansion has been refurbished with an elegance which compliments the original building perfectly.

The ambience is reminiscent of an English Country House at its very best. The service is that which you would expect from a hotel of such distinction. The welcome is warm and the service friendly but discreet.

There are 92 bedrooms including 11 suites, five of which have four posters. The rooms are beautifully furnished and include all modern amenities to make your stay totally relaxing. The library, bar and dining room are rich with Oak panelling and have open log fires during the winter months, creating a warm welcome for guests. The hotel, also has its own punts, 9 hole par 3 golf course, croquet lawn, billiards room and fishing rights. During the Summer, champagne boat trips are a common occurrence.

The Oakleaf Restaurant is known for miles around and offers a table d'hote lunch and dinner and a six course Gourmet Menu as well as an a la carte menu. During the summer, light lunches and afternoon tea are served on the terrace overlooking the river.

The tranquillity of Oakley Court contrasts the excitement which surrounds it, nearby are the historic sights of Windsor and Eton and of course Windsor Safari Park, with its large collection of big cats and other animals from the African plains, is only a short drive away.

London, with all its sights and theatres, is 40 minutes away. Major sporting centres such as Wentworth or Sunningdale for golf; Ascot, Windsor and Newbury for horseracing; Henley for boating and Twickenham for rugby, are all at close hand.

Oakley Court
Windsor Road
Water Oakley
Windsor
Berkshire
SL4 5UR
Tel: (0628) 74141
Fax: (0628) 37011

WESTBURY FARM VINEYARD

Westbury Vineyard was started in 1968 as an additional farm enterprise when it was realised that not only had the vine been grown successfully in England since Roman times, but that the Thames Valley had always been famous for growing the best wines.

Only a mile away from us, at Tidmarsh, there was a well-known vineyard, which had its origins in Roman times and continued until the Middle Ages. The Abbots of Reading had extensive vineyards in the district, which were as well known as those of the King at Windsor.

The Westbury Vineyard is now over 16 acres which is one of the largest established vineyards in the country.

All vines are grown on the Geneva double curtain system. This method of training was devised by Professional Shaulis of Cornell University, New York State. It is the first advance to be made in the science and art of training and pruning the vine for over a century, requiring less labour, increasing the yield and, most importantly, improving the quality of the wine.

The vineyard is gravel over chalk on the banks of the Thames. Our maritime climate gives the wines a particular freshness and fruitiness that overseas growers find remarkable.

We have many varieties of grape, carefully chosen from the best in Europe, producing a wide range of white wines, and a fine Rosé.

Our red wine was the first commercially made in England since 1914 and is made mainly from the Pinot Noir grape, a classic variety used in the production of Burgundy.

Our Westbury sparkling champagne is produced by the Methode 'Champenoise', using the traditional grape varieties, Pinot Noir, Pinot Meunier and Chardonnay.

People are welcome to pay a visit at any time for a casual walk around the vineyard. For groups of 25 or more a talk on viticulture and wine appreciation can be arranged, followed by a simple but excellent 'vineyard meal'.

Westbury Farm Vineyard
Westbury Lane
Purley-On-Thames
Reading
Berkshire RG8 8DL
Tel: (0734) 843123

THE THAMES & CHILTERNS

PLOUGH AT CLANFIELD, Clanfield, Oxfordshire. Tel: (0306781) 222
Set in the village centre this intimately small hotel is comfortable, pretty and delightfully 16th century.

RANDOLPH HOTEL, Oxford, Oxfordshire. Tel: (0865) 247481
This is a recently restored Victorian hotel which is spacious and comfortably furnished. There are good sized bedrooms with en suite bath or shower rooms. There is a coffee shop below and above, a more formal restaurant.

ROYAL OAK, Yattendon, Berkshire. Tel: (0635) 201325
A delightful, 16th century inn in the village of Yattendon, the Royal Oak has well appointed and comfortable bedrooms offering excellent accommodation. The restaurant offers imaginative cuisine in intimate surroundings and there is also a popular bar, offering good pub food.

SHILLINGFORD BRIDGE, Wallingford, Oxfordshire. Tel: (0491) 36665
This hotel makes the most of its superb setting on the River Thames in Oxfordshire. All rooms are well furnished and comfortable, with a traditional English feel.

SOPWELL HOUSE, St Albans, Hertfordshire. Tel: (0727) 864477
Close to Woburn Abbey and Hatfield House this elegant Georgian Manor House was once the house of the Mountbattens. It settles in 12 acres of private grounds overlooking the beautiful Hertfordshire countryside.

SPRINGS HOTEL, North Stoke, Oxfordshire. Tel: (0491) 36687
Swans, wild ducks and kingfishers inhabit the lake beneath the restaurant and the hotel itself commands 30 acres of gardens right in the heart of the breathtaking and historic Thames Valley.

ST MICHAEL'S MANOR HOTEL, St Albans, Hertfordshire. Tel: (0727) 864444
Set in 5 acres of beautiful grounds, at the heart of Roman Verulamium this 16th century manor house boasts an Elizabethan plastered ceiling with fleur-de-lys and floral bosses as part of the original Tudor structure.

STUDLEY PRIORY, Horton-cum-Studley, Oxfordshire. Tel: (086735) 203/254
This beautifully preserved Elizabethan Priory rests on 13 acres which offer breathtaking views of the surrounding countryside. Broughton Castle, Blenheim Palace, Waddesdon and Milton Manors are just some of the fascinating sights nearby.

UPPER REACHES HOTEL, Abingdon, Oxfordshire. Tel: (0235) 22311
This excellent hotel was built on the site of an old corn mill and the restored waterwheel provides an attractive backdrop. Bedrooms are furnished to a high standard and many afford splendid views of the Thames.

The Mill House

MOORE PLACE

When Francis Moore built his elegant Georgian mansion in the tranquil Bedfordshire village of Aspley Guise in 1786 he could never have imagined it would be such a focal point for hospitality 200 years later. Thoughtfully renovated and extended, the original house now has a Victorian style conservatory restaurant, and a collection of new bedrooms which create a courtyard effect, featuring a rock garden and water cascade. The hotel's attractive day rooms – including an airy, glass roofed reception and relaxing bar-lounge – are decorated and furnished in handsome period style.

The 54 prettily decorated bedrooms all have ensuite bathrooms, direct dial telephone, colour television, tea and coffee making facilities and hairdryer.

There are 3 private function rooms in this charming Georgian house, where banquets and conferences are well provided for. The rooms are traditionally decorated, yet equipped with full audio-visual facilities.

The highly acclaimed restaurant is an outstanding success. Accomplished cooking in the modern mode can be enjoyed in the beautiful, picture windowed restaurant. Excellent cuisine is complemented by a good selection of fine wines. Moore Place is surrounded by interesting places to visit, such as the Duke of Bedford's Woburn Abbey, Dunstable Downs and Whipsnade Zoo. Woburn golf course is also nearby.

Moore Place,
Aspley Guise,
Nr Woburn, Beds MK17 8DW
Tel: (0908) 282000
Fax: (0908) 281888

THE THAMES & CHILTERNS

THE WARRENER, Warren Row, Berkshire. Tel: (062882) 2803

This delightful restaurant is found in a pair of pink and white country cottages. The food here is quite superb and the set menu offers imaginative six course meals. The wine list is good. There are five bedrooms, each with its own individual character.

WEST LODGE PARK, Hadley Wood, Hertfordshire. Tel: (081) 440 8311

This family run hotel stands in 34 acres of Green Belt, 12 miles from central London. Filled with antiques and old masters the hotel offers every modern comfort and convenience.

WESTON MANOR, West on the Green, Oxfordshire.

This 14th century manor house, once a monastery, is now a charming hotel. The imposing entrance hall has stone floors and carved oak furniture. There is a unique oak-panelled restaurant with minstrels' gallery. The bedrooms are very comfortable, with their unique character offering period charm.

WHATELY HALL, Banbury, Oxfordshire. Tel: (0295) 263451

Fine ecclesiastical architecture and restrained decoration still reflect the original 17th century vicar, William Whateley. Opposite Banbury Cross of nursery rhyme fame.

WOODLANDS MANOR, Clapham, Bedfordshire. Tel: (0234) 363281

A Victorian manor house set in well tended grounds and woodlands provides great comfort and relaxation. It is ideally located for Bedford, Woburn Abbey, the RSPB at Sandy and the Shuttleworth collection of aeroplanes.

WYONTON HOUSE HOTEL, Wyonton St Mary, Oxfordshire.

Beautifully restored to link three 17th century village houses, a clocktower wing and conservatory lounge, this delightful hotel is built of local honeyed stone.

YE OLDE BELL HOTEL, Hurley, Berkshire. Tel: (062 882) 5881

Originally a guest house to a Benedictine monastery, built around 1135. The fascinating architecture begins with the Norman archway leading to the heavily beamed bar. Overall it provides comfortable and charming accommodation.

ACCOMMODATION OF MERIT

THE COTTAGE, Birchanger, Hertfordshire. Tel: (0279) 812349

Delightful 17th century listed house with oak-panelled rooms and romantic conservatory dining room overlooking beautiful gardens. The quiet village of Birchanger is convenient for Cambridge, London and East Anglia.

Rushmere Manor

THE THAMES & CHILTERNS

DRAKES BARN, Woodrow, Buckinghamshire. Tel: (0494) 722366
Made up of two 17th century listed barns grouped around a courtyard, this property has an incredible view over the Chilterns. Set in 3 acres, this atmospheric home is close to Milton's cottage, Cambridge, London and Windsor.

GROVE FARM, Grove, Bedfordshire. Tel: (0525) 372225
Built in 1890, and set in two and a half acres of gardens, this farmhouse looks out over 30 acres of paddocks with thoroughbred horses grazing. With its heated pool, this house is perfect for visiting Dunstaple, Downs, Woburn, Whipsnade, Windsor and more.

THE MILL HOUSE, Olney, Buckinghamshire. Tel: (0234) 711381
An elegant Georgian mill house on the River Ouse, once owned by Henry VIII. The historic market town of Olney was home to the poet William Cowper and to the vicar who composed 'Amazing Grace'. Ideally situated for exploring Oxford, Cambridge and Stratford. (See photograph).

THE OLD RECTORY, Middle Claydon, Buckinghamshire. Tel: (0296) 730557
Set in beautiful grounds, this classical Georgian house, with its peaceful library retreat, is an excellent base from which to explore many historical sites in Aylesbury, the Chilterns and the Downs.

RUSHMERE MANOR, Leighton Buzzard, Bedfordshire. Tel: (052523) 336
Attractive private George I house, located opposite the wooded Rushmere Park estate and furnished in keeping with its period. People are welcome to stay by prior arrangement and explore Woburn Abbey, Luton Hoo and many other fascinating sites. (See photograph).

ST MARY'S HOUSE, Kintbury, Berkshire. Tel: (0488) 58551
An unusual converted Victorian schoolhouse originally built in 1853. This comfortable house is situated next to the parish church, close to the River Kennet, and within easy reach of fascinating historical sites in Bath, Oxford, Salisbury and Stonehenge.

SWALCLIFFE MANOR, Swalcliffe, Oxfordshire. Tel: (029578) 348
The oldest Oxfordshire stone manor house, built in 1200s and set beside the church. Architecturally fascinating with its rare mediaeval undercroft, Tudor Great Hall and Georgian drawing room. Lovingly tended Cotswold gardens provide a peaceful retreat after touring Stratford and Oxford. (See photograph).

VENUS HILL FARM, Venus Hill, Hertfordshire. Tel: (0442) 833396
A beautiful example of a black and white 300 year old farmhouse. It is set in two acres of pretty gardens, nestling amongst open farmland. The outdoor heated pool provides wonderful relaxation at the end of a long day exploring the surrounding country.

Swalcliffe Manor (The Undercroft)

THEO FOSSEL - STICKMAKER

Theo Fossel studied forestry and has always been deeply interested in the countryside. From boyhood he has whittled sticks from hedgerows and has found his life gradually taken over by his hobby.

This led to running his own company specialising in the supply of all forms of sticks and also components to other stickmakers. During the winter months, when not actually out cutting or making sticks, he organises regular training classes all over Britain and the U.S.A., has appeared several times on TV and on Radio, and in 1984 became founding Chairman of the British Stickmakers Guild. The Guild has achieved 1000 members from all over the world.

Theo now has two offices in the United States, one in Shreveport, Louisiana, handling his book and video; and another in Alexandria, Virginia, to distribute his range of components, tools and other aids to cane carving.

In 1988 The International Stick Society was formed as an information exchange for collectors and Theo was elected its first President. He has also contributed a number of articles on the subject to various magazines. In 1986 he wrote and published his own book on the making of sticks, which continues to be a best seller and is now a standard work of reference. A sixty minute video on stickmaking and carving is now also available.

In 1990 he was commissioned to produce a very special stick for presentation to the Queen Mother on the occasion of her 90th birthday.

For further details please write: (Callers by appointment)

Theo Fossel
119 Station Road
Beaconsfield
Bucks HP9 1LG
Tel/Fax: (0494) 672349

U.S.A. addresses:
Books, Videos & General Enquiries
P.O. Box 5775
Shreveport
LA 71135-5775

Components & Stickmaking Materials
P.O. Box 6894
Alexandria
VA 22306-0894

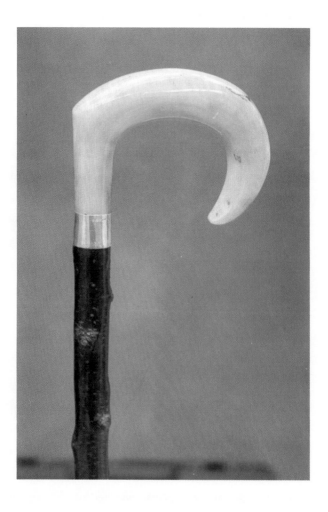

THE THAMES & CHILTERNS

INNS OF CHARACTER

BARLEY MOW, Clifton Hampden.
Ships' timbers, low beams, oak settles and old engravings characterize this quaint deep thatched 13th century inn. The favour it found with Jerome K Jerome has not changed today. Traditional bar food and good ales complement this characterful pub.

THE BLUE BOAR, Chieveley, Berkshire.
In 1644 this thatched inn served as a resting place for Cromwell on the eve of the Battle of Newbury. Today little has changed amid the rambling rooms with their old-fashioned style. Fine ales and many whiskies complement the traditional food here.

THE BULL, Stanford Dingley, Berkshire.
Excellent food and fine ales can be enjoyed at this attractive 18th century red brick country pub. The atmosphere is relaxed and friendly, the interior is red quarry tiled with heavy black beams and there are many charming old-fashioned furnishings.

THE COCK, Broom, Bedfordshire.
Attractively situated overlooking the village green, this lovely little pub combines rustic simplicity with outstanding management. This popular pub is a definite 'must', not only for its beautiful setting and old-fashioned atmosphere, but also for its well-priced bar food and well kept ales.

KING'S ARMS, Amersham, Buckinghamshire.
A mellow atmosphere prevails within the original alcoves, beams and oak flooring of this handsome rambling Tudor inn. Decent food and ales make this pub well worth a visit.

LIONS OF BLEDLOW, Bledlow, Buckinghamshire.
Heavy low beams abound in this 16th century pub set on the village green. The atmosphere here is very relaxed. A good selection of food and ales can be enjoyed at this genuinely friendly inn.

THE ROYAL STANDARD OF ENGLAND, Forty Green, Buckinghamshire.
One of England's oldest at over 900 years, this characterful inn is dominated by blackened oak beams, finely carved panelling and stained glass. The rambling rooms once hid Charles II during his flight from the Battle of Worcester and it remains popular today, with excellent food and ales.

WHITE HART, Fyfield, Oxfordshire.
This charming inn was originally built to house priests in about 1450. Huge stones and low ceilings are in keeping with its history, itself depicted on the wall. Excellent food and a wide range of fine ales may be enjoyed at this friendly village pub.

Foley Lodge

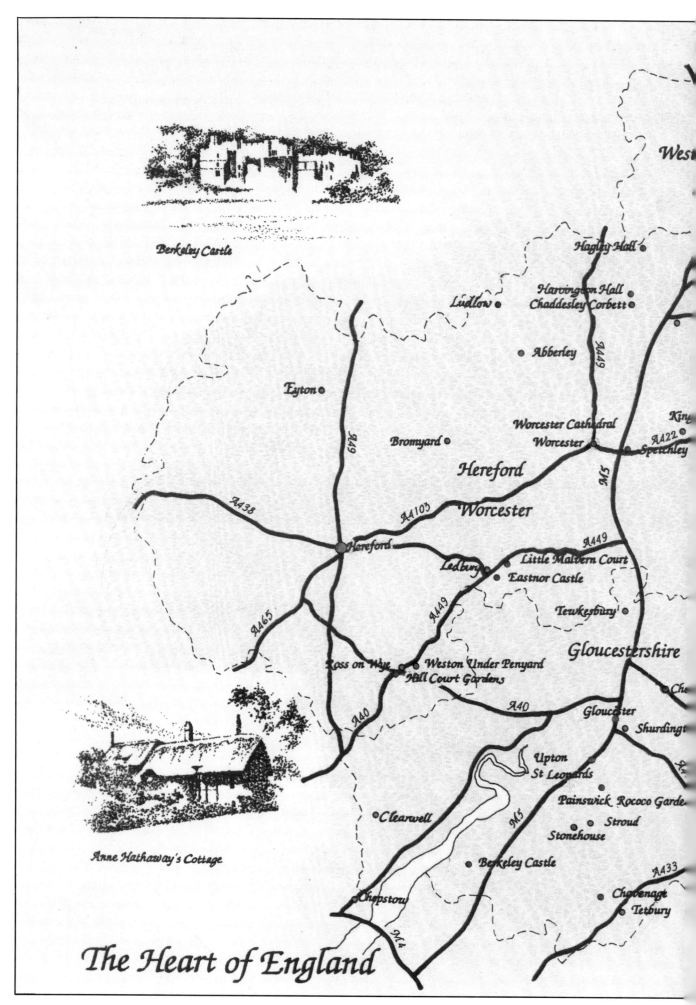

Berkeley Castle

West

Hagley Hall

Harvington Hall
Ludlow
Chaddesley Corbett

Abberley

A449

Eyton

Worcester Cathedral
Worcester

King

A22

Bromyard

Spetchley

Hereford

A438

A4103

Worcester

A465

A449

Hereford

A449

Little Malvern Court

Ledbury

Eastnor Castle

Tewkesbury

A449

Gloucestershire

Ross on Wye

Weston Under Penyard
Hill Court Gardens

A40

Gloucester

Ch

A40

Shurdingt

Upton
St Leonards

Clearwell

M5

Painswick Rococo Garde

Stroud

Stonehouse

Berkeley Castle

A433

Chepstow

Chavenage

M5

Tetbury

M4

Anne Hathaway's Cottage

The Heart of England

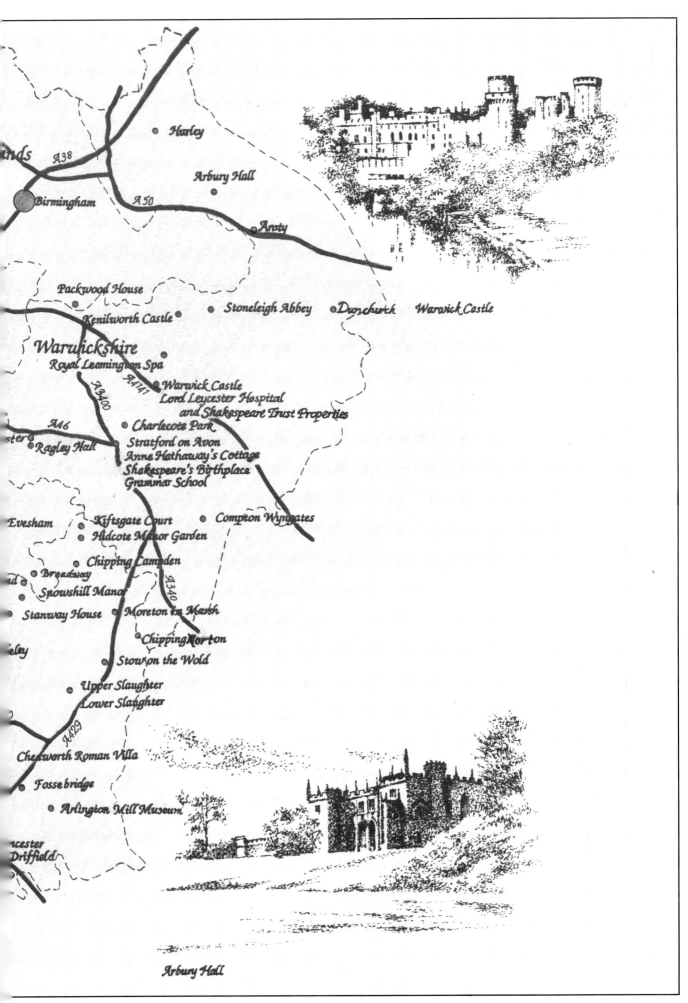

Hurley

Arbury Hall

A38

Birmingham

A50

Ansty

Packwood House

Stoneleigh Abbey • Dunchurch   Warwick Castle

Kenilworth Castle

Warwickshire

Royal Leamington Spa

A4141

A3400

Warwick Castle
Lord Leycester Hospital
and Shakespeare Trust Properties

A46

Charlecote Park

Ragley Hall

Stratford on Avon
Anne Hathaway's Cottage
Shakespeare's Birthplace
Grammar School

Evesham   Kiftsgate Court   • Compton Wynyates

Hidcote Manor Garden

Chipping Campden

Broadway

A340

Snowshill Manor

Stanway House   Moreton in Marsh

Chipping Norton

Stow on the Wold

Upper Slaughter

Lower Slaughter

A429

Chedworth Roman Villa

Fosse bridge

Arlington Mill Museum

ester
Driffield

Arbury Hall

155

THE HEART OF ENGLAND

THE COTSWOLDS

The Cotswold Hills extend from north of Bath to Tetbury to Cirencester, onto Burford through Stow on the Wold to Chipping Camden and to Cheltenham in the West. Famous for its stone which has been used in so many of the traditional buildings of the area, much of the land rises to 800 feet above sea level offering fine views of the surrounding landscape.

The City of Gloucester and the spa town of Cheltenham stand either side of the M5 motorway, part way between Bristol and Birmingham. Gloucester has been growing and developing for hundreds of years but recently major changes have been taking place especially in the docks area; where redundant Victorian warehouses have been refurbished and converted into offices, museums and leisure facilities for all to enjoy. Work on Gloucester Cathedral commenced in 1089, taking 30 years to complete; it was altered and extended in the 14th century. Edward II who was murdered in 1327 at nearby Berkeley Castle, is buried here and his ornate tomb as well as the east end were remodelled by London sculptors on instruction of his son, Edward III. A magnificent collection of Iron Age treasures and other items are to be found in the City Museum and Art Gallery.

George III and the Duke of Wellington popularised the medicinal effects of a well found in the 1700's in Cheltenham. Consequently there was Regency building on a magnificent scale, with fine buildings along the Promenade, around the Imperial Gardens and the Royal Crescent. Many of the original houses are now occupied as offices and in Montpellier Walk, shops, banks and restaurants dominate.

Elsewhere in the town, visit the composer Gustav Holst's birthplace which is now a museum displaying many of his original works; and the classical Pittville Pump Room which stands in its own magnificent setting. Built in the 1820's, there is a gallery overlooking a great hall, entered by an Ionic colonnade.

Leave Cheltenham on the B4632 north towards Winchcombe, where there are magnificent views to the Vale of Evesham and off to the east at Belas Knap, the remains of a Roman Villa.

Once the home of Queen Katherine Parr, **Sudeley Castle** near Winchcombe dates from the 12th century, although much refurbishment work was carried out in the 19th century (featured later).

Close by at Stanway, is **Stanway House**, built in the 7th century by the Tracys, a Norman family; the house has changed ownership only once since that time. Its Jacobean gatehouse, built in Cotswold limestone, is a masterpiece of local architecture, as is the 14th century tithe barn, said to be one of the finest in the country. Inside, family portraits hang on the walls and original furniture graces the splendid rooms, all of which are used daily by the owners. Of particular interest is the Great Parlour, the Great Hall and Audit Room, where estate tenants gather to pay their rent on the usual quarter days. Four acres of landscaped gardens and large grounds give spectacular views to the Malverns and Wales beyond. The grounds include the village cricket pitch, a fine pavilion designed by J.M. Barrie, who was a regular visitor.

The pretty Cotswold villages of Stanway and nearby Stanton with their beautiful cottages offer superb walks through hilly countryside and open farmland.

Nearby is **Snowshill Manor**, 3 miles south west of Broadway, a Tudor House dating from around 1700. No ordinary Cotswold manor house, it is full to the brim with Charles Wade's collection of craftmanship from all over the world. Wade himself lived in a cottage in the grounds and created the charming cottage garden. It has a fascinating collection of toys and dolls, clocks, musical instruments and samurai armour.

Further north beyond Chipping Camden off the B4081 is one of the most beautiful gardens in England, **Hidcote Manor Gardens**. The American horticulturalist Major Lawrence Johnston and his mother bought the manor house and 280 acres of farmland in 1905. For over seven years he toiled to transform 10 acres of the land into a magnificent profusion of colour, with formal compartments separated by walls and hedges - one of which is entirely red - and informal landscaped areas. Lawrence travelled to South Africa and China in the 1920/30's and many of the exotic and unusual shrubs and plants were brought back by him at this time. From the end of the long grass walks with their colourful herbaceous borders there are splendid views out over the rolling Cotswold countryside. A mile or two away is **Kiftsgate Court**, with its wonderful displays of old fashioned roses and unusual shrubs and plants.

Heading south by Bourton on the Hill, there is the impressive Norman Church of St Lawrence with its circular columns to the nave and a perpendicular font reminiscent of the times. The bustling market town of Stow on the Wold is an ideal spot for the visitor to take time off and browse around the antique shops and picture galleries.

At Chedworth, the **Church of St Andrew** is also of Norman origins, although the intricately detailed pulpit dates from the 15th century and the nave roof is even later.

Close by are **Chedworth Roman Villas**, 3 miles north west of Fossebridge, probably the best preserved Roman Villas in the country. Covered by silt until rediscovered in 1864, the beautiful mosaic floors to the dining room and communal baths show scenes of Bacchus and the four Seasons. Probably occupied from the 2nd century until the fall of the Roman Empire in the 5th century, this location close to the prosperous farming town of Cirencester is also near to the Fosse Way which runs between Exeter and the river Humber. Today the buildings may be entered and the treasures from the site viewed in the museum.

THE SEVERN ESTUARY/CIRENCESTER

The Severn Road Bridge and the Severn Rail Tunnel cross the Mouth of the Severn to link England and Wales. The Forest of Dean to the north provides good walking country through heathland and forest, whilst to the south, the Vale of Berkeley is fertile low lying land.

Built in traditional local stone, the **Court House** at Painswick is so called because Charles I used part of this manor house as a courtroom. Three miles north of Painswick on the A46 near Cranham is **Prinknash Abbey and Pottery**, situated in one of the beauty spots of England, with breathtaking views of the Vale of Gloucester. The Abbey was designed and built for a

Benedictine Monastic Community, who welcome visitors to the church and grounds. In 1928 the old house was made over to the Order by the 20th Earl of Rothes - the new monastery was completed in 1972. The Pottery stands in the grounds of the Abbey, where the guides conduct visitors on a tour of the Pottery factory - an ideal venue to obtain distinctive gifts.

Close by in this southern part of the Cotswolds lies **Haresfield Beacon**, an Iron Age fort with spectacular views across the Vale of Berkeley to the Severn and the Forest of Dean beyond.

Set in the Vale of Berkeley stands the 12th century **Berkeley Castle**, still the home of the famous family who gave their name to Berkeley Square in London. It was here that Edward II was murdered in 1327 (featured later).

Join the A4135 at Dursley towards Tetbury to visit **Chavenage House**, a magnificent Elizabethan house remodelled in 1576 by Edward Stephens. Stephens added the porch and wings to an earlier manor house, by using stonework from other buildings - one stone by the porch is said to be from the Horsley Priory altar. Currently the home of the Lowsley-Williams family, who were related to the Stephens by marriage, there are splendid collections of exquisite furniture, 17th century tapestries and pictures. Cromwell is said to have stayed here in the Main Hall and there are numerous treasures from this period. The early 19th century Chapel is set in fine gardens, with an earlier tower conceived as a folly.

Now take the A433 to the Roman city of Corinium Dobunnorum, now called **Cirencester**. The Corinium Museum displays mosaics and everyday Roman items found in the vicinity. The late 15th century additions to the Norman **Church of St John the Baptist** are considered to be a splendid example of Perpendicular tracery to the south porch and west tower.

The old 17th century flour mill at Arlington on the B4425 houses a museum of agricultural machinery and rural crafts.

HEREFORD AND WORCESTER

One of the most rural counties of England, Hereford and Worcester sits on the Welsh border and boasts some of the most fertile farming land in the country.

The old Saxon town of Hereford finally fell to the English in 1645, after one of numerous battles fought with the Welsh as a direct result of its border location.

Offa, the King of Mercia beheaded Ethelbert, the Christian King of East Anglia, who is buried in the salmon coloured stone Cathedral of St Mary and St Ethelbert the King. Although altered many times over the centuries, parts of the Cathedral date from the 11th century. Of particular interest is Richard of Haldingham's Mappa Mundi, which dates from around 1300, and is one of the most detailed in existence. Also the magnificent chained library where 1500 printed and handwritten books, some dating from before 1500, are chained together as they were originally to prevent them from being stolen.

The Museum and Art Gallery have some fine Roman relics from Kenchester (called Magna in Roman times) and The Old House, dating from 1621, is a superb example of a black and white Jacobean Timber house and now houses a museum.

The County Cricket Ground in ancient Worcester is one of the most picturesque in England, standing by the River Severn, overlooked by Worcester Cathedral and its 14th century tower. Much of the Cathedral dates from this time, although there has been a building here since 680. Inside, the Romanesque Crypt dates from the 11th century and the marble Tomb of King John dates from around 1216.

Originally a hospital, The Commandery, with its superb timber hall, is a fine Tudor house and well worth a visit, as is The Royal Worcester Porcelain Works and The Dyson Perrins Museum, where china from 1751 to the present day is on display.

THE MALVERN HILLS

Lying to the south of Worcester, the Malvern Hills stretch from west of the Victorian spa town of Great Malvern to the East of Ledbury. Famous for the Malvern Water, visitors can walk by St Anne's Well, on their way to the Worcestershire Beacon, standing 1400 feet above sea level overlooking the relatively flat surrounding land.

Off the B4228 at Hom Green, near Ross on Wye is **Hill Court Gardens** set in magnificent grounds of a fine William and Mary mansion, approached through an avenue of white limes. A walk in the 18th century ornamental gardens is particularly pleasing, as is the water garden, gazebo and display of roses. In association with the integral garden centre one of the compartmented walled gardens is set out to allow the visitor to select suitable shrubs and plants for their own garden.

Travelling north east on the A449 to Ledbury the A438 takes

Prinknash Pottery

THE HEART OF ENGLAND

the visitor to **Eastnor Castle**. The Castle, designed in 1812 by Sir Robert Smirke, with spectacular views over the Malvern Hills, is a fine example of the Norman and Gothic revival architecture of this period (featured later).

Close by off the A4104 near Great Malvern is **Little Malvern Court**. Although the main rooms were altered and added to by Hansom in Victorian times, the original building was built as a 12th century Benedictine Priory. Since the Dissolution to this day, it has been the family home of the Beringtons, whose family portraits and paintings hang on the walls. In addition there are some fine European paintings and furniture and a wonderful collection of 18th and 19th century needlework. There are splendid views to the Malvern Hills across the lake and lovely displays of old fashioned roses and spring bulbs in the former monastery grounds, now a 10 acre garden.

Take the A449/A422 towards Worcester then Stratford-upon-Avon to **Spetchley Park** standing over 20 acres of mature parkland with numerous ornamental trees and roaming Red and Fallow deer. The gardens are particularly beautiful in spring and early summer when the rare plants and exotic shrubs are at their most colourful.

MEDIEVAL WARWICK

Warwick Castle is one of Britains most beautiful castles dating from the 14th century. Built on the site of a Norman castle it has a commanding site of the River Avon (featured later).

Kenilworth is situated between Coventry and Warwick in an area known as the Heart of England. It is a charming area with lots of pretty half timbered houses dating from the fifteenth century. There are fascinating remains of an Augustinian Abbey in Abbey Fields and the magnificent Norman doorway of the mainly perpendicular parish church of St Nicholas.

Kenilworth Castle, however, is the town's greatest glory, made famous by Sir Walter Scott in Kenilworth, his historical novel of Elizabethan England. The castle was used as a setting for many of his books. Situated north west of the town it is referred to as the grand fortress ruin in England, because of its size. It was built on an original Saxon site by the Norman de Clinton family in the 12th century. In the fourteenth century John of Gaunt re-modelled the castle and from the seventeenth century onwards it fell into ruin. Although damaged by parliamentary forces during the civil war the massive keep with its walls over seventeen feet thick still stands.

After visiting Kenilworth, you can easily travel to Stoneleigh Abbey which is four miles east of Kenilworth. This Italian mansion, built around the remains of an abbey and completed in 1726 has been restored, following a fire. The splendid state rooms have all been immaculately refurbished and are well worth a visit. Stoneleigh is well known as the site of the Royal Agricultural Society of England's showground, venue for the 'Royal Show' each July and many other farming and country events.

Lord Leycester Hospital was founded in 1571 by Robert Dudley, Earl of Leicester, who was Elizabeth I's favourite. The buildings had been used as Guildhall, Council Chamber and Grammar School before this time. Robert Dudley arranged for their renovation and extension. They were then used by men wounded in the service of the Queen and her successors. To this day it has been the home of ex-servicemen.

Charlecote Park, 6 miles south of Warwick has been the home of the Lucy family from 1247. Sir Thomas Lucy completed the house in 1558. Set in the middle of a beautiful and extensive wooded deer park grazed by Fallow and Red Deer it is here that our great William Shakespeare was caught poaching! The house sums up Elizabethan England with its rose-coloured brickwork that turns gold in the sun. Elizabeth I spent two nights here in 1572. There are many lovely portraits and pieces of furniture to see. The house has been altered and is shown as it would have been a century ago, complete with Victorian kitchen and utensils. The breadhouse which was in operation until the 1890's can be seen in the outbuildings along with the washhouse and a coach which displays family carriages throughout the years. The park landscaped by 'Capability' Brown has a formal garden adorned with clipped yew and urns filled with colourful flowers either side of the steps which are a nineteenth century addition. All in all Charlecote is a wonderful place to see.

Also owned by the National Trust is **Packwood House** which is 2 miles east of Hockley Heath on the A34. This magnificent Tudor house is surrounded by gardens and parkland with panoramic views from the lakeside walk. It has a famous yew garden, which is thought to represent the Sermon on the Mount. The house itself contains a connoisseurs collection of fine textiles and tapestries, with wonderful panelling and furniture to reflect the spirit of the age.

Arbury Hall is set in large grounds with beautiful landscape gardens, the hall is built on the site of an Augustinian priory. It was here that the novelist George Eliot was born (featured later).

SHAKESPEARE'S AVON

Famous as William Shakespeare's birthplace, Stratford-Upon-Avon is a charming old market town with much to see. This medieval and Georgian town is now only second to London as a tourist attraction.

The country's first national theatre was built from a public fund in 1932. At night it looks stunning as the floodlights reflect on its riverside position, it is here that the world famous Royal Shakespeare company perform.

The house in Henley Street is Shakespeare's actual birthplace. Restored to the way it was it typifies middle class of its time. Upstairs you can visit the room in which the playwright was born. Scratches on the walls and ceiling, even the glass in the windows are from visitors such as Walter Scott, Robert Browning, Issac Walton and other literary figures. You can see treasures such as a sword and ring, his school desk, documents, portraits and many more.

Halls Croft was the home of an eminent doctor who married Shakespeare's older daughter Susanna. It is the most impressive medieval house in Stratford. The walled garden is beautiful and it is from here you see the house at its best. Shakespeare's direct line of descendants came to an end when Susanna's daughter Elizabeth died in 1670.

Nash's house, a lovely half timbered building, takes its name from Thomas Nash who was the husband of Shakespeare's

THE HEART OF ENGLAND

granddaughter Elizabeth Hall. It is now used as a museum telling Stratford's history since pre-historic times and gives an accurate record of England in Shakespeare's time.

The beautiful **Holy Trinity Church** stands in tranquil grounds besides the River Avon. There is a bust of Shakespeare in the channel set in a wall above his gravestone. He rests here with his wife on one side and his daughter Susanna on the other.

Ann Hathaway's cottage is situated two miles from the centre of Stratford in the village of Shottery. The Hathaway family lived here until 1892. Shakespeare married Ann Hathaway in 1582. This beautiful 15th century building looks like a typical English Cottage with a country garden, it is kept as in their day. In one of the bedrooms is an oak bed over 400 years old with fascinating carved heads at its head.

Ragley Hall is one of the earliest and loveliest of these great Palladian country houses in England. Home of the Marquess and Marchioness of Hooke it was designed in 1680 by Robert Hooke. Except for the elaborate portico added in 1780 by Wyatt the architecture remains unchanged. The state rooms are outstanding with beautiful furniture and porcelain and an important art collection. The magnificent hall has moulded 18th century plasterwork. Ragley Hall is set in 500 acres of parkland with extensive gardens and lakes. Children will enjoy an adventure wood and other amusements. The grounds were landscaped by Capability Brown.

The Heart of England is perhaps best known as the birthplace of English literatures' greatest playwright. There is nothing erronean in such an assumption but visitors should expect to be pleasantly surprised by a wealth of other attractions, all worthy of inspection and all a source of interest and pleasure.

Berkeley Castle

SUDELEY CASTLE

In the beauty of its Cotswold surroundings, and in its rather intimate scale for a castle, Sudeley has a special charm. It has seen magnificent times, when it was a favour in the gift of the Crown, and it has seen dire times when it lay pillaged, ruined and neglected.

Once the property of Ethelred the Unready, the castle was rebuilt by Boteler, created Baron Sudeley in 1441. Much of his work is seen today including St Mary's Church, the stately Banqueting Hall, now in ruins, the Tithe Barn, the Portmane Tower and the Dungeon Tower. During the Wars of the Roses the castle was sold to the Crown, and eventually given to Sir Thomas Seymour.

The year was 1547, the most momentous year in the history of Sudeley Castle, and the high point of its splendour. Brother to Henry VIII's third wife, Jane Seymour, Thomas was one of the most attractive men of his day. Immediately Henry died, Seymour turned his attention to the widowed Queen Katherine Parr, who had been his lover before she became Henry's sixth wife. Thomas and Katherine were married within weeks of the King's death, and he began to prepare Sudeley Castle for the Queen Dowager, and the enormous household she brought with her.

The following year Katherine died shortly after giving birth to a daughter, and the next year saw Thomas in the Tower as a result of his insatiable ambition, where he was beheaded in 1549. Sudeley Castle then passed to Lord Chandos in 1554 and under the 6th Lord Chandos became a Royalist headquarters during the Civil War. In the absense of Lord Chandos the Castle surrendered to the Roundheads in 1643. There followed terrible plundering of its contents and desecration of its church.

For two centuries the ruins of Sudeley lay neglected and left to the ravages of the weather and looters took whatever remained of its former glory. In 1810 the castle was bought by the Marquess of Buckingham and used as stables and a public house.

In 1837 the Victorian era brought rescue for Sudeley Castle in the shape of the the Dent brothers, John and William, who bought the estate and, with their cousin, set about its restoration. A major programme of work was undertaken, assisted by

a number of architects including the eminent Sir Gilbert Scott, whose main contribution was to the church. By 1840 a large part of the building was again habitable, although certain parts including the Banqueting Hall were left in a ruined but strengthened condition. It is to the Dent's credit that their restoration was so faithful to the original, and that they resisted any temptation to 'Victorianise'. Unfortunately all three Dents died within about a year of each other, but their nephew who inherited had married a remarkable lady, and it is to Emma Dent that Sudeley Castle owes the wealth of its treasures. On her death in 1900 the castle passed to her nephew and has remained in the same family ever since, restoration continuing periodically up until about 1930.

Sudeley boasts an impressive collection of the treasures of centuries, from fine furniture to arms and armaur; the Needlework Corridor filled with the work of many generations of industrious fingers; paintings including masterpieces by Van Dyck, Rubens and Turner. Perhaps the most celebrated of Sudeley's treasures is the historic painting of the Tudor Succession, an allegorical work by Hans Eworth.

Sudeley's magnificent gardens were laid out during the 19th century restoration and the formal Queen's Garden forms its centrepiece. Based on the original Tudor parterre, the remains of which were discovered by the Dents, it is substantially the same as it would have appeared to Katherine Parr. The terraces provide a delightful walk with fine views of the majestic old trees in the Home Park and the Cotswold Hills beyond.

The ruined Tithe Barn, covered by wisteria, stands beside the ornamental pond stocked with large carp. To the east is the Moat Pond where ornamental water fowl duck and dive. The principal feature of St Mary's Church, restored in 1863, is the marble tomb of Katherine Parr.

The Old Kitchen Restaurant serves delicious lunches and tempting cream teas, and is available for private functions such as wedding receptions. The castle shop shows the Sudeley Crafts Collection and stocks a wide range of lovely gifts including antiques (some from the attics at Sudeley itself!)

BERKELEY CASTLE

Berkeley Castle, that most romantic of castles overlooking the Severn and Welsh border, is an enchanted castle in spite of its massive solidity. In 1153 Lord Maurice Berkeley completed his fortress at the command of Henry II, and ever since it has been the home of the Berkeley family. For 839 years 24 generations have preserved this ancient castle and gradually transformed a savage Norman fortress into a stately home full of treasures including paintings by English and Dutch masters, tapestries, fine furniture, silver and porcelain.

From the Inner Courtyard a Norman doorway leads into the Keep and the room where the unfortunate King Edward II met his death in 1327. In one corner of the room is a deep hole like a well, twenty-eight feet deep, which is the Dungeon. It was the barbarious custom to throw the rotting carcasses of cattle down into this pit, when the stench of putrefaction would eventually asphyxiate the hapless prisoner in the room above. It appears that the King's robust constitution resisted the pestilential vapours and he was most brutally murdered in his bed by his jailers.

The magnificent Great Hall was built in the 14th century within the 12th century curtain wall on the site of the original hall c.1340. The walls are hung with a fine series of Oudenarde tapestries and the 16th century screen retains its original painted decoration. Here one can see a well-preserved example of a five-sided Berkeley Arch.

The Morning Room, once the Chapel, has a timbered roof painted with verses translated from the book of Revelation by John Trevisa, the Castle chaplain, and thought to be one of the earliest translations. There is a magnificent series of early Brussels tapestries.

The Long Drawing Room and the Small Drawing Room are elegantly furnished with gilt chairs and sofas, superb wall mirrors and another series of fine Brussels tapestries. The Dining Room houses part of the famous Berkeley collection of silver and its walls are hung with family portraits, many depicting Berkeley men resplendent in the distinctive yellow jackets of the Berkeley hunt.

The Castle is surrounded by terraced lawns bordered by low growing plants and specimen shrubs with climbing plants clinging to the Castle walls. The Bowling Alley is flanked by ancient yews once clipped into the shape of elephants, and below the Alley is a long pond across which waterlillies float. What appears to be an 18th century country house amongst the trees is the stable and kennels of the Hunt.

The best view of the Castle is from the meadows stretching away towards the Severn. Its massive 'pot-pourri' coloured walls, a mix of rose and lavender, take on different hues around sunset and the great Castle turns almost purple - a truly impressive sight.

EASTNOR CASTLE

Commanding glorious views of the Malvern Hills, dramatic Eastnor is a castle in the Medieval style, built in 1812 for Lord Somers. It was designed by Sir Robert Smirke to replace an old house which the Somers family had owned for 200 years and which was thought to be a little old fashioned and inconvenient. This was a period in England's history when trade and agriculture were booming and elegant new homes were springing up everywhere. It was the age of Wordsworth, Coleridge and Byron and the romantic feeling of the time is reflected in Smirke's design with its battlements, turrets and trefoil-shaped main towers.

It was also the time of the Napoleonic wars which caused large timbers to be in short supply. Smirke therefore decided to use cast iron stanchions instead of timber roof trusses, thought to be the first time a roof was constructed in this way. Other plans for the castle were on a lavish scale, although some were curtailed by the tragic death of the eldest son in action against the French in the Peninsular War.

In later years the 2nd Earl employed A.W.Pugin and George Fox to redecorate parts of Eastnor, whilst the 3rd Earl spent much time abroad where he collected beautiful pictures, furniture and tapestry to decorate his house. He seems to have had a strong affinity with Italy.

The Great Hall, redecorated by Fox in a design based on an altarcloth from Toulouse Cathedral, houses an impressive collection of arms and armour from Europe, India, Turkey, Africa and Persia. There are 33 three-quarter suits of armour which were probably worn by the bodyguard of an Italian prince, complete suits and a magnificent full equestrian suit, deeply etched and gilded. The two most important suits, in the Inner Hall, date from 1520 and were probably looted by Napoleon from Bavaria. A third French example of the 17th century bears its proof mark - a dent where a bullet was shot at it.

The Gothic Drawing Room was decorated by Pugin in 1849 and shows Victorian flamboyance at its most elaborate with fan tracery and gilding everywhere. Above the fireplace is the Somers family motto which Pugin appears not to have read - Be useful rather than conspicuous.

The Staircase Hall is dominated by five frescoes, painted by the famous Victorian artist George Watts, and rescued from the Somers' London house in Carlton Terrace. Eastnor also has a very fine collection of works by Van Dyck, Lely, Kneller, Reynolds, Romney, Angelica Kaufman and many others, lovely tapestries and needlework panels and an interesting series of photographs by Julia Cameron, the eminent Victorian photographer. The 500 acre deer park and huge lake provide Eastnor Castle with a wonderful setting. The arboretum has an outstanding number of mature specimen trees.

WARWICK

The first castle at Warwick was built by William I over 900 years ago in order to safeguard the Midlands while he turned his attention to the troublesome North. Since 1068 it has slowly developed from mighty stronghold to grand mansion.

The original motte and bailey castle was sited on a solid sandstone bluff overlooking the River Avon and was a timber construction, later replaced by stone. Parts of the octagonal keep still survive within the present framework of the castle. The major reconstruction at Warwick was begun in the 14th Century by Thomas de Beauchamp, a notable military commander and was eventually completed by his son, also Thomas. The dramatic changes which they brought about included two mighty towers - Caesar's Tower which dominates the river and Guy's Tower named after Thomas senior's father; 'The Black Cur of Arden' as he was known to his enemies. Between the towers they built the gatehouse and barbican and a curtain wall which made Warwick virtually impregnable.

In 1445 the title and estates passed by marriage to the renowned 'Kingmaker' Richard Neville during the Wars of the Roses. When he was killed in battle the title passed, again through the female line, to his son-in-law who was put to death in the Tower of London, a fate which also befell his son. The title then lapsed. Consequently, when Sir Fulke Greville came to Warwick in 1604, the castle was in a state of disrepair, a situation he set about to remedy at a cost of £20,000.

In 1621 the Grevilles acquired the title of Baron Brooke followed by Earl Brooke in the 18th Century and finally became Earls of Warwick in 1759. During this time, the castle became grander with the addition of state apartments and some fine new windows to give an altogether more imposing appearance.

The Great Hall is the largest room in the castle; 40 feet high and 62 feet long. Originally 14th Century, it was severely damaged by fire in 1871 but completely restored to its former state by Anthony Salvin in just four years. This is where Warwick Castle's peerless collection of arms and armour is shown to great effect; over 1,000 pieces which include the shield of Bonnie Prince Charlie and a set of child's armour made for the son of the Earl of Leicester.

The first of the great State Rooms, the Red Drawing Room, takes its name from the red lacquered panelling bordered with gold. The pictures here are particularly fine and include works by Lely, Sidney and Kneller. The painted panels are Italian and are the oldest paintings to be found in the castle. The furniture is mostly French and Italian.

The Cedar Drawing Room is possibly the grandest in the house. The rich cedar wood panelling is intricately carved and the elaborate white and gold plaster ceiling is 17th Century Italian. The room glows with the light from five beautiful chandeliers, all of them English except the central one which is Irish Waterford Crystal. The magnificent Aubusson carpet was woven in one piece and incorporates elements from the Warwick and Greville crests - echoing the swan which is also worked into the ceiling.

The Queen Anne Bedroom, so called because it now holds her magnificent state bed brought from Windsor, holds some of the most valuable treasures in the castle. These are exquisite

Delft tapestries signed and dated: Franciscus Spiringius 1604. They depict the gardens of a medieval palace and the minute detail of animal, insect and flower is remarkable.

Warwick castle is no longer a family home, having been acquired by Madame Tussaud's in 1978. In the former family apartments a weekend house party of 1898 has been faithfully recreated to the last detail. A dozen or so rooms are filled with servants and guests including the Prince of Wales, later Edward VII all dressed in costumes from the period. It is a fascinating experience to wander through this elegant party.

When Sir Fulke Greville came to restore his newly-acquired castle in 1604 much of the roof had fallen in and parts of the castle were in use as the county Gaol. He was forced to occupy the Watergate Tower where he had a study and a bed chamber. These rooms are simply and somberly furnished with heavily carved oak pieces of the period. He is said to haunt his study where he was murdered by his man servant in a most unpleasant manner. The finest medieval castle in England would not be complete without a dungeon. It lies deep at the base of Caesars's Tower reached by a flight of narrow stone steps.

The grounds at Warwick are simple and informal, consisting mainly of natural parkland in the style of 'Capability' Brown whose only major change was to raise the level of the courtyard by some eleven feet. The 18th Century conservatory with its gothic style windows is the focal point of the garden and was built specifically to house the celebrated Warwick Vase, now part of the Burrell Collection in Glasgow. From the conservatory the large lawn, known as the Pageant Field, sweeps gently down to the river flanked by a variety of trees including fine old Lebanese Cedars which lead the eye down to Shakespeare's Avon and the parkland beyond. Some 35 peacocks roam the grounds at will and have, on occasion, been seen strutting down Warwick High Street.

In 1868 the Victorian Rose Garden was laid out to the design of Robert Marnock but by the end of the Second World War it had all but disappeared. Fortunately, two of Marnock's drawings survived, enabling a faithful reconstruction to be carried out in 1984. The roses are all old fashioned varieties popular with the Victorians and during June and July, their delicate blooms and scents are at their best. The small rock garden with its pond, rill and cascade was added in 1900.

In 1785 Lord Torrington wrote of the Governor of Warwick Castle '....and who was famed for his hospitality to pilgrims and visitors.' Those traditions of welcome and hospitality make the castle the ideal choice for corporate entertaining. Situated in the heart of England, only two miles from junction 15 of the M40, Warwick offers a variety of impressive settings for events large and small, grand or informal, indoors and outdoor. The elegant State Dining Room, the vaulted Undercroft, the baronial splendour of the Great Hall or the light and airy Conservatory all present a unique opportunity to select something a little different.

ARBURY HALL

Warwickshire is one the favoured settings for the work of Nuneaton's most famous daughter George Eliot, born on the Arbury Estate in 1819. The 'Cheverel Manor' of 'Scenes of Clerical Life' is, in fact, Arbury, and 'Sir Christopher Cheverel', its benevolent and cultivated owner, Sir Roger Newdigate. His transformation of the house from Elizabethan to Gothick, in the eighteenth century is described in 'Mr Gilfil's Love-Story' as simply - 'Cheverel Manor was growing from ugliness into beauty'. An operation sufficiently impressing to be able to influence a young woman born thirteen years after the death of Newdigate himself. Arbury remains one of the most effectively handled transformations of its type, and although its architecture is largely Gothick Revival, traces of the Elizabethan background still survive, as does one of Sir Christhopher Wren's few works outside of London. But Arbury is more than simply a haven for Gothick revivalists, containing a notable collection of paintings, furniture and other works of art accumulated down the centuries by successive generations of the Newdigate family.

The visiting public are guided to the open rooms via the vaulted corridor known as the Cloisters, the walls decorated with trophies of arms and portraits of Royalty. The Chapel is a remarkable and beautifully preserved example of late seventeenth century decoration, particularly the rich plaster ceiling by Edward Martin, and panelled walls.

Adjoining the Chapel and facing east is the Schoolroom, formerly the Chaplain's Bedroom. Beyond this is the Little Sitting Room with groined ceiling and exuberant gothic decoration. It also contains a collection of interesting paintings, mostly family portraits and a set of Jacobite and Georgian drinking glasses.

Onto the Saloon, the principal east-front room lit by a projecting bow window. A lofty and elaborately fan-vaulted ceiling looks down onto a distinguished set of Chippendale Gothic chairs as well as other notable furniture pieces.

The Drawing-Room is where the eye-catching elaborate Gothick chimney piece is notable as being based on the design of the thirteenth century tomb of Aymer de Valence in Westminster Abbey.

The culmination of Sir Roger's gothic transformation of Arbury

is the Dining-Roon, considerably higher than most of the other rooms, allowing for even more enthusiastic fan-vaulting. Copies of famous classical statues watch from canopied niches and a veritable gallery of portraits hang from the walls, pride of place going to to a striking depiction of Queen Elizabeth I by John Bettes.

Returning via the Cloisters, one finds oneself in the Long Gallery, filled with still more fascinating paintings, furniture and curios. A chair and table share the unusual history of being used by Henry Grey, Duke of Suffolk and father of the unfortunate nine-day queen, Lady Jane Grey, when he was hiding in a hollow oak tree at Astley, shortly before his betrayal and execution in 1554. Architecturally the gallery is the only part of the house to retain some original Elizabethan features, notably the chimney piece and its painted overmantel.

Outside the house itself, the visitor still has to visit the stables at the north of the forecourt, the porch of these was designed by Wren and a letter from him to Newdigate in 1674 mentions the design and 'hopes that it will fit his worke', and then wander on into the gardens. Again these are largely the responsibility of Sir Roger, the strict formal planting swept away to make room for the rolling lawns, serpentine paths cascade, and an artificial lake. A good example of the later change in mood. Stretching away from the house for quite a distance is the park. Originally a deer park until the beginning of this century, a few of the original Forest of Arden oaks can still be seen among the more recent woods and plantations.

The beginnings of Arbury are similar to those of most great country houses. Built as an Augustinian monastery in Henry II's reign it was confiscated by the Crown in 1536 when Henry VIII's break from Papal Rome led to his dissolution of the monasteries. John Newdegate exchanged his Middlesex home, Harefield Place, for Arbury, leaving it to his son, another John in 1592. The plot thickens - he had married a certain Anne Fitton in 1587, whose younger sister, Mary, a lady of great beauty and a notable lack of morals, was Maid-Of-Honour to Elizabeth, and has sometimes been suggested as the mysterious 'dark lady' of Shakespeare's sonnet devotions. But back to Arbury, the house finally passed to Sir Roger in 1734 from whom, in work spanning 1750-1805, it gained its present character and appearance.

THE HEART OF ENGLAND

If England had a heart it would beat somewhere midway between Malvern and the Cotswold Hills. I have little understanding of the corpse, but if the heart is full of happy memories then Gloucestershire and Warwickshire would seem a suitable area to place that vital organ.

Gloucestershire is one of the most beautiful and varied counties in England. The Cotswold Hills contrast with the forests and green vales of this Shire, brimming with history. Its country lanes lead into the most enchanting villages where the legacies of Saxons and Romans are immediately apparent. The area grew very rich as a result of the wool trade and a number of the old store houses have now been converted into hotels of great beauty and character. The mellow limestone is soft to the eye, the yellowy hues turning pink in the evening sun.

The Cotswolds are extremely popular and as a result can be very busy, full of visitors enjoying the sights and the hospitality. Pubs, inns and bed & breakfasts can all be found in vast numbers and the visitor has more than enough choice. The Cotswolds are also famous for the antique shops found in almost every village. Although you are unlikely to find a bargain, it is always worth having a rummage. You never know what you might stumble across.

In contrast to the mellow limestone, Hereford and Worcester's trademark is 'black and white' villages. To the west of this area lies the Black Forest, which in turn has stunning views over the River Wye. Sir Edward Elgar was born and bred in the Malvern Hills and many of his works have been played in the three great Cathedrals of Hereford, Worcester and Gloucester. An inspiring place!

Britain's most famous bard William Shakespeare made Stratford his home and the town pays tribute to him and his many famous works. Despite being a haven for tourists, the town remains very pleasant and there are many hotels here, each with a history of their own. Bed & breakfasts also play a large part with a supporting role played by the many pubs and inns in the surrounding area.

It is clear then, whether you are a Shakespearean enthusiast or a lover of pomp and circumstance, you will be enthraled by your visit to the area. England's heart continues to beat strongly.

HOTELS OF DISTINCTION

ANSTY HALL, Ansty. Tel: (0203) 612222
This red-brick Caroline house offers gracious well proportioned rooms overlooking 8 acres of gardens on the edge of the village. Comfort is foremost and the cuisine is imaginative.

ARROW MILL, Alcester, Warwickshire. Tel: (0789) 762419 765170
First written up in the Domesday Book when it was a flour mill, the wheel is still turning in the restaurant. Flagstones and beams remain but the curtains have been replaced. Step outside to find local coarse and game fishing, and clay pigeon shooting.

BILLESLEY MANOR, Billesley, Warwickshire. Tel: (0789) 400888
A delightful country mansion situated three miles west of Stratford in the heart of Shakespeare country, Oak panelling, log fires and beautiful grounds include a topiary garden. Elegant dining room and comfortable bedrooms.

BREDON MANOR, Bredon, Gloucestershire. Tel: (0684) 72293
Parts of Bredon Manor date back to 1455 and the hotel is quite charming surrounded by its own beautiful gardens. All rooms are well appointed and the bedrooms each have their own personal character.

BROADWAY HOTEL, Broadway, Gloucestershire. Tel: (0386) 852401
An ex-monastic guesthouse dating from 16th century and now with the mellowed stone that has a welcoming glow typical of this lovely area. Simple and immaculate accommodation.

BROCKENCOTE HALL, Chaddesley Corbett, Hereford & Worcester Tel: (0562) 777 876
A magnificent hotel set in 70 acres of grounds with a lake, gatehouse and half-timbered dovecote. It is conveniently located for Birmingham and for touring Worcestershire.

BUCKLAND MANOR, Broadway, Gloucestershire. Tel: (0386) 852626
A fine manor house dating back to the 13th century and now an award-winning country house hotel. The hotel is set in an idyllic Cotswold valley and offers numerous sporting facilities.

CHARINGWORTH MANOR, Chipping Campden, Gloucestershire. Tel: (038678) 555
The ancient manor of Charingworth was mentioned in the Domesday Book and the present building dates back to the 14th century. Set in 50 acres of gardens and grazing land the hotel offers stunning views. Ideally located for the Cotswolds.

CLOSE HOTEL, Tetbury, Gloucestershire. Tel: (0666) 502272
The Close Hotel dates back from the 16th century. The rooms are elaborately furnished with antiques and the bedrooms full of character. The restaurant is famous for attention to detail and the wine list is distinctive.

CORSE LAWN HOUSE HOTEL, Corse Lawn, Hereford & Worcester. Tel: (045278) 479/771
An elegant Queen Anne listed building set in 12 acres of grounds in an unspoilt hamlet. The hotel offers friendly personal service and many sporting facilities, and is within easy reach of the Cotswolds.

COTSWOLD HOUSE, Chipping Campden, Gloucestershire. Tel: (0386) 840330
Dating back to the 17th century this Cotswold House has been recently restored and boasts a magnificent Adam staircase and elegant antique furniture. It provides an ideal base for exploring Shakespeare country and the Cotswolds.

CRUDWELL COURT HOTEL, Cirencester, Gloucestershire Tel: (0666) 77194/5
A beautiful 17th century rectory set in 3 acres of Cotswold walled gardens, Crudwell Court provides a relaxed country house atmosphere and is an ideal base to visit Bath, Bristol, Lacock Abbey and the Cotswolds.

WYCK HILL HOUSE

Wyck Hill House dates from 1720 but has recently been completely restored and modernised so that it now offers to the discerning visitor the highest levels of 20th century comfort, service and facilities. Set in 100 acres of formal gardens, woods and parkland, this gracious country manor house commands magnificent views over the picturesque Windrush Valley and is surely one of the Cotswolds' most striking and impressive hotels.

There is a total of thirty luxuriously furnished and beautifully appointed bedrooms, including twelve in the tastefully converted Coach House and Orangery. The high standard of accommodation, both in the bedrooms and the welcoming public rooms such as the Library, Lounge and Cocktail bar, is complemented by the superb cuisine of award-winning chef, Ian Smith. Wines, too, are a great strength with a comprehensive list showing a wide range from around the World with some exciting and memorable examples, particularly amongst the clarets.

Croquet and, (by prior arrangement) clay pigeon shooting are available within the grounds. Golf, riding and tennis can be enjoyed locally.

Exclusive conference facilities for up to 30 delegates, syndicate rooms and all audio visual equipment are available. There are superb private dining facilities and wedding receptions for up to 200 are catered for in an elegant marquee set on the croquet lawn.

The hotel forms the ideal location for exploring the many fascinating Cotswold villages and local antique shops or for a visit to the Royal Shakespeare Theatre at Stratford Upon Avon, Blenheim Palace or Sudeley and Warwick Castles.

The ambience is more of a home than an hotel but with the essential and underlying professionalism that typifies the very best of British Hotel Keeping. The hotel is open all year round and a perfect choice for business or pleasure.

Wyck Hill House
Stow on the Wold
Gloucestershire
GL54 1HY
Tel: Cotswold (0451) 31936
Fax: (0451) 32243

THE HEART OF ENGLAND

DIAL HOUSE HOTEL, Bourton-on-the-Water, Gloucestershire. Tel: (0451) 22244
Once a 17th century farmhouse, now a carefully and prettily converted hotel. Lovely garden with croquet, and set in wonderful countryside.

DORMY HOUSE, Broadway, Hereford & Worcester. Tel: (0386) 852711
A 17th century farmhouse converted into a delightful hotel whilst retaining many original features. Ideally located for Indcote Manor Garden and Sudeley Castle with Stratford-upon-Avon and Cheltenham Spa nearby too.

DUN COW, Dunchurch, Warwickshire. Tel: (0788) 810233
Almost a parody of itself, this is a fine old English inn with everything in. From spreading ivy to cosy wood corners; from beams and panelling to whitewash and creaky sign, this place has a character that bursts out of the walls. Check out the legend of the Dun Cow.

ELMS HOTEL, Abberley, Hereford & Worcester. Tel: (0299) 896666
Built in 1710 by a protege of Sir Christopher Wren, The Elms is an elegant Queen Anne mansion set in extensive gardens and grounds. Superb accommodation is available in both the main building and in the adjacent Coach House.

ETTINGTON PARK HOTEL, Alderminster, Warwickshire. Tel: (0789) 740740
This majestic Gothic mansion is decorated throughout with a fascinating collection of antiques and original paintings and commands an impressive view of forty acres of breathtaking Warwickshire parkland.

FALCON HOTEL, Bromyard, Hereford & Worcester. Tel: (0885) 483034
Brought back from terrible disrepair, and now a fine example of a 16th century timber framed building restored to show off lovely panelling. An excellent restaurant complements this lovely building.

FOSSEBRIDGE INN, Fossebridge, Gloucestershire. Tel: (0285) 720721
There has been a 'watering-hole' on this spot since Roman times. This ivy-clad inn stands square to the original Fosse way, just at the crossing of the River Coln.

FOWNES HOTEL, Worcester. Tel: (0905) 613151
Once a glove factory, the building was only converted into a luxurious hotel in 1985. It is conveniently situated on the ringroad but despite its location offers restful accommodation for business guests and holiday makers alike.

GRAFTON MANOR COUNTRY HOUSE HOTEL, Bromsgrove, Hereford & Worcester. Tel: (0527) 579007
Dating from 1567 and set in 11 acres of gardens this hotel cleverly combines modern comfort with faded grandeur, having been painstakingly restored in traditional style. It is within easy reach of Birmingham.

HATTON COURT HOTEL, Upton St Leonards, Gloucestershire. Tel: (0452) 617412
Close to the historic town of Bath and fascinating Stratford-upon-Avon, this beautiful ivy-clad manor house nestles in 37 acres of picturesque gardens and pastures, preserving the charms of a more elegant age.

HOPE END HOTEL, Ledbury, Hereford & Worcester. Tel: (0531) 3613
This individual Georgian hotel provides total peace and relaxation in lovely rural surroundings. It has award-winning cuisine based on home-grown produce and makes a good base for exploring the Cotswolds and Wales.

LORDS OF THE MANOR HOTEL, Cheltenham, Gloucestershire. Tel: (0451) 20243
Decorated inside with antiques and fine paintings, this 17th century hotel lies on the edge of one of England's most unspoilt villages, right in the heart of the Cotswolds. Historic Bath, Warwick Castle and Blenheim Palace are all nearby.

LOWER SLAUGHTER MANOR, Lower Slaughter, Gloucestershire. Tel: (0451) 20456
A delightful Cotswold stone manor house furnished with fine paintings and antiques and providing an ideal retreat from which to explore the Cotswolds. The hotel offers traditional cuisine and many sporting facilities.

LYGON ARMS, Broadway, Gloucestershire. Tel: (0386) 852255
The Lygon Arms is a magnificent Tudor building meticulously restored to retain its wealth of original features, such as 17th century oak panelling and minstrels' gallery. Offering numerous leisure facilities, it is well based for Oxford and Shakespeare country.

MALLORY COURT, Leamington Spa, Warwickshire. Tel: (0926) 330214
One of the original country house hotels, and still one of the best examples, Mallory Court holds an air of luxury and refinement. The panelled dining room is a successful and attractive restaurant in its own right.

MANOR HOUSE HOTEL, Moreton-in-Marsh, Warwickshire. Tel: (0608) 50501
A beautiful 16th century manor house with its own priesthole and secret passages. The Manor House Hotel offers traditional English cuisine and many leisure facilities, and is an ideal base for exploring Stratford-upon-Avon, Warwick, Cheltenham, Oxford and Bath.

MARSH COUNTRY HOTEL, Eyton, Hereford & Worcester Tel: (0568) 613952
A charming little country hotel, small and personal with cosy bedrooms. The oldest parts of the building date back into the 14th century and the original timbered banqueting hall enjoys a new lease of life as a tastefully converted lounge.

NOEL ARMS HOTEL, Chipping Campden, Gloucestershire. Tel: (0386) 840317
Recent major updating to this historic old inn has meant increased and improved bedrooms, and much renovated public rooms. The Cotswold countryside is just on the doorstep.

OAKES, Stroud, Gloucestershire. Tel: (0453) 759950
Built in the early 19th century, this mellow Cotswold house is

now home to an excellent restaurant. The cuisine here is imaginative with many specialities complemented by the extensive wine list.

PUCKRUP HALL HOTEL, Tewkesbury, Gloucestershire.
Tel: (0684) 293293
Just west of the hotel, the River Severn makes its way towards the beautiful Tewkesbury Abbey. Not far from Shakespeare country this imposing country house commands 114 acres of idyllic parkland.

SNOOTY FOX, Tetbury, Gloucestershire. Tel: (0660) 502436
The honey coloured Snooty Fox dates back to the 16th century. Originally a coaching inn it is now a very comfortable and cosy hotel.

STONEHOUSE COURT HOTEL, Nr Stroud, Gloucestershire.
Tel: (0453) 825155
This 17th century Grade II listed building commands 6 tranquil acres of gardens and parkland whilst the interior is complete with oak panelling and open space fireplaces.

STRATTON HOUSE HOTEL, Cirencester, Gloucestershire.
Tel: (0285) 651761
The main house once belonged to a wool merchant, and this part of the hotel is by far the best, with glowing honey coloured stone exterior and elegant reception rooms. Walled garden and Jacobean bar.

THE GREENWAY, Cheltenham, Gloucestershire. Tel: (0242) 862352
A peaceful oasis in private parkland in the heart of the Cotswold countryside this lovely house combines elegance and modern comforts. Well located for Cheltenham and the Cotswolds.

THE BELL, Tewkesbury, Gloucestershire. Tel: (0684) 293293
This half-timbered hotel is situated in the town centre. The interior is charming and bedrooms well appointed and comfortable.

Blackwell Grange

THE HEART OF ENGLAND

WHARTON LODGE, Weston-under-Penyard, Herefordshire. Tel: (0989) 81795
In 15 acres of parkland surrounded by idyllic Herefordshire countryside this gracious Georgian house has been in the owner's family for four generations. The picturesque market town of Ross-on-Wye is nearby.

WHITE SWAN, Stratford-upon-Avon, Warwickshire. Tel: (0789) 297022
This is a traditional inn, dating back to the 15th century, set in the heart of Shakespeare country with plenty of interest and character. The bedrooms are well furnished and very comfortable with some interesting period furniture.

WYCKHILL HOUSE, Stow-on-the-Wold, Gloucestershire. Tel: (0451) 31936
Set in 100 acres and dating from early 1700's, reputedly on the site of a Roman settlement, the interior of this hotel is furnished with antiques. The cedar-panelled library is a particularly peaceful room.

ACCOMMODATION OF MERIT

BLACKWELL GRANGE, Blackwell, Warwick. Tel: (060882) 357
Dating from 1603 this attractive stone house is atmospheric with its low ceilings, inglenook fireplace and flagstone floors. With spectacular views from the house and pretty cottage gardens of the Ilmington Hills this is a romantic place from which to tour Middle England. (See photograph).

ETTINGTON MANOR, Ettington, Warwickshire. Tel: (0789) 740216
The oak panelled drawing room with its original Elizabethan fireplace is just one of the classic features which enchant in this small Tudor Manor. Stratford is within easy reach to explore Shakespeare's heritage and the famous RSC Theatre.

GROVE HOUSE, Bromsbarrow Heath, Hereford. Tel: (0531) 650584
13 acres of field and gardens surround this delightful 15th century home. Near the Malvern Hills this beamed and panelled house is ideal for visiting the Cotswolds, Wales, Stratford, Worcester, Shropshire and many wonderful places of heritage.

HALEWELL, Withington, Gloucestershire. Tel: (024 289) 238
'Holy Well' feeds a five acre trout lake and this Cotswold stone house, dating from 15th century and originally a farming mastery. Part of a 50 acre estate, on the edge of a quiet village, it has good facilities for the disabled.

LEASOW HOUSE, Laverton Meadows, Worcestershire. Tel: (038673) 526
Situated near some of the best known picturesque towns in the Cotswolds, this recently renovated 17th century stone farmhouse is wonderfully convenient for touring the Vale of Evesham and all places of heritage in the Midlands.

Postlip House

PUCKRUP HALL

Standing in just over one hundred acres of lawns and rolling parkland between the Cotswold and Malvern Hills, Puckrup Hall is a grand Regency house offering the ideal location for a touring base, quiet break or management retreat. To the north are Worcester and Great Malvern, while to the east the Vale of Evesham lads to Shakespeare country. Just to the west of the hotel the great river Severn meanders for three miles to Tewkesbury and its magnificent Abbey.

The emphasis at Puckrup Hall is on a relaxing and luxurious stay. There is a remarkable air of light and spaciousness throughout the hotel, perhaps influenced by the design and decor of the delightful Orangery and Conservatory. Leading off from the elegant hallway is the Worcester Room, a beautifully proportioned meeting or dining room for up to 16 guests and an integral part of the original house. The magnificent Ballroom is second to none and can cater for up to 200 people for private dining or company entertaining.

Each of Puckrup Hall's delightful, well appointed en suite bedrooms is individual, both in shape and interior design. This is reflected in that each of the twelve double or twin bedrooms is given a name, after the month of the year, while the four suites, including two with four poster beds, are named after the four seasons, with interior designs to catch the colours of the year.

The gourmet will certainly not be disappointed with the cuisine at the hotel. Dining in an atmosphere of soft intimate colours, be prepared for imaginative menus which are changed daily and a much acclaimed a la carte menu which changes with each season, emphasising the freshness and quality of the best from the Vale of Evesham and the finest produce available at the time.

For a memorable stay in an idyllic country setting, Tewkesbury Hall is hard to beat. The hotel is just two miles north of Tewkesbury Centre on the A38 and only a few minutes from junction 8 of the M5, via junction 1 of the M50, making it easily accessible from Birmingham, Bristol and South Wales.

Puckrup Hall
Puckrup
Tewkesbury
Gloucestershire GL20 6EL

Tel: Tewkesbury (0684) 296200   Fax: (0684) 850788

THE HEART OF ENGLAND

LONGDEN MANOR, Shipston-on-Stow, Warwickshire. Tel: (060882) 235

Polished flagstones, fine Jacobean staircase and walled gardens all create a romantic atmosphere in this Elizabethan Manor, built on the edge of the Cotswolds. It is a working farm which offers a perfect retreat from a hectic day's touring.

MANOR FARM HOUSE, Abbots Lench, Worcestershire. Tel: (0789) 205889

Oak beams, flagstone floors and extra thick stone walls all add to the classic style and character of this 16th century, half-timbered house. Shakespeare's and Edward Elgar's haunts are easily reached, along with many other fascinating places.

POSTLIP HOUSE, Winchcombe, Gloucestershire. Tel: (0242) 602390

Built in 1878 by the local papermill owner this attractive Cotswold stone manor house, surrounded by beautiful gardens and woodlands, provides overnight accommodation. Also available are the recently restored stables and coach house for holiday cottage accommodation. Central for touring Cheltenham, Stratford and Oxford. (See photograph)

UPPER COURT, Kemerton, Gloucestershire. Tel: (038689) 351

Behind the church, this member of the National Garden Scheme lies within beautiful and interesting grounds with lake, tennis court, croquet lawn, stables and productive vegetable garden. Close to the M5 this 18th century Cotswold Manor is easily accessible.

UPTON HOUSE, Upton Snodsbury, Worcestershire. Tel: (090560) 226

A black and white Tudor Yeoman's house set in two acres of pretty garden, with its complement of ducks. Worcester Cathedral, Cotswolds, Dyson Perrin Museum, Stratford and Warwick are all within a stones throw of this elegant beamed cottage.

INNS OF CHARACTER

THE BEAR INN, Bisley, Gloucestershire.

Four fine columns support this predominantly 16th century former Court House. The atmosphere here typifies gentle Cotswold life. Fine ales and reliable bar food are served at this elegant village inn.

THE CASTLE INN, Edge Hill, Warwickshire.

The octagonal castellated folly that forms part of this historic inn was built in 1749. Interior decorations commemorate the first battle of the Civil War. Perched on a steep slope the pub is distinctly atmospheric and straightforward bar food and ales can be enjoyed.

THE FEATHERS, Ledbury, Hereford & Worcester.

Poet Laureate John Masefield described Ledbury, his birthplace, as 'pleasant to the sight, fair and half timbered houses, black and white'. Built in 1565 this pub is a typical example. Inside, the spreading beams and timbers create a relaxed atmosphere. Excellent bar food and many fine ales can be enjoyed.

FLEECE INN, Bretforton, Hereford & Worcester.

This medieval building was converted from a farmhouse to a beerhouse in 1848. Much of the unique original furniture still remains since it was bequeathed in 1977 to the National Trust after 500 years of family ownership. This fine traditional pub has a marvellous reputation.

HOLLY BUSH, Priors Marston, Warwickshire.

This delightful 15th century golden stone pub, set in beautiful countryside offers a friendly rambling atmosphere. Real ales and traditional food are additional attractions.

KINGS ARMS, Ombersley, Hereford & Worcester.

This rambling black and white, half timbered Tudor pub dates back to 1411. Among the delightful rooms, one has Charles II's coat of arms moulded into the ceiling - he reputedly stayed here in 1651. Delicious wide-ranging food and finest ales are available here.

THE OLD MINT, Southam, Warwickshire.

Originally a monks' hospice this pub's medieval heritage is evident from the irregular stonework and mullioned windows. Many well kept ales and good food are other delights at this elegant old inn.

THE PLOUGH, Ford, Gloucestershire.

This former old Court House is yet another of England's oldest inns. Interestingly the front of this delightful pub holds a plaque reputedly engraved by William Shakespeare. Excellent food and fine ales are served within its rambling atmospheric walls.

ROSE AND CROWN, Ratley, Warwickshire.

Much of this 12th century inn remains in its original condition - beams, stone walls and flagstone floor are the dominant characteristics. Well kept ales and traditional bar food may be enjoyed at this popular pub.

THE TROUT, Lechlade, Gloucestershire.

Back in the 13th century an Augustinian hospital occupied this site. This later became a priory and eventually an inn. Low beams and flagstones are among its many charms. Good food and fine ales are here to be enjoyed.

THE SWAN INN, Southrop, Gloucestershire.

Green creepers cover this cosy, picturesque village pub dating back to 1645. Once the premises of the local coffin maker this delightfully located pub offers outstanding food and a fine selection of wines.

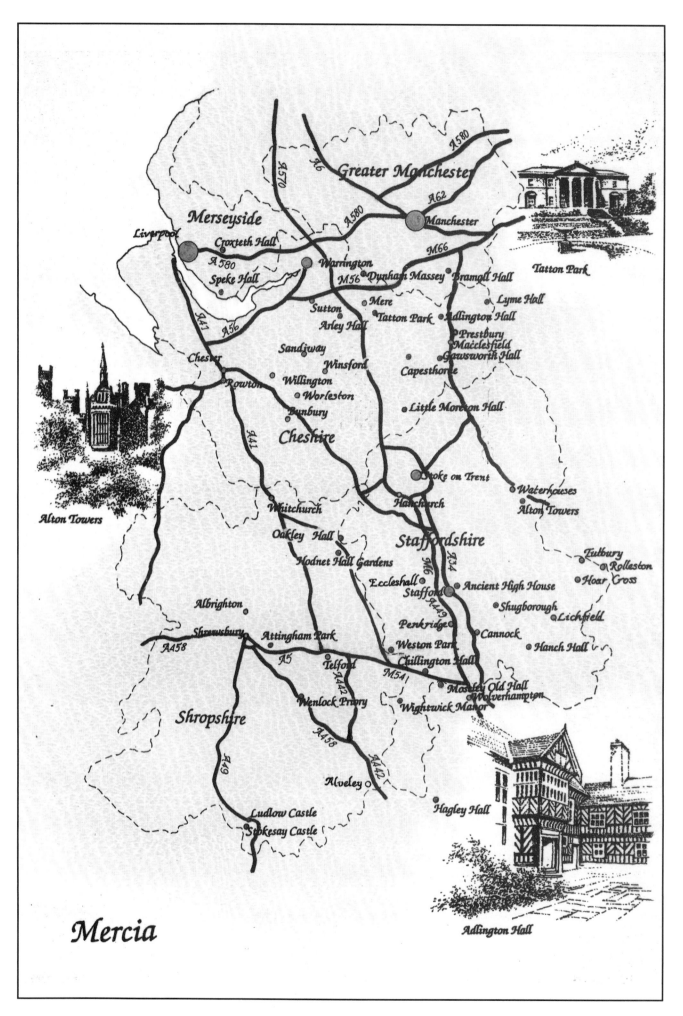

Mercia

MERCIA

THE CHESHIRE PLAIN

The countryside and character of the Cheshire Plain are hugely varied. Macclesfield and Stalybridge are centres for the textile industry, salt has been Winsford's lifeblood and Crewe prospered around its railways. Chester has been an important stronghold and the coastlines of the Wirral lie close to the heavy industry of Birkenhead and Ellesmere Port. **Arley Hall and Gardens** situated at Northwich was built around 1840 by the owner's great great grandfather, Rowland Egerton-Warburton. It is a beautiful Victorian Jacobean style house with many interesting features (featured later).

Knutsford became famous as the Cranford of Mrs Gaskell's novel, and nearby **Tatton Park**, with its magnificent gardens, is one of the National Trust's finest properties (featured later). Home of the Leghs of Adlington from 1315 to the present day, **Adlington Hall** was built on the site of a Hunting Lodge which stood in the Forest of Macclesfield in 1040. The Hall is quadrangular in shape and was at one time surrounded by a moat. The present house presents two completely different faces to the world. Two sides of the Courtyard and the east wing were built in the characteristic half-timbered 'Black & White' Cheshire style in 1581. The south front and west wing were added between 1749 and 1757 and are built of red brick with a handsome stone portico with four huge columns on octagonal pedestals. The centre from which the house grew is the Great Hall with its lofty proportions beneath a splendid hammerbeam roof, richly moulded with finely carved angels at the terminals of each hammerbeam. Built around 1480, two oak trees with their roots still in the ground support the east end of the Hall and are all that remain of the original Hunting Lodge. Between the trees is an organ, once played by Handel, which is the largest 17th century organ in the country. It was built around 1670, incorporating the console of a pre-Cromwellian instrument, and stands on a gallery with a beautifully carved balustrade beneath elaborately carved and gilded angels and a unicorn.

The gardens were landscaped in the middle of the 18th century in the style associated with 'Capability' Brown. At that time there were a number of small temples, a Chinese bridge over the river Dean, a Hermitage and even a mock castle. Jodrell Bank, the huge radio telescope, can be seen nearby.

Gawsworth Hall, three miles south of Macclesfield, is a lovely 15th century timbered house, again with literary connections. It was the home of Mary Fitton, maid to Elizabeth I and supposed mysterious 'dark lady' of Shakespeare's sonnets.

Nearby Disley is dominated by **Lyme Park**, which is made up of 1,300 acres of deer park, wild moorland scenery and fabulous formal gardens as well as Lyme Hall, a classically styled house remodelled by Giacomo Leoni. The park and house were given to the National Trust in 1946. Be sure to see the lovely Dutch walled garden, and the imposing Cage, built as a hunting tower in 1524 and commanding a splendid view over the estate.

Capesthorne Hall six miles north of Congleton is worth a visit, as is the fine timber **Bramall Hall** near Stockport and the ruined **Beeston Castle.**

Little Moreton Hall is a charming example of the timber-framed architecture for which Cheshire is famous. Approached by a bridge over its moat, the great hall is the oldest part of the house which has fine early panelling and some lovely fireplaces. The hall is set within a pretty knot garden of the 17th century design.

Goyt Valley, now partly flooded to form the Errwood Reservoir, is a lovely spot for picnics or walking, and you can walk up the valley to the ruins of Errwood Hall, a picturesque spot which gives a good of the area's natural beauty. Alderley Edge is lovely for its views, and the Alderley Old Mill is an interesting piece of local industrial history.

CHESTER

One of Britain's most picturesque cities is Chester, with its timbered houses, and Roman city wall, which remains virtually intact. Places of interest there include the Water Tower, King Charles' Tower, Bishop Lloyds House, Stanley Palace and the Grosvenor Museum. The Cathedral is also a must, and leave some time to potter along the Rows, galleried walks along the tops of the ground floor shops, whose origin is not very clear, but which adds much to the charm of this pretty town.

Speke Hall, despite its close proximity to Liverpool's airport, is a delightful, almost unaltered Tudor manor, surrounded by gardens and woodland. Built between 1490 and 1615 for the Morris family, the half-timbered, black and white house surrounds a cobbled courtyard with two ancient yew trees. Besides a splendid Elizabethan plaster ceiling, an impressive Tudor fireplace and fine oak furniture, the house boasts a network of secret passages and priest's holes. Speke has belonged to the National Trust since 1944. **Rofford Old Hall** remains virtually unaltered from the 15th century. **Croxteth Hall** and Country Park, with wonderful Edwardian room settings is well worth a visit. It is the former home of the Earls of Sefton and has many breeds of rare animals in its farm.

Liverpool is a bustling city, connected by its two tunnels and its ferries to Birkenhead. The Liver Building dominates the city's skyline, each of its two towers being topped by the mythical Liver birds from which the city apparently takes its name. Both its cathedrals are worthy of an extended visit.

SHREWSBURY AND THE SHROPSHIRE HILLS

The county of Shropshire is full of pretty towns with celebrated black and white houses. Shrewsbury itself is full of interesting places to see. The Castle, Library and Museum are worth a visit, and the Square has a lovely Market Hall. Many churches, including the Abbey Church, and the famous public school, whose past pupils include the 'hanging' Judge Jeffries and Charles Darwin, are of interest.

Weston Park is situated on the site of the original medieval Manor House with beautiful parkland that has been matured over several hundred years into a true masterpiece of unspoiled landscape (featured later).

Not far from Shrewsbury are **Stokesay Castle** and **Ludlow**, both of which have much to offer their visitors. Just south of Ludlow, Stokesay Castle was built in 1280 and has some fine examples of fireplaces and panelling. The town of Ludlow, nestling on a hill overlooking the Teme, is surely one of England's prettiest. The Castle was once the home of the Lords

MERCIA

President of the Marches who ruled the border country and Wales. Plays and poetry recitals are still performed there. Do wander round the town, too, and take in its other lovely buildings.

Hodnet Hall Gardens, are beautiful landscape gardens that surround a large Elizabethan style house (not open to the public). The gardens were begun in 1922 by Brigadier Heber-Percy who spent the next thirty years creating the sixty acres of gardens. There are lakes, pools, sweeping lawns in a perfect setting for the rare shrubs and trees, colourful displays of rhododendrons and azaleas. Market Drayton is known as the birthplace of Robert Clive, better known as Clive of India, and **Attingham Park**, the last surviving example of the work of George Stewart, was built for Lord Berwick in 1783. In 1807 John Nash added a picture gallery for the 2nd Lord Berwick, it still has pictures hung in the 19th century manner. The octagon room and the round boudoir have fine painted and moulded Adam style ceilings.

Other houses of interest in the area include Wythenshaw Hall, a lovely half-timbered house set in parkland and noted for its 17th century furniture and pictures; **Heaton Hall**, designed by James Wyatt which has some lovely 18th century pieces and an organ by Samuel Green; and **Platt Hall**, which boasts an interesting collection of English costume.

The area around Ironbridge is famous for its place in England's economic history. The famous iron bridge, the first of its kind in the world, makes an impressive sight. It was cast in specially enlarged furnaces at nearby Coalbrookdale.

The Ironbridge Gorge Museum in Telford is fascinating and warrants a day trip. It consists of six separate museums graphically illustrating the history of the area and the industries that grew up there. The museum has won many awards, including European Museum of the Year in 1977, and more projects are planned for the 90's.

Hodnet Hall Gardens

MERCIA

Benthall Hall, near Broseley, is known for its fine staircase and ceilings, and near Much Wenlock, we find the ruins of **Wenlock Priory**, once a nunnery.

Shipton Hall, also in Much Wenlock is definitely worth visiting. This delightful Elizabethan Manor was built c.1587 and Georgian additions were made later on. The Roccoco and Gothic plasterwork by T.F. Pritchard is of particular interest, another interesting feature is the Georgian stable block where you can witness working pottery. The garden is not to be missed with a medieval dovecote and parish church all dating from the late Saxon period.

THE CITY OF MANCHESTER

The origins of the city of Manchester are Roman, but it was little more than a market town until the industrial revolution transformed it into the main trading centre for Lancashire cotton. It is also interesting to note that Manchester, despite being totally landlocked, is one of England's busiest ports. This came about following the completion of the Manchester Ship Canal in 1894, which ensured the continuing prosperity of the city.

The city's skyline is dominated by its Perpendicular Gothic Cathedral, and the central library is an interesting rotunda style building with Corinthian columns. Manchester has many interesting art galleries, a very good shopping centre - though many of its prettier winding streets were destroyed by bombing - and a good variety of cultural activities through its theatres and cinemas. Do visit the Royal Exchange Theatre, a star-

Ironbridge Gorge Museum

tling piece of new architecture within an old building, which shows how new uses can be found for lovely old exteriors.

To the north of the Greater Manchester area lies Bolton where you will find **Smithills Museum** which is one of the earliest and most important examples of a Lancashire Manor house. Just outside Bolton, features include the restored 14th century Great Hall with carved family portraits in the oak linenfold panelling of the 16th century withdrawing room. The grounds contain a nature trail and trailside museum. Nearby is **Halli'th Wood Museum** which is a typical medieval Lancashire Merchant's House and the home of Samuel Crompton in 1779 when he invented the spinning mule.

STAFFORDSHIRE

The county of Staffordshire and the thought of potteries are inseparable in most people's minds, and with good reason. For some 300 years, the area's prosperity has been closely tied in with china and clay. Local resources such as clay, coal and water made the area ideally able to take advantage of the growing fashion for fine china. The development of the network of canals helped to transport its precious wares more cheaply and efficiently, both nationally and internationally, bringing fame to Josiah Wedgwood, Josiah Spode and numerous others.

Stoke on Trent, interesting for those keen on local history, was formed in 1910 as an amalgamation of the five towns made famous by Arnold Bennett.

City Museum

The Church of St Peter commemorates the great potters of the area, and Josiah Wedgwood is buried here.

Elsewhere in the town, there are countless reminders of the crafts, which continue to bring prosperity to the region. The Gladstone is an early Victorian pottery, now restored as a working museum. Enthusiasts can also visit the potteries of Spode, Minton, Royal Grafton, Royal Doulton and others.

The county town of Stafford and the brewing centre and historic town of Burton on Trent are at the centre of Staffordshire. The **City Museum** at Hanley, Stoke on Trent houses one of the world's finest collections of English pottery and porcelain. An award winning museum, it has fine exhibits including natural history, social history, archaeology and the decorative arts.

Stafford has many fine Norman buildings including the **Church of St Chad** and the **Ancient High House** in Greengate Street, the largest timber framed town house in England, where Charles I and Prince Rupert were sheltered in 1642 (featured later). **Stafford Castle**, one and a half miles southwest of the city, is now in ruins.

To the south, on the doorstep of the Black Country, is Cannock Chase, the remains of the vast hunting ground which covered much of the county in Norman times.

Shugborough is a beautiful white colonnaded mansion, seat of the Earls of Lichfield. You can reach it by a bridge across a landscaped lake and there are many garden ornaments includ-

ing a Chinese House (featured later).

Guided tours of **Hanch Hall** a fine red-brick house are usually conducted by members of the family who are busy restoring it. Dating from the 13th century, the house displays a variety of collections including christening gowns.

The Cathedral at Lichfield has three sandstone spires which tower above the city. They are known as the Three Ladies of the Vale. The city is also famous as being the birthplace of Samuel Johnson, who is now honoured with a museum.

The towns of Stone, Uttoxeter and Tutbury are also very pretty, as is the village of Swynnerton.

For a break with the history of the area, you could spend a day at **Alton Towers**, a huge fun park with all manner of attractions for all the family (featured later).

THE BLACK COUNTRY

Wolverhampton, known as the Capital of the Black Country, is an important economic centre, four miles north of which is **Moseley Old Hall**. Built around 1600 it was the home of the Whitgrave family for over 300 years. The gardens and grounds have been recreated in the style prevalent at the time. Nearby **Wightwick Manor** is Jacobean in style though it was not built until 1887. It contains unusual stained glass, as well as fine examples of the designs of William Morris, and some very in-

Smithills Hall

teresting paintings.

BIRMINGHAM - BRITAIN'S SECOND CITY

The West Midlands is dominated by the city and suburbs of Birmingham. Hundreds of industries are based there, and it is hard to think that, until the industrial revolution, the city was overshadowed by its neighbour, the ancient city of Coventry; or that the thickly wooded forest of Arden covered much of the area.

The city is the centre of a very complicated network of roads, known as 'Spaghetti Junction', and also of the region's canal network. It boasts some fine architecture, although many newer additions will not be to everyone's taste. The Town Hall is a neo-classical copy of the Temple of Jupiter Stator in Rome, the Council House is in Italian High Renaissance style and the city museum and art gallery has an enviable collection of paintings.

St Philip's Cathedral includes windows designed by Burne-Jones and made by Morris, and the Central Library has more than a million books.

Hagley Hall, a fine Palladian mansion was built for Sir George Lyttleton in the 1750's by Sanderson Miller and replaced an older house. The rather severe exterior hides wonderful rococo interiors, designed around a set of Soho tapestries of 1720. The park is dotted with some fine buildings including a Greek temple by Charles 'Athenian' Stuart.

Edgbaston is well known to all cricket fans, but is also worth a visit for its botanical gardens, which are more than 100 years old and are considered second only to Kew for their specimens of plants and trees.

Blakesley Hall to the east of Birmingham houses a museum of local history, and **Bourneville**, four miles to the south, is a famous example of 'capitalist benevolence towards the workers'. It was built by the Cadbury family in 1879, and is a chocolate factory set in a garden - considered to be a model for municipal housing and welfare.

From the industrial cities of Manchester and Liverpool to the beautiful countryside of the Cheshire Plain and Shropshire Hills, the counties of Mercia provide the traveller with a variety of pleasures to savour.

Shipton Hall

ARLEY HALL & GARDENS

In 1469 Piers Warburton decided to move his principle seat from Warburton to Arley, a site which was high enough to command fine views yet close enough to the Arley Brook to supply fresh water. There were pools to serve as fish ponds, woodland to provide fuel and building materials, good supplies of clay for bricks and deer to hunt - everything a Tudor gentleman required for a desirable residence. Some hundred years later an Elizabethan wing was added forming a square around a large internal courtyard.

In 1758 Sir Peter Warburton felt that the time had come to stop patching and mending the external timber framework of the house through which the chill winds whistled. He encased the entire house in brick, removed the massive Tudor chimneys and finished his new walls with stucco to give a neo-classical appearance. The courtyard broke out in a rash of pinnacles and spires - a gothic extravaganza.

Not everyone was happy with this extraordinary external facelift. Letters mention the stench of the drains, old Lady Warburton felt that 'the noisome steams of boilings in the kitchen wing' had somehow affected the timbers and rats had the run of the house. Nothing was done until Rowland Egerton-Warburton brought his young bride, Mary, to Arley in 1831.

Rowland was proud of the history of his inheritance and, influenced by the Romantic movement, determined to build a house that would enshrine the antiquity of his ancestors and be healthy and comfortable for his family and at the same time reflect his social position. This was no simple task - the house was still swarming with rats. Piers, their son, wrote 'My mother used to hear them in troops running down the old passages and wondered what the noise was, though she was no novice in the art of rat catching.'

Rowland also felt that it should not be too expensive and was

assured by his architect George Latham that 'a superior mansion might be erected with from £5 - 6,000'. This proved wildly optimistic and the final cost was nearer £30,000 - building styles may have changed since Victoria's day but seemingly little else has. Between 1832 and 1845 the old house was pulled down and replaced by the one we see today, with fine wood panelling, beautiful plaster ceilings and Latham's marvellous Grand Staircase. The Emperor's Room (so named because Napolean slept here) contains a charming collection of watercolours by Piers Egerton-Warburton.

Adjoining the Hall is a very fine Chapel built in 1846 and designed by Anthony Salvin.

The fine gardens at Arley, extending over 12 acres are worthy of separate mention. Rowland Egerton-Warburton and his young wife Mary designed much of what we see today between 1840 and 1860, apparently without professional assistance, and five generations of their descendants have cared for and added to it. This remains essentially a family garden, attached to a home, and an integral part of a country estate.

The most important feature is the double herbaceous border, one of the first of its kind in England, separated along its length by yew buttresses. On a fine sunny afternoon its skilful blend of form and colour typifies an old English garden at its very prettiest - an English summer at its very best. The delightful Tea Cottage, a half-timbered building formerly used for tea-parties in the garden, is surrounded by shrub roses; the Fish Garden with its goldfish pond has seven stones engraved with Rowland Egerton-Warburton's epitaphs to his favourite horses. A Walled Garden, Kitchen Garden, Herb Garden, The Grove, The Rootree, the unusual Ilex Avenue, a Scented Garden; any one of these is a plant-lovers paradise. This is not a garden to rush but a treat to enjoy - and a notebook is essential.

TATTON PARK

Set in incomparable Cheshire countryside, Tatton Park, former home of the Egerton family, paints a vivid picture of life in a large country household since 1760. The magnificent Georgian Mansion, built in the Neo-Classical style by Samuel and Lewis Wyatt between 1785 and 1813, has the most sumptuous state-rooms containing all the original family collections. There is outstanding Gillow Furniture, fine paintings and wonderful chandeliers - each room evoking a different atmosphere.

The Entrance Hall is formal and grand with a large painting of The Cheshire Hunt showing Wilbraham Egerton, who was largely responsible for Tatton's rebuilding. Grandeur is replaced by warmth in the Music Room and Drawing Room. Here the walls are hung with cherry red silk from nearby Macclesfield, complemented by elegant French "boulle" furniture in the Music Room and the ornate gilded furniture of the Drawing Room. The intricately patterned and gilded ceiling in the Drawing Room is by Lewis Wyatt and among the paintings are two by Canaletto. The harpsichord in the Music Room is over 200 years old and one of the finest in England. The comfortable library, mostly used by the gentlemen, was designed by Gillows of Lancaster around 1811 and houses some 12,000 books. The lovely informal Yellow Sitting Room contains some of the oldest and finest pieces of Gillow furniture together with many family portraits. There are 24 elegant bedrooms and a wonderful bath on castors which was moved from room to room. Filled with hot water by maids who had the advantage of the first electric lifts in the country to bring up the buckets of water, which was kept hot by a charcoal fire in a box beneath the bath.

In stark contrast the servants' quarters provide an insight into a very different life. The scullery and kitchen contain row upon row of enormous iron cooking pots and gleaming copper pans, reflecting the toil and bustle of service in such a large house.

In the Old Hall one steps back over 500 years to 1520 when the Hall was first built by Sir Richard Brereton, Lord of Tatton. Dimly lit, the rush-strewn hall is furnished with simple trestle tables and benches. All but the Lord and his family would have slept on the floor around the central fire. In the later Stuart wing, built around 1614, the servant's room contains simple wooden truckle beds, their lumpy straw mattresses supported by ropes. The Master bedroom has the luxury of its own fire-place and a four poster bed with a fine feather mattress and snug curtains against the draughts.

In the eighteenth century barn one can discover just how hard life on the land really was by threshing and winnowing using the original basic tools. In the gamekeeper's cottage of around 1900 and the estate workers' cottage of 1958, faithfully recreated, the journey back from medieval times is complete. The Home Farm has changed little in 60 years and reflects life on a typical mixed working farm of the 1930s inhabited by original breeds. Hens strut freely and the Red Poll cows chew contentedly. An excellent ice-cream is made from their milk in the summer months. 'Horses at Tatton' celebrates the role of the horse at work and for pleasure.

The spectacular gardens at Tatton Park are as much a part of the Estate as the mansion itself. There have been gardens and gardeners here since 1715, six generations of Egertons in fact. Set within 1,000 acres of deer park landscaped by Humphry Repton there are 50 acres of hidden pathways, unusual features and delightful surprises, spiced with exotic trees and colourful shrubs. The last Lord Egerton planted Tatton's famous rhododendrons and azaleas which blaze with colour during early summer. His wife was especially fond of the Rose Garden which is planted with roses from the Edwardian period.

The long 'L' shaped herbaceous border is divided by buttresses of clipped yew, each section having its own colour scheme. There is a formal Italian Garden designed by Joseph Paxton in 1865, an Arboretum of rare trees, an Orangery, a maze and a Fernery. Perhaps the most stunning feature is the cool and shady Japanese Garden - totally authentic and planted by workmen from Japan in 1910. A central focal point is the Golden Brook which surrounds the beautiful Japanese Shinto Temple.

Now owned by the National Trust but managed and financed by Cheshire County Council, Tatton Park, with its splendid mansion and superb grounds, offers a wonderful setting for special events. From prestigious outdoor shows to intimate candle lit dinners, any occasion is sure to be a success. There is easy access from the M6 (junction 19) and M56 (junction 7) and Manchester Airport is only 20 minutes distant.

WESTON PARK

The mellow brick house at Weston Park was built in 1671 on the site of a medieval manor and exemplifies the early classical style favoured by its designer, Lady Wilbraham. In the 18th Century the house passed twice through the female line, first to the Newport family and in 1762 to the Bridgemans, later Earls of Bradford, who altered and improved both the house and its park.

Altogether, the house has undergone three major periods of refurbishment, the last being in 1961. The 6th Countess had the intention of restoring the interior to its original and so create a more sympathetic setting for Weston's fine paintings which include works by Gainsborough, Reynolds and Stubbs, a Holbein and several Van Dycks.

The Countess was extremely successful in her endeavours, the present house is a model of elegant restraint. The only two rooms which remain as they were in the 18th Century are the Library and the Tapestry Room. The Library, hung with family portraits, glows with the patina of richly polished wood and the warm subtle shades of the velvet sofas and drapes. Among the books is Lady Wilbraham's copy of Palladio's First Book of Architecture. Her notes in the fly-leaves provide a fascinating insight into the building of Weston. Titles such as The American Peerage hide two secret doors. The Tapestry Room is quite exquisite. Its Gobelin tapestries depict Les Amours de Dieux in large medallions, surrounded by swags of softly coloured flowers and bordered by gold frames on a beautiful rose background.

Weston Park extends to almost a thousand acres bounded by some eight miles of wall. The classical Orangery, linked to the house by an arcade, was heated by fires stoked from below to produce tropical fruit for the household. The fine stable block now houses the gift emporium, ice-cream parlour and museum as well as the Old Stables Bar and Restaurant.

Weston and its Park offer unparalleled facilities for both corporate and private entertainment. This gracious house has become the perfect amalgam of 17th Century style and 20th Century business technology. Some 30 minutes from the centre of Birmingham, seven miles from the M6 and three from the M54, Weston is an inspired choice for residential conferences and seminars, product launches and promotions, private lunches or dinner parties and wedding receptions. The Old Stables, Orangery and the House itself provide prestigious settings for any function and the present Earl's years of experience ensure that the catering is always to exacting standards. To wander through the historic house at will, enjoy fine wines and delicious food in the magnificent Grand Dining Room is to share Country House Party hospitality at its best.

Among the outdoor activities offered are clay pigeon shooting, go-karting, rally driving, hovercraft driving, archery, ballooning (champagne included) and quad biking. For the less energetic there is fishing and treasure hunting - the really lazy can even travel by golf buggy.

After dark, choose from theme evenings; Elizabethan, Casino and Murder evenings are popular, here often rounded off with fireworks.

ALTON TOWERS

Situated within the magnificent grounds and gardens of what was once the largest private house in Europe, Alton Towers, former home of the Earls of Shrewsbury, now sets the scene for what must be the most original and unique corporate hospitality location in the country.

The internationally famous theme park, combined with the best in modern conference and business amenities, results in the ultimate mix of business with pleasure. Perhaps less well known is the fact that the gardens, created in the 19th century by the fifteenth Earl, are among the finest in England.

The house itself, although now in ruins, provides an impressive backdrop for these tranquil gardens. Designed by Augustus Pugin in the new gothic style, its multitude of towers, turrets and battlements provides the gardens with a quiet dignity.

Charles, 15th Earl of Shrewsbury was an extremely wealthy man and lavished huge sums of money on transforming the site in the valley of the River Churnet into a rich tapestry of form and colour. He began with few natural advantages and had to overcome the problems created by the steepness of the site and the very poor quality of the soil. The Churnet was dammed to create lakes and ponds and fountains. Vast numbers of trees and shrubs were planted and buildings in various styles were built all around the gardens. Particularly fine are the conservatories with their beautiful glass domes. There is a Grecian temple dedicated to the Earl, a Chinese pagoda, a Gothic tower, a Roman colonnade and even a miniature Stonehenge. Her Ladyship's Garden is planted with a lovely collection of roses and in the late spring the magnolias and rhododendrons form a dazzling display.

Well away from the peace of the gardens the pleasure grounds burst with the most exciting and exhilarating rides to delight the young - and the young at heart. A whole host of stunning new sensations tests nerve and stamina as you loop the loop - backwards! Enjoy plunging fifty feet into the total darkness of the Black Hole and then getting soaked at the end of the largest Log Flume in Europe. These are just some of the thrills (or terrors) in store at Alton Towers.

One of the most popular forms of corporate hospitality here is the Company Activity Day as there is something for the whole family to enjoy, and the Alton Towers approach is one of total flexibility. Conferences and seminars, exhibitions, concerts, banquets, wedding receptions, theme balls are just some of the functions offered. Alton Towers has established a wide range of catering facilities throughout the 500 acres of grounds. Over 50 restaurants cater for everything from fast food to a la carte, from hot dogs to smoked salmon. Picnic hampers may be produced and marquees erected for special occasions. Alton Towers is easily accessible from the M1 and M6 motorways which are a 40 minute drive.

SHUGBOROUGH

Set in beautiful parkland close to Cannock Chase, the 18th century seat of the Earls of Lichfield almost competes for attention with the wealth of fine historic buildings within its own park. The present house was begun in 1693 by William Anson who built the simple three-storey central section and in 1740 Thomas Anson extended the house by adding the elegant pavilions on each side. Between 1790 and 1806 Samuel Wyatt gave the main front its classic portico and most of the interiors are his work.

Much of the work carried out by Thomas Anson was made possible by considerable financial help from his younger brother, Admiral Lord Anson, who acquired great riches after capturing a Spanish galleon laden with treasure. The pavilions have delicate rococo plasterwork by Vassali, and Wyatt's entrance hall is an unusual oval shape encircled by scagliola marble columns based on ones which were discovered at Delos.

The most elegant of Wyatt's rooms is the Red Drawing Room. The coved ceiling is richly ornamented in the Neo-Classical manner by Joseph Rose and from it is suspended an exquisite

Irish cut glass chandelier. The house contains a collection of fine 18th century ceramics, family portraits, silver and 18th century English and French furniture.

In the Servant's Quarters the Staffordshire County Museum has recreated 19th century servant life and the Kitchens, Butler's Pantry, Laundry and Brew House have all been restored. There is a Victorian Schoolroom and a collection of horse-drawn vehicles in the Coachhouse. Shugborough Park Farm is a working farm museum with rare breeds, demonstrations of traditional farming methods and a working flour mill. Built in 1805 as a Home Farm for the Estate, butter and cheese making are some of the skills practised here.

Thomas Anson landscaped the park and commissioned James 'Athenian' Stuart to build a series of temples and pavilions around the park all with a classical Greek theme popular at the time. There are eight in all, each of great architectural merit in its own right. Within the park, 18 acres of formal gardens were laid out bordered by the River Sow.

THE ANCIENT HIGH HOUSE

Built in 1595, the Ancient High House is not only a splendid example of Elizabethan architecture, but is also the largest surviving timber-framed town house in England from this date. Recently restored to its former glory, the High House is now a heritage centre, and is also home to the Stafford's Tourist Information Centre.

Over the centuries, the High House has played an integral part in Stafford's rich and historic past - its height singling it out as one of the town's landmarks.

Although the house has been inhabited for nearly 400 years, it has witnessed various changes during this time, being in turn a home, a prison during the civil war, a school, shops and offices, and now a heritage centre. These changes are reflected in different period room settings, in which notable events or characters in the house's history are presented.

A Civil War tableau depicts a visit made to the house by Charles I in 1642, whilst breaking his journey from Uttoxeter to Shrewsbury to recruits troops. Of the same period is a magnificent Stuart bedroom, authentically furnished with a beautifully carved tester bed complete with period hangings.

A Regency dining room and a Victorian sitting room demonstrate different period furnishing styles, whilst an Edwardian office is dedicated to the life and business activities of one of the houses most colourful characters - Mr William Albert Marson, who owned the house from 1876-1908.

The exciting discovery of numerous 18th and 19th century wallpapers was made during the restoration of the house. These are particularly worth seeing as wherever possible they have been left 'in situ', giving visitors a rare insight into the decorating methods of our predecessors.

Situated in the heart of busy county town, the Ancient High House is easily accessible by bus, rail or road (car parks are close by). The house is open to visitors all year round,(except Christmas and New Year), Monday to Friday - 9.00am - 5.00pm Saturday 10.00am - 4.00pm (April - October), 10.00am - 3.00pm (November - March). Admission charges include a video presentation telling the story of the house and a heritage shop is open for the sale of souvenirs. Guided tours and evening supper tours are available by appointment for parties of 15 or more.

For further details contact:-
The Ancient High House
Greengate St
Stafford ST16 2JA
Tel: (0785) 40204/223181 ext 352

SHRIGLEY HALL

Shrigley Hall is a four star Regency Style Country House Hotel set in the 262 acre estate of Shrigley Park in one of the most beautiful parts of Cheshire.

The estate was the seat of the Downes family for over five centuries and was bought by William Turner the High Sherriff of Cheshire in 1821. He built the present hall in 1825 which was desighed by Thomas Emmett. Shrigley Hall was passed by marriage into the Lowther family until 1929, when it was sold to the Salesian order of missionaries, with whom Shrigley remained until the 1980's. Guests can now enjoy it as a hotel of remarkable splendour and luxury.

The hotel has been restored to its original grandeur, with many of the Neo Classical features of the original architecture retained. The sumptuous Oakridge Restaurant offers a superb choice of dining with the finest cuisine and service, and guests can relax in the individually designed bedrooms, many having magnificent views over the estate and the Cheshire Plains. For those who prefer a more informal atmosphere, meals can also be enjoyed in the relaxing Wine Bar and Leisure Club.

The former church building now houses the Country Club, offering truly magnificent facilities in luxurious surroundings. Guests can take advantage of a glorious indoor heated swimming pool, squash, tennis, snooker, gymnasium, saunas, solarium, steam room and beauty therapy. For the golfer, a round of golf can become a very special experience. The rolling landscape of the course and the spectacular views of Cheshire and the Peak District can be admired whilst enjoying the challenges of the hotel's own 18 hole golf course, designed by the internatioally renowned golf architect Donald Steel.

Guests to Shrigley Hall of an active persuasion can take in the many other activies and attractions on offer nearby, such as walking, sailing, climbing and riding. If guests come together as a large party,activities can be arranged, including clay pideon shooting, skirmish, archery, hot air ballooning and many others.

For a Country Club atmosphere and a refreshing break away from the stresses of every day life, Shrigley Hall provides the perfect answer.

Shrigley Hall
Shrigley Park
Pott Shrigley
Nr. Macclesfield
Cheshire SK10 5SB

Tel: (0625) 575757   Fax: (0625) 573323

MERCIA

Shropshire is many things to many men. Above all else, it was the birthplace of the Industrial Revolution. When Abraham Derby discovered how to smelt iron from coke he started an unprecedented growth of construction and development of industry. This belies the many more rural areas of the county which, have endured much havoc in their history.

The English, the Welsh and the Romans all wanted control of Shropshire because of its strategic position. The ruined castles and fortifications are reminders of these tempestuous times. Offa's Dyke is a particularly spectacular defence. There are a number of memorable towns to visit and Ludlow and Shrewsbury are two good examples. The towns and countryside boast numerous watering holes of variety and distinction. One finds excellent hotels in the country manor style, while some of the finest inns in the country grace the Shropshire towns.

Cheshire also has its share of delightful architecture and Chester is a fascinating mixture of periods with many Roman remains and some delightful streets punctuated by handsome black and white galleried buildings. There are some outstanding hotels in the town and this emphasises the popularity of Chester, often used as a staging post to destinations further north.

Turning southward, through dramatic moorland scenery, we come to the delights of Cannock Chase. Returning to a more industrial vein we must consider the potteries as here you will find the factories of Royal Doulton, Minton and Spode. The town of Burton-On-Trent is better known for its breweries than its ceramics and there are a multitude of public houses in which to whet your whistle.

Further south one finds the sprawl of Birmingham. But before you retreat rapidly, consider a number of the villages that surround the city. They are far from urbanised and provide an ideal place to take a break should you so wish.

The Kingdom of Mercia is full of spectacular contrast. From the borders of Wales to the Mersey and from the Trent and Severn it combines a fascinating cocktail of culture, revolution and countryside.

HOTELS OF DISTINCTION

BROOKHOUSE HOTEL, Burton-upon-Trent, Staffordshire. Tel: (0283) 814188
An attractive William and Mary Grade II listed farmhouse set in beautiful grounds beside a brook. The Shugborough estate, Calke Abbey, Hadden and Kedleston Halls are all nearby, as are the Derbyshire Dales.

BROXTON HALL COUNTRY HOUSE HOTEL, Broxton, Cheshire. Tel: (0829) 782321
A Tudor half-timbered building, Broxton Hall is set in 5 acres of beautiful gardens south of the historic walled city of Chester, with its Roman and medieval architecture.

CHESTER GROSVENOR, Chester, Cheshire. Tel: (0244) 324024
Rest from the serious tourism of Chester - this is luxury behind a black and white facade. Racing and romance star alongside excellent food in the Arkle Restaurant.

CRABWALL MANOR, Chester, Cheshire. Tel: (0244) 851666
One of the finest country house hotels in England, Crabwall Manor's history goes back to Saxon times with the present Grade II listed building dating from the early 19th century. It offers a relaxed ambience and fine cuisine.

DINHAM HALL, Ludlow, Shropshire. Tel: (0584) 6464
Newly restored Georgian house which has already become a renowned restaurant with its own local and further afield specialities. The bedrooms vary in size and there are some four-posters.

FEATHERS AT LUDLOW, Ludlow, Shropshire. Tel: (0584) 875261
An inn since 1670, this Grade I listed building is one of the best known timber framed buildings in the country. With a wealth of antiques and old beams, it is an ideal base from which to tour the Marches.

FROGG MANOR, Broxton, Cheshire. Tel: (0829) 782629
A superb Georgian manor house decorated in traditional style with period furniture. The hotel is set in 9 acres of gardens in the Buxton hills and commands rolling views to Wales.

HOAR CROSS HALL, Hoar Cross, Staffordshire.
Tel: (028375) 671
A health resort in a Grade II listed stately home, Hoar Cross Hall is a first rate health spa specialising in hydrotherapy whilst retaining all the grace and charm of a luxurious country house.

HORNCHURCH MANOR, Hornchurch, Staffordshire.
Tel: (0782) 643030
Built in the early 19th century, this gracious Tudor-style country house is a Grade II listed building and boasts an impressive architecture with its stone-mullioned windows and projecting gables.

MADELEY COURT HOTEL, Telford, Shropshire.
Tel: (0952) 680068
This 16th century manor house has recently been restored to further complement the fascinating stone and half-timbered walls, wood panelling and oak spiral staircase. Ironbridge Gorge, Powys Castle and other historic sites are all nearby.

MILL HOTEL, Birds Green, Shropshire. Tel: (0746) 780850
Set in beautiful gardens, great care has been taken to display the mill workings visible in the bar. By contrast, the bedrooms are large and modernly decorated.

NAILCOTE HALL HOTEL, Berkswell, Warwickshire.
Tel: (0203) 466174
A charming Elizabethan house in 8 acres of gardens and parkland, sympathetically restored to retain its original character. This hotel is conveniently situated for Stratford-upon-Avon, Warwick and the Cotswolds.

NUNSMERE HALL, Sandiway, Cheshire. Tel: (0606) 889100
In the heart of rural Cheshire, with three sides surrounded by a 60 acre lake, this country house is set in 10 acres of woodland, and provides perfect tranquility for the discerning visitor.

MERCIA

OLD BEAMS, Waterhouses, Staffordshire.
Tel: (0538) 308254

This attractive 18th century house is the location for a charming restaurant. The menu is imaginative and is complemented by an outstanding wine list. Six bedrooms have now been added so you can enjoy the atmosphere a little longer.

ROOKERY HALL, Nantwich, Cheshire. Tel: (0270) 626866
This 200 year old Grade II listed chateau overlooks the Cheshire Plain and is one of the finest houses in the area. Luxuriously decorated, the hotel offers excellent cuisine and many sporting facilities.

ROWTON CASTLE, Shrewsbury, Shropshire.
Tel: (0743) 884044

Destroyed in 1282, and rebuilt in the 17th century, this Grade II listed building with oak-panelled restaurant stands on the original site of an ancient Roman fort.

SHRIGLEY HALL, Pott Shrigley, Cheshire.
Tel: (0625) 575757

This four star Regency Style Country House Hotel is set in the 262 acre estate os Shrigley Park. The hotel has been restored to its original grandeur with many of the neo-classical features of the original architecture retained.

ST GEORGE HOTEL, Eccleshall, Staffordshire.
Tel: (0785) 850300

This charming 17th century coaching inn manages to keep the original character with old beams and inglenook fireplace, while at the same time supplying the 20th century comforts the modern visitor has come to expect.

SUTTON HALL, Sutton Weaver, Cheshire. Tel: (02605) 3211
Formerly a 16th century stately home, this inn now caters for those mortals who enjoy log fires, exposed timbers and fine furniture. Each bedroom boasts a four-poster and has modern facilities.

SWINFEN HALL, Swinfen, Staffordshire. Tel: (0543) 481494
Built in 1755, the galleried entrance hall of this hotel is as impressive as the oak panelled banqueting hall and other public areas. Food in the wooden dining room is also excellent.

WILD BOAR HOTEL, Bunbury, Cheshire. Tel: (0829) 260309
A 17th century building houses this fine restaurant, while all the modern comforts are available in the adjacent recent hotel, with good sized and well appointed bedrooms.

WILLINGTON HALL HOTEL, Willington, Cheshire.
Tel: (0829) 52321

Close to historic Chester and Beeston Castle, this country house was converted to a hotel by a descendant of the original owner. Set in parkland, it offers stunning views across the Welsh mountains.

YE OLDE DOG & PARTRIDGE, Tutbury, Staffordshire.
Tel: (0283) 813030

Parts of this inn date back to the 15th century. Located in the middle of this charming village, the hotel is both traditional and homely and there is a choice between the comfortable Carvery or the more formal Grill Room. Some of the bedrooms are beamed, others are in the elegant Georgian annexe.

ACCOMMODATION OF MERIT

THE CITADEL, Weston-under-Redcastle, Shropshire.
Tel: (063084) 204

A fascinating and unusual sandstone castellated house built in the 19th century, with views of the Welsh Hills, Hawkstone Park golf course and its own rhododendron filled gardens. Historic Shrewsbury, Chester, Staffordshire's Potteries, and Ironbridge are all worth visiting.

THE LODGE, Ludlow, Shropshire. Tel: (0584) 872103
Still lived in by the same family that built it in 1740, this pretty country house is set in a large garden within beautiful rural surroundings. The Medieval town of Ludlow is closeby; as are a variety of fascinating historical sites.

THE MOAT HOUSE, Longnor, Shropshire. Tel: (074373) 434
Surrounded by its own 700 year old water-filled moat, this unique timber framed 14th century manor house offers a look back in time. Architecturally fascinating, the open dining hall has carved timbers and a massive stone fireplace. Ludlow, Shrewsbury and Ironbridge are all nearby. (see photograph).

NEEDHAMS FARM, Werneth Low, Cheshire.
Tel: 061-368 4610

A small working farm originally built in the 1500s. Beautifully placed just outside the Peak National Park, between Werneth Low Country Park and Etherow Valley, it is an ideal base from which to explore, not only Cheshire, but Derby, Stafford and Yorkshire too.

OLD FURNACE FARM, Greendale, Staffordshire.
Tel: (0538) 702442

Overlooking the Dimmingsdale Valley, this tastefully restored Victorian farmhouse provides a wonderful retreat after a day visiting Alton Towers or the Potteries. Also convenient for exploring Ironbridge's Heritage sites and Derby.

THE OLD RECTORY, Hopesay, Shropshire. Tel: (05887) 245
Attractive 17th century family house in two acres of gardens, tended by an enthusiastic host. A perfect place from which to explore the Welsh Marches, Ironbridge and Ludlow and close to Stokesay and Ludlow Castles.

PETHILL BANK COTTAGE, Bottomhouse, Staffordshire.
Tel: (05388) 277

Whitewashed former farmhouse set in half an acre of landscaped gardens, this cottage lies in the Low Peak National Park. The inside is quaint with its solid beams, low ceilings, and thick stone walls. Close to Potteries.

INNS OF CHARACTER

BELLS OF PEOVER, Lower Peover, Cheshire.
This warm country pub is a long-standing favourite for locals and visitors alike. The paved terrace faces a beautiful black and white 14th century church while the lawn beyond the old coachyard rolls down through trees to a small stream. Excellent food and friendly service within an attractive original styled interior have further enhanced its reputation.

MERCIA

COMBERMERE ARMS, Burleydam, Cheshire.
A warm atmosphere pervades this rural pub, reputedly dating back 450 years. Fine ales on handpump, well-priced bar food and a friendly restaurant combine to make delightful surroundings.

THE GOAT'S HEAD, Abbotts Bromley, Staffordshire.
This attractive black and white half-timbered inn dates back to the 17th century. Overlooking the picturesque village, this popular pub offers a wide range of food and ales.

HORSE SHOE, Llanyblodwel, Shropshire.
This rambling 16th century Tudor inn nestles in pretty country surroundings, beside the River Tanat. Black and white timber on the exterior and low beams inside give this quaint pub its traditional feel. Simple food and fine ales are available.

RISING SUN, Tarporley, Cheshire.
Low ceilings and beamed rooms together with creaking 19th century mahogany furniture give this cosy pub considerable character. Good value lunchtime food and fuller evening meals tempt the discerning palate, while local ales are on hand-pump.

ROYAL OAK, Cardington, Shropshire.
Low beams, old standing timbers and little alcoves dominate this 15th century typical village pub. Set in a tiny picturesque area, it offers traditional home-made bar food and fine ales. A warm atmosphere is in keeping with its surroundings.

SMOKERS, Plumley, Cheshire.
A remnant salvaged from the Houses of Parliament during World War II, an Edwardian print and a large collection of antique copper kettles provide a historical setting in this 16th century thatched pub. Home made bar food, a wide selection of wines and a remarkable collection of 25 malt whiskies represent excellent value at this atmospheric inn.

YEW TREE, Cauldon, Staffordshire.
This marvellous village pub is as old as the yew tree outside, dating back to the late 17th century. Ancient guns, penny farthings, polyphons, symphonions, crank handle telephones and Staffordshire pottery are just a few of the charms here. With traditional food, fine ales, interesting malts and a friendly atmosphere, this is a particularly welcoming place to stop and rest.

The Moat House

CRABWALL MANOR

Crabwall Manor, one of the few hotels in Britain where you will feel totally at home as soon as you arrive.

Set in 11 acres of park and farmland, yet only two miles from Chester, the Manor was renovated and opened as a hotel in May, 1987, but still retains the original Tudor/Gothic castellated frontage which dates back to the 16th Century. The renovation has been so sympathetically carried out that it is impossible to distinguish original from new building.

Crabwall is expertly managed by Julian Hook, who works closely with Head Chef, Michael Truelove, previously at the famous Box Tree Restaurant at Ilkley. The menus change weekly and offer only fresh seasonal produce. For lunch or dinner there is a table d'hote menu, but it is complemented in the evening with an extensive a la carte menu. The wine list, consisting of some 375 wines, has been carefully assembled by Carl Lewis the Managing Director, who is himself a Restaurateur and collector of fine wines.

The decor at Crabwall is timeless, the light airy lounges boast subtle fabrics which are carried through into all the bedrooms.

Crabwall has 42 twin or double bedrooms and 6 suites to choose from, each individually designed with special touches to make your stay even more memorable.

Crabwall has been awarded 3 red stars by the A.A., 4 black stars by the R.A.C. and is one of Britain's Prestige Hotels.

Crabwall Manor Hotel
Mollington
Chester CH1 6NE
Tel: (0244) 851666

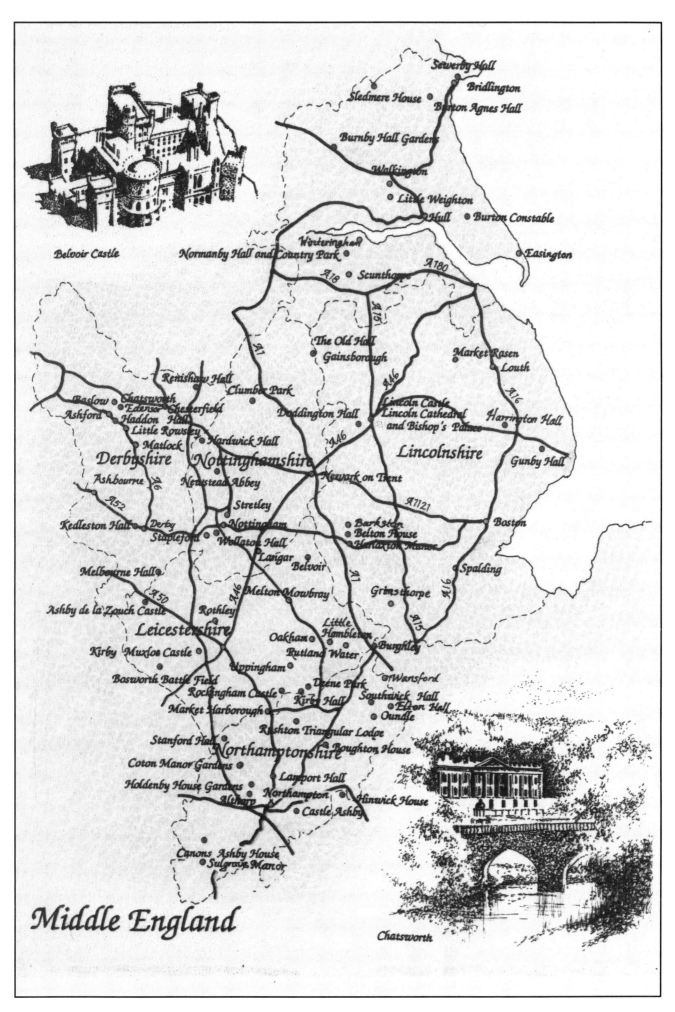

Sewerby Hall

Sledmere House • Bridlington
Burton Agnes Hall

Burnby Hall Gardens

Walkington

Little Weighton

Hull • Burton Constable

Winteringham • Easington

Belvoir Castle
Normanby Hall and Country Park

A180

A18 • Scunthorpe

A161

The Old Hall
Gainsborough

A1

Market Rasen
Louth

A46

A16

Renishaw Hall

Clumber Park

Baslow • Chatsworth
Ashford • Edensor • Chesterfield
Haddon Hall
Little Rowsley

Doddington Hall

Lincoln Castle
Lincoln Cathedral
and Bishop's Palace

Harrington Hall

A46

Matlock

Hardwick Hall

Derbyshire   **Nottinghamshire**   **Lincolnshire**

Gunby Hall

Ashbourne A6

Newstead Abbey

Newark on Trent

A1121

Boston

A52

Stretley

Kedleston Hall • Derby
Stapleford
Nottingham
Wollaton Hall

Barkston
Belton House
Harlaxton Manor

Langar

Melbourne Hall

Belvoir

A6 A50

Melton Mowbray

Grimsthorpe

Spalding

A46

A1

A16

Ashby de la Zouch Castle
Rothley

Leicestershire

Little
Hambleton

Burghley

A15

Kirby Muxloe Castle

Oakham

Rutland Water

Bosworth Battle Field

Uppingham

Deene Park

Wansford

Rockingham Castle

Southwick Hall

Market Harborough

Kirby Hall

Elton Hall

Oundle

Stanford Hall

Rushton Triangular Lodge

Boughton House

Northamptonshire

Coton Manor Gardens

Holdenby House Gardens

Lamport Hall

Althorp • Northampton • Hinwick House

Castle Ashby

Canons Ashby House
Sulgrave Manor

Middle England

Chatsworth

MIDDLE ENGLAND

The counties of Derbyshire, Leicestershire, Lincolnshire, Northamptonshire and Nottinghamshire form the centre of England. Each county has its own landscape, history and character, and each has different attractions for local and visitor alike.

DERBYSHIRE

Derbyshire is a county of contrasts. from rugged peaks and purple heather moorlands to scenic valleys and pretty towns and villages. Buxton originated as a spa town, but the waters are still bottled as drinking water and are widely available. The Crescent is a colonnaded promenade built on the site of a Roman bath and boasts a fine Opera House. The surrounding towns, villages and dales have delightful names, steeped in history - Wildboarclough, Chapel-en-le-Frith, Chee Dale, Miller's Dale and Water-cum-Jolly Dale.

Ashbourne, like Buxton famous for its water, stands on the fringe of the Peak District National Park. **Ashbourne Hall**, which used to be the family seat of the Cokaynes, has been altered greatly and is now the county library.

Dove Dale is a beautiful two mile stretch of the river Dove, with spectacular rock formations in its caves, called **Jacob's Ladder** and the **Twelve Apostles**.

Edale a very pretty old village, makes an excellent base for walking through the Vale of Edale along the Pennine Way and is an especially lovely spot. Castleton, by contrast, is high up in the peaks, and also makes a good centre for touring. It is well-known for its ruined **Peveril Castle**.

The area around Castleton is rich in caves, including the Blue John Caves, the Peak Cavern and the Speedwell Cavern.

Hathersage is an old village, and is the supposed birthplace of Robin Hood's henchman Little John.

Bakewell, famous for its tarts, is a typical dales village with a market hall, town hall and **Holme Hall**, a mansion built in 1626.

About a mile from Bakewell is **Haddon Hall**, dating mainly the 14th century. It was built for the Vernon family, but passed to the Manners family in Tudor times, and has a reputation for romance, following stories of the elopement of Dorothy Manners with her lover. It is the most complete surviving Medieval manor house in England standing on a limestone slope surrounded by the River Wye. After 200 years of Haddon Hall being uninhabited, the 9th Duke of Rutland in 1912 decided to make Haddon Hall his home and the restoration, his life's work. The medieval Great Hall and kitchens, the Tudor parlour and the magnificent Elizabethan Long Gallery have been preserved re-creating the original grandeur and charm. the gardens are beautiful, with rose gardens and clipped yew trees being just two of its many attractive features.

Haddon Hall

MIDDLE ENGLAND

Matlock, in the vale of the Derwent, is rich in craggy scenery and old buildings. The town was a spa in Victorian times, but you can climb up to High Tor, or visit the ruins of **Riber Castle**. **Chatsworth House**, 'palace of the peaks' is one of England's most splendid stately homes. It was built in the classical style in 1707 for the first Duke of Devonshire, onto a much earlier building designed by his ancestor, Bess of Hardwick, who has associations with **Hardwick Hall**. Chatsworth still belongs to the family and houses a splendid collection of paintings, sculpture, furniture and manuscripts. The grounds are also quite splendid (featured later).

Kedleston Hall near Derby is a superb Robert Adam house, built in 1759 for the 1st Lord Scarsdale. Many rooms have fine Adam ceilings and the circular saloon is based on a Roman temple, housing a wonderful display of sculpture. The magnificent state bed has posts carved in the form of palm-trees. **Melbourne Hall** is another treat, with its famous collection of pictures and furniture, and one of the best formal gardens in Britain.

Taking a brief look at the county's larger centres, the twisted spire of Chesterfield is certainly the towns most famous landmark and Derby is a very ancient town on the River Derwent. Here, Bess of Hardwick is buried, and the cathedral was built by James Gibb, who was also architect of St Martin-in-the-Fields in London.

ROYALISTS AND ROUNDHEADS

The south Midlands can claim to have played a key role in shaping the destiny of England. The many battles fought across its lands have earned it the name 'cockpit of England'. The Wars of the Roses came to an end at **Bosworth Battle Field** when Henry Tudor was crowned king and the Lancastrians routed the Yorkists. The Civil War began at Powick near Worcester and was won at Naseby in Northamptonshire. Many other battles were fought across the plains of the Midlands - at Evesham, Northampton, Tewskesbury, Bosworth and Worcester.

Leicestershire was originally famous as a hunting area, and still provides a home for the Cottesmore, the oldest hunt in England. Its small towns are famous for many and varied reasons. Uppingham is known for its public school, and has some lovely Georgian architecture and bow fronted shops, Melton Mowbray is famous for its pork pies and Stilton, the King of Cheeses, and Market Bosworth is a lovely stone-built town near the famous battlefield of Bosworth which is well worth a visit.

Belvoir Castle, the seat of the Duke of Rutland, stands in the northern tip of the county, west of Grantham (featured later), and **Stapleford Park**, east of Melton Mowbray, is a fine mansion with attractions including a miniature railway.

Leicester, the county town, stands on the Soar, and has an interesting park with a lake and the remains of the **Abbey** at its centre. **Ashby de la Zouch** is a charming old town on the edge of the vast Charnwood Forest which dominates the region. Ashby is certainly worth a detour. There are several good half-timbered houses and the ruins of the old castle where Mary Queen of Scots was a visitor. The 15th century castle, with its huge Hastings Tower added during the Wars of the Roses, was an important Royalist stronghold during the Civil War and was besieged by Roundhead forces in 1644.

The main attraction at Long Whatton is **Whatton House** and its 25 acre park, with its lovely Chinese garden. The picturesque ruined castle at **Kirby Muxloe** is worth visiting. This moated fortified mansion, begun by Lord Hastings, was never completed but the striking patterns of the brickwork are visible on the gatehouse walls. **Stanford Hall**, which was built in the 1690s and has a good collection of pictures, antiques and family costumes (featured later).

Bosworth Battle Field

MIDDLE ENGLAND

LINCOLNSHIRE

Many are surprised to hear that Lincolnshire is England's second largest county after Yorkshire. It is perhaps most famous for its fenlands, with areas like Spalding which attract many visitors in springtime when the famous local bulbs are in bloom.

In the city of **Lincoln** the triple-towered **Cathedral** looms up above the skyline, encompassing an extraordinary variety of architectural styles. It rises to a height of 365 feet and has many treasures -literally and metaphorically, including a copy of the Magna Carta. Almost facing the western approach to the cathedral is the castle, though all that now remains of the fortress founded by William the Conqueror are the outer walls and some towers.

As you leave Lincoln, it is worth paying a visit to **Doddington Hall**, an Elizabethan mansion built in 1600 by Robert Smythson. Its gardens and maze are very attractive and it contains elegant Georgian rooms, fine pictures, textiles and porcelain.

Grantham, Lincolnshire's second city, has a pretty market square and some lovely old coaching inns, highlighting the importance of the Great North Road in the town's economy over the ages. **Grantham House**, built in the 14th century and enlarged in the 16th, is now a National Trust property. **Harlaxton Manor**, built in the early 19th century by Anthony Salvin, is now run as a college, and boasts the East Midlands' largest conservatory, which is stocked by Kew Gardens.

Belton House, Park and Gardens, also near Grantham, contains some important collections and has mementoes of the Duke of Windsor. Home of the Brownlow family, this late Stuart house has been described as a 'perfect house from the age of Wren', and remains relatively unaltered. Of particular note is the large family chapel with its magnificent carved vervets.

Stamford is a lovely old town dating back to Roman times. **Burghley House**, about a mile to the south east, was built by William Cecil and has famous painted ceilings, Italian painted ceilings, lovely tapestries and silver fireplaces (featured later).

Gunby Hall near Spilsby features interesting contemporary wainscoting and has glorious formal walled gardens. This Wren styled house, home of the Massingberd family, has fine 17th century furniture and portraits by Joshua Reynolds. Do visit the beautifully preserved medieval manor house of **Gainsborough**, with its original kitchen, Great Hall, tower and Richard III exhibition.

Harrington Hall is a warm 17th century red brick house set in beautiful grounds, it is the house in Tennyson's poem 'Maud come into the garden Maud', you will find it a mile east of Somersby.

Boston is a lovely old town on the river Witham, but was surprisingly a flourishing seaport in the 13th century. The marshy land around the fens has been gradually drained to provide very fertile land, making many previously coastal areas into inland regions. Much of the flat area around Boston is dominated by the 'Boston Stump', the octagonal tower of **St Botolph's Church** which rises 272ft above the river. There are some towns and villages to be found, and miss **Tattershall Castle**, the 15th century fortified house now owned by the National Trust.

Sulgrave Manor

MIDDLE ENGLAND

NORTHAMPTONSHIRE

Though mainly agricultural, the county of Northamptonshire has its fair share of stately homes and buildings of interest. The marriage of Lady Diana Spencer to the Prince of Wales brought her family home at **Althorp** into the international spotlight. The house merits a visit in its own right, quite apart from the newer royal interest. Built in 1508 by Sir John Spencer, it contains a splendid collection of paintings and porcelain (featured later).

Sulgrave Manor, is a superb example of a modest manor house and garden of the time of Shakespeare and was home to the ancestors of George Washington. In 1539 Henry VIII sold the original manor to Lawrence Washington who built the present house, and whose family lived there for the next 120 years, when Colonel John Washington set sail for America to take up land in Virginia which later became Mount Vernon. His great grandson became the first President of the United States of America and the Washington arms is said to have been the inspiration for the American flag.

In 1914 Sulgrave Manor was presented to the peoples of Great Britain and the United States to mark a century of peace between the two nations and is now as much American as it is English.

It is difficult to believe that the great George Washington never actually lived here himself, as he gazes down from the walls of the Parlour and the Great Hall. He is portrayed as Colonel by Archibald Robertson and Charles Wilson Peale and as revered statesman by Gilbert Stuart, and it is this portrait by America's greatest portrait painter which takes pride of place.

Coton Manor

One of the most fascinating rooms is the fully furnished 18th century kitchen, complete with open hearth, pots and pans and much curious equipment - we have indeed come a long way, thanks in part to the inventiveness of our American cousins.

One of the most attractive features of the Manor is the garden. To the east is the rose garden where lavender, that most English of plants, grows in profusion. Many thousands of bags of its scented flowers have survived the crossing to the New World.

Boughton House, at Geddington, is a 500 year old monastic building which has been gradually enlarged and has amassed an outstanding collection of 17th and 18th century art treasures, furniture and tapestry. The house has a very strong French feeling, and as it was very much a second home, remains virtually as it was at the beginning of the 18th century. The new fashion for 'Versailles' parquet floors is thought to have originated here.

The 14th century manor house of **Southwick Hall** near Oundle has exhibitions of Victorian and Edwardian costumes, and Elizabethan enthusiasts will be interested to visit **Kirby Hall**, an outstanding example of a large stone-built manor of the period with rich architectural detail.

Castle Ashby will also interest Elizabethan fans. Its interiors are noted for its 17th century woodwork including chimney pieces and moulded ceilings. The house is surrounded by a lettered stone parapet (featured later).

Canons Ashby House is also worth a look for its Elizabethan wall paintings and Jacobean plasterwork.

Deene Park

MIDDLE ENGLAND

The gardens at **Coton Manor** are quite outstanding and include lakes, waterfalls and rose gardens. The gardens themselves date back to 1926 and have a wonderful homely feel to them. The grounds cover ten acres with beauty enhanced by the creative use of trees, shrubs and roses. The stream is wonderful and you can see a variety of water features including flamingo's and waterfowl.

Hinwick House is a lovely Queen Anne house displaying costume from 1840 to 1940 and tapestries and lace. the fine paintings include the works of Lely, Kneller and Van Dyck.

Holdenby House Gardens, the largest private house during the reign of Elizabeth I, is most noted today for its wonderful gardens which include a silver border and a fragrant border.

Deene Park near Corby is famous as the home of the 7th Earl of Cardigan who led the Charge of the Light Brigade. Deene is a largely 16th century house incorporating a medieval manor (the only visible remnant an arch of c.1300). Built around a courtyard with important rooms added during the reign of George III, the house has belonged to the Brudenell family since 1514 and was the seat of the Earls of Cardigan. The 7th and most famous Earl led the celebrated charge at Balaklava and the house is filled with mementoes of his Crimean exploits, together with many family portraits, fine period furniture and beautiful paintings.

The heart of the house is the Great Hall with its spectacular sweet-chestnut hammerbeam roof - a complex structure of single alternating with double hammerbeams. The magnificent carved panelling in the Oak Parlour has only been in place since 1919 when it was brought here from Yorkshire, and this room contains some exceptional portraits as does the Bow Room. This is the first of a series of three lovely Georgian Rooms, all elegantly furnished, and houses the library, most of which belonged to the 1st Earl. He was infuriated when his whole library was unjustly taken away by Cromwell's troops, but his anger knew no bounds when, after the War, he had to pay to ensure, their safe return.

In the period leading up to the last war and during it when the house was occupied by soldiers Deene became painfully shabby and uncomfortable. There was no heating or electricity and the kitchen was so far away that the present owner's mother rode there on a bicycle. After selling furniture and silver the daunting task of putting the house to rights was begun - with quite amazing results.

The garden also has been reclaimed and improved, with lawns which dip down to the canal and its beautiful 17th century stone bridge. The octagonal summer house was built for the 7th Earl who wanted a secluded retreat to indulge in flirtations without fear of interruption.

Lamport Hall, seat of the Isham family since 1560 features rare examples of the work of John Webb, and is set in lovely wooded gardens.

Of special interest is **Rockingham Castle** near Market Harborough. It was built by William the Conqueror on the site of an earlier fortress and its collections on view include one of Rockingham china (featured later).

Also of great interest is the **Rushton Triangular Lodge**, a unique building dating back to the late 16th century and comprising three sides, three floors, trefoil windows and three gables on each side, to represent the Holy Trinity.

SHERWOOD FOREST AND ROBIN HOOD

Everyone associates the county of Nottinghamshire with its folklore hero, Robin Hood, and the natural landscape with the vast woodlands of Sherwood Forest makes it very easy to picture him with his band of merry men.

However, the county has rather more substantial treats for its visitors than the legends surrounding Robin Hood.

Nottingham is a very ancient city, but really came to prosperity during the Industrial Revolution. **Nottingham Castle** may have associations with the hooded man, but its roots are firmly grounded in history. It was built in the 17th century on the site of a medieval royal castle and is now a very interesting museum.

Wollaton Hall is an interesting example of Elizabethan domestic architecture built by Sir Francis Willoughby in 1580 to 1588. It now houses the county's museum of Natural History.

Henry II built **Newstead Abbey** for the Augustinians in 1170 as an atonement for the murder of Thomas a Becket at Canterbury. After the Dissolution, it became the home of the Byron family and is now owned by Nottingham Corporation and used to display many items to the poet Byron and his family.

Newark has a very famous **Castle**, whose ruins still overlook the Devon River, having been destroyed by the Parliamentarians in the Civil War after King Charles I ordered its surrender.

These counties that make up Middle England, with varied landscapes and abundance of historical attractions are well worth visiting.

Newstead Abbey

CASTLE ASHBY

Castle Ashby House the sixteenth century home of the Marquess of Northampton. The house occupies a magnificent position in its typically English Park. The present house was built in 1574 by Henry, 1st Lord Compton, amid 200 acres of unspoilt parkland at the heart of a 10,000 acre estate.

In 1599 Henry's son brought great wealth into the family. He married Elizabeth, daughter of the rich Sir John Spencer, totally against her father's wishes, having carried her from her family home in a baker's basket. A reconciliation was effected by Queen Elizabeth I upon the birth of their first son and when Sir John died in 1610 his wealth passed to his son-in-law who was created Earl of Northampton in 1618. During the next few years many improvements were made to the house, including the addition of the parapet of stone lettering around the top of the house in 1624.

In 1635 the open side of the E-shaped house was closed when Inigo Jones built the South Screen linking the two Elizabethan wings. Since that time any alterations were restricted to the park until the late 18th century when the Long Gallery, Big Hall, Smoking Room and Chapel were redecorated and greatly improved by the 4th Marquess, a title granted to the family in 1812.

To the north of the house the park slopes down to the peaceful prospect of the ornamental lakes, stretching almost a mile and beyond. Against the steep rise of plantations stands the Temple designed by 'Capability' Brown in 1760. Four large terraces surround the house, decorated by stone fountains with lettered balustrading echoing that around the top of the house.

Castle Ashby House is available for 'Exclusive Use' and is centrally situated in Northamptonshire, just 12 miles from the M1. It offers the perfect setting for both indoor and outdoor functions including Exhibitions, Conferences, Banquets, Private Dinner Parties and Wedding Receptions. This centre for all occassions offers facilities for 10-150 covers, and to satisfy larger numbers the central castle courtyard can accommodate a marquee structure for up to 400 covers.

Accommodation is available in 26 beautiful ensuite bedrooms furnished with elegant antique furniture and paintings. The Castle offers many delights of country living such as Clay Shooting, Archery, Falconry, Cricket, Croquet and Golf nearby. This private home offers guests for business and social occassions twentieth century facilities in the glorious environment of a more generous age.

CHATSWORTH

The magnificence of the vast house at Chatsworth is matched only by the rugged natural beauty of its moorland setting and the cultivated splendour of its own immense gardens. Majestic, at the head of a series of watercourses and fountains, it has been the seat of the Cavendish family since 1552 when building was begun by Bess of Hardwick and her husband Sir William Cavendish. Their son was created Earl of Devonshire in 1618 and the 4th Earl was rewarded for his part in bringing William of Orange to the throne with a Dukedom in 1694. It was he who was responsible for the rebuilding of Chatsworth, beginning with the South Front. This accomplished, he found building so much to his taste that he was unable to stop. The East Front followed. Then new outbuildings and a grand, formal garden with a cascade and a temple from whence the water springs. Satisfied, he commissioned a drawing to record these changes only to feel once more the irresistible urge to build. The rebuilding of the West Front was rapidly followed by that of the North Front. A hill was removed to make way for the Canal Pond - nothing it seems would stop this resourceful man.

The 2nd Duke set about filling the house with suitably fine paintings and drawings - presumably he had seen quite enough of building during his youth. The 4th Duke wrought further sweeping changes to the park and gardens. Having decided that his house should be approached from the west, he pulled down the stables which obscured the view and razed the cottages which made up the village of Edensor which were then in his line of vision. New stables were erected up the slope to the north-east. The course of the river was changed and James Paine designed a fine new bridge. What little was left of Edensor village was enclosed within the park and remains so today. 'Capability' Brown removed most of the 1st Duke's formal garden in order to return the park to a more natural state so popular at the time.

The 5th Duke has been the subject of many books concerning certain activities including a 'menage-a-trois' with his wife's best friend by whom he had two children. Despite all this, he still found the time to redesign the private drawing rooms at Chatsworth.

The 6th Duke engaged Sir Jeffry Wyatville to build the long North Wing and was forced to sell most of the town of Wetherby in Yorkshire to finance the venture. He became intensely interested in gardening and appointed Joseph Paxton as head gardener at Chatsworth in 1826. Together they embarked on what is probably the most ambitious garden project ever attempted. The results were quite spectacular and can be seen in the present garden as it is today.

Generations of alterations and additions have resulted in a truly great house with over 175 rooms; 24 are open to the public, and of these, five form the grand State Apartments. Richly carved and decorated with painted ceilings they were designed to display furniture and pictures rather than for comfort. However, the rooms were occupied between 1939 and 1946 by the girls of Penrhos College.

The 6th Duke actually considered them a waste of space and wrote of ' ...this dismal, ponderous range of Hampton-Court like chambers.' The largest of the State Rooms, the Dining Room is unchanged since the 1st Duke's time. Looking carefully at the ceiling, painted by Verrio, visitors will see that The Fury is in fact a portrait of Mrs Hacket, the 1st Duke's House-keeper whom the artist disliked.

The Chapel is the only part of the house which remains completely unaltered by time and Dukes. Laguerre and Ricard painted the walls and ceilings with scenes from the life of Christ. Verrio painted Doubting Thomas over the alter piece of carved local alabaster. The pervasive smell comes, not from lingering incense but from the cedar wainscot, richly carved. Two rows of ornate high-backed chairs bear the names of family and friends responsible for working their needlepoint seats and chair backs for the 6th Duke.

It would be impossible to give more than a suggestion of the treasures housed at Chatsworth. Furniture by William Kent and Boulle, paintings by Lely, Rembrandt, Van Dyck, Tintorretto, Giordano, Breugel, Landseer and Sargent; tapestries from Mortlake and Brussels; sculpture by Canara and Cibber. The Devonshire tradition of collecting the best of contemporary art is maintained by the present Duke who has acquired works by Vanessa Bell, Jacob Epstein, Gwen and Augustus John, L. S. Lowry, Lucian Freud and Angela Conner.

STANFORD HALL

Stanford Hall is an outstandingly pretty William and Mary house set amidst parkland on the banks of the River Avon. The present Hall was built for Sir Roger Cave in the 1690s and is the home of Lady Braye, descendant of the Cave family.

In 1430 Peter Cave occupied the Manor House at Stanford-on-Avon, in the county of Northamptonshire, as a tenant and in 1540 his great-grandson Sir Thomas bought the Manor from Henry VIII. In 1690 the family decided to pull down the old Manor House and rebuild on a higher and drier site across the river on the Leicestershire bank. Sir Roger Cave commissioned the famous William Smith and his sons, of Warwick, to build the present Hall which is a wonderful example of their work. Sadly, Sir Roger did not live to see his lovely house finished, but his son Sir Thomas completed the Hall. The next Cave to build at Stanford was the 5th Baronet, also Sir Thomas, who erected the fine Georgian stable block and courtyard, and added much to the Stanford collection of manuscripts including the Peck Collection.

The fine panelled Library contains many interesting papers of Tudor, Jacobean and Georgian times including an eye-witness account of the Trial and Execution of Charles I. The Marble Passage, Oak Gallery and Grand Staircase are hung with fine portraits, many of them members of the family, and the bedrooms have fine 17th century Flemish tapestries and bed hangings.

The old Dining Room contains some of the furniture from the old Manor House including Charles I chairs and a refectory table, and the Green Drawing Room has some lovely Queen Anne and Hepplewhite pieces.

The Ballroom, with its wonderful acoustics, is a beautifully

proportioned room with a coved ceiling with four panels painted when the house was restored for the 5th Lord Braye in 1880 by F. Joubert. Most of the portraits in this room form part of the collection belonging to Henry Stuart, Cardinal Duke of York, last of the royal line of Stuarts who died in Rome in 1807. His collection was subsequently bought by Sarah, 3rd Baroness Braye, together with other Stuart relics which form part of this important collection.

The house was restored in Victorian times by the 5th Lord Braye whose son Adrian, aided by his father's grooms and two ferrets, wired the Hall for electricity. Anxious to avoid ripping up the beautiful floorboards, he hit upon the marvellous idea of making two holes at opposite ends of a room and tying the flex to the ferrets collar. Down one hole was placed a piece of rather smelly rabbit and down the other went the ferret. In no time the flex was in position and the ferret had his reward. Several rabbits later the house was fully wired.

Adrian, later 6th Lord Braye, was a close friend of Lieutenant Percy Pilcher, the first man to fly in England, and helped to fly some of the earliest machines. Tragically Pilcher was killed while flying at Stanford in 1899. The Pilcher Aviation Museum in the Stable block, housing a replica of his flying machine 'The Hawk', is a tribute to his courage and achievement.

Behind the stables is a lovely walled Rose Garden and a Nature Trail runs around the park through which the River Avon winds its gentle course. There is a Restaurant/Tea Room and the Ballroom, Old Dining Room and Stable block are available for conferences, lunches, dinners and incentive days. Stanford Hall is only 5 miles from the M1 (junction 20) and 6 miles from the M6 (junction 1).

BELVOIR

Perched high above the Vale of Belvoir, this romantic castle commands spectacular panoramic views which fully justify its name which means literally 'beautiful view.'

However, the siting of the original castle was probably more strategic than aesthetic. Built by Robert de Todeni, Standard Bearer to William The Conqueror, it was one of a string of castles intended to subdue the recently vanquished English and has remained the ancestral home of the Dukes of Rutland ever since the time of Henry VIII.

The original Norman fortification was extensively damaged during the Civil Wars of both the 15th and 17th centuries. It would appear that this corner of England has always been staunchly royalist and therefore not always on the winning side. Each time the castle was rebuilt it was in a different style to suit the incumbent of the time.

In 1816 the castle was again destroyed, this time by fire. That Belvoir rose so rapidly from the ashes is largely due to the driving force of Elizabeth, 5th Duchess, aided by the notable architect of the day James Wyatt. The new Belvoir was much less a military fortress and much more obviously a grand and comfortable house. Among the treasures with which Elizabeth and subsequent members of the family have embellished the castle are works by Rubens, Reynolds, Holbein and Poussin; fine furniture and porcelain; delicate silks from China; Gobelin and Mortlake tapestries. All of these reflect her energy and determination, but most of all her fine taste.

As if to attest to the castle's former bellicose history, it is home to the 17th/21st Lancers Museum housed in the magnificent Guardroom. The outstanding and comprehensive collection of weapons, armour and uniforms are displayed to great effect. The serried row upon row of muskets and swords, bugles and drums, a tattered battle standard, cannot fail to stir echoes of the many campaigns, won and lost, which must have set forth from Belvoir.

To wander through the Statue Gardens restores a sense of peace and tranquillity. The garden is set into the hillside below the castle and has been planted to provide colour and interest throughout the changing seasons, the lovely walks and terraces punctuated by the works of Caius Cibber, sculptor to Charles II.

This very grand castle, lying to the west of the A1, six miles from Grantham is an ideal location for seminars, banquets, product launches, Christmas parties and clay pigeon shooting. A visit to Belvoir offers a unique opportunity to study a fascinating chapter in English History.

The landscaped parkland surrounding the castle is a delightful place to picnic and Belvoir also has a licensed self-service restaurant which provides a cold-carved buffet and teas. There is also a gift shop, nature trail and adventure playground. Special events are held throughout the summer months and perhaps the most popular of these is Medieval Jousting, when the castle comes alive to the colourful carnival atmosphere of jugglers, minstrels and pedlars and richly clad ladies watch noble knights locked in combat to win their favours. And the evil Black Knight is vanquished - yet again.

BURGHLEY HOUSE

One of the largest and grandest Elizabethan houses, **Burghley** stands tribute to the power, wealth and vision of Sir William Cecil, Lord High Treasurer to the Court of Queen Elizabeth I.

Set amidst rolling parkland studded with ancient limes its herd of fallow deer graze peacefully, despite being only a mile from the Great North Road and the fine old town of Stamford. Only when seen from a distance - and preferably from the North West - can Burghley's massive scale be fully appreciated. Huge coupled chimneys; a multitude of cupolas and turrets around the simpler clock tower; loops of ornate balustrading break the skyline in an ever changing pattern depending on one's exact viewpoint. It is a sight to linger on.

Built on the sight of a 12th Century monastery, Burghley House with its triple Italianate facades, was constructed from local Barnack rag between 1555 and 1587 to plans drawn up by William Cecil who later became the first Lord Burghley. His elder son was later to become Earl of Exeter.

As would befit a man of such high office, the house contains some 240 rooms including 18 staterooms regularly occupied by Royal visitors and a cavernous kitchen to cope with the demands of such a lofty household. Turtle soup seems to have been a firm favourite with guests here.

The house has remained largely unchanged externally, although the interior was extensively refurbished in the late 17th Century by John, the 5th Earl, who embarked on the 'Grand Tour' and began collecting on the 'grand scale', culminating in one of the finest private collections of Baroque art in the world.

The first floor State Apartments contain an almost bewildering array of fine furniture, portraits and tapestries, porcelain and silver, and intricate wood carvings, each room vying in splendour with the one preceding it. The bedrooms, some with silver fireplaces and all with sumptuous bedhangings are par-

ticularly fine. A closer inspection may reveal the presence of carefully concealed doors leading into the screens passage which connects all these rooms to bathrooms installed in the 19th Century.

The South Front houses the Great State Rooms or George Rooms, rearranged for the proposed visit of the Prince Regent, later George IV, and possibly the grandest of all. For here, the 5th Earl indulged his passion for Italian art to the limit and commissioned Antonio Verrio to paint a series of six elaborate ceilings. Sadly, the rooms were never occupied by their intended guest. However, Queen Victoria and Prince Albert did occupy this opulent suite much later, although what she thought of the ample cherubs remains a matter for conjecture.

Back to earth in the shape of the Great Hall, passing briefly through 'hell' on the way, where the relative simplicity of this former banqueting hall forms a dignified backdrop for the concerts and social events held here. Among the members of this distinguished family, the most famous in recent times was the 6th Marquess who won an Olympic Gold medal in 1928 for the 400 metres hurdles and whose commitment to sport in general was lifelong. His comprehensive collection of rare Oriental snuff boxes may be seen in the Heaven Room.

Burghley Park has undergone many changes according to prevailing fashion. Much of the formal terraces, ponds and maze beloved of Elizabethan gardens disappeared when the 9th Earl employed 'Capability' Brown to bring Burghley in line with the more natural style of the times. He retained the mile-long Queen Anne Avenue of 1200 lime trees and constructed a 22 acre lake and the Lion Bridge in 1775. The Bottle Lodges, so aptly named, were built in 1801 by the 1st Marquess.

Nearby Stamford, with which the Cecil family continues to have close ties, is an unspoilt town of charm and character well worth visiting.

ROCKINGHAM CASTLE

Rockingham Castle dominates the local landscape. Nestling in the hillside on the edge of the Welland Valley, it is protected on three sides by natural inclines and ravines, and on the fourth by man-made stone walls - the perfect defensive site. Surrounded by dense forest, the castle, built by William the Conqueror, became a favourite with subsequent kings for its excellent hunting.

In 1544 Edward Watson was granted a lease on the Royal Castle and Park and began converting the now derelict medieval castle into a comfortble Tudor residence. He started by adding the Gallery Wing and went on to divide the Great Hall into two rooms with bedrooms above. In all the work took him thirty years to complete. His grandson, Sir Lewis Watson, bought the castle from James I in 1619 and rebuilt the Gallery Wing in 1631, only to see much of it demolished twelve years later during the Civil War. The previously unassailable castle was captured by Parliamentary forces and held against repeated Royalist attacks. After the War Sir Lewis returned to the empty and vandalised shell of the castle (the Keep and most of the walls had been demolished) and spent the rest of his life trying to restore it and extract compensation from the Government.

Throughout the 18th century the castle was not used regularly as a family home, but in 1836 Richard Watson embarked on a major modernisation programme. He employed Anthony Salvin to renovate the interiors, and at this time the towers were castellated and the Flag Tower added to the Gallery Wing.

Once inside, it is possible to imagine the self-sufficient life of a large castle. The picturesque cobbled street was the hub of domestic activity for the community, with the laundry and its clock tower, brewhouse and bakery, game larder and dairy.

The Great Hall still retains a strong Tudor atmosphere, although the occupying Roundheads removed or destroyed much of the original furniture. The Panel Room, created when Edward Watson divided the Great Hall, contains a wide variety of impressionist and modern paintings. There are works by Augustus John, Robert Colquhoun, Sickert and Barbara Hepworth.

The finest room is the Long Gallery, where the castle's major paintings are hung including works by Lely, Zoffany and Reynolds. Originally much longer than its present ninety feet, it was shortened by Lewis Watson during the Restoration after the Civil War, using the panels from his broken four poster bed for the door! Charles Dickens, a close family friend and frequent visitor produced and acted in plays here. The fine furniture includes a Louis XV writing desk and commodes, and of particular note are the semi-circular tables hand painted by Angelica Kaufman.

The Flag Tower rewards the effort of the steep climb up its spiral steps with magnifcent views across four counties. The room at the top of the stairs, known as the Armoury, was used by Dickens as the model for 'Mr Tulkinghorn's Chamber' in 'Bleak House', and contains a collection of weapons.

The sweep of the lush parkland and meadows has replaced the dense forests of the Middle Ages, and Rockingham Castle is now surrounded by twelve acres of delightful gardens ranging from the formal circular Rose Garden, on the site of the Old Keep, to the Wild Garden in the Ravine. The church has some fine marble memorials in the Chancel and Chapel. From the tiny churchyard there are lovely views of Rockingham village as it tumbles down the hill and the Welland Valley beyond.

ALTHORP

The Northamptonshire home of the Spencer family began as a red-brick Elizabethan house with a moat and formal gardens. Built around 1508 by Sir John Spencer it was remodelled, improved or altered several times in its transformation to the elegant house which is still the home of the Earls Spencer.

In 1650 the inner courtyard disappeared when Dorothy, 1st Countess of Sunderland, used the space to create the Saloon and Great Staircase. In 1732 the grand stable block was built to a design by Roger Morris, but the most extensive remodelling, which gave Althorp much of its present atmosphere and character, was carried out in 1786 for the 2nd Earl Spencer.

He engaged the services of Henry Holland who filled in the moat and refaced the old red bricks with the far more fashionable grey-white bricks seen today. He asked Samuel Lapidge, assistant to 'Capability' Brown, to work on the gardens which were greatly improved at this time. Althorp is renowned for its fine art collection, one of the finest in a private house in the country. Begun by the 2nd Earl and augmented by successive generations, one of the magnificent rooms was specifically designed for part of the collection. The entrance hall, or Wooton Hall, is the work of Roger Morris in collaboration Colen Campbell. This elegant Palladian hall, with its beautiful plaster ceiling, is the setting for a collection of equestrian paintings by John Wooton which fit the walls exactly.

The house is rich with a remarkable variety of fine furniture and porcelain and many family treasures were inherited from Sarah, Duchess of Marlborough. In the room named after her are portraits by Reynolds and Gainsborough; the Great Staircase is hung with many fine portraits of the Spencer family and throughout the house there are works by Rubens, Lely, Van Dyck and many other famous artists.

The lovely gardens date from 1860 when they were designed by the architect W.M. Teulon. Althorp is available for concerts, buffets, cocktails parties, lunches and seminars.

Normanton Park Hotel

BARNSDALE LODGE

Barnsdale Lodge is a substantial, beautiful and recently-restored 17th century farmhouse, set in the heart of the ancient county of Rutland amongst unspoiled countryside overlooking Rutland Water - one of the largest man-made lakes in Europe.

At Barnsdale Lodge, guests can enjoy the luxury and warmth of an English country house with all the charm and splendour of a bygone era.

The hosts, Robert Reid and the Hon. Thomas Noel, welcome guests to the gracious living of times gone by in the seventeen bedrooms, each furnished in Edwardian style and with private facilities. Guests can relax in style and comfort and enjoy the traditional English cuisine and fine wines in the dining rooms. Elevenses, buttery lunches, afternoon teas and suppers can be taken in the bar, drawing rooms, or on the terrace. There are three fully-equipped conference rooms and parties and wedding receptions are catered for in the Barn/Marquee which can accommodate up to 220 guests.

This haven of rural peace is only two miles from the tranquil market town of Oakham, and within easy reach of the historic town of Stamford and historic attractions such as Burghley House, Belvoir and Rockingham Castles, and cathedrals at Ely and Peterborough. Rutland Water is of great interest both to the sports enthusiast and to nature lovers. Guests can take a trip on 'The Rutland Belle', the Water's passenger cruiser, or take advantage of the dinghy sailing and wind-surfing available.

The keen fisherman will find himself in heaven - trout fishing is available from the shore or hire boats, and the 350 acre nature reserve offers the opportunity for birdwatching, guided tours and a nature trail.

Barnsdale Lodge provides all those traditional qualities of English service so often forgotten, together with a welcome second to none. The hotel is situated on the A606 Oakham to Stamford road.

Barnsdale Lodge
The Avenue
Rutland Water
Near Oakham
Rutland LE15 8AH
Tel: (0572) 724678
Fax: (0572) 724961

MIDDLE ENGLAND

England's 'middle' is all too often avoided by travellers heading north and south. This is a tragic error and something all lovers of the nation's heritage should immediately rectify.

The Peak District of Derbyshire, Britain's first National Park was described by Byron as 'having everything but the sea.' The Dales are a delight to behold and even their names bring a smile to the face. Water-cum-Jolly Dale is a particularly splendid example. There are all manner of first class hotels to be found and cottages and bed & breakfasts galore tempt the tourist to stay a little longer here.

Buxton, renowned for its waters and international opera, is a delightful town but there are many other attractive towns and villages. The numerous pubs here are full of character and are very welcoming after a long hike.

Leicestershire is celebrated hunting country, the Quorn being one of the most famous of packs. The Vale of Belvoir, where Leicestershire meets Nottinghamshire, is an area rich in history, bearing the scars of the Civil War. There are many good pubs and country house hotels in this area making it the ideal stopping place off the A1 or M1.

East of the A1, one finds Lincolnshire with its curious combination of coast and countryside. It remains one of the least populated regions in the country and there are relatively few hotels and inns as a result. What it lacks in numbers it makes up for in quality and one glorious inn is The George at Stamford. Lincolnshire is the land of Tennyson and of the Pilgrim Fathers. It is a quiet county, centred on its Cathedral City of Lincoln. Cobble stones and ancient streets are the norm here and the triple towered Cathedral is majestic. Returning west of the Great North Road, we venture toward Rockingham Forest.

Northamptonshire is another county of contrasts and it offers innumerable places of interest, together with a spattering of welcoming hotels and small country pubs. The town of Northampton is renowned for its shoe making and there are reminders of this throughout the town.

Middle England is an expanse of countryside which will appeal to those seeking to combine rural England with any number of pleasant hotels.

HOTELS OF DISTINCTION

BARKSTON HOUSE, Barkston, Lincolnshire.
Tel: (0400) 50555
The hospitable restaurant of this charmingly converted old Georgian farmhouse also has two comfortable bedrooms available, in case the excellent wine list becomes a little too tempting.

BLACK HORSE INN, Grimsthorpe, Lincolnshire.
Tel: (077 832) 247
Once a farmhouse, the old world character of this inn is charmingly maintained with exposed beams, stone walls and a log fire in the comfortingly traditional public bar.

CALLOW HALL, Ashbourne, Derbyshire. Tel: (0335) 43403
Callow Hall is situated in woodland with commanding views over the valleys of the Bentley Brook and the River Dove, with fly fishing available. Elegantly restored and with an emphasis on home-made food the hotel is both relaxing and comfortable.

CAVENDISH HOTEL, Baslow, Derbyshire.
Tel: (0246) 582311
A late 18th century hotel set on the Duke and Duchess of Devonshire's estate at Chatsworth. Hardwick Hall, a late 16th century 'prodigy house' and Haddon Hall are nearby too.

FISCHERS, Baslow, Derbyshire. Tel: (0246) 583259
Built in 1907 of Derbyshire stone with gables and mullioned windows, Baslow Hall is renowned for its superb cuisine. It is well situated for exploring the Peak National Park, Buxton, Matlock and Bakewell.

THE GEORGE HOTEL, Melton Mowbray, Leicestershire.
Tel: (0664) 62112
A former coaching inn, the George, this popular establishment is located in the middle of the town. Traditional furnishings add to the atmosphere and the bedrooms are comfortable and cosy, some with four-posters.

THE GEORGE, Stamford. Tel: (0780) 55171
Parts of this splendid building housed Norman pilgrims some one thousand years ago. Timbers, heavy beams and massive stonework are the norm here providing a genuinely unspoilt atmosphere. Outstanding food and wines are other attractions of this popular venue.

HAMBLETON HALL, Hambleton, Leicestershire.
Tel: (0572) 756991
This is a fine Victorian mansion, set in its own native grounds on the edge of Rutland Water. The atmosphere is sophisticated and comfortable at the same time and the furnishings outstanding restaurant is elegant and always first class.

HASSOP HALL HOTEL, Hassop, Derbyshire.
Tel: (062987) 488
A mention in the Domesday book for this splendid site, on which an enormous and these days exquisitely appointed hotel welcomes visitors. Luxury, you can play croquet, tennis and land your helicopter! The Bakewell Tart is a local delicacy.

IZAAC WALTON HOTEL, Dovedale, Derbyshire.
Tel: (033 529) 555
With magnificent views over the majestic Thorpe Cloud and stunning Dove Valley, this 17th century farmhouse was the perfect location for Izaac Walton to amass material for the 'Compleat Angler'.

LAKE ISLE, Uppingham, Leicestershire. Tel: (0572) 822951
Burghley House and the castles of Rockingham and Belvoir are just a short drive from this friendly town house in the famous market town of Uppingham, with its renowned Public School.

LANGAR HALL, Langar, Nottinghamshire. Tel: (0949) 60559
Built in 1830 and still in the core of the original family. This country house retains its antique furnishings in beautiful rooms, all with impressive views of the gardens, park and moat.

LANGAR HALL

This charming small country House Hotel & Restaurant in the village of Langar, 12 miles S.E. of Nottingham is set in quiet seclusion overlooking the Vale of Belvoir and ancient trees in the park. It is the family home of Imogen Skirving and although it is fully staffed and managed as an hotel the atmosphere is still that of having the run of someone's country house.

There are three superb double rooms in the front of the house (including two four-posters) & four comfortable double rooms in the wing. (Three of the rooms have adjacent single rooms). There are a further two rooms in the recently converted stable including one named after Desert Orchid. All the bedrooms have ensuite bathrooms/shower, direct dial telephone, tea making facilities, clock radio and lovely views over the garden & parkland.

Head chef Frank Vallat runs the kitchen with the help of two talented under chefs. The emphasis is on fresh ingredients cooked to order and served with sauces. His style of food is an individual expression of his taste & talents combined with the experience gained from working in star restaurants and are slanted towards customers coming for a special night out & to cheer the traveller at the end of a tiring day.

The Butler, Crispin Harris (actor/playwrite/musician) runs a popular restaurant and sometimes plays the piano. On the last Friday of the month he produces after dinner theatre: 1/2 hour plays written or adapted for the dining room & performed by 'Scoundrels' a local professional theatre company. This makes an amusing evening without interfering with the 'serious' appreciation of the food.

The wine list is written & chosen by James Seely author of 'Great Bordeaux Wines' and 'The Loire Valley & it's wine'.

Langar Hall makes an ideal venue for private meetings & conferences (Max 25).

Children and Dogs welcome by arrangement.

Whole house bookings taken for private parties/weddings.

Langar Hall
Langar
Nottinghamshire
NG13 9HG
Tel: (0949) 60559
Fax: (0949) 61045

MIDDLE ENGLAND

NEW HALL, Sutton Coldfield, West Midlands.
Tel: 021-378 2442
Built in the 12th century and reputedly the oldest moated manor house in England, New Hall is set in 26 acres of gardens, orchards and shady groves and is close to historic Warwick, Kenilworth and Stratford.

NORMANTON PARK HOTEL, Rutland, Leicestershire. Tel: (0780) 720315
This award winning, Grade II listed building is a beautifully restored Georgian coach house. On the south shore of Rutland Water it is ideal for exploring Cambridge, Calke Abbey and the numerous surrounding National Trust properties.

THE OLD VICARAGE, Ridgeway, Derbyshire. Tel: (0742) 475814
Fine gardens set off this stone, former Vicarage where the chef/owner creates her own particular specialities. The restaurant is formal and attractive and to accompany the often home grown produce there is a stunningly good wine list.

PEACOCK HOTEL, Rowsley, Derbyshire. Tel: (0629) 733518
If local patronage is a good sign, then this is a restaurant worth visiting. The building is 17th century with antiques in the main house. Bedrooms offering more modest accommodation are available in the cottage annexe.

RIBER HALL, Matlock, Derbyshire. Tel: (0629) 582795
A listed Elizabethan manor house with a delightful walled garden and orchards, this hotel is finely furnished with antiques. Acknowledged for its outstanding restaurant this hotel is the perfect base for visiting Chatsworth House.

RIVERSIDE COUNTRY HOUSE HOTEL, Ashford-in-the-Water, Derbyshire. Tel: (0629) 814275
A rather special hotel with superb cuisine, set in mature gardens on the River Wye. Beautifully furnished with antiques and silver this pretty hotel is well located for visiting Chatsworth House, Haddon and Hardwick Halls.

ROTHLEY COURT, Rothley, Leicestershire.
Tel: (0533) 374141
Formed round an originally 13th century manor house with 17th century and more modern additions. The better accommodation is in the main block with further rooms in the former stables. There are six acres of grounds.

STAPLEFORD PARK, Stapleford, Leicestershire.
Tel: (057284) 522
Once belonging to the six Earls of Harborough, this hotel, the most important privately owned stately home/hotel in England, stands in 500 acres of gardens, wood and parkland. Grinling Gibbons, England's greatest wood carver, was responsible for the fine dining room.

THE TALBOT HOTEL, Oundle, Northamptonshire. Tel: (0832) 273621
This is a historically very interesting building based, and recently restored, round a courtyard. The narrow stepped staircase is said to have been transported from nearby Fotheringay where Mary Queen of Scots met her end. The bedrooms are spacious and pleasing.

THREE SWANS HOTEL, Market Harborough, Leicestershire. Tel: (0858) 466644
The Three Swans has been a coaching inn for 500 years and is steeped in history. Renovated to a high standard the hotel offers relaxation combined with excellent cuisine. An ideal base for visiting Rockingham Castle, Althorpe and the Grand Union Canal.

WHIPPER-INN HOTEL, Oakham, Leicestershire. Tel: (0572) 756971
This is an intriguing antique furnished, 17th century inn. the atmosphere is appealing and the welcome one receives is just right. The restaurant proudly serves good British food and the service is excellent. Each bedroom is individually styled and has character.

ACCOMMODATION OF MERIT

ASHEN CLOUGH, Chinley, Derby. Tel: (0663) 750311
Overlooked by the peak District hills, this yeoman's home built in the 1500's stands in an acre of colourful gardens. A multitude of classic country houses are within easy reach - Chatsworth, Haddon Hall, Hardwick Hall.

BOURNE EAU HOUSE, Bourne, Lincolnshire. Tel: (0778) 423621
Close to A1, this wonderful Elizabethan/Georgian country house is a delightful place to stay in. A stone's throw from Hereward the Wake's castle ruins and next to a 12th century abbey. Burghley, Belton and Belvoir are also near.

DUNSTON MANOR, Dunston, Lincolnshire.
Tel: (0526) 20463
Made of local stone in 1750, this manor house has walls nearly three foot thick. Ideal for exploring Lincoln with its castle and Cathedral, plus halls such as Doddington, Gainsborough and Harrington. Close too are Belvoir, Belton and Burghley.

FULFORD HOUSE, Culworth, Oxfordshire.
Tel: (029 576) 355
A charming and comfortable 17th century country house with large gracious rooms, peaceful old fashioned gardens and glorious views. Very close to Sulgrave Manor and perfectly positioned for excursions to Warwick, Oxfordshire and Northamptonshire. Only eight minutes from Junction 11, M40. (see photograph).

PEACOCK FARM, Redmile, Nottinghamshire.
Tel: (0949) 42475
Perfectly situated with stunning views of Belvoir Castle, this two hundred and eighty year old farmhouse offers both accommodation and an excellent restaurant. A romantic house to return to after visiting the numerous local historical sites.

SHELTON HALL, Shelton, Nottinghamshire.
Tel: (0949) 50180
Fine early 18th century Georgian hall, with early 19th century uplift. Set in four acres of well laid out grounds. This is Robin Hood country with numerous castles and halls all within striking distance.

SYCAMORE FARM, Bassingthorpe, Lincolnshire.
Tel: (0476 85) 274
Spacious peaceful Victorian farmhouse, just four and a half

miles from A1 yet within easy reach of Belton House, Burghley House, Belvoir Castle and Lincoln. Accommodation is in three attractively furnished bedrooms all with modern amenities and lovely views over open countryside.

THE MALTINGS, Aldwincle, Northamptonshire.
Tel: (08015) 233

The traditional walled garden, complete with plants of special interest, are open to the public twice a year. The former farmhouse is 500 years old with solid beams and inglenooks. Many historical places lie within a short drive away.

THE OLD RECTORY, Hallaton, Leicestershire.
Tel: (085889) 350

Imposing, listed, stone rectory with huge windows and lofty ceilings all creating the effect of light and space. The beautiful countryside around is full of fascinating castles and houses worth visiting with Rutland Water also nearby.

INNS OF CHARACTER

ABBEY INN, Derby.
Once a significant 11th century monastery, this pub has recently undergone thoughtful restoration but has not lost its historical character. Combining imaginative good value barfood and well kept fine ales, its location opposite the park and a weir on the River Derwent makes it definitely worth a visit.

ANGEL, Wainfleet, All Saints, Lincolnshire.
This Georgian-fronted building, full of sturdy settles and traditional cast iron-framed tables, has been an inn since the 18th century. Undeniably good bar food and fine ales are served within a refreshingly friendly atmosphere.

THE BELL, Nottingham
Low beams, panelling and timbers are in keeping with the tradition of this popular 15th century Elizabethan building. Excellent food and fine ales are very popular and add to the pub's attraction.

BOAT INN, Stoke Bruerne, Northamptonshire.
This pretty 17th century thatched limestone cottage sits on the tow path of the Grand Union canal. The interior with its low ceilings and tiled floor depicts traditional barge life. The atmospheric pub offers good food and fine ales.

BUL'I'TH THORN, Buxton, Derby
This characterful 14th century hall has an extremely friendly atmosphere. Popular with locals and passers-by, it offers sensibly priced bar food well kept local ale on handpumps and is definitely worth a stop.

Fulford House

MIDDLE ENGLAND

CHESHIRE CHEESE, Hope, Derby.
Oak beams, local photos and coal fires are the characteristics of this quaint 16th century village pub. Good value, traditional bar food and local fine ales enhance the attraction of this popular pub.

THE COCK, Sibson, Leicestershire.
Heavy black beams, ancient wall timbers, latticed windows and low doorways dominate this thatched and timbered black and white pub dating back to 1250. Traditional bar food and fine ales make this an attractive stop.

THE CROWN, Old Dalby, Leicestershire.
Outstanding food, excellent fine ales and numerous malts are some of the delights of this unspoilt pub. Black beams, oak settles and rustic prints characterise the interior. In the spirit of its popularity the atmosphere continues to be relaxed.

CROSS KEYS, Upton, Nottinghamshire.
Generously served good bar food and many fine ales can be enjoyed at this heavy framed 17th century inn. The atmospheric rambling interior is full of little alcoves and fine furnishings.

THE FALCON, Fotheringay, Northamptonshire
A fine stone building is a fitting complement to a beautiful village full of history in the shape of a 12th century castle and lovely church. Delightful traditional food and good ales can be enjoyed at this wonderful location.

THE OLD BARN, Glooston, Leicestershire.
This characterful 16th century pub has a tremendous range of well kept ales. Good fresh barfood is also served at this charming village.

THE THREE CONIES, Thorpe Manderville.
Close to Sulgrave Manor (George Washington's ancestral home) this 17th century pub is popular for its genuinely homemade food. The traditional furnishings of the low-beamed bar make for a most homely atmosphere.

Hambleton Hall

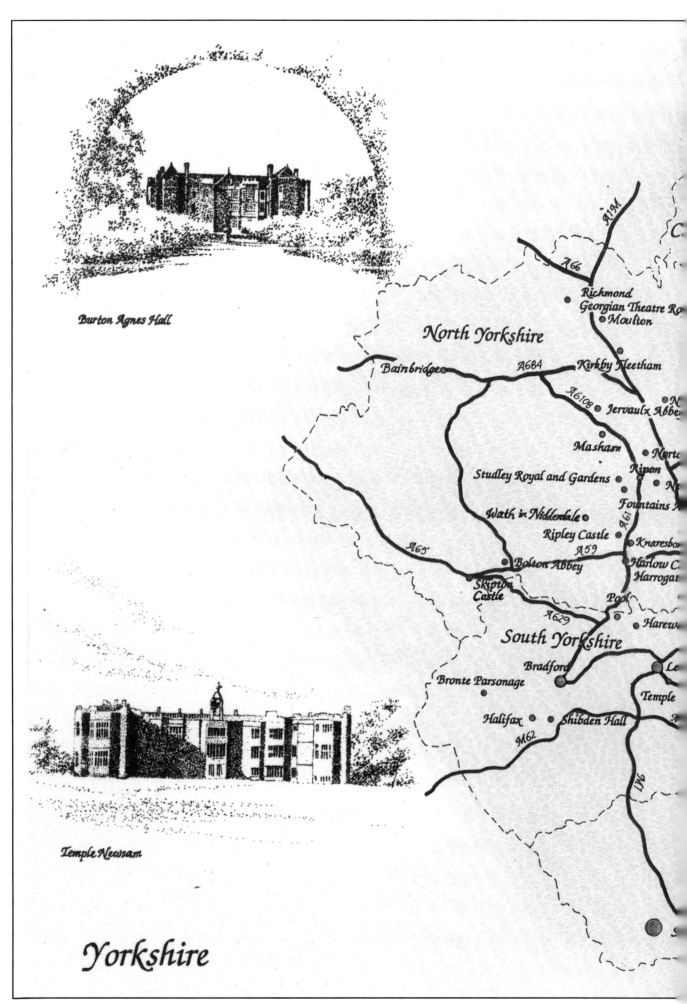

Burton Agnes Hall

Temple Newsam

Yorkshire

North Yorkshire

A66

Richmond
Georgian Theatre R
Moulton

Bainbridge
A684
Kirkby Fleetham

A6108
Jervaulx Abbe

Masham
Nort

Studley Royal and Gardens
Ripon
N

Wath in Nidderdale
Fountains

A65
Ripley Castle
Knaresbo
A59
Harlow C
Bolton Abbey
Harrogat
Skipton
Castle
Pool

A629
Harewe

South Yorkshire

Bradford
Le

Bronte Parsonage
Temple

Halifax
Shibden Hall

M62

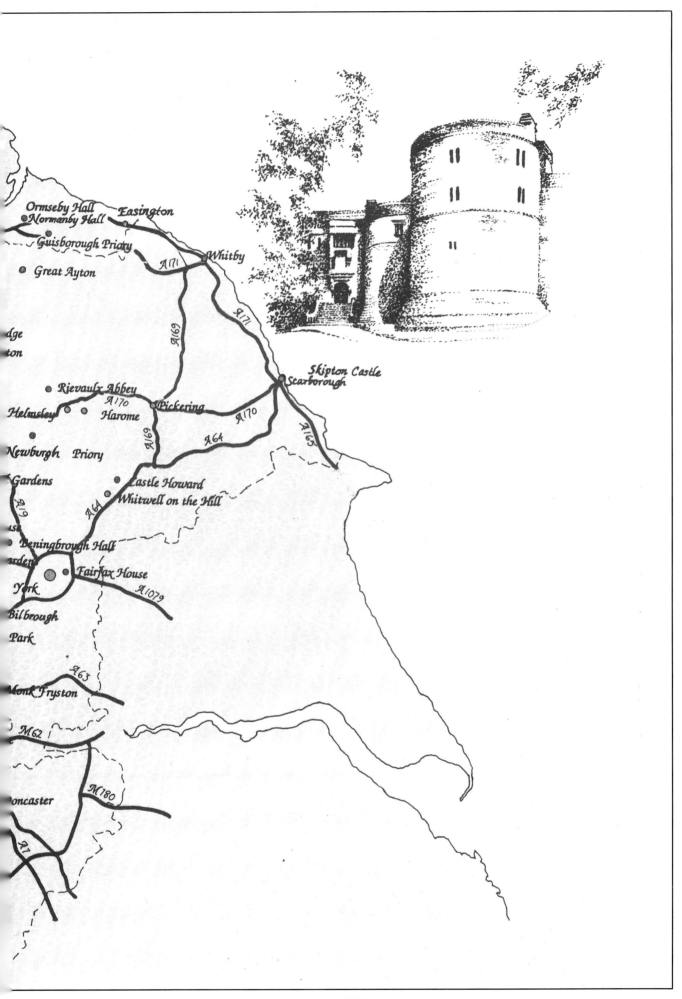

Ormseby Hall   Easington

Normanby Hall

Guisborough Priory

Whitby

A171

Great Ayton

dge

ton

A169

A171

Skipton Castle

Rievaulx Abbey

Scarborough

Helmsley   Harome   Pickering

A170   A170

A169

Newburgh   Priory

A64

A165

Gardens

Castle Howard

A64   Whitwell on the Hill

A19

Beningbrough Hall

rden

Fairfax House

York

A1079

Bilbrough

Park

A63

Monk Fryston

M62

M180

oncaster

A1

209

YORKSHIRE & HUMBERSIDE

What lovelier county could there be than Yorkshire, with its rolling hills, glorious dales and wild moors? As well as its natural beauty, the county also boasts a marvellous selection of stately homes, churches, gardens and famous houses.

To the south of Yorkshire, Humberside is steeped in history. Its coastlines are ever-changing, eroding at a rate of two to seven feet per year low clay cliffs are beaten by the savage North Sea.

THE NORTH SEA COAST

On the banks of the Humber lies Hull, or Kingston Upon Hull to give it its correct title, Britain's third largest fishing port, and very important economically for the region. Definitely worth a detour is nearby **Burton Constable Hall & Country Park**, which was built in 1570 for the Constable family and is the home of the 46th Lord Paramount of the Seigniary of Holderness, a title which has been held by the family since the 16th Century. This large twin-towered house, with battlements and turrets built of mellow medieval brick, was remodelled in the 18th Century and now contains some of the finest examples of the works of Thomas Chippendale and Robert Adam.

Besides being a traveller and collector of fine paintings, William Constable was also a scholarly man whose particular interests included Botany, Geology and the Sciences in general. The Science Museum Room contains a fascinating collection of natural history specimens and scientific instruments.

It seems that William Constable may have been reluctant to leave his home for he is said to visit the gold bedroom on occasions and was last seen by the present owner's grandmother who, undeterred by his appearances, always used this room. His is not the only presence felt at Burton Constable. Sometimes, the fleeting impression of a nun is said to move quickly down the Long Gallery and across the Staircase hall, always avoiding the Priests' hole. Nocturnal activity seems to be a regular feature at the house where Nurse Dowdall has also been seen walking around the North Tower in search of her charges - she was a nanny to the Clifford Constable children. Whether she lost them or what befell the children we do not know, but it cannot have been too awful as she was held in such high esteem by the family that she was buried in the family mausoleum after her death.

The woods surrounding the road which runs along the top of the drive have also been heard, resounding to the sound of marching feet. For anyone fortunate to see it, the sight of an approaching Roman Legion must be awesome.

The 20 acres of surrounding parkland were landscaped by Lancelot Brown and of particular interest is the fine Georgian stable block and Orangery.

Towns such as Beverley are of great interest to the tourist. Beverley describes itself as a gracious market town, and boasts a splendid variety of architecture. Georgian buildings predominate, but the medieval Minster with its twin towers dominates this lovely town. Beverley would also make an excellent base for exploring the region.

One of the area's more popular bathing resorts is Bridlington, whose Old Town is charming. The Priory was founded in 1113.

Its ruins now include a **Museum of Antiquities**, housed in the **Bayle Gate**. Five miles south west of Bridlington is **Burton Agnes Hall**, seat of the Boynton family and a fine example of Elizabethan architecture, with the added interest of being reputedly haunted by the daughter of the first owner (featured later).

Another attraction near Bridlington is **Sewerby Hall**, **Park & Zoo**. As its name suggests its attractions are manifold - a zoo, an aviary, an English Walled Garden, activities and train rides into Bridlington. Always a popular stop for all the family.

Burnby Hall and gardens at Pocklington is famous for its sensational collection of water lilies, which is claimed to be Europe's finest. There are over 60 species and in mid-summer their shades of pink, yellow and crimson are a glorious sight.

The Stewart Collection of sporting trophies was made by Major PM Stewart, a noted big game hunter and fisherman.

Scunthorpe is perhaps best known as a steel town, but its attractions for tourists include nearby **Normanby Hall**, a Regency mansion built by Sir Robert Smirke, whose other claims to fame include the design of the British Museum. The hall is set in 350 acres of parkland, with lovely gardens, a deerpark, and many attractions, including a golf-course and swimming pool.

Near Driffield is **Sledmere House**, the home of Sir Tatton Sykes. This attractive Georgian house was begun in 1751. Tragically the entire building was burnt to the ground in 1911, the furniture and sculptures were saved by the locals. The building was splendidly restored by architect Walter Brierley during the First

Sledmere House

YORKSHIRE & HUMBERSIDE

World War. It contains Chippendale, Sheraton and French furnishings, and gardens designed by 'Capability' Brown.

Cliff Mill at Hessle has interesting displays on the history of milling and offers access to the **Humber Bridge Country Park** which has fine views onto the massive bridge dominating the area, both visually and economically.

BRONTE COUNTRY

Yorkshire is famous for many things, but the Brontes have done more than anyone to attract interest to their homeland. What schoolgirl has not dreamed of rushing across the rugged moors of Wuthering Heights with Heathcliff?

The Bronte's home at Haworth is a mecca for tourists, and is as important a literary attraction as Anne Hathaway's cottage in Stratford on Avon. The Bronte family came to live at Haworth in 1820, and were all profoundly influenced by the Yorkshire moorland that surrounded their home. Charlotte Bronte's 'Jane Eyre' and Emily Bronte's 'Wuthering Heights' were both written here, and the house contains an important collection of paintings, letters and manuscripts as well as their personal treasures. The Black Bull Inn at Haworth is reputedly where Branwell Bronte drank himself to death.

The area has many other claims to fame. There are many picturesque towns and villages, and there is much evidence of the importance of the woollen trade in the history of the region's prosperity. The canals and their locks and towpaths are a picturesque feature, and these owe their existence to the need to transport wool and other commodities. Bradford is dominated by its Wool Exchange, and smaller towns such as **Hebden**

Bridge are fine examples of the architecture of their time - with a central wool mill being surrounded by terraces of workers' cottages. Huddersfield has some excellent Victorian buildings, especially its Classical-styled station buildings.

Leeds, a major centre for the woollen trade, has much to see. Nearby Kirkstall Abbey contributed much to the foundation of Leeds, and **Temple Newsam House**, three miles to the east, is mainly Jacobean and is now a museum, its attractions extending to its 935 acre park (featured later). **Shibden Hall**, near Halifax is a lovely 15th century mansion, now a museum. **Allerton Park** is one of the grandest homes, the great hall and dining room are some of the finest carved wood rooms in England. The house was designed by George Martin with some of the interior rooms by Benjeman Baud. You can see a very interesting collection of mechanical music machines and luxury antique motor cars. Allerton has also been the setting of TV films.

HILLS, DALES AND MOORS

The landscape of Yorkshire is wonderfully varied, as are the treasures it offers its visitors. York is a delightful city. Wander along its quaint little streets and yards and visit the lovely shops and tearooms. **York Minster**, the fifth church to have occupied its site, is a worthy cathedral for the city, and the **Castle Museum** contains an entire street of reconstructed shops. The city also boasts a wonderful **Railway Museum**, and the newer **Jorvik Viking Centre**, which will whisk you back 1,000 years to Viking Age Jorvik.

In the Vale of York - the lowland areas to the east of York - there are literally hundreds of things to see and do. **Skipton** is

Allerton Park

YORKSHIRE & HUMBERSIDE

quite often regarded as The Gateway to the Dales, it is essentially a market town, with the introduction of textile manufacturing in the 18th century. Skipton Castle built by the Normans in the 12th century suffered extensive damage in the 13th century and was rebuilt by the Clifford family. It is a fine example of a medieval fortress (featured later).

Harewood House, the seat of the Earls of Harewood has lovely gardens, again designed by 'Capability' Brown (featured later). Both Harrogate and Knaresborough, perching on the River Nidd, are fun to visit.

Harrogate was best known as a spa town, and its visitors travelled miles to take its waters. It is full of fine Victorian architecture, and features a 200 acre grassland, known as The Stray, which extends right into the town centre. **Harlow Car Gardens** are the home of the Northern Horticultural Society and are worth a visit, as are the **Valley Gardens**. After your exploits, pop into Betty's famous tearooms to watch life go by.

Knaresborough is rich in Georgian architecture and its sights include the **Dropping Well** where lime deposits have petrified all sorts of objects.

The Devil's Arrows at Boroughsbridge are three massive stone monoliths dating back to 1500 to 2000 BC and Northallerton has medieval roots. **Beningbrough Hall**, built in 1716, has a permanent exhibition of portraits from the National Portrait Gallery and an exhibition of 19th century domestic life in the Victorian Laundry.

Ripon has plenty to see. Its Cathedral includes a replica of the tomb from which Jesus arose from the dead and dates back to 672 and the woodcarvings and misericordes are 500 years old.

Fountains Abbey, founded by the Cistercian monks in 1132 is Britain's largest monastic ruin, located on the banks of the river Skell and **Studley Royal** is one of the few surviving examples of a Georgian green garden, famous for its water garden, ornamental follies and lake, and with a 400 acre deerpark.

Newby Hall is one of Yorkshire's most famous Adam houses, and has lovely 18th century interiors and the famous Gobelins Tapestry Room. Other points of interest are its miniature railway and woodland discovery walk (featured later).

Norton Conyers is a beautiful house which is best known by its connection with Charlotte Bronte who visited the house in 1839. She was very impressed by the family legend of the mad woman who had been confined to an attic room in the previous century. It is hard to believe that when Charlotte came to write' Jane Eyre' eight years later she did not base the mad Mrs Rochester on Norton Conyers very own mad woman. The house belonged to the same family for over 360 years and has a very warm and appealing atmosphere. The first mention of the property is in the Domesday Book (1086), when it belonged to a Norman family called Conyers. The earliest ports of the house go back to the mid 14th century and there are many lovely rooms to see in this enchanting house. You will also be able to discover the fascinating family history of the Graham family who since 1624 and to this present day own Norton Conyers. There is a pretty garden and a small garden centre, specialising in unusual and old fashioned hardy plants.

Ripley Castle, family home of the Inglebys since the 1320s has a wonderful library, a medieval Knight's Chamber, Geor-

Ripley Castle

212

gian Rooms, gardens by 'Capability' Brown and lovely views over the deerpark.

Of all the people who have lived in this house, Charles Gregory, 9th and last Viscount Fairfax has had the greatest influence. In 1750 he bought **Fairfax House** and completely remodelled the interior for his beloved daughter Anne, his sole surviving child. His three sons had died in an epidemic of smallpox, and his wife and two of his daughters died shortly afterwards. The house, described as a classical architectural masterpiece of its age and certainly one of the finest fully-furnished Georgian town houses in England, was saved from near collapse by the York Civic Trust and restored to its former glory between 1982 and 1984.

In addition to the superbly decorated plasterwork, wood and wrought iron, the house is now home for an outstanding collection of 18th century furniture and clocks formed by the late Noel Terry. All the major English clockmakers of the late 17th and early 18th century are represented.

The Library, Dining Room and Great Staircase have superb stuccoed ceilings and much of the elegant furniture is in the style of Chippendale. A particularly fine piece is the dining table richly decorated on the frieze with swags and vines. The kitchens have been authentically recreated with a great 18th century range and oven, complete with a spit driven by a fan within the chimney. Food was a very important part of Georgian life and Viscount Fairfax paid his cook accordingly - £2 per year more than his housekeeper.

The Drawing Room and Saloon have walls hung with rich damask to provide a backdrop for some outstanding furniture and a collection of paintings by the 19th century York artist, William Etty.

Kirkham Priory is a beautiful spot - the ruins of a 12th century priory nestling next to the river Derwent as it wends its way into the Vale of York. Its setting is enhanced by the cherry and copper beech trees around it.

The town of Malton, on the Derwent, has a lovely market square and a Norman church and nearby is **Castle Howard**, one of England's finest houses. Designed by Sir John Vanbrugh, the house is set in magnificent parkland, with a vast lake and beautiful rose gardens. It forms a landmark for miles around and would be an essential element to any visit to the area (featured later).

Landseer's painting of **Bolton Abbey** has helped bring attention to the ruins of this 12th century priory whose nave has been restored and is now used as the local parish church. A quick scramble across **Brimham Rocks** will certainly blow away those cobwebs. The site offers glorious views across the neighbouring areas, and certainly merits a detour. There is so much to see in Yorkshire, it is hard to know where to stop. The Yorkshire Pennines along the western dales are a place of 'infinite loneliness' and the upland moors in the **Yorkshire Dales National Park** sweep to summits of more than 2,000 feet which are wild and windswept. Here lie Richmond and Wensley, two very pretty towns. Further west, we find such spectacles as the majestic **Rievaulx Abbey**, founded by the Cistercians in 1125 and now shrouded by wooded hills.

Helmsley Castle is 12th century and is surrounded by a double ditch and **Newburgh Priory** is a very interesting house to visit, it was originally built in 1145 with alterations in 1568 and between 1720 and 1760. The house has been the home of one family and its descendants since 1538, it also contains the tomb of Oliver Cromwell. The grounds are beautiful with a water garden and rare alpines and rhododendrons.

INTO THE CLEVELAND HILLS

The coast running up from Scarborough to Whitby is of great interest. Whitby has its associations with the sinister Count Dracula, who landed here in Bram Stoker's book and Robin Hood's Bay plunges spectacularly into the sea, steeped in its associations with smuggling days gone by. The 13th century ruins of Whitby Abbey stand on a headland dominating the skyline, and the popular fishing village and seaside resort of Scarborough boasts a splendid 12th century Castle.

Inland is Great Ayton, a pretty village where Captain James Cook was schooled, and Ormesby Hall, acquired by the Pennyman family in 1600 has a splendid first floor gallery, fine plasterwork and a display of 18th century costumes. No trip to the Cleveland Hills would be complete without a visit to **Guisborough**, a charming market town with a medieval priory.

Fairfax House

YORKSHIRE & HUMBERSIDE

The Georgian Theatre Royal in Richmond is well worth a visit. The oldest theatre in England, it houses much interesting theatrical memorabilia.

Near Richmond, we find **Easby Abbey** and the 14th century Carthusian monastery of **Mount Grace** also nestles in the Cleveland Hills.

TO THE SOUTH

Sheffield predominates economically in the south of the counties of Yorkshire, and the importance of its history is plain to see. Famous as the city of cutlers and steelmakers, the Cutlers Hall dominates the town centre and there are some lovely Georgian houses and an interesting Cathedral. Its industrial history is celebrated at nearby Abbeydale Industrial Hamlet.

Goole is interesting as being of our furthest inland seaports, and **Pontefract's Castle** has an interesting history, having witnessed the murder of Richard II in 1400 and many other bloody battles.

Penistone is a pretty little town, and nearby **Gunthwaite Hall** is a spectacular half-timbered building which has stood for more than 500 years. Selby boasts a famous Norman Abbey, and **Conisborough Castle**, five miles north east of Rotherham still has a 90 foot high buttressed keep, and is the only surviving circular keep in Britain.

With some of the most magnificent countryside and places of natural beauty along with its important historical heritage, Yorkshire and Humberside will always remain great favourites with many a traveller.

Newburgh Priory

BURTON AGNES HALL

Burton Agnes Hall is a house of immense charm and character which has suffered little from alterations or additions in its history. A magnificent example of late Elizabethan architecture, the beautiful proportions of the Hall confirm the hand of a professional in its design. The architect was Robert Smithson who built the house in 1598 for Sir Henry Griffith on the site of a Norman Manor House. Built of brick which has weathered to a pleasing dusty pink, Smithson retained the perfect symmetry by placing the entrance door at the side of one of the projecting bays. His original mullioned windows have been replaced by sash windows in the centre and Palladian windows were added to each end of the Gallery in the 18th century. There are wonderful carvings, lovely furniture and a very fine collection of modern French and English paintings of the Impressionist Schools together with porcelain and bronzes.

The Elizabethan carving, plasterwork and panelling in the Great Hall is matchless. The screen and massive chimney piece are alive with tier upon tier of elaborately carved allegorical figures in alabaster. The furniture is of the same period as the decor and includes a magnificent Nonsuch Chest.

The Red Drawing Room has a further outstanding example of the Elizabethan woodcarvers skill in the form of a gruesome Dance of Death in the chimney-piece. The gilded Elizabethan panelling blends with the French furniture and a beautiful collection of 18th and 19th century European and English porcelain.

The Staircase is one of the most remarkable features of the house. The wide sweep of the stairs is flanked by a series of arches, all lavishly carved.

By contrast the Upper Drawing Room is light and elegant containing some of the finest furniture, particularly the satinwood commode with its pair of companion tables, delicately inlaid and attributed to Chippendale.

The State Bedrooms with their beautiful plasterwork ceilings, richly carved panelling and original beds were once witness to a sad and chilling chapter in the history of the house. Anne Griffith, daughter of Sir Henry had watched the house being built and talked of nothing but its beauty. When it was almost finished she was attacked and robbed by ruffians whilst visiting friends. She was brought home to Burton Agnes and some days later, in 1620, died of her injuries in the Queen's State Bedroom. Sometimes delirious, she had told her sisters that she would never rest unless some part of her remained 'in our beautiful home'. She made them promise that upon her death her head should be severed and preserved at the Hall. The sisters agreed, but Anne was buried with her head firmly on her shoulders. But her ghost terrified her sisters until they brought her skull into the house. Once it was thrown away, once it was buried in the garden and each time Anne reappeared with tremendous noise and upheaval. The skull is still in the house, built into one of the walls. No one knows for sure just where it is, but the ghost walks no more.

The Long Gallery has in recent times been restored as faithfully as possible to its former glory and now holds many treasures; graceful 18th century furniture; oriental, continental and English porcelain; fine bronzes and Georgian chandeliers; and many more fine paintings.

The gardens provide a perfect setting for this historic house. Clipped yew hedges, fountains and statuary form the framework whilst herbaceous borders, roses, clematis and campanulas add variety and colour from spring to late summer..

TEMPLE NEWSAM

Temple Newsam, during the first hundred years after it was begun in around 1500 was associated with the central figures of English history. Henry V111 and Elizabeth 1 both confiscated it in revenge for Catholic intrigue, and in the interim it was owned by the Earl and Countess of Lennox whose son, Lord Darnley, husband of Mary Queen of Scots, was born in the house. Settled times came with its purchase in 1622 by Sir Arthur Ingram, a highly successful financier and courtier. More than most houses Temple Newsam reflects the fortunes of its owners.

The estate was originally owned by the Knights Templar and was given to the Darcy family by Edward 111 in 1337. The house was begun by Thomas, Lord Darcy who was second in importance in the north to the Earl of Northumberland and his house reflected his exalted position - it is by far the largest of its date in Yorkshire. Darcy was executed in 1537 and after Lord Darnley was assassinated in 1567, the house eventually came to Sir Arthur Ingram whose family lived here for almost 300 years, relatively peacefully, becoming the Viscounts Irwin after the Civil War. Sir Arthur set about rebuilding Temple Newsam, demolishing most of the Tudor Darcy house, retaining one wing as the central block, and adding two long wings with large centred bay windows. A stone balustrade unites the old and new roof sections. Substantial alterations were made to the interior in the rococo style of the mid-18th century when the south wing was remodelled. The cupola was added in 1788.

After the death of the 9th Viscount the house passed through the female line to the Dowager Lady Hertford who created some notable Regency interiors. The Hon. Emily Maynell Ingram made some spectacular Victorian improvements and in 1922 her nephew, the Hon. Edward Wood (later Earl of Halifax) sold the house to the City of Leeds. Despite the sale of many of the furnishings at the time, the basis of the contents of Temple Newsam today is still the family collection, added to over the years to create one of the finest publicly-owned collections of English decorative art outside London.

One of the most celebrated pieces in the house is the beautiful library writing table in the elegant green and gold Edwardian Library. It was made by Thomas Chippendale for Harewood House in about 1770.

The Chinese Drawing Room shows Lady Hertford's taste of 1827-28 almost undisturbed. The walls are hung with hand-painted Chinese wallpaper, a gift from the Prince Regent in 1806 and embellished with birds cut out from the first volume of Audubon's celebrated Birds of America.

The Tudor Room in the original part of the house has arched doors, windows and fireplace. The panelling and magnificent bed, although made for another house, are contemporary with the fabric of Temple Newsam and give some idea of how the room might have looked in about 1530. The Georgian Library is a Palladian masterpiece. Classic Corinthian columns support a beautifully delicate plasterwork ceiling and in the centre is the original library table, returned in 1988 after a public appeal.

The house also contains famous furniture by Thomas Chippendale, Old Master paintings, a large collection of Leeds Creamware and spectacular silver.

The 900 acre park was landscaped in 1762 by 'Capability' Brown and was intended to reflect the gentle serenity of a landscape painting. The imposing Palladian stable block was built in 1742 and the home farm is now a haven for rare breeds of livestock.

Today there are seven lovely gardens at Temple Newsam including a herb garden, a spring garden of bulbs, an Italian garden, and laburnum and rhododendron walks winding through broad beds of azaleas to the lakes and arboretum.

Beside the upper lake there is a bog garden and the walled kitchen garden is planted with roses and wide herbaceous borders. The conservatory is set against a 'fire wall' built in 1788 to ripen pineapples and other exotic fruit.

SKIPTON CASTLE

Skipton Castle is one of the most complete and well-preserved medieval castles in England because, unlike its fellows, it survived Cromwell and the Victorians and its appearance today is similar to that of 450 years ago.

The first castle at Skipton was built about 1090 on a site well chosen - standing on rock with the ground rising from the south and then falling away sharply in a sheer cliff face to the north. In 1310 King Edward II granted Skipton Castle to Robert de Clifford who built the strongest parts of the Castle seen today, including the massive round towers and Main Gate. The history of the Castle is inextricably linked with the great fighting House of Clifford who distinguished itself on many a far-flung battle-field.

Under Thomas, the 8th Lord, Skipton entered the Wars of the Roses, but on the Lancastrian side which proved disastrous for the Cliffords. Thomas was killed in 1455 and his son in 1461, but not before he had earned himself the name of 'The Butcher' for severing the head of the Duke of York and placing it over the gates of York are among many unsavoury deeds. On his death his estates were confiscated by the enraged Yorkists and his widow, fearful for their son's safety, sent the boy into the wild Cumberland fells. There he tended sheep until restored to his estate by Henry VII after the Battle of Bosworth in 1485. Thus Henry, the 10th Lord and son of 'The Butcher' became known as 'The Shepherd'.

The 'Shepherd Lord' built the beautiful Conduit Court right at the heart of the castle, the safest place he could find. Built in the style which flourished after the Wars of the Roses, it was so named because it provided the castle's water supply. Inumerable doorways and staircases lead off this central area whose mullioned windows gave safe light to many rooms whose massive walls had only narrow slits or arrow loops.

His son, created Earl of Cumberland by his close friend King Henry VIII, built the Tudor Wing with its Long Gallery in 1536, in anticipation of the marriage of his son to the King's niece.

The 3rd Earl of Cumberland became Champion to Queen Elizabeth I and was a great sailor; he fought against the Spanish Amarda and undertook many hazardous voyages.

The strength of Skipton Castle, on its fine cliff-top site, was proved during the Civil War when it withstood a three-year siege. It was, in fact, the last castle in the North of England to hold out for Charles I. The Earl's daughter, Anne Clifford, planted the now-famous yew in the Conduit Court to celebrate the restoration of the castle following the War and rebuilt the damaged parts of the castle. On completion of her task she added the parapet with the Clifford motto over the Main Gate. Because Skipton Castle has remained fully roofed there are many rooms to explore, the most important of which are the Banqueting or Great Hall, the Withdrawing Room or Great Chamber and the Kitchen.

HAREWOOD HOUSE

Harewood House has become the treasure house of Yorkshire, much more than just the magnificent stately home of the Earl and Countess of Harewood. In 1759 Edwin Lascelles, whose family settled in Yorkshire after the Norman Conquest, instructed John Carr to build this noble house. Robert Adam was charged with designing the interiors with a gentle reminder that "I would not exceed the limits of expense that I have always set myself. Let us do everything properly and well, mais pas trop." The sugar plantations in Barbados were obviously thriving, but Edwin Lascelles was, after all, a Yorkshireman. Adam commissioned the finest craftsmen and artists to execute his wonderfully delicate designs and Thomas Chippendale to produce the furnishings. Harewood contains the richest collection of Chippendale furniture anywhere in the world, along with some of Adam's finest ceilings and an art collection of international renown.

Many of the portraits were acquired by Edward Lascelles who became 1st Earl of Harewood in 1812. Louisa, wife of the 2nd Earl called in Sir Charles Barry who added an additional third floor and sadly, altered or removed some of Adam's work. The early Victorians showed little respect for the past, but more recent refurbishments have been carried out in a manner much more sympathetic to Robert Adam's original themes.

The imposing Entrance Hall, never intended by Robert Adam as a place in which to linger, is now dominated by Jacob Epstein's Adam, the most important addition in recent years.

The lovely China Room was converted from a small library, the cabinets now displaying beautiful examples of gold and white Crown Derby and Sevres which form only a part of the collection of porcelain throughout Harewood.

Princess Mary's (mother to the present 7th Earl) Sitting Room contains some of the finest pieces of Thomas Chippendale's furniture - a secretaire and two commodes - the larger of which is inlaid with ivory and is justly famous. This room also houses part of a remarkable collection of watercolours of Harewood and its surroundings. Few houses can have been painted so often or by such eminent watercolourists as Varley, Malton, Turner & Girtin. The Gallery extends over the whole west of the house and 'presents such a show of magnificence and art

as eye hath seldom seen and words cannot describe.' Today the Gallery is the setting for the Italian pictures collected by the 6th Earl after the 1914-18 war and contains works by El Greco, Veronese, Tintoretto and Titian amongst many, many more, together with the famous Harewood Chinese porcelain.

To crown Thomas Chippendale's achievement here - a celebrated feature of the room - are the pelmets, intricately carved and painted, to give the impression of heavy folds of draped material. They are the only 'curtains' the room was intended to have.

In 1772 'Capability' Brown arrived and stayed for 9 years, turning the park into 'one of the most delectable of landscapes', with plantations and gently undulating vistas where before there had been fields and pasture. His method was to take inspiration from the natural contours of the land, although he would employ hundreds of men to shift tons of earth if nature's plan did not agree with his own.

The very formal Terrace was added by Barry and Lady Harewood in the 1840's and commands spectacular views across the lake. The Italian theme represents folded ribbons in a series of parterres around a central fountain with a modern bronze of Orpheus. There have been rhododendrons at Harewood for over a century. Princess Mary had a passion for these beautiful shrubs, shared by her husband the 6th Earl, who subscribed to pre-war expeditions to the Himalayas in search of new species. As a result there are over 100 different species and many more hybrids which create a dazzling display of jewel-bright colour along the lakeside walks in summer.

The Harewood Bird Garden, active in the conservation of rare species, is set beside the lake on gentle slopes amidst fine old trees. A more recent extension to this is the Tropical Rain Forest, recreated as authentically as possible.

There are restaurants and gift shops and a fine stable block has been converted to form an ideal setting for private and business functions. Harewood is easily accessible from the A61 Leeds-Harrogate road, 7 miles north of Leeds, and 8 miles from the M1.

NEWBY HALL

Newby Hall, home of Mr and Mrs Robin Compton, was built by Sir Edward Blackett during the 1690s in the style of Sir Christopher Wren. The estate was bought by the Weddell family in 1748 and the next twenty five years were to see great changes at Newby.

William Weddell, a man of great taste, commissioned John Carr to alter and enlarge the house, primarily to house his collection of classical sculpture (he returned from the Grand Tour with nineteen chests) and for the set of Gobelins tapestries he ordered in 1766. Carr added the two wings to the east of the house, remodelled much of the main block and designed the Statue Gallery, but not to Weddell's entire satisfaction. In 1767 Robert Adam was commissioned to complete the gallery and to decorate the Tapestry Room and some of the other main rooms. How Weddell must have loved the beauty and elegance of the result!

In 1792 the house passed to his cousin, the 3rd Lord Grantham, who felt the house lacked a large, sunny sitting room, and that the library was too small for all his books. An amateur architect himself, he decided to turn Adam's south-facing dining room into a library and build a new dining room, the Regency Dining Room, much of which he designed himself. His grandson added the Billiards Room above the Dining Room and the Victorian Wing.

The Robert Adam interiors, redecorated with great knowledge and flair by Mrs Compton, are excellent examples of his classical style, none more so that the Statue Gallery and the Tapestry Room. The Gallery, William Weddell's joy, was designed in the style of a Roman interior - the perfect setting for his famous collection. In three sections, two square rooms and a central, domed rotunda, the plasterwork ceilings are finely executed. Some of the pedestals for the sculptures were also designed by Adam.

The Tapestry Room is one of the marvels of 18th century decoration in England. The tapestries, depicting the 'Loves of the Gods', were one of only five sets made for English patrons. The Newby set is the only one to have a dove-grey and not a rose pink background. The chairs and sofas, by Thomas Chippendale, are unique as they are upholstered in their original tapestry, each one having different sprays of flowers. The lovely painted panels of the ceiling are by Antonio Zucchi.

The house is filled with fine English and French furniture, family portraits and paintings and porcelain including a unique collection of chamber pots from all over Europe and the Far East. Ranging from rough peasant ware of the 16th century to fine examples of 18th and 19th century china, many are extremely rare.

The gardens at Newby Hall cover some twenty-five acres, bordered by the River Ure. The great double herbaceous borders, flanked by yew hedges, form a magnificent vista from the south front of the house down to the river. Off this main axis are a series of formal gardens, each attaining perfection in different seasons of the year. There is a Woodland Discovery Walk through Bragget Wood, Adventure Gardens and a miniature railway runs alongside the river.

CASTLE HOWARD

Rolling up from the Vale of York, the Howardian Hills are the framework for Castle Howard, home to the Howard family from the day it was built, since when it has also been open to the public. Castle Howard grew from the imagination and vision of three men, Charles, 3rd Earl of Carlisle, Sir John Vanbrugh and Nicholas Hawksmoor.

Charles Howard, 3rd Earl of Carlisle was a man of immense power and ambition. At the time a considerable number of grand country houses were being built, and in 1699, he commissioned the building of a new house on the site of Henderskelfe Castle. His choice of architect was an unlikely one, for though John Vanbrugh was a man of easy charm and wit, as an architect he was untried. He consulted Nicholas Hawksmoor whose training and experience took over where Vanbrugh's imagination left off. The design of Castle Howard took shape as it was built; when the first stones were laid there was as yet no dome envisaged. Perhaps his very lack of training left Vanbrugh free to use with such exuberance the wealth of super-imposed detail which enlivens Castle Howard.

When Vanbrugh died in 1726 the West Wing was still unbuilt and was completed for the 4th Earl by his brother-in-law Sir Thomas Robinson. Unfortunately the Palladian wing bears little relation to Vanbrugh's design. In 1940 two thirds of the South Front and the entire dome were destroyed by fire. George Howard, later Lord Howard of Henderskelfe, restored the dome in 1960 and in 1981 he built the Garden Hall, followed in 1983 by the Library. Both these rooms are in the style of Vanbrugh and complement the house rather than detracting from it.

The Great Hall is the centrepiece of the house, a splendid justification of the 3rd Earl's choice of Vanbrugh as his architect. Its arches, niches, columns and capitals, vigorously carved are interspersed by Pellegrini's depictions of the Four Elements. Scrolling elaborately up the stairs, across the balcony and round the Gallery above is the wrought iron work of John Gardom. Rising 20 feet, the Hall is crowned by its gilded dome.

Portraits of the Earls of Carlisle hang on the walls of the Grand Staircase which leads to the China Landing. Here a magnificent

china cabinet holds Crown Derby, Chelsea, Meissen, Derby and Minton porcelain. The Antique Passage is one of Vanbrugh's many innovations and was designed to be a feature of the house rather than a utilitarian corridor and is a perfect example of his theatrical style. The majority of the antiquities in the house were collected by Henry, 4th Earl and the Passage provides the perfect setting for mythical Gods intermingled with portrait busts and funeral urns.

The Long Gallery, at 192 feet, is probably the longest room in a private house. The North and South Ends are separated by the Octagon which houses rare books ranging from the 16th century to the present day.

The 5th Earl of Carlisle was an avid collector of paintings and acquired at least ten by Reynolds. Throughout the house are works by Holbein, Rubens and Gainsborough, together with paintings by Dutch and Italian artists, fine furniture and beautiful ceramics.

As important as Castle Howard itself is the setting in which it is found. In the centre of Vanbrugh's curtain wall, with bastions, mock fortifications and eleven different towers is his Gatehouse with a massive arch and pyramid, and wings added by Thomas Robinson in 1756. Set back from the avenues of limes are the Stables built in 1781 to the design of John Carr, and now home to the Castle Howard Costume Gallery, the largest private collection from the 17th century to the present day.

The Great Lake, ponds and New River provide an informal contrast to the Walled Garden, lawns and gravelled paths. Recently two Rose Gardens have been planted, one with old-fashioned varieties, the other with more modern hybrids.

The terraced walk to the Temple is awash with daffodils in the spring. The Temple of the Four Winds, high on its promontary was Vanbrugh's last work. The magnificent Mausoleum, with its classical white and gold interior, is a fine example of the work of Nicholas Hawksmoor, a fitting climax for one of the great works of landscape and architecture.

Harewood House

BILBROUGH MANOR

Whether you are enjoying the Sport at York's famous 'Champagne Course' or visiting our charming city and countryside at any time of year you will find Bilbrough manor your perfect House in the Country, complete with a butler to attend to your every need and a chef whose consummate flair has brought him major awards and an international reputation.

Standing in wooded grounds extending to 100 acres, the Manor was the ancestral home of the prominent Fairfax Family, the most famous of whom, General 'Black Tom' Fairfax, commander of Cromwell's New Model Army, is buried in the churchyard next door. The Manor House and grounds have been extensively refurbished to create one of the finest Country House Hotels in the North of England: few could believe the transformation that has been wrought by the resident proprietors, the Bell family and their team of craftsmen. Every aspect of the gracious stone mansion has been enhanced and the considerable new work involved was matched perfectly to the old to provide a setting of mellow panelling, warming fires and imaginative soft furnishings, ideally suited to comfortable relaxation, or indeed executive business meetings.

Accolades have been heaped on Bilbrough Manor from all directions; from appreciative guests, loath to leave the log fires and attentive butler, from the present Lord Fairfax and other dignitaries, and from the international Press, including Egon Ronay's Guide.

So what is Bilbrough's secret? It is evident that no expense has been spared in providing every comfort for visitors, who indeed are treated as family guests. Fixtures and fittings are of the highest quality, every bedroom is en suite and individually furnished with impeccable taste. The dining room is oak panelled and elegant, the public rooms sumptuous and magnificent, at the same time exuding an atmosphere of warmth and welcome.

Every comfort is catered for, encouraging guests to relax, unwind and enjoy to the full this taste of gracious country living. Bilbrough has the best of both worlds, only 3 miles West from the City of York but situated in an attractive conservation village and enjoying glorious views over the Vale of York.

With such surroundings and with such conscientious care for their guests' welfare, how could the Bells fail to make Bilbrough a resounding success.

The promise they saw has been fulfilled. Bilbrough Manor's reputation is only just beginning, but it will go on to be one of the legendary hotels in the land.

Bilbrough Manor
Bilbrough
Nr York YO2 3PH
Tel: (0937) 834002

YORKSHIRE

Although Yorkshire is split into separate areas, it remains, for the sake of its cricket team, a single entity and in this part of the world that carries far more weight than any Departmental directive wishing to move the county borders.

The major cities of Yorkshire are concentrated to the south of the Shire whilst to the north and east lie the Dales and the sea.

This is a county which boasts sea cliffs, acres of National Parkland and a mystique all of its own. This is the county of Captain Cook, Emily Bronte, James Herriot and Geoffrey Boycott to name but a few illustrious Yorkshire folk.

The White Rose flies proudly over Yorkshire and no matter what the weather throws at you, you are sure to find some quiet corner from which to enjoy the scenery and heritage of the county - the pubs are numerous and the ale second to none!

The city of York is quite beautiful and one which deserves a visit. Rich in heritage, there are some first class hotels within its medieval city walls and if you have only got the time for a short visit to Yorkshire then York City must be at the top of the list.

Outside York, the moorlands stretch away, covered in clouds of purple heather - quite a sight. The Pennines also play their part for this county. The backbone of England, the Pennines are home to many wild flowers and animals as well as friendly pubs and inns. Hotels also cater for the traveller seeking Castle Howard or the ruins of once great Abbeys.

Yorkshire has a bloody heritage. It was here that Dick Turpin roamed the countryside holding up coaches passing through the county.

A county of infinite variety to many, Yorkshire has a peculiar sense of loneliness in the hectic 20th century but perhaps this is its greatest attraction.

HOTELS OF DISTINCTION

AYTON HALL, Great Ayton, North Yorkshire. Tel: (0642) 723595
Ayton Hall is a Grade II listed building of special architectural and historic interest. Built on foundations dating back to 1281, the Hall claims strong connections to Captain James Cook FRS. Set in 6 acres of landscaped gardens, the Hall offers many sporting facilities.

THE BELL, Great Driffield, Yorkshire. Tel: (0377) 46661
Not only has this historic coaching inn been tastefully renovated but the owners have lovingly restored the adjacent Old Town Hall to serve as a conference centre. Comfortably furnished with antiques.

BILBOROUGH MANOR HOTEL, Near York, North Yorkshire. Tel: (0937) 834002
Elegantly set in a village the bedrooms here have a modern feel. The restaurant serves good French and English cooking and the hotel is within easy driving distance of York with its wonderful Minster and ancient buildings.

THE BLACK SWAN, Helmsley, North Yorkshire. Tel: (0439) 70466
Originally an Elizabethan coaching inn, this hotel has now spread to encompass a Georgian house and a Tudor rectory. The interior is very traditional with heavy timbers and low ceilings.

CHARNWOOD HOTEL, Sheffield, South Yorkshire. Tel: (0742) 589411
This Georgian mansion is a listed building dating from 1780 and boasts a library and two new restaurants. It is a mere 10 minutes drive from the stunning Peak National Park.

DEAN COURT, York, Yorkshire. Tel: (0904) 625082
Many of the rooms here enjoy views of York's spectacular Minster. The hotel is attractively furnished to provide comfortable accommodation in delightful surroundings.

DEVONSHIRE ARMS COUNTRY HOUSE HOTEL, Bolton Abbey, North Yorkshire. Tel: (076671) 441
Originally a coaching inn, now enlarged and with many antiques, this hotel is both traditional and comfortable. Beautiful countryside and the best-of-British shopping are at Harrogate nearby.

DOWER HOUSE, Knaresborough, North Yorkshire. Tel: (0423) 863302
A listed, former dower house, this ivy-covered building retains a traditional charm while still providing guests with modern conveniences. The interior decor is complete with Georgian staircase and period furniture.

THE FEVERSHAM ARMS HOTEL, Helmsley, North Yorkshire. Tel: (0439) 70766
A luxuriously modernised, historic coaching inn set in over an acre of walled gardens, this hotel offers every comfort and is perfect for exploring the Moors, Dales, East Coast and the medieval city of York.

THE GEORGE HOTEL, Clifton, North Yorkshire. Tel: (0904) 644744
This carefully restored hotel rests close to the ancient city walls of the city of York. Beautiful antique furniture decorates the interior of this elegant Regency town house.

THE GRANGE, York, North Yorkshire. Tel: (0904) 612453
This is a beautiful Regency building of York stone located near the centre of York. The building has been beautifully restored to create an elegant yet comfortable hotel with bright, well furnished rooms. The excellent Ivy Restaurant is another good reason for visiting.

GRANTS HOTEL, Harrogate, North Yorkshire. Tel: (0423) 560666
This friendly hotel is perfectly located for exploring the Yorkshire Dales and Harrogate itself with the Royal Pump Room Museum and Baths Assembly Rooms where you can soak up the fascinating history.

HOLDSWORTH HOUSE, Halifax, West Yorkshire. Tel: (0422) 240024
Now a Grade II listed building, the hotel first appeared in 1633. Little has changed on the outside, and the interior has been

KIRKBY FLEETHAM HALL

Set amidst thirty two acres of private parkland, yet within easy reach of the A1, Kirkby Fleetham Hall is a splendid Georgian house which has been sympathetically turned into a luxury 22 bedroom country house hotel with strong emphasis placed on the creation of a homely atmosphere.

In the elegant dining room one may enjoy modern English cuisine prepared by a brigade of highly talented chefs led by David Alton. A wealth of local produce compliment the fruit, vegetables and herbs grown in the walled Victorian kitchen garden to help produce a memorable food experience. From the freshly baked breads to the tempting desserts, even the most discerning appetites are satisfied, especially after a most exhilarating day at the races.

Each of the bedrooms has its own distinctive decor and is exquisitely furnished, All rooms have a direct dial telephone, colour television, radio and delightful view.

Under the watchful eye of Manager Stephen J. Mannock, all the staff are committed to the well being of their guest. To stay in this tranquil country house hotel is to experience gracious living in a way that Herriot country land owners did in more

relaxing times. It is without doubt a house for all seasons.

If you prefer something more exciting then Kirkby Fleetham Hall still has the answer. In association with "Special Events" a company who mirror Kirkby Fleetham's own high standards of customer well-being and attention to detail, the grounds of the hotel are offered as an ideal venue for Clay Pigeon Shooting, Fly Fishing, Archery and off the road Buggie driving. Arrangements can also be made for guests to have hands on experience of flying by microlight, private plane or glider.

Kirkby Fleetham Hall is ideally located between the North Yorkshire Moors and the Dales. Both areas offer a host of leisure and sightseeing activities to suit every taste, with more than its fair share of beautiful scenery, Stately Homes, Cathedrals Castles and fascinating towns and cities.

Children are welcome at Kirkby Fleetham Hall, though under 7's are not allowed in the dining room at dinner.

Dogs by prior arrangement.

Open all year.

Kirkby Fleetham Hall
Kirkby Fleetham
Northallerton
North Yorkshire
DL7 0SU
Tel: (0609) 748711
Fax: (0609) 748747

YORKSHIRE

beautifully restored to complement the open beams and fine panelling.

HOLBECK HALL HOTEL, South Cliffe, North Yorkshire. Tel: (0723) 374374
Close to the fascinating medieval city of York and to Castle Howard, this splendid late Victorian mansion is set in 3 acres of grounds which boast a romantic rose garden and natural woodland.

JERVAULX HALL, Masham, North Yorkshire. Tel: (0677) 60235
A 19th century manor house adjacent to the ruined 12th century Jervaulx Abbey. Offering a high standard of comfort and cuisine, it is ideally situated for visiting Middleham Castle, Bramham Park, Castle Howard, Harrogate, Ripon and York.

JUDGES LODGING, York, North Yorkshire. Tel: (0904) 638733
An 18th century, Grade I listed building, the Judges Lodging is set in the middle of York amidst its own well kept gardens. The atmosphere here is welcoming and all rooms are of a good size. There is an old cantilever staircase, still in good condition, in the entrance to the hotel.

KILDWICK HALL, Kildwick, West Yorkshire. Tel: (0535) 632244
An extraordinary mish-mash of architecture comprises this fine Jacobean mansion-hotel. It is never quite elegant, but then its interest value far outweighs any strict design faults it might have.

KIRKBY FLEETHAM HALL, Kirkby Fleetham, North Yorkshire. Tel: (0609) 748711
In the heart of James Herriot's country, between the Yorkshire Moors and Dales, this beautiful Georgian hall is set in its own 30 acre estate and adjoins an impressive 12th century church.

THE MANOR HOUSE, Northlands, North Humberside. Tel: (0452) 881645
Just on the outskirts of the Yorkshire Wolds, this beautiful 19th century manor house is the perfect retreat, with bedrooms overlooking 3 acres of private tree-lined grounds.

MIDDLETHORPE HALL, York, North Yorkshire. Tel: (0904) 641241
Built in 1699 and home to the diarist Lady Mary Wortley who lived here in the 18th century. Close to historic York and commanding 26 acres of parkland, Middlethorpe is perfect for exploring the Fountains and Rievaulx Abbeys.

MONK FRYSTON HALL, Monk Fryston, North Yorkshire. Tel: (0977) 682369
A mellow old manor house dating back to the Middle Ages and of great architectural interest. This luxury hotel offers period elegance with modern facilities and fine traditional cuisine.

MOUNT ROYALE HOTEL, York, North Yorkshire. Tel: (0904) 628896
The elegant combination of two beautifully restored William IV houses with an acre of old English gardens has created this gracious hotel only minutes away from the historic city of York.

NIDD HALL, Harrogate, North Yorkshire. Tel: (0423) 771598
An imposing country mansion in 45 acres of grounds, Nidd Hall combines grandeur with comfort. It offers many facilities, including a leisure club and fishing and is conveniently located for visiting York.

THE PHEASANT, Helmsley, North Yorkshire. Tel: (0439) 71241/70416
A charming family-run hotel, brightly decorated and offering traditional Yorkshire hospitality and cuisine. Ideally situated for the abbeys of Byland and Rievaulx, Castle Howard and York.

POOL COURT RESTAURANT WITH ROOMS, Pool Bank, West Yorkshire. Tel: (0532) 84288
This Georgian mansion prefers to be known for the restaurant it has built its fine reputation on. The original cellar rooms, with vaulted ceilings and old stonework provide the perfect atmosphere for the small meeting.

ROSE AND CROWN HOTEL, Bainbridge, North Yorkshire. Tel: (0969) 50225
The Bainbridge Horn still guides the weary and lost traveller on cold winter evenings in the heart of the lovely Yorkshire Dales, but take your maps as well. Famous for good cheese and good cheer, this is the heart of farming Yorkshire, where cricket is discussed with passion.

ROWLEY MANOR, Little Weighton, Humberside. Tel: (0482) 848248
A gracious Georgian manor with a Grinling Gibbons panelled study and a unique water temple, this hotel is set in 15 acres of grounds. All the rooms have superb views and the restaurant offers delicious country cooking.

THE SPORTSMAN'S ARMS, Wath-in-Nidderdale, North Yorkshire. Tel: (0423) 711306.
This 17th century building resting in beautiful Nidderdale is home to an excellent restaurant. Enjoy pre-dinner drinks in the bar before moving into the restaurant to enjoy Ray Carter's cuisine. The cooking is English, with game, salmon and other seafood a speciality.

MCCOY'S, Straddle Bridge, North Yorkshire. Tel: (0609) 82671
The 1920's, 30's and 40's are lovingly combined with this extraordinarily atmospheric and original abode. Splendid antiques adorn the bedrooms and the restaurant, which is equally stylish and one of the first in England.

WHITWELL HALL, Whitwell-on-the-Hill, North Yorkshire. Tel: (065381) 551
A Tudor-Gothic style, ivy clad manor house with mullioned windows. Impressive entrance hall with stone floors and porches. The pleasant homely feel of the rooms which are filled with good antique furniture.

WOOD HALL, Linton, West Yorkshire. Tel: (093)767271
Predominantly Georgian, with a Jacobean wing, this hotel commands 100 acres. Nearby are stately homes and the rolling Yorkshire Dales, and guests may fish for trout in a private stretch of the river Wharfe.

THE MOUNT ROYALE HOTEL

The hotel is the result of the tasteful blending of two beautiful William IV detatched houses. The proprietors, Richard and Christine Oxtoby, have spent a good deal of effort on restoring the former glory of these buildings and their efforts have been well rewarded.

Any traveller having an interest in English history must surely rank the fascinating city of York at least alongside London. The capital of the north and second city of the realm, it began its long and fascinating life around AD71 as a fortress to protect the Roman 9th Legion. The marauding Vikings gave the city its name, derived from Jorvik or Yorwik. This period of history has been magnificently captured in the Jorvik Viking Centre, one of the most entertaining museums in the country. The Minster or Cathedral is the largest medieval structure in Britain. There has been a Minster on the site since the 7th century, the present one is the fourth and was started about 1220, taking 250 years to complete. The city is still protected by ancient city walls, guarded by defensive bastions, working portcullis' and barbican at the Walmgate bar.

Wander around the Micklegate bar, where traitors' severed heads were displayed or visit the National Rail Museum.

Staying in York involves mixing with some of the most fascinating sights in the world. Relaxing afterwards in the intimate cocktail bar of the Mount Royale, or enjoying a delicious meal in the restaurant overlooking the delightful garden, enhances the whole experience. Enjoying the gracious beauty of the hotel, the style and antiquity of much of the furnishings, or slipping into the secluded heated swimming pool is the perfect way to pamper the body as well as the mind.

The hotel is ideal for the small conference or private dinner party, and is only a short drive from the rolling Yorkshire Dales. The perfect base, offering peace and tranquility, practically in the heart of this wonderful city.

Mount Royale Hotel
The Mount
York YO2 2DA
Tel: (0904) 628856

YORKSHIRE

WREA HEAD COUNTRY HOUSE HOTEL, Scalby, North Yorkshire. Tel: (0723) 378211

Furnished with paintings and antiques, with panelled walls and inglenook fireplaces, this Victorian country house, built in 1871, commands 14 acres of grounds on the edge of the North Yorkshire Moors National Park. Historic York is nearby.

ACCOMMODATION OF MERIT

BRAFFERTON HALL, Brafferton, North Yorkshire.
Tel: (0423) 360352

Nestled on the Swale this attractive house, built in 1780's offers generous hospitality to those who wish to explore Harrogate, York, the Moors and Dales, Coast and the many historical houses. Only four, very rural, miles from the A1. (see photograph).

DUNSLEY HALL, Dunsley, Yorkshire. Tel: (0947) 83437

An elegant country house in peaceful four acre ground, complete with oak panelled rooms and unusual carved billiard room. Ideal touring base for North and East Yorkshire, including Captain Cook country, Herriot country, the Heritage Coast and York.

ELMFIELD HOUSE, Bedale, North Yorkshire.
Tel: (0677) 50558

In the heart of 'Herriot Country', Elmfield House sits in its own secluded grounds with uninterrupted views. Golf, riding and fishing are all within easy reach, as are York and Ripon racecourses.

HOLGATE HEAD, Kirby Malham, North Yorkshire.
Tel: (07293) 376

A delightful old stone house, with wonderful views over Malhamdale, in the heart of the Yorkshire Dales. Warm 17th century oak panelling in the hall-sitting room with open fireplace make this hotel with its large gardens and woodland a comfortable touring base.

LITTLEBURN, Thoralby, North Yorkshire.
Tel: (0969) 663621

Facing south over Bishopdale, this classic mid-Georgian country house is a comfortable base from which to tour the Dales, and all of Yorkshire, being halfway between M1 and M6. Previous guests have included Lord Nelson and the Duke of Wellington!

LOW HALL, Dacre, North Yorkshire. Tel: (0423) 781457

A Small Dales Manor House, dating from 1635, complete with classic stone mullions, oak beams and log fires, and set in delightful gardens. Rivaulx and Fountains Abbey, Skipton, Settle, Grassington and Ripon are all within easy reach.

THE MANOR HOUSE, Flamborough, East Yorkshire.
Tel: (0262) 850943

Records of a manor on this site can be found in the Domesday Book, but the current house is a well-proportioned Georgian residence. The Heritage coast, RSPB reserve, Castle Howard and York are all within easy reach.

Brafferton Hall

THE GRANGE HOTEL

THE GRANGE
YORK

The Grange is a classical Regency Townhouse situated within four minutes walk of the world famous Minster.

The hotel opened in 1990 after extensive restoration and within the year was awarded 'Best Newcomer in the North' and three Red Stars by the AA - a unique achievement.

The Grange is decorated in the comfy style of an English Country house with fine paintings and antique furniture. The flower filled Morning Room is especially warm and welcoming where one may relax in one of the deep sofas in front of the blazing log fire.

Within the hotel, the Ivy Restaurant has already established a reputation as one of the very best in the North of England under the direction of Cara Baird who came from Le Gavroche in London. Because York is exceptionally well placed near both sea and moorland, the menu offers a wide range of fresh fish and game according to the season.

There is also The Brasserie in the old brick vaulted cellars, full of atmosphere and charm which provides light gourmet dishes with interesting wines at reasonable prices.

For private dinners or parties the grand panelled Library and Drawing Room provide the perfect setting.

But the Grange is very proud that several of the leading guidebooks have marked out for special distinction the friendliness and efficiency of the staff. It is their aim to ensure that you have a memorable stay and to assist wherever possible.

The Grange Hotel
Clifton
York
YO3 6AA
Tel: (0904) 644744
Fax: (0904) 612453

WHITWELL HALL

The setting of this impressive Tudor Gothic mansion, with its gardens full of flowers and views over the Vale of York, is spectacular.

The grand welcome of the hall, with its red-carpeted, cantilevered staricase leading up to the arched gallery, is memorable.

Some of the bedrooms are spacious, and all have antique chests, attractive colour schemes, direct-dial telephones and well-fitted bathrooms.

With an indoor swimming pool and sauna, and an attractive orangery, the house affords a wonderful sense of space and light.

The chef, Rodney Yorke, has made Whitwell Hall very popular for light lunches, and the a la Carte menu in the evening has excellent venison and very good fish from Whitby. The table d'hote menu is good value.

You feel you are staying in a house rather than an hotel, and Sallie and Peter Milner ensure that you enjoy your stay.

A good round of golf can be had at nearby Ganton, and York racecourse is just 20 minutes away. There are more abbeys in this area than anywhere else in the country; Castle Howard is five minutes away, and there are other stately homes and National Trust properties within half an hour's drive.

Historical and beautiful York, with its superb Minster, is just down the road, which makes this delightful country house hotel one of the nicest places to stay in the North of England.

Whitwell Hall Country House Hotel,
Whitwell on the Hill,
York YO6 7JJ.
Tel: (065 381) 551
Fax: (065 381) 554

JERVAULX HALL

Set amidst the beautiful scenery of the Yorkshire dales and standing adjacent to one of England's most resplendant ruins, Jervaulx Abbey, there could be no better or more unique place from which to tour the surrounding countryside than this friendly and well run hotel.

Bought in 1979, the idea was to create a splendid hotel from this imposing country house. Eight acres of delightful gardens and mature woodlands surround the house which lies midway between the quaint market towns of Masham and Middleham.

It is essentially a quiet and peaceful hotel in which to relax and enjoy beautiful surroundings. The gardens are a delight and can be explored. Over 120 species of wild flowers have been recorded in a single season in the grounds of Jervaulx. The Abbey, founded in 1156 by the monks who gave Wensleydale Cheese its name, is also well worth visiting - its walls are a spectacular riot of marjoram and wall flowers.

The original character of the house interior has been preserved.

The hotel has ten double bedrooms, bathrooms en suite. One bedroom is situated on the ground floor with its own doorway opening on to the garden, making it particularly suitable for the elderly or disabled, or guests with dogs.

The hotel also offers a residential and table licence. Fresh vegetables and soft fruits, local lamb and game are offered on the menu when in season. The hotel's balanced menu and good wines will thus add to the enjoyment of one's stay at Jervaulx. Having lingered a while in the superb setting of Jervaulx it might be as well to get out and about to sample the rest of the area. Castle Howard, Harewood House, Fountains Abbey, York, Harrogate, Richmond and Ripon are all places that should not be missed.

With all of Yorkshire's eleven racecourses conveniently near and the A1 only 20 minutes away, this haven of peace and tranquility is a splendid place to ponder after a day's racing or golf.

Jervaulx Hall Hotel
Jervaulx
Nr Masham
Ripon HG4 4PH
North Yorkshire
Tel: (0677) 60235

YORKSHIRE

THE OLD HALL, Jervaulx Abbey, North Yorkshire. Tel: (0677) 60313
A mellow stone house once the servants' quarters of the nearby manor is placed in four acres of land complete with courtyard and stabling. Perfectly situated for visiting the abundance of historical sites throughout Yorkshire.

THORNTON RUST HALL, Leyburn, North Yorkshire. Tel: (0969) 663569
The new part of this manor was built in 1702 but it was begun in 1675. Sloping beamed ceilings, three foot thick walls, walled garden, fullsize billiard room, a panelled dining room and indoor heated pool are all delightful features.

INNS OF CHARACTER

ALTISIDORA, Bishop Burton, Humberside.
This picturesque 400 year old pub overlooking a pretty duck pond on the lovely village green offers good value bar food and fine ales. Traditional low beams are the hallmark of this comfortable inn.

BLACKSMITHS ARMS, Lastingham, North Yorkshire.
Stone walls and oak beams abound at this typically traditional Yorkshire village pub which some years ago was kept by the village parson! Traditional food, fine ales and malt whiskies are all to be recommended here.

GREEN TREE, Hatfield Woodhouse, South Yorkshire.
A feeling of warmth meets the visitor to this sixteenth century ale house. Simplicity and comfort combined with good food and fine ales retain the popularity of this cheerful pub.

QUEENS ARMS, Litton, North Yorkshire. Nowhere is the character of the Dales more apparent than at this scenic 17th century inn. Excellent food and fine ale can be enjoyed within the traditional surroundings of stone walls and beams.

SHIP INN, Saltburn-by-the-Sea, Cleveland.
Tiled floors, rough wooden tables and an open fire dominate this cosy Victorian pub. Situated on the beach and surrounded by small boats, local fresh seafood and good ales are the main delights.

SHOE, Ellerton, Humberside.
This unspoilt and unpretentious 16th century cottage is well worth visiting for its comfortable and friendly atmosphere. Fair priced bar food and well kept ales are in keeping with its overall charm.

TAN HILL INN, Tan Hill, North Yorkshire.
Remote and isolated on the moors, Britain's highest pub was built in 1737 to cater for local coal miners. Simple but extremely cheerful it continues to draw visitors from far afield.

TRITON, Sledmere, Humberside.
This welcoming 18th century inn is quite a charmer, with stately cushioned settles and a traditional lounge bar making for a pleasant atmosphere. Good food and fine ales encourage a visit to this rural spot.

Middlethorp Hall

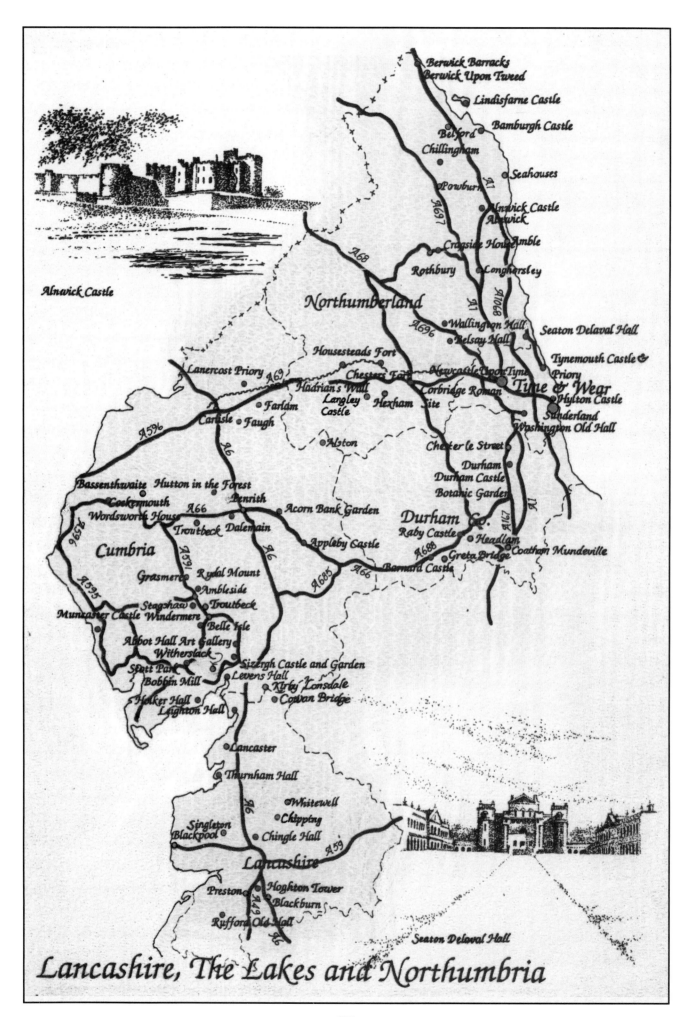

Berwick Barracks
Berwick Upon Tweed
Lindisfarne Castle
Bamburgh Castle
Belford
Chillingham
Seahouses
Powburn
Alnwick Castle
Alnwick
Cragside House Amble
Rothbury
Longhorsley

Northumberland

A697
A1
A1068

Wallington Hall
Seaton Delaval Hall
A696
Belsay Hall
Housesteads Fort
Tynemouth Castle &
Lanercost Priory
A69
Chesters Fort
Newcastle Upon Tyne
Priory
Hadrian's Wall
Corbridge Roman
Tyne & Wear
Farlam
Langley
Hexham
Site
Hylton Castle
Castle
Sunderland
Carlisle
Faugh
Washington Old Hall
A596
A6
Chester le Street
Alston
Durham
Durham Castle
Botanic Garden
Bassenthwaite
Hutton in the Forest
Cockermouth
Penrith
Durham Co.
Wordsworth House
Acorn Bank Garden
Raby Castle
Headlam
A66
Troutbeck
Dalemain
A1(M)
A596
Coatham Mundeville
Cumbria
A592
Appleby Castle
A688
Greta Bridge
A6
Grasmere
Rydal Mount
A685
A66
Barnard Castle
A595
Ambleside
Stagshaw
Troutbeck
Muncaster Castle
Windermere
Belle Isle
Abbot Hall Art Gallery
Witherslack
Stott Park
Sizergh Castle and Garden
Bobbin Mill
Levens Hall
Holker Hall
Kirby Lonsdale
Leighton Hall
Cowan Bridge

Lancaster

Thurnham Hall

Whitewell
Chipping
Singleton
Blackpool
Chingle Hall
A6
A59
Lancashire
Preston
Hoghton Tower
A49
Blackburn
A6
Rufford Old Hall
Seaton Delaval Hall

Alnwick Castle

Lancashire, The Lakes and Northumbria

LANCASHIRE, THE LAKES AND NORTHUMBRIA

The traveller visiting Cumbria for the first time has a rare treat in store. Cumbria claims to be 'the most beautiful corner of England' and it is not an empty claim. Cumbria's reputation is dominated by the Lake District, the country's largest National Park with 866 square miles of mountainous countryside and glorious scenery. The area is a walker's paradise, offering gentle strolls by the lake, or challenging hikes across the rugged moorlands and climbs up the rocky mountains. The less energetic can settle for a boat trip on the lakes, or an amble around one of the area's many museums or stately homes. The scenery can be little changed since Wordsworth was inspired by it over 150 years ago.

AROUND THE SOUTHERN COAST

Much of the Lake District is designated as being 'of outstanding natural beauty'. This includes the area around the pretty seaside town of Arnside, where uniquely varying countryside includes limestone pavements, salt marshes and fenland, with woodland on the higher ground. National Trust Properties which are worth a visit in the area include **Arnside Knott**, 211 acres with lovely tress and rare flowers, overlooking Morecambe Bay. Kirkby Lonsdale is one of the District's most beautiful towns, set on a hill above the river Lune, with the imposing Devil's Bridge spanning the river to the south of the town. The bridge probably dates back to the 13th century. Worth a visit while you are there are the Norman St Mary's Church, the 17th century manor house and the 18th century Fountain House.

Kendal is an interesting town, despite being known as 'the old grey town' because of its abundance of grey limestone buildings. The ruined castle was once the home of Catherine Parr, and also take a look at **Abbott Hall**, a lovely Georgian mansion which now houses an art gallery which includes sculptures and ceramics. The 13th century church with its extraordinary peel of bells is definitely worth a detour.

Five miles south of Kendal is **Levens Hall**, a lovely Elizabethan House with splendid oak carvings and pictures, and a topiary garden (featured later). Close by is **Sizergh Castle**, which has grown over the years from being one of the many 14th century peles (towers within a protective stockade) which littered the border country at that time. It is now an amazing collection of buildings through the ages and has an estate of 1,500 acres.

On Morecambe Bay, the town of Cartmel is interesting as it is effectively a cathedral town in miniature, with a fine priory church, formerly known as 'the Cathedral of the Lakes' and a splendid gateway. A little to the north is **Holker Hall**, dating from the 16th century, and boasting lovely gardens and a huge deer park (featured later).

Stott Park Bobbin Mill at Finsthwaite, built in 1835 has been restored as a working industrial monument, with original machinery including a turbine and a steam engine.

Furness Abbey was founded in the 12th century by Stephen, Count of Boulogne and Martain, and later king of England, and its ruins give a good impression of the size and splendour of its former buildings.

WORDSWORTH AND THE LAKE DISTRICT

Windermere is the largest lake in England and is the Lake District's centre for sailing. The towns of Windermere and Bowness form a small settlement on the eastern side of the lake, and many lovely walks and boat trips can be had from here.

In terms of marine heritage the **Windermere Steamboat Museum** is a world class titan. It incorporates everything that a visitor could hope for in a museum, while preserving not only a unique form of transport, but also a way of life. The museum has probably the finest collection of steamboats in the world, and the oldest has perhaps the most fascinating history. Built in 1850, Steam Launch Dolly is the oldest working mechanically-powered boat in the world. Part of the fascination of the museum is hearing stories of how the boats were salvaged. The oldest boat in the collection is a 26 foot lugsail yacht, carvel built in 1780 of pine and oak. Detective work led to her discovery near Southport, upside down, in use as a henhouse.

Ambleside's 200 year old **Bridge House** is worth a visit, as are **Stagshaw Gardens**, a woodland garden on a steep slope overlooking Lake Windermere.

Despite its size, Windermere has only a handful of islands. Of these, **Belle Isle**, is the largest. The 39 acre island is owned by the Curwen family. It includes the first completely round house to be built in England. It is named after Isabella Curwen who bought it for £1,700 in 1776, including the round house which

Windermere Steamboat Museum

had been built by the previous owner at a cost of £5,000, but he decided to sell it when his friends laughed at the design.

In addition, try and make time to visit **Rydal Water**, the smallest of the lakes, and many believe the loveliest. It has the merit of having reputedly been Wordsworth's favourite too. **Lake Grasmere** is also really beautiful, and also inspired Wordsworth - indeed many of his finest poems are said to have been composed here.

Dove Cottage & Wordsworth Museum, where the poet lived between 1799 and 1808 remains as it was when the poet lived there, and contains several original manuscripts and portraits of Wordsworth and his family. From 1813 until his death, Wordsworth lived at **Rydal Mount**, a 16th century farmhouse with 18th century additions, and containing many mementoes of the poet and his family. The poet's garden is quite lovely, laid out in its original formal manner. The Wordsworth Memorial is at Grasmere Church, where he is buried in the southeast corner of the churchyard. His early life, however, was spent at Wordsworth House in Cockermouth, further north. This is where the poet was born, and the garden is referred to in his 'Prelude'. It is now run by the National Trust.

Another famous name associated with the Lakes is Beatrix Potter, whose illustrated children's tales have enchanted generations. Her home, Hill Top Farm at Sawrey, and much of the land surrounding it was bequeathed to the National Trust when she died.

Coniston is a pretty village on the edge of Coniston Water, where Donald Campbell made his ill-fated attempts on the world water speed record.

Keswick is one of the Lake District's best known towns, on the banks of the River Greta near the northern shore of Derwent Water. In its main street, visit **Moot Hall**. The novelist Sir Hugh Walpole is buried at St John's Churchyard, and other literary connections include stays by both Coleridge and Shelley at Greta Hall, now part of Keswick School.

The area around Keswick is full of treasures of natural beauty. The celebrated Falls of Lodore occupy a beautiful ravine named Castlehead or Castlet, this is all that's left of the volcano which originally created the Lake District and is worth a visit for its lovely views and the chance to glimpse the mysterious Floating Island. The Borrowdale Stone is a huge 'ship' of alien stone, probably carried down from Scotland by glaciers and now balancing precariously on the lower slopes of Grange Fell; and **Castlerigg Stone Circle** is believed to be even older than Stonehenge.

Keswick also forms a useful base for walking in the fells, but do treat the fells with respect, and make sure you go properly dressed and equipped for the drastically changing weather and terrain.

AROUND PENRITH

The ancient town of Penrith, gateway to the Lakes from the north, has had a turbulent history. It has been ransacked and invaded many times and was the scene of fighting during the Civil War. The many castles and fortifications in its district are reminders of this history.

Penrith Castle was built in the 14th century as a defence against the Scots and was lived in by the Duke of Gloucester,

Hutton-in-the-Forest

LANCASHIRE, THE LAKES AND NORTHUMBRIA

later King Richard III. The ruins are now in a public park. The ruined 17th century **Brougham Castle** was once visited by James I, and the huge Keep and Gatehouse are well preserved. The castle is reckoned to be one of the most interesting in Northern England. **Lowther Castle** was once 'one of the stateliest homes in England' though now only the ruins remain.

Hutton-in-the-Forest is the historic home of Lord & Lady Inglewood, lying in the magnificent woodland of the medieval forest of Inglewood at the northern tip of the Lake District, only 3 miles from the M6 (Exit 41 on B5305). Legend has it that this was the site of the Green Knight's Castle in the Arthurian tale of Sir Gawain and the Green Knight. The oldest part of the house is the medieval Pele Tower which was extensively added to in the 17th century. An outstanding feature of the house is the Cupid Staircase which dominates the Hall. Dating from the reign of Charles II it is heavily carved with a rich design of acanthus leaves and winged cherubs. The Gallery is a rare feature in Northern houses and provides an imposing setting for the fine portraits, mostly of members of the family.

In Victorian times the house underwent considerable alterations to its interior, mostly the work of Anthony Salvin, and the Library is a good example of his restrained hand, in complete contrast to the Drawing Room which is very evocative of the almost indiscriminate arrangement of a whole variety of objects beloved of the Victorians. The house contains some very fine tapestries and china and a recently acquired contemporary painting of John Peel the legendary huntsman, who was employed by Sir Frederick Vane. In 1830 his hounds established a run of 70 miles, one of the longest ever in the history of fox-hunting. Another of John Peel's lesser known talents

was to give virtuoso displays of drinking after dinner.

The house looks out over the Topiary Terraces which were originally laid out in the 17th century to an extensive woodland garden beyond - magnificent in early summer when the rhododendrons are in full bloom. The Walled Garden, laid out in the Georgian period, has topiary work of a later date which can best be admired from the gazebo windows of the Gallery.

Dalemain House, home of the Hasell family for over three centuries, is a house full of surprises. The early Georgian facade of soft pink sandstone embraces an earlier Elizabethan manor house, which itself was built on the site of a 12th century pele-tower. The house has evolved, its shape dictated by domestic considerations or simply by the fashion of the day. As a result, some parts of the house are a glorious confusion of winding passages, quaint stairways, unexpected rooms - the sort of house that children love to play in. Indeed much of Dalemain's charm is that it is still very much a family home, yet the richness of its furnishings and portraits is exceptional for a house of its size. There are also grand public rooms including the magnificent Chinese Room. The walls are papered with exotic pheasants hand painted in China with butterflies, insects and more birds added once the paper was in place. The chairs are Chinese Chippendale and the lovely porcelain is 18th century Nanking.

Throughout the house there are works by well know artists including Van Dyck, Lely and Zoffany; one of a pair by Van Dyck which hangs in the hall is the charming Catherine, Lady Aubigny who carried messages for Charles I in her ringlets.

Stepping into the Nursery one is convinced that the children

Dalemain House

LANCASHIRE, THE LAKES AND NORTHUMBRIA

will rush back in at any moment. The Georgian dolls house door is left open ready to resume play; the animals are filing into Noah's Ark; and Hornby trains and 'Dinky' toys spill across the floor under the watchful eye of Peter Rabbit. The framed poem by Kipling, 'The Children's Song', hangs on the wall and the windows are especially low to allow the children to look onto the courtyard.

The Housekeeper's Room is equally charming with its simple furnishings. Its occupant reigned supreme below stairs where once there would have been some 15 servants living in.

The Norman pele-tower houses the Museum of the **Museum of the Westmoreland & Cumberland Yeomanry** who saw action in the Boer War.

The gardens at Dalemain are a delight and have developed around the simple herb garden of Norman times. To the north of the house is the Tudor Knot Garden, laid out to reflect the pattern of the ceilings in the house, and at the top of the High Garden there is a brick gazebo, also Tudor, with mullion windows looking out across Dare Beck, where once monks from the nearby monastery fished. In the orchard, apple trees planted in 1782 still bear fruit, and shrub roses scramble up old walls and tumble over rustic arches in scented profusion. The lovely fountain is Italian Travatine marble and the lawn to the front of the house is dominated by an ancient Tulip Tree.

Appleby Castle Conservation Centre is worth a visit. The grounds have been beautifully preserved and now provide a home for rare breeds of British farm animals, and the castle includes an 11th century Norman Keep and a splendid Great Hall.

Also near Penrith, and well worth a visit, is **Acorn Bank Garden,** the National Trust's most comprehensive collection of medicinal and culinary herbs, with unusual trees and a very pretty walled garden.

Kendal Castle was built on high ground overlooking the town and was the birthplace of Catherine Parr, and **Naworth Castle** is a historic border fortress worth a visit for its Great Hall with Gobelin Tapestries, pre-Raphaelite Library and Lord William's Tower.

Muncaster Castle and gardens has been the home of the Pennington family since the 13th century and the pele tower stands on Roman foundations. Interesting furniture, tapestries and paintings are complemented by the castle being the headquarters for the British Owl Breeding and Release Scheme.

The energetic who climb to the top of the 3,210 foot Scafell Pike will be rewarded by spectacular views from this wild and desolate spot.

To the north, and away from the main 'Lake District' is the border city of Carlisle, which is the administrative centre for Cumbria. The red sandstone cathedral is interesting, and its castle keep houses a Border Regiment Museum.

LANCASHIRE

The county of Lancashire is divided quite clearly into the seaside resorts to the west, and the more industrial section of the east.

In the West, Preston was born as a cotton town on the Ribble,

Towneley Hall

LANCASHIRE, THE LAKES AND NORTHUMBRIA

and has some interesting Georgian buildings. **Houghton Tower**, near Preston, is definitely worth a detour, standing on the top of a 300 foot escarpment and looking like a miniature castle through the approach of its fortified gatehouse. **Scarisbrick Hall** is an interesting example of Gothic architecture, and **Rufford Old Hall** is a lovely late medieval house with a hammer beam roof and a huge moveable screen.

The famous resorts of Lytham St Anne's and Blackpool could not be more different from each other, but each offers attractions in their own inimitable style. Further along the coast are Thornton Cleveleys, Fleetwood, Morecambe and Heysham, which each attract good numbers of visitors.

Leighton Hall is a lovely mansion with an interesting collection of furniture and pictures (featured later).

The county town of Lancaster stands on the Lune, with an interesting castle perched up on the hill overlooking the river. Its associations with John of Gaunt are celebrated by 'John of Gaunt's Chair', a turret which was among the many additions he made to the existing structure.

Since 1902, the ancient home of the Towneley family has been **Burnley's Art Gallery and Museum**. The house itself dates from the 14th century with many later additions and alterations, including a splendid baroque entrance hall dating from the 1720's by Franceso Vassalli and Martino Quadri and the Regency drawing room and dinning room by Sir Jeffry Wyatville. The 16th century chapel and long gallery are furnished with 17th century oak furniture and the kitchen appears as it might have been in the mid 19th century. There are also two 20th century top lit art galleries displaying Victorian oil paintings, English water colours and a full programme of changing exhibitions. Throughout the building there are displays of local history, ceramics, glass and archaeology. The illustration shows a water colour of **Towneley Hall**, painted by J.M.W.Turner in 1790.

Set in the surrounding park are the **Museum of Local Crafts and Industries** in the former brewhouse and the **Natural History Centre and Aquarium** in the walled garden.

East Lancashire is physically and economically quite different. Chorley is a cotton-weaving and engineering town, notable for **Astley Hall**, an Elizabethan mansion to which the rhyming description 'more glass than wall' can be appropriately applied with reference to its southern entrance wing.

The **Ribchester Museum**, north west of Blackburn, occupied the site of the Roman Fort of Bremetennacum and has some interesting Roman remains.

Also worth a visit in East Lancashire is **Gawthorpe Hall**, a National Trust Jacobean property, which was the home of the Shuttleworth family for many years but is now let to a local college of education and houses a remarkable collection of textiles and embroideries, celebrating the Shuttleworth family and their locality.

The Lake District is renowned as possessing some of Britain's most scenic and dramatic landscapes. Such fame is more than justified and draws unparalleled numbers of visitors, particularly during the heady summer months. Newcomers to the region are understandably drawn to the more famous beauty spots, but would do well to pause awhile - Lancashire and Cumbria possess a wealth of splendid and varied attractions, each as worthy of inspection as the spectacular Lakeland.

NORTHUMBRIA

Northumbria, the Saxon name for this region, includes some of Britain's most spectacular scenery. The area has had a turbulent history, often at the hands of various conquerors, and it has an important place in the history of Christianity in Britain.

Its modern appearance bears witness to this, with a landscape that is rich in castles and fortifications, monasteries and churches.

Hadrian's Wall, built between 122 and 130 AD was the frontier of the Roman Empire in Britain, and has been granted World Heritage Status. Keen ramblers walk the 73 miles from Wallsend on the Tyne through Northumberland and Cumberland to Bowness on Solway. Much of the wall still stands, a solemn reminder of the area's strategic importance throughout history. The area is also rich in natural beauty, with miles of uncrowded yet beautiful beaches, and many interesting cities, towns and villages.

THE PENNINE WAY

The Durham Moors offer some of the loveliest and most rugged scenery to be found along the Pennine Way. The Durham Moors are relatively flat and high, and suffer from severe weather conditions in winter, and sometimes in summer too. Ramblers must treat the area with respect, and be prepared for harsh weather and tough terrain. In return they will be rewarded with stunning views, especially of the reservoirs and spectacular waterfalls which pepper the area.

DURHAM AND ITS DALES

The lovely market town of **Barnard Castle** makes a useful base for exploring the upper dales of west Durham.

The ruined castle overlooks the River Tees. Its remains include a 14th century Great Hall, a three storeyed keep and a round tower which provided the inspiration for Sir Walter Scott's 1813 work 'Rokeby'. Charles Dickens stayed at the King's Head in the marketplace while on a visit to study Yorkshire's schools, described in 'Nicholas Nickelby'

Whilst at Barnard Castle, take the opportunity of visiting the **Bowes Museum**, one of the county's best. It is housed in an ornate mansion, built in the style of a French Chateau from 1869 to 1892 for John Bowes and his French wife, the Countess of Montalbo.

Its period rooms display an excellent collection of paintings and European art, including porcelain, textiles and ecclesiastical art. It also devotes some rooms to displays on Teeside's rural life in earlier centuries.

Near **Langdon Beck**, a three and a half mile footpath leads to **Caldron Snout**, the highest waterfall in England. Those who make the trek will be rewarded by seeing the Tees drop more than 100 ft by a series of cascades, into a wild ravine.

LANCASHIRE, THE LAKES AND NORTHUMBRIA

The countryside is full of lovely spots with exceptional views. **Blanchland** has a well-earned reputation for being one of Britain's unspoilt villages, planned in the early 18th century, after the 12th century plans of the White Canon monks. **Derwent Reservoir** is a pretty place to stop for a picnics, or a sail; **Hamsterley Forest**, a 5,000 acre Forestry Commission area provides car parks and picnic areas; some of the country's rarest alpine plants are to be found near **Cow Green Reservoir**; and a fine tudor mansion dominates the large green at **West Auckland**. The drive to West Auckland will take you along the boundary of the ancient deer park at **Raby Castle**, the battlemented castle is one of the finest 14th century castles in England, with splendid gatehouses and massive corner towers. It originally belonged to King Canute, but is now the home of Sir Henry Vane's descendants and contains a fine collection of Meissen porcelain and Hiram Power's statue of a naked, manacled slave girl which caused more than a few raised eyebrows when it was first on show.

THE CITY OF DURHAM

This university city is one of the most interesting and historic in England. Even its setting is spectacular, with the older part of the city standing on the summit of a high peninsular which is almost enclosed by a loop in the River Wear. The city is dominated by its Norman cathedral and its castle, prompting Sir Walter Scott to comment that Durham has a strangely dual aspect, 'half church of God, half castle 'gainst the Scot'. On the religious side, **Durham Cathedral** is thought by many to be our finest Norman church. It houses the tombs of St Cuthbert and the Venerable Bede, and many other important early Christian relics.

Across the broad Palace Green is **Durham Castle**, founded by William the Conqueror, now forming part of the University.

The University, through its various colleges, exhibits many important and interesting artifacts. The **Gulbenkian Museum** has a fabulous collection of oriental art and archaeology, and many of the university's buildings and gardens are interesting in themselves. The city generally is a lovely place to wander around, and is well worth a visit.

Sunderland is County Durham's largest town, a bustling seaport, famous for its shipbuilding yards. In its suburbs is **Hylton Castle**, which has a huge towerhouse dating back to 1400 and a detached 15th century chapel. Although in ruins, carved figures and heraldic shields can still be seen in the walls.

BORDER POSTS

The tempestuous history of Northumberland's border districts is obvious from the number and splendour of the fortresses within it.

Berwick-on-Tweed is a lovely old port and fishing town on the north bank of the Tweed. Originally in Scotland, it changed hands no fewer than 13 times from 1147 to 1482. However, it now forms part of Northumberland and is worth a visit for its Elizabethan bridge and its nearby **Royal Border Bridge**, built in 1847 by Robert Louis Stephenson the famous railway engineer.

The main market town on the river Aln, **Alnwick** makes a great base for touring. **Alnwick Castle** was originally built in the 12th century, but has been impressively restored and proudly displays the Canaletto painting of its vista (featured later). The seaport of **Alnmouth**, four miles away, is also well known as a golfing centre. Nearby **Warkworth** also boasts a medieval castle, which looks most splendid from the medieval bridge.

From Seahouses, a pretty fishing village, visit Holt Island where **Lindisfarne Priory** commemorates the birth of Christianity in the North of England. St Aiden established a bishopric there in 635 and the ruins include a 12th century church, and various domestic buildings.

Rising above the bay stands Lindisfarne Castle, built in about 1550. The island is well worth a visit, but is accessible for only about five hours during low tide. For the rest of the time, the causeway across the sands is underwater. Watch the notices, once on the island, to avoid having to stay longer than you intended!

Nearby **Bamburgh Castle** completely restored in 1900, now displays its collections of china, porcelain, furniture, paintings, arms and armour.

While at Bamburgh, do visit the **Grace Darling Memorial**, which was placed at the highest point in St Aiden's churchyard in order to be visible from the sea. Her story dates back to 1838, when a storm blew up which was so strong that the lifeboatmen refused to launch their boats. Twenty-three year old Grace persuaded her father, keeper of the Longstone Lighthouse, to row out with her to the ship Forfarshire, which had been shipwrecked off the great cliffs. Nine survivors were rescued and tended at the lighthouse. A small **Memorial Museum** was built next door to her home, where she had died of consumption four years later.

Chillingham Castle is a medieval fortress with Tudor additions. Its exhibits include a torture chamber - not for the fainthearted, woodland walks, and an Elizabethan topiary garden. The National Trust is now caring for **Wallington**, a delightful 17th and 18th century house, which has one of England's best collections of porcelain, and Ruskin paintings adorning its great hall.

Another National Trust property is **Cragside House and Country Park**, to the east of Rothbury. It was the first house to be lit by electricity generated by water power, and incidentally has a fabulous display of rhododendrons which are a wonderful sight if you visit when they are in bloom in early summer.

The grounds of **Belsay Hall** are also quite lovely. The house is in the Neo-Classical style and built in the grounds of a 14th century tower-house to a design by Sir Charles Monck. Close to **Otterburn**, a pretty village in the upland valley of the Rede.

Kielder Water, at Falstone, is an impressive sight. It claims to be the largest man-made lake in Europe and is certainly worth a detour.

HADRIAN'S WALL

What scholar can forget learning about Hadrian's Wall? This massive feat of engineering, was erected by the Emperor

LANCASHIRE, THE LAKES AND NORTHUMBRIA

Hadrian to keep the marauding Scots where they belonged - well away from his Roman Empire in England. The ruins of Hadrian's Wall are our most spectacular relic of Roman Britain, and are much visited by tourists and scholars alike.

The wall runs across the width of northern England for 73 miles from Wallsend near Newcastle to Bowness on Solway. Some of the surviving portions are 14 feet high, punctuated by ruined turrets, milecastles and forts. If walking the full length seems a little daunting, pick out some of the more interesting sights along the way. Much of the wall is accessible from nearby roads. **Chester's Roman Fort** at **Chollerford**, for example, was originally built for 500 cavalrymen and contains the finest military bathhouse in Britain. A little further along, the **Corbridge Roman Site** is one of the wall's principal museums. **Corstopitum**, to give it its Roman name, was once a prosperous town and a supply depot for Hadrian's Wall. Extensive Roman remains can be seen. **Heddon-on-the-Wall** offers a fine stretch of 280 yards of wall with circular chambers and a medieval kiln; while **Housesteads Roman Fort** at Haydon Bridge is the best preserved and most impressive of the Roman forts.

TYNE & WEAR

Tyneside conjures up for many an image of industry. It is true that there are many signs of the coal, iron and steel that have given prosperity to the area, but there is much more on offer. Newcastle is the industrial and commercial centre for the region. Splendid bridges carry travellers into the city - the New Tyne Bridge and Stephenson's High Level Bridge.

Panoramic views of the city can be gained from the **Castle Keep**, one of the best surviving examples of a Norman keep. The medieval **Church of St Nicholas** is the fourth largest parish church in England and forms an outstanding landmark.

The Central Railway Station is also a splendid building, and the centre of Newcastle is one of England's most interesting - a fine example of Victorian planning and containing an impressive selection of museums, art galleries and a very good shopping centre. The nearby Metrocentre, a new shopping and leisure centre at Gateshead is also well worth a trip.

From 1183 to 1288, **Washington Old Hall** was the home of George Washington's ancestors, indeed it was from this manor house, restored in 1936, that the family took its name.

Tynemouth Castle and Priory dating from the 7th century stands on a headland at the mouth of the river. The Priory is enclosed by a curtain wall and the castle has a late 14th century barbican and gatehouse. Tynemouth itself is a pleasant seaside town, and a popular stopping point, along with Whitley Bay, for beach seekers. While in this area, John Vanbrugh's masterpiece **Seaton Delaval Hall**, which was built in 1718 to 1929 should not be missed (featured later).

The **Beamish North of England Open Air Museum** in Durham and **Preston Park** in Cleveland offer unforgettable experiences of life as it used to be in the region, looking forward to a bright future, but rightly cherishing its past.

The **Captain Cook Birthplace Museum** in Stewart Park, Marton, situated about 200 yards from the site of Cook's birth, in one and a quarter acres of outstanding Victorian parkland with ornamental lake, wildfowl ponds and rare trees. The conservatory houses plants from the South Seas. Inside the museum you can trace Captain Cook's life from his birth to the sights and sounds of his early seafaring career in Whitby and to his great voyages of discovery.

Northumbria boasts an outstanding combination of breathtaking scenery and historic importance. The delights of **Dunstanburgh Castle** on the National Trust land of Northumberland are a splendid and haunting example of the region's turbulent past, while the sea views are a constant reminder of its sheer unspoilt beauty. From historic Durham through moorland and rivers Northumbria beckons, it remains one of the most delightfully unspoilt areas of Britain.

Captain Cooks Birth place Museum

LEVENS HALL

Levens Hall, much-loved home of the Bagot family, is a mainly Elizabethan house built around an earlier pele tower by the Bellinghams between 1510 and 1590. When James Bellingham inherited Levens he completely refurbished the rather grim medieval structure and installed the comforts required in a gentleman's residence. The original great hall still stands, with its staircase tower and the base of the pele, all facing the river and the ford. James Bellingham added a separate dining room and servant's hall, drawing rooms and kitchens. All the rooms were panelled using local oak or hung with tapestry and ornamented with fine plasterwork.

In 1603, Bellingham was knighted by King James I, but in 1686 his grandson gambled away the entire estate which was bought by a kinsman, Colonel James Grahme two years later. He added the south wing and brew hall and much of the fine furniture seen today. The house also contains silver, paintings by Rubens, Cuyp and Lely and mementoes of the family links with important figures such as the Duke of Wellington.

The main rooms are notable for the rich panelling and intricately moulded plasterwork from James Bellingham's time. The Drawing Room is a particularly good example and in addition has a magnificently carved overmantel dated 1595 which incorporates the arms of Elizabeth I. The furniture is mainly of the Charles II and William and Mary periods, but the fine harpsichord is of a later date.

The Dining Room contains a magnificent set of Charles II walnut dining chairs, considered to be the finest in the country. The walls are covered in rich Cordova leather and there is another finely carved overmantel. The collection of early 18th century silver includes a lovely silver-gilt christening cup made in 1746.

Displayed in the hall are a collection of very old glasses including the great Levens Constables, used for drinking Morocco ale - a home-brew which matured for twenty-one years! In Colonel Grahme's day during the 'Radish Feast', held at the start of Milnthorpe Fair, guests were required to cross the bowling green in a straight line after drinking a glass of the potent ale. If they succeeded they were given another glass - no-one was known to make the return journey successfully.

The gardens at Levens are also one of the Colonel's legacies. He commissioned Monsieur Beaumont in 1690 to design the grounds and the topiary garden which is one of the best examples still intact in its original design. During the later part of the 18th century the garden became delightfully overgrown, with honeysuckle, sweet smelling mignonette and roses everywhere, so that the next head-gardener had to replant nine miles of box edging to restore order once more.

In the park is a herd of Bagot goats and black fallow deer and local superstition has it that, should a white fawn be born, some change will befall the house.

Levens Hall also boasts a fine collection of steam engines. The main collection illustrates the development of steam power from 1820 to 1920.

HOLKER HALL

The history of Holker Hall goes back to the early 16th century. It has never been bought or sold, but has belonged to three families, the Prestons, the Lowthers and the Cavendishes, all related by marriage. Each family has left a lasting impression by adding, embellishing or rebuilding.

The Prestons were substantial local landowners who, in the 1550s, bought part of the Cartmel Priory Estates. George Preston is thought to have built the first house on the present site in 1604, but the estates were lost by his son Thomas who entertained Royalist troops at Holker in 1644. He regained possession after paying fines imposed by the Parliamentarians and on his death in 1697 he left his estates to his daughter Catherine. In the same year she married Sir William Lowther and the house remained in his family until 1756.

Sir Thomas Lowther married Lady Elizabeth Cavendish, daughter of the 2nd Duke of Devonshire and in the 1720s much of the house was reconstructed. Their son William, a great friend of Sir Joshua Reynòlds, died unmarried in 1756 leaving Holker to his cousin, Lord George Augustus Cavendish, the second son of the 3rd Duke of Devonshire. From that date to this the house has been in the possession of the Cavendish family.

Lord George Augustus engaged the architect John Carr and between 1783 and 1793 made additions to the house in an 'elegant modern gothic' style. He also made extensive alterations to the grounds, sweeping away formality in favour of the fashionable natural landscape. His latter years were spent peacefully at Holker, often in the company of his two brothers, by all accounts a delightful trio known as ' the three old Lords'. In the summer after an early dinner, they would often saunter down to the summer house where they would sit and eat cockles and drink punch.

Between 1838 and 1842 William Cavendish, 2nd Earl of Burlington and later 7th Duke of Devonshire, altered the entire house. By adding tall ornamental chimneys, gables and mullioned windows it was given a gothic appearance. Disaster struck in 1871 when in the space of a few hours the entire west wing was destroyed by fire. The destruction was devastating. Furniture, statues, numerous paintings and valuable books were lost forever.

Undaunted the 7th Duke began plans to rebuild on a grander scale with the help of architects Paley and Austin of Lancaster. It covered the same site as the previous wing, and although in Elizabethan style, it is unmistakably Victorian. It is this New Wing which is open to the public, with its distinctive furniture, historic paintings, photographs and family treasures which add a delightful lived-in atmosphere. There are no ropes or barriers at Holker and visitors are encouraged to wander at will.

The library is said to be one of the finest in the North. Many of the books survived the fire and others were subsequently brought from Chatsworth, and among them are works by Henry Cavendish, who discovered nitric acid, the properties of hydrogen and calculated the density of the earth. His microscope can also be seen in this room. His mysogynism was legendary; in his London home he had a special staircase built to avoid seeing his servants and should he catch sight of a maid, the poor creature was instantly dismissed.

The craftsmanship of the linenfold panelling, of which there are four variations in the Hall, and the plaster ceiling are of excellent quality as they are throughout the house. Electricity was installed in 1911 with the lighting and switches carefully concealed. In this room the switches are behind imitation books, each bearing a humorous title. In the Drawing Room the walls are covered with the original silk and the furniture includes Hepplewhite sofas and chairs, a Chinese Chippendale table and a Chippendale silver table. There is a beautiful collection of Meissen and other china and fine pictures by English and Continental artists including some from the notable collection of Sir William Lowther.

Holker Hall is situated amongst the most beautiful of English countryside with gardens merging into parkland - with hills on one side and the expanse of Morecambe Bay on the other. To the north lies the dramatic lakes and craggy fells of the Lake District.

The Pleasure Grounds are 23 acres of formal and woodland gardens. A large Monkey Puzzle by the fountain was grown from seed brought back from Chile in 1844. Some 40 years later it blew down and was re-erected with the help of seven shire horses and its roots embedded in concrete. The Rose Garden is reached by a curved pergola, heavy with Wisteria, Honeysuckle and Chinese Schisandra. Many of the Cavendish ladies have been gifted gardeners and have introduced many rare and beautiful shrubs and trees.

In the spring throughout the woodland garden there are great drifts of crocus, aconites, snowdrops, daffodils, primroses and bluebells. In summer the magnolias, azaleas and rhododendrons are a glorious sight. From the great Turkey Oak and stately plumes of Victorian Pampas to the formal summer garden and recently created cascade, there is evidence of many generations of gardeners.

LEIGHTON HALL

Few houses could be more beautifully situated than Leighton. Lying low in its densely wooded park, the house is framed against the spectacular natural backdrop of the Lakeland mountains rising into the distance beyond.

The facade of white limestone, in the neo-Gothic style of about 1800, has an almost theatrical quality and was superimposed on the Adam style house built in 1763 on the ruins of an older house. The new south wing was added in 1870.

In 1822 Leighton Hall became the home of the Gillow family, famous furniture makers of Lancaster, and remains a much loved and lived-in family home with a fine collection of 18th century Gillow furniture, paintings, clocks and objects d'art.

The Entrance Hall is an exceptionally fine example of the early Gothic revival, with a beautifully curved stone staircase framed by delicate pillars. The interesting eight-winged table known as a 'Daisy Table' is by Gillow, as are the chairs, wine chest, sideboard and table in the Dining Room. Particularly significant is the large expanding table thought to be the prototype of all leafed tables. A fine portrait of Richard Gillow, son of the founder of the family firm, presides over the room.

Leading from the lovely small Library, the Drawing Room contains some of the most important and valuable pieces of Gillow furniture, particularly the fine early 18th century games table,

the satinwood writing table and the lady's work box, almost certainly made for Mrs Richard Gillow in 1820. A case on the French desk contains buttons and a lock of James II's hair set in gold, given by the Old Pretender to an ancestor of the present owner during the Jacobite Rising of 1745. Among the many interesting pictures are works by Poussin, Wouverman, Morlands and Guardi. This room also has a splendid view of the Lakeland mountains.

The gardens at Leighton Hall are delightfully informal. A lawn extends the full length of the kitchen garden wall over which hang great cascades of roses. At its feet the long herbaceous border provides pools of soft colour, punctuated here and there by dazzling reds - a wonderful sight on a hazy summer afternoon.

A monument in the grounds marks the site of the former burial ground. Every owner of Leighton but one has been a Roman Catholic and at times when burial in consecrated ground was denied them, many landowning Catholic families had their own private cemeteries. The sundial on the rose lawn near the pond is the sole relic of pre-Jacobite Leighton.

Leighton Hall now houses the largest collection of birds of prey in the North of England and is also home to 'Falconaide' which takes care of sick or injured birds.

ALNWICK CASTLE

This magnificent border fortress dates back to the Norman Conquest when the earliest parts of the present castle were constructed by Yvo de Vescy, first Baron of Alnwick. It was considered at the time to be very strongly fortified and was of substantially the same design as at present; a circular keep composed of a series of towers surrounding a courtyard with two outer baileys, and was one of the earliest to assume this somewhat larger form. The Percy family came into ownership in 1309 and without interfering with the general design Henry, 1st Lord Percy, proceeded to rebuild and strengthen still further the greater part of the castle. The Percys, distinguished on the battlefield, were one of the most powerful landowning families in the country and these were troubled times. His son the 2nd Lord Percy was ordered by his King, Edward III to fortify and provision Alnwick Castle to guard the north eastern march; the castle played a vital role in repelling any advance from north of the border. Hostilities with the Scots continued intermittently. The 4th Lord Percy fought bravely and was created 1st Earl of Northumberland. His son, Hotspur, was immortalised by Shakespeare in Henry IV. While still skirmishing with the Scots the Percys became caught up in one of the most turbulent periods in England's history - the Wars of the Roses - pitching their considerable military might on the side of Lancaster. Earls one, two and three all died, albeit courageously, in battle and the 4th Earl was murdered by a mob for his part in raising an unpopular tax.

When relative peace returned during the reign of Henry VIII the Percys forsook their border stronghold for the comforts of one of their London houses and the pleasures of life at court. The 6th Earl was unfortunate enough to fall in love with the beguiling Anne Boleyn which brought him to the attention of his King. During the dissolution of the monasteries the Earl's brothers led a revolt against the King and were confined to the Tower and in order to placate his sovereign Percy left his estates to the Crown. He died in 1537 in dire poverty and stricken with grief at the ruin of his family, once so great and powerful.

Twenty years later the estates were restored and began the rise to their former eminence when in 1766 the 1st Duke of Northumberland was created. It was he who began to restore Alnwick employing Robert Adam who adopted the style known as 'Strawberry Hill' Gothic or 'Gingerbread', reputedly not the Duke's choice (who was noted for his fine taste) but that of his Duchess. The main restoration work was carried out by the 4th Duke during the reign of Queen Victoria.

The rugged medieval exterior belies the richness of the interior, decorated in the classical Italian Renaissance manner which replaced most of Robert Adam's work. During his travels in Italy the 4th Duke had conceived a great admiration for Italian art and it was his ambition to introduce the best examples to this country. Work was begun in 1854 under the direction of Salvin, while the interior decoration was entrusted to the celebrated Italian Caniva.

The great door of the Keep leads through a simple entrance hall which does little to prepare one for the sheer magnificence of Alnwick; the first taste of what the castle holds in store can be had by gazing up the Grand Staircase, an ascending blend of Carrara marbles beneath a groin vaulted ceiling with stucco decoration. Each step is a single piece of stone twelve feet wide and the landing consists of one piece twelve feet square, leading to the Guard room. This impressive room has a pavement

of Venetian mosaic and a deeply panelled stucco ceiling in the octagonal design characteristic of many of the castle's ceilings. Paintings by Van Dyck and Canaletto adorn the white and gold walls and in the centre of the room stands a beautiful circular gaming table with decorative swags giving the room an air of both opulence and restraint.

The warmly elegant Library occupies the whole of one floor of the Prudhoe Tower. The two tiers of bookcases are oak inlaid with maple with a gallery running along the upper tier. The exquisite ceiling is divided into four sections in which are coffered panels with carved trophies representing History, Painting, Poetry and the Sciences all richly gilded. Three fireplaces, inlaid with white marble, support busts of Shakespeare, Bacon and Newton.

The Music Room, with its richly gilded ceiling suggestive of St Peters in Rome, contains some fine examples of French furniture and has works by Canaletto and Van Dyck. The gold gives way to crimson in the Red Drawing Room which was intended to be the most splendid of all. The two 'pietra dura' cabinets made for Louis XIV are especially fine.

The elegant Dining Room is dominated by a large double portrait of the 1st Duke and Duchess and there are two magnificent Meissen dinner services.

From the terrace the wild landscape stretches northwards to the River Aln, tamed somewhat by the skilled hand of 'Capability' Brown, but nevertheless a reminder that this sumptuous mansion was once a mighty fortification against an ever present threat of invasion.

SEATON DELAVAL HALL

The splendid English baroque house that Sir John Vanbrugh built for Admiral George Delaval between 1718 and 1728 is as dramatic and theatrical as one might expect of a playwright turned architect. So too is the history of the house and its original owners that it might almost have been written by Sir John himself. Twice burnt, left roofless for fifty years, damaged by troops during the first world war and requisitioned again during the second, the house described as 'one of the glories of the North' was in danger of becoming totally derelict.

Extensive restoration work was begun in 1950 including the removal of the hundreds of pigeons for whom Seaton Delaval was home. A series of photographs in the great entrance hall charts the progress of the work and illustrates how much was achieved in just ten years. The house is now resplendent behind the huge portico of the south front, with fine pictures and furnishings.

The mahogany room of 1726 survived the fire and is probably the best room in the house. The use of mahogany for panelling is unusual. One of the most impressive features of the house is the stable block in the East wing, described as 'cathedral like'. It is indeed very grand with vast stone stalls and every comfort provided for the fortunate occupants.

Sadly Admiral George Delaval did not live to see his fine house completed. He died as a result of a fall from his horse in 1723; the spot where he fell is marked by an obelisk. Delaval Hall then passed to his nephew Francis Blake-Delaval who had already inherited Ford Castle, on condition that, should he also succeed to Seaton Delaval, he would return Ford to his mother's sister. However, Francis simply placed the Delaval crest, a stone ram's head, above the door at Ford. One day 'this Ram's head, in the hearing of the steward and all the family, spoke out in clear tones and predicted that, so long as the Ford Estate was united with that of Seaton Delaval, no male of the family should die 'in his bed'. It then remained silent'. Neither Francis Blake-Delaval, nor seven of his eight sons, nor his grandson, died in bed; the last surviving son died peaceably abed at the age of eighty five - but only after Ford Castle had been bequeathed to his great-niece.

Besides his eight sons Francis also had five daughters, the 'gay Delavals', renowned for their generosity and brilliance, particularly Sir Francis who entertained on a lavish scale. 'Seaton Delaval was like an Italian palace, and the grounds were a perfect fairyland of light, beauty and music.' Guests at Seaton Delaval would find their beds lowered into baths of icy water in the middle of the night or the partitions of their rooms would disappear to reveal some member of the opposite sex in a state of undress. Yet this elegant dilettante rushed to enlist when the invasion of France was imminent and acquitted himself with great valour. Little wonder that he did not die in his bed!

It is from this time, the early Georgian period, that the legend of the 'white Lady of Seaton Delaval' springs. Some say that she awaits the return of a lover, others that she will continue her lonely vigil until an heir is born within the walls of the famous ruins, and others maintain she is a mere reflection of the sun. Perhaps a glance up at the north-east room on the first floor will reveal the truth - for she is still seen from time to time.

LANCASHIRE, THE LAKES & NORTHUMBRIA

The Ribble flows cheerfully through Lancashire and its banks are bordered by some beautiful countryside. Lancashire is a most romantic county, the old mill towns contrasting dramatically with the rolling countryside of the Forest and hills of Bowland, the Ribble Valley and Pendle Hill. The Forest of Bowland has provided rich hunting grounds for many centuries whilst Pendle Hill looms above, strange and mischievous. It sweeps, broomstick like, into the horizon. This is the home of witches, visit if you dare. On a more friendly note, there are innumerable pubs in which to stay, together with some outstanding inns. The luxurious country house hotel is harder to find but bed and breakfasts in this area are of a high standard and are easier to locate.

There could be no finer contrast to the grey textile towns than the Lake District of Cumbria. The mountainous terrain is interspersed with lakes and tarns, mountain streams and valleys cut deep into the rock by the moving ice. We should not forget the splendid coastline here too, all too often it is ignored for the magnificent splendours of the Lakes themselves. The dramatic scenery is a huge draw and during the summer the fells are a hive of activity with walkers, mountaineers and tourists. The Lakes has a marvellous selection of hotels, bed & breakfasts, pubs and self-catering accommodation to cater for its visitors.

Although it is the scenery which draws the majority of people here, there are numerous other delights to behold. Castles cottages and gardens are interspersed with quaint villages and dramatic landscapes. Rise early and enjoy the changing hues of the mountains and later, as the sun rises, return for a hearty Lakeland breakfast.

To the east lies Northumbria, embracing the counties of Durham, Cleveland, Tyne & Wear and Northumberland.

Durham is the land of the Prince Bishops and at one time, to all intense and purposes, acted as a tiny independent state with armies and lands protected by the castle stronghold perched high on the banks of the River Wear. The home of the Prince Bishops for over 800 years, Durham is where you find one of the most beautiful buildings in Europe, Durham Cathedral on Palace Green which dominates the city and neighbouring cas-

tle. There are a number of good hotels in the city and several nearby country houses have been renovated and converted into impressive hotels.

The surrounding countryside is riddled with castles, some ruined, some still occupied. Nearly all are a legacy from England's attempts to protect her northen territory from the Scottish during the many border raids.

Northumbria is an area of contrast, but the Dales and moorland are some of the most remote and most beautiful in England. High Force, England's highest waterfall, is just one of the many natural monuments that are dotted around this pleasing part of the country.

In total contrast to the moorland, Cleveland is better known for its steel works and heavy industry. This, however, is not the county's most attractive face which, without doubt, is the spectacular coastline. There are some delightful villages to be found and captain James Cook was born inn this area - a testimony, if any were needed, to the seafaring heritage of Northumbria.

Heading further north, we find Tyne and Wear. This is an area rich in industrial heritage with the collieries and the shipyards playing a large part in the birth of the city and the history of Newcastle and surrounding countryside.

Northumberland is England's border county and one of her most beautiful. As you would imagine, there is much history here and most is entwined with the Scots in some way. The most famous landmark is Hadrians Wall, built by the Romans in 122 AD, a remarkable feat of engineering still standing as testament to the strength of the feeling which ran between the Scots and the English. It never fails to impress.

To the Cheviots and the coast; Lindesfarne, Bamburgh, Alnwick the list of castles and stately homes is long and varied.

Northumbria remains one of Englands most unspoiled areas and any visitor will marvel at its beauty, its heritage and the unrivalled welcome of the native Geordie (even if they can't understand a word!)

HOTELS OF DISTINCTION

ABBEY HOUSE HOTEL, Barrow in Furness, Cumbria. Tel: 90229) 838282
This impressive red sandstone building is the work of the architect Sir Edwin Lutyen. Abbey House offers impeccable accommodation, with English and French a la carte cuisine in the Abbey restaurant.

ARMATHWAITE HALL, Near Keswick, Cumbria. Tel: (059681) 551
Once a Benedictine nunnery, the restrained and grand feel to this stately home full of history and dark panelling, surrounded by a deer park rewards the visitor with memories of grand living. Fishing, croquet, tennis and luxurious beauty treatment are all available.

AYNSOME MANOR HOTEL, Cartmel, Cumbria.
Tel: (05395) 36653

A small family run hotel dating from the sixteenth century, Aynsome Manor makes an ideal base for exploring the Lake District or coastline. Set in its own grounds, this hotel is a charming and peaceful retreat.

BLUE BELL HOTEL, Belford, Northumberland. Tel: (0668) 213543
A renowned coaching inn tastefully refurbished in Georgian style and set in three acres of gardens. The Blue Bell is ideally located for the historic coastal area of Northumberland, including Farne Island, Lindisfarne and Berwick.

CROSBY LODGE HOTEL, Crosby-On-Eden, Cumbria. Tel: (0228 73) 618
An elegant country mansion combining a tasteful collection of antiques with fine furniture in both private and public rooms. The restaurant serves delicious food and is open to non residents.

245

FARLAM HALL

Farlam Hall is situated in an area that is one of the most peaceful and unspoilt parts of the country, and yet was once so violent and war torn that it was named 'The Debatable Lands'.

The legacy that is left today of those years of border warfare is a wealth of fortifications, castles, houses and ruined abbeys that date back to Roman times. Many of the towns, Carlisle included, were sacked and burnt on more than one occasion, but now the castle, cathedral and museums can be enjoyed in peace. The history of the area combines with the beauty of lush farmland, open moors and hidden river valleys to produce an area so varied that it has few equals.

Farlam Hall itself reflects the changes of the years as it has grown from a small fortified farm house in the 1700's to the large elegant, mainly Victorian border home it is today.

Owned and personally run by the Quinion and Stevenson families since 1975 it is now recognised internationally as a haven of fine food and comfort.

It is an ideal base from which to explore, with Hadrian's Wall stretching eastwards from only 4 miles away. Along its path are exhibitions and museums which help to explain the years of occupation.

The only debate today in these lands is whether or not you can spare enough time to explore in full its beauty and history.

Farlam Hall
Country House Hotel
Brampton, Cumbria CA8 2NG
Tel: 06977-46234
Fax: 06977-46683

246

LANCASHIRE, THE LAKES & NORTHUMBRIA

FARLAM HALL HOTEL, Brampton, Cumbria. Tel: (06976) 234
Dating back to the 17th century, Farlam Hall is set in four acres of grounds with a lake and offers great comfort. It is ideally located for visiting Hadrian's Wall, Naworth Castle and Lanercost Priory.

GIBBON BRIDGE COUNTRY HOUSE AND RESTAURANT, Chipping, Lancashire. Tel: (0995) 61456
An atmosphere of warmth and tranquility fills this cosy, family-run country house hotel which rests in charming landscaped gardens set on the banks of the beautiful River Loud.

GRINKLE PARK HOTEL, Easington, Co Durham. Tel: (0287) 40515
The atmosphere of a more gracious age rests quietly in the rooms of this elegant Victorian manor house. Peaceful lounges with rich panelling and old stone fireplaces give way to the airiness of the cane-filled Camellia room.

HALL GARTH COUNTRY HOUSE, Coatham Mundeville, Co Durham. Tel: (0325) 300400
A charming, rambling, informal hotel, dating from 1540, set in 67 acres of splendid grounds. Ideal for touring the northern sites of Raby Castle, Washington Hall, Durham Cathedral, Herriot Country and the Dales.

HEADLAM HALL, Darlington, Co Durham. Tel (0325) 730238
A magnificent Jacobean mansion set in three acres of formal gardens including a small private trout water. The hotel has many sporting facilities and provides excellent traditional English cuisine.

INN AT WHITEWELL, Whitewell, Lancashire. Tel: (02008) 222
Belonging to the Queen as part of the Duchy of Lancaster, this whitewashed, stone mullioned manor has Georgian and Victorian extensions housing an art gallery and wine merchant. Excellent food and well kept ales can be enjoyed within a delightfully traditional atmosphere.

LANGLEY CASTLE, Langley-On-Tyne, Northumberland. Tel: (0434) 688888
A real castle, restored from ruins at the beginning of the century, with a fascinating display of historical features. The outer walls, for example, are seven feet thick.

LEEMING HOUSE, Ullswater, Cumbria. Tel: (07684) 86622
This is a charming country house hotel enjoying a beautiful setting on the edge of Lake Ullswater within its own landscaped gardens. The home cooking in the elegant restaurant is well recommended.

LINDEN HALL HOTEL, Morpeth, Northumberland. Tel: (0670) 516611
An impressive Georgian mansion set in 300 acres of park. The hotel is beautifully furnished with antiques and period features, and benefits from many varied amenities.

LONGDALE CHASE, Windermere, Cumbria. Tel: (05394) 32201
With its position on the shore of glorious Lake Windermere, this enchanting hotel is perfect for visitors to the homes of Wordsworth, Ruskin, Beatrix Potter and England's oldest narrow-gauge railway.

LORD CREWE ARMS HOTEL, Blanchland, Co. Durham. Tel: (0434) 675251
A small, extremely solid, stone built and possibly haunted hotel, dating from the 13th Century when the Abbot's robes swept across the flagstones. Consett is now world renowned as the home of the travelling Phileas Fogg.

LOVELADY SHIELD COUNTRY HOUSE HOTEL, Alston, Cumbria. Tel: (0434) 381203
The Lovelady Shield nestles in 3 acres of riverside gardens within easy reach of the Pennine Way, Hadrian's Wall and the Lake District. The hotel has a welcoming atmosphere and a variety of tempting cuisine.

LUMLEY CASTLE HOTEL, Chester-le-Street, Co Durham. Tel: (091) 3891111
Originally a real 13th century castle, now a high quality, comfortable and elegant hotel with a large library. All sorts of goodies by way of four poster beds, antiques and courtyards, plus a snooker room.

MAINS HALL COUNTRY HOUSE, Singleton, Lancashire. Tel: (0253) 885130
A privately owned Grade II listed house overlooking the River Wyre, Mains Hall is steeped in history. The hotel offers many leisure facilities including fishing and badminton.

MICHAELS NOOK, Grasmere, Cumbria. Tel: (09665) 496
A gracious stone built Lakeland house overlooking the Grasmere Valley. This hotel is beautifully furnished with antiques and offers memorable high quality cuisine. It is a perfect base for exploring the Lake District.

MILLER HOWE HOTEL, Windermere, Cumbria. Tel: (09662) 2536
John Tovey's delightful lakeland hotel enjoys stunning views of Windermere and the fells. All rooms are tastefully furnished, with fine paintings, flowers and porcelain all adding to the homely charm. The food is quite superb and the 5 course (no choice) dinner is served to all guests simultaneously. All in all, a first class hotel with many little extras which add to a memorable visit.

MORRITT ARMS HOTEL, Greta Bridge, Co Durham. Tel: (0833) 27232
The lounge bar in this jolly old inn sports an antique barrel organ and miniature traction engine. The famous Dickens Bar depicts various characters from the well-loved novels.

OLD CHURCH, Watermillock, Cumbria. Tel: (07684) 86204
This is a popular hotel on the edge of Lake Ullswater. Large picture windows afford a spectacular view of the lake. The four-course menu changes daily and despite the restricted choice the cuisine here is first class.

OLD VICARAGE COUNTRY HOUSE HOTEL, Witherslack, Cumbria. (Tel: (044852) 381
This is a charming Georgian hotel set in pretty gardens. Rooms are tastefully furnished with antiques and fresh flowers. The restaurant here offers a superb 5 course set menu with imaginative dishes prepared to a very high standard.

CROSBY LODGE

Crosby Lodge was purchased by the Sedgwick family in 1970, and has been skilfully restored and converted into the romantically beautiful Country House Hotel it is today.

The front door opens into an enormous welcoming log fire, with an oak staircase leading to the bedrooms. Each bedroom is decorated and designed individually, with en suite bathrooms. Various period pieces such as half-tester beds, have been retained, whilst at the same time, the hotel provides first class modern amenities. Crosby Lodge has an established reputation for excellence and the large spacious rooms, full of antiques and elegantly furnished, welcome guests with a comfortable and relaxed atmosphere. Overlooking tree-lined parkland, the delightful dining room, with its beamed ceiling, gleaming cutlery and long windows, is a haven for the connoisseur of good food and wine. Deliciously exciting menus feature authentic continental cuisine alongside the very best of traditional British fare. The four course Table d'hote menu has a vast choice and is complimented by a smaller A la carte menu providing such delights as steaks, scampi and Dover sole. The Crosby Lodge sweet trolley is renowned far and wide, and coffee and delicious home-made sweetmeats can be taken in the charming lounge and cocktail bar. Chef Proprietor Michael Sedgwick produces exciting dishes using fresh, mainly local ingredients, ensuring everything is to the highest standard.

To the visitor, Crosby Lodge offers untold days of pleasure with the Lake District and Scottish Lowlands so near at hand. Historic Hadrians Wall, stunning Cumberland and Northumberland country and the ancient border city of Carlisle await the visitor, and travelling further afield, yet returning to Crosby Lodge in the evening, one can reach Edinburgh, a city steeped in history and culture. Featured in Egon Ronay, Michelin, with three AA stars and a British Tourist for crown hotel, Crosby Lodge is fully deserving of the praise it receives. With an emphasis on comfort, relaxation, good food, traditional courtesy and old-fashioned hospitality, Michael and Patricia Sedgwick, son James and staff will ensure that you have a memorable stay and every assistance with your arrangements.

Crosby Lodge
Country House Hotel and Restaurant
Crosby-on-Eden
Carlisle
Cumbria CA6 4QZ

Tel: (0228) 573618
Fax: (0228) 573428

LANCASHIRE, THE LAKES & NORTHUMBRIA

OLDE SHIP HOTEL, Seahouses, Northumberland. Tel: (0665) 720200
This is a proud, family run hotel which overlooks both the quiet harbour of Seahouses and the Farne Islands. There is an assortment of bars and a collection of model ships on view. The bedrooms and bathrooms are spotless and in keeping with the whole ambience of the hotel.

PHEASANT INN, Bassenthwaite Lake, Cumbria. Tel: (059681) 234
A first class inn, long established, renowned and with the patina of long use by people enjoying themselves near the lakes. Rustic outside and relaxing inside.

REDWORTH HALL HOTEL, Redworth, Co Durham. Tel: (0388) 772442
This seventeenth century manor house commands 25 acres of park and woodland. Reputedly haunted, a bounty of £5,000 is offered to the guest who can prove its ghostly rumours.

ROTHAY MANOR. Ambleside, Cumbria. Tel: (05394) 33605
An elegant Georgian manor house in one and a half acres of grounds close to Lake Windermere. The hotel offers luxury accommodation and leisure facilities, including trout fishing. Several stately homes, Wordsworth's cottage and a steam railway are nearby.

SHARROW BAY, Howtown, Cumbria. Tel: (07684) 86301/ 56483
Set on the shore of the magnificent Lake Ullswater, the hotel is elegantly furnished throughout with 'objets d'art', antiques and many pictures, and is superbly placed for exploring the natural beauty of the surrounding area.

STRING OF HORSES INN, Carlisle, Cumria. Tel: (0228) 70297
A late 17th century inn, the String of Horses is a must for antique lovers, it is a true Aladdins Cave of furniture. There is a well equipped leisure centre and the hotel is only a short distance from Hadrian's Wall.

TUFTON ARMS HOTEL, Appleby-in-Westmoreland, Cumbria. Tel: (07683) 51593
A distinguished Victorian coaching inn totally refurbished to provide great luxury and comfort. With a wide ranging menu and extensive wine list, the Tufton Arms is an ideal base for tours of the Lakes, Dales and Pennines.

WATEREDGE HOTEL, Ambleside, Cumbria. Tel: (05394) 32332
The homely feel of the original fishermen's cottages remains in this very comfortable hotel, which benefits from the wonderful Windermere air, fresh and bright furnishings. Nearby is the wonderful Abbey with its famous Roman Catholic school.

Aydon Grange

ABBEY HOUSE HOTEL

This most impressive red sandstone building is a superb and slightly unusual example of the work of the eminent English architect, Sir Edwin Lutyens. It was completed in 1914 as a business guest house and, in its, conversion to a graceful hotel of the very highest calibre, virtually all of the magnificently-proportioned rooms have adapted to their new role with minimal disturbance. There is an inherent grandeur and quiet dignity about the hotel equalled only by the fourteen acres of grounds, comprising a beautifully balanced mixture of formal gardens and wooded copses. Beyond these lies a splendid vista of mature woodland and meadow interspersed with established walkways which lead to the ruins of nearby Furness Abbey. For too long Furness Abbey has remained part of England's 'Hidden Heritage'. Every year, crowds of visitors make Pilgrimages to Glastonbury, Fountains and Rievaulx Abbeys, yet Furness remains relatively unknown; such was not the case in Medieval Times for the Abbey of St. Mary of Furness was one of Britain's great Religious Houses. Now it is your turn to re-live those great years by visiting Furness to see one of the last remaining unspoilt Abbeys. Also nearby are Holker Hall, Muncaster Castle, Conishead Priory and many more Stately Homes and glorious gardens.

In less than half-an-hour's drive you are in the centre of the English Lake District with all the historic and picturesque places of interest in and around Grizedale Forest.

Barrow-in-Furness lies on a peninsula with a road bridge to the Isle of Walney, and some tiny isolated islands in and around sheltered bays; Sailing craft complete the coastal picture. Inland excursions bring you to the tarns, fells and pikes of the Cumbrian Mountains.

Abbey House offers impeccable accommodation for business and holiday visitors alike, and the finest a la carte English and French cuisine of the Abbey Restaurant is available to residents and non-residents.

Excellent conference and banqueting facilities can be provided. Special discounted rates to Parties from 4-40 persons.

Abbey House Hotel
Abbey Road
Barrow in Furness
Cumbria LA13 OPA
Tel: (0229) 838282
Fax: (0229) 820403

LANCASHIRE, THE LAKES & NORTHUMBRIA

WHITE MOSS HOTEL, Grasmere, Cumbria. Tel: (09665) 295
An attractive 18th century house overlooking Rydal Water, and once owned by Wordsworth. The comfortable rooms are furnished with antiques, and the restaurant is famed for its imagination and style.

WILD BOAR HOTEL, Crook, Co Durham. Tel:(096 62) 5225
This early-Victorian coaching inn, complete with blackened beams and log fires, reputedly guards in the spot where Westmoreland's last wild boar was killed, back in the reign of King John.

WORDSWORTH HOTEL, Grasmere, Cumbria. Tel: (09665) 592
In the heart of Lakeland, this first class, four star hotel has a reputation as one of the area's finest. It offers comfortable bedrooms and many leisure facilities, together with superb cuisine.

ACCOMMODATION OF MERIT

AYDON GRANGE, Corbridge, Northumberland. Tel: (0434) 632169
Enchanting house with friendly family atmosphere standing in extensive, mature gardens. A peaceful haven from which to tour Hadrian's Wall, Newcastle, Durham and the surrounding countryside. It is advisable to book in advance. (see photograph).

HIPPING HALL, Cowan Bridge, Cumbria. Tel: (05242) 71187
Set in 4 acres of walled gardens near Kirby Lonsdale, this handsome 17th century country house is an ideal base from which to tour both the Cumbrian Lakes and Yorkshire Dales. An unusual (and enjoyable!) feature - guests dine together, dinner party style, in the Great Hall. (see photograph).

KITTY FRISK HOUSE, Hexham, Northumberland. Tel: (0434) 606850
A beautiful family home, originally built in the early 1900's as a gentleman's country residence. It stands in 3 acres of garden and woodland and is a quiet haven. The unspoilt Northumbrian countryside and Hadrian's Wall are within easy reach.

LITTLE HOLMSIDE HALL, Burnhope, Durham. Tel: (0207) 284740
A restored Elizabethan manor house dating from 1668 and set in pretty gardens with beautiful views across the local countryside. An atmospheric place from which to visit Durham City, Beamish Museum and other fascinating historical sites.

LOW BARNS, Thornborough, Northumberland. Tel: (0434) 632408
An attractive 18th century farmhouse surrounded by open countryside but within its own 2 acres of garden and paddock. Walking the Roman Wall and discovering rural Northumberland and its heritage are easy from this welcoming environment.

Hipping Hall

SHARROW BAY COUNTRY HOUSE HOTEL

Evidence of our heritage surrounds the Sharrow Bay and the beauty of its location has been brought inside where antiques and soft furnishings, together with fresh flowers and the aroma of the cooking, create the feeling of established comfort associated with our country houses.

Nestling beneath Barton Fell, Sharrow Bay Country House Hotel - which is reputed to be the first 'Country House' hotel to be created in Great Britain - is on the shore of Lake Ullswater, the waves actually lapping the terrace wall of soft grey stone.

The views - of lake, woods and mountains - are legendary, constantly changing and as inspirational today as they were for the poets who are part of the history of this area. There are twelve acres of gardens and woodlands and half a mile of lake shore (complete with a private jetty) where guests can wander in total peace. The bedrooms are as one would expect; luxuriously cosy and full of porcelain, pictures, antique furniture, books and games.

In the main hotel there are twelve bedrooms, eight with private bathroom. There is also a garden cottage and a charming Quaker cottage in the village of Tirril, four miles from the hotel. The Edwardian gatehouse at the entrance to the hotel, has an additional room and three superb suites - ideal, as are many of the rooms, for honeymoons.

In addition, the hotel has a converted Elizabethan farmhouse, a mile and a quarter further along the lake from the main house. Bank House is approached by a sweeping drive which takes one up onto the fell-side where the views are unbelievable. All of the seven bedrooms look down on Ullswater and the superb refectory breakfast room has breathtaking views. Guests join those at the main house for dinner but this is the only time they need leave the tranquil surroundings.

Because guests are genuinely cared for, comfort is the key word associated with Sharrow. There are two lounges in Bank House, as there are in the main house, where soft sofas jostle for space with antique chairs and freshly cut flowers and numerous lights make even grey days light. It is an oasis where one can escape from the world and one's own problems.

The cuisine has become internationally renowned and the emphasis is on traditional British dishes, created with imagination and served with graciousness and care by the excellent staff, some of whom have been at Sharrow for over twenty five years. 1992 will see the commencement of Sharrow's 44th season under the present proprietors.

A haven for those who wish to relax completely in peaceful surroundings, guests will find echoes of the Italian lakes, and will understand why Sharrow was given an award by the AA for having the best view of any hotel in the United Kingdom. In the immediate vicinity, guests can enjoy boating, fishing, and of course walking or climbing. Alternatively, the market town of Penrith lies seven miles to the east - a friendly little town full of atmosphere and ideal for shopping. On the outskirts of the town there is a fine golf course with wide views of the Fells. The area also offers a variety of places of archaeological interest which can be visited, such as Hadrian's Wall east of Carlisle, or Long Meg stone circle near Penrith.

Just six miles from the M6 motorway, and with modern high speed electric train links from Carlisle to London and the North, Sharrow Bay, with its delightful atmosphere and outstanding vistas, is a rare treat.

Sharrow Bay Country House Hotel
Lake Ullswater
Pooley Bridge
Penrith CA10 2LZ
Tel: (07684) 86301
Fax: (07684) 86349

LANCASHIRE, THE LAKES & NORTHUMBRIA

LOWICK HOUSE, Lowick Green, Cumbria.
Tel: (022985) 227
Two miles from the foot of Coniston Water, amidst beautiful gardens with a trout beck, this attractive 1730's house provides romantic accommodation for those touring the Lake District with its abundance of heritage.

NEW CAPERNWRAY FARM, Capernwray, Lancashire.
Tel: (0524) 734284
A 17th century country house providing three charming bedrooms with ensuite/private facilities. Low ceilings and old oak beams make a romantic setting for excellent candle-lit dinners. Five minutes from A6/M6 Exit 35. Close to Holker, Leighton, Levens, Thurnham Halls, Lancaster and Sizergh Castle. (see photograph).

THE OLD VICARAGE, Orton, Cumbria. Tel: (05874) 210
An attractive early Victorian House, two and a half miles from the M6, close to Ullswater and Hawkswater, and convenient for touring the Lake District. Appleby, with its castle, and Gypsy Horse Fair are both near to this pretty fell village.

ORREST HEAD HOUSE, Windermere, Cumbria. Tel: (09662) 4315
Located in 3 acres of garden this Lakeland style house commands spectacular views over Windermere and towards the mountains. Partly 17th century this house provides tranquil accommodation for exhausted explorers of local heritage.

TUGGAL HALL, Chathill, Northumberland.
Tel: (066589) 229
A welcoming, stone-built, 17th century family house, set in ten acres of private land, clad in colourful Virginia creeper. Home grown produce is a delicious feature at mealtimes, while the hotel is convenient for Alnwick Castle, Holy Island, Farne Islands, Cheviot Hills and Hadrian's Wall. (see photograph).

WALKER GROUND MANOR, Hawkshead, Cumbria. Tel: (09666) 219
This 16th century house was part of Furness Abbey until 1532, and offers home cooked food, log fires and four posters. Hawkshead, once a Viking settlement, is convenient for visiting Brantwood, Hill Top, Muncaster, Sizergh and Levens. No smoking, young children or pets.

INNS OF CHARACTER

ANCIENT UNICORN, Bowes, Co Durham.
This unpretentious 16th century coaching inn and its village have a close connection with Charles Dickens' novel 'Nicholas Nickleby'. Rustic simplicity is very much the character of this old pub with its reliable bar food and good ale.

BOOT, Burnmoor, Lancashire.
Beauty and tranquility characterise the setting of this charming 16th century family-run pub nestling within a hamlet at the highest point of the Ravenglass and Eskdale light steam rail-

New Capernwray Farm

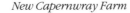

MICHAELS NOOK HOTEL

A gracious, stone-built Lakeland home, with a wealth of mahogany woodwork, Michaels Nook is quietly tucked away overlooking the Grasmere valley and surrounded by well-kept lawns and beautiful trees. It was opened as a hotel over twenty years ago by owner Reg Gifford, a respected antique dealer, and furnishings, enhanced by an abundance of flowers and plants, reflect his appreciation of English furniture, antique rugs, prints and porcelain. The Hotel retains the mellowness of the private home, and a hint of pleasing eccentricity, accentuated by the presence of a Great Dane and some exotic cats.

There are twelve, lovely, individually-designed bedrooms, all with en suite bathrooms, and two magnificent suites. Each room has colour television and direct dial telephone, and is provided with many thoughtful extra touches, such as fresh flowers, fruit, and mineral water. Full room service is available.

In the Restaurant, polished tables gleam, set with fine crystal and porcelain, and only the best fresh ingredients are used for dishes memorable for their delicate flavour and artistic presentation. Different choices are offered each day. A very extensive

Wine List offers selections from all the best wine-producing areas, and makes for fascinating reading, as well as excellent drinking. The panelled Oak Room, with handsome stone fireplace and gilt furnishings, hosts Director and Senior Manager meetings and private celebrations.

Spectacular excursions, by car or on foot, start from the doorstep of this delightful house, and encompass some of Britain's most impressive scenery. Dove Cottage, Wordsworth's home during his most creative period, is close at hand, and Beatrix Potter's farm at Sawrey only a short drive away.

The Hotel itself has three acres of landscaped grounds, and a further ten acres of woodland and wild fell, plus a speciality rhododendron garden covering four acres of nearby hillside. Guests are also welcome to make use of the heated swimming pool, and other health facilities of The Wordsworth Hotel, less than a mile away, and under the same ownership. Both Hotels offer special arrangements with Keswick Golf Club, and enjoy a close proximity to some of the excellent northern links courses.

Michaels Nook
Grasmere
Ambleside
Cumbria LA22 9RP
Tel: (05394) 35496
Fax: (05394) 35765

LANCASHIRE, THE LAKES & NORTHUMBRIA

way. In keeping with rural tradition good bar food comes in generous portions. There are extensive walking opportunities in this scenic area. Rooms are also available.

COOPERAGE, Newcastle-Upon-Tyne, Tyne and Wear.
This heavily timbered and beamed Tudor inn with its exposed stonework is popular and atmospheric. An extensive list of regular and guest ales plus good value bar-food are sure to please visitors to one of the city's oldest pubs.

EAGLE AND CHILD, Wharles, Lancashire.
17th century oak armchairs and a magnificent Jacobean settle are among the many distinctive antique charms here. Excellent home and guest ales are in keeping with the traditional atmosphere. No food, but there are picnic tables outside.

GROTTO, Marsden, Tyne and Wear.
This unique pub is noted for its atmospheric position, built within the cliff caverns and requiring a lift to descend to the bar and restaurant. Although not 'olde-worlde' this unconventional inn is worth a fascinating visit. Real ales and excellent food are here to be enjoyed.

KINGS ARMS, Hawkshead, Cumbria.
An old fashioned inn perched above a delightful Elizabethan village. Fine ales and generous portions of traditional food can be enjoyed sitting at the old teak seats and oak cask tables of this splendidly located pub.

LORD CREWE ARMS, Blanchland, Northumberland.
Originally built in 1235 for Premonstratension Canons, this inn was formed from the Abbot's lodgings and has lost little of its ancient character. The original cloister and crypt still stand amid the heavy stone walls. Traditional bar food and fine ales are in keeping with the delightful antiquity of this village pub.

MORTAL MAN, Troutbeck, Cumbria.
A charming and historic country inn, the Mortal Man enjoys beautiful views over Lake Windermere.

MORRITT ARMS, Greta Bridge, Co Durham.
Beautifully situated, overlooking the River Gieto, this 18th century inn claims Dickens, Cotman and Turner amongst its previous guests. Visitors today can appreciate a lifesize Pickwickian mural and other traditional decoration at this charming pub. Food and ales are excellent.

THE OLDE SHIP, Seahouses, Northumberland.
Low beams, teak and mahogany dominate this old seaside inn with its nautical memorabilia. Locally caught fish, traditional food and fine ales are the norm at this delightfully atmospheric pub.

ROYAL OAK, Appleby, Cumbria.
Particularly good food, a well chosen wine list and a wide range of ales are the main benefits of this delightful pub overlooking the village church. Once part of a 14th century posting house, oak panels and heavy beams preserve its cosy atmosphere.

THE STAR, Netherton, Northumberland.
Built at the turn of the century, this village inn stands in bleak and isolated countryside. There are few concessions to the modern era here as there is no bar - just a serving hatch for food! The excellent beer, tapped from the cask, merits a visit to this no-nonsense establishment.

SUN, Coniston, Cumbria.
Lakes and fells provide a breathtaking setting for this lovely old stone inn. Good food, real ales handpumped from the 16th century granite cellar and a range of rare malt whiskies add to the attraction of this warm, informal pub. Accommodation is also available.

WHITE BULL, Ribchester, Lancashire.
Four, 1400 year old Tuscan columns rescued from a nearby Roman site support the porch of this rustic 17th century pub. Refurbishment has not deprived the pub of its charming old character. Good food and real ales are a couple of other attractions.

Tuggall Hall

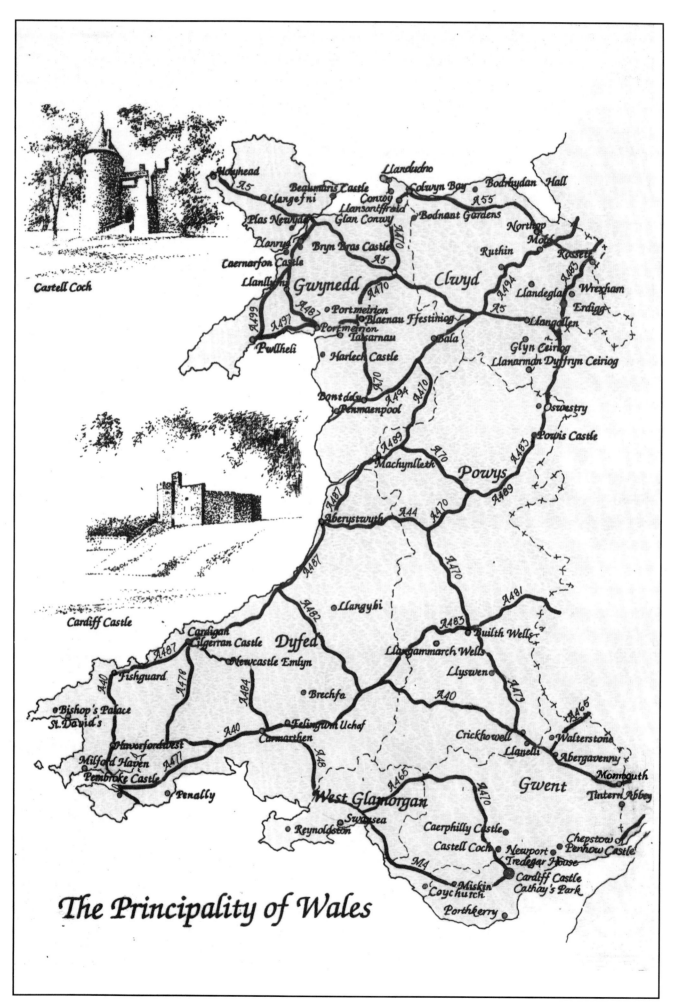

The Principality of Wales

THE PRINCIPALITY OF WALES

The Mercian king, Offa, who reigned in the latter half of the 8th century is generally credited with the construction of **Offa's Dyke** to define the boundary between his kingdom and Wales. From Prestatyn, near Rhyl, through the border counties of Wales and England to the mouth of the River Wye, near Chepstow, sits the great dyke built of earth and stone. Forests, long since gone, leave gaps in the earthworks where the woodlands themselves would have provided sufficient deterrent to raiders. Nowadays there is no such barrier to enter Wales - except perhaps the Severn Bridge - and visitors flock to the Principality.

Its male voice choirs and rugby union are as much a part of the cultural heritage of this land, once 'famed' only for the depressing scenes of collieries and coal tips towering over villages and towns. Today many of the mines have closed and the valleys are being returned to their former beauty, undoing over 100 years of industrial endeavour.

Whilst much of the heavy industry is based around the M4 spine through Newport, Cardiff, Swansea, Port Talbot and Milford Haven, there are also beautiful coastal walks through Pembrokeshire, Cardigan Bay, with its long stretches of sandy beaches and sand dunes set against towering cliffs and close by is Bontddu, where gold is mined to this day for Royal wedding rings.

The Isle of Anglesey and the north coast seaside towns of Bangor, Llandudno, Colwyn Bay and Rhyl are popular destinations for visitors. Scattered around the coastline are the magnificent castles at St David's and Harlech; Tintern Abbey on the border; the Brecon Beacons National Park and the magnificent Cambrian Mountains, with its lakes and reservoirs, forests and moorlands; and - most intriguingly - the narrow gauge railways to take visitors to many of the peaks.

DYFED, GLAMORGAN, GWENT

Consisting of Pembrokeshire, Carmarthenshire, Breconshire, Glamorgan and Monmouthsire - the old counties long since gone - South and West Wales offers a variety of contrasting sights from **the Pembrokeshire Coast National Park** with its winding path around a spectacular coastline, to **the Brecon Beacons National Park** with its woodlands and reservoirs; from the bustling cities of Cardiff, Newport and Swansea to the holiday towns of Tenby and Cardigan; from the industrial towns of Port Talbot and Milford Haven to the now green valleys of the Rhondda.

THE PEMBROKE PENINSULA

North of Fishguard with its regular ferry services to Ireland, lies Cardigan on the A487 over the River Teifi. Here the picturesque ruins of **Cilgerran Castle**, dating from the 13th century, is one of the most often painted and photographed fortresses in the land, standing proudly above a deep gorge overlooking the river.

Driving south on the A487 the Preseli Hills lie to the south and it was from here in 2000 BC that the 'blue stones' were taken to build Stonehenge along what was the road between Ireland and Salisbury.

Near St David's Head is **St David's Bishop's Palace**. Built between 1280 and 1350, the imposing Bishop's Palace stands within the Cathedral Close and houses a display showing the resourcefulness of the churchmen who built cathedrals at this time. The intricate detailing of the medieval carved heads and animal figures to the wings of the palace and the entrance to the Great Hall are testament to the power of the Church and the bishops. Further south, off the A4139 is **Lamphrey Bishop's Palace** where the bishops of St David's retreated when their work was done, their country residence!

The River Pembroke and its banks form a natural defence to **Pembroke Castle**, the birthplace of Henry VII, standing over the medieval town of the same name. Here in 1648, Cromwell's troops destroyed the castle after laying siege to it for six weeks. Works to the castle commenced in the latter part of the 11th century, with the impressive circular Keep and Gatehouse dating from around 1200. Much of what visitors can see today is from the 13th century when curtain walls were built to add to the castles defences.

THE RHONDDA VALLEY

Travel back towards **Cardiff**, now the capital of the Principality of Wales, mainly through the growth of its docks instigated by the Marquess of Bath during the 19th century. The docks area is now being transformed into a marina, housing, retail and business space with the help of the Cardiff Bay Development Corporation, and includes the Welsh Industrial and Maritime Museum sited on a former dock basin exhibiting the development of industry and transport in Wales. The architecturally praised Cardiff Bay Visitor Centre is well worth a visit to see the proposals for the area's development. **Cardiff Castle** dates back to Roman times although the Norman keep dates from the 12th century and replaced an earlier wooden structure (featured later). Close by is the National Museum of Wales with its interesting history of Wales and the Welsh people, and in addition superb displays of porcelain and bronze works. The Roman Fort in the town centre was reconstructed by Lord Bute to afford the visitor a view today of what the fortress would have been like in the 3rd century.

North of Cardiff is **Castell Coch,** a unique fairytale castle built to the designs of William Burges for Lord Bute, as a weekend retreat from Cardiff Castle. The architect and owner - there is a wonderful exhibition to be viewed of the two men - allowed their imaginations to run wild to create an imaginative medieval castle with intricately detailed walls and ceilings depicting birds, monkeys and butterflies and scenes from Aesop's Fables.

The 4th Marquess of Bute carried out extensive restoration work to **Caerphilly Castle** and this work has been continued by Welsh Historic Monuments. Built in 1271, to an innovative design, the Castle, set in 30 acres with its large lakes was able to withstand the fiercest onslaught by the dreaded military catapult.

THE MOUTH OF THE SEVERN

The M4 Motorway leads towards Newport and **Penhow Castle** seven miles north of Newport is the oldest 'lived in' castle in Wales, with a magnificent 15th century stone hall. Originally built in the 13th century, much restoration work has ben carried out recently by the owner Stephen Weeks. Jane Seymour, a descendant of the original family who built the

Castle, became Henry VIII's third wife and gave him a son, later to become Edward VI.

The seat of the Morgans for over 500 years, the imposing **Tredegar House** standing in over 90 acres was rebuilt in red brick in the 17th century. This fine house with magnificently decorated State Rooms furnished in period style has been lovingly refurbished, since ceasing to be a school in 1974. Of particular interest to the visitor are the 'below stairs' rooms of the kitchen and servants hall where domestic appliances of the time can be seen.

The original medieval walled garden layout survives on two sides of the house, although only one avenue of oaks and chestnuts remain as a result of Mickle's 18th century replanning. The architecturally rich stable block and other outbuildings now house craft workshops and the parkland is home for a variety of rhododendron and other plants.

Set in wonderful countryside is **Chepstow Castle,** part of which dates from the 11th century. Standing high above the River Wye it guards one of the most important border crossings from England to Wales. Further north in the Wye Valley, stands the spectacular ruins of **Tintern Abbey**, founded in 1131 by Cistercian Walter de Clare. It fell into disrepair after the Dissolution of the Monasteries under Henry VIII in the 16th century. The splendid **Raglan Castle** near Raglan, is set in a beautiful border location. The ruined hexagonal tower and drawbridge built in the 15th century are in a style more usually found in Northern France.

The A40/A465 leads towards Ebbw Vale where the 1992 Garden Festival of Wales will take place in October. Nearby at Brynmawr, there is a unique underground tour and exhibition of 19th century coal and iron mines which give an insight into the working conditions and way of life for the mining communities.

Beyond Merthyr Tydfil is the Brecon Mountain Railway which allows the visitor to take a trip on a vintage steam locomotive into the Brecon Beacons National Park - mainly over 1000 feet this is a picturesque area with woodland and reservoirs.

POWYS

Cambrian Mountains, the heart of Wales contains ancient prehistoric treasures, imposing medieval castles and abbey ruins. From Cardigan Bay to Tremadog Bay there is spectacular coastline, with sandy beaches, clifftop walks and inland, winding mountain roads over the Cambrians, gentle moorland, with reservoirs and lakes and border forests.

Powis Castle, near the market town of Welshpool, is a medieval fortress overlooking the Severn Valley. Once the seat of the Upper Powis princes, it has been the home of the Herbert family since 1587. With ornately decorated ceilings and murals, this elegant castle has many fine paintings and tapestries, and the Clive of India Museum. Clive's son married into the family in the early 19th century and there is an enormous collection of Indian art and memorabilia.

The formal gardens were laid out in a Dutch style, almost 300 year ago, with terraces, balustrading and lead statuary. Exotic plants and shrubs grow in the less exposed areas below the terraces, and some fine trees can be seen in the grounds beyond.

From the remains of **Montgomery Castle** there are spectacular views of the surrounding countryside. Built in 1223 by Henry III, on the site of an earlier Norman fort, it is an early example of a twin towered gatehouse; the 70m deep well is of particular interest. Follow the A483 to Newtown, where the WH Smith Museum is located. A compact display, photographs, models and memorabilia depict an engrossing chronicle of WH Smith from its beginning in 1792. There are many features of the museum, including a selection of photographs of WH Smith wholesale houses which show their development from the opening of the first one in 1850 to the present day modern look of some 100 wholesale houses. When railway mania was at its height in 1848, WH Smith opened its first bookstall - at Euston Station. The museum is situated on the first floor of the Newtown branch of WH Smith, the shop has been completely restored to its 1927 appearance, when the branch first opened. It has the original oak shop front, tiling and mirrors, plaster relief decoration and other details. There will be a special celebration for WH Smith when they reach their Bicentenary (1792-1992).

Take the A489/470/4120 to **Devils Bridge** where three bridges cross the Rivers Rheidol and Mynach, overlooking impressive waterfalls in a deep gorge. The lowest bridge dates from the 12th century and is said to have been built by the monks of Strata Florida Abbey close by. The Cistercian monks lived in this peaceful countryside from 1164 and encouraged the use of the Welsh language and writings. The middle bridge is built of stone and dates from the mid 18th century; the highest is an iron bridge from the early part of this century. The Vale of Rheidol Light Railway runs from here, past the Rheidol Power Station to the seaside resort and university town of Aberystwyth, on Cardigan Bay.

Heading north on the A487 lies Dyfi Furnace, with its spectacular waterfall, which turned the bellows to smelt iron ore in the 18th century. Near Merrion Mill, is Port Minllyn, a twin arched bridge, almost overgrown with vegetation, built by the Rector of Mallwyd in the early 17th century.

At Llanelltyd take the A496 to Barmouth, then north along the sandy coastline to **Harlech Castle** built over 700 years ago (featured later). To the east is the southern part of the Snowdonia National Park.

Portmeirion is a unique fairy tale village situated on the rocky tree clad peninsular of Cardigan Bay. This dream village was built by Welsh architect Sir Clough Williams-Ellis amidst beautiful scenery. Gwyllt Gardens are considered to be one of the finest wild gardens in Wales and include wonderful displays of rhododendrons, hydrangeas, azaleas and other subtropical flora. It was in Portmeirion that 'Noel Coward' wrote his comedy Blithe Spirit. We mustn't forget Portmeirion pottery, famous worldwide (featured later).

GWYNEDD & CLWYD

From Anglesey and Holyhead through the Cambrian Mountains and Snowdonia National park, to the holiday resorts of Llandudno and Colwyn Bay, to the industrial town of Wrexham this is a land of contrasts. From the highest point on Snow-

THE PRINCIPALITY OF WALES

donia through the valleys of Conwy and Clwyd and the fourteen mile long Menai Strait, there are spectacular views to the twin lakes of Llyn Padarn and Llyn Peris, impressive waterfalls and woodland.

ANGLESEY AND SNOWDONIA

The Lleyn Peninsula stretches into the Irish Sea to Bardsey Island where a Christian monastery was visited by pilgrims in medieval times. At Plas yu Rhiw, which dates in part from the 10th century, there is a splendid subtropical and exotic garden.

Taking the road north the **Snowdonia National Park** lies to the east, with Snowdon summit at 3559 feet the highest mountain in England and Wales. From the summit it is possible to descend - or ascend if you wish - on the narrow gauge rack and pinion railway powered by the original engines since 1896 back to Llanberis, with wonderful views of the mountains and Anglesey.

Close by is the Neo-Romanesque **Bryn Bras Castle** built around the 1830s on the site of an earlier building. Inside there are some beautiful stained glass windows, elegantly panelled family rooms and ornate ceilings and period furniture. The splendidly landscaped gardens are set in grounds of over 30 acres, with woodland and mountain walks offering magnificent views.

Caernarfon Castle is the most important of Edward I's castles (featured later). The Menai Strait separates the **Isle of Anglesey**, the 'Mother of Wales', from the mainland, and is crossed by a road and by a road/rail bridge. Telford's cast iron road bridge with a central span of nearly 100m was completed in 1826. Stevenson's bridge was built in the late 1840s, of five huge red sandstone piers, three of which stand in the Straits - destroyed by fire in 1970 it was reconstructed as a combined road and rail bridge.

Adjacent to the Menai Strait is the fine 18th century James Wyatt house at **Plas Newydd** with unrivalled views of the Straits and Snowdonia. There is a beautiful display of flowers and shrubs in the springtime, an interesting military museum and Whistler exhibition.

The moated **Beaumaris Castle**, built for Edward I in 1290 but never completed, standing on flat, open ground is perfectly symmetrical with a five metre thick curtain wall. History from Victorian times ranges from the courthouse and jail, with its wooden treadmill, to the museum of childhood.

The island has many prehistoric remains including the standing stones at Tregwehelydd and the Presaddfed Burial Chamber. From Holyhead on Holy Island ferries sail to Ireland as they have since the middle of the 16th century. The dramatic cliffs and coastline is home to a variety of birds, including puffins and choughs and seals.

Conwy Castle is close to Telford's suspension road bridge over the River Conwy next to Stephenson's tubular rail bridge. Built in the 1280s, it is a considerable feat of medieval military design. South on the A470 are **Bodnant Gardens**, originally laid out in 1875, with magnificent displays of rhododendrons, azaleas and magnolias. A Pin Mill, transferred from Gloucester in 1938, sits proudly at the end of the lily canal and is used as a summerhouse. Henry Pochim's daughter and her husband, Lord Aberconwy, extended the gardens before donating them to the National Trust in 1949.

THE VALE OF CLWYD

Further along the A55 at Rhyl is **Bodrhyddan Hall**, a fine 17th century manor house (featured later). Nearby is the ruin of **Rhuddlan Castle** built by Edward around 1280, with its moat, twin gate house and concentric curtain walls.

South of Wrexham is **Erddig**, a late 17th century house, with later additions, standing in formal gardens with splendid fruit trees. Restored by the National Trust over the last 20 years, it was the home of the Yorke family between 1733 and 1973 before it fell into disrepair. A fascinating array of servants quarters include the laundry, bakehouse, sawmill and blacksmith, all restored to their original state, together with old photographs and paintings of servants during the Yorke's time in the house.

Wales, and its people, offer the opportunity for a quiet, relaxing break amid splendid scenery with history dating from prehistoric times through the ages to the recent transformation in the valleys and indeed to the capital and its docks.

W H Smith Museum

CARDIFF CASTLE

Cardiff Castle, in the heart of the City, has a history stretching back over 1900 years. The Romans first built a fort on this site, and the remains of the massive ten feet thick walls are visible in places. They were followed many centuries later by the Normans who built a castle, much of which survives including the Keep, and which was added to by medieval Lords. The castle passed in and out of royal ownership and possession was granted to several powerful families, each of which left their mark. They built stronger defences, for this was frontier land, and they created more gracious living quarters for their families. Much of their work remains despite the castle coming under attack in the Anglo-Welsh and English Civil Wars.

It was the Butes, last of the great families to occupy Cardiff Castle, who carried out the most ambitious changes. They brought power and prosperity to Cardiff, turning it from a sleepy backwater into one of the greatest coal ports in the world. In 1778 the 4th Earl of Bute embarked upon an ambitious plan to landscape the grounds and modernise the lodgings but the project was not completed.

In 1865 the 3rd Marquess of Bute invited William Burges to report on the state of the Castle and this was the beginning of a momentous partnership; an unlikely one perhaps between the handsome, shy, young aristocrat and the middle aged, worldly, extrovert who transformed the Castle into an extravaganza of whimsy, colour and rich architectural detail. Both men shared a delight in all things medieval and drew much of their inspiration from this rich source.

Lord Bute ordered the setting up of the Bute Workshops, employing the finest Welsh craftsmen to work on many aspects of the building. He paid the closest attention to every detail and every design passed through his hands.

Burges built the Clock Tower between 1869 and 1874, it was designed as a suite of bachelor apartments with Winter and Summer Smoking Rooms, and Bachelor Bedroom and Bathroom. Each room is built one above the other and the austere outward appearance of the Tower belies their glorious decoration based upon one theme - the passing of time.

Within the Castle, Lord Bute built a Chapel in memory of his father on the site of the room in which he died. It is richly decorated with paintings and sculpture and a memorial bust of the 2nd Marquess.

During the 1870's when Burges extended the lodgings he was told to build upwards and not outwards. He built upwards in such a way as was to become his own, and Cardiff's glory; gleaming chivalric towers with rooms rich in glowing colour. Work started on the Bute Tower with its private apartments all richly decorated. In the Bedroom the chimney piece is a bronze gilt and jewelled statue of St John and the Bathroom is lined with sixty different types of marble. The Tower is topped off by a Roof Garden with fountain and pool.

The Herbert Tower contains the Arab Room. This beautiful Islamic room, has walls lined with cedarwood and marble, and the golden stalactite ceiling is said to have been a favourite of Lord Bute. In the Guest Tower may be seen the Fairytale Nursery with a hand painted frieze depicting characters from Arabian Nights, Hans Anderson and the Brothers Grimm.

The Banqueting Hall is built on the site of the old medieval Hall. The timber vaulted ceiling is ablaze with heraldic devices tracing the Bute ancestry and carved angels gaze down from above. The stained glass windows depict the Lords of the Castle through the ages, and the medieval theme is carried through to the huge castellated chimney piece complete with knights and trumpeters.

Burges died in 1881 and his work at Cardiff Castle was completed by his assistant, William Frame. A collection of over 2,000 of Burges's drawings is available for research, forming a remarkable record of his restoration. In 1947 the Castle was given to the City of Cardiff.

CAERNARFON CASTLE

Caernarfon Castle is a supreme example of medieval military architecture at its most sophisticated. Begun in 1283 by Edward I, Caernarfon is the nearest building Wales has to a Royal Palace having been owned continuously by the Crown ever since.

The castle was constructed with east and west bailleys and walls which encircled part of the town for safety. During the uprising of 1294 the Welsh breached the town walls and entered the castle from its weaker northern side. The English response was to rebuild with mighty walls and soaring towers. The awesome curtain wall is twenty feet thick at its base and is strengthened by thirteen towers, each one different, spaced at intervals along its length. These many sided towers are the only remaining ones of this type in Wales. The varying bands of decorative stone were modelled on the walls of Constantinople.

The main entrance from the town is through the King's Gate over a drawbridge across a deep ditch. Any intruder who had come this far would then have to negotiate the most ingenious and elaborate series of narrow passages, right angle bends and portcullises, while all the time arrows rained down from all sides. The entrance to the eastern bailly was through the Queen's Gate.

In 1284 the new seat of government for North Wales was the birth place of its new English Prince, the ill-fated King Edward II. Legend says it was here that King Edward I showed his baby son to the Welsh people as 'the native-born Prince who could speak no English'.

Caernarfon Castle earned a place in modern history on 1 July 1969 when another Prince of Wales was presented to his subjects at the Investiture of HRH Prince Charles. The Castle also witnessed the Investiture of Prince Edward in 1911 when King George V invested his son. Since then Caernarfon has seen many Royal Tours and has received King George VI and Queen Elizabeth (the present Queen Mother) in 1937; Her Majesty Queen Elizabeth II after her coronation in 1953 and more recently the Prince of Wales and his new Princess in 1981.

There is a haunting beauty about Caernarfon today, as striking as its protective strength of yesterday.

HARLECH CASTLE

The soaring walls and towers of Harlech Castle are challenged for supremacy only by the purple mass of distant Snowdonia. These rugged peaks played a large part in determining Harlech's siting as one of the so-called 'iron-ring' of nine fortresses built by Edward I to impose his authority over the vanquished Welsh.

The Castle was constructed largely between 1283 and 1289 and represents a high point in medieval castle-building. It appears almost to have been carved out of the cliff face itself as it towers above Tremadog Bay. Two rectangular walls, one built within the other, are strengthened by round towers at each corner. In places the walls are over nine feet thick and the views from the battlements extend from the high peaks of Snowdonia, across the waters of the Bay and Lleyn Peninsula beyond.

The great glory of the castle is its massive twin-towered Gatehouse which gives Harlech its air of impregnability. In the inner bailly the domestic buildings vital to the day to day life of the garrison, particularly during times of siege, were situated. These would have included a well, kitchens, bakehouse, granary, a great hall and a chapel.

The garrison successfully withstood a siege during the Welsh uprising in 1294, but in 1404 the Welsh attacked again, this time under the leadership of their proclaimed Prince, Owain Glyndwr. The battle was long and hard-fought, and Wales won the day. Some years later the English returned with their own Prince of Wales, Henry V, and Harlech was retaken.

During the Wars of the Roses the castle was a great Lancastrian stronghold, the last remaining in North Wales, until it was forced to surrender to the Yorkists - but only after a long and bloody battle lasting seven years. That most stirring of battle hymns, 'Men of Harlech', was written as a tribute to the bravery of the garrison among whom was Henry Tudor, still only a boy but destined to become King Henry VII and founder of the House of Tudor.

In the Civil War of the 17th century the castle played a less dramatic role, although it was the last Royalist stronghold in Wales and withstood a siege by Roundhead forces, but later surrendered. This is perhaps why it was not rendered powerless by the Parliamentarians as was usually the case. The castle slowly collapsed into ruin, but now its fabric is maintained as a truly great monument to the history of both England and Wales.

PORTMEIRION POTTERIES

Back in the 1950s Euan Cooper-Willis and his wife, Susan Williams-Ellis, a designer and illustrator who had gained her considerable expertise studying under the esteemed artists Henry Moore and Graham Sutherland, founded a small business selling pottery in the gift shop in Portmeirion, the pretty little tourist village in North Wales created by Susan's father, Sir Clough Williams-Ellis. Some of this collection was designed exclusively for the Portmeirion shop by Susan. The pottery was manufactured elsewhere by a small Stoke-On-Trent businesss. Later the pair bought this up and the design and manufacture of the famous "Portmeirion" pottery products began.

The products are now exported to some 34 countries worldwide, and indeed the company was granted the Queen's Award for Export Achievement in 1990. The success of the designs is hardly surprising. There must surely be few people who do not recognise the famous "Botanic Garden" design pictured in the photograph above. Created and shaped by Susan in 1972, its original and distinctive design proved extremely popular, and highly collectable, featuring thirty varieties of plants as well as numerous butterflies, bees and ladybirds. This of course is only one of the main designs, the others are equally impressive. 'Birds of Britain', for example, boasts over forty different birds in its collection.

The attraction of Portmeirion for most people is its freshness of approach, breathing a healthy new air into a contemporary market full of tired shapes and non-committal designs. Portmeirion's are always robust and classical, most inspired by eighteenth and nineteenth century natural history illustrations. Of course there is also the versatility; knowing full well that there is little point in collecting a range of beautiful pottery only to store it away for special occasions, the Portmeirion collections are dishwasher, microwave and freezer safe. Moderately priced and yet beautiful to use and display, they suit every occasion, as formal or informal as you desire.

To complement the range of pottery, a range of accessories has also been produced, such as place mats, aprons, cushions, chopping boards and cutlery. Presently available in the Botanic Garden range and the relatively new Pomona design, all have been designed and produced to the same artistic and practical standards.

With their interest in the classical concerns of striking designs and high quality material, the group has already been commissioned by the National Trust for two exclusive designs and is also responsible for the British Heritage Collection, a quite stunning range of jugs and vases, based on antique pottery moulds, some of which date back to the 1830s.

With such pride and personal attention lavished on it, it is hardly surprising that the value of the beautiful Portmeirion pottery only continues to rise.

Portmeirion Potteries Ltd
London Road
Stoke-on-Trent ST4 7QQ
Tel: (0782) 744721

BODRHYDDAN HALL

Bodrhyddan Hall, the home of Lord Langford and his family, was built in the 17th century by John Conwy on the site of a much earlier house, probably dating from the Tudor period. A typical example of the William and Mary style, it consisted then of two storeys of mellow red brick with the Great Hall as its central feature.

Towards the end of the 18th century, a fairly major addition was made in the form of the Big Dining Room, although the exact date is not known. For the next hundred years or so no further changes were made until, in the early 1870s Lord Langford's grandfather decided that the house simply was no longer big enough for his large Victorian family. With the aid of the architect Robert Nesfield he built a new entrance, redesigned the west front in the Queen Anne style and enlarged the house to its present size.

The front hall contains an impressive collection of arms and armour, most of which dates from the Civil War, although there are Italian, German and Oriental pieces.

The Egypt Room contains two mummy cases and many other small treasures brought home by Lord Langford's intrepid great grandmother Charlotte Rowley. In recent times it was found that one of the cases still contains the original occupant, which is now on display.

The White Drawing Room, once the library whose carvings were painted a dark and dismal brown, now has an elegant white and gold scheme to create a fitting setting for the notable collection of china and wheel-back Hepplewhite chairs.

The Big Dining Room has become the family portrait gallery and contains works by Hogarth and Sir Joshua Reynolds. In the Great Hall there are two fine portraits by de Troy.

The front of the older part of the house is a formal pattern garden in the French manner with clipped yew walks radiating from a fountain. In the Pleasuaunce, a semi-wild woodland garden, is St Mary's Well, holy from pagan times and housed in a small octagonal sandstone pavilion by Inigo Jones. Local legend has it that the well house was used for clandestine marriages.

GLIFFAES COUNTRY HOUSE

A thoroughly charming Victorian country house hotel, Gliffaes boasts fine gardens and parkland, situated in the National Park yet only one mile off the main A40 road. It offers peace and tranquillity as well as being easily accessible.

The house, which faces due south, stands in its own 29 acres in the beautiful valley of the River Usk, midway between the Brecon Beacons and the Black Mountains. Built in 1885 as a private residence, it has been ideally adapted to provide spacious comfort in the country house tradition. There are 22 bedrooms with private bathrooms or showers and all are individual in decor and furnishings, including three in the converted lodge.

The downstairs rooms include a large, comfortable, panelled sitting-room which leads into an elegant regency style drawing-room. From here, french windows open into a large conservatory with double doors on to the terrace. The dining-room and comfortable bar also open on to the terrace, with the glorious views of the surrounding hills and River Usk one hundred and fifty feet below. The billiard room has a full sized table and provides an additional sitting-room with something of a club atmosphere.

Breakfast is served from a sideboard, lunch is a cold buffet with soup and a hot dish. Dinner is either table d'hote or a la carte. In fact, country house standards of the old order are carefully maintained by the resident owners; the Brabner family have held sway here since 1948.

External facilities include fishing for salmon and trout in the part of the Usk which the hotel overlooks, tennis, bowls, putting and croquet. There is an extensive range of short walks in the vicinity and a nearby riding and pony trekking establishment where horses and ponies can be hired.

The hotel is justly proud of its in-house cooking and remains open from the middle of March to the end of the year.

Gliffaes Country House Hotel
Crickhowell
Powys
Wales NP8 1RH
Tel: (0874) 730371 Fax: (0874) 730463

WALES

In recent years, the standard of accommodation in Wales has improved in leaps and bounds. Country houses exude charm and small wayside inns have been lovingly restored to cater for the many nomadic visitors who are discovering the hitherto unexplored delights of the country.

Its countryside varies enormously, rich farmland in the south, spectacular coastlines, Snowdonia National Park and all manner of winding rivers and streams cutting through remote uplands and moorlands. Downstream, the valleys echo with the sound of the male voice choirs. The history of Wales is saturated with song and poem.

To the south, the visitor finds many castles, Abbeys and numerous country house hotels. The Brecon Beacons and the Black Mountains are dotted with small towns of character whilst Pembrokeshire is one of the most beautiful places in Britain.

Sheep take centre stage in Mid-Wales and this, together with ancient ruins, quiet villages and delightful moorland reflect some of the most unspoiled acreage in the country. The area is popular with walkers and is a delightful escape for lovers of the countryside.

There are numerous fortifications along the Welsh border. None more impressive than Offa's Dyke. It dates from 750 AD and was built by the King of Mercia to control the marauding Welsh. Castles date from a later period but are equally impressive to view. The coast is also remarkably unspoilt and the beaches are a delight.

North Wales is a land of mountains, rivers, valleys and seaside with lovely fishing villages nestling along the cliffs above the sea. The Welsh language is still spoken here and as tradition has it, the locals are fiercely proud and independent. Indeed, north Wales has always resented the conquering Kings of England. And who can blame them? The dramatic coastal castles of Harlech and Caernarvon are spectacular but as the visitor soon discovers there is much more to Wales than meets the eye!

HOTELS OF DISTINCTION

THE BEAR, Crickhowell, Powys. Tel: (0873) 810408
Heavy oak beams, a large open fireplace and characterful furniture add further charm to this 15th century country inn which is the focal point of a beautiful market town. Bedrooms are charming and the food is most enjoyable.

BERTHLWYD HALL HOTEL, Llechwedd, Gwynedd. Tel: (0492) 592409
Overlooking historic Conwy in the Snowdonia National Park, this delightful Victorian manor retains much of its old charm with oak panelling, galleried landing and staircase, carved fireplaces and beautiful stained glass windows.

BODIDRIS HALL, Llandgela, Clwyd. Tel: (0978) 88434/479
Reputedly haunted, Bodidris features in many legends of the Welsh heroes. A fortified building has held the site since 1100 and the Hall retains a prison cell and a priest hole.

BODYSGALLEN HALL, Llandudno, Gwynedd. Tel: (0492) 584466
Furnished with antiques, the hotel stands in beautiful grounds which include a rare seventeenth century knot garden, rose garden, a refreshing cascade and offers breath-taking views of Snowdonia.

BONTDDU HALL, Bontddu, Gwynedd. Tel: (034149) 661
Set in some of the finest natural scenery in Britain, in the Snowdonia National Park, this historic Victorian mansion is ideally placed for exploring local castles and the gold mine in Bontddu.

CAER BERIS MANOR, Builth Wells, Powys. Tel: (0982) 552601
The former owner, Lord Swansea, has left his mark in the family's heraldic crests which adorn the oak-panelled dining room of this Elizabethan manor, set in the heart of beautiful Wales.

THE CASTLE VIEW, Chepstow, Gwent. Tel: (02912) 70349
This ivy-clad hotel which dates from the 17th century has a fine setting opposite the castle ruins. Original stone walls, beams and a delightful oak staircase add to the atmosphere. Bedrooms are comfortable and well equipped.

COED-Y-MWSTWR HOTEL, Coychurch, Mid-Glamorgan. Tel: (0656) 860621
This typically elegant late Victorian mansion is set in 17 acres of beautifully kept grounds which boast many delightful species of trees and shrubs. The oak panelled restaurant maintains an excellent reputation.

CWRT BLEDDYN, Llangybi, Gwent. Tel: (0633) 49521
This small country manor house has been sympathetically extended in recent years. The grounds and neighbouring villages are beautifully picturesque. Antiques combine with modern additions making for a hotel of real quality.

EGERTON GREY COUNTRY HOUSE HOTEL, Porthkerry, South Glamorgan. Tel: (0446) 711666
This nineteenth century former rectory is Egon Ronay's 'definitive country house hotel for South Wales'. The interior is furnished with antiques, open fireplaces, original Victorian baths and brass work, with rooms boasting mahogany and oak panelling.

FAIRYHILL, Reynoldston, West Glamorgan. Tel: (0792) 390139
A remote beautifully situated 18th century mansion surrounded by glorious woodland and parkland on the Gower Peninsular. 11 comfortable bedrooms, friendly service and first class meals. An ideal place for complete relaxation.

GEORGE III HOTEL, Penmaenpool, Gwynedd. Tel: (0341) 422525
The bar at this pleasant inn, situated at the head of the Mawddalh Estuary, boasts stone walls and heavy wooden tables. Slate stones, beams and attractively converted bedrooms are further attractions at this cosy hotel.

GLIFFAES COUNTRY HOUSE HOTEL, Crickhowell, Powys. Tel: (0874) 730371
Dating from 1885, this distinctive hotel is set in 29 acres of private gardens with private fishing and offering stunning views of the surrounding National Park and River Usk.

WALES

GOLDEN PHEASANT, Glyn Ceirios, Clwyd. Tel: (069172) 281

An hotel with the character of an inn which enjoys beautiful country views. The tranquillity is perhaps the major attraction but there are all manner of other touches which make for a really pleasant atmosphere in which to stay.

HAND HOTEL, Llanarmon Dyffryn Ceirios, Clwyd. Tel: (069176) 666

A pleasant situation for this 16th century inn which is beautifully maintained. It is a particularly peaceful place to stay and for those of us who wish to escape telephones and televisions this is the place to go.

HOTEL MAES-Y-NEUADD, Talsarnau, Gwynedd. Tel: (0766) 780200

Close to numerous historic castles, this tranquil fourteenth century manor house rests peacefully in 8 acres of landscaped mountainside. The architecture varies from early beams and dormers to the later elegance of Georgian full height windows.

THE LAKE COUNTRY HOUSE, Llangammarch Wells, Powys. Tel: (05912) 202

Complete with open fireplaces and antiques, this riverside hotel is set in 50 acres of beautiful lawns, woods, fascinating walks and a private lake where guests may fish for trout.

HOTEL PORTMEIRION, Portmeirion, Gwynedd. Tel: (0766) 771331

Portmeirion, thanks to Sir Clough Williams Ellis, is a delightfully presented peninsular in South Wales. The hotel is a mixture of magnificent themes and tastes and the bedrooms in the main house are exquisite.

KING'S HEAD, Monmouth, Gwent. Tel: (0600) 2177

A comfortable family-run 17th century inn which stands in the heart of historic Monmouth in Agincourt Square. An oak beamed bar, cottage style bedrooms and some excellent eating make for an ideal place to stay.

LLANGOED HALL, Llyswen, Powys. Tel: (0874) 754525

A splendid house which was the first major commission of architect Sir Clough Williams-Ellis. Sir Bernard Ashley has bestowed similar love in its restoration and the bedrooms are simply marvellous. Food is also outstanding. Extensive gardens complete a delightful picture.

THE OLD RECTORY, Llansantffraid, Clwyd. Tel: (0492) 580611

Elegant antiques, Victorian watercolours and other delights can be seen in this early Georgian hotel. The restaurant is especially appealing and the bedrooms are stylishly decorated. Good food; fine views of the Conwy estuary are further treats to behold.

LLYNDIR HALL, Rossett, Clywd. Tel: (0244) 571648

A Victorian house with real charm and welcome. Individually designed bedrooms are particularly pleasing. The whole house is homely and the restaurant boasts some really first class cuisine. A delightful place to stay when exploring North Wales.

LLYWN ONN HALL, Wrexham, Clwyd. Tel: (0978) 261225

Originally an eighteenth century manor house, the hotel is set in charming parkland with the fascinating Chirk Castle, Erddig Hall and Chester nearby.

MISKIN MANOR, Miskin, Mid-Glamorgan. Tel: (0443) 224204

Once used by the future King Edward VIII, this charming old house rests peacefully in 20 acres of beautiful parkland. The interior boasts panelled walls, ornate ceilings and open fireplaces - all complemented by rich drapery.

PALE HALL, Llandderfel, Gwynedd. Tel: (06783) 285

An imposing 19th century mansion with delightful oak panelling and galleried staircase. A bath used by none other than Queen Victoria is an unexpected and unusual treasure. There are many added extras to make a stay both luxurious and memorable.

PENALLY ABBEY, Penally, Pembrokeshire. Tel: (0834) 3033

This elegant country house rests in five acres of gardens and woodland on the edge of the Pembrokeshire National Park, overlooking Camarthen Bay and Caldey Island.

PLAS BODEGROES, Pwllheli, Gwynedd. Tel: (0758) 612363

A delightful setting for an elegant restaurant with some cosy, comfortable bedrooms. A Grade II manor house with a Georgian heritage. The cooking, which makes the most of fresh local produce, is outstanding.

PLOUGH INN, Felingwm Isaf, Dyfed. Tel: (0267) 290220

The restaurant, for which you must book, is the main attraction of this most appealing house. Elaborate dishes are worth travelling many miles for. Accommodation in a cottage across the way is a bonus.

RUTHIN CASTLE, Ruthin, Clwyd. Tel: (08242) 2664

A real find for lovers of historic houses. A medieval castle surrounded by 30 acres. Swords, crossbows, huge fireplaces add to the charm. This is a fascinating place to stay and thoroughly recommended.

ROYAL GEORGE, Tintern Abbey, Gwent. Tel: (0291) 689205

Situated in the picturesque Wye valley, overlooking the Abbey, this former inn dates back to the 17th century. The bedrooms in the main house are extremely characterful and enjoy pleasant views.

SEIONT MANOR, Llanrug, Gwynedd. Tel: (0286) 76887

An old farmhouse forms the nucleus of this delightful hotel. The bedrooms are particularly impressive and the hotel boasts some fine modern facilities which do not distract from its overall charm.

TRE-YSGAWEN HALL Llangefni, Gwynedd. Tel: (0248) 750750

A recently opened and delightfully restored late Victorian stone built mansion; four-poster beds, fine furnishings and a really sumptuous restaurant make for a tremendously relaxing hotel in which to stay and enjoy elegance and excellence.

TY MAWR, Brechfa, Dyfed. Tel: (0267) 202332

This is a delightful unspoilt hotel. Rugs cover quarry tiles, beams and stone walls add further to the atmosphere. Bedrooms are well equipped and pleasantly decorated. Pleasant gardens are further attraction.

WALES

WALNUT TREE INN, Abergavenny, Gwent. Tel: (0873) 2797
This is a first class restaurant set in an unpretentious but airy establishment. The cellar boasts more heritage than many in the world and if you are a lover of good food, then visit Llandewi Skirrid for a real treat.

WARPOOL COURT HOTEL, St Davids, Pembrokeshire. Tel: (0437) 720300
Famous for its antique armorial and pictorial file collection, the hotel lies on a remote peninsula, commanding a scene of wild beauty and offering stunning views of the Atlantic.

WEST ARMS, Llanarmon Dyffryn Leirios, Clwyd. Tel: (069176) 262
An extremely friendly characterful village inn which dates from the 16th century. Ancient flagstones and a large inglenook fireplace are two attractions. Bedrooms with more recent fittings are in total contrast but similarly appealing.

YNYSHIR HALL COUNTRY HOUSE HOTEL, Eglwysfach, Powys. Tel: (0654) 781209
Once used by Queen Victoria, this charming Georgian manor house rests in twelve acres of delightful landscaped gardens, whilst the inside is decorated with works of art, including many by the resident owner/artist.

ACCOMMODATION OF MERIT

EISTEDDFA, Criccieth, Gwynedd. Tel: (076652) 2104
Sensitively enlarged 17th century stone Welsh farmhouse now the comfortable home of Lloyd George's grandson. In the 1800s Tony Armstrong-Jones's great-grandfather lived here. This 'Resting Place' is steeped in history and perfect for touring Wales.

THE CROWN AT WHITEBROOK, Whitebrook, Gwent. Tel: (0600) 860254
Award winning cuisine is one feature of this comfortable hotel. Accommodation is also of a high standard and guests are always assured of a warm welcome. Racing and golf are among the many local attractions.

CWMIRFON LODGE, Llanwrtyd Wells, Powys. Tel: (05913) 217
Large Victorian sporting lodge, complete with two and a half miles of private fishing on the Irfon and three acres of grounds. Delightful part of Wales, great for forays into Welsh Lake District and Abergwesyn Valley.

THE DOLMELYNLLYN HALL, Ganllywd, Gwynedd. Tel: (034 140) 273
Golf, fishing and Stately Hall fans are well catered for at this elegant Country House Hotel. Of particular local note are the castles of Erddig and Powis, whilst the rivers Mawddach and Wnion are sure to keep eager anglers occupied.

DRAGON HOTEL, Montgomery, Powys. Tel: (0686) 668359
This popular hotel can provide both active and relaxing holidays to suit every taste. A wide range of facilities are available, including swimming, tennis and a well-equipped gym, whilst the surrounding countryside offers many scenic and historic attractions.

THE FOUNTAIN INN, Tintern, Gwent. Tel: (0291) 689303
The Fountain is a lovely old inn situated just off the Wye Valley in a designated Area of Outstanding Natural Beauty. Simple but comfortable accommodation is available, as well as excellent food and a fine selection of wines and beers.

GOLDEN GROVE, Llanasa, Clwyd Tel: (0745) 854452
Handsome grade 1 listed Elizabethan Manor, set in large formal gardens, overlooking the largest Welsh Bronze Age tumulus and Moel Fammau. Nearby are Chester, Vale of Clwyd, Conwy and Snowdonia and a perfect break en route to Ireland via Holyhead.

LLANWENARTH HOUSE, Govilon, Gwent. Tel: (0873) 830289
Nestled in the Brecon Beacons National Park, this beautiful 16th century manor stands in its own pretty grounds. Cordon Bleu food and relaxing atmosphere make this a great place from which to tour Wales and its heritage.

The Old Rectory

WALES

THE OLD RECTORY, Llansanffraid, Gwynedd.
Tel: (0492) 580611
Dramatic vistas of Snowdonia, Conwy Castle and Estuary are enjoyed from this elegant Georgian house set in two and a half acres of gardens. Close to Bodnant Gardens and World Heritage historic Conwy, gourmet food (Egon Ronay). Antiques, paintings abound. Luxury draped bedrooms. (see photograph).

RHAGATT HALL, Corwen, Clwyd. Tel: (0490) 2308
Georgian mansion with grounds that roll down to the River Dee, through beautiful woodland. The rear of this stunning house was built as far back as the 1300's and it all provides an excellent base for Welsh Heritage tours.

SANT-Y-NYLL HOUSE, St Brides-Super-Ely, Glamorgan.
Tel: (0446) 760209
One of the attractive features of this Georgian house is the spectacular view over the Vale of Glamorgan. Set amidst extensive grounds it is an ideal base for touring South Wales, and St Fagan's Welsh Folk Museum.

ST TUDNO HOTEL, Llandudno, Gwynedd.
Tel: (0492) 874411
This award-winning hotel provides accommodation of the very highest calibre and is equally renowned for it's fine cuisine. Golf, fishing and various castles and homes are all within easy travelling distance.

TREGYNON COUNTRY FARM, Pontfaen, Dyfed.
Tel: (0239) 820531
Standing in extensive grounds, with oak woodlands, overlooking the Gwaun Valley in Pembrokeshire National Park. This 16th Century beamed farmhouse provides delightful accommodation. Breathtaking 200 foot waterfall and Iron Age Fort are also within the farm's estate.

UNIVERSITY COLLEGE OF NORTH WALES, Bangor, Gwynedd. Tel: (0248) 351151, Ex 2561
Clean and comfortable accommodation is available from July to September in these Halls of residence. Each residence has a dining room and a multitude of university facilities are at the disposal of guests.

INNS OF CHARACTER

ABBEY HOTEL, Llanthony, Gwent.
This pub's setting is one of the most beautiful of any in Britain. Part of the graceful ruins of Norman Priory founded in 1108, its lawns stretch among the lofty crumbling arches.

BLUE ANCHOR, East Aberthaw, South Glamorgan.
This creeper-covered pub dates back to 1380 and has been lovingly preserved, even the thatched roof. Low beamed alcoves and coal fires make it particulary cosy.

BOAT, Erbistock, Clwyd.
Sharing a peaceful spot on a bend of the river Dee with a church, this 14th century pub boasts a charming garden where guests may sit surrounded by flowers, weeping ash and clear birdsong.

DINORBEN ARMS, Bodfari, Clwyd.
Contains an ancient well complete with a spell cast over it 1300 years ago. Children ducked in it should never cry again. The garden has tastefully arranged furniture and beautiful views.

DRUIDSTONE, Broad Haven, Dyfed. Tel: (043 783) 221
A family-run hotel in an enviable position alone above the sea, with a steep path down to a long and virtually private beach, where the inn runs its own land yachts.

DYFFRYN ARMS, Cwm Gwaun, Dyfed.
So old-fashioned it still celebrates New Year on January 13th, a custom generally abandoned back in 1752! The popular pastime here is draughts, so much so, the tables are inlaid with marquetry draughtboards.

HAND, Chirk, Clwyd.
Victorian New Testament parable tiles hang over one fireplace and horse brasses decorate dark beams in this old three-storey coaching inn with a stately Georgian facade.

MAENAN ABBEY HOTEL, Llanrwst, Gwynedd.
Built in 1850 as a medieval style country house, this attractive steep-gabled building with battlemented tower is set in grounds of conifers and beech, with picnic space available.

MERMAID, Mumbles, Swansea.
A picturesque little pub in the fascinating sea-side town of Mumbles. The renowned Welsh poet and drinker, Dylan Thomas, would apparently practise both arts here, and the memorabilia on the walls celebrates the fact. By a curious co-incidence the present manager's name is also Dylan Thomas.

OLDE BULL'S HEAD, Beaumaris, Anglesey.
Parts of this friendly inn date back 500 years and its courtyard is closed by the biggest single hinged door in Britain. The oak-beamed lounge has an impressive display of cutlasses on one wall and a preserved ducking stool.

PEN-Y-GWRYD, Nr Llanberis, Gwynedd.
Isolated among high peaks, this pub was used as a training base by the 1953 Everest team who scrawled their signatures across one ceiling. The climber's bar doubles as a mountain-rescue post.

PRINCE OF WALES, Kenfig, Mid-Glamorgan.
Reputedly haunted and electronically 'proved' in 1982, this pub became the Guildhall when the town was swamped by sand-storms in 1607. The badge of office, the alderman's mace, is still kept.

SALUSBURY ARMS, Tremeirchion, Clwyd.
The oak-beamed lounge bar of this charming little shuttered cottage was originally the stable area of a building dating back to 1350 and includes timbers removed from St Asaph Cathedral.

SERJEANTS, Eglwyswrw, Dyfed.
This is one of the few British inns to still have Petty Court sessions on its premises. The ancient building has heavy black beams set into the dark smoke-stained ceiling.

SKIRRID, Llanfihangel Crucorney, Gwent.
Dating back to 1110 and possible the oldest in Wales, this pub once doubled as the area's courthouse. Between then and the 17th century over 200 people were hanged here.

WELSH RAREBITS

Wales is a distinctive country. And Welsh Rarebits is a unique collection of distinctive hotels. Welsh Rarebits has established a worldwide reputation for welcome, service, standards and value for money.

Like all the best hotel listings, Welsh Rarebits is largely - and unashamedly - a subjective one. These hand-picked hotels offer personal service, imaginative and tasteful decor, attention to detail, that indefinable sense of atmosphere and character, and those important little touches that separate the best from the rest.

There's no likelihood that you will confuse one Welsh Rarebits hotel with another - we are the complete opposite of the standardised, homogenised, interchangeable international hotel chain. Welsh Rarebits encompasses everything from old coaching inns to some of Britain's most luxurious country house hotels.

The only common features you will find amongst Welsh Rarebits members are desirable ones. All are small and privately owned, which helps explain their genuine hospitality, warm welcome and high standards. Comfortable - and, in some cases, superluxurious - accommodation is also a shared characteristic, together with quality cuisine. Most Welsh Rarebits hotels are already acknowledged for the excellence of their cooking. Wales' top chefs work at some of the hotels; many establishments appear in the 'good food' guides.

The variety of places to stay is enormous - you're bound to find something that's just right for you. Each hotel has its own personality and its own strengths. There's also a great variety of prices. But whatever the rate, you'll find that every hotel offers exceptional value for money.

Welsh Rarebits
Pentre Bach
Montgomery
Powys SY15 6HR
Tel: (0686) 668030
Fax: (0686) 668029

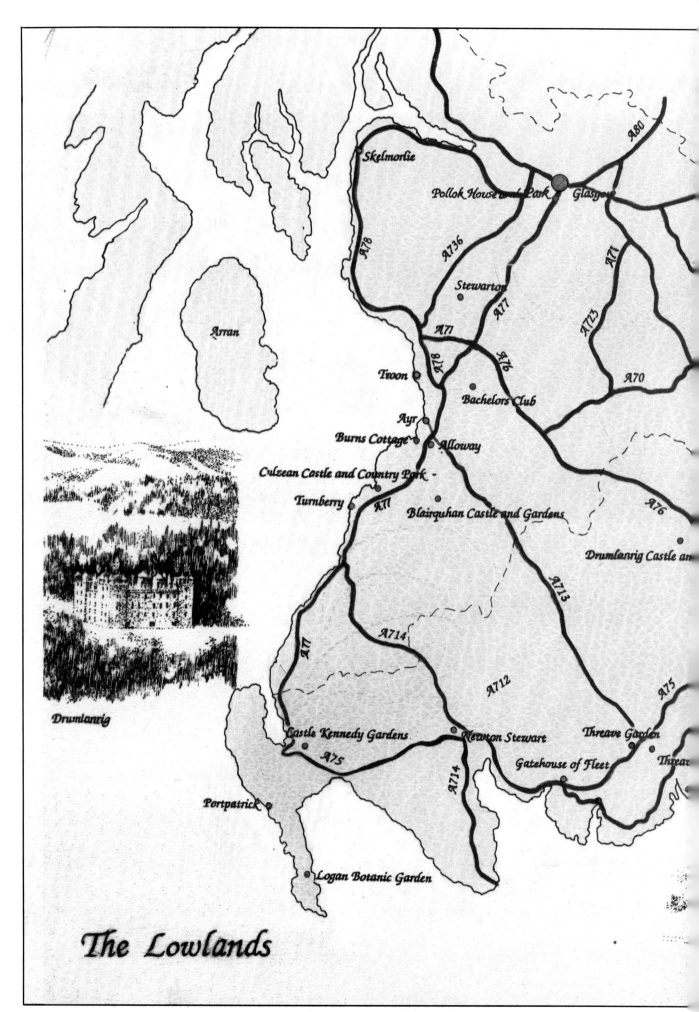

Skelmorlie

Pollok House and Park • Glasgow

A80

A78

A736

Stewarton

A77

A71

A723

A71

A70

Troon

A78

A76

Bachelors Club

Ayr

Burns Cottage • Alloway

Culzean Castle and Country Park

Turnberry

A77

Blairquhan Castle and Gardens

Drumlanrig Castle an

A76

A713

Arran

A77

A714

A712

A75

Drumlanrig

Castle Kennedy Gardens • Newton Stewart

Threave Garden

A75

Gatehouse of Fleet • Threav

Portpatrick

A714

Logan Botanic Garden

The Lowlands

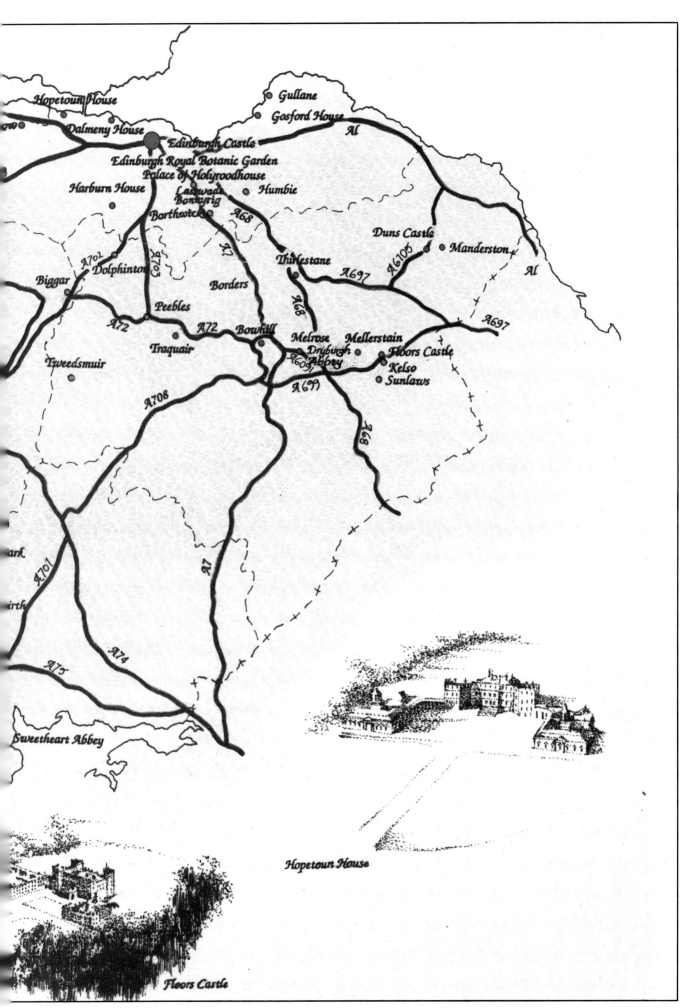

Hopetoun House

Floors Castle

THE LOWLANDS

The Lowlands are generally accepted as being that part of Scotland to the South of the Highland Boundary Fault, which runs diagonally across the country from the Firth of Clyde to Stonehaven on the east coast.

The dramatic rolling border hills, moorlands and forests of the Scottish Borders and Dumfries and Galloway are for many visitors, arriving from the south by road, their first and last sight of Scotland. Further north the Lowland corridor runs between the Firth of Clyde and the Firth of Forth and includes Scotland's capital, Edinburgh, and its largest city, Glasgow. This is the industrial heartland of the country and although much of the traditional industries such as shipbuilding, steel making and car manufacturing are in decline, they are being replaced by a new and cleaner working environment. North of the Forth, is the Kingdom of Fife and Angus, where the picturesque fishing villages and towns with their working harbours are dotted along this windy but sunny east coast. 'Historic Scotland' maintain many properties throughout the Lowlands where visitors are made most welcome (featured later).

THE BORDERS

The Scottish Borders lie to the south east of Scotland, where the rolling hills of Lammermuir, Moorfoot and Pentland look out north towards the Forth Valley and the forests and woodlands of Ettrick, Eskdalemuir and Craik offer splendid walks. Testament to the area's bloody past are the sites of various battles with both the invading English and inter-family feuds; the now peaceful and impressive ruined **Abbeys of Dryburgh**, **Jedburgh**, **Kelso** and **Melrose** (where the heart of Robert the Bruce was buried) were looted and plundered by the English; and the hilltop pele towers and rugged castles. Throughout the Borders there are examples of stately homes and castles designed by some of the best known architects of the time.

THE VALLEY OF THE TWEED

The River Tweed enters the North Sea at Berwick-upon-Tweed in England but for much of its length to a point west of Coldstream forms the natural border between Scotland and England. It is said that armies crossed the Tweed at **Coldstream**, which gave its name to the famous Guards, founded in 1659 where the local museum preserves the regiment's treasures from various campaigns. Close by Coldstream is the Hirsel, the home of the Douglas-Homes; the Homestead Museum is housed in old farm buildings and the splendid rhododendron display should not be missed. This valley offers a wonderful array of churches, abbeys and chapels, castles and houses, towers, monuments and obelisks with spectacular views to the countryside beyond. The **Union Suspension Bridge**, the first of its type in Britain, built in 1820 by Samuel Brown, links Scotland with England two miles south of Paxton.

The fine Edwardian Country House of **Manderston** is set in formal and woodland gardens. It was designed by John Kinross at the turn of the century for Sir James Miller, the wealthy racehorse owner, whose horses won the Derby and lived a pampered life in the luxurious stables. An enormous amount of money was spent on the construction of this Georgian style mansion and much of the lavish interiors are modelled on Lady Miller's family home in Derbyshire, Kedleston Hall by Robert Adam. The grand ballroom ceiling is decorated in Sir James' racing colours of primrose and white.

Duns Castle is the private family home of Alexander Hay and is not open to the public except by special arrangement. The castle was built in 1696 by the Earl of Tweedale for his son William Hay and the Hays have lived here ever since. Built in 1320 a Pele Tower given by Robert the Bruce to the Earl of Moray, the castle has been remodelled over the years but still retains detailed panelling, plasterwork and fireplaces.

The trophies of the world champion racing car driver Jim Clark, who was killed in 1968 and buried nearby at Chirnside, can be seen in the market town of Duns.

Thirlestane Castle near Lauder, is one of Scotland's oldest and finest castles built originally in the 13th century as a fort, it was rebuilt in the 16th century to defend the main approaches to Edinburgh from the south. The seat of the Earls and Dukes of Lauderdale it remains the home of the Maitland family to this day. The richly decorated rooms contain many treasures including some superb plaster ceilings which were added to the State Rooms in the 17th century. Children are able to entertain themselves browsing through the enormous toy collection now housed in the old nurseries. Close by is the **Border Country Life Museum** which is well worth a visit to explore the history of the area.

Mellerstain House, home of the Earl of Haddington, is set in magnificent grounds and is a fine example of Adam family architecture, as both father and son were involved. The beautiful decoration and plasterwork together with the unique collections of 18th century furniture and Old Masters make it perhaps one of the best Georgian houses in Scotland. The splendid library is possibly Robert Adam's masterpiece of interior design.

Close by, off the B6404, is the isolated **Smailholm Tower** with spectacular views to a loch below and countryside beyond. The tower now exhibits the costumes and tapestries of the characters in Scott's 'Minstrelsy of the Scottish Border'.

Standing on John Rennie's bridge (built in 1803) over the Tweed at Kelso affords a magnificent view of **Floors Castle**. Built in the early 18th century Floors Castle, the family seat of the Dukes of Roxburgh, commands spectacular views over the castle ruins of old Roxburgh to Kelso, the River Tweed and the Cheviot Hills beyond.

Originally designed by William Adam, (father of Robert Adam) but extensively remodelled by William Playfair on the instructions of the 6th Duke in 1838, the Castle houses a magnificent collection of French 18th century furniture, carpets and tapestries from France and Belgium (featured later).

There are fine Georgian buildings in Kelso, in addition to the ruined Abbey ravaged in 1545 by the English.

THE CHEVIOT FOOTHILLS

Jedburgh Abbey, by Jed Water, also plundered by the English in the 1540s, stands complete, except for its roof. The imposing red sandstone abbey with its Norman Tower houses a museum containing medieval treasures and a history of the Augustinian Canons from France who founded the monastery in the 12th century. In the town a Museum of Methods of 19th Century Imprisonments is housed in what was the county

THE LOWLANDS

prison. This Georgian building built in 1823 stands on the site of the old Jedburgh Castle, built in the 12th century as a home for Scotland's kings, but later demolished by the Scottish parliament as it was too difficult to defend from attack by the English. Visit the tragic Mary, Queen of Scot's House which stands in gardens and contains mementoes from the Queens's life.

Travel north to Dryburgh on the A68, a scenic tourist route from the south past the Waterloo Monument and site of Anerum Moor battlefield, to visit **Dryburgh Abbey**. Once a holy place for Druids, large parts of the Abbey still stand including the 13th century portal and cloister buildings. Sir Walter Scott is buried in the abbey grounds.

Melrose sits between the main A7 and A68 trunk roads and this prime location has lead to much bloodshed over the years, especially during the Wars of Scottish Independence. The ruins of the famous **Melrose Abbey** suggest a fine 15th century building with detailed stonework and features, which was the inspiration to many of Sir Walter Scott's romantic works.

Bowhill, the Borders home of the Duke of Buccleuch and Queensberry, K.T., dates from the early part of the 19th century and is set in extensive grounds with lochs, rivers and woodlands and a wonderful adventure playground. In the fine rooms, world famous collections of furniture, porcelain and paintings, including works by Canaletto, Claude, Gainsborough and Holbein can be found. An interesting feature is the portraits and manuscripts of Sir Walter Scott, who lived nearby on a farm on the bank of the Tweed in the early part of the 19th century. Scott created the romantic image of Scotland and had **Abbotsford House** built at this place, west of Melrose which

now houses many personal mementoes and treasures. Beyond Selkirk stands his statue in the market place.

Over one thousand years old **Traquair House** on the bank of the Tweed is said to be the oldest, continuously inhabited, family home in Scotland. It has been visited by twenty seven monarchs of Scotland and England and has associations with Mary, Queen of Scots and the Jacobites. Traquair's mysterious past is evident in the secret rooms and passageways. The Bear Gates have been closed since 1745 when Bonnie Prince Charlie passed through - not to be reopened until a Stuart returns to the Throne (featured later). Close by is Innerleithen, which became a wealthy spa town in the last century (the Well on the hillside above the town can be visited and the health giving waters can still be taken) and is remembered in Sir Walter Scott's novel 'St Ronan's Well'. This is Sir Walter Scott's country for all visitors to enjoy.

DUMFRIES AND GALLOWAY

Mostly to the west of the busy A74, in the south west of the country, the peaceful Dumfries and Galloway has dramatic south facing coastline overlooking the Solway Firth. From **Gretna Green**, where eloping couples from England were married by local blacksmiths until 1940, to the birthplace of Scottish Christianity at Whithorn, at present an archaelogical dig, there is much to see and do. Inland, visit the **Scottish Leadmining Museum** at Wanlockhead, Scotland's highest village, where in nearby Leadhills the source of the River Clyde exists, before descending on the A76 past **Drumlanrig Castle** to Dumfries.

Edinburgh Castle

THE LOWLANDS

Drumlanrig Castle built in the late 17th century is the Dumfriesshire home of the Duke of Buccleuch and Queensberry, K.T., set in fine grounds on the site of a medieval Douglas fortress (featured later).

Dumfries 'the Queen of the South' sits on the River Nith, and was home to Robert Burns for the last 5 years of his life - both he and his wife are buried in a Mausoleum behind St Michael's Church. Eight miles south of Dumfries is **Caerlaverock Castle** which, with its moat, turrets and towers, is probably what is expected of a medieval fortress. The marshland and mudflats of the National Nature Reserve is home to breeding toads and flocks of geese and wildfowl. Close by is the delightful New Abbey Corn Mill and the ancient Sweetheart Abbey.

THE GARDEN OF SCOTLAND

The mild south westerly winds allow exotic plants and wildlife to grow and inhabit interesting gardens and nature reserves throughout the region.

The daunting **Threave Castle** ruins, set on an island in the River Dee (ring a bell and the keeper will row you across!), give some indication of the development of Scottish secular architecture in the later medieval and early modern period. 'The Tall Forbidding Tower House' was built in the latter part of the 14th century for Archibald The Grim, for the 'Black Douglases', one of Scotland's most powerful families.

Over the last twenty years the National Trust for Scotland has developed the 60 acre **Threave Gardens**, one mile away. Renowned for its plant location and interesting layout, it has, in addition to the traditional walled garden, greenhouses and vegetable collection, magnificent seasonal displays of daffodils - some 200 varieties in a spectacular springtime display - roses, heathers and conifers. Nearby on the Dee, ducks and geese flock to the **Threave Wildfowl Refuge** in the winter months (open November/March).

The home of the present Earl and Countess of Stair is Lochinch Castle built in 1867 to replace **Castle Kennedy** which was razed to the ground in 1716, although it had been in existence since before 1482. The internationally famous gardens around

Dalmeny House

THE LOWLANDS

the ruins are set between two lochs in 35 hectares featuring beautiful rhododendrons, azaleas, magnolias and monkey puzzle trees.

Almost surrounded by the sea and benefiting from the warm breezes of the Gulf Stream **Logan Botanic Garden** capitalises on its unique location by nurturing the growth of plants not normally associated with this part of the world. Originating from the turn of the century, it is now owned by the Royal Botanic Garden in Edinburgh. Further south at Logan Bay, a tidal fish pool 10 metres deep was constructed in 1788 to supply the Lairds of Logan with cod; the fish can be fed by hand today.

Back inland, north of Moffat, near the Borders is the National Trust owned Grey Mare's Tail Waterfalls. The spectacular waterfalls are set in over 2000 acres in which herds of wild goats roam amongst interesting wild flowers.

The coastline, inland walks and pleasant climate make Dumfries and Galloway a varied and interesting place to visit.

LOTHIAN

Lothian is made up of the Forth Valley with its impressive bridges across the Forth, the birthplace of Mary, Queen of Scots at the **Linlithgow Palace** and canals, mines and railways from the industrial past; West and Mid Lothian bounded to the south by the Border hills; east Lothian with its sandy beaches and unspoilt coastline; and Edinburgh.

Gosford House on the A198 near Aberlady, stands in a spectacular seaside location overlooking the Firth of Forth with views to both the Forth Rail and Road Bridges and Edinburgh Castle. Frances Charteris, who was to become the 7th Earl of Wemyss bought the House in 1781 in order to play golf on the sandy shores nearby and avoid travelling to his then home at Annsfield near Haddington. However he never moved into this new house and during the 18th century much improvement and alteration was to take place.

The Classical house, designed by Robert Adam, was greatly altered and his grandson demolished both wings whilst adding to the 'old house' adjacent to the Adam stables.

Haddington was the birth place of the founder of the Presbyterian Church, John Knox, who spent much of his life in Europe, before returning to Edinburgh to establish the new Protestant religion with the blessing of the Scottish parliament.

EDINBURGH - THE ROYAL MILE

The architectural quality of the elegant Georgian New Town with its wide streets, Crescents and Circuses, contrasts with the Old Town crammed around the Royal Mile and together with the historical monuments and statues gave rise to Edinburgh's nickname 'the Athens of the North'. Probably Scotland's best known landmark, **Edinburgh Castle** stands on what was an extinct volcano and the fortress provides a spectacular setting for the annual military tattoo, part of the annual festival of arts (featured later). From the castle the Royal Mile leads to the **Palace of Holyroodhouse** and the **Abbey Ruins**, founded by King David I in 1128. One hundred and eleven portraits of

Carnegie Birthplace Museum

THE LOWLANDS

Scottish Kings hang in the splendid picture gallery in the Palace of Holyroodhouse, built for Charles II in 1671, which is still used by members of the Royal Family today. Mary, Queen of Scots lived here for six years during her reign and witnessed the murder of her secretary David Rizzio, by her over protective husband.

Along **the Royal Mile**, where some of the buildings were built before the 1700s, the visitor can find St Giles Cathedral dating from the 14th century; Lady Stairs House containing original works by Robert Burns, Sir Walter Scott and Robert Louis Stevenson, possibly the oldest house in Edinburgh, built in 1490 where the reformer John Knox lived in the 16th century; the 'noisy' Museum of Childhood; and The Canongate Tollbooth which now houses the Dunbar collection of Highland dress and tartans.

James Playfairs' mid 19th century building in Princes Gardens houses **The National Gallery of Scotland** with its fine collection of paintings, including distinguished works by Scottish artists. Close by, the enormous **Scott Monument**, built in 1840 has a statue of Sir Walter Scott below its arches. **Princes Street** opposite is the only 'one sided' shopping street in the country.

To the north is the **Royal Botanic Gardens** famed for its rhododendron collection. **The National Gallery of Modern Art**, with its works by Henry Moore and Barbara Hepworth, is housed in Inverleigh House set in the Garden and surrounded by the spectacular landscaping and Heath, Peat Woodland and Rock Gardens.

At Edinburgh University, Arthur Conan Doyle studied medicine in the 1880s before becoming a novelist and Alexander Graham Bell, who later invented the telephone in America, studied sciences.

The Drum is Edinburgh's largest private house with over 60 rooms and has been the home of the More Nisbetts for over 130 years. Set in 500 acres of wooded parkland but only 20 minutes from Princes Street, the main house was built by William Adam in 1715, and adjoins an earlier 15th century keep where the family now live. The splendid Entrance Hall has the only known example of William Adam's plastering and this splendour is maintained in the plasterwork in the State Apartments. The 400 year old avenues of cedars point north, south, east and west - the summer solstice sets down the north avenue and is directly in line with the Dining Room. The 18th century garden has been recreated by the More Nisbetts with splendid walks through azaleas and rhododendrons. There is a troop of polo ponies, Highland cows, Charolais cattle and ponies for disabled riders.

THE FORTH VALLEY

To the east of the Forth Bridges stands the present **Dalmeny House,** built in 1815 by William Wilkins - alternative proposals by Robert Adam and others are on display in the House - it is Scotland's first Tudor Gothic Revival house and the Primrose family, the Earls of Roseberry, have lived here for over 300 years. Inside the house the Rothschild Collection was brought from Mentmore in Buckinghamshire, the home of the present Earl's grandmother and includes magnificent French 18th century furniture, tapestries and other works of art. The contents of the Napoleon Room, collected by the 5th Earl, includes period furniture used by him at the height of his glory and the basics he used when exiled to St Helena - the Duke of Wellington's campaign chair adds a touch of irony to the situation. Scottish portraits, 17th century furniture, 18th century portraits by Reynolds, Gainsborough, Raeburn and Lawrence and racing objects from the Mentmore stud, which produced seven Derby winners, make up the Roseberry collection.

Outside, the landscaped garden and shoreline walk offer fantastic views across the mud flats and sandy beaches, where many varieties of sea birds can be seen, to the Forth Road and Rail Bridges beyond. On an island in the Firth of Forth opposite Aberdour stands Incholm Abbey.

Hopetoun House is Scotland's greatest Adam mansion, standing on the shores of the Forth, to the west of the Forth Bridges. originally designed by Sir William Bruce (architect of Holyrood Palace) for the 1st Earl of Hopetoun, it was enlarged some 20 years later in 1721 by William Adam, whose sons John, Robert and James completed the interior after their father's death in 1748. Although the family no longer own the house (it is a charitable trust for the benefit of the public) the Marquess of Linlithgow has a home in part of the house. Of particular interest are the red and yellow furnished drawing rooms, the original furniture, tapestries and paintings including works by Rubens, Van Dyke, Titian and Canaletto, and ceramics dating from the mid 18th century. There is a superb nature trail through part of the 100 acre woodlands, where fallow and red deer roam and St Kilda sheep (with 4 horns) can be seen (featured later).

Linlithgow Palace is best known as the birth place of Mary Queen of Scots, born on the 8th of December 1542. The magnificent ruins of the Palace stand proudly by the shore of the Loch and replaced an older Castle razed to the ground in 1424. The splendid quadrangle with its finely detailed 16th century ornamental fountain is a beautiful setting for the late 15th century Great Hall and Chapel.

Harburn House is a splendid Georgian house built in 1807 after the original mansion was blown up by Oliver Cromwell, with only the stables from the old house remaining and in use today. The estate extends to some 3000 acres of woodland and farmland. The house is hidden away in parkland with views over lakes to the Pentland hills beyond. This country residence offers total seclusion for private use for business entertaining, yet is only a few minutes from the M8 motorway and easy access to both Edinburgh and Glasgow. Visitors to the Lothians should try to visit Edinburgh during 'The Festival' to enhance an already enthralling experience into Scotland's past.

FIFE

Scotland's ancient Capital **Dunfermline** is situated just to the north of the Forth Road Bridge. Here in the town centre is the **Andrew Carnegie Birthplace Museum** which comprises the original weaver's cottage and the adjacent memorial hall which gives an impression of Carnegie's early life and his later achievements. It is said that in his lifetime and indeed since his death he and his trusts have donated hundreds of millions of pounds to deserving causes throughout the world.

For golf fanatics and even those who do not play this 'religion', the clubhouse on the **Old Course, St Andrews**, is one

THE LOWLANDS

of the most famous sights in the world. Whilst an exact date for the birth of golf still causes a certain amount of controversy, golf was played here in the 15th century. In 1754 the Society of St Andrew's Golfers was founded by 22 'diehards' and in 1834 King William 1V allowed the society to become **the Royal and Ancient Golf Club**, now the game's governing body. A walk along 'The Scores' overlooking the seafront takes the visitor to St Andrews Castle, built in 1200 to repel raiders and home of the Bishop of St Andrew's. The unpleasant 24 feet deep bottle dungeon and secret passage are well worth a visit. Once an important religious town, the Cathedral built in 1160 and consecrated in 1318, welcomed medieval pilgrims to pray at the 31 altars and shrine of St Andrew in the sanctuary. Close by are the ruins of the 12th century Church of St Rule, who brought St Andrew's relics to this place and there is a spectacular view from the church tower (108 feet high) which takes in the town and the harbour to the east. The Scottish flag ('satire') comes from the cross of St Andrew, the patron saint of Scotland and dates from around the 13th century.

St Andrew's is Scotland's oldest university founded in the 15th century and still an important seat of learning today, whose students can be seen attending church each Sunday in traditional red robes. In the 16th century John Napier, the mathematician who devised logarithms and the earliest calculator of ivory pieces, was a student here.

The National Trust for Scotland now administers on behalf of Her Royal Highness Queen Elizabeth II the **Royal Palace of Falkland**, the country residence of the Stuart kings and queens where wild boar and deer were hunted. The original castle and palace dates from the 12th century but the present palace was built between 1501 and 1541 by James IV and James V who was responsible for decorating the south and east ranges in the Renaissance style with medallions of figures from classical mythology. 19th century restoration work to these ranges by the Marquess of Bute and more recent work by the Trust has allowed visitors to view the Chapel Royal, Library, Keeper's Apartments and the King's Bedchamber. The oldest Real

Culzean Castle

THE LOWLANDS

(or Royal) Tennis Court in Britain, still playable to this day, built in 1539 is situated in the splendid gardens. The picturesque 17th to 19th century town of Falkland, with its cobbled streets, was Scotland's first conservation area in 1970.

THE WEST OF SCOTLAND

The West of Scotland comprises the southern part of the vast Strathclyde Region, the western part of the Lowland corridor and Glasgow.

Glasgow has come a long way since its 6th century beginnings by the missionary St Mungo, whose small timber church stood on the site of what is now the 12th century **Cathedral** in St Mungo's memory. Close by the Cathedral, is the Necropolis with its fascinating array of statues, temples and monuments to the dead, where the important Victorian fathers of the city are buried. From this humble beginning much hard work has resulted in the successful Garden Festival in recent years and in 1990 the city was the 'European City of Culture'. The University was founded in 1451, the second oldest in Scotland, by Bishop William Turnbull and relocated from the High Street to Kelvingrove Park in 1870 to Victorian Gothic buildings designed by Sir Gilbert Scott. Nearby is the **Glasgow Art Gallery and Museum** with its superb collection of Old Masters and Modern Art including works by Rembrandt, Rubens, Van Gogh, Cezanne and Dali. **The Hunterian Museum** has an important coin collection, geological and archaeological finds, together with treasures bought back from the South Sea Islands by Captain Cook and a model of a James Watt engine. At Kelvin Hill a fascinating collection of tramcars and other modes of transport is on display at the **Museum of Transport**. In the 17th century the Merchants of Glasgow were responsible for much of the new building of hospitals and public buildings. In the early part of the 19th century the architect David Hamilton designed various buildings including Hutcheson's Hospital in 1802 and part of Royal Exchange Square, including Stirling's Library in 1829. Alexander 'Greek' Thompson was the architect responsible for several churches; the Caledonian Road Church, built in 1857, and St Vincent Street Church built 2 years later, are both fine examples of the Grecian style. The School of Art, the Willow Tea Rooms in Sauchiehall Street and Hill House at Helensburgh were by the Scottish art nouveau architect and interior designer Charles Rennie MacIntosh, who is perhaps best remembered for his high backed chairs. **The Burrell Collection** is housed in a purpose built gallery in Pollok Country Park. Sir William Burrell, who died in 1958, collected magnificent 19th century French pictures, medieval art, Chinese ceramics, tapestries and stained glass, jades and bronze from his travels around the world.

Pollok House Mansion was built by William Adam in 1752, set in superb grounds overlooking the River White Cart. It houses the Stirling Maxwell Collection of Spanish and other European paintings, together with wonderful displays of furniture and decorative arts (featured later).

The Clyde Valley to the south east of Glasgow is steeped in history with a major Roman base near Crawford, where today their early work on the land allows soft fruit and tomatoes to be grown. William Wallace's statue at Lanark marks the spot where his men gathered before going into battle and close by is New Lanark, an important industrial archaeological site, founded by Robert Owen to give his cotton mill workers homes,

a school, canteen and shops.

The David Livingstone Centre in Blantyre gives an insight into the missionary's work in Africa, where he died, whilst searching for the source of the Nile.

BURNS COUNTRY

Burns Country is centred around the county town of Ayr where the Bard Rabbie Burns was born on the 25th January 1759 in the nearby town of Alloway. To Scots all over the world his birthday is celebrated annually on 'Burns Night' with the traditional supper of tatties, neeps and haggis washed down with whisky, and reminiscing and recollecting the words of many of his 350 or so poems and songs. **Burns Cottage** was built by the poet's father in 1757 and is now open to visitors who come from all over the world to see the relics of his life. **The Burns Museum** is adjacent to the cottage and contains original manuscripts and books and close by is the **Burns Monument**, erected in 1820, where sculptures of characters from his poems stand in the grounds. The original **Tam o'Shanter Inn** in Ayr now houses a Burns Museum and is the starting point for the annual Tam's ride as depicted in the poem of the same name. His First Edition of poems was published chiefly in the Scottish dialect and made Burns instantly famous. 'Auld Lang Syne', 'Tam O'Shanter' and 'My Love's Like a Red Red Rose' are perhaps the best known of his works. The village of Darbotton became Burns' home for his late teens and early twenties after his father moved to the farm of Lochlea. With friends he founded a debating club in 1780, **the Bachelor's Club**, now owned by the NTS and joined the Freemasons in 1781. At Leglen Wood it is said that his hero William Wallace, a Scottish nationalist and patriot, took refuge in the 13th century. Burns visited this area often and wrote a poem whose opening line is 'Scots wha hae wi Wallace bled',which is now a kind of rallying call to Scots.

Travel south from Ayr on the A77 to Maybole then take the B7023/B741 to **Blairquhan Castle**, built in 1820. The 3rd Baronet, Sir David Hunter Blair, commissioned William Burn to carry out the work to replace an earlier castle built in the 14th century. The Hunter Blairs still live here today, the building remains largely unaltered and many of the original fittings and fabrics are still in use. John Tweedie designed the gardens to the compliment the 3rd Baronet's beautiful landscaped grounds, which has a fine collection of mature trees. It is believed that the 4th Baronet planted a spectacular Sequoia Gigantea in 1860, from seeds brought on the SS 'Great Britain' from America. The visitor may be interested in Tweedie's Regency greenhouse, where it is possible to light fires in the specially designed chimneys to protect the fruit trees in cold weather.

The gardens and grounds of **Culzean Castle** are off the A719 overlooking the Firth of Clyde (featured later).

Close by at Turnberry, Prestwick and Troon there are some of the world famous golf courses where many Open Championships have been played.

The Lowlands covers a large part of the country where the vast majority of Scots live and offers the visitor varied excursions to enjoy fine country houses and parks, magnificent castles, superb gardens and the opportunity to enjoy some of the best golf and sailing in the world.

FLOORS CASTLE

Overlooking the Tweed, one of Scotland's finest salmon rivers, Floors Castle occupies an outstandingly beautiful setting. Reputed to be the largest inhabited house in Scotland, it is home to the Duke of Roxburghe and his family.

When it was built for the 1st Duke in 1721 to a design by William Adam it bore little resemblance to the grand castle seen today. Adam's design was for a plain Georgian house. The 6th Duke called upon William Playfair to enlarge and embellish the castle in 1841 and he let his imagination and his talent run riot. The results are dramatic with two vast embracing wings and an exotic roofscape of pepper pot spires and domes.

There have been no external alterations since the 6th Duke's time of any note. Internally the story is quite different as many of the rooms were completely tranformed by the 8th Duke's American wife. The castle contains an outstanding collection of tapestries and French 17th and 18th century furniture, much of which were brought to Floors by the 8th Duchess.

She created the Drawing Room in Louis XV style to accommodate the magnificent set of late 17th Century Brussels tapestries brought from her family's Long Island mansion. The Louis XV gilt suite of eight chairs is covered in Beauvais tapestry.

The Needle Room, said to be a copy of a room at Versailles, was decorated by Duchess May in the style Louis XVI and the French furniture includes several important pieces of this period. The walls are hung with the Duchess' collection of modern post-impressionist paintings including works by Henri Matisse, Pierre Bonnard, Odilon Redon, Augustus John and Sir Matthew Smith.

The Ballroom, one of Playfair's additions, was also modified by Duchess May for more of her wonderful tapestries, in this case a set of 17th Century Gobelins. Besides fine paintings and an impressive collection of English, French and Italian furniture this room contains a spectacular collection of Chinese porcelain.

The gardens at Floors are informal with extensive herbaceous borders and rose beds. For many years the castle has been famous for the quality of its carnations; several new varieties have been propagated here.

Floors Castle provides an unrivalled location for corporate entertaining, offering exclusive style, service and privacy in elegant surroundings.

TRAQUAIR HOUSE

Almost a thousand years old, Traquair is the oldest inhabited house in Scotland. The River Tweed, famous for its salmon fishing, runs at the back of the house, and the wooded hills of the Border landscape provide the perfect peaceful setting for this romantic house. Traquair was originally used as a hunting lodge for Scottish monarchs who took part in their favourite pastimes of hunting, hawking and fishing. Then the forests abounded in game, small and large.

In 1478 the Earl of Buchan, an uncle of the King, bought the house for the paltry sum of £3.15s and in 1491 he bestowed it to his son, James Stuart, who became the first Laird of Traquair. James had plans for extending his house, but before this could be done he fell alongside his King, James IV, at Flodden Field in 1513. During the 16th century, Traquair began a gradual process of transformation under successive generations to the stately mansion seen today, practically untouched since the end of the 17th century.

Traquair became one of the great bastions of the Catholic faith, and at the top of the house in a room commanding a view of the approaches Mass was celebrated in secret. The concealed staircase at the back of a cupboard, connecting with one from the Museum Room was constructed at this time as Traquair became a refuge for Catholic Priests in times of terror. The Stuarts of Traquair suffered for their religion and their Jacobite sympathies without counting the cost. Imprisoned, fined and isolated for their beliefs, Traquair became the Jacobite centre of the South.

When the 5th Earl of Traquair bade farewell to this guest, Prince Chalres Edward Stuart, on his long march south to claim the throne, the famous Bear Gates were closed behind him. The Earl promised that the gates would not be reopened until a Stuart King was returned to the throne. The gates have remained shut ever since.

Besides the fine furniture and paintings, the house contains collections of manuscripts, books, letters, silver and needle-work. A particularly fine collection of Jacobite drinking glasses includes the famous Traquair 'amen' glass engraved with a Jacobite verse and a portrait glass showing the head of Bonnie Prince Charlie.

In the peaceful grounds an active craft centre flourishes, there is a maze to wander through and enchanted woods to explore. Ale has been brewed at Traquair since Mary Queen of Scots visited in 1566, and no doubt fortified Prince Charles Edward Stuart before he left on his long journey. Visitors may once again sip Traquair Ale, brewed in the old brewhouse, with a light lunch.

After 19 Lairds and 8 Earls, the present owner is Catherine Maxwell Stuart, 21st Lady of Traquair.

DRUMLANRIG CASTLE

Drumlanrig Castle is the ancient stronghold of the Douglas family and Dumfriesshire home of the Duke of Buccleuch and Queensberry. The castle, of local pink sandstone, is set on a hill at the end of a long ridge with beautiful views across Nithsdale to rolling hills and woodlands. William Douglas, 1st Duke of Queensberry, began to build in 1679 around an open court-yard, with a circular staircase tower in each corner. Four square towers with twelve turrets form the outside angles. Drumlanrig is one of the first and most important renaissance buildings in the grand manner in Scottish domestic architecture.

Almost 700 years ago the Douglases were staunch supporters of Robert Bruce, King of Scotland. When he died in 1329 his heart was entrusted to Sir James Douglas, or 'Black Douglas', who would take it on the next crusade and thus fulfill his King's ambition. While fighting in Spain he fell mortally wounded and hurled the heart in its silver casket with the cry 'Forward, brave heart'. To this day the Douglas motto is 'Forward' and their striking crest, a winged heart surmounted by Bruce's crown is emblazoned all over Drumlanrig in stone, lead, iron, wood and even woven into the carpeting.

The graceful curves of the horseshoe staircase and the arches of the lower colonnade contrast with the hard straight lines of the main structure; the rich carvings over the windows and the charm of the little cupolas further help to soften the sense of fortress-like severity. Drumlanrig is steeped in history and filled with treasures, greatly enriched by the merger of the three families Montagu, Douglas and Scott in the 18th century.

Within the entrance hall there is an immediate sense of civilised living - fine oil paintings, a magnificent French longcase clock, a rare Italian statuette and 17th century chairs all set against a wall covering of Douglas hearts stamped on gilded leather. A fine piece of needlework is believed to be the work of Mary Queen of Scots and her ladies.

The oak staircase and balustrade is one of the first of its kind in Scotland. The oak panelling is adorned by eight curved giltwood sconces in the style of Thomas Chippendale and some out-standing paintings. The most notable are Holbein's 'Sir Nicholas Carew', Leonardo da Vinci's 'Madonna with the Yarnwinder' and Rembrandt's 'Old Woman Reading'. The mgnificent silver chandelier in the staircase gallery has sixteen branches in the form of dolphins and mermaids and was made in about 1670.

The well proportioned drawing room with its fine Grinling Gibbons carvings contains some magnificent works of art. They include two French cabinets of outstanding merit, believed to have been presented by King Louis XIV to King Charles II. Both were made for Versailles c. 1675. The Boulle table with red tortoiseshell and brass inlay is also of the Louis XIV period, as are the pair of kneehole writing tables. Above these are a mag-nificent pair of late 17th Century mirrors.

Drumlanrig's builder, the 1st Duke of Queensberry, was a little concerned at the cost he incurred. He might well have felt happier about his investment had he been able to see for him-self the contribution his castle now makes in our history.

EDINBURGH CASTLE

Edinburgh Castle rises majestically from its rocky cliff high above the Firth of Forth, dominating the beautiful town which sprawls around its feet. The Castle, an active army garrison until 1923, is approached across an open, sloping parade ground known as the Esplanade which terminates at the Gatehouse and drawbridge. Here the impressive spectacle of the Edinburgh Military Tattoo is held against the backdrop of the flood-lit castle, when the parade ground echoes once more to the sound of marching feet and the skirl of the pipes.

This side of the Castle is fortified by gun emplacements or batteries, the most impressive of which is the Half Moon Battery, built in 1574 and jutting out over the easterly quarter above the town below. Within the Castle walls are barracks, the 18th century Governor's House and a military hospital which now houses the Scottish United Services Museum. Most of the older buildings are found in an area known as the Citadel. Grouped around Crown Square at its southern end are the Palace, the Great Hall and the Scottish National War Memorial.

By far the oldest building in the Citadel, indeed it is the oldest in Edinburgh, is the tiny St Margaret's Chapel dating from the 12th century. Its main features, the rounded interior within rectangular walls and the carved chancel arch, are characteristically Norman.

Within the wall of the Half Moon Battery are the remains of David's Tower, a great square Keep which dominated the Castle until it was destroyed during the 'Long Siege' of 1571-1573. The Castle was bombarded and besieged many times during the centuries when England was at war with Scotland and changed hands on more than one occasion.

The Great Hall, with its splendid hammer beam roof, was built by James 1V and extensively restored in the 1880s and now displays a fine collection of weaponry. The Palace, also built in the 15th century but greatly remodelled in 1617, was the royal residence of the Stuart monarchs and the royal arms and ciphers can be seen in several places. Mary Queen of Scots gave birth to her son, the future James V1 in a small chamber of the royal apartments in 1566. It was he who united the two warring factions in 1603 when he became King James I of England.

The last great siege of the castle took place in 1659 when it was held for the deposed James II against William and Mary; the last defence of all was in 1745 when Bonnie Prince Charlie and his Jacobite supporters ineffectively blockaded the castle.

For over a hundred years after the Act of Union in 1707 the Honours of Scotland had disappeared. They were discovered in 1818 hidden in a chest in the Crown Chamber and are now on display. Part of the crown, the oldest in the United Kingdom c1540, is said to date from the time of Robert the Bruce. The jewels include pearls fished from the River Tay. The sword and sceptre were both gifts to James 1V, while the sword belt, lost in the 17th century when the Honours were being hidden from Cromwell was found in a wall and finally restored to the castle in 1893. The Honours were last used during the Queen's visit after her Coronation in 1953.

HOPETOUN HOUSE

The site for Hopetoun House was well chosen, affording fine views over the deer park to the shores of the Firth of Forth and the hills of Fife beyond. The house was designed for Charles Hope, 1st Earl of Hopetoun, by Sir William Bruce and built between 1699 and 1707. Enlargements were made by William Adam and completed by his three sons after his death in 1748. The interior decoration was completed largely under John Adam's supervision between 1752 and 1767 and much of the original decorations and furniture survives today. In effect Hopetoun House is two buildings in contrasting styles, one designed by Sir William Bruce and the other by William Adam, linked by the Entrance Hall.

The front staircase is one of the outstanding decorative features of the Bruce house. The pine-panelled walls, frieze, cornice and panel borders are carved with flowers, fruit, wheatears and peapods. The murals within these framed panels are modern, painted in 1967 by William McLaren as a memorial to the wife of the 3rd Marquess. The Cupola painting depicts angels and cherubs supporting the Hope crest and coat-of-arms and although painted early in the 18th century is perfectly in harmony with the modern panels.

The Bruce Bedchamber, designed for the young 1st Earl contains a magnificent gilt four-poster bed hung with red damask and a unique Pattern Chair. This was made to display various forms of carving to enable the 2nd Earl to select which style he preferred for the State Apartments. The panelled Garden Parlour has a portrait of the 4th Earl wearing the uniform of the Company of Archers of which he was Captain-General in 1822, when he entertained George IV at Hopetoun. He had had a distinguished military career and was responsible for the completion of the State Dining Room, and for the purchase of several important pictures.

The State Apartments were created by William Adam and executed by his eldest son, John. The Yellow Drawing Room, its walls hung with glowing yellow silk damask, was originally the dining room. The magnificent furniture was made by the noted rococo cabinet maker and upholsterer James Cullen, a contemporary of Thomas Chippendale.

The Red Drawing Room has a beautiful coved ceiling with an enriched cornice and frieze which is one of the finest examples of rococo decoration in Scotland. The furniture, again by James Cullen, is arranged in the 18th century manner known as 'Parade' style, with all the furniture placed around the walls.

The State Dining Room was created from two rooms in the early 19th century and represents a fine example of a Regency room as practically everything in it dates from that period, including the cornice, chimneypiece, elaborate curtains and golden wallpaper. This room contains a wonderful collection of family portraits and exquisite Meissen and Dresden porcelain. To ensure that food arrived from the distant kitchens piping hot it was packed in a steam-heated container and trundled along a railway track and up in a lift to a warming oven in the specially created Serving Room, and the waiting footmen. In the South Pavilion the elegant Ballroom is hung with eight late 17th century Aubusson tapestries. Nowadays the Ballroom provides an impressive setting for special functions including gala dinners, concerts and balls.

From the roof-top viewing platform the gardens and grounds can be fully appreciated. In the 18th century formal gardens were laid out on the west lawn, and although the Parterre is no longer there, the intricate outlines are still visible some 250 years later, and the 'large bason of water' (the Round Pond) still remains. The 'Terras' is now the Bastion or Sea Walk and a walled kitchen garden occupied the site of the present Garden Centre. It had an ingenious heated hollow 'firewall' against which were grown the luscious peaches and nectarines for this grand household.

In early spring drifts of daffodils flutter on the slopes above the Bowling Green; primroses, bluebells and many other wild flowers carpet the lovely woodland walks. In early summer the soft shades of spring give way to iridescent azaleas and rhododendrons; later still berries of all kinds and many types of fungi may be seen. The large lawned areas are excellent for a host of outdoor events, and everywhere the views are spectacular.

Only 12 miles from Edinburgh on the A904, Hopetoun has excellent facilities for both business and private entertaining. The Scottish Gala Evening in particular provides a taste of the finest entertainment 'north of the border', and can be rounded off by the stirring ceremony of Beating the Retreat.

CULZEAN CASTLE AND COUNTRY PARK

Standing proudly on the Ayrshire coast overlooking Arran, the Mull of Kintyre and Ailsa Craig, Culzean Castle is one of Robert Adam's most spectacular achievements. Built between 1772 and 1792, its Gothic style is less familiar than Adam's more usual Classicism.

Robert Adam was commissioned by the 10th Earl of Cassilis and began to remodel the south front to incorporate an older mansion. Work on the north front followed and then the impressive round tower, which was linked to the south front by Adam's imaginative oval staircase, was completed. In the 19th century an entrance hall was added, but most of the lovely Adam interiors are relatively unchanged.

The splendid Round Drawing Room and Oval Staircase are lavishly furnished and decorated with ornate plasterwork friezes,

fireplaces and finely moulded ceilings. As was his practice, much of the fine furniture was designed by Adam himself to complement a particular room and the carpets were often made to echo the design of the ceiling. The house also contains some very fine family portraits, silver and porcelain.

The magnificent Country Park extends to some 560 acres including the Swan Pond, formal walled gardens, quiet woodlands and 2½ miles of picturesque coastline. The walled garden is entered through a Victorian camellia house which is a wonderful sight in summer filled with exotic blooms. Inside the walled garden is the grotto and the formal fountain garden has terraces and herbaceous borders planted with an ever changing show of colour as the summer days lengthen. There is a varied programme of guided walks along the coast. There are excellent facilities for conferences and seminars.

POLLOK HOUSE AND BURRELL COLLECTION

Pollok House   (Alan Crumlish)

Some time after England fell to the Normans in 1066, Edgar the Atheling led a band of Saxon Thanes to Scotland. Among these were said to have been one Maccus, ancestor of the Scottish Maxwells. It was about the year 1269 that Sir John Maxwell, a great-grandson of Maccus, became the first knight of Pollok in Renfrewshire. Throughout the seven centuries that followed, his descendants continued to live at Pollok, weathering political and financial uncertainty. When the 10th Baronet, Sir John Stirling Maxwell, died on 30th May 1956 aged almost ninety, the baronetcy fell into abeyance as he had no son. At this stage, Pollok could so easily have gone the way of the many lost houses of Scotland. Instead it was preserved for all to enjoy by an act of exceptional generosity on the part of Sir John's daughter, Mrs Anne Maxwell Macdonald, and her family. In 1966 Pollok House, together with its internationally famed collection of paintings and 361 acres of parkland, was given to the City of Glasgow. Since that time it has been administered as a branch of the city's Museums and Art Galleries Department. The parkland provided an ideal setting for the Burrell Collection and it was exploited to great effect by the three young architects, who in 1972 won the architectural competition for the design of the building. Barry Gasson, John Meunier and Brit Anderson created an environment of considerable sensitivity. The continuous interaction of the objects on display with the natural world beyond the glazed walls is intended to stimulate the visitor's appreciation of the Collection, which is wide-ranging and diverse: Ancient Civilizations, Chinese ceramics and metal work, European decorative arts from the 12th to the 18th centuries and fine Art - paintings, prints, drawings and sculpture - emphasizing French and Dutch work of the 19th and early 20th centuries.

Burrell Gallery, Glasgow Museums

Pollok House and Burrell Collection
Pollok Park
Glasgow G43
Pollok House, Tel: 041 632 0274
Burrell Collection, Tel: 041 649 7151

HISTORIC SCOTLAND

Historic Scotland looks after over 300 historic properties throughout the length and breadth of Scotland, from Dumfries and Galloway in the south to Shetland in the north.

Edinburgh and Stirling Castles are the most famous but there are many other fascinating sites waiting to be discovered, covering five and a half thousand years of Scotland's colourful history. There are the majestic Border abbeys of Melrose, Jedburgh, Kelso and Dryburgh; the outstanding pre-historic monuments of Orkney including the stone-age village of Skara Brae, and there are reminders of the nation's more recent industrial past in the iron furnace at Bonawe in Argyll and Dallas Dhu Distillery by Forres.

Historic Scotland welcomes over two million visitors a year, a number that has increased steadily as interest in the built heritage grows. Of these visitors, over 28,000 have become our Friends - members of Friends of Historic Scotland that is.

For an annual fee Friends gain unlimited access to Historic Scotland sites, a guidebook listing all properties, a quarterly newsletter with news on conservation, archaeology and new facilities at properties. Special guided tours are arranged for Friends, and English Heritage and Welsh Cadw sites can be visited for half price in the first year of membership, free in the second.

Visitors can join at any Historic Scotland property or through headquarters at 20 Brandon Street, Edinburgh EH3 5RA, telephone: 031-244-3099.

Also available from Historic Scotland sites is the Explorer Ticket. This gives unlimited entry to all properties for a seven or fourteen day period and is excellent value for money. It is available at adult, family, pensioner or student rates.

Here is a selection of Historic Scotland sites around the country:

Stirling Castle

Guarding the route between the Highlands and the Lowlands, this magnificent fortress has been at the forefront of Scottish History. It was constantly fought over during the Wars of Independence with the English.

But Stirling Castle was also a favoured royal palace and much fine building work went on there. The Great Hall of James IV is currently being restored to its regal splendour. The Renaissance Palace of James V and the Chapel Royal of James VI are other highlights of a tour.

The regimental museum of the Argyll and Sutherland Highlanders is here, and there are also displays of 18th and 19th century military life in the Queen Anne casemates and Nether Bailey.

Inchcolm Abbey

On an island in the Firth of Forth opposite Aberdour and reached by ferry from South Queensferry. The remains of the 12th-century abbey, often called the Iona of the East, are remarkably complete, including the 13th-century chapter house. Inchcolm is a delightful island with a varied bird and seal life. There are the remains of World War I fortifications too.

Fort George

This complete 18th-century artillery fort was built following Culloden to make sure there was never another Highland uprising. The fort, which covers 42 acres and has a mile-long rampart, succeeded in its aim without ever firing a shot in anger. Still a working army barracks, the fort also contains reconstructed barrack rooms of the 18th and 19th century and has a fine collection of cannon, mortars and other armaments.

New Abbey Corn Mill

This delightful 18th-century water-powered oatmeal mill has been restored to full working order and is in the picturesque Dumfries-shire village of New Abbey. Close by is the ancient Sweetheart Abbey founded by the Lady Devorgilla who was buried there with the heart of her husband, John Balliol.

For more information on Historic Scotland properties and opening times telephone 031-244-3101.

LOWLANDS

As you would imagine, much of Scotland's rich heritage comes as a direct result of its desire for independence from English rule. Robert The Bruce did rout the English at Bannockburn but more often tales of tragedy and bloodshed are the only lasting outcome of the frequent clashes. The history of Scotland's Clans is powerful and compelling and feuds between these 'families' form a rich part of Britain's history.

Argyll, The Islands and Ayrshire are a peculiar mixture of heather, hills and coastline and there are a great variety of inns and hotels to cover every budget.

Although many people see the Highlands and Perthshire as true Scotland, this is to miss out on some of the most delightful countryside and friendliest people. The borderlands stretch from the foothills of the Cheviots, through the Tweed Valley. The border towns have a celebrated history of their own and each has individual appeal. Melrose, Selkirk and Hawick are particularly pleasant. The area is thick with textile mills and the towns lie in the shadow of many ruined Abbeys, castle and towers. South west of this area, Dumfries and Galloway is an area of delightful coastline and rolling hills. Whilst the Borders

are the land of Sir Walter Scott, Ayrshire is the home of Robbie Burns.

One of the beauties of Scotland is space - rarely are crowds a worry here, except perhaps in Edinburgh, or Glasgow when Rangers play a home game.

Edinburgh is beautiful and too richly endowed with a fascinating history to afford to miss it. Quaint streets are dominated by the grey Castle perched above and the bustle of Princes Street with restaurants, hotels and ancient pubs makes the city positively buzz. Glasgow too has tremendous character.

The roads that lead ever northward run through some breathtaking scenery and at Loch Lomond, where the Lowlands meet the Highlands, the views are such you will never forget.

From Peebles to Perthshire and Ayrshire to the ancient Kingdom of Fife, Scotland is a treat. To tour the land will only make the visitor hunger for more. From the Borders to the tip of the Highlands, it is a wonderful mixture of heather and heritage, history and hospitality.

HOTELS OF DISTINCTION

AIROS, Port Appin, Strathclyde. Tel: (063173) 236
An idyllic setting overlooking Loch Linnhe is one attraction of this impressive hotel. Extremely comfortable interiors and delightfully cosy bedrooms add to the peace of your stay. The restaurant serves traditional Scottish fare and is outstanding.

ARDANAISEIG, By Toynuilt, Argyll. Tel: (08663) 333
Built in 1834 and ideal for touring the West Coast, this hotel is set in 32 acres of gardens on the shores of Loch Awe, beneath the craggy peaks of Cruachan.

ARDFILLAYNE HOTEL AND RESTAURANT, Dunoon, Argyll. Tel: (0369) 2267
A Scotland's Heritage Hotel built in 1535, originally the retreat of the romantic novlist A D Fillan, it rests in the seclusion of acres of wooded grounds with views over West Bray and Dunoon.

ARDSHEAL HOUSE, Kentallen of Appin, Argyll.
Tel: (063174) 227
Built in 1760 as the home of the Stewarts of Appin, the house rests in 900 acres, high on a peninsula overlooking Loch Linnhe and the Morvern mountains. The interior boasts open fires, oak panelling and many antiques.

BALHOUSIE CASTLE, Bonnyriss, Lothian. Tel: (0875) 20153
This turreted castle dates to the 13th century and much of the house's history is intact. Dungeons are a particularly interesting feature. Bedrooms are well furnished and offer further charm.

BARJARG TOWER, Auldgirty, Dumfriesshire.
Tel: (0848) 31345
Commanding 40 acres of magnificent grounds, this 16th century tower house has been superbly refurbished to retain all the charm of its period features such as the open fireplaces and beautiful oak panelling.

BARON'S CRAIG HOTEL, Rockcliffe, Kirkcudbrightshire.
Tel: (055663) 225
Close to Castle Douglas and New Abbey this late 19th century mansion house is set in glorious heather and woodland overlooking the Solway and the Rough Firth.

BORTHWICK CASTLE, North Middleton, Edinburgh.
Tel: (0875) 20514
Built in 1430 and described by Sir Walter Scott as 'the finest example of a twin-tower keep', it has been the refuge of Mary Queen of Scots and husband Boswell, and later besieged by Cromwell.

BURNS BYRE RESTAURANT, Alloway, Strathclyde.
Tel: (0292) 43644
Lovers of the poetic heritage of Scotland must surely make a pilgrimage to Alloway. The village is alive with Burns. The cattle byre is now a delightful restaurant and makes for a happy port of call for all lovers of fine food.

BURTS, Melrose, Borders. Tel: (089682) 2285
A converted townhouse which dates from the early 18th century, the house has huge appeal and arcitectural interest, and is a delightfully cosy place in which to stay when visiting the Borders of Scotland.

THE CALEDONIAN, Edinburgh, Lothian. Tel: 031 225 2433
The Caley stands at one end of Princes Sunset and is proudly overlooked by Edinburgh Castle. Built of red sandstone in 1903 the hotel is a famous landmark. Bars, excellent restaurants and some bedrooms make this a perfect place to stay in delightful Edinburgh.

CALLY PALACE HOTEL, Dumfries, Galloway.
Tel: (0557) 814341
This restored 15th century country house commands 100 acres of forest and parkland. The interior is on a grand scale with marble pillars and fireplaces, ornate ceilings and fine furniture.

SUNLAWS HOUSE

Sunlaws House stands in the heart of Scotland's beautiful Border country, in 200 acres of gardens and mature parkland along the banks of the Teviot, three miles from the historic town of Kelso.There has been a house on the same site at Sunlaws for nearly 500 years and from its beginnings it has always been a Scottish family house – and that, to all intents and purposes, is how it will stay!

Sunlaws has a place in history, from the faint echoes of ancient strife when English armies of the 15th and 16th centuries came marauding through Roxburghshire and the Borders, to the Jacobite rebellion of 1745. Indeed Prince Charles Edward Stuart is reputed to have stayed on November 5th 1745 and to have planted a white rose bush in the grounds.

Sunlaws hope that their guests will find that in the intervening year there have been some welcome changes. Its owner, the Duke of Roxburghe, has carefully converted Sunlaws into the small, welcoming but unpretentious hotel of comfort and character that it is.

There are 22 bedrooms, which include the splendid Bowmont Suite and six delightful rooms in the stable courtyard, all furnished with care to His Graces' own taste and all with private bathroom or shower, colour television, radio and direct-dial telephone. Disabled guests too are provided with the amenities they need.

The spacious public rooms are furnished with the same care and elegance, which adds to the overall atmosphere of warmth and welcome with log fires burning in the main and inner hall, drawing room, library bar and dining room, throughout the winter and on cold summer evenings.

Flowers and plants, from the gardens and the conservatory, will be found all over the house; herbs too are grown for the kitchen and will be found in many of the traditional dishes that are prepared for the dining room. Not only is Sunlaws right in the heart of Scotland's beautiful Border Country, it is also the perfect centre for a host of holiday activities. Sporting and cultural interests are well served, too.

Salmon and trout fishing, and a complete range of shooting are available at the Hotel, with golf, horse-riding, racing and fox hunting all nearby.

Sunlaws is the perfect location for touring the Borders, with great country houses including Abbotsford, the home of Sir Walter Scott, and a number of abbeys and museums all within easy reach.

Sunlaws House Hotel
Kelso
Roxburghshire
Scotland
Tel: (05735) 331 Fax: (05735) 611

LOWLANDS

CHAPELTOUN HOUSE, Stewarton, Ayrshire.
Tel: (0560) 82696
The original owners were a Scottish and English couple and thus the ornate plasterwork and masonry incorporates a romantic theme of thistles and roses. The Burrell collection, Dean Castle and Royal Troon are nearby.

CRINGLETIE HOUSE HOTEL, Peebles, Borders.
Tel: (07213) 233
This turreted Baronial style mansion commands 28 acres of beautiful gardens and woodland. Its interior boasts an impressive panelled lounge with carved oak and marble fireplace and painted ceilings.

THE CROOK INN, Tweedsmuir, Borders. Tel: (08997) 272
A splendid situation in the Tweed Valley for this delightful inn which dates from 1604. The interior of the hotel has a homely air and the traditional furnishings further enhance the memories of your visit.

CROSS KEYS, Kelso, Borders. Tel: (0573) 23303
Kelso is one of Scotlands marvellous border towns. The Cross Keys is one of the countrys oldest walking inns and one of its most welcoming. This is an ideal point from which to explore the Borders.

DALHOUSIE CASTLE HOTEL, Bonnyrigg, Edinburgh.
Tel: (0875) 20155
Built around 1450 for the Ramseys of Dalhousie this hotel now rests in 12 acres of gardens. Ornate plasterwork, fine panelling, stone walls and rich drapes are carefully preserved, whilst ancient dungeons are a unique setting for dinner.

DOLPHINTON HOUSE HOTEL, Nr West Linton, Peebleshire. Tel: (0968) 82286
Started in 1801 and set in 160 acres of land the hotel is complete with the unexcavated remains of an Iron Age fort. The interior is peaceful and relaxing with crackling log fires in the lounge.

EDNAM HOUSE HOTEL, Kelso, Roxburghshire.
Tel: (0573) 24168
One of the finest examples of Georgian architecture in the country, Ednam House lies in 3 acres of gardens overlooking the River Tweed. The local area, made famous by Sir Walter Scott, is rich with open country houses.

ENMORE HOTEL, Dunoon, Argyll. Tel: (0369) 2230
Built in 1785 as a summer house for a wealthy cotton merchant and family, the Enmore, with its interesting features, overlooks the Clyde.

FERNIE CATLE, Letham, Fife. Tel: (033781) 381
An imposing 14th century castle surrounded by its own grounds. The keep bar with arrow slit walls and vaulted ceiling lends a particular atmosphere. Facilities are superb and this is an excellent point from which to explore central Scotland.

THE GEORGE, Edinburgh, Lothian. Tel: 031-225 1251
The Hotel is particularly convenient for Princes Street which makes it extremely popular. The grand foyer makes an excellent impression on entrance and the restaurants and bars continue this effect.

GLENFEOCHAN HOUSE, Kilmore, Strathclyde.
Tel: (063177) 273
There are only three double rooms at this elegant turreted mansion but they are delightful as the rest of the house, with its sumptuous interior. The restaurant is also well considered and for those looking to stay in a classic Scottish house Glenfeochan is an outstanding choice.

HOUSTON HOUSE HOTEL, Uphall, West Lothian.
Tel: (0506) 853831
Originally a 17th century laird's fortified tower, the hotel now enjoys 20 peaceful acres of wooded grounds. The vaulted bar dates from 1737 with a huge log fire to complement the range of malt whiskies.

THE HOWARD, Edinburgh, Lothian. Tel: (031) 557 3500
A splendidly appointed, elegant hotel situated in the city's Georgian new town area. There are a number of memorable features. A mural and domed stairwell ceiling are two examples. A handy base from which to explore the historical capital.

INVERCRERAN COUNTRY HOUSE HOTEL, Appin, Argyll.
Tel: (063173) 532
Offering breathtaking views of mountainous Glen Creran, the Invercreran stands in 25 acres of shrub garden and woodland. The marble-floored dining room is highly impressive while Oban and Fort William are nearby.

ISLE OF ERISKA, Eriska, Strathclyde. Tel: (063172) 371
This is a Baronial style mansion which has been superbly converted to a country house hotel. Bedrooms are quaintly old fashioned, while the restaurant is excellent and the peace of the Isle and the house is positively wondrous.

JOHNSTOUNBURN HOUSE, Humbie, East Lothian.
Tel: (087533) 696
At the foot of the Lammermuir Hills, close to Edinburgh, Tantallon Castle, Abbotsford and Traquair House, this 17th century stone-walled hotel is warmed by open fires, and has a beautiful wood-panelled lounge.

KIRROUGHTREE HOTEL, Newton Stewart, Dumfries and Galloway. Tel: (0671) 2141
Regarded as one of Britains most luxurious country house hotels, the elegant Kirroughtree has stood since 1719 and still maintains much of its traditional character.

KNOCKINAAM LODGE, Port Patrick, Wigtownshire.
Tel: (077681) 471
Set in 30 acres of rocky grassland the hotel has gardens and a private beach. Churchill chose the Lodge for a secret meeting with Eisenhower in World War II. Open fires and antiques add to the luxury.

MANOR PARK HOTEL, Skelmorlie, Ayrshire.
Tel: (0475) 520832
Built in 1840, the Manor has retained much of its elegance with oak staircase, imposing portraits and log fires. The fascinating Cowal Room is where Churchill and Eisenhower chose to plan the D-Day landings.

INVERCRERAN HOTEL

The Invercreran is a stylish mansion house, now an outstanding small country house hotel. It rests in 25 acres of mature shrub gardens and woodlands beyond which, the view extends over the beautiful Glen Creran - its beautiful tree-lined meadows interspersed with walks to the River Creran surrounded by impressive mountains.

Viewed from the outside, it is difficult to imagine that the Invercreran has only 7 guest rooms. However, once one steps inside any of the bedrooms, bathrooms or public rooms it becomes easier to see why. With an unashamed emphasis on luxury the sheer spaciousness of the rooms is one of the most striking first impressions, on top of which the bedrooms all have en suite bathrooms and offer all the facilities the discerning guest would expect from such a hotel. They all enjoy commanding views too.

The lounge has been specially designed to curve to the contour of the hill. It boasts a freestanding marble fireplace, where the warm glow of logs under a copper canopy further enhances the relaxing, friendly atmosphere for which the hotel is especially renowned.

The hotel is run by the Kersley family and their sons. Tony is the chef, cooking exquisite Scottish fare to order. The menu is wide and varied, with the emphasis on local landed seafood, selection of finest Scottish meat, game and fresh vegetables. All complemented with an outstanding cellar of specially chosen wines.

Invercreran Country House Hotel
Glen Creran
Appin
Argyll PA38 4BJ
Tel: (063173) 414 and 456
Fax: (063173) 532

LOWLANDS

THE NORTON HOUSE HOTEL, Ingliston, Edinburgh.
Tel: (031333) 1275
Dating back to 1861 and situated in 55 acres of parkland, a former stable block has been converted into a tavern of this splendid Scottish Victorian mansion.

ONE DEVONSHIRE GARDENS, Glasgow. Tel: (041339) 2001
Voted Best City Hotel by Scottish Hotel Guide 1989, this hotel is set amidst the Victorian Mansions and graceful terraces of Western Glasgow, and is ideal for exploring the fascinating historic city itself.

PIERSLAND HOUSE, Troon, Strathclyde. Tel: (0292) 314747
Built in the late 19th century for the heirs of Johnnie Walker of distilling fame. The grounds include a Japanese Garden which is overlooked by a pleasing conservatory. Bedrooms are tastefully decorated and extremely comfortable.

SHIELDHILL HOTEL, Biggar, Lanarkshire. Tel: (0899) 20039
This 12th century mansion house boasts extensive grounds. The oak-panelled sitting room, dining room and other public rooms are reputedly haunted by the 'Grey Lady of the Old Keep'.

SUNLAWS HOUSE HOTEL, Kelso, Roxburghshire.
Tel: (0573) 5331
Owned by the Duke of Roxburgh and resting in 200 acres of beautiful gardens beside the Tevrot, this hotel boasts a fine library bar with open log fire and leather bound tomes.

TIRORAN HOUSE, Tiroran, Strathclyde. Tel: (06815) 232
This is a delightful hotel in a remote setting. Splendid views, luxurious public rooms and bedrooms exude character, while the dining room is first class and the welcome second to none.

TURNBERRY, Turnberry, Strathclyde. Tel: (0655) 31000
Turnberry is one of the outstanding hotels in Britain. High ceilings, marvellous views over historic links and all around real luxury and perfect service. The building itself is most impressive - all in all, a delightful place at which to stay.

ACCOMMODATION OF MERIT

COMLONGON CASTLE, Clarencefield, Dumbartonshire.
Tel: (038787) 283
Magnificent Border castle, set in 50 acres of mature gardens and woodland. Reputed to harbour a 16th century ghost it is a beautiful base for exploring Scotland. There is golf and fishing nearby plus many sites of heritage.

COSSES, Ballantrae, Ayrshire. Tel: (046583) 363
Converted farmhouse in a quiet valley surrounded by woodland and gardens totalling 12 acres. Home grown produce is a feature at meal times. Ideal for visiting Robert Burns' birthplace, and the many historic houses and gardens.

THE DRUM, Gilmerton, Edinburgh. Tel: 031 664 7215
This is Edinburgh's largest private house, a grade 1 listed 15th century castle, extended by Willian Adam in 1726. It provides sumptuous surroundings from which to tour Edinburgh with its centuries of history.

FORBES LODGE, Gifford, East Lothian. Tel: (062081) 212
Attractive 18th century house, only 18 miles from Edinburgh, whose hostess' family have lived in the picturesque village since

1188. Wonderful place to stay whilst touring the many historical sites of Southern Scotland.

HART MANOR HOTEL, By Langholm, Dumfriesshire.
Tel: (0387) 373217
This friendly establishment is a popular with touring holiday makers. Fishing is available on the White Esk only three hundred yards from the hotel and Bowhill at Selkirk regualarly proves another local favourite.

HOEBRIDGE INN, Gattonside, Melrose. Tel: (0896 82) 3082
This locally renowned restaurant comes highly recommended. Enjoy a freshly prepared meal of local game and fish, a vegetarian dish or one of the Italian specialities in a friendly informal atmosphere. Managed by Chef proprietor Carlo Campari and his wife Joy, the restaurant is only ten minutes from Melrose and Galashiels.

KIRKTON HOUSE, Cardross, Dumbartonshire.
Tel: (0389) 841 951
This comfortable guesthouse is within easy reach of the thriving city of Glasgow and its huge array of attractions. Pollock House and the fantastic Burrell collection will be of particular interest to many patrons.

THE LEY, Innerleithen, Peebleshire. Tel: (90896) 830240
Unusual looking but beautiful Victorian house set in mature gardens amidst a 30 acre estate. The wool town of Innerleithen is nearby, as are the market town of Peebles and the fascinating Neidpath Castle and Traquair House.

NORTHFIELD HOUSE, Annan, Dumfries. Tel: (0461) 202851
A Georgian house situated in 12 aces of mature grounds plus its own stretch of river with fishing. It is a perfect haven for eager historians and game sportsmen as the Borders are full of fine houses, Abbeys and excellent water for fishing.

SIBBET HOUSE, Edinburgh, Lothian. Tel: 031 556 1078
Sibbet House was built in 1809 and is generously furnished with antiques and draperies. An elegant, but comfortable Georgian family home, Sibbet offers well-appointed guest rooms with private facilities.

SOLWAYSIDE HOTEL AND RESTAURANT, Auchencairn, Castle Douglas. Tel: (0556) 64280
A comfortable, family run hotel offering good food and superb sea and country views. Amongst the many local attractions are Dundrennan Castle, Sweetheart Abbey and Threave Garden and Castle. Excellent local fishing is also available and the hotel provides freezing facilities and a drying room.

STUART HOUSE, Edinburgh, Lothian. Tel: 031 557 9030
Stuart House is a lovely Georgian-style Town House located in the refined elegance of New Town, Edinburgh. All bedrooms are en-suite and also feature direct-dial telephone, colour television and tea/coffee hospitality tray.

INNS OF CHARACTER

BENNETS BAR, Edinburgh., Lothian
An elaborately decorated Victorian bar, where arched and mahogany pillared mirrors are surrounded by tiled cherubs. Ornate moulded beams support a high maroon ceiling and 'art nouveau' stained glass windows complete the picture.

CULCREUCH CASTLE

Culcreuch Castle, the home of the Barons of Culcreuch since 1699 and before this the ancestral fortalice of the Galbraiths and indeed Clan Castle of the Galbraith chiefs for over three centuries (1320 to 1630), has now been restored and converted by its present owners into a most comfortable family-run country house hotel, intimately blending the elegance of bygone days with modern comforts and personal service in an atmosphere of friendly informal hospitality. The eight individually decorated and furnished bedrooms all have en suite facilities, colour television and tea and coffee making facilities. Most command uninterrupted and quite unsurpassed views over the 1600 acre parkland grounds, described by the National Trust for Scotland as a 'gem of outstanding beauty', and beyond a kaleidoscope of spectacular scenery of hills, moorlands, lochs, burns and woods comprising the Endrick valley and the Campsie Fells above.

All the public rooms are decorated in period style and furnished with antiques giving the aura and grace of a bygone age. Log fires create warmth and intimacy and the candlelit evening meals in the panelled dining room make for most romantic occasions, well complemented by freshly prepared local produce and a carefully selected wine cellar.

Of all the historic rooms within the Castle, perhaps the most unique of all and within the old fortress is the haunted Chinese Bird Room, so called because its walls are covered in hand-painted Chinese wallpapers whose designs depict colourful birds and exotic palms which were painted onto paper rolls in China and brought over to Scotland in 1723. The paper was hung in the same year in this bedroom and is still in position - over two hundred and sixty years later! It is believed to be the only surviving example of genuine antique Chinese wallpaper in Scotland and visitors come to Culcreuch especially to view it. The room is full of antique ornaments and furniture - mainly French and made of satinwood, including a half-tester double bed. The original garde-robe, built into the six feet thick walls, has been tastefully converted into a small bathroom. In addition there is a private shower room along the corridor. Not

surprisingly, requests come from all over the world from guests wishing to reserve the Chinese Bird Room.

Beware, however, a stay at Culcreuch is not for the faint-hearted. Time after time unsuspecting visitors report experiencing strange and inexplicable phenomena during their stay - experiences which have uncanny similarities with stories handed down from previous generations and which fall into three clearly distinguishable categories known as the three 'ghosts' of Culcreuch. Almost all experiences appear to take place whilst the visitors are within the six feet thick walls of the original 1296 fortress and lead one to suggest that they are connected to persons or events which took place before additions were made to the original castle in 1721. None of the three 'ghosts' are apparitions of a human form - two being abstract and one an animal. The regularity and consistency of these reports by unconnected persons is, however, uncanny and unnerving.....

Whether for either business or pleasure Culcreuch is a most convenient centrally positioned base for visiting Edinburgh (55 minutes by motorway), Glasgow (35 minutes) and Stirling (25 minutes). For business clients there is no comparable venue for entertaining and the Castle specialises in offering its unique facilities for small meetings.

From Autumn to Spring, reduced terms for off-season breaks are offered, together with House Parties over the Christmas and New Year Holidays' and during these cooler months the log fires offer a cheerful welcome on your return from a day out in the Trossachs.

The location of Culcreuch is rural but not isolated, and with the fresh air of the countryside, the space, grace, comfort, good wholesome food and that unique warmth of friendship and hospitality offered from a family run home from home, a stay here is most conducive to shedding the cares and pressures of modern day life and utterly relaxing.

We look forward to your company. — The Haslam Family

Culcreuch Castle
Fintry
Stirlingshire G63 OLW
Tel: (036 086) 228
Fax: (0532) 390093
Telex: 557299

LOWLANDS

BLACK BULL, Moffat, Dumfries and Galloway.
Burns once scratched a verse on one of the windows here, a witty piece concerning his girlfriend and her mother. Unfortunately the window in now in a Moscow museum, but the bar is still well worth a visit.

GLOBE, Dumfries.
Robert Burns wrote of the Globe, '... for these many years has been my Howff (Scottish for 'regular haunt')'. At the back is a little museum to the poet, with some of the verses he scratched in the window. Long ago, the barmaid here, Anna Park, bore his child.

GORDON ARMS, Mountbenger, Borders.
A hundred and fifty years ago, the poet James Hogg, the - 'Ettrick Shepherd' recommended that this lonely moorland inn be allowed to keep its licence. Fortunately, the justice at the time was Sir Walter Scott who knew the inn, and so it was granted.

HAWES, Queensferry, Lothian.
This old inn has something of an atmosphere about it, probably the very air that inspired Robert Louis Stevenson to use it as a setting in 'Kidnapped'. Rumour has it he began writing the book whilst staying in the hotel itself.

INVERARNAN INN, Inverarnan, Central.
Scotland is well in evidence here, the barman wears a tradi-tional kilt; the furniture is covered with tartan and deerskins, while bagpipes, horsecollars and Highland paintings decorate the wall.

MURRAY ARMS, Dumfries and Galloway.
The town itself took its name from this inn, originally called the gatehouse. With its striking tower it dates back to the 17th century and includes within it the 1661 tollhouse for the road. The national poet himself composed in the Burns room in 1793.

PRINCE OF WALES, Aberdeen, Grampian.
Boasting the longest bar in the city, this pub has a cosy back lounge area complete with log fire, wooden pews and furniture, all reached by a tiny, twisting cobbled alley.

TIBBIE SHIELS INN, St Mary's Loch, Borders.
This beautiful and remote old inn offers free fishing on its adjoining loch to residents. The name is that of the original owner, a sharp-tongued woman who would embarass the literary figures of the day, Hogg, Scott and Stevenson, with her pertinent questions. Her photograph is on the wall.

TWEEDDALE ARMS, Gifford, Lothian.
The 13th century ruin in the grounds of this comfortable old inn was supposedly the model for Goblin Hall in Scott's 'Marmion'. With a tastefully decorated lounge, this inn boasts wonderful views over wooded hills and greens.

GLENFEOCHAN HOUSE AND GARDENS

Glenfeochan House is a listed, turreted, Victorian Country Mansion at the head of Loch Feochan, built in 1875 and set amidst a 350 acre Estate of Hills, Lochs, Rivers and Pasture. The House is surrounded by a mature 6 acre Garden (open to the Public) with a 1½ acre Walled Garden with herbaceous borders, vegetables fruit and Herb beds.

The house has recently been carefully restored with family antiques and beautiful fabrics. All the main rooms have high ceilings with original ornate plasterwork. The intricately carved American Pine staircase with beautifully Pargeted canopy lead Guests to three large comfortable bedrooms with ensuite bathrooms. The views over the Garden and Parkland through to Loch Feochan are spectacular. This is a really peaceful setting for a holiday.

The Victorian Arboretum is "One of the Great Gardens of the Highlands". Many rare shrubs and trees, some planted in 1840, make a wonderful canopy for the tender Rhododendrons and other rare shrubs including a large Embothrium and Davidia which abounds with "White Handkerchiefs" in the Summer.

Carpets of Snowdrops, Daffodils and Bluebells herald the Spring. Many tender Acers love this sheltered garden. The Herbaceous Borders are a blaze of colour in the summer and provide many of the flowers for the house. The walled garden has one of the old Victorian heated walls. This gives shelter to a huge Magnolia, Eucryphia and a Ginkgo. All the vegetables for the house are grown here. There is a large greenhouse entirely for white

and yellow peaches and nectarines. Salmon and Sea Trout fishing on the River Nell and wonderful bird and otter watching make Glenfeochan a unique place to stay.

Glenfeochan House and Gardens
Kilmore
Oban
Argyllshire PA34 4QR
Tel: (063 177) 273

Blair Castle

Highlands and Islands

Sco

Ulla

Inverewe Garden

A832

A890

Dunvegan Castle

Kyle of Lochalsh
Eilean Donan Ca

A87

Ferrindonald
Kilmore
Mallaig

Arisaig   A830

Old
Fort

Glenborrodale

Kentalle

A28

Eriska
Tiroran   Port Appin   Invereraran

A828

Mull

Oban
Ardanaiseig   A85

A816   A819

Inveraray
Castle

Crarae Lodge Gardens

Ardrishaig

Dunoon

Tarbert

A83

Arran

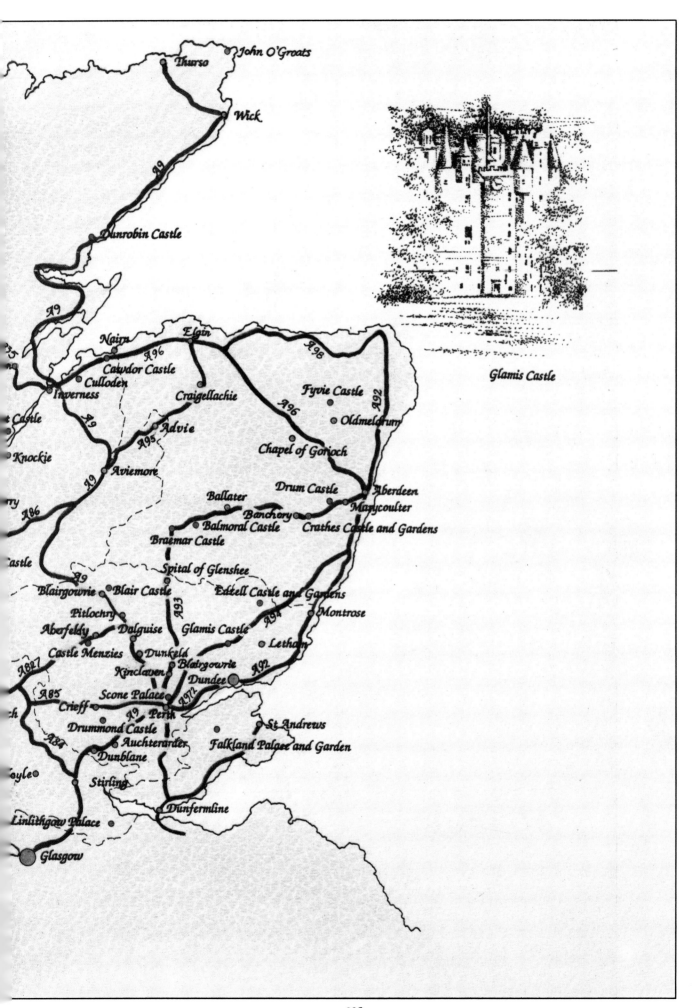

John O'Groats

Thurso

Wick

A9

Dunrobin Castle

A9

A95

Nairn
A96
Elgin
A98
Cawdor Castle
Culloden
Craigellachie
Fyvie Castle
A92
Inverness
A96
Oldmeldrum
A9
Advie
A95
Chapel of Gorioch
Knockie
Aviemore
Drum Castle
Aberdeen
A86
Ballater
Banchory
Maryculter
Balmoral Castle
Crathes Castle and Gardens
Braemar Castle
Castle
Spital of Glenshee
A9
Blairgowrie
Blair Castle
Edzell Castle and Gardens
A94
Pitlochry
A93
Montrose
Aberfeldy
Dalguise
Glamis Castle
A94
Castle Menzies
Dunkeld
Letham
A827
Kinclaven
Blairgowrie
A92
Scone Palace
A972
Dundee
A85
Crieff
A9
Perth
Drummond Castle
St Andrews
A84
Auchterarder
Falkland Palace and Garden
Dunblane
oyle
Stirling
Dunfermline
Linlithgow Palace
Glasgow

Glamis Castle

295

THE HIGHLANDS AND ISLANDS

The Highlands and Islands are located to the north of the Highland Boundary Fault Line and normally divided to comprise the Central Highlands and the Northern Highlands and Islands. The Central Highlands stretch from the Trossachs and Loch Lomond west to Argyll and its Islands, north to Inverness, Fort William and Aberdeen. Caithness, Sutherland, Ross and Cromarty, Skye, Western Isles, Orkney and Shetland form the Northern Highlands and Islands. From the large and small islands in the Firth of Clyde and the west beyond, the Central Highlands include the most westerly point on the British mainland at Ardnamurchan. With the magnificent splendour and history of Stirling and Perth, the Great Glen to the north and the fishing ports of Fraserburgh and Peterhead on the shoulder of Scotland, this is perhaps a region that has everything. Historic Scotland looks after many historic properties throughout the area where visitors are most welcome (featured later).

ARGYLL

North and west of the Firth of Clyde sits Argyll, with its lush green hills descending to hundreds of miles of rugged coastline. No matter where the visitor travels in this area superb scenery is assured from Campbelltown on the south tip of the Kintyre peninsula (Scotland's longest); to the Isles of Arran and Bute in the Firth of Clyde (reached by ferry from Ardrossan or Wemyss Bay); the Atlantic coast islands of Islay, Jura and Gigha; and Mid-Argyll and the Cowal Peninsula (reached by ferry from Gourock) with Loch Fyne between.

LOCH FYNE

Near the head of the loch is **Inveraray Castle** built in the latter half of the 18th century, the home of the Duke and Duchess of Argyll. Designed by Roger Morris and decorated by Robert Mylne, the style of Robert Adam is to be seen in his role as clerk of works. The turreted Gothic revival exterior gives way to a splendid decorative interior which now houses the family's magnificent collection of pictures and tapestries, over 1300 pieces of armour, French 18th century furniture and Continental china. Numerous walks in the woodlands offer spectacular views, none better than from the top of the Inveraray Bell Tower, some 126 feet high.

Inveraray Jail in the town centre is worth a visit to get some idea of the conditions prisoners were kept in during the last century. The 18th century courtroom is of architectural and historical interest and in addition has a real life period trial with jury on display.

Further south on the north bank of the loch is **Crarae Forest and Lodge Gardens** with its splendid displays of azaleas, rhododendrons and exotic shrubs, set in a beautiful glen. Driving south through Lochgilphead and Ardrushaig, the pretty fishing village of Tarbert not only lands the famous Loch Fyne herring but also plays host to a tremendous variety of sailing events, with yachts from all over the world enjoying the local hospitality.

The Isle of Arran can be reached by ferry from Claonaig to Lochranza, where the ruins of Lochranza Castle is said to be the landing point for Robert the Bruce on his return from Ireland. This is splendid walking and climbing country, particularly high above Brodick Bay and Brodick Castle, Garden and Country Park with fine views from Goat Fell to the mainland.

The Dukes of Hamilton owned the castle, built in the 13th century, which now houses fine paintings, silver and porcelain. North from Inveraray the A819 and A85 lead to **Oban** where a regular ferry service sails to the Western Isles and **Iona**, where St Columba landed from Ireland in 563. The original monastery has been destroyed but remains of the later 13th century nunnery and monastery, from where followers were sent to convert Scotland to Christianity, survive today. Sitting by the bustling harbour with its pleasure and fishing boats and commercial ferries there are splendid views of the Island and Sound of Mull.

CENTRAL AND TAYSIDE

The Heartlands of Scotland consist of Loch Lomond, Stirlingshire, Perthshire and the Trossachs leading to the Gateway to the Highlands. This is the land of Sir Walter Scott and Rob Roy MacGregor with castle strongholds shrouded in mystery, and breathtaking scenery over hills and lochs.

Stirling, the Gateway to the Highlands, is so called due to its central location in the country - it sits by the River Forth, overlooked by the Ochil Hills and has in the past been the scene of many battles, including Bannockburn where Robert the Bruce defeated the English in 1314. **Stirling Castle**, standing high above the town, was the scene of much fighting between the Scots and the English until it became the home of the Scottish kings from 1370 to 1603. Both Mary Queen of Scots and James VI (James I of England) lived here and James II and James V were born in the Castle (featured later).

A short drive from Glasgow is Britain's largest lake, **Loch Lomond** 24 miles long and in the shadow of the majestic Ben Lomond, 3194 feet high, which the healthy visitor can climb from the 'bonnie bonnie banks' of the loch. From Balloch in the south, the traditional cruise ship 'Countess Fiona' sails to Inversnaid and around the islands of Inchmurrin and Inchcailloch where the ruins of a castle and nunnery can be seen. Take the A811/A81 to Aberfoyle and the Trossachs, where on Loch Katrine steamer trips are available on the SS 'Sir Walter Scott'. Scott's poem 'The Lady of the Lake' is said to be set in the lochs and hills of this area of outstanding natural beauty. North on the A84, at Balquhidder, is the grave of Rob Roy MacGregor, who died in 1734, near his house at Inverlochlarig. At Lochearnhead the A85 west to Crieff passes the Melville Monument, set 859 feet above sea level from where there are breathtaking views of the countryside. In nearby Comrie is the Museum of Scottish Tartans, where the history of every tartan, clan and surname can be traced.

Drummond Castle, south of Crieff, dates from the 15th century although Cromwell attacked and destroyed most of this structure in 1745. The old tower remains and now houses an interesting collection of armour. A well tended formal Italian garden is set in the grounds with a multiple sundial dating from 1630.

THE FINEST SALMON WATERS IN THE WORLD

Take the A851/A827 by the Falls of Dochart at Killin, beyond the region's highest mountain Ben Lawers (3984 feet) - with views to both the North Sea and the Atlantic - along the banks of Loch Tay, 14 miles long and reputedly the **Finest Salmon Waters in the World**.

THE HIGHLANDS AND ISLANDS

From the Firth of Tay east of Perth the River Tay can be traced to Scone, Regorton and Almondmouth, to Stanley with its craggy glen; by the River Isla; to Dunkeld where sea trout have improved in recent years. Here in the 9th century the Scots and the Picts came together in what was then the religious centre of Scotland at the Cathedral of Columba. Part of Shakespeare's Macbeth is set in Birnham Woods to the south of the town. The River Lyon enters the Tay downstream from Kenmore where the autumn scenery is spectacular in this stretch to Aberfeldy.

Castle Menzies, west of Aberfeldy, has recently been restored by the Menzies Clan Society, and houses the Clans Museum. The turrets and finely detailed dormers were added in 1577 to this magnificent early 16th century fortress after the original castle was burnt to the ground by the Wolf of Badenoch.

From Ben Lui the clear streams collect at Fillan Water, near Crianlarich, then to Loch Dochart with its ruined castle, to Glen Dochart and its river where the Lochay joins at Killin, at the west end of Loch Tay. From its source in these high, deserted mountains of Perthshire to the Firth these majestic waters travel over 100 miles to provide spectacular - and frustrating - fishing.

Blair Castle off the A935 miles north of Perth, was built in the 13th century and since the mid-19th century has been home to the Earls and Dukes of Atholl (featured later). South of Blair Castle, through the Pass of Killiecrankie, where in 1689 the Jacobites defeated the Government's army, there are some fine walks through woodlands following the Tunnell Nature Trail. Here the Pitlochry Power Station and Dam, part of the hydro electric system, allows visitors to view salmon through windows in the fish ladder.

The A924 to the Bridge of Cally - where skiers for Glenshee travel north - and on to Couper Angus, where the A94 takes the visitor to **Glamis Castle** west of Forfar. Glamis Castle has been the home of the Lyons family since the 14th century, Princess Margaret was born here in 1930 (featured later).

Further east beyond Brechin to the north is **Edzell Castle and Garden**, off the B966, an early 16th century tower house and late 16th century castle, with an unusual walled garden, in the Renaissance style, designed in 1604 by Sir David Lindsay. The recesses in the walls are filled with flowers and highlight the sculptures of various coats of arms.

Scone Palace was built in 1803 on the site of an ancient church dating back to the 6th century and earliest days of Scottish history (featured later). The Fair City of Perth, with its Georgian houses on both banks of the Tay and colourful past, was once Scotland's capital. The famous Black Watch has its museum containing regimental honours in Balhousie Castle and the tiny Branklyn Gardens, at less than two acres, has been described as the finest private garden in the country.

GRAMPIAN AND THE HIGHLANDS

The Grampian Region in the north east of the country stretches from a point east of Nairn on the Moray coast, with its sandy beaches and picturesque fishing villages; around the shoulder of Scotland, where the Moray Firth meets the North Sea, with its breathtaking views out over rugged cliffs, natural wildlife, and historic castles; beyond Aberdeen to Deeside, where the

Dee provides some of the best salmon fishing in the country. Inland, there is good farmland, spectacular views to the Cairngorm Mountains, the River Spey, the ruins of Elgin Cathedral and, believe it or not, a Scotch Whisky Trail. The City of Aberdeen, Scotland's third largest, is an important staging post for the worlds' oil companies and their offshore operations in the North Sea - but there is much more to this granite city and its 'northern lights'. William the Lion granted Aberdeen the royal charters in the 12th century and it has been an important sea port ever since, first trading tea with China, then in the 19th century, trawling fish. The 18th century chapel, at the Kings College University buildings built in 1494, is a particularly important example of a medieval college church. The Art Gallery and Maritime Museum contain some interesting paintings and models depicting the city's traditions with the sea - as does the early morning daily auction at the local fishmarket.

THE MALT WHISKY TRAIL

Take the A947 north from Aberdeen by the Dyce airport to **Fyvie Castle**, some 25 miles away, a fine example of Scottish baronial architecture dating from the 13th century. Each of the five towers is named after one of the five families who have owned the Castle through the centuries. Recently refurbished to the Edwardian style, created by the first Lord Leith of Fyvie, the great wheel stair, panelling and plaster ceiling in the 17th century Morning Room are of particular interest. Fine portraits by Raeburn, Romney, Gainsborough and others hang in the principle rooms. There are interesting walks through the landscaped woodlands around Loch Fyvie. Fyvie Castle is part of Scotland's only Castle Trail, which includes eight other interesting castles in the Grampian Region, but for those more inclined to have 'a wee dram', rejoin the A96 and A941 to Dufftown. Here in beautiful Speyside are eight distilleries where the visitor can learn more of the skills and mysteries behind the making of malt whisky. Smoking peat fires dry locally harvested barley, water is added then distilled in copper stills and left to mature in oak casks - simple isn't it! The Malt Whisky Trail allows visits to the distilleries making Glenfiddich (Dufftown), Strathisia (Keith), Glenfarcas, Cragganmore, the Glenlivet and Tamnavulin (Tomintoul). From here head south through the Lecht Ski Area to Balmoral and Braemar.

Balmoral Castle has been used as a summer holiday residence of the Royal Family since purchased by Prince Albert in 1852, and is the private residence of the Queen. Queen Victoria's consort had much of the castle rebuilt in a Scottish baronial style in white granite with its 100 foot tower, turrets and battlements. When the Royals are not in residence visitors can walk through the Garden, designed by Prince Albert, with its rare conifers and trees. Also on view is Queen Mary's sunken garden and Queen Victoria's garden cottage. Close by is Crathie Church, where the Royals worship when in residence.

Braemar Castle, an impressive fortress built in 1628 by the Earl of Mar as a bulwark against the rising power of the Farquharsons, was destroyed in 1689 by the Black Colonel, John Farquharson of Inverey. The castle remained an uninhabited ruin for 60 years until after the defeat of Bonnie Prince Charlie at Culloden in 1746, when the English troops, with the help of John Adam, made good the earlier damage and used the castle as a garrison. Later, the Farquharsons of Inverey purchased and restored the castle and it is still used to this day as their private home. The iron 'yett', newel staircase and the Lairds

Pit - an underground dungeon - together with the daunting fortification and central round tower allow the visitor to imagine the past mystery and intrigue of the castle. The famous Braemar Highland Gathering is held annually at the nearby village where, at a cottage in Castleton Terrace, Robert Louis Stevenson wrote 'Treasure Island'.

Take the A93 back towards Aberdeen via **Crathes Castle,** near Banchory. Crathes Castle was built in the later half of the 16th century in Scottish baronial style, although it was extended during Queen Anne's reign. A spiral staircase leads the visitor from the impressive entrance door to the main floor, well above ground level. From here, the ornate Elizabethan fireplace in the Great Hall the beautiful painted ceilings in the Chamber of Nine Nobles and the Long Gallery should not be missed. However, those of a nervous disposition may wish to avoid the Green Lady's Room with its biblical inscriptions on the crossbeams - it is said to be haunted!

The spectacular lime avenues and thick yew hedging were planted in the early 18th century and each section of the garden has a particular colour theme - purple foliage with red and yellow flowers in the Pool Garden.

THE CAIRNGORM MOUNTAINS

The Cairngorm Mountains lie to the east of the Grampians and straddle the boundary with the Highland Region. Here in this rugged but beautiful part of the country are some of Britain's highest mountains with Ben Macdui 4296 feet and Cairn Gorm 4084 feet. There are numerous fascinating walks and climbs for the visitor of every ability, although, as always on mountains care should be taken, as the weather can change quite suddenly. In the Cairngorms National Nature Reserve, the country's largest eagles and stags can be seen in their natural habitat, whilst to the north at the Glen More Forest Park, now owned by the Forestry Commission, the visitor should be on the lookout for eagles and ospreys, and reindeer brought from Scandinavia 30 years ago. Travelling south from Scotland's premier ski resort of Aviemore -the skiing actually takes place on the northern slopes of Cairn Gorm - is the Highland Wildlife Park in the Spey valley where wild horses and goats, red deer, bison, grouse and many other animals can be seen. Nearby at Loch Insh, eagles, ospreys and other rare birds are protected by the RSPB ownership.

Heading north on the A9 towards Inverness, there stands the ruins of a medieval castle on Loch Moy. Taking the B851/B9006 to Newlands, the exposed moorland is the place where the last battle on mainland Britain, in 1746, was fought at **Culloden** between Bonnie Prince Charlie and the Duke of Cumberland. The Scots were outnumbered two to one and suffered appalling casualties and 1200 deaths both during and after the surrender, earning the Duke his nickname 'Butcher' Cumberland. Old Leanach Cottage, at the centre of the battlefield , now houses a museum run by the National Trust for Scotland. In 1881 a cairn to the dead was erected by the side of the road and across the road are scattered stones marking the names of the clans involved in the fighting. The Cumberland Stone in the adjacent Field of the English, where only 76 of the Dukes troops perished, is said to mark the spot from where the Duke orchestrated the slaughter. The circular burial chambers and upright stones of the Clava Cairns are about 3500 years old and are an important prehistoric monument to Scotland's past.

After Culloden, **Fort George** was built to ensure that there was never another Highland uprising.

Continue on the B9006/B9090 to Cawdor to find **Cawdor Castle** made famous by Shakespeare with its Macbeth overtures (featured later). In Inverness, only Cromwell's Clock Tower remains of the large monument built by his army, the remainder was destroyed when Charles II regained the throne. Standing on the banks of the River Ness, the town has been the capital of the highland region for many a day, its Castle dating back to the 12th century. In front of the present Castle, built in 1834, is a statue of Flora Macdonald, who assisted Bonnie Prince Charlie to escape from Cromwell's army.

THE GREAT GLEN

Running from Inverness to Fort William is Glen Albyn or Glen Mor, a natural fault often referred to as **The Great Glen**. The engineer Thomas Telford constructed the Caledonian Canal in the 19th century to link the North Sea and the Moray Firth with the Atlantic Ocean and Loch Linnhe by a series of locks and gates. Take the scenic B862 south to Fort Augustus and look across to **Castle Urquart** standing on the bank of Loch Ness overlooking Urquart Bay. Although a ruin today, the visitor is able to imagine the mystery and romance of this beautiful location. Keep an eye out for 'Nessy' the Loch Ness Monster as you travel the 24 mile length of the loch and if unsuccessful take a trip to the Drumnadrochit Monster Centre - unfortunately on the other side of the loch! Fort William stands in the shadow of Britain's tallest mountain, Ben Nevis - although not visible from the town, some 4406 feet above sea level, where on good days the visitor can walk the well worn paths to the summit. The West Highland Museum contains many items belonging to Bonnie Prince Charlie and Flora Macdonald and is an interesting visit for those now coming to terms with this period of Scotland's history.

The A82 south to Ballachulish takes the visitor to **Glencoe** country, a spectacular skiing, walking and climbing destination for people from all over the world. With the bleak Rannoch Moor to the south and isolated Rannoch railway station accessible only from the east by road, the area gives a fabulous insight into the past. It was here in the winter of 1692 that the tragic massacre of Glencoe took place, when the visiting Campbells turned on their hosts, the Macdonalds, to murder men, women and children -many of those who fled died in the cold February weather. On the old road, near the Clachaig Inn, stands a memorial to the Macdonalds and the Signal Rock where, it is said, the word was given by King William III to the Campbells to proceed with the massacre - the Clachaig is to be recommended for the thirsty traveller!

THE NORTH

If the first stop for visitors travelling from Inverness is to be the spectacular Rogie Waterfalls, near Contin, by the Victorian Spa town of Strathpeffer, then the Black Isle has been bypassed. This quiet peninsula, with its attractive villages and gently sloping hills is worth discovering, as is the 18th century geologist Hugh Millers cottage in Cromarty. Macbeth is said to have been born in the country town of Dingwall on the Cromarty Firth, where a journey along the A862 reveals an extraordinary scene of huge oil rigs moored in the Firth for repairs against the rolling hills behind. Beyond the Clan Ross Museum in Tain and

THE HIGHLANDS AND ISLANDS

the Cathedral in Dornoch is **Dunrobin Castle,** by Golspie. The seat of the Countess of Sutherland, one of the seven ancient Earldoms of Scotland, it was built around the early 1300s, overlooking the Moray Firth, but with various extensions in 1650, 1780 and 1845, the latter by Barry, who designed the Houses of Parliament. The house has been continuously inhabited since then. In 1915 Sir Robert Lorimer redesigned the main Barry rooms which were destroyed by fire. The contents of the Castle have been collected by the owners over six centuries and provide an important insight into the life of the Dukes of Sutherland. The magnificent display of furniture, pictures, china and ceremonial costumes can be seen by visitors in the Library, Drawing Room, Queen Victoria's Room, where she slept during her stay in 1872, and other State Rooms. The original Summer House was converted and extended to a Museum which now houses hunting trophies and other mementoes of the Sutherland family and their friends. Charles Barry also designed the splendid Gardens in 1848, with terraces and fountains modelled on his love of Versailles.

This is the wilderness of North Britain with fresh, clean air, rugged cliffs and beautiful beaches, crystal clear sea, lochs and streams making up perhaps the most dramatic scenery in the country between John O'Groats and Cape Wrath.

The picturesque town of Ullapool allows for cruising to the Summer Isles, whilst there are unbelievable views form Corrieshalloch Gorge on the A832.

Inverewe Gardens, north of Poolewe by Gairloch, were created in 1865 by Osgood Mackenzie who began to plant a garden in the grounds of his house overlooking Loch Ewe. However, before a proper start could be made he had to establish the right conditions by importing soil and by planting tree breaks to provide shelter from the salt winds from the Atlantic. The warm air of the Gulf Stream allowed rare and precious exotic plants from all over the world to flourish. Of particular interest to the many visitors nowadays are the giant ferns and eucalyptus, the quaint forget-me-nots and colourful rhododendrons.

The lush green hills, rugged coastline, deserted beaches and single track roads with passing places make this part of the country a delight for the visitor. The castle ruins at Strome and the scenic harbour at Plockton, with its warm Gulf breezes and palm trees are magnificent. Set by lochs Duich, Long and Alsh is **Eilean Donan Castle**. The causeway approach to the islet where Eilean Donan Castle stands is somewhat overshadowed today by the construction of a second bridge across Loch Long. Built in 1220 by Alexander II of Scotland to prevent attacks by invading Danes, it was captured by Spanish Jacobites from Clan MacKenzie in 1719 and subsequently shelled by the English battleship Worcester. It has recently been rebuilt after 200 years of neglect and contains many interesting treasures.

THE ISLANDS

The Isle of Skye can be reached by ferry from the Kyle of Lochalsh and Mallaig. With over 900 miles of craggy coastline, the spectacular Cullin Hills rising to a ridge over 3000 feet high and picturesque villages such as Portree, the visitor, like Bonnie Prince Charlie who fled to this place, will not be disappointed.

Dunvegan Castle, set in a magnificent location on the Isle of Skye has been the home of the Clan Macleod chiefs since 1200;

the present owner is the 29th Macleod to inhabit the castle in almost 800 years. This long association with one family is the stuff of legends and mystery, none more so than the 'Fairy Flag of Dunvegan' said to protect both the Clan and the Chief. It still hangs in the 18th century Drawing Room which once was the Great Hall of the Keep. Before its major restoration in the 19th century, a 15th century dungeon and 16th century tower were added - presumably a sign of the times.

The warm sea breezes so common to this area, have allowed a splendid collection of azaleas and rhododendrons to establish themselves, which provide a perfect adjunct to the two magnificent natural waterfalls. Take a boat trip from the castle jetty to the nearby seal colony, where seals breed in their natural habitat. Otters can be seen at Kylerhea and numerous species of birds from sea eagles and peregrine falcons to mallards and eider ducks are to be found by the avid birdwatcher.

The Western Isles or **Outer Hebrides**, made up of five main islands of Lewis and Harris, North Uist, Benbeala, South Uist and Barra, are unbelievably beautiful and peaceful. Separated from the mainland by up to a six hour ferry trip, their Gaelic character and culture has been preserved to provide the visitor with unspoilt sandy beaches on the west and craggy cliffs and inlets on the east. The standing stones at Callanish, Lewis, west of the main town of Stornoway and nearby Giarynahime, are said to date from 2000 BC and are to this day surrounded with mystery and legend.

St Kilda, being 60 miles west of Harris is a National Nature Reserve with puffins, fulmars and gannets inhabiting this remote, picturesque outcrop in the Atlantic.

The enormous natural harbour of Scapa Flow protected by the mainland, Hoy and South Ronaldsay, in the **Orkney Islands** provided the Royal Navy with natural shelter in both world wars. Only a few miles north of the mainland, the numerous islands are linked by car and passenger ferries. Here visitors are impressed by the solitude and scenic beauty and over one million seabirds in nine RSPB reserves. The prehistoric village of Skara Brae, the Stones of Stenness and the burial ground at Maes Howe, dating from around 2000 BC are some of the most historically important sites in Europe. At one time ruled by the King of Norway's representative, it has since the 15th century been part of Scotland.

Lying almost as close to Norway as to Scotland, the Shetland Islands are made up of over 100 separate islands. The Viking heritage has been retained in language and culture, and can be studied at the **Shetland Museum** in Lerwick. The giant Sullom Voe oil terminal has been constructed in the last 20 years to take advantage of the Island's proximity to the North Sea oil industry. Here, like Orkney, there are numerous nature reserves for thousands of birds around cliff tops and solitary islands, sea trout in clear lochs and seals and otters along the magnificent coastline.

The Highlands and Islands of Scotland are probably the least populated areas in Britain offering the visitor peace and tranquility with beautiful scenery, breathtaking views and interesting treasures into the areas heritage.

GLAMIS CASTLE

Glamis Castle, framed by the majestic Grampian Mountains, is one of the most beautiful and historic of Scotland's great castles. It is the family home of the Earls of Strathmore and Kinghorne and has been a royal residence since 1372. It is also the childhood home of Her Majesty Queen Elizabeth The Queen Mother, the birthplace of Her Royal Highness The Princess Margaret and the legendary setting of Shakespeare's Macbeth.

The thaneage of Glamis was granted to Sir John Lyon in 1372 by King Robert II of Scotland. Four years later Sir John married the King's daughter and founded a line of feudal barons, and later earls, which still flourishes and dwells at Glamis. The King made his son-in-law Chamberlain of Scotland and Sir John began to construct a new house befitting a great officer of state and a royal princess. Much of what he built is incorporated in the present castle, a five-storey 'L' shaped tower block of sandstone not dissimilar in colour to the heather-covered mountains beyond. Sir John's castle was a simple tall, narrow building, with an entrance hall on the first floor reached by outer stairs with the Great Hall above it and bedchambers above that. Although never intended as a fortress, it would have been fairly impregnable to attack.

Patrick Lyon was created Earl of Kinghorne in 1606 and in 1677 the 3rd Earl added Strathmore to the title, and continued the extension and improvement of the castle begun by his grandfather. This was an amazing achievement by the young Earl since, when he came into his inheritance, he found debts totalling £400,000 - a monumental sum in those days. It took 40 years of determination and strict economies, but he restored the estate to solvency.

He added two wings to the castle, remodelled the Great Hall and decorated the chapel. During this period the castle assumed its present fairy-castle appearance with turrets, towers and spires everywhere, causing Daniel Defoe to liken it to a city.

The Crypt and the eerie Duncan's Hall are little changed since medieval times. The Crypt contains numerous big game heads and arms and armour, some of which dates from the 15th century. A secret chamber is thought to be located within the massive thickness of the walls. Here, it is said, one Lord of Glamis and the Earl of Crawford played cards with the Devil on the Sabbath. So great were the resulting disturbances that the room was permanently sealed. Duncan's Hall is by tradition where Macbeth murdered his cousin King Duncan.

The Chapel was richly decorated by the 3rd Earl who commissioned Jacob de Wet to paint the beautiful panels on the walls and ceiling, making this one of the finest small chapels in Europe.

The Great Hall was transformed into an elegant Drawing Room. The bare stone walls were plastered, the ceiling was stuccoed in the Italian manner and a frieze was added. The soft pink wash on the walls makes a perfect background for the many family portraits, notably the enormous painting of the 3rd Earl and his sons, who looks down on his favourite room in the castle.

King Malcolm's Room is not the actual room where the King died in 1034, but is close to where it was in the original hunting lodge. The glory of this room is its plasterwork ceiling, and the arms of the 2nd Earl picked out in full heraldic colours.

Following Lady Elizabeth Bowes Lyon's marriage into the Royal Family in 1923, her mother, the Countess of Strathmore, arranged the Royal Apartments for the couple whenever they visited Glamis. The suite of three rooms is comfortable rather than grand and filled with family portraits, photographs and personal mementoes. The bedhangings in the Queen Mother's Bedroom bear the embroidered names of the children of the 14th Earl and Countess including 'Elizabeth 1900'. Also in this room is a copy of the lovely portrait by de Laszlo of the Queen Mother when she was Duchess of York.

A grand tree-lined drive leads down through the lush Angus landscape to the castle and its gardens. The Dutch garden was laid out in the 1890s in the form of low box hedges containing a profusion of roses. The Queen Mother's parents adapted part of the shrubberies to form the Italian Garden, two acres enclosed within high yew hedges, with herbaceous borders, a fountain and two attractive 17th century style gazebos.

A 21 foot high 17th century sundial dominates one of the castle lawns. Placed three degrees west of the Greenwich Meridian by the 3rd Earl, it was extremely accurate. There are lovely woodland walks among the massive Douglas firs where the peace of Glamis can be enjoyed to the full. A licensed Restaurant provides light lunches and teas, there are Gift Shops and a Picnic Area and the picturesque village of Glamis lies 5 miles west of Forfar on the A94. Glamis Castle is available for a variety of social and sporting functions from cocktail parties and champagne receptions to archery and clay pigeon shooting. The magnificent setting, excellent food and wines and resident piper make dinner parties at Glamis very special.

SCONE PALACE

Scone is at the very centre of Scotland, both geographically and historically. It is the ancient crowning place of Scottish kings, including the legendary Macbeth and Robert the Bruce, and one time home of the Stone of Scone. The chroniclers tell us of Druids, of fantastic glimpses of kings and king-making and of the high kings of the Picts in the 'Kingdom of Scone'. In 1296 the Stone was removed by King Edward I and placed beneath the Coronation Chair in Westminster Abbey, upon which Queen Elizabeth II was crowned in 1953.

Without the Stone the Royal City of Scone began to lose prestige and in 1559 the Abbey of Scone was destroyed and what remained of the Palace was given to the Gowrie family. Their part in the 'Gowrie Conspiracy', when the life of King James VI was threatened but saved by Sir David Murray, led to their downfall. Thus, in 1604, Sir David was rewarded with the Palace and lands of Scone. He was also created Lord Scone and later Viscount Stormont. In 1776 William Murray, son of the 5th Viscount was created Earl of Mansfield, whose descendants continue to live at Scone.

The Palace, as we see it today, was adapted and enlarged for the 3rd Earl by the architect William Atkinson in 1802. The restrained Gothic style is well suited to the monastic history of Scone. Throughout the house there are fine collections of furniture and works of art, porcelain and needlework.

The beautiful Drawing Room, whose walls are hung with Lyons silk, contains some excellent pieces of French boulle furniture, together with an important set of French armchairs covered in superb needlework. An exquisite little writing table was made for Marie Antoinette and bears her cypher. A portrait of the 1st Earl of Mansfield by Reynolds shows him in the robes and wig of Lord Chief Justice of England - a position he held for over 32 years. He was instrumental in the beginning of the Abolition of Slavery and respected as the greatest lawyer of all time.

In the Dining Room the fabulous Ivories, collected mostly by the 4th Earl, are displayed. Carved in elephant and walrus tusk, they came from Bavaria, Flanders, Italy and France.

The enchantingly pretty Ante-Room, painted in white, gold and silver is the perfect setting for a set of Chinese Chippendale chairs and a portrait of Sir David Murray, first Lord Scone.

The Library bookcases have been taken over by the exceptional collection of fine and rare Meissen, Sevres, Ludwigsburg, Chelsea, Derby and Worcester porcelain. From the windows may be seen the mighty oak planted by James VI before 1603 and, across the silver ribbon of the Tay, the distant mountains around Ben Vorlich.

The Long Gallery, hung with many family portraits is of an unusual length for a Scottish home. Its magnificent floor is of Scottish oak inset with bog oak and has been trodden by many kingly feet. Here the comprehensive and unique collection of Vernis Martin is displayed.

The Duke of Lennox's Room contains very fine examples of needlework including a magnificent set of bed hangings worked by Mary Queen of Scots, mother of King James VI, and her ladies.

The beautiful grounds at Scone Palace are peaceful and informal. The Pinetum was first planted in 1848 with exotic coniferous trees, including a vast and very special fir. This was raised from seed sent to Scone by David Douglas in 1826. Douglas was born at Scone in 1798 and worked as an under-gardener until he joined the Botanical Gardens in Glasgow. During a trip to America he discovered the 'Douglas Fir' for which he is now famous.

Scone Palace, just outside Perth on the A93 Braemar road, provides a grand and historic setting for business and private functions, including Scone Palace Grand Dinners when Roast Palace Peacock may appear on the menu.

BLAIR CASTLE

The ancient fortress home of the Earls and Dukes of Atholl, situated in the wide Strath of Garry, commands a strategic position on the main route through the central Highlands, in a wild and rugged setting of wooded mountains and picturesque rivers. About a mile to the east the Tilt joins the Garry on its course to the Pass of Killiecrankie three miles away. The Banvie burn, which runs in front of the castle, tumbles through its narrow glen among giant larches, Scots firs, beeches and rhododendrons.

During its almost 700 years of history the castle has seen splendid royal visits, occupation by enemy forces on four occasions, and has withstood siege and partial destruction.

The main tower, known as Cummings Tower, is part of the original 13th century building, but the main part of the castle owes much of its present appearance to the 2nd Duke who began an ambitious scheme of alterations. He was interrupted by the Jacobite revolt in 1745, but in the more peaceful times that followed he remodelled the castle in the style of a grand Georgian house. There are now thirty two rooms of infinite variety displaying beautiful furniture, fine collections of paintings, arms and armour, china, costumes, lace and embroidery, masonic regalia and a host of other treasures from the 16th century to the present day.

The Picture Staircase, made in 1756, and the Dining Room are notable examples of the extensive work carried out for the 2nd Duke. Both have particularly fine stuccoed ceilings, and the striking overmantel in the Dining Room is in the form of a trophy of arms of all periods - a fitting subject for Blair Castle.

The magnificent Drawing Room, its walls hung with crimson damask, has perhaps the most beautiful ceiling and above the white marble fireplace the charming portrait of the 3rd Duke and Duchess with their seven children by Zoffany. Amongst the wealth of furniture are two gilt settees and twelve chairs, their covers finely worked by Lady Charlotte, the pretty girl holding the wreath in the Zoffany picture. For how many long hours she patiently stitched we do not know, but the castle is filled with the industry of many of the ladies who have lived here.

The Tapestry Room is hung with a fine set of Brussels Tapestries made for Charles I. The magnificent William and Mary bed, with rich silk hangings beneath great sprays of ostrich plumes belonged to the 1st Duke of Atholl.

In the Tullibardine Room a much simpler Tent Bed is covered with tartan over 200 years old, said to come from an earlier circular bed in which slept the seventeen sons of Sir David Murray of Tullibardine. Somewhat ahead of its time, it was presumably this shape to avoid small boys going bump in the night.

The China Room, Costume Room and Treasure Room contain many rare and beautiful things - fortunately generations at Blair did not discard items which became unfashionable.

Blair Castle is approached from the little village of Blair Atholl (off the A9 Perth - Inverness road) along a great avenue of limes which lead up to the castle through thickly wooded parkland. The 4th Duke was especially fond of trees, larch in particular, and planted great forests of them together with a wide variety of other trees, which provide a simple majestic setting for Blair - a setting which is perfect for special lunches, weddings, Highland Balls, equestrian events. The list if endless.

CAWDOR CASTLE

The magical name of Cawdor, romantically linked by Shakespeare with Macbeth, is steeped in the history and legend of the turbulent times of medieval Scotland. Periods of peace came and went, but to a family such as the Thanes of Cawdor, a stout defendable home meant survival itself. Quarrels and feuds were the rule, not the exception, and black and bloody deeds were not uncommon. During one such feud the infant daughter of the 8th Thane was kidnapped by the Earl of Argyll. For future recognition she was branded on the hip by her nurse with a red hot key, and the top joint of her left little finger was bitten off. In 1510, at the age of 12, she was married to the Earl's younger son, Sir John Campbell. The happy conclusion to this violent beginning was a union from which the present Campbells of Cawdor are descended.

The central 14th century tower, approached across a drawbridge, is the oldest part of the castle, which was protected on one side by the Cawdor Burn and on the others by a dry moat. During the 17th century this small defensive fort was transformed into a large family mansion. A massive building programme was carried out without the use of plans or drawings, the Thane of the day supervising the work as it proceeded. Amazingly they all seem to have favoured the same style - mellow sandstone with crow-stepped gables and slated roofs. In the 18th century a separate house was built and incorporated into the main building in the 19th century, again with no loss of harmony.

Whether Macbeth actually lived here or not, once over the drawbridge one can easily imagine that he did. The Tower Room, once the old entrance hall, is built around the ancient trunk of a thorn tree. The legend is that a certain Thane was told in a dream to build his new castle wherever a donkey laden with gold lay down to rest for the night. He would then prosper for evermore. The tree, and therefore the Tower, has been dated by modern scientific methods to 1372.

In the depths of the Tower is a small 'bottle' dungeon probably used to conceal ransomed prisoners - it boasts a privy - or for hiding women and children in times of danger. The only access was through a trap-door from the room above.

Cawdor is not simply a monument to the past, but a splendid house and a lived-in home filled with fine furniture and paintings, ceramics and beautiful tapestries. In the heart of the Tower is the cosy, flower-filled Yellow Sitting Room which is typically Jacobean in character. The Family Bedroom, with its Venetian bed draped in crimson velvet, is hung with Flemish tapestries made in 1682 specially for the room.

The elegant Drawing Room has a fine collection of family portraits including Sir Henry Campbell painted as a young man in the uniform of the Green Jackets. In later life he was advised by his doctor to drink a little brandy for his health, whereupon he told the poor man that every night on top of pints of champagne, claret and port, he was accustomed to drinking at least five large glasses of brandy. He was wise enough to employ a retired prostitute to guide him home in London, and to ward off the Ladies of the Night. Throughout their long history the Cawdor Campbells seem to have done nothing by halves.

There are three gardens to enjoy at Cawdor Castle, all of them beautiful in different ways and in different seasons. Hedges, fruit, flowers, shrubs and herbs framed by aged walls and mighty trees, which have been lovingly tended for thirty decades. And beyond the sweeping lawns and the babbling burn, the majestic Cawdor Wood.

There is a licensed restaurant and gift shop as well as a putting green and mini golf. As Shakespeare said 'This castle hath a pleasant seat; the air nimbly and sweetly recommends itself unto our gentle senses.'

NATIONAL TRUST FOR SCOTLAND

Fyvie Castle

The National Trust for Scotland is an association of more than 200,000 people, all with a common love for Scotland, her heritage and stunning countryside. The Trust was founded in 1931 by a small number of prominent Scots concerned at the seemingly endless destruction of much of the country's priceless heritage of landscape and architecture. Its raison-d'etre is to promote the preservation and upkeep of fine buildings, historic places and beautiful countryside.

The Trust has grown into a trusted and influential body and today cares for more than one hundred properties, covering some 100,000 acres. They include castles, gardens, historic sites, islands, countryside, little houses, coastline, waterfalls and the birthplaces of several famous Scots. The North East of Scotland contains many particularly fine Trust properties. One of the most notable is Castle Fraser, sixteen miles west of Aberdeen. This magnificent castle belongs to the same period of architectural achievement as Crathes Castle and Craigievar Castle. Begun in about 1575 by the sixth Laird, Michael Fraser, Castle Fraser was not completed until 1636. Craigievar Castle offers a similarly spectacular spectacle for visitors, and is often described as having a fairy-tale aura. The castle, completed in 1626 by William Forbes, features magnificent plaster ceilings, turrets, cupolas and corbelling. It has much in common with nearby Crathes Castle whose Royal historic associations date from 1323. Crathes also has some remarkable, late sixteenth century painted ceilings and visitors also benefit from extensive gardens that provide a wealth of colour throughout the summer months. The five towers of Fyvie Castle enshrine five centuries of Scottish history, each being named after one of the five families who owned the castle. The oldest part dates from the thirteenth century and Fyvie is now probably the grandest example of Scottish baronial architecture.

Other particularly notable Trust properties in this part of the world include Drum Castle, with it's great, square tower and unique walled garden of historic roses, Haddo House, Leith Hall, Pitmedden Garden and Provost Ross's House. In actual fact, visitors to all parts of Scotland will almost inevitably come across properties owned by The National Trust for Scotland during their stay, all painstakingly restored and maintained to their former glories. Scotland's heritage is indeed in good hands but the future of both it and the Trust are very much dependent on continuing public support, whether in the form of membership, donation or legacy.

National Trust for Scotland
Grampion Regional Office
Rose Lane, Market Place
Inverurie
Aberdeenshire AB51 9PY
Tel: (0467) 22988
Fax: (0467) 25404

HIGHLANDS

Witches and goblins, whisky and heather, castles and crofts. The Highlands of Scotland are a dramtic backdrop for those seeking some of the most fascinating houses in the whole of Britain's heritage. The wild nature of much of the land has precluded development and that is in essence, the reason for its remoteness, isolation and peace. But the Highlands have not always been peaceful and have lain witness to some of the bloodiest battles and feuds throughout history when the mountains rang to the sound of clashing steel upon steel.

Today, there are more tranquil times to be had and a whole variety of historic houses and castles depict the changing history of the lands as families, clans and chiefs are remembered. The Scottish Highlands also boast a collection of some of the finest country house hotels in Britain. Former baronial castles and family seats have been transformed into luxurious guesthouses and hotels, enabling the travellers to experience Scottish hospitality in style and to enjoy some of the cuisine for which the country is famous.

Inevitably, a stag will peer down thoughtfully from a stone wall and a huge log fire will crackle in the inglenook as you consider times gone by and what it must have been like in those far off days of bloody Chieftans.

The Grampians are home to some magnificent salmon rivers and Speyside is dotted with celebrated distilleries. The banks of the Dee and the Don reveal a number of castles and houses. Balmoral on Deeside is the most famous but the ruin of Kildrummy is also breathtaking. Many of the towns are built in the sombre granite and along the coast, fishing villages peek cheekily from the neighbouring links. Cawdor Castle and Culloden are two of the most famous and haunting spots in Scotland. The former, the castle made famous by Shakespeare and his witches and the latter, a reminder of the bloodiest battle.

The eerily beautiful Glen of Glencoe is another bloody reminder of the passion and pride of the native clans. Still haunting, the land is a haven for wildlife and you may well see a stag or spot an eagle soaring into the skies.

The scenery and the history of the Highlands are varied, but always dramatic, and for the visitor, around every corner another piece of history or a change in landscape will draw you further into its fascinating past.

HOTELS OF DISTINCTION

ALTNAHARRIE HOTEL, Ullapool, Grampian. Tel: (085483) 230
A cocktail of sea breezes precedes dinner at one of the most remote but finest restaurants in Britain. Bedrooms are charming and the location is stunning. The cooking takes centre stage and is unforgettable.

ARDOE HOUSE, Aberdeen, Grampian. Tel: (0224) 867355
There are some magnificent architectural features at this 15th century mansion which is built in the Scottish Baronial style. Bedrooms are also pleasing and the house is a splendid location for visiting Grampian.

ARISAIG HOUSE, Arisaig, Highland. Tel: (06875) 622
Lochs and mountains surround this spectacular house. The gardens in which this stone mansion is situated are also delightful. The restaurant is first class and the attractive bedrooms add further elegance.

BALBIRNIE HOUSE, Markinch, Fife. Tel: (0592) 610066
Meor Keilre Castle and the Scottish Deer Centre, this 18th century former ancestral mansion of the Balfours of Balbirnie commands 416 acres of parkland and is flanked by Balbirnie golf course to which guests have access.

BALFOUR CASTLE, Shapinsay, Orkney Islands. Tel:(089671) 282
Originally built in 1848 the hotel holds sway over extensive wooded grounds and boasts the splendour of panoramic, searing views, with much of the food cultivated in its own gardens, the restaurant is just one part of the castle which benefits from the careful combination of modern amenities with its colourful past.

BALLATHIE HOUSE HOTEL, Kinclaven by Stanley, Perthshire. Tel: (025083) 268

Fronted by a splendid French baronial facade the hotel overlooks its beautiful lawns which slope to the riverside. It is ideally situated for exploring Perth, Blairgowrie, Scone Palace or nearby Edinburgh.

BUNCHREW HOUSE, Inverness, Grampian. Tel: (0463) 234917
A 17th century house which delights in its grounds and heritage. Gardens and woodlands overlook Beauly Firth. Elegance pervades throughout the first class bedrooms and outstanding restaurant. A wonderful place to 'live' Scotland.

CASTLETON HOUSE HOTEL, Glamis by Forfar, Angus. Tel: (030784) 340
Glamis Castle is only 3 miles from this hotel set in 11 acres of gardens and woodland in the heart of the tranquil Angus countryside.

CLIFTON, Nairn, Grampian. Tel: (0667) 53119
The house dates from 1874 and today boasts a splendid interior of antiques and 'Objet d'art'. Open fires and fresh flowers are extremely welcoming as are the bedrooms. The restaurant is also outstanding.

COUL HOUSE HOTEL, Contin, Ross-shire. Tel: (0997) 21487
This traditional Highland hotel offers a number of fascinating breaks which include visits to Loch Ness, Cawdor Castle, Glenfiddich Distillery and Culloden battlefield. Golf and fishing holidays are also available.

CRAIGELLOCHIE HOTEL, Banffshire. Tel: (0340) 881204
At the confluence of the Fiddish and Spey rivers, in a beautiful Moray village, lies this elegant Victorian hotel, complete with blazing log fires and early morning Scottish piper.

CROMLIX HOUSE, Dunblane, Central. Tel: (0786) 822125
A marvellous mix of Victorian and Edwardian architecture reveal one of the most delightful hotels in Scotland it is surrounded

BALFOUR CASTLE

Balfour Castle was built in 1848 and was purchased from the last of the Balfour line in 1961 by the Zawcedzki family - they opened the Castle to a limited number of paying guests some fifteen years ago. Set in an extensive acreage of wooded grounds, and with panoramic views over the sea and neighbouring islands, the Castle remains very much as it was in its Victorian heyday — and contains its original furnishings.

The woods, an unusual feature for Orkney, are a naturalist's paradise, from the bluebells in springtime to the birdlife which abounds. The two acres of walled gardens are still fully and traditionally cultivated, providing fruit and vegetables which are picked daily throughout the year. Milk, butter, cream, cheese, eggs, poultry and pork are all home produced. With the finest of fresh ingredients, the traditional menu is outstanding - complemented by scallops, crab, salmon and game from the Island.

Household arrangements are very informal, and a family atmosphere prevails. Guests' bedrooms are individual in character, with canopy and four poster beds, all with modern en suite bathrooms. A family room is available.

Our guests have full use of the oak panelled library, the drawing room with its relief plaster-gilded ceilngs and adjoining conservatory and snooker room.

The island of Shapinsay is tranquil and beautiful with clean sandy beaches, wild flowers and dramatic coastal walks. Our speciality is wild life excursions in our speed boat to the seabird cliffs, seal colonies and uninhabited islands. Orkney's wild life has to be seen to be believed!

Additionally, Shapinsay is only a 20 minute boat ride from Kirkwall, from where numerous archeological sites can be visited. There is an inter-island ro-ro ferry service.

We offer personal hospitality, and the natural friendship of the Orkney people, something which will stay with you and draw you back again.

Balfour Castle
Shapinsay
Orkney Islands KW17 2DX
Tel: (085671) 282
Fax: (0856) 5039

by a huge estate and the interior is equally impressive. Bedrooms are marvellous and the restaurant is exquisite - a rare treat in every way.

CULLODEN HOUSE HOTEL, Inverness. Tel: (0463) 790461
Historically linked to Bonnie Prince Charlie, this impressive Georgian House commands 40 acres of garden, parkland and tranquil woodland. Cawdor Castle, the Clara Cairns and Culloden Battlefield centre are nearby.

DALMUNZIE HOUSE, Blairgowrie, Perthshire. Tel: (0250) 85224
Standing in its own 6000 acre estate in the Scottish Highlands the hotel can offer turreted bedrooms, antique furnishings and even the highest 9-hole golf course in Britain.

DUNAIN PARK, Inverness. Tel: (0463) 230512
Decorated inside with antique furnishings, oil paintings and relaxing log fire, this elegant, listed Georgian country house rests peacefully in 6 acres of gardens and woodlands.

THE EDDRACHILLES HOTEL, Scourie, Highlands. Tel: (0971) 2080
This listed, 200 year old former manse rests in 320 acres on beautiful Badcall Bay, only minutes away from the haunted Sandwood Bay and the tallest waterfalls in Britain at Eas Coul Alin.

FARLEYER HOUSE, Aberfeldy, Tayside. Tel: (0887) 20332
Formerly the dower house of Castle Menzies this fine hotel is a sylish comfortable dwelling in which to stay. Bedrooms are particularly attractive and the restaurant an ideal place to end a day exploring Tayside.

GLENBORRODALE CASTLE, Glenborrodale, Highland. Tel: (09724) 266
One of the most beautifully located hotels in Britain. This is a supremely luxurious hotel with fine furnishings throughout. Bedrooms are beautifully decorated. Leisure facilities are impressive as is the splendid restaurant.

GLENEAGLES, Auchterarder, Tayside Tel: (07646) 2231
This is an outstanding hotel in every way it has an aura and history that positively excites it visitors. Principally a leisure hotel if offers all manner of sporting facilities. Service is outstanding and a visit is always special.

INVERLOCHY CASTLE, Fort William, Highland. Tel: (0397) 2177
Renowned as one of the most superb hotels in Britain. As the you would expect there are grand interiors, excellent staff and a fine restaurant. Queen Victoria loved the estate and with its situation at the foot of Ben Nevis it is easy to appreciate why.

INVERY HOUSE, Royal Deeside, Kincardineshire. Tel: (03302) 4782
Set in 40 delightful acres this early 19th century mansion house has fishing rights on several beats of the River Dee. The interior boasts fine antique furniture and beautiful fabrics.

KILDRUMMY CASTLE, Kildrummy, Grampian. Tel: (09755) 71345
A castellated country house in superb grounds which overlook the ruins of a 13th century castle. The interior is wonder-

fully fashioned and the bedrooms are well appointed - a superb hotel in which to stay.

KINGSMILL HOTEL, Culcabeck Road, Inverness. Tel: (0463) 237166
Built in 1785 this historic hotel nestles in 3 acres of tranquil gardens adjacent to Inverness golf course. Nearby are the fascinating places of Loch Ness, Culloden and Candor Castle.

KINLOCH HOUSE HOTEL, By Blairgowrie, Perthshire. Tel: (0250) 84237
Inside this beautifully preserved Scottish country home is a stunning galleried hall with an ornate glass ceiling. The rest of the hotel is decorated with many fine paintings and antiques.

KINNAIRD, Dunkeld, Perthshire. Tel: (079682) 440
A spectacular country mansion at the heart of the Kinnaird Estate makes home for a splendid hotel which will not fail to impress. Delightfully refurbished and marvellously stylish. The restaurant is set to become one of the finest in Scotland.

KINTAIL LODGE, Glenshiel, Ross-shire. Tel: (05998) 275
Eileann Donan castle is close to this former Georgian shooting lodge which rests in 3 private acres at the foot of the Five Sisters of Kintail.

KNOCKIE LODGE HOTEL, Whitebridge, Inverness-Shire. Tel: (04563) 276
Close to the famous Loch Ness, where the fishermen may cast for salmon, is this former shooting lodge built in 1789. The interior is distinctly furnished with antique furniture and family paintings.

MANSION HOUSE HOTEL, The Haugh, Moray. Tel: (0343) 548811
Built in the 19th century this impressive baronial mansion overlooks the River Lossie. Nearby in the Moray countryside are many places of interest including the famous whisky trail and the historic town of Elgin.

MELDRUM HOUSE, Old Meldrum, Grampian. Tel: (06512) 2294
A grey stone Scottish hotel provide a thoroughly appealing place in which to stay. The surrounding grounds are also impressive while the fine restaurant completes the picture.

MURRAYSHALL COUNTRY HOUSE HOTEL, Scone, Perthshire. Tel: (0738) 51171
The beautiful restaurant is hung with Dutch paintings to compliment the traditional furnishings of this magnificent country house, set in 300 acres of stunning parkland and wooded hillside.

PARKLODGE HOTEL, 32 Park Terrace, Stirling. Tel: (0786) 74862
Overlooking Stirling Castle and Campside Fen Hills this fine Georgian country house boasts luxurious furnishings and decor that matches the graceful elegance of the traditions it maintains.

PINE TREES HOTEL, Pittlochry, Perthshire. Tel: (0796) 2121
This distinctive Victorian mansion, built in 1892, is set amidst a garden of pine trees in the heart of the Scottish Highlands. The famous Festival theatre and Blair Castle are both nearby.

MURRAYSHALL COUNTRY HOUSE HOTEL

The Murrayshall Country House Hotel and Golf Course is only 4 miles from Perth, set in 300 acres of parkland. Deer stroll the wooded hillside, pheasants and peacocks call from the greens. The natural beauty and splashes of colour in the garden are complemented by the mellow stone of the main house with its crow stepped gables.

The hotel, completely refurbished, is elegantly furnished in a traditional style but with the use of the wonderful fabric designs available today. The bedrooms all have en suite facilities, self dial telephone and colour television.

The aptly named Old Masters Restaurant has walls hung with Dutch Masters and table settings befitting the artistry of master chef, Bruce Sangster. The restaurant has received various culinary accolades and Bruce Sangster held the 'Scottish Chef Of The Year' title for 1989/90. Vegetables and herbs from the hotel's walled garden and an abundance of local produce form the basis of the menus which have a Scottish flavour with a hint of modern French cuisine. A well balanced wine list is complemented by the finest of rare malt whiskies.

The 6420 yard, 18 hole, par 73 course is interspersed with magnificent specimen trees lining the fairways, water hazards and white sanded bunkers to offer a challenge to all golfers. Buggies and sets of clubs are available for hire. Neil Mackintosh, our resident professional, is pleased to give tuition, from half an hour to a week's course. Perth is ideally situated for Scotland's courses. Golfers can relax in the newly refurbished club house which overlooks the course and provides informal dining.

Other sporting activities include tennis, croquet and bowls. However, situated only a few miles from the famous Salmon Waters of the River Tay, even closer to Perth Race Course, Murrayshall is uniquely placed to make it an attractive venue for whatever might bring you to this area of Scotland.

Private dining and conference facilities are available in both the hotel and club house. Conference organisers, requiring the best of service and attention for their senior delegates, will find Murrayshall the ideal conference haven.

Murrayshall is one of three group golf courses, the other two are Westerwood and Fernfell. Westerwood Golf Course was designed by Seve Ballesteros and Dave Thomas and is located at Cumbernauld, near Glasgow. The 47 bedroomed Hotel and Country Club opened in April 1991. Fernfell Golf and Country Club is located just out of Cranleigh, 8 miles from Guildford in Surrey. Corporate golf packages are offered at all three courses with the opportunity to place your company name and logo on a tee and to reserve the course for your company golf day. Golf Societies and Green Fee Payers are welcome.

Murrayshall Country House Hotel and Golf Course
Scone
Perthshire PH2 7PH
Tel: (0738) 51171
Fax: (0738) 52595

HIGHLANDS

PITTODRIE HOUSE, Pitcaple, Aberdeenshire
Tel:(04676) 444
Dating back to 1490, and owned by the present family since 1896, the hotel basks in the grandeur of its original country house atmosphere tastefully blended with extensive modernisations to provide the highest standards of comfort. Complete with an excellent restaurant and extremely well stocked bar.

RAEMOIR HOUSE HOTEL, Banchory, Grampian.
Tel: (03302) 4884/4923
Set on a 3500 acre estate this 18th century mansion house lies sheltered by the historic Hill of Fare. The famous Ha' House, dating back to the 16th century is now part of the hotel. Balmoral castle is nearby.

TULCHAN LODGE, Advie, Highland. Tel: (08075) 200
A sporting lodge which has been beautifully converted into a country house hotel. The drawing room and dining room are wonderfully relaxing and the bedrooms are superb - one offers a friendly ghost as an option.

TULLICH LODGE, By Ballater, Grampian. Tel: (03397) 55406
Offering the complete experience of country house living, this hotel, the former residence of a Victorian gentleman, is ideally placed for exploring the surrounding castle ruins and the Straths of Dee and Dod.

ACCOMMODATION OF MERIT

AUCHNAHYLE, Pitlochry, Perthshire. Tel: (0796) 2318
Situated outside Pitlochry and its Festival Theatre this lovely 18th century farmhouse is secluded in acres of farmland. Blair Castle and other major places are within easy reach of the friendly house.

BHEINNE MHOR, Birnam, Dunkeld. Tel: (03502) 779 from spring 1992 (0350) 727779
This charming, Victorian turreted house offers four comfortable guestrooms with modern amenities. Features include an attractive guest TV lounge and good home-cooking, together with a splendid setting in the heart of Perthshire.

BLERVIE, Forres, Morayshire. Tel: (0309) 72358
A charming 18th century stone house standing in pretty gardens surrounded by fields. Museums, castles, distilleries, Culloden and the West Coast are all easily accessible from here. Local produce and game (in season) are featured at dinner.

CONTIN HOUSE, Contin, Ross-shire. Tel: (0997) 21920
Dating from 1794, this attractive family home on the Blackwater is only twenty minutes from Inverness. Picturesque fishing villages, golf courses, Inverewe gardens and the Distillery Trail are all nearby. Even game fishing and shooting can be arranged. (See photograph).

CUILL BARROCH, Lochailort, Invernesshire.
Tel: (06877) 232
Oaktrees and rhododendrons create a fine setting for this attractive imposing stone mansion. Large windows look out over the sea loch from where Bonnie Prince Charlie sailed. The islands with all their rugged beauty are easily reached.

CUNNOQUHIE, Letham, Fife. Tel: (033781) 237
Large country manor house, with beautiful walled garden, commanding spectacular views, to the south. The Georgian/Victorian setting is the perfect atmosphere to retire to after visiting the nearby historical places or St Andrews for golf.

EDEN HOUSE, Banff, Aberdeen. Tel: (02616) 282
High in a Devonshire valley, secluded in acres of wood and parkland, this beautiful listed house provides delightful food and accomodation convenient for golfers and those following the Whisky Trail or visiting various Scottish castles.

GLENGARRY CASTLE HOTEL, Invergarry, Invernessshire. Tel: (08093) 254
A range of comfortable accommodation is available at this highly recommended hotel. All rooms are furnished to a high standard and offer relaxing comfort after a day's energetic tennis or fishing.

KLIBRECK GUESTHOUSE, Aberdeen, Grampian. Tel: (0224) 316115
Situated in a quiet, residential area in the west end of the city, Klibreck offers comfort and service and is within easy reach of many places of interest such as Drum Castle, Crathes Castle, Fyvie Castle, Fraser Castle and Craiievar Castle.

POLMAILY HOUSE HOTEL, Drumnadrochit, Invernessshire. Tel: (04562) 343
Polmaily House is a small, comfortable Country House Hotel situated on the slopes of Glen Urquhart. Great golf can be played at Dornoch and Nairn, fishing is available locally while Cawdor and Brodie are nearby stately homes.

SKIPNESS CASTLE, Tarbert, Argyllshire. Tel: (08806) 207
Built on the foundations of its Victorian predecessor, which burned down in 1969, this very attractive house has spectacular sea views. Set beside an imposing Norman Keep from Robert the Bruce's era, it is very convenient for visiting the Isles.

BROUGH HOUSE, Milton Brodie, Morayshire. Tel: (034385) 617
A charming family house, only eight miles from the market town of Elgin, set in beautiful gardens and countryside yet only a mile from the coast. Perfect for visiting Cawdor and Brodie Castles, Fort George or the Whisky Trail.

TIGH-NA-CLOICH HOTEL, Pitlochry. Tel: (0796) 2216
Hospitality, comfort, good food and beautiful views typify this small, highly-recommended Highland hotel. Bedrooms are thoughtfully and pleasantly furnished while the traditional Scottish dishes are prepared using the best local produce.

INNS OF CHARACTER

ACHNASHEEN HOTEL, Achnasheen, Highland.
Set in a wonderfully desolate location, a bleak and windswept valley surrounded by heather and rough pasture, this hotel stands almost alone, except for the company of one or two small houses.

PITTODRIE HOUSE

Pittodrie House dates back to 1490 when it was originally owned by the Erskine Family. The house and estate was originally bought by the Grandfather of the present owner in 1895 and was converted by his Grandson Theo Smith to a Hotel in 1977.

The house was extensively modernised internally to bring it up to a high standard of comfort. A lot of time has been spent trying to retain the atmosphere of a Country House. All the rooms abound in antiques, paintings and family portraits.

A five course dinner is served nightly in the restaurants with the emphasis on fresh local produce. The menu changes daily. We have an impressive wine list with over 200 wines from 19 different countries. The bar is also well stocked with over 80 different malt whiskies and over 50 liqueurs.

We offer people at Pittodrie a chance to relax in comfortable surroundings. It is possible to take leisurely strolls in the 5 acre walled garden or a more energetic walk up Bennachie - the hill behind the house. There are also 2 squash courts, tennis court, snooker table, croquet, table tennis and clay-pigeon shooting.

The Pittodrie House Hotel
Pitcaple
Aberdeenshire
AB5 9HS
Tel: (04676) 444
Fax: (04676) 648

HIGHLANDS

ARDVASAR HOTEL, Ardvasar, Isle of Skye.
The area around here can offer some of the most spectacular sunsets in Scotland. A beautiful place to rest while exploring the Sleat peninsula.

CROWN AND ANCHOR, Findhorn, Grampian.
Originally an 18th century coaching inn, this friendly pub still serves the jetty where sailing ships used to take Highland customers down to Edinburgh.

HOTEL EILEAN IARMAIN, Isle Ornsay, Isle of Skye.
A fascinating pub where it seems most of the customers converse in Gaelic with the staff; even the menu is in two languages. Beautiful wall panelling and brass fittings.

PLOCKTON HOTEL, Plockton, Highland.
The whole of this beautiful village is owned by the National Trust for Scotland. Interesting partly panelled and partly bare stone lounge bar. Good view over Loch Carron.

PRINCE OF WALES, Aberdeen, Grampian.
Boasting the longest bar in the city, this pub has a cosy back lounge area complete with log fire, wooden pews and furniture, all reached by a tiny, twisting cobbled alley.

SKEABOST HOUSE HOTEL, Skeabost, Isle of Skye. Tel: (047 852) 333
This hotel owns fishing rights to Loch Snizort, considered by many to be the best salmon river Skye can offer. The grounds here include a beautiful water garden, putting green and 9-hole golf course.

STEIN INN, Stein, Isle of Skye.
This charming little inn was opened in 1787 as part of 'British Fisheries' plan to turn the area into a fishing centre. Unfortunately the herring shoals moved away soon afterwards. A copy of the original village plan hangs on the walls.

Contin House

Blarney House

Kylemore Abbey

Malahide Castle

Bushmills
Portrush
Coleraine
Rathmullan
Londonderry
Glenveagh Castle Gardens
Larne
Carrickfergus
Dunadry **Newtownards**
Belfast
Mount Stewart
Donegal **Omagh**
Rossnowlagh
Ballyshannon
Castle Ward
Armagh
Enniskillen **Castle Coole**
Annalong
Lissadell House **Newry**
Rosses Point **Florence Court**
Sligo
Riverstown
Ballina **Dundalk**
Crossmolina **Charlestown** **Carrichmacross**
Newport
Roscommon
Malahide Castle
Skerries
Cong **Mullingar** **Dublin**
Kylemore Abbey **Beech Park**
Letterfrack **Powerscourt Gardens**
Ballynahinch
Cashel **Japanese Gardens** **Killruddery House**
Moycullen **Mount Usher Gardens** **Rathnew**
Dunguaire **Birr Castle** **Emo Court & Gardens** **Wicklow**
Castledermot
Carlow
Knappogue Castle **Altamount Gardens** **Booris**
Newmarket on Fergus
Bunratty Castle
Limerick
Adare
Glin Castle **Clonmel** **Rosslare**
Castle Matrix **Mount Congreve** **Waterford**
Kilcoran
Tralee **Anne's Grove Gardens** **Lismore Castle**
Midleton
Killarney **Blarney Castle** **Cork**
Parknasilla **Blarney House**
Waterville **Kenmare** **Inishannon**
Bantry
Creagh Gardens
Dunmanus Bay **Durrus**

Northern Ireland and Eire

IRELAND

Ireland has a character which is quite different from that of the other British Isles. It would surely be an understatement to say that its history has had a profound impact on the country as we find it today. The country's heritage in terms of music, literature and art is also very strong and to discover Ireland is to discover a treasure trove of cities, towns, villages, rolling countryside, bustling ports and magnificent houses and gardens in all styles, shapes and sizes.

While Ireland is different from its neighbouring countries, it would also be stating the obvious to say that the North is dramatically different from the South. Though Northern Ireland covers only a sixth of the country in terms of size, over a third of the country's population lives there.

The province has literally hundreds of ruined castles and historic monuments, and over a thousand early Christian farmsteads or 'raths', 'cashels' or stone-built defended homesteads, and 'crannogs' artificial islands in shallow lakes. There are Neolithic tombs, churches and towers, early crosses, monasteries and primitive churches, castles, mills...you name it!

The city of Belfast has many interesting buildings. Visit the **City Hall**, where George V opened the first Northern Ireland parliament; the **Linen Hall Library**, an 18th century building which houses an interesting Irish collection; **St Anne's Cathedral** an Hiberno-Romanesque building which is the burial place of Lord Carson, leader of the opposition to home rule; the **Ulster Museum**, and the **Botanic Gardens** and **Palm House**; the **Transport Museum** with exhibits showing more than 200 years of Irish transport and the Crown Liquor Saloon, a former railway hotel which is decorated in a very flamboyant style. Four miles to the East of Belfast is **Stormont**, the former parliament building, and one of the Northern Counties' landmarks which is most often seen on foreign television.

There are many historic houses and castles around the six counties. Near Belfast is **Carrickfergus Castle**, built by John de Courcy in 1180. Carrickfergus has interesting literary connections. William Congreve and Jonathan Swift both have roots there as does the poet Louis MacNeice. American president, Andrew Jackson was also born there. The village of Hillsborough has many fine Georgian townhouses.

County Down is famous as the landing place of St Patrick, and among the interesting buildings there is **Kirkistown Castle**, actually more of a fortified townhouse than a castle, one of many built between the 15th and 17th centuries by local landlords - often as protection against each other.

Mount Stewart, home of Viscount Castlereagh, is one of the National Trust properties in the county, with a garden created by Edith, Lady Londonderry, which is reckoned to be among the National Trust's top six. Treasures in the house include paintings by Stubbs, and many items of political interest (featured later).

Castle Ward is an extraordinary piece of architecture. Half Classical and half Gothic, the division of styles is carried throughout the house, giving an eccentric mixture of moods (featured later).

North of Downpatrick, the ruins of **Inch Abbey** are to be found overlooking the Quoile river. **Rowallane Gardens** at Saintfield,

run by the National Trust, have a lovely display of rhododendrons, azaleas and herbaceous plants and **Castlewellan Arboretum** is the showpiece of Castlewellan Forest Park.

County Armagh contains Lough Neagh, the largest lake in the British Isles, and focus for much of the area's leisure activities.

Armagh, the county's main centre, is the seat of both the Anglican and the Roman Catholic archbishops of Ireland, with the two cathedrals, which are both dedicated to St Patrick, dominating the city. There are however, many other buildings of note - the County Museum, Armagh Friary, the ruins of Ireland's longest church, the Planetarium, Navan Fort, and the Royal School founded by James I in 1608. Nearby do visit The Argory, an National Trust property built in 1824 for Walter McGeough, and now a kind of time capsule showing life as it was at the turn of the century. **Ardress House** is also interesting for its plasterwork and lovely 18th century furniture, as well as a fine collection of paintings.

County Fermanagh contains the ancestral home of the US president Ulysses Simpson Grant, commander of the victorious armies in the American Civil War.

Enniskillen, nestling on an island between Upper and Lower Lough Erne, has a ring of castles around it which were built to control this strategic stretch of shore. Lough Erne contains nearly 100 islands, many of which have attractions for the tourist.

Florence Court and Castle Coole are two lovely properties owned by the National Trust near Enniskillen. **Castle Coole** is a magnificent neo-Classical house designed by James Wyatt, and now the family home of the Earls of Belmore. It has a

Tyrone Crystal

IRELAND

marvellous Regency Saloon and a lavish state bedroom, and its fine woodlands and Lough Coole provide a perfect setting.

Florence Court has one of the loveliest situations in Northern Ireland, nestling in the mountains. The house was formerly the home of the Earls of Enniskillen and is an interesting example of 18th century Irish architecture, with a lovely walled garden and an adjoining Forest Park.

To the north-west, in Londonderry, do make a detour to Springhill and Wellbrook. **Springhill** is a 17th century Plantation House, which was the Lenox-Conynghams' family home until it was given to the National Trust in 1957, and is reputed to be the prettiest in Ulster. It has an extensive costume museum, and memorabilia from the family and even its own friendly ghost.

Wellbrook Beetling Mill has a huge water mill and is a working display of the final process for finishing linen, battering the cloth as it passes under the wooden hammers of the beetling engine. Moneymore is a very pretty plantation town, the first of many settlements to be built by the Draper's Company, and the first town in Ulster to have piped water in 1615. It was sadly destroyed, but many Georgian buildings remain.

John Nash, who was responsible for some of the landscaping and terraces of Regent's Park in London, was the architect of Killymoon Castle, a Norman-revival castle.

A good general view of the emigration of Irish men and women to the United States of America can be gleaned from the Ulster-American Folk Park outside Omagh, where an exhibition explores the exploits of the individuals and groups who set off to the 'New Country'.

Londonderry City , with its 17th century walls and magnificent Guildhall and cathedrals, is an interesting centre for the visitor.

The north coast of Antrim has been a popular haunt for tourists for hundreds of years, thanks to the Giant's Causeway, with its tall colonnades of volcanic rock lending a dramatic beauty to the coastline. The ruins of **Dunlace Castle** with its nearby sea cave which can only be visited in calm weather, are fun to see, and **Kinbane Castle** also offers spectacular views, perching on the clifftops. Those who suffer from vertigo should avoid the Carrick-a-Rede rope bridge, which swings 80ft above the sea to a small island. It is definitely not for the faint-hearted!

EIRE

The visitor to Eire is in for a treat every bit as much as the visitor to Northern Ireland. The country has a rich variety of countryside, cities, towns and coastlines, and is as fiercely proud of its history and heritage as its neighbour.

The 'Fair City' of Dublin is rich in history for the tourist. A beautiful and atmospheric city, it is full of reminders of its famous sons and daughters. The **Abbey Theatre** was primarily established by the poet W B Yeats, though the original which opened in 1904 was burned to the ground after a performance of Sean O'Casey's 'The Plough and The Stars' in 1951. It was re-opened in 1966.

Other literary luminaries associated with the city include the poet and playwright Lady Gregory, playwrights J M Synge and

The Oak Room, Malahide Castle

314

IRELAND

George Bernard Shaw as well as Samuel Beckett, Oscar Wilde and James Joyce.

Dublin's history goes back to a 4,000 year old burial site in Phoenix Park, and the city's castle and the Cathedrals of St Patrick (Roman Catholic) and Christ Church (Protestant) are all worth a visit.

The National Gallery has many fine exhibits; and the old and new Parliament Houses are of architectural importance (the old one is now the Bank of Ireland and the new one at **Leinster House** is better known as Dail Eireann). **Trinity College** has many important documents including the Book of Kells, and the Chester Beatty Library also has an interesting collection of manuscripts which have been bequeathed to the nation.

The Four Courts, arranged around a central courtyard, front the river and are very impressive.

Dublin is lovely to explore on foot, with many interesting buildings, squares and bridges. It also has some excellent shops, bars and restaurants, and in particular **Powerscourt Town House** in South William Street, a family town house built in the 18th century and now converted into an award-winning shopping centre.

Around the county of Dublin, many more treasures are to be found. **Malahide Castle** is the oldest to be continually inhabited by the same family, its history dating back virtually unbroken to 1185. The only break was a period when Cromwell evicted the family. It also boasts the only surviving original medieval great hall and a beautifully landscaped garden (featured later).

Newbridge House, at Donabate, was designed in 1737 by George Semple, and contains a fine Georgian drawing room with a good collection of paintings and an eclectic collection of objects from the Cobbes' family travels.

James Joyce Tower, at Sandycove, is one of the earliest of a series of martello towers built along the east coast as a defence against the threat of a Napoleonic invasion. The tower, where Joyce stayed as a boy and whose memory he draws on in the opening pages of 'Ulysses', now houses a James Joyce museum and often hosts events or lectures about the writer.

Fernhill Gardens at Sandyford, have giant redwoods, a Victorian laurel lawn and magnificent springtime blooms, as well as a rare enclosed Victorian vegetable and flower garden. Many of the estate's trees and plants date back 200 years.

Beech Park at Clonsilla, Co Dublin, is the walled garden of a Regency house and contains a wonderful collection of herbaceous and alpine plants.

THE EASTERN COUNTIES

The road from Dublin to **Slane Castle** was reputedly straightened to speed George IV's visits to his mistress Lady Conyngham. Either way, the castle certainly merits a visit. The castle was begun in 1785 and finished by the First Marquess Conyngham, husband of the King's mistress. The gothic revival castle has a wonderful ballroom with filigree vaulting, and enjoys a dramatic setting overlooking the river Boyne, now sometimes used for rock concerts.

Also in Meath, is **Tullynally Castle and Gardens**, the largest castellated house in Ireland, which also includes one of the earliest central heating systems and many interesting 19th century gadgets.

The **Irish National Stud** is the unlikely home of one of the oldest Japanese gardens in Europe. The gardens were laid out by Tasa Eida tracing the life of man from the cradle to the grave and on to eternity, in the Japanese tea garden style, with symbolic features in stone and sand.

Castletown House at Celbridge, was the country's first Palladian mansion and is still important for its baroque staircase and charming 18th century printroom. The architect, Edward Lovett Pearce, also designed the old Parliament House in Dublin.

Killruddery House and Gardens at Bray, Co Wicklow, is one of Ireland's earliest surviving gardens. A pair of long canals reflect the sky and a high beech hedge encircles a pool and fountains. Some splendid statues and a Victorian conservatory are among the other delights.

Garden enthusiasts must also visit **Mount Usher Gardens** at Ashford, which date back to 1868 and now include more than

Castletown House

IRELAND

5,000 species of plants gathered from all corners of the world by the Walpole family. Weirs, waterfalls and unusual bridges complete the picture (featured later).

The Sugar Loaf Mountain looks down on **Powerscourt Gardens** and Waterfall at Enniskerry. These elaborate gardens, which were influenced by the Villa Butera in Sicily, include a circular pond and fountain, Italian statues and patterned ramps, and elaborate ironwork. The waterfall is set in parkland a few miles away, in a beautiful, rocky yet verdant valley.

County Offaly is home to the beautiful **Birr Castle** Demesne, whose park and gardens date back to the 18th century and buildings date to the 16th century (featured later).

The domed rotunda at **Emo Court** in County Laois is reckoned to be one of Ireland's most impressive rooms. The house was designed by James Gandon who also designed the Custom House.

ACROSS THE SOUTHERN COUNTIES

The lovely southern counties of Ireland are manna from heaven for the tourist, with their lovely scenery, beautiful coastlines and interesting places to visit. **Johnstown Castle** Demesne in Murrintown, Co Wexford, is a fabulous gothic revival castle, which is reflected in its own ornamental lake. An agricultural museum in the farmyard has displays of rural transport and antique implements. Further into the county, at New Ross, is the **John F Kennedy Arboretum**, which will inspire gardeners from far afield. It was opened in 1968 by Coillte Teoranta, the Irish Forestry Board, and is also a centre for plant research.

Annes Grove Gardens

Powerscourt Gardens

IRELAND

Altamount Gardens at Tullow, Co Carlow, was planted in 1850, and has many fine tress and shrubs including a handkerchief tree, a tulip tree and a fern-leaved beech. The lane with inviting small islands and water lilies can be seen beyond the sweeping lawns. the winding paths round the lake take you beyond the glen which is carpeted with bluebells and ferns, then through the ancient mossy oak woods to the beautiful River Slaney. The Altamount Garden Trust hold a series of mid week garden courses for visitors who would like to increase their knowledge while holidaying in beautiful surroundings, the courses end with a farewell banquet in Altamount House.

Lismore Castle Gardens, at Lismore, County Waterford, are delightful. The original castle dated from 1185, but the present castle was built in the 19th century and is the Irish home of the Duke of Devonshire. The lovely gardens include an ancient yew walk. Also, don't miss **Mount Congreve**, in Co Waterford, a plantsman's garden on the grandest of scales with endless rare plants which really does warrant a tour.

The city of Cork dominates the southern coast in terms of population, being the second largest city in the Republic and the third largest in Ireland as a whole. The name means marsh in Irish, and the Anglo-Norman walled town occupied a pair of islands between the north and south channels of the River Lee, most of which have now been reclaimed to support the modern city. Cork is rich in interesting old buildings, churches, quaywalls and bridges. The Protestant church of St Anne Shandon is worth a visit, and the old custom house now forms part of the modern Crawford Municipal School of Art. The Catholic Church of St Mary Shandon, known as the North Chapel, had its interior rebuilt in 1820 by George Richard Pain. The Courthouse, many of the University buildings and the Cork Steam Packet Company building in Penrose Quay are among the other buildings of note.

Nearby **Riverstown House** contains fine examples of the work of the Italian stuccadores Paolo and Filippo La Francini, which enhance the dining room ceilings and walls. It was enlarged and extended, and has been restored quite recently with the help of the Georgian Society. **Liscarrol Castle** is one of the largest 13th century castles in Ireland.

Fota House, at Carrigtwohill, is one of Ireland's finest Regency houses. It includes a neo-classical hallway and a fine collection of Irish landscape paintings. Fine period furniture, Adam fireplaces, and a rare 1880 barrel organ are among the treats for visitors to **Dunkathiel** at Glanmire, and don't miss **Annes Grove Gardens** at Castletownroche, which were inspired by the 19th century Irish gardener William Robinson. The gardens feature plants grown to unusual sizes and gathered from many parts of the world, and there are riverside walks and a cliff garden. Another garden to take advantage of Co Cork's mild climate is **Creagh Gardens**, at Skibbereen, where many exotic plants usually found only in greenhouses can be seen in the lovely displays.

Surely one of Ireland's most famous legends must be that of the **Blarney Stone**, which has given the English language a new word. Visitors are invited to kiss the stone, and also to visit the **Blarney Castle** which is one of Ireland's oldest and most historic castles. An ancient stronghold of the MacCarthy's, Lords of Muskenny, it is one of the strongest fortresses in Munster, with walls over 15 feet thick in places. It was built in 1446 by Carmal MacCarthy in the form of a massive four storey keep added on to an earlier tower. It changed hands during the Civil and Williamite Wars and was used as a prison for the protestants of Cak. During the reign of Queen Elizabeth I Dermot MacCarthy was determined not to lose the castle again. Possessed of the gift of 'plamas', the Irish word for soft talking flattery, he tried to talk his way out of handing over Blarney as an agent to the Queen.

After much Irish prevarication the Queen declared 'I will hear

Altnamount Garden

no more of this Blarney talk.' A new word passed into the English language and the legend persists, that anyone who kisses the famous stone high up in the battlements will be endowed with lifelong eloquence.

Blarney House is one of the most elegant and gracious of the great houses of Ireland. A family home now tastefully restored to its former splendour, it was built in 1874 overlooking the beautiful Blarney Castle. It contains a collection of early furniture, family portraits, tapestries and fine paintings.

The picturesque gardens known as Rock Close were laid out by the Jeffreyes family in 1759.

Bantry House near the western coast of County Cork, was built around 1740, and has been added to since. It now houses an extensive art collection and some interesting tapestries.

Muckross House and Gardens at Killarney, County Kerry, has become a folk life and visitor centre as well as enjoying a lovely setting against the mountains, and visitors to **Dunloe Castle** Hotel Gardens will be rewarded by such sights as the aromatic-leaved headache tree and the Chinese swamp cypress.

Damer House at Roscrea, Co Tipperary, now houses various exhibitions of local heritage, and also boasts a magnificent carved pine staircase similar to the one at Cashel Palace.

AROUND THE WESTERN COUNTIES

Limerick is one of the oldest centres along the western coast. Like many of its seaboard neighbours, the city has Viking foundations. It is divided into the English Medieval town on an island in the Shannon, Irishtown on the mainland and Newton Pery, the late 18th century development.

The castle is interesting. Nearly square in shape it retains its north and south walls, and St Mary's Cathedral is one of Ireland's most historic Medieval examples. The Custom House in Irishtown was designed by Davis Ducart, and the Catholic Cathedral of St John, off St John's Square, was built in 1856-1861. Newton Pery also has many notable buildings.

Castle Matrix, at Rathkeale, takes its name from the sanctuary of Matres, the Celtic goddess of love and poetry, on which it stands, and the castle is thought to have been an inspiration to the poet Spenser who wrote 'The Faerie Queene'.

Glin Castle stands on the site that has been the home of the Fitz-Geralds for 700 years. The Georgian house became a castle in 1785 when crenellations were added, and the castle is guarded by three sets of toy fort lodges.

Lough Gur is one of Ireland's most important archaeological centres, with the remains of burial chambers, stone circles and many other remnants from a major Neolithic settlement.

Those with a taste for the unusual will be interested in **Cratloe Woods House** in County Clare, which has a ghost and the only surviving 17th century longhouse which is still a home.

Craggaunowen is a collection and recreation of homesteads and artefacts planned by late art historian, John Hunt, one of the worlds leading experts on medieval art (featured later).

Bunratty Castle and Folk Park boasts three murder holes through which boiling water was poured onto the attackers below. The Castle gives an insight into the lives of 15th and 16th century Irishmen and the crafts and skills of the farming community are remembered in the nearby Folk Park (featured later).

Dunguaire Castle at Kinvara, Co Galway, takes it name from the ancient fort of Guaire, King of Connaught. The castle was built in 1520 and was occupied by Guaire's descendants, the O'Hynes before passing into the hands of the Martyns of Galway in the 17th century, who owned the castle until this century. Dunguaire was bought and repaired in 1924 by Oliver St John Gogarty, the famous surgeon and literary figure. The restoration was completed in 1954 when Dunguaire was acquired by Christobel Lady Ampthill. With 13 centuries of Irish history from the skirmishes, battles and sieges that characterise its colourful past through to the literary revival of the early 20th century. Today this magnificent castle, fully restored, gives an insight into the lifestyle of the people who lived there from 1520 to modern times.

In medieval Ireland, a nobleman's standing was measured not just on his possessions or conquests but on the level of hospi-

Dunguaire Castle

IRELAND

tality he offered to friends and strangers alike. He would ensure that all who called to his house were greeted at the gates, wined and dined in lavish style, entertained by musicians and singers, finally to depart, no doubt singing the praises of their hosts. You can enjoy these wonderful medieval evenings at Knappogue, Bunratty and Dunguarie. Reservations are necessary, these can be made through any tourist office, travel agent or Shannon Medieval Castle Banquets, Tel (010 353 61) 61788 or (010 353 91) 37108.

Thoor Ballylee in Co Galway was the home of the poet W B Yeats and his wife, and visitors can climb the stairs to the top of his tower, and roam the gardens to find his initials still carved in one of the copper beeches.

Knappogue Castle near Quin was the pride of forty two castles built by the McNamara family who dominated the area for over 1000 years. Knappogue was built in 1467 and has survived over five troubled but colourful centuries of Irish history. It has been beautifully restored in 15th century style retaining its unique medieval character and atmosphere.

Kylemore Abbey, has an idyllic setting on the lakes of the Kylemore Valley surrounded by the forests and mountains of Connemara and Doughruagh. The castle is now a girl's convent school, though part of the abbey and its lovely chapel, based on the design of Norwich Cathedral, are worth visiting.

Lissadell House at Drumcliffe, Co Sligo, has mementoes of the extraordinary Gore-Booth family, whose exploits are colourful enough to warrant a book all of their own.

Up in the North-Eastern corner of Ireland, at Churchill in County Donegal, don't miss the **Glenveagh Castle Gardens**, which were created by Henry McIlhenny from Philadelphia and form part of the national park.

Ireland is a country of many and varied pleasures, whose character and pace of life are as varied as could possibly be imagined. The visitor who has yet to discover this country is lucky indeed.

Blarney Castle

MOUNT USHER GARDENS

Initiative and knowledge, handed down through four generations of Walpoles, has seen Mount Usher grow from a potato patch in 1860 to one of Ireland's finest gardens. Laid out along the banks of the River Varty the gardens represent the epitome of the Robinsonian style of informality and natural design. The sea is about three miles distant and the climate is mild and inclined to be humid. Snow is rare and the thermometer seldom registers more than ten degrees of frost. For this reason many plants grow here in the open, which normally require the protection of a glasshouse. Lime is entirely absent from the soil and the location is very favourable for the acclimatisation of semi-exotic trees and shrubs from many parts of the world.

Mount Usher was originally a mill, though it is unknown when it was started. Around 1868 corn milling was in decline and Edward Walpole took over the mill and one acre of land, a patch which grew potatoes. Walpole grew flowers in their stead and the giant sequoia seen today was planted. In 1875 Edward Walpole transferred his interest in the property to his three sons: George and Edward were keen plantsmen and Thomas was an engineer, the many lovely bridges and weirs at Mount Usher recall his memory.

Over a number of years new plots of land were acquired, trees and shrubs were planted and the Azalea Walk created. The gardens are laid out in the style of William Robinson who believed that trees and shrubs should be allowed to grow more or less naturally. George and Edward Walpole were his disciples and applied his methods to Mount Usher.

Trees and shrubs from all over the world, spectacular in their flowering season, are planted in grass naturalised by bulbs and wild flowers. There are shade-loving plants bordering the river banks and every changing season brings new delights. There are some 4,000 species covering over 20 acres, and to professional and amateur gardener alike, a visit to Mount Usher is sure to be a memorable one.

BUNRATTY CASTLE

Bunratty Castle is situated in the picturesque country-side of County Clare and is the most authentic and complete medieval castle in Ireland. The great square keep was built around 1450 by the MacNamaras on the site of several earlier castles.

The castle has had a dramatic and bloody history. Its strategic position on the River Shannon always attracted interest and envy from unfriendly quarters. It changed hands many times, usually violently, during the periods of friction between the native Irish of Thomond and the Norman and Norman-Irish intruders. The Castle has been destroyed at least eight or nine times and it has seen many bloody murders.

Today, however, there is little evidence of all this death and destruction. The Castle stands peacefully in delightful grounds, the houses and cottages of the Folk Park spread out at the foot of its massive walls, much in the way that the cottages and crofts of old would have clustered around its base. Bunratty was in its great days the Manor of the Great Earl of Thomond, an Elizabethan aristocrat and President of Munster, and he saw to it that his house reflected his elevated position.

The modern visitor to Bunratty Castle approaches along a section of ancient paved road, across the remains of a moat which once surrounded the castle, and through a door in the 'bawn' wall into the courtyard before mounting steps to a drawbridge.

The banquets at Bunratty are magnificent, you will share with up to 140 other guests a banquet with the great Earl of Thomond toasting an era of Great Irish taste with excellent food, fine wines and honeyed mead. You will be entertained by the renowned Bunratty Singers with enchanting melodies to the music of harp and violin. This is a memorable occasion full of fun and good humour.

The Folk Park offers a glimpse of an entirely different era. The buildings and atmosphere date from around the year 1900 when the influence of the towns was just beginning to percolate through to rural communities.

This was a time when news of the horseless carriage had reached the countryside; electricity was known in the towns, as was the telephone- although only in large government departments and big businesses- but the new technological revolution had not noticeably affected country life.

A visit to Bunratty Castle and Folk Park offers the opportunity to experience, with the help of a little imagination, what life was like in these two fascinating periods of Irish history.

MOUNT STEWART

Mount Stewart is the former home of Viscount Castlereagh who became Foreign Secretary and Leader of the House of Commons in 1812. The house was extended by his father, the first Marquess of Londonderry, who added the west wing designed by George Dance in 1804. Most of the house seen today, however, is the work of William Vitruvius Morrison who carried out extensive rebuilding for the third Marquess between 1825 and 1835. His design reulted in a restrained symmetrical facade in the same dark stone as the earlier house with a balustrade running around the roof. A huge Ionic portico, wide enough to take a carriage, was added to the entrance.

The interiors are richly decorated with fine Irish and English furniture, collections of classical sculpture and porcelain and portraits of members of the family and their racehorses.

The spacious drawing room was created by Morrison from three smaller rooms and contains a fine Austrian inlaid walnut writing desk, Aubusson carpets and portraits of Viscount Castlereagh and his wife. In the dining room are the 22 Empire chairs used by the delegates at the Congress of Vienna in 1815. They are beautifully embroidered with the arms of those present and the nations which they represented.

The Castlereagh room is devoted to the great statesman, whose portrait by Lawrence hangs above the fireplace. There are engravings of his contemporaries in the Irish Parliament, caricature statuettes and busts of political figures of the day, and many of his most important documents are on display. The set of 18th century angle chairs are Goanese and made from padouk wood.

On the staircase hangs one of the finest paintings in Ireland, Hambletonian by George Stubbs, painted after beating Diamond at Newmarket in 1799. There are also family portraits by Batoni, Mengs and de Lazlo.

The lovely gardens at Mount Stewart were created by Edith, Lady Londonderry, in the 1920s. An arched walk, heavy with wisteria in early summer, leads to the Tasmanian Blue Gum Trees of the Fountain Walk. The huge Irish Yews look down onto the Italian Garden which contains mainly herbacaus plants since roses proved unsuccessful. It is enclosed by the Dodo Terrace recalling a club founded by Lady Londonderry during the First World War. The west front of the house overlooks the Sunken Garden designed by Gertrude Jekyll and surrounded on three sides by a stone pergola. In the Shammrock Garden there is a topiary harp and a bed in the colour and shape of the Red Hand of Ulster.

The Temple of the Winds enjoys wonderful views across Strangford Lough to the distant mountains of Mourne. It was built by James 'Athenian' Stuart in 1783 as a banqueting house for the first Marquess, and is a masterpiece in miniature. Except for its balconies it is a faithful copy of its namesake in Athens. A cantilevered spiral staircase rises under an elegant coffered ceiling in the rear turret. The scallops and scrolls of the plasterwak ceiling exactly mirror the design of the inlaid wooden floor, and the offices where the servants assembled the food are linked to the vaulted basement by a concealed passage.

MALAHIDE CASTLE

Malahide Castle is one of the oldest and most historic castles in Ireland. For almost 800 years it has been the home of the Talbot family who arrived in Ireland with Henry II about 1174 and were granted the lands of Malahid in 1185 by his son, Prince John. From that time onwards Malahide and the fortunes of the Talbots seem to have become inseparable.

In 1654 the lands were confiscated when the Talbots found themselves on the wrong side in the Civil War. Malahide was given to Myles Corbet who had the misfortune to have been one of four signatories to the death warrant of King Charles I. His tenure of Malahide, and his life, were predictably short, for at the Restoration he lost both and John Talbot was restored to his lands in 1655. In 1831 the family was raised to the peerage and Mrs Margaret Talbot became Baroness Talbot de Malahide.

The original Anglo-Norman castle has given way to time and changing fashions. The oldest part of the present house is a keep-like tower dating from the 14th century. A circular stairway and three walls are still standing.

The next addition was the Great Hall which dates from the time when King Edward IV gave the incumbent Lord and his heirs the title of Admiral of Malahide and the Seas Adjoining in 1475. Although re-roofed and re-windowed, the original walls and supporting undercroft make this the only essentially medieval hall still in use in Ireland. There are many family portraits and handsome furniture, but look for Puck's Doorway - the residence of the Ghost of Malahide.

The imposing Oak Room takes its name from the 16th century panelling dominated by the Flemish carving of the Coronation of the Virgin. Tradition states that the carving disappeared when Cromwell siezed the estate and miraculously reappeared when the Talbots were reinstated. Also in this room is a set of six 17th century panels of Dutch or Flemish origin, carved to depict incidents from the Bible. The furniture shows the contrast of styles before and after the Restoration.

The most striking feature of the Library is the gilt and hand-painted leather wall hangings, probably Flemish, and dating from the 1700s. There are two Irish mahogany library chairs, each with a swing reading easel. The two charming Drawing Rooms are in complete contrast to the rest of the house, and are in an elaborate, almost rococo style with lovely plaster ceilings. Among the furniture is a pair of French gilt settees of about 1700 and a magnificent pair of carved, gilt and lacquered side tables, almost certainly Irish of about 1740.

The portraits in Malahide Castle, before the sale of collection, were regarded as the most complete record of any one family still in Ireland. As a result the National Gallery of Ireland purchased 31 of these portraits which centre round Richard Talbot, titular Duke of Tyrconnell, who with other members of the family were James II's most faithful followers. Indeed, on the morning of the Battle of the Boyne in 1690 some 14 cousins sat down to breakfast at Malahide and all were dead by nightfall.

Accordingly, to underline the importance of these portraits, Wycke's large portrait of the Battle of the Boyne hangs in the Great Hall.

To these the National Gallery have added historic battle, sporting and other pictures to create a panaroma of Irish life over the past centuries. Malahide Castle makes the perfect historic setting for this collections.

CASTLE WARD

Bernard Ward, First Viscount Bangor, and his wife Anne could not agree, especially when it came to the architectural style of their home. More fortunate than most, their house was of suitably large proportions for a sensible compromise to be reached. Lady Anne got the Strawberry Hill Gothic home she had always wanted, while the Viscount was well-pleased with his Classical mansion.

The house is an architectural wonder of about 1760: the front facade reflects the Viscount's Classical taste, while the back of the house satisfies his wife's fanciful Gothic preference. The result - marital, if not architectural, harmony. The division of styles is carried right through the house, which is filled with furniture, pictures and personal objects as if the family still lived there. The Music Room is in the severe classical style with Davic columns and finely worked plaster freeze. The whimsical Gothic

boudoir has a spectacular fan-vaulted ceiling and an altogether more feminine touch.

The wily Viscount got one up on his wife, however. The grand staircase is a masterpiece of classic simplicity, but it was Lady Anne who had the last word. She eventually left her husband for good. The stable yard vividly recalls life below stairs in Victorian times. The laundry is full of equipment and clothes of the period, and the farm yard, with mills and slaughterhouse, evokes life on a Victorian estate.

There are lovely walks through the estate past the peaceful shores of Strangford Lough and a display in the Barn highlights the Lough's importance. Many species of indigenous birds can be studied in the walled garden beside the early 18th century landscape of the Temple Water.

BIRR CASTLE

Birr Castle dates in part from 1120 when Sir Lawrence Parsons was granted the estate and built a 'dwelling house' over and around the gatehouse of the original fortress. This forms the centre of the present castle which had two flanking towers on either side. A generation later these towers were incorporated into the house.

In 1642 the Molloys, Coghlands and Ormonders set fire to the town of Birr, 'blew upon their bagpipes and beat upon their drums and fell a dauncinge in the hills'. The castle was beseiged and finally capitulated when a mine was placed beneath it. Some 50 years later, when Birr was garrisoned by the Williamites, it was besieged by the army of the Duke of Berwick. Cannon balls flew through the parlour window leaving marks which can be seen today. Lady Parsons was forced to give up the lead cistern used for salting beef which was melted down for bullets and the siege was lifted.

Despite these disturbances the beginnings of the beautiful Formal Gardens were laid out at this time and the famous box hedges were planted. The wives and daughters of the house grew herbs and collected medicinal remedies which must have proved extremely useful in such troubled times. They wrote recipes for preserving their fruits and vegetables such as 'chicking frigasee' and 'hartichoake pie'. One can only hope their cooking was an improvement on their spelling!

Peace returned in the 18th century. Sir Lawrence the fifth baronet became well known as a patriotic statesman, but in the early 19th century he gave up politics to devote his life to literature and building and the castle begain to take its final form.

He turned the old house back to front to face the park, heightening and crenellating it in the new Gothic style and adding the great Gothic Saloon whose windows look down on the waterfalls of the Camcor.

In 1807 Sir Lawrence inherited the title of Earl of Rosse from his uncle. He disapproved of sending his children away to school and they were educated by tutors in an atmosphere of great enlightenment for that time. They were skilled in the principles of building and engineering and during this time the suspension bridge was built over the Camcor, described in 1826 as a 'curious wire bridge which hangs as it were suspended in the air just under the castle'.

The second Earl's eldest son constructed the giant telescope whose tube can still be seen inside the Gothic walls in the middle of the park. He designed and built it himself and was able to see further than anyone had before and attracted world-wide interest.

The magnificent gardens and grounds at Birr are laid out around a lake and along the banks of two adjacent rivers, covering 100 acres and containing 1000 different species of trees and shrubs. The gardens are particularly noted for their spring flowering magnolias, cherries and crab apples, autumn colouring maples, chestnuts and weeping beech; also for the formal gardens, hornbeam alleys and box hedges acknowledged as the tallest in the world. The present Earl and Countess still take part in expeditions to remote corners of the world to add to the collection of rare specimens.

CRAGGAUNOWEN & THE HUNT MUSEUM

A basic pattern to early Irish life began to establish itself as far back as the Stone age, five or six thousand years ago. In a small country of such rich agricultural land, the ancient Irish never really adopted the nomadic life-style and instead slowly began to settle and develop farms and homes. Craggaunowen is a collection and re-creation of homesteads and artefacts, carefully planned as a step back of over a thousand years by the late art-historian, John Hunt, one of the world's leading experts on medieval art. A living example of life in ancient Ireland and a vibrant testimony to the ancestors of these fascinating people.

The castle at the centre of the Craggaunowen complex is one of thousands of such towers built from 15th-17th century by Gaelic lords who did not want a good night's sleep to be disturbed by anything unpleasant, such as a large axe in the back of the head. The tower is typical, four storeys high, decorated throughout with fascinating period artefacts, gathered together, not as typically representative, but, more interestingly, as a general overview of relevant items of the time. Naturally during its more domestic days it would have been a good deal sparser. It was built around 1550 by John MacSheeda MacNamara, Lord of East Clancullen, noted in the 'Annals of the Four Masters' as 'nobel and majestic, the favourite of women and damsels on account of his great mirthfulness'. Following the Cromwellian Wars, the castle followed the fate of other Gaelic family properties, confiscated and rendered indefensible by the removal of its battlements. It was partially restored by a certain 'Honest Tom Steele', who grew rather fond of it following his return from the Spanish Wars.

The 'crannog' is possibly the most striking of the features at Craggaunowen. A virtually man-made island created by piling stones into a lake and laying logs, branches and brushwood over the top, it became the base for one or two houses, protected by a timber palisade. The ramp joining it to the shore is for the convenience of today's visitors, unlikely to be a feature of the ancient originals, detracting as it does from the defence of the island. If no causeway existed or was built, access would be limited to some form of boat, a wooden dug-out or skin-covered vessel. Both houses on the crannog are typically 'wattle and daub', consisting of woven branches covered with clay. There are cooking fires in the huts, but no chimneys, and no windows - only a door for light. A few tools and basic pieces of furniture are found here, but life for the farmer was simple.

The ring-fort in the castle grounds belongs to the same period. A farmstead rather than a fortification, it was essentially a circular enclosure, an earthern bank surrounded by wooden fence, or possibly stone if there was a need for, and access to it.

The 'souterrain' here is a feature of ancient ring-forts, a man-made underground passage easily maintained at a fairly even temperature and used for food storage or possibly refuge in dangerous times. The cooking-place recreated at Craggaunowen is an example of a large and elaborate one built for frequent use. Such 'fulachta fiadh' were used throughout the country from the end of the Stone Age to the 17th century AD. They consisted of a stone or wood-lined boggy pit in which heated stones were used to boil the water that slowly seeped in, until straw-wrapped meat could be easily cooked.

Nearby is a wooden trackway, part of those built to facilitate transport across the marshy ground during the time spanning roughly 500 BC-500 AD, the heroic Iron Age - time of CuChulainn and the famous Red Branch Knights when the land was considerably wetter than today. This particular 'trochar' was built in the spring or summer of 148 BC in Co Longford, corresponding with 'The Annals' which records the building of a great road across Ireland at this period. Close by, as part of the site, is the unique 'Brendan', an exact reconstruction of the legendary, tiny wood-and-oxhide boat which St Brendan the Navigator apparently used to cross the Atlantic to land in America during the 6th century AD, a 1000 years before Columbus.

When John Hunt began his Craggaunowen project in 1973 he envisaged its focal point being an interpretative and display centre, whose diverse contents would further illustrate the lifesyles of our remoter ancestors. However, the Hunt collection is so extensive that, at present, there is not room enough to display it in its entirety. Thus part of it is housed in a special museum gallery in the University of Limerick. The museum collection is fascinating enough for a feature of its own, but since it is impossible to do justice to such a remarkable display in so short a space it seems fairer to admit defeat and suggest only that it is a vital part of Craggaunowen, together a fascinating example of not only the mysterious world of the ancient past, but also of a new approach to archaeology, the re-creation of the old for the education of the new.

PARK HOTEL KENMARE

Welcome to a hotel of unrivalled charm, elegance and splendour. Welcome to the Park Hotel Kenmare. Step over the threshold and take a step back in time. Surrender to the gracious living of a forgotten age. Allow us to attend to your every need, let your senses succumb to the allure of our hospitality, commitment and dedication to service. From the moment you arrive we are ever-mindful of your individual desires and are unwavering in our resolve to fulfil them to your satisfaction.

Treat your eye to antiques from all over Ireland and Europe which create the magnificent furnishings in our guests bedrooms and the classical elegance of our dining room. Treat your palate to our innovative culinary delights from a cuisine judged among the highest in the land.

Spend your nights at the Park Hotel Kenmare, in comfort and splendour. Spend the day in outdoor pursuits of croquet, walking, tennis, golf or fishing - so rich and varied is the terrain of the Emerald Isle.

Based at Park Hotel Kenmare, you can choose to play golf at

Killarney's 36 holes - it's famous courses of Mahony's Point and the newer Killeen sited on the shore of the Lakes of Killarney -or at Waterville - one of the largest courses in Europe and one of the greatest golfing tests.

A little further afield is Ballybunion, a glorious links course on the Atlantic shore regarded as one of the world's best. Closer to home, adjacent to the hotel is an executive 9 hole course, ideal for our guests.

If fishing is more your line you are spoilt for choice. In the Rivers Waterville and Comeragh and lakes Currane and Caragh you can fish for trout and salmon in one of Ireland's most beautiful regions. In the stretch of water around Bearon Island, an angler can catch ray, conger, flatfish and dogfish. As this could entail boat-fishing the Park Hotel Kenmare would prepare your packed lunch.

The Park Hotel Kenmare bids you an eternal welcome.

Park Hotel Kenmare
Kenmare
Co Kerry
Ireland
Tel: (010 353 64) 41200
Fax: (010 353 64) 41402

ELEGANT IRELAND

Glin Castle

The Irish have always had a reputation for providing a memorable welcome; as far back as 1683 Tadhg Rody described them as 'very much addicted to hospitality'. Imagine the delight of experiencing, not only the warmth and friendship of that period, but indeed, the very same houses it was extended from.

Elegant Ireland is literally the key to the history of one of the world's most fascinating countries. Through this most prestigious of tour operators it is possible to discover at first hand the wonders that lie behind the doors of some of the most beautifully preserved country houses, mansions and castles. By special arrangements they have made it possible for the discerning guest to live in such places, either by renting the entire property, or as part of a party of select house guests.

This is the 'Unknown Ireland' - that Ireland that many have heard of, yet few have seen. Visitors are taken away from the beaten tourist tracks and familiar well-trodden sights to an altogether different world of custom-made itineraries, gaining admission into private places not normally open to the visitor, and provided with accomodation in historic castles, gracious mansions and spreading country estates; the homes of writers, academics, lords and ladies. For example, take some time to live the prominent history of Glin Castle, home to the Knight of Glin since the twelfth century; or choose to be the personal guest of the Earl of Inchiquin, direct descendant of the eleventh century King Brian Boru.

Naturally the standard of living and comfort they offer embrace a dimension which can only be experienced to be appreciated. Decorations are family heirlooms, now valuable antiques, paintings, furniture with a personal history, and the collections of books that symbolise this country of folklore and legend, storytellers and poets.

Birr Castle

ELEGANT IRELAND

Thomond House

Ross Castle

The history of the country embraces anyone who sets foot on it, but it is only certain visitors who may gain the insight of the expert guides - doubling as chauffeurs - the carefully arranged tours, the specialist lectures, and of course, access to houses, gardens and art collections not available to the general public. Unique, special-interest tours can be arranged; architecture, gardens, history, literature, folklore and modern Ireland are just a few of the more popular. Naturally, everything is organised for you, all you have to do is arrive, leisurely unpack and change before a pre-dinner drink with your amiable and talkative host.

It would be a crime in such a country not to sample the many sporting delights for which it is so justly famous. Elegant Ireland can arrange specialised packages for the country sportsman, or indeed combine a business and sporting break for the corporate market. For the golfer, Ireland is a paradise. There are more courses per square mile here than anywhere else in the world, as such it is virtually impossible to get more than 25 miles from one. The play is year round, and the breath-taking scenery of rolling Atlantic coastline, or the wide open lakes and rivers of the inland courses can only enhance your game. Relax while we arrange bookings and tee-off times to suit your schedule. For the fisherman Ireland boasts some of Europe's cleanest water, spread over 14,000km of rivers feeding over 4000 lakes. Almost every stream has a resident stock of brown trout, while the salmon you catch are wild from the Atlantic. As for the sailor, the famous American writer Don Steel puts it in perspective: 'This place is astonishing. Despite its long sailing tradition, it's still the new European cruising ground, uncrowded, unspoilt and welcoming, with great sailing off a wonderful coast.' Indeed, with almost 6,000 km of coastline to be challenged, not to mention the choice of inland waters, sailing in Ireland is a truly memorable experience. If shooting is your game, then again Ireland has a quite incredible selection, from driven pheasant, duck, snipe and woodcock, rough and walk-up shooting with ghillie and dog, to pigeon shooting and hunting fallow deer. Some of the properties you may stay in have their own sporting facilities on private estates, or if not, they are easily arranged locally.

Lisnavagh

Whether it be a dinner for six or a week-end for sixty, a private party in some of the most magnificent surroundings in the world, or a murder mystery week-end in the country, the choice is entirely yours. One thing is certain though, whatever you choose and wherever you decide to go, everything we do for you will be conducted with care and attention to detail and the backdrop of literally thousands of years of the vibrant magic and history that is Ireland.

Elegant Ireland
15 Harcourt Street
Dublin 2
Ireland
Tel: (01) 751632/751665
Fax: (01) 751012

THE EMERALD ISLE

Back in medieval Ireland a nobleman's standing was measured not simply by the violence of his conquests, or the gaudy grandeur of his possessions, but more simply, by his ability to entertain his guests. His quickness to welcome friends and strangers alike, and extend his arms and home in hospitality was a measure of his true worth. Tradition is something which dies hard in Ireland.

The Celtic blood has always led to a strange development, creating a race unique in the history of the British Isles. A race of warrior-poets, where the ability to pen a line or compose a song was as important as the ability to wield a sword. Thus, to set foot in Ireland is to enter a country rich in the fortified strongholds and beautifully preserved castles of a once-warring nation, but also, perhaps paradoxically, the home of artists whose work has spanned not centuries, but thousands of years, and produced some of the most influential in history. For a country so small to have produced three Nobel Prize winning writers would lead one to think there is more than a little something special in the air.

Ireland, above all else, is a land of people; not the hordes of people who crowd the streets of the cities, but people who have retained the art of a gentler life, simply looking to share a conversation, a song, a little laughter and perhaps a drink or two. The welcome is spontaneous, the unsuspecting visitor could well find himself dragged unwittingly into an impromptu singing session amidst the warmth and cheers of an Irish pub.

There is a certain magic in Ireland, perhaps in the air, perhaps in the light that has streamed over the country through the ages, lighting the colours of this island where there are truly forty shades of green. Not a wash of watercolours here, but a penetrating vibrancy that seems to change in harmony with the movements of the sun.

The story is a long one, of a culture steeped in legends that are still being made. Ancient standing stones and the earthern castles of the early Celts have stood as monumental guards since long before the far-off eastern pyramids were heaved into existence. The battles to protect the land from the marauding Vikings and Normans built the gaunt structural history that survives to this day. The relative piety of the Middle Ages led to the periods of study and monastic patience that were to produce

Kilkenny Castle and Gardens

THE EMERALD ISLE

such masterpieces as the 8th/9th century 'Book Of Kells', now housed at Trinity College, Dublin, and arguably the most beautiful book in the world.

Ireland is a land steeped in the shrouds of legend and the magic of Celtic faery. It is still the land of the four-leaved clover, the pot of gold at the rainbow's end, the shadowy world of the 'little people', where the man with the sharp eye and the open mind can catch and hold one of the elusive leprechauns until he reveals the location of his hoard of hidden treasure. The writings of the mythological sagas date back to the 5th century, chronicling events from 300 years before the birth of Christ, the exploits of Cuchulainn, the most powerful of the mighty Red Branch Knights of Ulster. The 'Book of the Dun Cow' still survives, almost 900 years old, to recount the Tain Bo Cualainge, originally recorded in the 7th century, the massive raid by Queen Maeve of Connacht, to secure the Brown Bull of Ulster. But this is the land of tall tales and fireside bards, and these are never those to let the facts spoil a good story. Consider Finn Mae Cool, the legendary warrior-giant, so strong he could put his hand into his back pocket and lift himself into the air! Warriors

and poets blend again in more recent times. James Joyce's 'Ulysses' ranks as one of the world's most influential novels, tracing the journey of the hero around the streets of Dublin - a journey still followed today - echoing the adventures of the legendary hellenistic hero in an epic example of the power of language at the height of its intensity. A use of lingual experimentation which influenced Samuel Beckett, Nobel Prize winner and one of the most original writers of modern times. The choice for lovers of literature is almost endless; from the rolling beauty of W.B Yeats, to the wit of Jonathan Swift and his travelling Gulliver, to the plays of Oscar Wilde and G.B Shaw, to 'The Vicar of Wakefield' and Bram Stoker's 'Dracula', boiling up to the outstanding modern poetry of Seamus Heaney.

Ireland is a country rich in almost everything, history, culture, beauty and, not least of all, people. They have a saying here; there's no such thing as a stranger, but only a friend you have yet to meet. A 'Cead Mile Failte' - a hundred thousand welcomes - is the least you can expect from the colourful inhabitants of this most fascinating of kingdoms.

Rock of Cashel, Co. Tipperary

THE HIDDEN IRELAND

For accommodation in Private Country Houses, the Hidden Ireland is a unique organisation offering the more adventurous visitor a chance to sample Irish country life at its very best, in a way not usually experienced by the ordinary tourist.

Tourist Board approved, our houses are most definitely not hotels, guesthouses or the average B & B. They are all houses of architectural character and merit with owners to match who are prepared to share them and their way of life with those who appreciate such things. A warm welcome, family atmosphere and decanter of sherry on a tray might be some of the replacements for the reception desk, bar and residents' lounges of more impersonal establishments. Bearing this in mind, it is a good idea to inform your hosts of your time of arrival - otherwise they could well be in the depths of the garden or elsewhere. It would also be appreciated if you would advise your hosts if you cannot take up a reservation.

For the sportsmen there is access to the very best hunting, fishing, shooting and golf. For family holidays they provide tranquil havens where there are enough activities for all. But perhaps the greatest attraction is the ambience of being a guest at a country house party. There is an air of exclusivity and privacy; you will meet the people who actually live in the house and are a fund of local knowledge. The group include great houses designed by important architects, lived in and visited over the years by world famous figures; among our houses there are those that have belonged to the same family for 300 years or more, those that are haunted and those with outstanding gardens.

Prices vary considerably and on the whole reflect the type of house in which you wish to stay. From the charm of a small family run shooting lodge to the special ambience of the great ancestral house, all offer value for money, and above all, a truly Irish way of life. The price for bed & breakfast is per person sharing. If a single room is required a supplement may be payable.

Many of the properties are very suitable for small conferences or family groups and can be taken on an exclusive basis. Special rates can be arranged.

We will be happy to arrange itineraries and self drive or chauffeur driven cars.

The Hidden Ireland
PO Box 2281
Dublin 4
Ireland
Tel: (010 353 1) 686463
Fax: (010 353 1) 686578

IRELAND

To describe Ireland as a land of variety is as understated as describing it as beautiful. This is a country where scenic splendour forms a natural combination with the natural exuberance of its people-a country that welcomes visitors as its own and is proud to allow them an insight into its history and culture. If such a lavish appraisal smacks of naive exaggeration, there exists a multitude of visitors who will testify that Ireland is a holiday destination with few equals.

Northern Ireland is only just beginning to realise that it has a real contribution to make to the holiday market. First-time visitors are invariably surprised by both the beauty of much of the countryside and the cheerful disposition of its population-a far cry from the traditional and distorted media image.

From the cliffs and beaches of the North Antrim Coast to the shopping facilities of downtown Belfast, the Province makes for a stimulating and enjoyable stay, particularly for those en route for the south. Historic houses and castles abound, with Castle Ward a particularly notable example. Of even more stunning dramatic appeal is the Giant's Causeway, described in some quarters as the eighth wonder of the world and a required destination on the itinerary of any self respecting tourist.

Luxurious hotels are not exactly commonplace in Northern Ireland but those that exist can more than hold their own. The guesthouses and B&B's of the Province give further credence to the importance of quality rather than quantity.

Southern Ireland, in some respects, is the classic 'land that time forgot'-a country of hills as green as the lakes are blue, of rugged mountains and dramatic valleys, a constantly changing kaleidoscope of colour that is invariably a joy to behold.

The fair city of Dublin is a capital in which the country takes pride, a city of bustle and shops, entertainment and culture, as well as an appealing selection of hotels and other fine accommodation. It would be enormously wrong to think of Ireland only in terms of Dublin, even though a huge proportion of the country's population resides there. Crossing to the west coast, the Connemara and Donegal regions offer a less sophisticated way of life-a timeless quality that is characterised by some magnificently rugged landscapes.

Moving further down the coastline, long mountain peninsulas reach proudly into an Atlantic Ocean, helping to ensure a mild and relaxing year-round climate. Further inland the city of Cork offers a colourful range of attractions and some excellent accommodation.

Sandy beaches and glorious, unspoiled countryside are two of the many features of the south east of the country, a region that includes the beautiful medieval town of Kilkenny. Here, just as throughout Ireland, walkers, anglers, sailors and golfers will find unrivalled opportunities for sport and healthy relaxation.

Appetites and thirsts can be more than satisfied afterwards in one of the countless inns or restaurants, some of them incorporated within stately homes and even castles. Ireland has a long and proud history and its aftermath can be glimpsed today at almost every step. This is a country-and an experience-simply not to miss.

SOUTHERN IRELAND

HOTELS OF DISTINCTION

ABBEYGLEN CASTLE HOTEL, Clifden, Co Galway, Tel: (010 353 95) 21201
An impressive display of crenellations, towers and pointed-arch windows gives an individual personality to this old castle, complete with a peat fire and hessianed walls in the bar.

ADARE MANOR, Adare, Co Limerick, Tel: (010 353 61) 396566
Set in over 800 acres, this imposing gothic style manor house has many fascinating architectural features and traditional darkwood furnishings.

ARBUTUS LODGE HOTEL, Montenotte, Co Cork, Tel: (010 353 21) 501237
Set in award winning gardens this hotel dates back to the late 18th century, with a variety of Victorian extensions. It offers fine views over the city and the interior is stylishly decorated, complete with the work of modern Irish painters.

ASHFORD CASTLE, Cong, Co Mayo, Tel: (010 353 92) 46003
Part 13th century castle and part French-style chateau the exterior splendour of this magnificent hotel continues on into the inside, decorated with suits of armour, carved balustrade and huge fireplaces. A harpist plays nightly downstairs in the dungeon bar.

ASSOLAS COUNTRY HOUSE, Kanturk, Co Cork, Tel: (010 353 29) 50015
A charming little Queen Anne hotel adorned inside with family photos, bookcases and a cheerful log fire in the delightful drawing room. The bedrooms are in beautiful condition and furnished with antiques.

BALLYCORMAC HOUSE, Borrisokane, Co Tipperary Tel: (010 353 67) 21129
The interior of this 300 year old farmhouse is delightfully furnished with antiques and some fascinating curios. Standing in its own pretty gardens it is only 7 miles from the castle town of Birr.

BALLYLICKEY MANOR HOUSE, Bantry Bay, Co Cork, Tel: (010 353 27) 50071
A beautiful tranquil setting of delightful gardens and grounds is the position of this former, 17th century, shooting lodge, commanding spectacular views of Bantry Bay. Furnished with a stylish collection of antiques.

BANTRY HOUSE, Bantry, Co Cork, Tel:.(010 353 27) 50047
The 2nd Earl of Bantry filled this house with a collection of souvenirs and curiosities from his continental travels back in the 19th century. The building itself is one of the finest stately homes in all of Ireland.

BLACKWATER CASTLE, Castletownroche, Co Cork, Tel: (010 353 22) 26333
Looking across the wooded Blackwater Valley, this small 12th century castle offers antique furniture and an attractive lounge/library.

MOUNT JULIET

This magnificently restored 18th century house stands proudly on nearly 1,500 acres of unspoiled parkland and offers every possible comfort naturally beautiful surroundings. This beguiling combination of old and new cannot fail to leave an indelible mark on even the most discerning of guests.

The hotel is well suited for prestigious conferences - a perfect 'out of town' venue, supported by all the necessary modern facilities plus superb hospitality and a wide range of sporting and recreational facilities.

For the golfer, Mount Juliet boasts its own 18 hole golf course designed by Jack Nicklaus. His great talent, combined with the magnificent rolling expanses of the estate, has resulted in a first class parkland course. The 7,000 yard championship layout, set on some 180 acres, offers variety and a challenge to golfers of all standards. From water to specimen trees to vigilant bunkers, each hole has its own unique features.

Top class professional tuition is on hand at all times. In addition, there is the unique 3 hole teaching academy offering players the opportunity to improve every aspect of their game. The Clubhouse is unique too, an interesting blend of leisure facilities combined with the charm and character of old estate buildings.

The estate also has an equestrian centre with fully qualified instructors which caters for all levels from beginners to serious cross-country riders. The experienced angler, can fish both the River Nore and King's River, while instruction for novices is provided at the Fishing Academy. Clay Pigeon shooting and a driven shoot are also available on the estate as are tennis and croquet whilst for the less energetic, the estate's enormous woodlands and gardens are ideal for walking, cycling or bird watching .

Dining here is a delight. The Lady Helen is recognised as one of Ireland's most distinguished restaurants, while the Old Kitchen offers relaxed dining in more informal surroundings. Each of the 32 en-suite bedrooms has its own unique ambience. Overnight guests can choose between Presidential Suites, deluxe mini-suites and superior rooms.

Whether it is for business or pleasure, there are few places to rival Mount Juliet.

Mount Juliet
Thomastown
Country Kilkenny
Ireland
Hotel Tel: (056) 24455 Fax: (056) 24522
Golf Tel: (056) 24725 Fax: (056) 24828

PARKNASILLA HOTEL

The area of County Kerry is justly renowned for its natural splendour. Deep in its heart, guarding 300 acres of beautiful sub tropical parkland, the Parknasilla hotel commands breath-taking views over the magnificent Kenmare Bay.

Relaxed hospitality is traditional in Ireland, and it takes a certain skill to combine the friendly atmosphere with the professionalism found here. Many guests are regular visitors, tempted back by the open welcome and charm.

As for leisure facilities, the choice is almost endless. If you are feeling energetic, why not work out on the tennis courts. Improve your handicap on the private 9-hole golf course with tuition available for those trickier shots. If water-sports are your thing, then keep your hand in with old favourites or try someting new; facilities are available for windsurfing, sailing, waterskiing, as well as lake and deep-sea fishing. For the indoor type, snooker and table-tennis provide ample challenge. Or take life at a slower pace and borrow a bicycle or enjoy a gentle horse ride around the miles of surrounding forest paths, or just pack up a lunch and take off on foot. However you decide to spend your day, what could be better than relaxing afterwards in the indoor heated swimming pool, jacuzzi or private sauna.

Fortunately the hotel is more than prepared for the appetites of the active. The award winning Pygmalion Restaurant features the finest of modern cuisine in truly sophisticated surroundings, enhanced still further by wonderful views across the countryside and bay. Other public rooms, such as the lounges, bar and fascinating Shaw library offer further examples of elegance and relaxation.

All of the 84 bedrooms have private bathroom, direct-dial telephone, multichannel TV and radio. With all of the facilities under one roof the Parknasilla provides the perfect venue for the conference or incentive meeting. The completely re-furbished Derryquin suite can easily accomodate up to 80 people.

Parknasilla Hotel
Co. Kerry
Ireland
Tel: (010 353 64) 45122
Fax: (010 353 64) 45323

WATERFORD CASTLE

Waterford Castle's long history stretches back as far as the sixth century when the Island was occupied by a monastery. The strategic importance of the Island eventually drove the monks elsewhere.

However, it was during the Norman Invasion of Ireland in 1160 that Maurice Fitzgerald, cousin to Strongbow, the English Earl of Pembroke, landed on the Island and built the original castle.

It was from the Island that Edward, perhaps the most famous of the Fitzgeralds, completed his elegant translation of the Rubaiyat of Omar Khayyam.

The family's unbroken stewardship of the Castle, one of the longest recorded in Irish history, lasted until 1958 when Mary Fitzgerald married an Italian Prince and moved to Dublin, selling the Island as she left. The Island saw a number of owners until 1987, when Eddie Kearns moved in and restored this magnificent building to create the Hotel.

The Island's private ferry provides the only access to the Hotel. Once there, guests will find rooms of supreme elegance and luxury and enjoy exceptional cuisine in the oak-panelled majesty of the Great Dining Room.

The Castle boasts its own leisure club which offers tennis, an indoor heated swimming pool, gymnasium and sauna, while horse riding and clay pigeon shooting can also be arranged.

In April, Waterford Castle Golf Course will be ready for play. The Castle may be private, but it is not remote. Ryanair fly direct from Stansted to Waterford Airport, itself only ten minutes' drive from the Castle.

For tranquility and luxury inherited from the Island's monastic past, there is nothing quite like the Isle of Waterford Castle.

Waterford Castle - the Isle of the Castle
For further information and bookings, contact:
Geraldine Fitzgerald
Tel: (010 353 517) 8203
Fax: (010 353 517) 9316

IRELAND

CASHEL HOUSE HOTEL, Cashel, Co Galway, Tel: (010 353 95) 31001
With 35 acres of award-winning gardens, this highly hospitable hotel offers a fine degree of comfort and tranquility and boasts the patronage of Harold Macmillan and General De Gaulle.

COOPERSHILL, Riverstown, Co Sligo, Tel: (010 353 71) 65108
This elegant Georgian manor house has been in the same family since 1774 and commands 500 acres. Family portraits and hunting trophies adorn the walls, while the bedrooms are furnished with antiques.

DROMOLAND CASTLE, Limerick, Co Clare, Tel: (010 353 61) 71144
The ancestral home of the O'Brien family, the interior is decorated with portraits of the past. Beautifully architectured, this hotel slips right into fairyland, its reflection glancing back off the lake at its foot.

ENNISCOE, Ballina, Co Mayo, Tel: (010 353 96) 31112
This splendid Irish Georgian house rests in 300 acres of woodland which include a lake with isles boasting the ruins of a 15th century castle. An old yard behind the house is used by the local Historical Society as a Heritage Centre.

FITZPATRICK'S CASTLE HOTEL, Killiney, Co Dublin, Tel: (010 353 1) 851533
Dating from 1741, this impressive crenellated mansion is attractively decorated inside and boasts a fine dungeon bar with rough plaster and stone walls.

GREGANS CASTLE HOTEL, Ballyvaughan, Co Clare, Tel: (010 353 65) 77005
Once the home of the Prince of Burren, the impressive architecture of this hotel is further enhanced by rolling views of Galway Bay and the limestone hills of Burren. A peaceful library with leather-bound classics is a delightful room.

HOTEL DUNLOE CASTLE, Beaufort, Co Kerry, Tel: (010 353 64) 44111
A creeper-clad keep in beautiful wooded grounds is a reminder of the original castle. The spacious first floor lounge affords wonderful views of the gap of Dunloe.

LONGUEVILLE HOUSE, Mallow, Co Cork, Tel: (010 353 22) 47156
Resting in a 500 acre cattle and sheep farm this substantial Georgian hotel has a very relaxed and informal atmosphere, with a pretty collection of antiques to decorate the interior.

MARLFIELD HOUSE, Gorey, Co Wexford, Tel: (010 353 55) 21124
An 18th century mansion house set in beautifully maintained mature gardens. Stylishly decorated inside including a notable collection of antiques.

MOUNT FALCON CASTLE, Ballina, Co Mayo, Tel: (010 353 96) 21172
The relaxed atmosphere of this old Victorian mansion is probably one of its biggest attractions. The unique and entertaining Constance Aldridge has lived and held court here since 1932.

MOUNT JULIET, Thomastown, Co Kilkenny, Tel: (010 353 56) 24455
This handsome 18th century house holds sway over a 1400 acre estate which includes a stud farm and a Jack Nicklaus designed golf course. Beautifully designed inside, complete with moulded ceilings and marble fireplace.

NEWPORT HOUSE, Newport, Co Mayo Tel:(010 353 98) 41222
Superb ivy clad, bow fronted Georgian Mansion. The peaceful sitting room boasts a fine fireplace and overhead an enormous chandelier. An elegant twisting staircase leads to the galleried landing.

PARK HOTEL KENMARE, Kenmare, Co Kerry, Tel:(010 353 64) 41200
Originally a railway hotel dating from 1897 it boasts many beautiful antiques, including a fascinating cistern decorated with mythological figures and supported by gilded dolphin. A Pianist plays each evening in the beautiful hexagonal bar.

PARKNASILLA GREAT SOUTHERN HOTEL, Killarney, Co Kerry, Tel: (010 353 64) 45122
Resting in delightful shoreside woodland, this imposing 19th century house has strong traditional links with George Bernard Shaw, and keeps up to modern standards with fine refurbishments.

THE SHELBOURNE, Dublin, Co Dublin, Tel: (010 353 1) 766471
This one is a bit of a Dublin institution, boasting the history of having had the Irish Constitution drafted in one of its rooms. The Horseshoe Bar is too famous and established to be upgraded.

TINAKILLY HOUSE HOTEL, Rathnew, Co Wicklow, Tel: (010 353 404) 69274
A bird sanctuary overlooks this mid-Victorian Italianate mansion, set in ten acres of superbly maintained gardens. A real log fire burns in the marble fireplace while bedrooms have canopied and four-poster beds.

WATERFORD CASTLE, The Island Ballinakill, Co Waterford, Tel: (010 353 51) 78203
Set on a private 310 acre island and reached by ferry, this 18th century castle is beautifully tranquil and impressively decorated inside with stone walls, old panelling and a gorgeous ribbon plastered ceiling.

ACCOMMODATION OF MERIT

ANNESBROOK, Duleek, Co Meath, Tel: (010 353 41) 23293
A beautiful Georgian house set amidst park and woodland. The perfect place from which to explore Newgrange, Tara, Monasterboice and Boyne. It is very welcoming, with its spacious bedrooms and delicious local food in its historical surroundings.

AVONDALE HOUSE, Scribblestown, Co Dublin, Tel: (010 353 1) 386545
On the banks of the Tolka, this 18th century house was once a farm, and then hunting lodge for the Earl of Granard. Pleasant surroundings with interesting period architecture provides an ideal base for Dublin, whilst Phoenix Park is only a walk away.

CLOCHAMON HOUSE, Bunclody, Co Wexford, Tel: (010 353 54) 77253
A beautiful late 18th century country house in the Slaney Valley, with the Slaney River below, and panoramic views of Mount Leinster. Surrounded by dairy farmland, rare trees and plants

abound in the gardens. Meals feature home-grown and local produce.

CULLINTRA HOUSE, Inistioge, Co Kilkenny, Tel: (010 353 51) 23614
A charming two hundred year old house set at the foot of Mount Brandon in a very rural area. Relax here whilst touring Ireland. Rosslare and Waterford are not far away. Painting tuition for small groups and game fishing can be arranged.

DUNMHON COUNTRY HOUSE, Co Cork, Tel: (010 353 27) 67092
A warm welcome is assured in this lovely house. The food is outstanding with home-grown produce a feature. 'Escargots' are a speciality - the host is chairman of the Irish Snail Farmers Association - as are fresh local lobsters caught daily. Convenient for Glengarriff and Garinish Island gardens.

ELEGANT IRELAND, 15 Harcourt Street, Dublin 2, Tel: (010 353 1) 751632 / 751665
Elegant Ireland are an incoming Tour Operator who can offer a wide range of services to interested clients. In addition to securing all travel and accomodation arrangements, possibilities include Garden Tours, Stately Home Tours, Art Tours and Golf Tours - a comprehensive service indeed.

HAMWOOD HOUSE, Dunboyne, Co Meath, Tel: (010 353 1) 255210
Built in 1760 this house is owned by the seventh generation of Hamiltons. The gardens are beautiful and open to the public one day a month. Ideal for exploring the historical Boyne Valley and Westmeath Lakes.

LISMACUE HOUSE, Bansha, Co Tipperary, Tel: (010 353 62) 54106
The hostess' family have owned this classic country mansion since it was built in 1813. At the foot of the Galtee mountains and set in extensive grounds, it provides a beautiful setting for exploring Ireland's history.

LISVANAGH, Rathvilly, Co Carlow, Tel: (010 353 503) 61104
Situated in extensive tranquil parkland, this Victorian Gothic mansion, built in 1848, provides a friendly and historic setting for those who wish to visit Russborough House, National Stud and the Japanese Gardens. With the medieval city of Kilkenny nearby.

NORTHERN IRELAND

HOTELS OF DISTINCTION

BUSHMILLS INN, Bushmills, Co Antrim, Tel: (026 57) 32339
The bar in this charming inn has quiet gas lights and prints that fill it with character. All found in a town boasting the oldest licensed distillery in Ireland.

THE OLD INN, Crawfordsburn, Co Down, Tel: (0247) 853255
Providing hospitality to travellers since the seventeenth century, this thatched inn sits in one of Ireland's prettiest villages. Conveniently accessible from Belfast airport, its interior is decorated with oak beams, antiques and soft gas lighting.

BLACKHEATH HOUSE, Macduff's, Garvagh, Co Londonderry, Tel: (0265) 868433
Primarily a splendid restaurant, this late Georgian rectory also offers rooms and a relaxed and friendly welcome.

CULLODEN HOTEL, Holywood, Co Down, Tel: (023 17) 5223
Standing in 12 acres of private grounds and overlooking Belfast Lough, this Victorian gothic house provides a superb example of the period architecture, with pointed windows, ribbed arches and stained glass windows.

MAGERAMORNE HOUSE HOTEl, Larne, Co Antrim, Tel: (0574) 79444
This Victorian stone mansion commands forty-six acres of formal gardens and grounds. Besides the magnificent architecture, recent refurbishments mean a variety of modern facilities.

BAYVIEW HOTEL, Portballintrae, Co Antrim, Tel: (026 57) 31453
This fairly small but long building offers wonderful views over the fresh and picturesque Portballintrae Bay, complete with its tiny harbour.

LONDONDERRY ARMS HOTEL, Carnlough, Co Antrim, Tel: (0574) 885255
This charming Georgian coaching inn was built by Sir Winston Churchill's great-grandmother back in 1848. The atmosphere is warm and friendly in this family-run hotel.

DRUMNAGREAGH HOTEL, Glenarm, Co Antrim, Tel: (0574) 841651
Resting in private grounds this pretty hotel dates back to 1896. Its whitewased walls exude charm while the inside is prepared with the modern conveniences that the discerning traveller expects.

SYLVAN HILL HOUSE, Dromore, Co Down, Tel: (0846) 692321
This listed Georgian "one-and-a-half-storey" house dates back to 1781 and offers stunning panoramic views across the mountains of Mourne and Dromara. Log fires welcome you inside.

ACCOMODATION OF MERIT

HOLESTONE HOUSE, Doagh, Co Antrim, Tel: (09603) 52306)
This family owned Georgian mansion, set in beautiful gardens and woodland, retains its original character. A mere 13 miles from Belfast it offers delightful accomodation.

GLEN HOUSE, Crawfordsburn, Co Down, Tel: (0247) 852610
Glen House was built in 1710 on the edge of what is now Crawfordsburn Country park. It is a pretty, white country house, close to the beach and offering an ideal place from which to tour Northern Ireland.

TULLYHONA HOUSE, Florence Court, Co Fermanagh, Tel: (036 582) 452
Ideally situated near Florence Court National Trust House and Marble Arch Caves, this award-winning beef and sheep farm guesthouse provides delicious food and comfortable accomodation. In season lambing tours and game shooting can be arranged.

ENNISKEEN HOUSE, Newcastle, Co Down, Tel: (039 67) 22392
An attractive Victorian house set in extensive mature gardens and offering impressive views across the Shinna Valley to the Mourne Mountains. This country house hotel provides quality cuisine and comfortable accomodation.

MARLFIELD HOUSE

Marlfield House is a fine house set in thirty-five acres of woodlands and gardens and was the principle residence of the Earl of Courtown. It has been converted by its present owners, Ray and Mary Bowe, whose aim is to meet the demands of the more discerning guest who insists on the best country house atmosphere.

The award winning restaurant is a memorable experience and serves modern French cooking with a classical base. At the rear of the house is a spectacular conservatory. An inner, mirrored section reflects painted forest scenes and is snug in winter. An outer section opens to the gardens for summer dining. Vegetables, herbs and some fruits are grown in the kitchen garden and ali local produce is made use of in the kitchen.

Accommodation is in nineteen superb rooms, including five luxurious junior suites and one magnificent master suite. These are lavishly decorated using period furniture, and have huge marble en suite bathrooms, some with jacuzzis. Each of the junior suites has its own theme: Irish Georgian, French, etc.

Marlfield is only eighty kilometres from Dublin, in the heart of the countryside, situated on the Gorey to Courtown Road, just two kilometres from a golf course; sandy beaches; or there is also fishing and shooting available in the area. It provides an ideal setting for touring the beauty spots of Wicklow and the South East of Ireland.

Marlfield House
Gorey
Co. Wexford
Tel: (010 353 55) 21125
Fax: (010 353 55) 21572

DROMOLAND CASTLE

Once the seat of the O'Brien clan, Dromoland Castle has all the imposing stature you'd expect of the Kings of Munster. It stands proud on its own lakeside setting - a location that instantly highlights it as a very exceptional hotel indeed.

The warm red carpet in the expansive reception hall reflects the warmth of the Dromoland welcome - a genuine attitude further supported by a subtle combination of informality and efficiency.

The numerous lounges are of truly regal proportions, extremely comfortable with exquisite decor. A cosy bar and a relaxing snooker room are two additional options to help pass the evening hours.

The magnificence of the hotel is more than equalled by the quality of the French and indigenous cuisine. In 1990, the Earl of Thomond Room restaurant won an Egon Ronay star as 'Best Hotel Restaurant' in Ireland. With its expansive views, it's an ideal setting to while away some delightful hours accompanied by the finest of wines from one of the most extensive cellars in the country.

Golfing guests can enjoy the challenge of the hotel's own 18-hole golf course and for an even greater challenge the championship courses of Lahinch and Ballybunion are nearby.

Anglers are catered for with trout in the hotel's own lake and salmon and trout in the nearby Shannon. An hour away, the more adventurous can tackle some deep-sea angling on the West coast. hunting of a different kind starts on November 1st, for snipe, pheasant and duck.

With Shannon international airport only 8 miles away, it's not surprising that Dromoland has proved a very popular location for international conferences and seminars. Its prestigious reputation adds a unique status to any such event or management think-tank.

If the O'Briens of old returned to day, they could only but be impressed. The manicured lawns...the calm elegance...the finest in food and facilities. It's true what they say - there is only one Dromoland.

Dromoland Castle
Newmarket-on-Fergus
Co. Clare
Ireland
Tel: (010 353 61) 368144
Fax: (010 353 61) 363355

TINAKILLY HOUSE

This delightful hotel was originally built for Captain Robert Halpin, the man who, as Commander of the Great Eastern, laid the first telegraph cable linking Europe to America. Now fully restored by William and Bee Power, the blend of Victorian elegance, good service and Irish hospitality make a stay at Tinakilly a true country house experience.

The classical Victorian architecture is augmented by splendid furnishings from the same era. The kitchen prepares country house cuisine, with excellent fresh food including home-grown vegetables and legendary brown bread. Fish and Wicklow lamb in summer, and game in winter, feature on the resident chef's menu. Each bedroom has full central heating, bathroom en suite, automatic dial telephone and television.

Tinakilly offers an ideal place from which to visit Dublin, with its many historical and architectural delights. In addition, golfing, fishing and horse riding can be organised close by. For the keen golfer, the area should need no introduction - you are literally spoilt for choice. So whether you want a spot of peace and quiet in the Wicklow countryside, or a base from which to tour this fascinating part of Ireland, Tinakilly House, overlooking the Irish Sea, is a reminder of how calm and luxurious life can still be.

Tinakilly House Hotel
Rathnew
Co Wicklow
Ireland
Tel: (010 353 404) 69274
Fax: (010 353 404) 67806

Castle Coole   (National Trust)

NEWPORT HOUSE

Adjoining the town of Newport and overlooking the tidal river and quay the impressive country mansion of Newport House stands guard over the centuries of history that form the backbone to its grounds and the surrounding countryside. Once the home of a branch of the O'Donel family, descended from the famous fighting Earls of Tir Connell and cousins to 'Red Hugh' of Irish history, it is now a superb example of a lovingly maintained Georgian Mansion House.

Encircled by mountains, lakes and streams, Newport is within easy reach of some of Ireland's most beautiful rivers. Renowned as an angling centre, it holds private salmon and sea-trout fishing rights to 8 miles of the Newport River; and the prolific waters of the stunning Lough Beltra West are close by. Less than twenty minutes drive from the hotel are Lakes Mask and Corrib, while the nearby Loughs Feeagh and Furnace are the site of the Salmon Research Trust of Ireland.

The discerning golfer has the pleasure of the 18-hole championship course at Westport as well as the more relaxed 9-hole course near Mulrany.

Outdoor activities are numerous amidst the breath-taking scenery of County Mayo. Riding is easily arranged or try swimming and diving on wide and often empty beaches, while hanggliding is a relatively new sport gaining popularity from the local Achill Cliffs. One of the best recreations though is simply walking across the ever changing panorama of mountain, forest and sea.

Warmth and friendliness fill this beautiful hotel in a country already famed for its hospitality. The house is furnished with a tasteful collection of fine antiques and paintings and the elegant bedrooms are individually decorated. Food is taken seriously, with much of the produce collected fresh from the fishery, gardens and farm. Home-smoked salmon and fresh sea-food are specialites, and all the dishes are complemented by a carefully chosen and extensive wine list.

Many of the staff have been long in the service of the estate, up to forty years in one case. Combine this with the solid background of the house and there is a rare feeling of continuity and maturity so rare in modern hotels today.

Newport House
Co. Mayo
Ireland
Tel: (010 353 98) 41222
Fax: (010 353 98) 41613

LONGUEVILLE HOUSE

Longueville is set in the centre of a 500 acre private wooded estate, overlooking one of the most beautiful river valleys in Ireland, the Blackwater - itself forming the Estate's southern boundary, famous as one of Ireland's foremost salmon and trout rivers.

Longueville is three miles on the Killarney road ex Mallow; Killarney itself in the heart of scenic Kerry being less than one hour away. Cork airport is 24 miles distant and Shannon airport is 54 miles away. Guests can make day trips to the Dingle and Beara Peninsulas. Blarney, Kinsale and the Vee Gap are all less than one hour's drive. For stay-at-homes, Longueville offers three miles of game fishing on the famous Blackwater river. There is horse-riding at nearby stables and golf at a dozen courses closeby including Premier Championship courses at Killarney, Ballybunion and Tralee.

A games room with full sized billiard table is in the basement. The estate is quiet and peaceful for walking or jogging with idyllic paths through wooded ways and water meadows.

Built in 1720, Longueville is the ancestral home of your hosts. Their aim is to maintain the friendly atmosphere of a home rather than a hotel. The centre block and two wings were added in 1800 and the Turner Curvilinear Conservatory was added in 1862.

Inside, Longueville offers many beautiful ceilings, doors and items of antique furniture in the public rooms and bedrooms - but in the latter, whether it be antique or otherwise, the acme of comfort is the bed. All bedrooms have en suite bathroom, colour television, radio and direct dial telephone.

The aim of Longueville's hosts is to have guests relax and feel completely at home in the comfort of their beautiful house, a classic Georgian country house. Central to all this is the kitchen, the heart of Longueville, over which the O'Callaghans' son William, a French-trained chef, presides. In here three lovingly prepared meals a day are made, using only the fresh produce of the estate's river, farm and gardens.

To match the superb food, Longueville's cellar includes over 150 wines, both from the Old and New World. The family's interest in wine has led them to plant their own three acre vineyard - unique in Ireland - produced in years of favourable climate.

Longueville House & Presidents' Restaurant
Mallow
Co Cork
Republic of Ireland
Tel: (010 353 22) 47156/47306
Fax: (010 353 22) 47459

ASHFORD CASTLE

An historic Irish castle, dating back to the 13th century, Ashford is now one of the finest hotels in the world.

Enter the main reception hall and the feeling of genuine history is matched only by the warmth of the welcome. Solid oak beams and wood panelling reflect a more formal age, but the most modern facilities and comforts are reassuring signs that Ashford is very much a hotel of today. And it's that same sense of elegant luxury which has entitled Ashford to host former US Presidents, European royalty and international celebrities.

For the past three years, Ashford Castle has been nominated 'Best Hotel In Ireland' by Egon Ronay. Experience the finest food and wine in the George V dining room or in the Connaught Room gourmet restaurant where the most fastidious palate is treated to the exquisite delights of French cuisine.

Standing on the shore of Lough Corrib, Ireland's second-largest lake, it's no surprise that Ashford offers its guests some of the most sporting salmon, trout, pike and perch fishing in the West of Ireland. But if golfing is more your bag, the hotel grounds comfortably accommodate Ashford's own 9-hole golf course - and golf clubs are available. For variety and an even stiffer challenge two additional courses are less than fifty miles away. From November 1st, shots of a different kind abound as hunters go in search of duck and pheasant; with unlimited rough shooting.

With its spacious grounds offering their own calming air of quiet it's no surprise that Ashford is consistently chosen by national and international corporations and organisations for conferences and management get-togethers.

Seven centuries since the first brick was laid, the setting, atmosphere and discreet luxury have made Ashford Castle more than a unique hotel. It's an experience.

RELAIS &
CHATEAUX
IRELAND

Ashford Castle
Cong
Co. Mayo
Ireland
Tel: (010 353 92) 46003
Fax: (010 353 92) 46260

KEY

Opening Times

*	Open Bank Holidays only.
**	Open summer months only.
***	Open all year.
R	Restricted opening, advisable to ring.
G	Gardens only.
NT	National Trust.
EH	English Heritage.

Price Guide

A	under £1.50
B	£1.50 - £3.50
C	Over £3.50
D	Free
+	Children free

THE WEST COUNTRY

CORNWALL

Antony House (NT)
Torpoint
(0752) 812191
**R / B

Antony Woodland Garden and
Natural Woods Torpoint
**R / A

Chysauster Ancient Village (EH)
Madron
(0736) 61889
** / A

Cotehele House (NT)
Calstock
Liskeard 50434
** / C

Glendurgan Garden (NT)
Helford River
(0326) 311300
**G / B

Godolphin House
Helston
(0736) 762409
**R / B

Lanhydrock (NT)
Bodmin
Bodmin 73320
** / C

Launceston Castle (EH)
(0566) 2365
*** R / A

Lawrence House
LauncestoN
(0566) 2833
** / A

Long Cross Victorian Gardens
Port Isaac
(0208) 880243
**G / D

Mount Edgcumbe House and
Country Park
Plymouth
Plymouth (0752) 822236
** / B

Pencarrow House and Garden
Bodmin
(0326) 316594
** / B

Pendennis Castle (EH)
Falmouth
(0326) 316594
** / A

Poldark Tin Mine
Wendron
(0326) 573173
**

Prideaux Place
Padstow
(0841) 532411
** / B

Restormel Castle (EH)
Lostwithiel
(020887) 2687
*** / A

St. Mawes Castle (EH)
St. Mawes
(0326) 270526
*** / A

St. Michael's Mount (NT)
Marazion
Penzance 710507
** / B

Tintagel Castle (EH)
Tintagel
(0840) 770328
** / A

Tintagel - The Old Post Office
(NT)
Tintagel
** / A

Trelissick Garden (NT)
Truro
Truro 862090
** / B

Trelowarren House and Chapel
Mawgan-in-Meneage, Helston
(032 622) 366
** / A

Trengwainton Garden (NT)
Penzance
Penzance 63021
**G / B

Trerice (NT)
St Newlyn East
Newquay 87504
** / B

Trewithen House and Gardens
Probus, nr Truro
(0726) 882418
** / B

DEVON

A La Ronde
Exmouth
(0395) 265514
**R

Arlington Court (NT)
Barnstaple
Barnstaple (0271) 850296
*** / C

Avenue Cottage Gardens
Ashprington, Totnes
(080 423) 769
** / D

Bickham Barton
Roborough
(0822) 852478
**RG / A

Bickleigh Castle
nr Tiverton
Bickleigh (088 45) 363
** / B

Bowden House
Totnes
Totnes (0803) 863664
** / B

Bradley Manor (NT)
Newton Abbot
** R / B

Buckland Abbey (NT)
Yelverton
(0822) 853607
** / C

Cadhay
Ottery St Mary
Ottery St Mary 2432
** / B

Castle Drogo (NT)
nr Chagford
(064 73) 3306
** / C

Chambercombe House
Ilfracombe
(0271) 62624
** / B

Coleton Fishacre Garden (NT)
Coleton
(080 425) 466
** / B

Compton Castle (NT)
nr Paington
(0803) 872112
** / B

Darlington Hall & Gardens
Darlington
(0803) 862224
*** / B

Dartmouth Castle (EH)
Dartmouth
(08043) 3588
** / B

Endsleigh House
Milton Abbot, nr Tavistock
(0822) 87 248
**G /

Fursden House
Cadbury
(0392) 860860
** R / B

Hemerdon House
Plympton, Plymouth
(0752) 223816
R / B

Killerton (NT)
nr Exeter
(0392) 881345
** / C

Kirkham House (EH)
Paignton
(0803) 522775
** / A

Knightshayes Court (NT)
nr Tiverton
(0884) 254665
** / C

Marwood Hill
nr Barnstaple
(0271) 42528
***G / A

Okehampton Castle (EH)
Okehampton
(0837) 2844
*** / A

Overbecks Museum and
Garden (NT)
Sharpitor, Salcombe
(054 884) 2893
** / B

Powderham Castle
nr Exeter
(0626) 890 243
** / B

Saltram House (NT)
Plymouth
(0752) 336546
** / C

Tiverton Castle
Tiverton
(0884)253200
** / B

Torre Abbey
Torquay
(0803) 293593
** / A

THE HERITAGE DIRECTORY : ENGLAND

Totnes House (EH)
Totnes
(0803) 864406
*** / A

Ugbrooke House
Chudleigh
(0626) 852179
** / C

WESSEX

AVON

Barstaple House (Trinity
Almshouses)
Bristol
(0272) 265777
*** / D

Beckford's Tower
Bath
(0225) 312917
** / A

Blaise Castle House Museum
Henbury
(0272) 506789
*** / D

Claverton Manor
nr Bath
(0225) 460503
** / C

Clevedon Court (NT)
nr Clevedon
(0272) 872257
** / B

Dyrham Park (NT)
nr Bristol and Bath
Abson 2501
** / C

Georgian House
Bristol
(0272) 299771 ext 237
*** / D

Holburne Museum
Bath
(0225) 66669
*** / B

Horton Court (NT)
Horton
** / A

Little Sodbury Manor
Chipping Sodbury
Chipping Sodbury 312232
R / B

Museum of Costume
Bath
(0225) 461111 ext 2751

Number One, Royal Crescent
Bath
(0225)428126
* / R

Red Lodge
Bristol
(0272) 299771 ext 236
*** / D

Roman Baths Museum
Bath
(0225) 461111 ext 2785
***

Vine House
Henbury, Bristol
(0272) 503573
R / A

DORSET

Abbotsbury Gardens
Abbotsbury
(0305) 871387
** / B

Athelhampton
Athelhampton
Puddeltown (0305) 848363
**R / B

Chettle House
Chettle, Blandfor
(0258 89) 209
** / B

Chiffchaffs
Chaffeymoor, Bourton,
Gillingham
Bourton 840841
**RG / A

Clouds Hill (NT)
nr Wool
(0929) 463824
**R / B

Compton House
nr Sherborne
(0935) 74608
**R /

Cranborne Manor Gardens
Cranborne
(07254) 289
**RG

Deans Court
Wimborne
**RG / A

Edmondsham House and
Gardens
Cranborne, nr Winborne
(072 54) 207
*R / B

Fiddleford Manor (EH)
(0258) 72597
** / A

Forde Abbey and Gardens
nr Chard
(0460) 20231
** /R / B+

Hardy's Cottage (NT)
Higher Bockhampton
Dorchester 62366
** / B

Highbury
West Moors
Ferndown 874372
**RG / A

Kingston Lacy
Wimborne
(0202) 88342
** / B

Lullingstone Silk Farm
Sherborne
(0935) 74608
** / B

Minterne
Dorchester
(03003) 370
*G / A+

Parnham House
Beaminster
(0308) 862204
**R / B+

Priest's House Museum and
Garden
23 High Street, Wimborne
Minster
Wimborne 882533
** / A

Portland Castle (EH)
(0305) 820539
** / A

Sherborne Castle
Sherborne
(0935) 813182
** / B

Sherborne Old Castle (EH)
Sherborne
(0935) 812730
*** / A

Smedmore
Kimmeridge
Corfe Castle 480719
**R / B

SOMERSET

Barrington Court
Ilminster
(0460) 41480
**

The Bishop's Palace
Wells
(0749) 78691
**R / B

Brympton d'Evercy
nr Yeovil
(0935) 862528
**

Cleeve Abbey (EH)
Washford
(0272) 734472
*** / A

Coleridge Cottage (NT)
Nether Stowey, nr Bridgwater
Nether Stowey 732662
**R / A

Combe Sydenham Country
Park
Monksilver
Stogumber (0984) 56284
** / B

Dodington Hall
nr Nether Stowey, Bridgwater
(0278 74) 400
**R / A

Dunster Castle (NT)
nr Minehead
Dunster 821314
** / C

Farleigh Hungerford Castle
(EH)
(0272) 734472
*** / A

Glastonbury Abbey
Glastonbury
(0458) 32267
***

Glastonbury Tribunal (EH)
Glastonbury
(0458) 32949
*** / A

Hatch Court
Hatch Beauchamp
(0823) 480208
** R

Hestercombe House and
Gardens
Cheddon Fitzpaine, Taunton
(0823) 337222
*** / A

Lytes Cary Manor
Charlton Mackrell
(045822) 3297
**

Maunsel House
North Newton, nr Bridgwater
(0278) 663413
** / A

Montacute House (NT)
Yeovil
Martock 823289
** / C

Muchelney Abbey
Langport
(0458) 250664
** / A

Priest's House (NT)
Muchelney
(0458) 250672
*** / A

Stoke-Sub-Hamdon Priory (NT)
nr Montacute
*** / D

Tintinhull House Garden (NT)
nr Yeovil
**RG / B

Wookey Hole Caves
Wookey Hole
(0749) 72243
***

WILTSHIRE

Avebury Museum (EH)
Marlborough
(06723) 250
*** / A

Bowood House and Gardens
Calne
(0249) 81202
**

Chisenbury Priory Gardens
East Chisenbury
(0980) 70406
**RG / A

Corsham Court
Chippenham
(0249) 712214
*** / C

The Court's Garden (NT)
Holt
North Trowbridge
(0225) 782340
**G / A+

Fitz House Garden
Teffont Magna
072276 257
**G

Hamptworth Lodge
Landford, Salisbury
(0794) 390215
R / B+

Heale House Gardens
Middle Woodford
(072273) 207
**

Lacock Abbey (NT)
nr Chippenham
Lacock 227
** / B

Littlecote House
Marlborough
(0488) 84000
**

Longleat House
Warminster
(0985) 844551
***

Mompesson House (NT)
(0722) 335659
Salisbury
** / B

Old Sarum (EH)
Salisbury
(0722) 335398
*** / A

Old Wardour Castle (EH)
Tisbury
(0747) 870487
*** / A

Philipps House (NT)
Dinton
Teffont 208
R / A

Sheldon Manor
Chippenham
(0249) 653120
R

Shute Barton (NT)
Shute, Nr Axminster
(0297) 34692
** / A

Stonehenge (EH)
Amesbury
(0980) 23108
***

Stourhead (NT)
Stourton, nr Mere
(0747) 840348
*** / C

Wardour Castle
Tisbury
(0747) 870464
** R

Westwood Manor (NT)
nr Bradford-on-Avon
** / B

Wilton House
Wilton
(0722) 743115
** / C

Win Green Hill (NT)
Win Green Hill

THE SOUTHERN COUNTIES

HAMPSHIRE

Avington Park
Winchester
0962-78-202
**/ B

Beaulieu
Beaulieu
(0590) 612345
***/ C

Bishop's Waltham Palace (EH)
Bishop's Waltham
(048 93) 2460
***/ B

Breamore House
nr Fordingbridge
(0725) 22468
**R/ B

Broadlands
Romsey
(0794) 516878
** / C

Calshot Castle (EH)
Fawley
(0703) 892023
** / A

Exbury Gardens
Elson
nr Southampton
**RG

Fort Brockhurst (EH)
Elson
(0705) 581059
*** / A

The Hawk Conservancy
Weyhill
(0264) 772252
**

The Hillier Gardens and
Arboretum
Ampfield, nr Romsey
(0794) 68787
***G / B

Hinton Ampner (NT)
nr Alresford
(0962) 771305
** / B

Houghton Lodge
Stockbridge
** / B

Hurst Castle (EH)
Keyhaven
(0590) 2344
*** / A

Jane Austen's House
Chawton
*** / A

Medieval Wine Merchant's
House (EH)
Southampton
(0703) 221503
*** / A

Mottisfont Abbey Garden (NT)
Mottisfont
Lockerley 41220
**G / B

Netley Abbey (EH)
Netley
(0703) 453076
*** / A

Portchester Castle (EH)
Portchester
(0705) 378291
*** / A

Sandham Memorial Chapel
(NT)
Burghclere,
Nr. Newbury
Burghclere 394 or 292
**

Stratfield Saye House
Reading
(0256) 882882
** / B

Titchfield Abbey (EH)
Titchfield
(0329) 43016
** / A

Winchester Cathedral
Winchester
(0962) 840500
*** / D+

Wolvesley: Old Bishop's Palace
(EH)
Winchester
(0962) 54766
** / A

The Vyne (NT)
Basingstoke
Basingstoke 881337
** / C

ISLE OF WIGHT

Appuldurcombe House (EH)
Wroxall
(0983) 852484
*** / A

Carisbrooke Castle (EH)
Newport
(0983) 522107
*** / B

The Needles Old Battery (NT)
Totland Bay
Isle of Wight 754772
** / A

Newtown Old Town Hall (NT)
Newtown
**R / A

Osborne House (EH)
East Cowes
(0983) 200022
** / C

THE HERITAGE DIRECTORY : ENGLAND

Yarmouth Castle (EH)
Yarmouth
(0983) 760678
** / A

SURREY

Albury Park
Albury, Guildford
** / B

Chilworth Manor
nr Guildford
**G / A+

Clandon Park (NT)
nr Guildford
Guildford 222482
** / C

Claremont Landscape Garden
(NT)
Esher
***G / A

Coverwood Lakes
Peaslake Road, Ewhurst
(0306) 731103
**R / A

Farnham Castle
Farnham
***R / A

Farnham Castle Keep (EH)
Farnham
(0252) 713393
** / A

Guildford House Gallery
Guildford
(0483) 444741
*** / D

Hatchlands Park (NT)
East Clandon
Guildford 222787
** / B

Loseley House
Guildford
(0483) 571881
** / B

Painshill Park
Portsmouth Road, Cobham
(0932) 868113
**G / B+

Polesden Lacey (NT)
nr Dorking
Bookham 58203
***R / B

Winkworth Arboretum (NT)
nr Godalming
***G / B

Wisley Garden
Wisley
***G / B

Ventnor Botanic Gardens
Ventnor
*** / D

WEST SUSSEX

Arundel Castle
Arundel
Arundel 883136
** / C

Chichester Cathedral
West Street
Chichester 782595
*** / D

Coates Manor
nr Fittleworth
RG/ A

Gibside Chapel and Grounds
(NT)
Gibside
(0207) 542255
** / B

Goodwood House
Chichester
(0243) 774107
**

Hammerwood Park
nr East Grinstead
(0342) 850594
** / B

Leonardslee Gardens
Horsham
**G / B

Nymans Garden (NT)
Handcross
Handcross 440321
**G / B

Parham House and Gardens
Pulborough
(0903) 742021
** / B

Petworth House (NT)
Petworth
(0798) 42207
**/ B

St Mary's House and Gardens
Bramber
Steyning 816205
** / B

Standen (NT)
East Grinstead
(0342) 23029
**R/ B

Stansted Park
Rowlands Castle
0705 412265
**R/ B

Wakehurst Place Garden (NT)
nr Ardingly
(0444) 892701
***G / B

Washington Old Hall (NT)
Washington
(091) 4166879
** / B

The Weald and Downland
Open Air Museum
Singleton, nr Chichester
(024 363) 348
***R / B

THE GARDEN OF
ENGLAND

KENT

Bedgebury National Pinetum
nr Goudhurst
(0580) 211044
***G / A

Boughton Monchelsea Place
nr Maidstone
(0622) 43120
** / B

Chartwell (NT)
Westerham
Edenbridge 866368
**R / C

Chiddingstone Castle
nr Edenbridge
(0892) 870347
** / B

Chilham Castle Gardens
nr Canterbury
Canterbury 730319
**G / B

Deal and Walmer Castles (EH)
(0304) 372762 or 364288
*** / B

Doddington Place Gardens
nr Sittingbourne
(079586) 385
**RG / B

Dover Castle (EH)
Dover
(0304) 201628
*** / B

Dymchurch Martello Towers
(EH)
Dymchurch
(0303) 873684
*** / A

Finchcocks
Goudhurst
(0580) 211702
** / C

Hever Castle and Gardens
nr Edenbridge
(0732) 865224
**/ B

Ightham Mote (NT)
Ivy Hatch
Plaxtol 810378
** / B

Knole (NT)
Sevenoaks
Sevenoaks 450608
** / B

Leeds Castle
nr Maidstone
Maidstone (0622) 765400
** / B

Lullingston Roman Villa (EH)
Eynsford
(0322) 863467
*** / A

Maison Dieu Hall, Ospringe
(EH)
Faversham
(0795) 533751
** R / A

Milton Chantry, Gravesend
(EH)
Milton
(0474) 321520
** / A

Owl House Gardens
Lamberhurst
***G / B

Owletts (NT)
Cobham
**R / A

Penshurst Place
Tunbridge Wells
(0892) 870307
** / B

Quebec House (NT)
Westerham
Westerham 62206
** / B

Reculver Towers and
Roman Fort (EH)
(02273) 66444
** / A

Richborough Castle (EH)
Sandwich
(0304) 612013
*** / A

Rochester Castle (EH)
Rochester
(0634) 402276
** / B

St. Augustine's Abbey (EH)
Canterbury
(0227) 67345
*** / A

St John's Jerusalem Garden
(NT)
Dartford
**R / A

THE HERITAGE DIRECTORY : ENGLAND

Saltwood Castle
nr Hythe
(303) 267190
R

Scotney Castle Garden (NT)
Lamberhurst
(0892) 890651
**G / B

Sissinghurst Castle Garden (NT)
Sissinghurst
Cranbrook 712850
** / C

Smallhythe Place (NT)
Tenterden
Tenterden 2334
** / B

Sprivers Garden (NT)
Horsmonden
**RG / A

Squerryes Court
Westerham
(0959) 62345
** / B

Stoneacre (NT)
Otham
** / A

Temple Manor (EH)
Rochester
(0634) 718743
** / A

Walmer Castle
Walmer
(0304) 364288
*** / B

Upnor Castle
Strood
(0634) 718742
** / A

EAST SUSSEX

Alfriston Clergy House (NT)
Alfriston, nr Seaford
(0323) 870001
**R / B

Bateman's (NT)
Burwash
Burwash 882302
** / B

Battle Abbey (EH)
Battle
(04246) 3792
** / B

Bayham Abbey (EH)
Lamberhurst
(0892) 890381
** / A

Beeches Farm
nr Uckfield
*** / A

Bodiam Castle (NT)
nr Robertsbridge
(058 083) 436
** / A

Filching Manor
Jevington Road, Wannock, nr
Polegate
(0323) 7838/7124
** / B

Firle Place
nr Lewes
(079 159) 335
**R / B

Glynde Place
nr Lewes
(079 159) 337
**R / B

Great Dixter
Northiam
(0797) 2533160
**/ B

Haremere Hall
Etchingham
Etchingham 245
**R/ B

Lamb House (NT)
Rye
** / A

Monks House (NT)
Rodmell
** / B

Pevensey Castle
Pevensey
(0323) 762604
*** / A

Royal Pavilion
Brighton
(0273) 603005
*** / C

Sheffield Park Garden (NT)
nr Uckfield
Danehill 790655
**G / C

LONDON

Apsley house
Wellington Museum
071-499 5676
*** / B

The Bank of England
City of London
071-601 5545
*** / B

The Blewcoat School (NT)
Westminster
071-222 2877
*** / D

Boston Manor
Brentford
081-862 5805
**R / D

Capel Manor
Nr Enfield
(0992) 763849
R / B

Carlyle's House (NT)
Chelsea
071-352 7087
** / B

Carshalton House
(St. Philomena's)
Carshalton
R / B

Chapter House and Pyx
Chamber
Westminster Abbey (EH)
071-222 5897
*** / B

Chelsea Physic Garden
Chelsea
071-352 5646
**G / B

Chiswick House (EH)
Chiswick
081-995 0508
** / B

College of Arms
City of London
071-248-2762
*** / D

The Dickens House
WC1
071-405 2127
*** / B

Dulwich College
Dulwich
081-693 3737
***R

Fulham Palace
Fulham
071-736 5821
*** / B

Ham House
Richmond
081-940 1950
*** / B

Hampton Court Palace
Hampton Court
081-977 8441
*** / C

Heritage Centre
Honeywood, Carshalton
081-770 4745

Imperial War Museum
SE1
071-735 8922
*** / B

Keats House
Wentworth Place, Keats Grove,
Hampstead
071-235 2062
*** / D

Kensington Palace
Kensington
071-937 9561
*** / C

Kenwood, the Iveagh Bequest
(EH)
Hampstead
071-348 1286
** / D

Kew Gardens
Kew
081-940 1171
*** / B

Kew Palace (Dutch House)
Kew
**

Leighton House Museum
Holland Park
071-602 3316
*** /

Linley Sambourne House
Kensington
081-994 1019
** / B

Little Holland House
Carshalton
**R/ D

Marble Hill House (EH)
Charing Cross
071-892 5115
*** / D

Marlborough House
Pall Mall

Museum of Garden History
Lambeth
071-373 4030
** / D

Old Royal Observatory
Greenwich
*** / B

Osterley Park House
Osterley
081-560 3918
*** / B

Ranger's House
Charing Cross
071-853 0035
*** / D

Southside House
Wimbledon Common
081-947 2491
R / B

THE HERITAGE DIRECTORY : ENGLAND

Syon House
Brentford
081-560 0881
** / B

Syon Park Gardens
Brentford
081-560 0881
*** /

Tower of London
Tower Hill
071-709-0765
*** / C

Westminster Abbey/Cathedral
Westminster
071-222 5152
*** / B

Whitehall
Cheam
071-643 1236
***R/ B

EAST ANGLIA

NORFOLK

Beeston Hall
Beeston St Lawrence
(0692) 630771
** / B

Berney Arms Windmill (EH)
(0493) 700605
** / A

Blickling Hall (NT)
Aylsham
Aylsham 733084
** / C

Castle Acre - Priory and Castle
(EH)
(07605) 394
***/ A

Castle Rising Castle (EH)
Castle Rising
(055387) 330
*** / A

Felbrigg Hall (NT)
nr Cromer
West Runton 444
** / C

Grime's Graves (EH)
(0842) 810656
*** / A

Holkham Hall
Wells
(0328) 710227
** / B

Houghton Hall
Kings Lynn
East Rudham 569
**R / B

Mannington Hall Gardens
Saxthorpe, Norfolk
(026 387) 4175
** / B

Norwich Castle
Norwich
(0603) 611277 ext 279

Old Merchant's House and The
Row 111 Houses, Great
Yarmouth (EH)
(0493) 857900
** / A

Oxburgh Hall (NT)
Swaffham
Gooderstone 258
** / B

Rainthorpe Hall and Gardens
Flordon, nr Norwich
** / A

Raveningham Hall Gardens
Norwich
(050846) 206
**RG / A+

Sandringham House and
Grounds
Sandringham
(0553) 772675
** / B

Walsingham Abbey
Walsingham
Walsingham 820259
** / A

Welle Manor Hall
Upwell
(0945) 773333
***R / A

SUFFOLK

Blakenham Woodland Garden
Little Blakenham, nr Ipswich
**G / A

Euston Hall
Thetford
** / A

Framlingham Castle (EH)
(0728) 723330
** / A

Gainsborough's House
Sudbury
(0787) 72958
*** / A

Guildhall (NT)
Lavenham
** / A

Helmingham Hall Gardens
Ipswich
**G / B

Ickworth (NT)
nr Bury St Edmunds
Horringer 270
**R / C

Kentwell Hall
Long Melford
(0787) 310207
**R / C

Melford Hall (NT)
nr Sudbury
**R / B

Orford Castle (EH)
Orford
(039 44) 50472
*** / A

Otley Hall
nr Ipswich
*R / B

The Priory
Lavenham
(0787) 247417
***R / B

Saxtead Green Post Mill (EH)
(0728) 82789
** / A

Somerleyton Hall
nr Lowestoft
**R/ B

Wingfield College
Nr Eye
(037 984) 505
**R /

CAMBRIDGESHIRE

Anglesey Abbey (NT)
Nr Cambridge
(0223) 81120
**R / C

Botanical Gardens
Cambridge
*** / D

Clare College
Cambridge
*** / D

Denny Abbey (EH)
Chittering
(0223) 860489
** / A

Elton Hall
Nr Peterborough
(0832) 280468
**R / B

Kimbolton Castle
Kimbolton
R / A

Longthorpe Tower (EH)
Peterborough
(0733) 268482
** / A

Peckover House and Garden
(NT)
Wisbech
Wisbech 583463
** / B

Wimpole Hall (NT)
Nr Cambridge
(0223) 207257
** / C

Wimpole Home Farm (NT)
Nr Cambridge
** / C

ESSEX

Audley End House and Park
(EH)
Saffron Waldon
(0799) 22399
** / C

Castle House
Dedham
(0206) 322127
** R / A

Gosfield House
Halstead
** R / A

Hedingham Castle
Nr Halstead
(0787) 60261
** / B

Hyde Hall
Rettendon
(0245) 400256
G ** / A+

Paycocke's (NT)
Coggeshall
(0376) 561305
** R / A

Prior's Hall Barn, Widdington
(EH)
(0799) 41047
* / A

St. Osyth Priory
St. Osyth
(0255) 820492
** R / B

Tilbury Fort (EH)
Tilbury
(0375) 858489
*** / A

THE THAMES AND CHILTERNS

BEDFORDSHIRE

Bushmead Priory
St Neaots
(023 062) 614
* / A

Cecil Higgins Art Gallery &
Museum (EH)
Bedford
(0234) 21122
*** R / D

Chicksands Priory
Shefford
(0767) 315674
** R / D

Luton Hoo
Luton
(0582) 22955
** / C

Stagsden Bird Gardens
Stagsden
(023 02) 2745
*** / B

The Swiss Garden
Old Warden
Nr Biggleswade
(0234) 228330
** / B

Woburn Abbey
Woburn
(0525) 290666
** / C

Wrest Park House and Gardens
(EH)
Silsoe
(0525) 60718
* / A

BERKSHIRE

Basildon Park (NT)
Nr Pangbourne
(0734) 843040
** / C

Dorney Court
Windsor
(0628) 604638
** R / C

Frogmore Gardens
Windsor
R / A+

Highclere Castle
nr Newbury
(0635) 253210
**R / B

Littlecote
Hungerford
(0488) 84000
**

The Old Rectory
Burghfield
G R / A

Savill Garden
Windsor Great Park
*** / B

Valley Gardens (G)
Windsor Great Park
*** / D

Windsor Castle
Windsor
(0753) 868286
*** / B

BUCKINGHAMSHIRE

Ascott (NT)
Wing
(0296) 688242
** / C

Chenies Manor House
Chenies
Little Chalfont 2888
** R / B

Chicheley Hall
Newport Pagnell
(023 065) 252
R / C

Chiltern Open Air Museum
Nr Chalfont St Giles
(024 07) 71117
** / B

Claydon House (NT)
Middle Claydon
Nr Winslow
(0296) 730349
** / C

Cliveden (NT)
Maidenhead
(0628) 605069
** / B

Hughenden House (NT)
High Wycombe
(0494) 32580
** / C

Mentmore Towers
(0296) 662183
** / B

Milton Cottage
Chalfont St Giles
Chalfont St Giles 2313
** / B

Nether Winchendon House
Aylesbury
Haddenham 290101
** / B

Princes Risborough House (NT)
Princes Risborough
R / A

Stowe Landscape Gardens (NT)
Nr Buckingham
R

Stowe (Stowe School)
Buckingham
** / C

Waddesdon Manor (NT)
Nr Aylesbury
(0296) 651211
** / C

West Wycombe Park (NT)
West Wycombe
(0494) 24411
** / C

Winslow Hall
Winslow
(029 671) 2323
R

Wotton House
Nr Aylesbury
**

HERTFORDSHIRE

Ashridge Gardens
Berkhamstead
(044254) 3491
** / B+

Hatfield House
Hatfield
(0707) 262823
** R / C

Knebworth House
Knebworth
Stevenage 812661
** R / C

Moor Park Mansion
Nr Rickmansworth
(0923) 776611
*** R / D

Shaw's Corner (NT)
Ayot St. Lawrence
(0438) 820307
** R / B

OXFORDSHIRE

Ardington House
Nr Wantage
(0235) 833244
** / A

Ashdown House (NT)
Nr Lambourn
** R / A

Blenheim Palace
Woodstock
(0993) 811325
** / B

Brook Cottage
Alkerton
(029 587) 303 or 590
** G / A +

Broughton Castle
Banbury
(0295) 262624
** / B

Buscot Park (NT)
Nr Faringdon
(0367) 242094
B

Buscot Old Parsonage (NT)
Nr Lechlade
** / A

Chastleton House
Nr Moreton-in-Marsh
(0608 74) 355
** / B

Ditchley Park
Enstone
(060 872) 346
R

The Great Barn (NT)
Great Coxwell
*** / A

Greys Court (NT)
Henley-on-Thames
(04917) 529
** / B

Fawley Court
Henley-on-Thames
(0491) 574917
** R / B

Kingston House
Kingston Bagpuize
(0865) 820259
** / B

Mapledurham House
Nr Reading
(0734) 723350
**

Milton Manor House
Milton
(0235) 831287
** / B

Minster Lovell Hall and
Dovecote (NT)
(0993) 775315
** R / A

North Leigh Roman Villa (EH)
Charlbury
(0993) 881830
** / A

Nuffield Place
Nettlebed
(0491) 641224
** / B

Rousham House
Steeple Aston
(0869) 47110
** R /

Rycote Chapel (EH)
Thame
(08447) 346
*** / A

THE HERITAGE DIRECTORY : ENGLAND

Stanton Harcourt Manor
Stanton Harcourt
** R / B

Stonor Park
Nr Henley-on-Thames
(049 163) 587
** R / B

Waterperry Gardens
Nr Wheatley
(084 47) 226 and 254
*** R / A

THE HEART OF ENGLAND

GLOUCESTERSHIRE

Arlington Mill
Bibury
(028574) 368
*** R / A

Berkeley Castle
Nr Bristol
(0453) 810332
** R /

Blackfriars (EH)
Gloucester
(0452) 27688
** / A

Bourton House (G)
Bourton-on-the-Hill
(0386) 700121
** R / A+

Chavenage House
Tetbury
(0666) 502329
** R / B

Chedworth Roman Villa (NT)
Yanworth
Withington 256
*** R / B

Hailes Abbey (EH)
(0242) 602398
*** / A

Hidcote Manor Garden (NT)
Hidcote Bartrim
Mickleton 438333
** /A

Kiftsgate Court
Nr Chipping Campden
** G / B

Newark Park (NT)
Wotton under Edge
Dursley 842644
** R / A

Painswick Rococo Garden (G)
Painswick
Painswick 813204
*** R / B

Prinknash Abbey
Grantham
(0452) 812239
*** / B

Snowshill Manor (NT)
Nr Broadway
Broadway 852410
** R / B

Stanway House
Nr Broadway
038673 469
** R / B

Sudeley Castle
Winchcombe
(0242) 602308
** / B

Westbury Court Garden (NT)
Westbury-on-Severn
Westbury-on-Severn 461
** / B

HEREFORD & WORCESTER

Abberley Hall
Nr Worcester
(0299) 896634
** R / A

Berrington Hall (NT)
Leominster
Leominster 5721
** R / B

Burford House Gardens
Tenbury Wells
(0584) 810777
** R / B

Burton Court
Eardisland
Pembridge 231
** / A

The Commandery
Sidbury
(0905) 355071
*** / B

Croft Castle (NT)
Nr Leominster
Yarpole 246
** R / B

Cwmmau Farmhouse (NT)
Whitney-on-Wye
** R/ A

Eastgrove Cottage
Sankyns Green
(0299) 896389
** R / A

Eastnor Castle
Nr Ledbury
(0531) 2305 or 3318
** R / B

Goodrich Castle (EH)
Goodrich
(0600) 890538
*** / A

The Greyfriars (NT)
Worcester
(0905) 23571
** R / C

Hanbury Hall (NT)
Nr Droitwich
Hanbury 214
** R / B

Harvington Hall
Nr Kidderminster
(0562 777) 267
** / B

Hill Court Gardens
Hom Green
Ross 763123
*** R / D

Kentchurch Court
Hereford
Golden Valley 240228
** R / B

Kinnersley Castle
Kinnersley
(05446) 407
** R / A

Little Malvern Court
Nr Great Malvern
(0684) 892988
** / B

Lower Brockhampton (NT)
Bromyard
** R / A

Mortimer's Cross Water Mill
(EH)
Lucton
(056881) 8820
** / A

Spetchley Park
Worcester
** R / A

The Weir (NT)
Swainshill
*** R / A

Worcester Cathedral
Worcester
(0905) 28854
*** R / B

WARWICKSHIRE

Anne Hathaway's Cottage
Stratford-upon-Avon
*** R / B

Arbury Hall
Nuneaton
(0203) 382804
** R / A

Baddesley Clinton (NT)
Solihull
(056 43) 3294
** R / B

Charlecote Park (NT)
Warwick
(0789) 470277
** R / C

Coughton Court (NT)
Alcester
(0789) 762435
** R / B

Farnborough Hall (NT)
Nr Banbury
** / A

Honington Hall
Shipston-on-Stour
(0608) 61434
** / A

Kenilworth Castle (EH)
(0926) 52078
** / A

Lord Leycester Hospital
Warwick
(0926) 492797
*** R / A

Packwood House (NT)
Hockley Heath
(056 43) 2024
** R / B

Ragley Hall
Alcester
(0789) 762090
** R / B

Shakespeare's Birthplace
Stratford-upon-Avon
*** R / B

Hall's Croft
Stratford-upon-Avon
*** R / B

New Place/Nash's House
Stratford-upon-Avon
*** R / A

The Shakespeare Countryside
Museum
at Mary Arden's House
Stratford-upon-Avon
*** R / B

Upton House (NT)
Edge Hill
Edge Hill 266
** R / B

Warwick Castle
Warwick
(0926) 495421
***

THE HERITAGE DIRECTORY : ENGLAND

MERCIA

CHESHIRE

Adlington Hall
Macclesfield
Prestbury 829206
** / B

Arley Hall and Gardens
Nr Northwich
(0565) 777353
** R / B

Beeston Castle (EH)
(0829) 260464
** / A

Capesthorne
Macclesfield
(0625) 861221
** / B

Cholmondeley Castle Gardens
Malpas
(0829) 22383/203
** R / G / B

Dunham Massey (NT)
Altrincham
061 941 1025
** / C

Gawsworth Hall
Macclesfield
0260 223456
** / B

Handforth Hall
Handforth, nr Wilmslow
R

Hare Hill Gardens (NT)
Over Alderley
Alderley, nr Macclesfield
** / A

Little Moreton Hall (NT)
Congleton
(0260) 272018
** / B

Lyme Park (NT)
Disley, Stockport
(0663) 62023
** / B

Ness Gardens
Wirral
051 336 2135
*** / B

Nether Alderley Mill (NT)
Nether Alderley
(0625) 523012
** R / A

Norton Priory Museum
Runcorn
(0928) 569895
** / B

Peckforth Castle
nr Tarporley
(0829) 260930
** / B

Peover Hall
Over Peover, Knutsford
Lower Peover 2135
** / A

Quarry Bank Mill (NT)
Styal
(0625) 527468
*** / C

Rode Hall
Scholar Green, Stoke -on-Trent
(0270) 873237
** / B

Tatton Park (NT)
Knutsford
(0565) 54822
** / B

GREATER MANCHESTER

Bramall Hall
Bramhall
061 485 3708
** / A

Hall I' Th' Wood
Bolton
(0204) 51159
**

Heaton Hall
Prestwich
061 236 9422
** / D

Smithills Hall
Bolton
(0204) 41265
**

MERSEYSIDE

Croxteth Hall & Country Park
Liverpool
051 228 5311
*** / D

Speke Hall (NT)
Liverpool
051 427 7231
** R / B

STAFFORDSHIRE

Alton Towers
Alton
(0538) 702200
*** / B+

Ancient High House
Stafford
*** R / A

Chillington Hall
Nr Wolverhampton
Brewood 850236
** / A

Hanch Hall
Lichfield
(0543) 490308
** R / B

Moseley Old Hall (NT)
Wolverhampton
(0902) 782808
** / B

Shugborough (NT)
Stafford
(0889) 881388
** R / B

Wall (Letocetum) Roman Site
(EH)
Lichfield
(0543) 480768
*** / A

SHROPSHIRE

Attingham Park (NT)
Nr Shrewsbury
(0743 77) 203
** / B

Benthall Hall (NT)
Broseley
(0952) 882159
** / A

Boscobel House (EH)
Shifnal
(0902) 850244
*** / B

Buildwas Abbey (EH)
Much Wenlock
(095 245) 3274
*** / A

Dudmaston (NT)
Bridgenorth
Quatt 780866
** / B

Haughmond Abbey (EH)
Shrewsbury
(074 377) 661
*** / A

Hodnet Hall Gardens
Nr Market Drayton
(063 084) 202
** R / B

Ludlow Castle (EH)
Ludlow
(0584) 873532
*** / B

Lilleshall Abbey (EH)
Newport
(0952) 604431
** / A

Shipton Hall
Much Wenlock
(074 636) 225
** / A

Stokesay Castle (EH)
Craven Arms
(0588) 672544
*** / A

Wenlock Priory (EH)
Much Wenlock
(0952) 727466
** / A

Weston Park
Nr Shifnal
Weston-under-Lizard 207
** R / A

Wroxeter (Viroconium) Roman
City (EH)
Shrewsbury
(074375) 330
*** / A

WEST MIDLANDS

Blakesley Hall
Birmingham
021 783 2193
** / D

Hagley Hall
Nr Stourbridge
(0562) 882408
*** R

Wightwick Manor (NT)
Wolverhampton
(0902) 761108
*** R / A

MIDDLE ENGLAND

DERBYSHIRE

Bolsover Castle (EH)
(0246) 823349
** / A

Calke Abbey and Park (NT)
Nr Derby
(0332) 863822
** / B

Chatsworth
Bakewell
(0246) 582204
** R /

Haddon Hall
Bakewell
(0629) 812855
** / B

Hardwick Hall (NT)
Nr Chesterfield
(0246) 850430
** R / B

Melbourne Hall and Gardens
Melbourne
(0332) 862502
** R /

Peveril Castle (EH)
Castleton
(0433) 20613
*** / A

Sudbury Hall (NT)
Nr Derby
(028 378) 305
** / B

Winster Market House (NT)
Nr Matlock
(033 529) 245
** R / D

LEICESTERSHIRE

Ashby de la Zouch Castle (EH)
Ashby de la Zouch
(0530) 413343
*** / A

Belvoir Castle
Nr Grantham
(0476) 870262
** R / B

Bosworth Battlefield Visitor
Centre & Country Park
Market Bosworth
(0455) 290429
** R / A

Kirby Muxloe Castle (EH)
(0533) 386886
*** / A

Lyddington Bede House (EH)
Lyddington
(057282) 2438
** / A

Stanford Hall
Lutterworth
(0788) 860250
** / B

LINCOLNSHIRE

Belton House (NT)
Nr Grantham
(0476) 66116
** / C

Bishop's Palace (EH)
Lincoln
(0522) 27468
** / A

Burghley House
Stamford
(0780) 52451
** / C

Doddington Hall
Doddington
(0522) 694308
** / A

Gainsborough Old Hall (EH)
Gainsborough
(0427) 2669
*** / A

Grantham House (NT)
Grantham
** R / A

Grimsthorpe Castle and
Gardens
Bourne
** R / A

Gunby Hall (NT)
Burgh-le-Marsh
** R / A

Harlaxton Manor
Grantham
(0476) 64541

Lincoln Castle
Castle Hill
(0522) 511068
* / A

Sibsey Trader Mill (EH)
(0205) 750036
** / A

Tattershall Castle (NT)
Lincoln
(0526) 42543
*** R / A

Woolsthorpe Manor (NT)
Nr Grantham
(0476) 860338
** R / A

NORTHAMPTONSHIRE

Althorp
Northampton
(0604) 770006
*** / B

Boughton House
Kettering
(0536) 515731
** / A

Canons Ashby House (NT)
Canons Ashby
(0327) 860044
** / B

Coton Manor Gardens
Northampton
(0604) 740219
**

Deene Park
Nr Corby
Bulwick 278 or 361
**

Hinwick House
Nr Wellingborough
(0933) 53624
** R / B

Holdenby House Gardens
Northampton
(0604) 770786 or 770241
** / A

Kirby Hall (EH)
Nr Corby
(0536) 203230
** / A

Lamport Hall
Northampton
*** R / B

Lilford Park
Nr Oundle
(08015) 648
** / A

Lyveden New Bield (NT)
Oundle
(083 25) 358
*** / A

Priest's House (NT)
Easton-on-the-Hill
(0780) 62506
R

Rockingham Castle
Nr Corby
(0536) 770240
** / B

Rushton Triangular Lodge (EH)
(0536) 710761
** / A

Southwick Hall
Nr Oundle
(0832) 274064
R / B

Sulgrave Manor
Banbury
(029 576) 205
*** R / A

NOTTINGHAMSHIRE

Clumber Park (NT)
Nr Worksop
(0909) 476592
***

Newstead Abbey
Linby
Mansfield (0623) 793557
** R / A

Wollaton Hall
Nottingham
Nottingham 281333
**** / D

YORKSHIRE

NORTH YORKSHIRE

Aldborough Roman Town (EH)
Boroughbridge
(0423) 322768
*** / A

Allerton Park
Nr Knaresborough
(0423) 330927
** / B

Bolton Castle
Nr Leyburn
(0969) 23981 or 23674
**

Byland Abbey (EH)
Coxwold
(03476) 614
*** / A

Castle Howard
York
(065 384) 333
** / C

Clifford's Tower (EH)
York
(0904) 646940
*** R / A

Constable Burton Hall
Leyburn
Bedale 50428
** / A

Easby Abbey (EH)
Richmond
*** / A

Fairfax House
Castlegate
(0904) 655543
*** R / B

Fountains Abbey &
Studley Royal (NT)
*** R / A

Georgian Theatre Royal
Richmond
(0748) 3021
**

Gilling Castle
Helmsley
***

Harlow Car Gardens
Harrogate
*** / D

Helmsley Castle (EH)
Helmsley
(0439) 70442
*** / A

Hovingham Hall
York
** R / B

Kirkham Priory (EH)
(065381) 768
*** / A

Middleham Castle (EH)
Leyburn
(0969) 23899
*** / A

Mount Grace Priory (EH)
Northallerton
(0609) 83249
*** / A

Pickering Castle (EH)
Pickering
(0751) 74989
*** / A

Newburgh Priory
Coxwold
(034 76) 435
** / A

Newby Hall & Gardens
Ripon
(0423) 322583
** / C

Norton Conyers
Ripon
(076 584) 333
** / A

Nunnington Hall (NT)
Nr Helmsley
Nunnington 283
** R / B

Richmond Castle (EH)
Richmond
(0748) 2493
*** / A

Rievaulx Abbey (EH)
Helmsley
(043 96) 228
*** / A

Rievaulx Terrace (NT)
Helmsley
Bilsdale 340
** / A

Ripley Castle
Ripley
(0423) 770152
*** R /

Scarborough Castle (EH)
Scarborough
(0723) 372451
*** / A

Sheriff Hutton Park
York
(034 77) 442
*** / A

Sion Hill Hall
Kirby Wiske
(0845) 587206
** / A+

Skipton Castle
Skipton
(0756) 792442
*** / A

Stockeld Park
Wetherby
(0937) 66101
** / A

Sutton Park
Sutton-on-the-Forest
(0347) 810249
**

Treasurer's House (NT)
York
(0904) 624247
** / B

Whitby Abbey (EH)
Whitby
(0947) 603568
*** / A

SOUTH YORKSHIRE

Conisbrough Castle (EH)
Doncaster
(0709) 863329
*** / A

Cannon Hall
Cawthorne
Barnsley 790270
*** / D

Monk Bretton Priory (EH)
Barnsley
(0226) 204089
*** / A

Roche Abbey (EH)
Maltby
(0709) 812739
*** / A

The Sue Ryder Home,
Hickleton Hall
Nr Doncaster
R

WEST YORKSHIRE

Bolling Hall
Bradford
Bradford 723057
*** / D

Bramham Park
Wetherby
(0937) 844265
*** R /

Bronte Parsonage
Haworth
(0535) 42323
*** R / A

East Riddlesden Hall (NT)
Keighley
** R / A

Harewood House and Bird
Garden
Leeds
(0532) 886225
*** R /

Nostell Priory (NT)
Wakefield
Wakefield 863892
** R / A

Temple Newsam
Leeds
(0532) 647321
*** / A

HUMBERSIDE

Blaydes House
Hull
(0482) 26406
*** R / A

Burton Agnes Hall
Nr Bridlington
(0262 89) 324
** / B

Burton Constable
Nr Hull
(0964) 562400
** R

The Charterhouse
Hull
(0482) 20026
*** R

Elsham Hall Country Park
Brigg
Barnetby 688698
*** R

The Guildhall
Beverley
(0482) 867430
** / D

Maister House (NT)
Hull
(0482) 24114
*** / A

Normanby Hall and Country
Park
Scunthorpe
(0724) 720215
** R / A

Sledmere House
Driffield
(0377) 86208
* / B

Thornton Abbey
(0469) 40357
*** / A

CLEVELAND

Gisborough Priory (EH)
Guisborough
(0287) 38301
** / A

Ormesby Hall (NT)
Nr Middlesborough
** / B

**LANCASHIRE AND
THE LAKES**

LANCASHIRE

Appleby Castle
Appleby
(07683) 51402
** / B+

Astley Hall
Chorley
*** / A

Chingle Hall
Goosnargh
(0772) 861082
*** R / B

Gawthorpe Hall (NT)
Padiham
(0282) 78511
*** R / A

Hoghton Tower
Nr Preston
(025 485) 2986
** / B+

Leighton Hall
Carnforth
(0524) 734474
*** R / B

Rufford Old Hall (NT)
Rufford
(0704) 821254
** / B

Towneley Hall Art Gallery &
Museum and the Museum of
Local Crafts & Industries
Burnley
Burnley 24213
*** / D

CUMBRIA

Abbot Hall Art Gallery
& Museum of Lakeland Life &
Industry
Kirkland
(0539) 722464
***

Acorn Bank Garden (NT)
Penrith
** G / A

Brantwood
Coniston
(0966) 41396
*** / B

Brough Castle (EH)
Nr Appleby
(0930) 42191
*** / A

Brougham Castle (EH)
Penrith
(0768) 62488
*** / A

Carlisle Castle (EH)
Carlisle
(0288) 31777
*** R / A

Castletown House
Rockcliffe
(0228 74) 205
** / A

THE HERITAGE DIRECTORY : ENGLAND

Dalemain
Nr Penrith
(07684) 86450
**

Furness Abbey (EH)
Nr Barrow-in-Furness
(0229) 23420
*** / A

Hadrian's Wall (EH)

Holker Hall
Cark-in-Cartmel
(05395) 58328
**

Hutton-in-the-Forest
Penrith
(085 34) 449
** / B+

Kendal Castle
Kendal
(0539) 725758
** / B

Lanercost Priory (EH)
Brampton
(06977) 3030
** / A

Levens Hall
Kendal
(076 87) 72287
** / B

Muncaster Castle
Ravenglass
** / A

Rydal Mount
Ambleside
(05394) 33002
*** R / A

Sizergh Castle and Garden (NT)
Kendal
(05395) 60070
** / A

Stagsden Bird Gardens
Stagsden
(023 02) 2745
*** / B

Stott Park Bobbin Mill (EH)
Finsthwaite
(0448) 31087
** / A

Townend (NT)
Troutbeck
(05394) 32628
** / A

Wordsworth House (NT)
Cockermouth
(0900) 824805
** / B

NORTHUMBRIA

DURHAM

Barnard Castle (EH)
(0833) 38212
*** / A

Durham Castle
Durham

Finchale Priory (EH)
091 386 3828
*** / A

Raby Castle
Staindrop
(0833) 60202
** / B

Rokeby Park
Nr Barnard Castle
** R

NORTHUMBERLAND

Alnwick Castle
Alnwick
(0665) 510777
** / B

Aydon Castle (EH)
Corbridge
(043 471) 2450
** / A

Bamburgh Castle
Bamburgh
Bamburgh 208
** / B

Belsay Hall Castle and Gardens
(EH)
Nr. Newcastle-upon-Tyne
(066 181) 636
*** / A

Berwick Barracks (EH)
Berwick
(0289) 304493
*** / B

Brinkburn Priory (EH)
Rothbury
(066 570) 628
** / A

Chesters Fort (EH)
Chollerford
(043481) 379
*** / A

Chillingham Castle
(0227) 730319
** / B+

Cragside House &
Country Park (NT)
Rothbury
(0669) 20333
*** R / B

Corbridge Roman Site (EH)
Corbridge
(043471) 2349
*** / B

Dunstanburgh Castle (EH)
Alnwick
(066475) 231
*** / A

George Stephenson's Birthplace
(NT)
Wylam
(06614) 3457
** / A

Hadrian's Roman Wall (EH)
In Northumberland and
Tyne & Wear

Housesteads Roman Fort (EH)
Bardon Mill
(04984) 363
*** / B

Lindisfarne Castle (NT)
Holy Island
(0289) 89244
** / B

Lindisfarne Priory (EH)
Holy Island
(028989) 200
*** / B

Norham Castle
Berwick
(028982

Seaton Delaval Hall
Whitley Bay
(091) 2373040 or 2371493
** / A

Prudhoe Castle (EH)
Prudhoe
(0661) 33459
*** / A

Tynemouth Castle and Priory
(EH)
Tynemouth
(091) 257 1090
*** / A

Wallington House, Walled
Garden
and Grounds (NT)
Cambo
(067 074) 283
*** R / B

Warkworth Castle (EH)
Alnwick
(0665) 711423
*** / A

Warkworth Hermitage
Alnwick
(0665) 711423
** / A

TYNE & WEAR

Hylton Castle (EH)
Sunderland
*** / A

Gibside Chapel & Grounds
(NT)
Gibside
(0207) 542255
** / B

Tynemouth Castle and Priory
(EH)
Tynemouth
091-257 1090
A

Washington Old Hall (NT)
Washington
(091) 4166879
** / A

THE HERITAGE DIRECTORY : SCOTLAND

THE LOWLANDS

BORDERS

Abbotsford House
Melrose
**

Ayton Castle
Eyemouth
(089 07) 81212
** / A+

Bowhill
Nr Selkirk
(0750) 20732
** R / B+

Dryburgh Abbey
Dryburgh
(0835) 22381
** / A

Duns Castle
(0361) 83211
R

Floors Castle
Kelso
(0573) 23333
** / B

Hermitage Castle
Liddlesdale
** / A

THE HERITAGE DIRECTORY : SCOTLAND

Jedburgh Abbey
Jedburgh
Jedburgh 63925
** / A

Kailzie Gardens
Nr Peebles
** / A

Manderston
Duns
(0361) 83450
**

Mellerstain
Gordon
(057 381) 225
** R

Melrose Abbey
Melrose
** / A

Priorwood Garden
Melrose
(089 682) 2555
**

Robert Smail's Printing Works
(NT)
Tweedale
** R / D

Smailholm Tower
Nr Smailholm
** / A

Thirlestane Castle
Lauder
(05782) 430
** R / B

Traquair House
Innerleithen
(0896) 830323
**

DUMFRIES AND GALLOWAY

Broughton House
Kirkcudbright
**

Caerlaverock Castle
Nr Dumfries
(0387) 77244
** / A

Carlyle's Birthplace
Ecclefechan
(057 63) 666
** / A

Castle Kennedy Gardens
Stranraer
(0776) 2024
** / A

Drumlanrig Castle and
Country Park
Nr Thornhill
(0848) 30248
** R / B+

Sweetheart Abbey
New Abbey
** / A

Threave Garden
Nr Castle Douglas
(0556) 2575
** / B

FIFE REGION

Aberdour Castle
Aberdour
(-383) 860519
*** / A

Falkland Palace & Garden (NT)
Fife
(0337) 57397
** / B+

Hill of Tarvit (NT)
Nr Cupar
(0334) 53127
** / B+

Kellie Castle and Garden (NT)
Fife
(033 38) 271
*** R / A+

The Town House & The Study
(NT)
Culross
(0383) 880359
** / A

LOTHIAN REGION

Amisfield Mains
Nr Haddington
(08757) 201
R

Beanston
Nr Haddington
(08757) 201
R

Dalkeith Country Park
Nr Edinburgh
031-663 5684
** / A

Dalmeny House
South Queensferry
031-331 1888
**

Dirleton Castle & Garden
Dirleton
031-661 4445
*** / A

Edinburgh Castle
Edinburgh
031-225 9846
*** / B

The Georgian House
Edinburgh
031-225 2160
** / B

Gladstone's Land
Edinburgh
031-226 5856
** / A

Gosford House
East Lothian
(08757) 201
** / A

Harelaw Farmhouse
Nr Longniddry
(08757) 201
R

Hopetoun House
South Queensferry
031-331 2451
** / B

The House of the Binns
Linlithgow
** / B+

Inveresk Lodge and Garden
Inveresk
050-683 4255
*** / A+

Lamb's House
Leith
031-554 3131
***

Lennoxlove
Haddington
(062 082) 3720
** / B

Malleny Garden
Balerno
*** / A

Palace of Holyroodhouse
Edinburgh
031-556 7371
*** R /

Preston Mill (NT)
East Linton
(0620) 860426
** / A

Royal Botanic Gardens
Edinburgh
*** / D

Stevenson House
Haddington
(062 082) 3376
** / A

Winton House
Pencaitland
(0875) 340 222
R / B

STRATHCLYDE REGION

Bachelor's Club
Tarbolton
(0292) 541 or 940
** / A+

Blairquhan Castle and Gardens
Ayrshire
(065 57) 239
** / B

Botanic Gardens
Glasgow
*** / D

Bothwell Castle
Bothwell
*** / A

Brodick Castle, Garden and
Country Park (NT)
Isle of Arran
(0770) 2202
*** R / B+

Burns Cottage
Alloway
***

Culzean Castle, Garden and
Country Park (NT)
Maybole
(065 56) 274
*** R / B

Dumbarton Castle
Dumbarton
(0389) 32828
*** / A

Finlaystone House and Gardens
Langbank
Langbank 285
*** / A

Greenbank Garden (NT)
Glasgow
(041) 639 3281
*** / A+

The Hill House
Helensburgh
(0436) 3900
*** / B

Hutchesons' Hall (NT)
Glasgow
041-552 8391
*** R / D

Inveraray Castle
Inveraray
(0499) 2203
** R

Kelburn Country Centre
and Kelburn Castle
Largs
(0475) 568685
** / B

Pollok House & Park
Glasgow
041-632 0274
*** / D

Souter Johnnie's Cottage
Kirkoswald
(065 56) 603
** / A+

THE HERITAGE DIRECTORY : SCOTLAND

The Tenement House (NT)
Glasgow
041-333 0183
** / A

Torosay Castle and Gardens
Isle of Mull
(068 02) 421
*** R / A

Weaver's Cottage (NT)
Kilbarchan
** / A+

HIGHLAND & ISLANDS

CENTRAL REGION

Castle Campbell
Dollar
(0259) 42408
** / A

Linlithgow Palace
Linlithgow
Linlithgow 842894
*** / A

Stirling Castle
Stirling
(0786) 50000
*** / A

GRAMPIAN REGION

Balmoral Castle
Nr Ballater
(03397) 42334
** / A+

Braemar Castle
Braemar
(03397) 41219 or 41224
** / A

Brodie Castle (NT)
Nr Nairn Moray
(030 94) 371
*** R / B

Castle Fraser (NT)
Sauchen
(03303) 463
** / B

Craigievar Castle (NT)
Lumphanan
(033 98) 83635
** / B+

Crathes Castle & Garden (NT)
Banchory
(033 044) 525
*** R / A

Drum Castle
Nr Aberdeen
(033 08) 204
** / B+

Duff House
Banff
(02612) 2872
** / A

Elgin Cathedral
Elgin
(0343) 547171
*** / A

Fyvie Castle (NT)
Fyvie
(065 16) 266
** / B

Haddo House (NT)
Nr Methlick
(065 15) 440
** / B+

Huntly House
Huntly
(0466) 793191
*** / A

Kildrummy Castle Garden
Donside
(09755) 71264 or 71277
** / A

Leith Hall and Garden (NT)
Kennethmont
(046 43) 216
*** R / B

Pitmedden Garden (NT)
Udny
(065 13) 2352
*** / B+

Provost Ross's House
Aberdeen
(0224) 572215
*** / D

HIGHLAND

Cawdor Castle
Nr Inverness
(066 77) 615
** / B

Dunrobin Castle
Golspie
(0408) 633177
*** R / B

Dunvegan Castle
Isle of Skye
*** R / B

Eilean Donon Castle
Wester Ross
(059 985) 202
** / A

Fort George
Ardersier
*** / A

Hugh Miller's Cottage (NT)
Cromarty
(038 17) 245
** / A+

Inverewe Garden (NT)
Wester Ross
Poolewe 229
*** R / A

Urquhart Castle
Loch Ness
(04562) 551
** / A

TAYSIDE

Angus Folk Museum (NT)
Glamis
(030 784) 288
** /A+

Barrie's Birthplace (NT)
Kirriemuir
(0575) 72646
** /A+

Blair Castle
Blair Atholl
(079 681) 207
** / B

Branklyn Garden (NT)
Perth
(0738) 25535
** / A

Castle Menzies
Weem
(0887) 20982
** / A

Drummond Castle Gardens
Muthill
** / A

Edzell Castle & Gardens
Edzell
*** R / A

Glamis Castle
Glamis
030-784 242
** / B

House of Dun
Nr Montrose
(067481) 264
**

Huntingtower Castle
Nr Perth
** / A

Scone Palace
Perth
(0738) 52300
** / B

THE HERITAGE DIRECTORY : WALES

CLWYD

Bodelwyddan Castle
Bodelwyddan
(0745) 584060
*** / B

Bodrhyddan Hall
Rhuddlan
** / A

Chirk Castle (NT)
Nr Wrexham
Chirk 777701
*** R / B

Erddig (NT)
Nr Wrexham
(0978) 355314
** R / C

Gyrn Castle
Holywell
*** / A

Plas Teg
Pontblyddyn
(0352) 771335
*** / A

DYFED

Carreg Cennen Castle
Trapp
(0558) 822291
*** / B

Cilgerran Castle
Cilgerran
(0239) 615136
*** / B

Lamphey Palace
Lamphey
(064667) 2224
*** / B

Llawhaden Castle
Llawhaden
*** / B

Pembroke Castle
Pembroke
Pembroke 684585
*** / B

THE HERITAGE DIRECTORY : WALES

Picton Castle
Haverfordwest
Dyfed 751326
**

St Davids Bishops Palace
St Davids
(0437) 720517
*** / B

Talley Abbey
Talley
*** / B

SOUTH GLAMORGAN

Caerphilly Castle
Caerphilly
(0222) 465511
*** / B

Cardiff Castle
Cardiff
Cardiff 822053
*** / B

Castell Coch
Tongwynlais
(0222) 810101
*** / B

WEST GLAMORGAN

Weobley Castle
Weobley
(0792) 390012

GWENT

Caerleon Roman Fortress
Baths and Amphitheatre
Caerleon
(0633) 422518

Chepstow Castle
Chepstow
(0222) 465511
*** / B

Penhow Castle
Nr Newport
(0633) 400800
*** R / B

Raglan Castle
Raglan
(0291) 690228
*** / B

Tintern Abbey
Tintern
(0291) 8251
*** / B

Tredegar House
Newport
(0633) 815880
*** R / B

GWYNEDD

Aberconwy House (NT)
Conwy
(049259) 2246
** / A

Beaumaris Castle
Beaumaris
(0248) 810361

Bodnant Garden (NT)
Tal-y-Cafn
(0492) 650466
** / B

Bryn Bras Castle
Llanrug
(0286) 870210
** / B

Caernarfon Castle
Caernarfon
Caernarfon 77617
*** / B

Conwy Castle
Conwy
(0492) 592358
*** / B

Criccieth Castle
Criccieth
(0239) 615136
***

Harlech Castle
Harlech
*** / B

Penrhyn Castle (NT)
Bangor
(0248) 353084
** / B

Plas Newydd (NT)
Isle of Anglesey
(0248) 714795
** / B

Ty Mawr Wybrnant (NT)
Nr Penmachno
(06903) 213
** / A

POWYS

Gregynog
Newtown
(068 687) 224
** / A

Powis Castle (NT)
Welshpool
(0938) 554336
** R / C

Tretower Court & Castle
Crickhowell
(0874) 730279

THE HERITAGE DIRECTORY : IRELAND

REPUBLIC OF IRELAND

Annes Grove Gardens
Castletownroche
(022) 26145
** R / B

Bantry House
Bantry Co. Cork
(027) 50047
*** / B

Birr Castle Demesne
Co Offaly
(509) 20056
*** / B

Blarney Castle and Blarney
House
Blarney, Co Cork
*** R / B

Bunratty Castle & Folk Park
Bunratty, Co Clare
(061) 361511
*** R / B

Carrigglas Manor
Longford
(043) 45165
** / B

Castletown House
Celbridge,
Co Roscommon
(0907) 20014
***

Clonalis House
Castlerea,
Co Roscommon
(0907) 20014
**

The Craggaunowen Project
Craggaunowen,
Co Clare
(061) 61511
** / B

Cratloe Woods House
Cratloe, Co Clare
(061) 327028
** / B

Dunguaire Castle
Kinvara,
Co Galway
(091) 37108
** / B

Dunkathel
Glanmire,
Co Cork
** / A

Dunloe Castle Hotel Gardens
Beaufort,
Co Kerry
(064) 44111
** / D

Emo Court
Portlaoise,
Co Leix
(0502) 26110
*** / B

Fota
Fota Island,
Co Cork
(021) 812555
** / A

Glin Castle
Glin
Co Limerick
(068) 34173 or 34112

Howth Castle Gardens
Howth
Co Dublin
(01) 322624
*** / A

Japanese Gardens
Tully
Co Kildare
(045) 21617
** / B

Johnstown Castle
Wexford
Co Wexford
*** / B

Knappogue Castle
Quin,
Co Clare
(061) 71103
** / A

Kylemore Abbey
Kylemore
Connemara
(095) 41146 or 41113
** / D

Lismore Castle (G)
Lismore,
Co Waterford
(058) 54424
** / A

Lough Gur Visitor Centre
Lough Gur
(061) 85186
** / A

Malahide Castle
Malahide
452655 or 452371
*** / B

THE HERITAGE DIRECTORY : IRELAND

Mount Usher Gardens
Ashford
Co Wicklow
(0404) 40205
** / A

Muckross House and Gardens
Killarney,
Co Kerry
(064) 31440
*** R / B

National Botanic Gardens
Glasnevin
Dublin
***

Powerscourt Gardens &
Waterfall
Enniskerry,
Co Wicklow
(01) 867676/7/8
*** R / B

Powerscourt Townhouse
Centre
Dublin
(01) 687477
*** / D

Riverstown House
Glanmire,
Co Cork
*** R / A

Slane Castle
Slane
Co Meath
(041) 24207
** / B

Thoor Ballylee
Gort
Co Galway
(091) 31436
**

Timoleague Castle Gardens (G)
Bandon
Co Cork
(023) 46116 or 831512
** / B

Westport House
Westport,
County Mayo
(098) 25430 or 25141
** / B

NORTHERN IRELAND

Ardress House (NT)
Co Armagh
Annaghmore 851236
** / A

The Argory (NT)
Co Armagh
Moy 84753
** / A

Castle Coole (NT)
Co Fermanagh
Enniskillen 22690
*** R / D

Castle Ward (NT)
Co Down
Strangford 204
*** R / B

Downhill Castle (NT)
Londonderry
** / D

Florence Court (NT)
Co Fermanagh
Florence Court 249
*** R / A

Gray's Printing Press (NT)
Strabane
Strabane 884094
*** R / A

Hezlett House (NT)
Co Londonderry
Castlerock 848567
** / A

Mount Stewart House, Garden
and Temple (NT)
Co Down
Greyabbey 387
** R / A

Rowallane Garden (NT)
Saintfield
Saintfield 510131
*** R / A

Springhill (NT)
Co Londonderry
Moneymore 48210
** / A

Templetown Mausoleum (NT)
Co Antrim
*** / D

Wellbrook Beetling Mill (NT)
Cookstown
Co Tyrone
** / A

ANNESBROOK

Prized for its food and tranquility, Annesbrook is a Georgian house which combines the luxury of first-class accommodation with the informality of a country residence.

Although situated off the beaten track in secluded woodland, overlooking the royal pastures of County Meath, Annesbrook is uniquely situated in proximity to Ireland's most historic monuments, towns, city and golf courses: Newgrange (12km), Tara (17km), Monasterboice (17km), Mellifont (15km), Fourknocks (9km), Boyne Valley (9km), Slane (12km), Drogheda (9km), Baltray (12km), Portmarnock (35km), Dublin (35km), Dublin Airport (25km).

Behind the house, through an enchanted wood of redwoods, beech, chestnut and sycamore, is the walled garden where your host and cook Kate Sweetman tends her beds of organically grown vegetables, fruit, herbs and flowers.

A castellated stone arch with pocket houses frames the entrance to Annesbrook. The avenue, tunneling its way through an aisle of ash and cedar, abruptly rounds an old oak tree to afford the visitor a first glimpse of the historic portico of Annesbrook and the Moorish Ballroom erected for George IV's visit in 1821.

Below the house is the river of the Nanny's water referred to by Thackeray in his vignette of Annesbrook in "The Irish Sketch Book" (1842):

'We waited for the coach at the beautiful lodge and gate of Annesbrook; and one of the sons of the house coming up, invited us to look at the domain, which is as pretty and neatly ordered as any in England.'

Annesbrook is open from May to September, off season bookings for groups of six or more can be arranged.

Kate Sweetman
Annesbrook
Duleek
Co. Meath
Ireland
Tel: (010 353 41) 23292